P9-ARZ-396

Acclaim for Michàlle E. Mor Barak's
Managing Diversity

- Academy of Management's George R. Terry Book Award for the year's most outstanding contribution to the advancement of management knowledge

- *Choice* Award for Outstanding Academic Titles by the Association of Research and College Libraries

"An excellent resource to develop, theorize, and work out the inclusive workplace in a very comprehensive, encompassing, and interdisciplinary way. . . . Boxes, tables, graphs, and figures as well as practical examples and empirical illustrations . . . make the book very interesting for both the conceptual, pedagogical research interest and the practical, educational interest."
> —**Cordula Barzantny,** *Academy of Management Learning & Education Journal*

"*Managing Diversity* comprehensively addresses the corporate role for inclusiveness as part of workforce management as well as at community, state and federal, and international levels. Mor Barak has made a substantial contribution to the human resources and management literature."
> —**Gary Bess,** *Profiles in Diversity Journal*

"The viewpoint of the book is truly global. By integrating established knowledge on diversity issues with contemporary perspectives on inclusion and globalization, this book pioneers the next generation of scholarship on issues of workforce diversity."
> —**Susan J. Lambert,** *Journal of Sociology and Social Welfare*

"Authored by an extremely knowledgeable professor with a joint appointment in business and social work at the University of Southern California, this volume provides a thorough, well-written, and interesting resource on managing global workplace diversity that will be useful to both the practitioner and the conceptual researcher. All in all, this is a refreshing and compelling volume that will be useful to anyone in global business management. Highly recommended."
> —**T. Gutteridge,** *CHOICE Magazine*

"This is a timely book. The book's subject, managing diversity in a global workplace, portends the future for a growing area of social work policy and practice. . . . A valuable resource for social work practice in a global context, the book is also highly recommended as a text in social work education programs."
> —**John J. Stretch,** *Social Work Journal*

"*Managing Diversity* comprehensively addresses the importance of inclusiveness as part of workforce management, which is scalable from small community-based organizations to large multinational service agencies. . . . Practical relevance is threaded throughout the book. . . . This book is a must-read for social work management professionals and others committed to social justice in the workplace."
> —*Administration in Social Work*

"[*Managing Diversity*] is thorough, well-written, and filled with interesting information and case examples. It deals with an important issue in a very complete manner, providing both theoretical and conceptual content and outstanding practical information. It should be valuable and useful to anyone studying international business management."

—Sheila Akabas, Professor and Director, Center for Social Policy and Practice in the Workplace, Columbia University

"The book will be helpful for students and scholars in international business management, international HRM, diversity management, and cross-cultural management. It is a useful resource for conceptualizing and implementing an inclusive workplace agenda. It reflects a global perspective and will interest readers across countries. The book has demonstrated well that when diversity and inclusion are being practiced as business strategies, they help in providing competitive advantage."

—Debi S. Saini, *The Journal of Business Perspective*

"Over the past two decades organizations, government, and society have grappled with demands presented by increased diversity in nations and workplaces alike. . . . Mor Barak's book is one of the first to explore the synergies between international management and domestic diversity management."

—Kate Hutchings, *Asia Pacific Journal of Human Relations*

"This book has been structured excellently and covers a vast number of diversity issues. . . . This book would be of value to anyone with research interests in diversity management or cross-cultural issues."

—Sunil Kumar Singh, *IIMB Management Review*

"Professor Mor Barak's book provides a myriad of practical examples and case illustrations that bring the content to life. The concept of the Inclusive Workplace that she has originated and developed is particularly useful for managers and scholars alike. I highly recommend this book."

—Nissan Pardo, PhD, CEO/CFO, *Dynamic Home Care & Nursing*

Managing Diversity

Fourth Edition

Managing Diversity

Fourth Edition

Dedicated to my parents—
Sara and Advocate Peretz Barak, a blessed memory

And may they live a long life,
to my darling Shunit, Tomer, and Oz—
For a brave new future!

To Ysrael—
The wind beneath my wings

Managing Diversity

Toward a Globally Inclusive Workplace

Fourth Edition

George A.
Rawlyk Library
Crandall University

Michàlle E. Mor Barak

University of Southern California

Los Angeles | London | New Delhi
Singapore | Washington DC | Melbourne

FOR INFORMATION:

SAGE Publications, Inc.
2455 Teller Road
Thousand Oaks, California 91320
E-mail: order@sagepub.com

SAGE Publications Ltd.
1 Oliver's Yard
55 City Road
London EC1Y 1SP
United Kingdom

SAGE Publications India Pvt. Ltd.
B 1/I 1 Mohan Cooperative Industrial Area
Mathura Road, New Delhi 110 044
India

SAGE Publications Asia-Pacific Pte. Ltd.
3 Church Street
#10-04 Samsung Hub
Singapore 049483

Copyright © 2017 by SAGE Publications, Inc.

All rights reserved. No part of this book may be reproduced or utilized in any form or by any means, electronic or mechanical, including photocopying, recording, or by any information storage and retrieval system, without permission in writing from the publisher.

Printed in the United States of America

Library of Congress Cataloging-in-Publication Data

Names: Mor-Barak, Michàlle E.

Title: Managing diversity : toward a globally inclusive workplace / Michalle E. Mor Barak, University of Southern California.

Description: Fourth Edition. | Thousand Oaks : SAGE Publications, Inc., 2017. | Revised edition of the author's Managing diversity, 2013. | Includes bibliographical references and index.

Identifiers: LCCN 2016039310 | ISBN 978-1-4833-8612-6 (pbk. : alk. paper)

Subjects: LCSH: Diversity in the workplace.

Classification: LCC HF5549.5.M5 M662 2017 | DDC 658.3008—dc23
LC record available at https://lccn.loc.gov/2016039310

This book is printed on acid-free paper.

Acquisitions Editor: Maggie Stanley
Editorial Assistant: Neda Dallal
Production Editor: David C. Felts
Copy Editor: Talia Greenberg
Typesetter: C&M Digitals (P) Ltd.
Proofreader: Bonnie Moore
Indexer: Joan Shapiro
Cover Designer: Michael Dubowe
Marketing Manager: Ashlee Blunk

SUSTAINABLE FORESTRY INITIATIVE

Certified Chain of Custody
At Least 10% Certified Forest Content
www.sfiprogram.org
SFI-01028

21 22 23 24 25 10 9 8 7 6 5

• Contents •

• List of Boxes, Figures, and Tables •

Chapter 8

Chapter 9

Chapter 10

Chapter 11

Chapter 17

Chapter 18

• Preface and Acknowledgments •

No one is born hating another person because of the color of his
skin, or his background, or his religion. People must learn to hate,
and if they can learn to hate, they can be taught to love, for love
comes more naturally to the human heart than its opposite.

—Nelson Mandela, *Long Walk to Freedom*, 1995

In the decade since I completed the first edition of *Managing Diversity: Toward a Globally Inclusive Workplace*, the field of diversity management has blossomed from a nascent practice area into a burgeoning specialization within business, governmental, and nonprofit organizations. Most global organizations now have people in executive positions in charge of diversity. The term *inclusion* that was introduced and defined in the first edition has become mainstream, and most professionals now relate to the specialization as Diversity & Inclusion, or D&I for short. Many global organizations have corporate officers who are in charge of whole departments that oversee policies and practices that are more closely aligned with the strategic goals of the organization. Moreover, diversity management has become a recognized field of scientific inquiry, and there are increasing numbers of research articles published every year in academic journals. I am gratified to see that the concept of the *inclusive workplace* and the model that I introduced in the first edition of this book have gained recognition by practitioners and researchers alike. The main principle of the inclusive workplace is that inclusion relates not only to the organization itself but should also be applied to expanding circles that are relevant to the organization's life—the local community, the wider national sphere, and the global context (see Figure 18.1 in Chapter 18). Through the different editions of the book I have introduced the accumulating research highlighting the benefits of the inclusive workplace model to the organization and its employees as well as on the communities it is serving, its stakeholders, and (where applicable) its stockholders.

Yet, both globally and locally, diversity and intergroup relations are as tumultuous as ever before. Although more organizations are benefiting from the richness of ideas and talents that are introduced by a more diverse workforce, they operate in social environments that are increasingly more suspicious and even hostile to people who look and behave differently from the mainstream. In the public and political spheres, there is increasing talk about erecting walls, both physically and metaphorically. These walls refer to strengthening borders and national identities on the one hand, and to creating restrictions in access to rights and privileges, on the other hand, between groups such as members of racial or ethnic minorities, sexual and gender identity minorities, the poor and the affluent, and immigrants and nonimmigrants. In some countries the arena for intergroup hostilities is political and affects people's livelihoods and sense of community; in others—and more tragically—they result in military actions that take people's lives and destroy communities and cultures. There is more work to be done in order to remove barriers of misunderstandings, miscommunications, and suspicion in order to create more inclusive organizations and more inclusive societies. The increased recognition that inclusion is not only the right thing to do but also carries great benefits for individuals, organizations, and societies at large represents a ray of hope.

My original quest to examine and understand key diversity experiences in today's global society has led to interviews with employees and managers around the globe, several research projects, and three international conferences—all culminating in this book. When I began my research, I was intrigued by three things: First, the original concept of inclusion that emerged from my interviews with employees and leaders at all levels of the organization in my initial qualitative studies was quite new in the context of diversity, and there was no research—let alone any measures for assessment—at the time. This was the impetus for my work and for generating specific measures for diversity and for inclusion, measures that have since been used rather extensively by other researchers in the field (see Chapter 17). Second, I was interested in the global aspects of diversity management and in what we could learn from research and practices in different countries. Initially, diversity was mostly thought to be a uniquely American specialization, and even the terms to describe diversity were anchored in the racial/ethnic groupings that were established by the U.S. Census Bureau (e.g., Caucasian, Asian, African American, and Latino). In contrast, this book takes a truly global view of diversity—from the definitions of the concepts (see Chapters 6 and 7) that could apply to any country or regional context; through the demographic, legislative, and public policy overviews (see Chapters 2–5); to the specific examples embedded in descriptive boxes throughout the book. And third, there was not much research to document the "business case for diversity" that was touted by pioneer practitioners in the field. The inclusive workplace model, unique to this book, provides not only a new way to conceptualize diversity management but is also backed with updated research (see Chapters 11–16) that demonstrates the benefits, as well as the limitations, of diversity policies and practices.

This fourth edition provides new and up-to-date information on both practice and research in each of the chapters. This includes updated global demographic trends of diversity, new legislation and public policies in different countries, and new case examples throughout the book. In addition, there are three features that are new to this edition. First, there is a new chapter devoted to inclusive leadership (Chapter 11). Second, this edition includes a chapter devoted to surveys and measurement tools to help organizations assess their baseline and progress to becoming more inclusive (Chapter 17). And third, the book examines research and practices that generate a climate of inclusion in organizations and includes distinguishing definitions of *climate of inclusion* and *climate of diversity* (Chapter 11).

Over the years that I have been studying workforce diversity, many people have helped me gain insight into diversity experiences around the world. Although the responsibility for the contents of this book rests solely with me, I am deeply thankful to those who joined me on this exciting journey.

I am indebted to the many people who agreed to participate in my research projects over the years, and who so generously shared their thoughts and their concerns regarding diversity. In fact, the realization that inclusion was key to understanding diversity in organizations came during the preliminary stages of a diversity research project that I conducted about two decades ago. I was invited to carry out a study on diversity in a large, high-tech company with headquarters in Southern California and business contracts all over the world. I approached the project with great trepidation because I felt that I lacked "a hook," a key construct or theme to provide the anchor for the study; I was wondering what was the common concern shared by people who were different from the organization's mainstream.

As a first step, I asked the company's management for permission to conduct some interviews. They agreed, and several interviews were scheduled with employees of diverse backgrounds at different levels of the organization. I was deeply touched by the interviewees' willingness to open up and tell me about their experiences, their thoughts, and their feelings. Some felt they were an integral part of their work team and the organization, whereas others thought that their coworkers, their boss, or their subordinates could not get past a certain characteristic that made them different. Whether the interviewee was a woman manager, an African American supervisor, a Korean American engineer, or a Latina secretary, their statements were similar.

Invariably, employees who were more included in the organization's decision-making and information networks were more satisfied, more committed to the organization, and more productive than those who were not. After several interviews with women, men, members of diverse racial and ethnic groups, as well as people with disabilities and members of diverse sexual orientations—many repeatedly telling me how they felt—it finally dawned on me: *Inclusion* was the key!

In the years that followed, I expanded my research to other countries and interviewed employees in several regions of the world. The theme of organizational inclusion guided my research and led to the development of the *inclusive workplace* model. My scientific work has also yielded two research measures that have been used extensively in diversity research in different countries and have been translated into several languages. I am thankful to the people who agreed to be interviewed and to the colleagues who collaborated with me on these projects.

I wish to thank the Rockefeller Foundation, particularly Susan Seckler and Susan Garfield, for their generosity in providing the Bellagio Award and inviting me to organize and lead a conference on Global Perspectives of Workforce Diversity. The discussions at the conference, held in the summer of 2001 at the Rockefeller Foundation's Villa Severloni in Bellagio, Italy, were inspiring. I wish to thank my dear colleagues who participated in the meetings: Manolo I. Abella, International Labour Organization (ILO), United Nations, Switzerland; Nancy J. Adler, McGill University, Canada; Cordula Barzantny, Groupe Ecole Supérieure de Commerce, Toulouse, France; Jae-Sung Choi, Yonsei University, South Korea; Philomena Essed, University of Amsterdam, The Netherlands; Brigida Garcia, El Colegio de Mexico, Mexico; Ellen Ernst Kossek, Michigan State University, United States; Alan D. Levy, Tishman International, United Kingdom and United States; Stella Nkomo, University of South Africa; Harriet Presser, University of Maryland, United States; Martha Farnsworth Riche, Farnsworth Riche Associates, Maryland, United States; Maritta Soininen, University of Stockholm, Sweden; Hou Wenrou, Renmin University, China; and John Wrench, University of Southern Denmark, Denmark.

I am also grateful to the Borchard Foundation for generously providing funding for a colloquium on workforce diversity in the United States and Europe. I am particularly thankful to Dr. Beiling, the director of the Borchard Foundation, and his wife, Mrs. Beiling, for so graciously hosting the colloquium at the Foundation's Château de la Bretesche in Brittany, France, in the summer of 2003. Both Dr. and Mrs. Beiling have generously shared with the participants their wisdom—accumulated during their world travels and fascinating experiences—and enhanced the group's discussions. A decade later, the Borchard Foundation funded a second colloquium to examine the contact between multiculturalism and diversity management. This time, our gracious host was Dr. Kristen Beiling and her family. Our colloquium has benefited greatly from her wise input and from her warm hospitality. I am very grateful to Mr. Alan Levy, chairman and CEO of Tishman International, for his important contribution to both the Bellagio and the La Bretesche colloquia, for so generously sharing his unique perspective on diversity, and for keeping all of us honest with his real-world wisdom. I also wish to thank my dear colleagues who participated at the La Bretesche colloquium: Manolo I. Abella, International Labour Organization, United Nations, Switzerland; Sheila H. Akabas, Columbia University, United States; Cordula Barzantny, Groupe Ecole Supérieure de Commerce, Toulouse, France; Lena Domilelli, University of Southampton, United Kingdom; Paul Kurzman, Hunter College, City University of New York, United States; Lawrence Root, University of Michigan, United States; Jeffrey Sanchez-Burks, University of Michigan, United States; Abye Tasse, PhD, Institut du Developpement Social, France; and Gill Widell, Göteborg University, Sweden.

I wish to thank Marilyn Flynn for her steadfast support of my research and scholarly work. I am especially thankful to Dnika Travis, who contributed to this project almost from its inception—for providing background research and helpful feedback. Her contribution was consistent and particularly valuable. I wish to thank Gary Bess for providing ongoing support and assistance with several of the diversity projects that led to this book and for assisting with various stages of the manuscript. I am thankful to Shunit Mor-Barak for initial edits of the manuscript and helpful comments on style and structure. Ralph Fertig and Jennifer Joseph provided helpful comments on the international legislation chapter. I am also thankful to doctoral students and research assistants who helped with various stages of the manuscript—Jan Nissly and Jim Fredo for their wonderful contribution to the various case studies; MinKyoung Rhee, Hsin-Yi "Cindy" Hsiao, Erica Lizano, and Ahraemi Kim for their valuable assistance with the second and third editions of the book; Katie Bess Strautman for her assistance with the third and fourth editions of the book; Rebecca Lengnik-Hall and Kim Brimhall for their assistance with the fourth edition; and the students in my graduate seminars on global diversity management over the years who cheerfully agreed to utilize drafts of the manuscript's first, second, and third editions as the course textbook and provided helpful comments.

I wish to thank the editor of the first edition, Al Bruckner, who saw the value of this project from its inception and provided support and valuable assistance throughout my work on the book. Al has since tragically passed on, and he is truly missed. I am thankful to the wonderful team at SAGE—Lisa Cuevas Shaw, the executive editor of the second edition, for her support, astute input, and patience; MaryAnn Vail; Diane Foster; Robert Holm; Patricia M. Quinlin, senior acquisitions editor, for her guidance and support for the third edition; Katie Guarino for her valuable assistance in the production process; and Megan Markanich for copyediting the third edition. For their guidance and support for the fourth edition I wish to thank the SAGE editorial team: Maggie Stanley, acquisitions editor; Katie Ancheta, eLearning editor; and editorial assistant, Neda Dallal. I also want to extend my thanks to the production team: David C. Felts, senior project editor, and Talia Greenberg, copy editor.

I also wish to thank the following reviewers: Stefano Basaglia, University of Bergamo, Bergamo, Italy, and Diversity Management Lab, SDA Bocconi School of Management, Milan, Italy; Marilyn Y. Byrd, The University of Oklahoma; Dana M. Cotham, University of Nevada Las Vegas; Andri Georgiadou, Hertfordshire Business School, University of Hertfordshire; Paul H. Jacques, Rhode Island College; Keith James, Portland State University; Alexia Panayiotou, University of Cyprus; Renee L. Roman, The Chicago School of Professional Psychology; and Debra M. Seeberger, Towson University.

My family has been supportive through the long hours of working on this manuscript, and for that, I am deeply grateful. I wish to thank my parents for being their wonderful selves and for their continued support. I sorely miss them both, my mother for her wisdom, selfless giving, insightful perspective on human nature, and endless love, and my father for his courage and tenacity, for instilling in me the confidence to do the right thing and for his unconditional love.

To my beloved children, Tomer and Shunit, and the wonderful addition to our family, Oz; I am thankful to you all for your constant love and support and for engaging in interesting conversations that helped me think through some ideas I was struggling with and the insightful discussions around the dinner table during our Shabbat and holiday celebrations. To Tamar, Doron, Limor, Yoel, Shir, Nir, Inbal, and Eden, I am so grateful that you are all in my life. And to Jennifer, Ori, Mikah, Leah, Joseph, Naomi, Shay, Tzameret, Shir-Yam, Yinon, Yarden, Jonathan, Ramit, Or, Aviv, Yarden, and Leah, and to the memory of our beloved Tali, who continues to inspire us all. To my aunts, uncles, and cousins on four different continents who exemplify a *close-knit global* family. I feel fortunate to have you all in my life.

Most important, I wish to thank my husband, Ysrael Kanot, for helping me stay focused and on track—even at times when the task seemed overwhelming—and for his continued love, support, and enthusiasm for this project.

A test bank, PowerPoint slides, and more resources for instructors are available at study.sagepub. com/morbarak4e.

Introduction and Conceptual Framework

士	Shi	Scholars
農	Nong	Farmers
工	Gong	Artisans
商	Shang	Merchants

W hat makes a successful manager? Chinese tradition divides human beings into four classes, each with its own unique qualities: the *shi* (scholars) are learned and contemplate vision and ethics, the *nong* (farmers) work the land and can provide for basic human needs, the *gong* (artisans) are creative and strive for beauty and excellence, and the *shang* (merchants) have strong ambition and a drive to succeed and to accumulate wealth. According to Chinese ancient wisdom, it is only when one can combine the qualities of all four classes—the vision and ethics of the scholars, the appreciation and respect for basic human needs of the farmers, the creativity and drive for excellence of the artisans, and the merchants' ambition to make a profit—that one can become a successful manager.

When I interviewed him for this book, Mr. Kyung-Young Park, the chief vision officer (CVO) of Harex,[1] relayed this wisdom, which had been imparted to him by the honorary chairman of his company, Mr. Seo. After a long discussion on diversity management and the outsider's misconception of the homogeneity of both Korean and Chinese societies ("there are many differences among us that foreigners do not see—regional, for example"), he concluded that managers could learn a great deal about managing diversity from that Chinese teaching.

Indeed, effective diversity management should encompass these four principles: (a) like scholars, managers must adopt an ethical learned approach to diversity, always aiming to "do the right thing";

(b) like farmers, they must respect their employees' unique characteristics; and (c) like artisans, they must introduce creative solutions as they strive for excellence in diversity management. These qualities, combined with the last principle—(d) ambition to utilize diversity to promote business goals and profitability for the organization—lay the groundwork for sound management. These interactive qualities—vision, ethics, respect, creativity, business goal orientation, and striving for excellence—are, in essence, *the heart and soul of this book.*

The Challenge of Managing Diversity in a Global Context

Successful management of today's increasingly diverse workforce is among the most important global challenges faced by corporate leaders, human resource managers, and management consultants. Workforce diversity is not a transient phenomenon; it is today's reality, and it is here to stay. Homogeneous societies have become heterogeneous, and this trend is irreversible. The problems of managing today's diverse workforce, however, do not stem from the heterogeneity of the workforce itself but from the unfortunate inability of corporate managers to fully comprehend its dynamics, divest themselves of their personal prejudicial attitudes, and creatively unleash the potential embedded in a multicultural workforce.

The global economy moves diversity to the top of the agenda. Immigration, worker migration (guest workers), and gender, religious, and ethnic differences continue to dramatically change the composition of the workforce. There is a growing demand for equal rights for these workers and for other groups like older workers, workers with disabilities or nonaverage body weight, gays and lesbians, and workers with nontraditional gender expression. Even without globalization, population projections suggest that the trend to a diverse workforce will be amplified in the coming decades. For example, due to consistently low birthrates and increased longevity, virtually all the more-developed countries will need even larger waves of immigrants just to sustain their current ratio of workers to retirees. At the same time, developing countries are experiencing an unprecedented growth in the numbers of young people. The combination of push-and-pull factors is moving all countries toward the same outcome: a more diverse workforce (United Nations, 2011c).

Most large corporations in today's global economy are international or multinational, and even those that are not rely on vendors to sell to customers located outside their national boundaries. For example, Virgin Group, headquartered in the United Kingdom, provides services in sectors including hotel/travel/tourism, media/entertainment, computer/IT/telecom, and transportation, and has main offices in Australia, Japan, the United States, Singapore, and South Africa. With total revenues exceeding £13 billion (or $21 billion), Virgin employs more than 50,000 people in 34 countries around the world (Virgin Group, 2012).

In the context of the globalized economy, most large companies fall in the category of multinational companies (MNC). The literature on international management includes several typologies of MNC, which are useful for understanding, explaining, and conducting empirical studies about the functioning of—and the interplay between—multinational corporations, the countries in which they do business, and the challenges of managing in a global context (Bartlett & Beamish, 2010; Bartlett & Ghoshal, 1998, 2002b; Harzing, 2000; Hordes, Clancy, & Baddaley, 1995; Rašković, Brenčič, & Jaklič, 2013; Rugman, Verbeke, & Yuan, 2011). The specific strategies employed by different MNCs to handle the global-local tension are often the determinant of the extent to which the company makes national differences a virtue rather than a hindrance (Edwards, 2010).

The seminal typology offered by Bartlett and Ghoshal (1998; Bartlett, Ghoshal, & Beamish, 2007; Berndt, 2014) is helpful as a general framework for understanding unique corporate cultures relevant to global workforce diversity. The first is *international corporations* with headquarters in one country and operations in one or more other countries. Their strategy is based primarily on transferring and adapting the parent company's knowledge or expertise to foreign markets while retaining considerable influence and control. This category of companies is characterized by an organizational culture primarily influenced by the home country, particularly regarding human resource management.

The second category is *multinational corporations,* in which the central corporate office still has the dominant decision-making power but each national or regional operation has some autonomy in business decisions. These companies develop strategic capabilities that allow them to be very sensitive and responsive to differences in national environments around the world. The company's culture is less unified and rigid, compared with those of international companies, and less dominated by one national culture.

The third form is *global companies* with headquarters that may be located in a specific geographic region but with a team composed of managers across the globe jointly making major business decisions. These companies are driven by their need for global efficiency and typically treat the world market as an integrated whole (Bartlett & Ghoshal, 1998; Bartlett et al., 2007). The corporate culture in this type of company is not dominated by any one national culture.

In addition to strategic alliances and a wide-ranging business span, companies must be able to utilize the diversity of their human resources to become truly global. This means that they maximize human talents regardless of where their employees are located or their national origin. Soliciting input from employees from varied backgrounds, with different educations and life experiences, can positively impact a company's external outputs (products and customer service) and internal processes (company culture, management policies) (Patrick & Kumar, 2012). As a first step to utilizing diversity, companies must learn the human side of the global company. The training, orientation, and cultural understanding needed for the management and employees of any company—national, international, multinational, or global—include the deep understanding of individuals who live in other national and cultural contexts and the ability to work within a global team framework.

Tensions Posed by Global Workforce Trends

As a result of unbalanced fertility rates in different regions of the world, global demographic trends are projected to create unprecedented workforce tensions. For example, the United Nations expects that the working-age population of the more-developed countries (as currently defined) will barely grow due to low fertility rates. In countries such as Germany, Italy, Japan, or the Russian Federation, the United Nations expects fewer people ages 15 to 64, based on population projections for 2025 and 2050 (United Nations, 2011c). Even if fertility rates increase in these countries, the current deficit in young people cannot be replaced, except by immigration. To maintain their current working-age population levels to the year 2050, these countries will need a few hundred thousand immigrants every year. Historically, these relatively homogeneous societies have been resistant to immigration, yet their current practices, induced by workforce decline, indicate a tacit acceptance of it. Other developed countries, such as the United States, will have more people in those ages but not enough to keep up with the pace of rapid population growth throughout the developing world as today's "youth explosion" in those regions enters the working ages.

Given these contrasting growth rates, today's more-developed countries can expect their share of the world's working-age population to drop from over 20% to 15% over the first quarter of the century (see Chapter 4 of this book). In contrast, working-age populations will continue to swell in developing countries as the substantial youth bulges produced by high fertility rates in earlier decades reach working age. Developing countries have seen a spurt in the size of young-adult populations in recent decades reflecting the widespread adoption of the public health knowledge and practices of the mid–20th century that have rapidly reduced mortality, especially for infants and youth. Although many migrants are fleeing upheavals and even violence in their native lands, most are seeking economic opportunities. With or without the transformation of economies in an increasingly global context, it would be difficult for these countries to accommodate such a surge of young adults into their labor force.

In most countries, people have become accustomed to having children survive, and fertility rates have declined. So over the next 2 decades, this bulge should be absorbed virtually everywhere except in Africa, which may contain more than one in four of the world's children in 2025 (United Nations, 2011c). Consequently, Africa may be the last frontier of "excess" labor available for low-wage competition in its home countries, or to fill jobs in developed countries that have fewer working-age people (see Chapter 4 of this book).

Women's increased presence in the formal labor force has affected—and will continue to affect—not only the workplace but also family and community life. Increasing numbers and shares of women in the workplace may be the most important component of diversity at the national level in most of the world. In particular, the gap between women's and men's rates has been narrowing in most regions (International Labour Organization [ILO], 2011). Women's share in the workforce grew significantly in Latin America, Western Europe, and other developed regions during the past several decades. Historically, only a small proportion of women could afford to remain outside the labor force, no matter what their family responsibilities, but they tended to work as unpaid family labor, particularly in agriculture or the informal economy. Even in countries where women have traditionally been discouraged from working outside the home, they came to make up an increasing share of the measured labor force. As a result, women's economic activity rates are increasingly similar around the world, except in regions where society constrains women's roles outside the home. Women's increased presence is particularly evident in economies where higher educational attainments are allied with higher earning prospects in the formal economy. Thus, a country's scale of development is a major determinant of women's presence in the workplace (ILO, 2011).

A particularly relevant aspect of current workplace trends is that women increasingly migrate autonomously as workers, and women migrants equal or outnumber men in some parts of the world. They are even becoming common in Asia, largely as a result of more women workers migrating on their own. Rapid economic growth and structural changes in the labor market that began in the 1980s and continued into the 21st century have motivated women to independently migrate. Women migrants' earnings now represent an important source of income for their families at home. Contract labor migration is the most rapidly increasing type of international migration in Asia, and women migrants are concentrated in such female-dominated occupations as domestic helpers, entertainers, salespersons, hotel and restaurant employees, and assembly-line workers.

The global economic trends that generate increased or decreased demands for workers in different areas at different times create tremendous opportunities as well as hardships for work organizations, individuals, and families. For example, the technology industry's boom in the 1990s created increased demand for skilled workers, and developed countries' generally strong economies during those years created a multinational, multicultural workforce that included many foreigners. Conversely, the global economy's downturn in the early 21st century, particularly the 2008 global financial crisis, has displaced many immigrants from their jobs and placed them in limbo. Unable to extend their legal stay in their host countries because their work visas were often linked to their original employer-sponsors, workers were forced to return to their countries of origin, where there were no jobs for them.

Global legislative trends banning discrimination against women, immigrants, minorities, and other diverse groups in the labor force have required employers in most democratic and quite a few nondemocratic countries to institute policies that ensure fair treatment of all employees. Some countries have introduced public policies stemming from the ideology of compensating population groups that have been discriminated against in the past. Employers are required to provide designated groups of applicants, such as racial and ethnic minorities and women, with a competitive advantage by actively recruiting them for open positions.

Disregarding these economic, demographic, and legislative trends can be devastating to companies, their employees, and the communities surrounding them. Companies unable or unwilling to change their policies and practices may suffer dire consequences. They may experience intergroup conflicts among their employees; they may limit their access to the pool of potentially talented employees; they may miss opportunities for creating alliances with business organizations; and they may be vulnerable to expensive lawsuits or government sanctions resulting in serious damage to their earnings, their public image, and their access to investment. Their culturally and linguistically diverse workers, who use languages other than the language of management, may even suffer safety impacts including work-related injuries or illnesses (O'Keeffe, 2016).

All signs point to increasing heterogeneity in the workforce, even as countries throughout the world struggle with hostile intergroup relations, prejudice, discrimination, and even violence. Gender, ethnicity, language, social class, religion, or other distinctions may define group membership, as each culture determines the context of social exchange and reward allocations. In Europe, for example, immigrants from North Africa and the former Soviet Union experience prejudice and discrimination in obtaining jobs. Worldwide, these group divisions contribute to exclusion of underprivileged groups such as women members of ethnic, religious, racial, and sexual orientation minority groups; older workers; and people with disabilities from positions of power in the workplace and create barriers to job opportunities and promotion. They also stifle the economic growth that could come from these groups of workers and directly affect long-term corporate earnings.

As a result of the increasing heterogeneity in the workforce, countries throughout the world are struggling with a powder keg of hostile intergroup relations in the workplace. The impact of prejudice and discrimination can be more than just detrimental to businesses—it can even result in violence; but effective management of workforce diversity can create tremendous rewards for businesses.

Diversity and Exclusion: A Critical Workforce Problem

One of the most significant problems facing today's diverse workforce is exclusion—both its overt practice, as a matter of formal or informal policy, and the perception by employees that they are not regarded as an integral part of the organization (e.g., Choi & Rainey, 2010; Insch, McIntyre, & Napier, 2008; Lonsmann, 2014; Mor Barak, 2014, 2015; Nishii, 2013; Shore et al., 2011). Though diversity groupings vary from one culture or country to the next, the common factor that seems to transcend national boundaries is the experience of social exclusion, particularly in the workplace. Individuals and groups are implicitly or explicitly excluded from job opportunities, information networks, team membership, human resource investments, and the decision-making process because of their actual or employer-perceived membership in a minority or disfavored identity group. Applicants and employees alike may be subject to stereotype threat (Casad & Bryant, 2016). Inclusion in organizational information networks and in decision-making processes has been linked to better job opportunities and career advancement in work organizations (e.g., Cunningham, 2007; Shore et al., 2011), job satisfaction (e.g., Acquavita, Pittman, Gibbons, & Castellanos-Brown, 2009; Bortree & Waters, 2008), well-being (e.g., Mor Barak & Levin, 2002; Vakalahi, 2012), job performance, and organizational commitment (e.g., Ailey, Brown, Friese, & Dugan, 2016; Cho & Mor Barak, 2008; Shore et al., 2011), all of which are related to employees' intention to leave and actual turnover (e.g., Buttner, Lowe, & Billings-Harris, 2012; Mor Barak, Levin, Nissly, & Lane, 2006). Employees' experience of exclusion, therefore, may play a critical role in explaining the connection between the lack of opportunities for members of diverse groups and their discontent with their roles as employees in organizations. Work organizations, therefore, need to remove barriers to full participation of traditionally excluded groups such as racial, ethnic, and religious minorities; women; people with disabilities; those who are targets of weight bias "under-" or "over"-weight; and members of gender and sexual orientation minorities. They need to overcome social and economic tensions between majority and minority identity groups to become inclusive organizations. One way to combat exclusion, and move beyond merely "managing diversity," is for the work organization to create an inclusive climate (Nishii, 2013), resting on a foundation of fairly implemented employment practices and policies that eliminate bias, thereby flattening out perceived status levels among groups. The implications are far-reaching, as work organizations represent opportunities to bridge understanding and tolerance among peoples from around the globe.

Recent unprecedented global demographic trends have created ethnically diverse work environments that are often the backdrop for hostile relations, discrimination, and even hate crimes. If managed well, however, these differences could lead to increased harmony among the groups involved (e.g., Pettigrew & Tropp, 2006; Stotzer & Hossellman, 2012). In addition to race, gender, and social class that cut across different cultures as determinants of exclusion, other characteristics like ethnicity, language, or religion may define group membership, as each culture determines the context of social exchange and reward allocation (Hofstede, Hofstede, & Minkov, 2010). Worldwide, these group divisions contribute to exclusion of group members from positions of power in the workplace and create barriers to job opportunities and promotion.

On a global scale, a gradual shift has been taking place in research and theory development related to diversity, social identity, and multiculturalism in the 21st century. More cross-national collaborations have been taking place, creating a conversion of ideas, concepts, and theoretical formulations from different regions and national contexts around the world. Prior to this shift, the research and scholarly work on individual and intergroup differences in the workplace has largely been disjointed. Although there were similarities in areas of research (e.g., gender and intergroup relationships), they were often examined under different frameworks and using different terminology. Broadly speaking, social psychological theories regarding diversity, social identity, and intergroup relations have been developed primarily in two locations: North America and Western Europe. Beyond these two regions, little or no attention has been paid to issues of exclusion in the workplace. In a review of the workforce diversity literature, Jonsen, Maznevski, and Schneider (2011) concluded that the diversity research field itself is not very diverse. They note that there are not enough studies analyzing diversity at the organizational (rather than personal) level, not enough studies addressing a variety of cultural contexts in real-life organizations (rather than artificially constructed ones), and that conceptual frameworks guiding existing studies are dominated by U.S.-centric research.

Research into workforce diversity hailing from different regions of the world often uses different terminology and may not even use the word *diversity*. For example, European scholars and those from regions other than North America who publish in this area often identify their work under titles such as "gender studies," "demography of the workforce," "labor migration," and "guest workers." The difference has been more than a semantic preference and seems to have stemmed from different perspectives and worldviews. North American researchers have focused on diversity of the workforce (e.g., gender, racial, and ethnic differences), which emanated from the region's historical role in absorbing immigrants and a value system rooted in equal employment opportunity (EEO), antidiscrimination, and fairness paradigms. Their studies focus on the discrepancies between the ideals and realities of the traditional EEOs, antidiscrimination, and fairness paradigms in the dynamic and fast-changing American society. European research has centered on multiculturalism, immigration, worker migration, and gender work roles, and the inherent social and emotional difficulties in integrating immigrants and women into each country's relatively stable social fabric and gender roles. Their studies have focused on the social and emotional difficulties inherent in integrating immigrants and women into each country's relatively stable social fabric and gender roles. The increased movement of individuals and groups across national boundaries has triggered debates among European countries as well as in other regions of the world regarding the multicultural nature of their societies (Bertossi, 2010). Beyond these two regions—North America and Europe—little or no attention has been paid to issues of exclusion in the workplace, perhaps because jobs have been scarce for dominant groups as well. There is clearly a need to bridge this gap and develop a comprehensive knowledge base.

Within the organizational context, I have conceptualized the inclusion-exclusion construct as a continuum of the degree to which individuals feel a part of critical organizational processes, such as access to information, connectedness to coworkers, and ability to participate in and influence the decision-making process (Mor Barak, 2000b, 2011; Mor Barak & Cherin, 1998; Mor Barak et al., 2006). The importance of the inclusion-exclusion experience has its historical roots in basic human needs, and thus the employee's experience is the measure of a work organization's success at becoming a truly global company. Because people have always depended on one another for their livelihood and needed to work together in order to acquire food, shelter, and clothing, social inclusion has had an important survival function through the ages and across cultures (Baumeister & Leary, 1995; Leary & Baumeister, 2000; MacDonald & Leary, 2005; Vohs & Baumeister, 2010).

Research on organizational demography indicates that being in the minority has significant effects on individuals' affective experiences in the workplace, including feelings of isolation and lack of personal efficacy in team and in one-on-one relationships (Barlow, Louis, & Terry, 2010; Lopez, Hodson, & Roscigno, 2009; Mor Barak et al., 2006). Milliken and Martins (1996) indicated a strong and consistent relationship between diversity in gender, ethnicity, and age and exclusion from important workplace interactions. One of the most frequently reported problems faced by women and minorities in organizational settings is their limited access to, or exclusion from, informal interaction networks (Ely & Thomas, 2001; Gray, Kurihara, Hommen, & Feldman, 2007; McDonald, 2011; McDonald, Lin, & Ao, 2009). These networks allocate a variety of instrumental resources that are critical for job effectiveness and career advancement, as well as expressive benefits such as social support and friendship (Gray et al., 2007; Ibarra, 1993; McDonald, 2011).

The Inclusive Workplace Model

This book presents a comprehensive model for diversity management utilizing the inclusive workplace model (Mor Barak, 2000b, 2005, 2014). Work organizations need to expand their notion of diversity to include, in addition to the organization itself, the larger systems that constitute its environment. Viewed from an ecological and systems perspective (Ashford, LeCroy, & Lortie, 2009), the notion of organizational inclusion is utilized as a focal point for understanding and managing workforce diversity. The concept of the inclusive workplace presented here and elaborated on in later chapters refers to a work organization that accepts and utilizes the diversity of its own workforce—while also being active in the community, in state and federal programs that support immigrants, women, the working poor, and other disadvantaged groups—and that collaborates across cultural and national boundaries (Mor Barak, 2000b).

The inclusive workplace is defined as one that

- Values and utilizes individual and intergroup differences within its workforce
- Cooperates with, and contributes to, its surrounding community
- Alleviates the needs of disadvantaged groups in its wider environment
- Collaborates with individuals, groups, and organizations across national and cultural boundaries

Valuing and utilizing individual and intergroup differences within the organization's workforce refers to the organization's relations with its own employees. Whereas an exclusionary workplace is based on the perception that all workers need to conform to preestablished organizational values and norms (determined by its "mainstream"), the inclusive workplace is based on a pluralistic value frame that respects all cultural perspectives represented among its employees. It will strive to constantly modify its values and norms to accommodate its employees (see Box 1.1 for an example).

Box 1.1

HAI HA-KOTOBUKI JOINT VENTURE (VIETNAM): PROGRAMS FOR INCLUSION WITHIN THE COMPANY

Hai Ha-Kotobuki, a joint venture company between Vietnamese corporation Vinataba and the Kotobuki Group of Japan, is a food manufacturing company located in Hanoi, Vietnam. Hai Ha-Kotobuki produces candy, cookies, and fresh cakes for sale in Vietnam and other Asian countries, including Japan, Singapore, China, Russia, and Mongolia (Hai Ha-Kotobuki, 2012; Vietnam Business Forum, 2013). The company was one of two businesses selected to partner with the Vietnam Chamber of Commerce and Industry, CARE International, and the National AIDS Committee in a joint project to promote HIV/AIDS prevention and control. With the support of top management and the involvement of a large number of company staff, Hai Ha-Kotobuki developed an HIV/AIDS workplace policy that included implementing prevention programs, confidential testing and nondisclosure of results, discrimination prevention, flexible work conditions for staff with HIV, and care responsibility for staff with HIV (Pramualratana & Rau, 2001). Employees were surveyed regarding their knowledge of HIV/AIDS; staff (including all supervisors and managers) were trained; and equal opportunity programs were implemented to ensure nondiscrimination of HIV staff, equal access to all company benefits, and flexible work conditions (Asian Business Coalition on AIDS, 2003). As a result of this collaboration, the company enjoyed reputational benefits. As noted by its deputy director, "instilling public trust in a company's quality products and the procedures involved in providing the product to the public is vital to our success" (World Bank, 2012).

Cooperating with, and contributing to, local community refers to the organization's sense of being an integral part of its surrounding community, regardless of whether it derives profits from local institutions and stakeholders. An exclusionary workplace misses the connection between profits and its community because it focuses solely on its responsibility to its financial stakeholders. An inclusive workplace, by contrast, maintains a dual focus, simultaneously intrinsic and extrinsic, that comes from acknowledging its responsibility to the wider community (see Box 1.2 for an example).

Box 1.2

THE PORT AUTHORITY OF NEW YORK (UNITED STATES): PROGRAMS FOR THE HOMELESS IN THE LOCAL COMMUNITY

The Port Authority of New York and New Jersey is an agency that runs many diverse transportation-related facilities such as bus stations and the New York airports. The rising number of homeless people at the Port Authority's facilities caused increasing problems for the delivery of quality transportation services, as well as for its image (Harshbarger, 2015; Port Authority of New York and New Jersey, 2004). The Port Authority took action in 1988 by forming a homeless project team and spending $2.5 million to fund homeless centers. Since 1997, the program has provided assessment and referral services to homeless people through a program located in the midtown bus terminal known as Operation Alternative. The agency, in partnership with Urban Pathways, created the Open Door Center, located across from the Port Authority bus terminal, to provide food, shelter, and social services to homeless people. Outreach teams assist individuals in need along the Sixth Avenue corridor in Port Authority Trans-Hudson Corporation (PATH) train stations from 33rd Street to Christopher Street. Homeless individuals tend to gravitate to these stations because they are warm and clean. Members of the outreach team creatively engage many of these people and divert them from the station by providing transportation to drop-in centers, shelters, hospitals, and other appropriate facilities. Renewing the Port Authority's commitment to Operation Alternative in 2014 (Strunsky, 2014), police offer homeless people on-premises medical care and counseling, as well as placement services provided by the Bowery Residents' Committee, a nonprofit partner (Harshbarger, 2015). Port Authority police have been trained to interact sensitively and compassionately with homeless people in their facilities, and to contact the PATH team to assist them with engaging the person in need and transporting him or her to the appropriate facility (Urban Pathways, 2012b). The drop-in centers provide comprehensive services to homeless people and were the recipient of the 1999 Governor's Exemplary Community Service Award (Port Authority, 2000). As a result of this intervention, the homeless people in the community received much-needed food, clothing, shelter, medical care, and counseling, and the Port Authority of New York was able to provide better services to its customers and improve its image.

Alleviating the needs of disadvantaged groups in the organization's wider environment refers to the values that drive organizational policies with regard to the disenfranchised (e.g., the working poor and former welfare recipients). The exclusionary workplace views these groups as disposable labor, but the inclusive workplace perceives them as a potentially stable and upwardly mobile labor force (see Box 1.3 for an example).

Box 1.3

DELTA CAFÉS (PORTUGAL AND EAST TIMOR): PROGRAMS FOR DISADVANTAGED GROUPS

The Delta Cafés Group, an MNC based in Campo Maior, Alentejo, Portugal, is the Portuguese market leader for coffee, holding 48% of the market share and generating revenues of 160 million euros (World Business Council for Sustainable Development, n.d.). Founded in 1961, the company is one of the leading coffee distributors on the Iberian Peninsula, and in 2015 was named a finalist of the European Business Awards (EBA) in the import/export category. Its efforts on social accountability and community development started in 2000 when the government of East Timor approached Delta about establishing operations in the newly independent country to revitalize its dilapidated coffee industry and to help alleviate the pervasive poverty there. Delta saw the opportunity to develop new markets and help rebuild East Timor's economy while generating revenues. Working with the government of East Timor, the United Nations, and local nongovernmental organizations (NGOs), Delta began holding capacity-building seminars with local farmers and contracted to purchase the coffee grown—at a fair market price (Caria, 2012). In 2002, the Council on Economic Priorities Accreditation Agency honored Delta Cafés with its first "social responsibility" award for the company's partnership efforts, including work with the ILO, Human Rights Universal Statement, and United Nations Convention on the Rights of the Child (European Business Awards, 2011). Delta has since launched Delta Q, a high-quality capsulated coffee product that has resulted in Delta Cafés receiving several awards, including the 2011 European Business Award for one of the top 10 country representatives in Portugal. Multiple interviews with those who were responsible for the development of the Delta Q product indicate the company's commitment to its core values—integrity, sustainability, loyalty, quality, solidarity, social responsibility, and humility (Caria, 2012). The new brand has been profitable since 2007 and currently represents 14% of the company's annual revenue.

Finally, *collaborating with individuals, groups, and organizations across national and cultural boundaries* refers to the organization's positions with respect to international collaborations. The exclusionary workplace that operates from a framework of one culture is competition-based, and is focused on narrowly defined national interests. The inclusive workplace sees value in collaborating across national borders, in being pluralistic, and in identifying global mutual interests (see Box 1.4 for an example).

There is accumulating research evidence that such corporate practices constitute good business. The benefits include (a) cost savings due to lower turnover of employees, less absenteeism, and improved productivity; (b) winning the competition for talent by being more attractive to women, minority groups, and diverse workforce members; (c) driving business growth by leveraging the many facets of diversity, such as marketing more effectively to minority communities or to senior citizens; (d) improved corporate image, with a positive impact on the company's stock valuation; and (e) reaping the benefits of an increasingly global marketplace by employing workers from different nationalities in or outside their native countries (see the chapters 12-16 for specific research examples).

Box 1.4

LA SIEMBRA (CANADA): INTERNATIONAL INCLUSION PROGRAMS

La Siembra Co-op was incorporated in 1999 in Ottawa, Canada, as the first North Americanimporter, manufacturer, and distributor of fair trade cocoa products (La Siembra, 2015; La Siembra Co-Operative, n.d.-a; "25 Years, 25 Success Stories," n.d.). The company's products—hot chocolate, cocoa powder, sugar, and chocolate bars—are marketed under the name Cocoa Camino in natural health food and grocery stores in Canada and the United States. It was founded on the principles of equal and respectful trade relations, fair wages and working conditions, environmentally sound farming practices, and education. La Siembra sources its products from co-operatives of traditional family farms in the Dominican Republic and Paraguay. La Siembra notes that each of its suppliers is formally registered with the Fair Trade Labeling Organization (FLO) as a fair trade producer and that the organization works closely with its partner co-operatives of family farmers to ensure transparency, respect, and fairness in the supply chain (La Siembra, 2015). Furthermore, La Siembra has received fair trade certification by Fairtrade Canada, formerly TransFair Canada, the independent Canadian fair trade certification organization (Fairtrade Canada, n.d.; La Siembra Co-Operative, n.d.-d). The certification assures consumers that farmers receive higher than world market prices for their goods, often including organic and social premiums used for development programs (La Siembra Co-Operative, n.d.-d). Consumers and corporate peers alike have recognized the company's efforts. La Siembra received the 2002 Socially Responsible Business Award at the 18th Annual Natural Products Expo held in Washington, D.C. (New Economy Development Group, 2006), and in 2008 and 2009, La Siembra was named to WorldBlu's List of Most Democratic Work Places (La Siembra Co-Operative, n.d.-b). The United Nations declared 2012 the International Year of Cooperatives. Throughout the year, La Siembra has participated in many activities put on by the Canadian Co-operative Association (CCA), through CCA's strategic plan. La Siembra has played an important role in the co-operative movement (La Siembra Co-Operative, n.d.-b). Additional awards for La Siembra include Trader of the Year for 2015 and Co-operative of the Year for 2012 and 2013 by Fairtrade Canada.

Source: La Siembra (Canada) Ontario Co-operative Association, 2003

Conceptual Framework and Organization of the Book

For too long, the question posed by management in organizations has been "*Is* diversity good for business?" The conceptual model presented in this book suggests reframing the question to "*How* can diversity work for organizations and for their employees and their communities?" Successful and seamless inclusion is the desired outcome of good diversity management. Achieving this goal, however, is not an undertaking for companies and employers alone. It needs to be reinforced through national and international laws and policies, and infused into global workforce cultures, top to bottom, via educational efforts to increase tolerance and cross-cultural understanding, and through media attention to intergroup collaborations. This broad perspective guides the conceptual framework for the book (see Figure 1.1).

FIGURE 1.1 ● Conceptual Framework and Organization of the Book		
Macro Dimensions	*Micro/Mezzo Dimensions*	*Practice Applications*
Demographic trends	Individual and group aspects of diversity	Diversity management paradigms
Legislation	Theoretical explanations of intergroup relations	The inclusive workplace model
Public policy	Culture and communication	Practice applications for the model
Global economy	Interpersonal cross-cultural relations in the workplace	Cases for discussion

The book is divided into three parts. Part I presents the macro, or large-systems, perspective on diversity: global demographic trends, legislation, and public policies in different countries. Part II presents the micro/mezzo—or smaller systems—perspective on diversity: how diversity is defined in different countries, theories explaining diversity, interpersonal and cultural aspects, and communication in the workplace. Finally, Part III presents solutions or practical intervention approaches: diversity paradigms, the inclusive workplace model, and case studies demonstrating how corporations in different parts of the world can apply the model.

This book utilizes an interdisciplinary approach, drawing from different bodies of knowledge to provide the demographic, legislative, and theoretical background for understanding diversity from an international perspective. Applying the previously stated principles, the book also offers practical guidelines that can help managers generate an organizational culture that welcomes and utilizes the diversity of their workforce and ultimately create the inclusive workplace.

Summary and Conclusion

The focus on diversity in global business today is quite different from civil rights legislation and from affirmative action programs. It is no longer only a matter of righting past wrongs or of trying to achieve equality of opportunity by addressing underrepresentation of specific groups. Emerging diversity efforts are focused on managing and engaging a company's heterogeneous workforce in ways that give it a competitive advantage. The gradual expansion of diversity compliance may be viewed as a continuum: EEO legislation means that it is against the law to discriminate, affirmative action programs mean that companies need to take positive steps to ensure equal employment and promotion opportunities, and diversity programs are proactive and aim to achieve a diverse and heterogeneous workforce that values employee differences—and contributes to the local as well as global community.

It is important to state that diversity programs without the foundation of strong legislation and sound proactive public policy may be fleeting. Often-used slogans such as "diversity makes business sense" and "diversity is good business" reflect a superficial acknowledgment of the necessity of diversity management. Although these phrases do suggest a useful and practical direction, their use often precludes consideration of ethical practices and major long-term organizational changes that may not be immediately linked to the bottom line. If left to the business world's interpretation of "what is good for business," this trend could disappear—as others have in the past—when businesses decide that practicing diversity management no longer aligns with their financial goals. Understanding the full range of practical benefits of diversity management is an important motivator for corporations to invest additional resources in employee development concurrent with their business development; but in addition, the scholarly and public examination of this multifaceted issue has to include the important dimensions of morality, ethics, fairness, and respect for human dignity.

Given the growing acceptance of (though not necessarily adherence to) human rights as a value around the globe, promoting fairness and economic advancement for disenfranchised members of society is perceived as the right and ethical thing to do. It also constitutes good business by giving corporations a competitive advantage in recruitment, in customer relations, in marketing to the growing minority communities with purchasing power, and in developing a positive corporate image that translates into corporate profits. To alleviate both social and economic tensions in society as a whole, and as reflected within the workforce, work organizations must learn not only to remove barriers but to actively encourage full participation of members of diverse groups in society.

The premise of this book is that work organizations must create and sustain a culture that is accepting of individual differences—and one that encourages greater involvement in community, national, and international affairs. In other words, they need to become inclusive organizations inside and out.

Note

1. Harex is a Korean-based, high-tech company that developed, among other things, an innovative gadget called ZOOP, which replaces credit cards, tollbooth operators, and bank debit cards.

The Global Context for Diversity Management

PART I

Diversity Legislation in a Global Perspective

Equality and Fairness in Employment

All human beings are born free and equal in dignity and rights.
They are endowed with reason and conscience and should
act towards one another in a spirit of brotherhood.

—Universal Declaration of Human Rights (Article 1), adopted by the United
Nations General Assembly Resolution 217 A (III) of December 10, 1948

The second half of the 20th century witnessed an unprecedented global trend in antidiscrimination and equal opportunity legislation that continued into the 21st century. A growing number of countries around the world have instituted legislation providing their citizens with wider protections against discrimination and workplace harassment. This trend began with the United Nations (UN) 1948 Universal Declaration of Human Rights, continued with the equal opportunity movement in the United States and Western Europe in the 1960s, and blossomed in the 1980s and 1990s with constitutional revisions and a multitude of laws protecting the rights of individuals of diverse backgrounds around the world.

In order to ensure adherence to employment laws and regulations, to avoid penalties, and to reap the rewards of compliance with local rules in these different national and cultural contexts, managers must understand the legislative and business-related social policy practices of countries in which they are doing business. Moreover, to practice in today's global economy, managers need a framework for understanding human rights that transcends individual national contexts. This chapter begins with a discussion of an international and overarching framework for managing workforce diversity that has its roots in the UN Universal Declaration of Human Rights. Next, it presents different antidiscrimination legislation in several regions of the world and some discrepancies between laws and common practices. Finally, we present some practical implications for international business practices.

The International Bill of Human Rights and Employment Rights

In democratic countries, legislation and social policy stem from a value system that is shared by a people and thus represents their collective wish to enforce these values. In order to examine diversity legislation from a global perspective, one has to look for an authoritative representative body that can speak to the value system of the majority of people on the face of the earth. The United Nations, with all its shortcomings, is the organization that comes closest to representing all people around the world. In an ideal world, this body would be composed of democratically elected governments of all world countries and thus be truly representative of all people. In reality, the majority of the governments that participate and vote in the UN General Assembly and its numerous committees are not democratically elected. This being so, a good place to start examining global values with respect to workforce diversity is still the UN International Bill of Human Rights[1] and its statements with respect to employment rights and equality in the workplace. Given the diversity of geopolitical interests represented at the United Nations, one could argue that where there is consensus on issues of human rights, these pronouncements represent minimum standards to which civilized countries should adhere.

The International Bill of Human Rights consists of the Universal Declaration of Human Rights; the International Covenant on Economic, Social, and Cultural Rights; the International Covenant on Civil and Political Rights; and the two optional protocols. The chart depicted in Figure 2.1 provides a graphic representation of the International Bill of Human Rights and indicates the articles that are relevant to employment.

The Universal Declaration of Human Rights, the first component of the International Bill of Human Rights, was adopted by the UN General Assembly in its Resolution 217 A (III) of December 10, 1948. The declaration consists of a preamble and 30 articles, setting forth the human rights and fundamental freedoms without any form of discrimination to which all men and women, everywhere in the world, are entitled. (For the complete declaration, see Appendix 2.1.)

Article 1 of the declaration (cited at the very top of this chapter) lays down the philosophy on which the declaration is based: First, the right to liberty and equality is the birthright of every human being, and it cannot be alienated; and second, human beings, as distinguished from other creatures, are rational and moral. For this reason, human beings are entitled to certain rights and freedoms that other creatures do not enjoy. Article 2, which sets out the basic principle of equality and non-discrimination with respect to human rights and fundamental freedoms, forbids "distinction of any kind, such as race, colour, sex, language, religion, political or other opinion, national or social origin, property, birth or other status."

The declaration assures every person, as a member of human society, specific economic, social, and cultural rights (stated in Articles 22–27).[2] These rights are characterized as indispensable for human

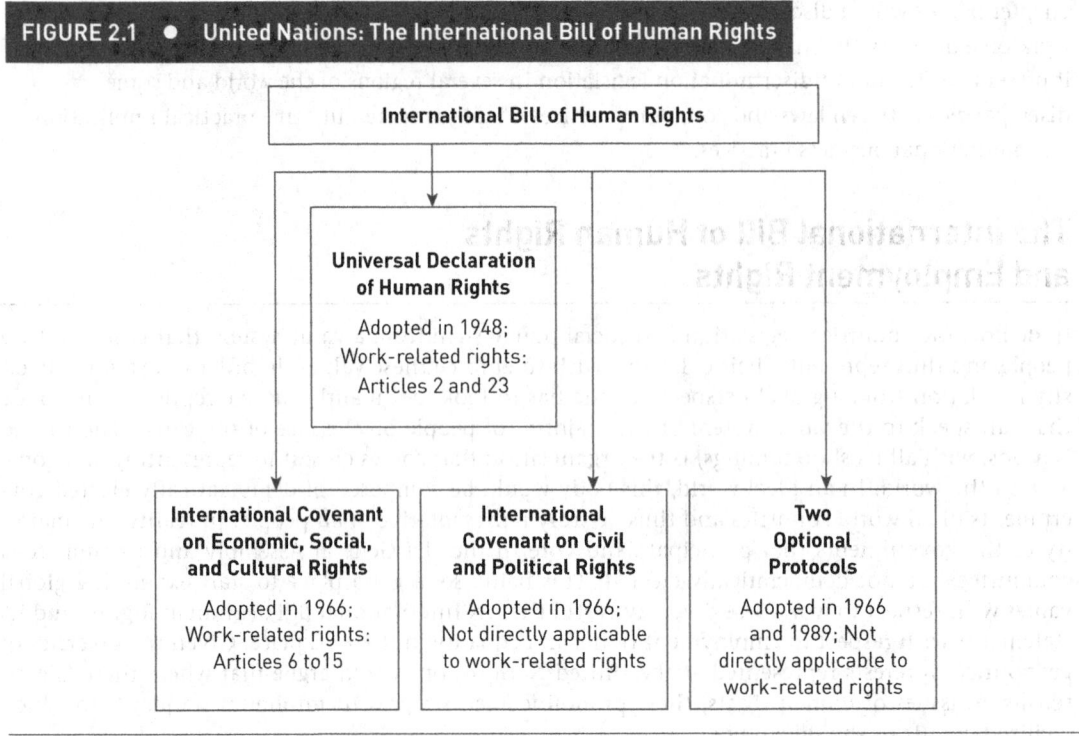

FIGURE 2.1 • United Nations: The International Bill of Human Rights

Source: Universal Declaration of Human Rights (1948).

dignity, and the Declaration indicates that they are to be realized "through national effort and international cooperation." The rights most relevant to employment include the following:

- The right to social security
- The right to work
- The right to equal pay for equal work
- The right to rest and leisure
- The right to a standard of living adequate for health and well-being

It is important to note that although the different articles under the declaration were designed to fit together harmoniously, there is potential tension between the articles that assure freedom of cultural and religious expression and those that guarantee equality, particularly as they apply to the workplace. For example, it is not uncommon in many cultures and religions around the world to have defined gender roles that specify behavioral expectations for women and men, not only within the family environment but also with respect to appropriate occupations and behaviors in the public arena. When these gender expectations create limitations on behaviors and communication patterns between men and women, they may challenge the principles of equality and fairness in the workplace. The debate over the ban on wearing religious attire in schools and in the workplace (the so-called "headscarf ban") demonstrates the potential tension between multiculturalism and human rights (McGoldrick, 2006; O'Niell, Gidengil, Cote, & Young, 2015; Vakulenko, 2007) (see Box 2.1).

Box 2.1

THE DEBATE OVER THE BAN ON WEARING OF RELIGIOUS ATTIRE AND RELIGIOUS SYMBOLS IN THE WORKPLACE

Historically, women in Turkey were prohibited by the Constitutional Court from participating in education and doing paid or unpaid work in public places while wearing a *hijab*, or the traditional religious head covering (Guveli, 2011). An example of how this impacted women was the case of Aysegul Yilmaz. Aysegul wanted to become a teacher after finishing college, but the 21-year-old student was not be able to do so while still practicing all elements of her religion. In Turkey, where Aysegul lives, it was illegal for Muslims to wear hijabs ("The Islamic Veil," 2011; Nelson, 2003). Predominantly Muslim, Turkey historically banned hijabs in schools, workplaces, and other public locations because of the principle of state secularism promoted by the founder of modern Turkey, Mustafa Kemal Atatürk, in the beginning of the 20th century (McGoldrick, 2006). For example, a female defendant was ordered to leave a Turkish court while her case proceeded because she refused to remove her hijab (Nelson, 2003). At Turkey's Ankara University, theology faculty failed 150 students who were not permitted to attend class because of their hijabs ("Theological Students," 2002). In a landmark case (ECtHR, 2004), the top European court of human rights set a precedent, determining that the ban on headscarves did not violate human rights. Leyla Sahin was a student at Istanbul University when she was refused access to written examinations and was not allowed to enroll in courses because she was wearing the hijab. The Strasbourg-based Grand Chamber European Court of Human Rights has upheld the ruling of the lower court that the headscarf ban in Turkey did not violate the rights to free-dom of thought, conscience, or religion guaranteed by an international human rights treaty. On February 9, 2008, the Turkish parliament passed an amendment to the constitution allowing women to wear the hijabs in universi-ties, only to have this amendment annulled by Turkey's Constitutional Court ruling on June 5, 2008, that removing the ban would run counter to official secularism (Birch, 2008; Immigration and Refugee Board of Canada, 2008). In 2010, after winning a referendum in September, the ruling AK Party supported students wearing the headscarf on university campuses. For the first time in Turkey's modern history, almost all universities across Turkey have per-mitted students to wear the headscarf on campus (Head, 2010). In 2013, Turkey amended its rules to allow women to wear headscarves in state institutions, with the exception of the judiciary, military, and police force.

Turkey is not the only country where hijabs, burkas, and other religious attire were or are prohibited. A number of other countries have also generated controversy in bans on wearing head coverings in public places (O'Niell et al., 2015). Furthermore, it is noted that national and international human rights organizations have criticized the ban as a human rights violation (Guveli, 2011). Similar bans are found in countries such as Belgium, Italy, Russia, Tunisia (which is also predominantly Muslim), and Germany, where hijabs are banned in schools in half of its 16 states (Browne, 2004; "German Courts," 2008; "The Islamic Veil," 2011, 2014; McGoldrick, 2006; Winet, 2012). In 2004, the French senate and parliament both overwhelmingly approved a law banning hijabs, yarmulkes (the Jewish skullcap), large crosses, the Sikh head cover, and similar conspicuous religious apparel (O'Niell et al., 2015; Richburg, 2004). France was the first country across Europe to ban women from wearing full-face Islamic veils in all public places, taking effect on April 11, 2011. Under the ban, any woman, French or foreigner, wearing a veil in public may be subject to a fine, and any person found forcing a woman to cover her face risks an even heavier fine ("The Islamic Veil," 2011; Leane, 2011). There are also different restrictions and various court rulings related to the ban on wearing the burkas and hijabs in other countries such as Italy, the Netherlands, Belgium, Great Britain, and Quebec (Head, 2010; Leane, 2011; O'Niell et al., 2015; Vakulenko, 2007).

In England, for example, a woman surgeon at Sheffield's Royal Hallamshire Hospital was confronted by another doctor for wanting to keep her headscarf on during surgery. The doctor claimed her headscarf contained blood from previous operations and would become a health and safety hazard. The woman refused to remove the headscarf and ended up walking out, requiring the hospital to find another person to do the surgery. The surgeon eventually left the hospital after an investigation backed the other physician's observations, and the

(Continued)

(Continued)

hospital enforced its strict dress code that religious headscarves are "excluded in areas such as theatre, where they could present a health and cross infection hazard" ("Top Doc," 2016).

Although opponents of these laws criticize them as limiting freedom of religion and religious expression, proponents claim that they promote a secular society and ensure freedom *from* religion in schools and in the workplace and therefore guarantee equality in the public arena. Some believe that banning the headscarf has hindered the opportunities for women to pursue advanced education, as many women choose (or are sometimes forced by their families) to forgo higher education because of these laws. This, in turn, could negatively affect the social and economic skills of women, as well as their social and psychological well-being. In addition, these laws might create barriers to women's full participation in society and make them rely on family members to support them (Guveli, 2011).

Opponents of these laws point to the restrictions on access to education and employment created by such bans, and the International Helsinki Federation for Human Rights, based in Austria, said it opposed the French bill because it believed it violated human rights ("Chirac on Secular Society," 2003; "The Islamic Veil," 2011). Most recently, approximately 2,000 women in Bosnia (a country with a more than 40% Muslim population) protested the headscarf ban in front of courthouses and other public institutions. The protest was in response to the court making a decision to ban "religious signs" in all judicial institutions. The headscarf ban in Bosnia continues to be condemned by religious leaders and Muslim politicians ("Bosnia Women Protest," 2016). Leane (2011) notes that these bans raise important questions regarding constitutional politics and legitimate social expectations of majority cultures, and that they would likely come to be seen in retrospect as incremental steps in breaching of minority religious and cultural freedoms. Defending the law, French president Jacques Chirac declared in his December 17, 2003, address to the nation: "Secularism guarantees freedom of conscience. It protects the freedom to believe or not to believe." He further stated,

> It is the neutrality of the public sphere which enables the harmonious existence side by side of different religions. Like all freedoms, the freedom to express one's faith can only have limits in the freedom of others, and in the compliance with rules of life in society. Religious freedom, which our country respects and protects, must not be abused, it must not call general rules into question, it must not infringe the freedom of belief of others. ("Chirac on Secular Society," 2003)

There has been a great deal of debate on the issues surrounding freedom of religious expression, female equality, secular traditions, and ethnic and religious minorities' assimilation and rights ("The Islamic Veil," 2011; Leane, 2011). In his highly publicized address to the Muslim world at the University of Cairo on June 4, 2009, U.S. president Barack Obama alluded to this controversy by stating,

> Moreover, freedom in America is indivisible from the freedom to practice one's religion. That is why there is a mosque in every state of our union, and over 1,200 mosques within our borders. That is why the U.S. government has gone to court to protect the right of women and girls to wear the *hijab*, and to punish those who would deny it. (*"Transcript,"* 2009)

In 2016, President Obama gave a speech at the Islamic Society of Baltimore in Maryland. He talked about the current state of the Muslim community in the United States: "[T]his is a time of concern and, frankly, a time of some fear. Like all Americans, you're worried about the threat of terrorism . . . you may also have another concern—and that is your entire community so often is targeted or blamed for the violent acts of the very few" (The White House, 2016). President Obama shared his values in protecting the right of women to wear hijabs and went on to talk about the importance of remembering America's core values, including the freedom of religion for all faiths (The White House, 2016).

Sources: (*The Washington Post*, 2009. Transcript: President Obama's Cairo Address to the Muslim World)

These declarations demonstrate different approaches to resolving the inherent conflict between Article 2—the basic principle of equality that forbids distinction of any kind such as race, color, sex, etc.—and Article 18—the basic principle of freedom of thought, conscience, and religion that ensures individuals' rights to manifest their religion and beliefs. The principles of secularism in the public arena (as in Turkey) and of freedom *from* religion (as in France) are used to justify a ban on prominent religious attire in schools and in the workplace, while the principle of freedom *of* religion (as in the United States) is used to justify the support for allowing prominent religious attire in schools and in the workplace. Different countries find their own balance among religion, education, and the workplace, and clearly, political considerations often influence these approaches (O'Niell et al., 2015; Smith, 2007).

Importance and Influence of the Declaration of Human Rights

The Universal Declaration of Human Rights is particularly relevant to the study of employment rights from a global perspective because no one country can serve as a model for other countries. The declaration is truly universal in scope, as it preserves its validity for every member of the human family, everywhere, regardless of whether or not governments have formally accepted its principles or ratified the covenants.

The International Covenant on Economic, Social, and Cultural Rights, which includes the employment-related nondiscrimination articles, entered into force on January 3, 1976. As of June 2012, the covenant had been ratified or acceded to by 164 states (United Nations, Human Rights, 2016):

Afghanistan, Albania, Algeria, Angola, Argentina, Armenia, Australia, Austria, Azerbaijan, Bahamas, Bahrain, Bangladesh, Barbados, Belarus, Belgium, Belize, Benin, Bolivia, Bosnia and Herzegovina, Brazil, Bulgaria, Burkina Faso, Burundi, Cabo Verde, Cambodia, Cameroon, Canada, Central African Republic, Chad, Chile, China, Colombia, Comoros, Congo, Costa Rica, Côte d'Ivoire, Croatia, Cuba, Cyprus, Czech Republic, Democratic People's Republic of Korea, Democratic Republic of the Congo, Denmark, Djibouti, Dominica, Dominican Republic, Ecuador, Egypt, El Salvador, Equatorial Guinea, Eritrea, Estonia, Ethiopia, Finland, France, Gabon, Gambia, Georgia, Germany, Ghana, Greece, Grenada, Guatemala, Guinea, Guinea-Bissau, Guyana, Haiti, Honduras, Hungary, Iceland, India, Indonesia, Iran (Islamic Republic of), Iraq, Ireland, Israel, Italy, Jamaica, Japan, Jordan, Kazakhstan, Kenya, Kuwait, Kyrgyzstan, Lao People's Democratic Republic, Latvia, Lebanon, Lesotho, Liberia, Libya, Liechtenstein, Lithuania, Luxembourg, Madagascar, Malawi, Maldives, Mali, Malta, Mauritania, Mauritius, Mexico, Monaco, Mongolia, Montenegro, Morocco, Myanmar, Namibia, Nepal, Netherlands, New Zealand, Nicaragua, Niger, Nigeria, Norway, Pakistan, Palau, Panama, Papua New Guinea, Paraguay, Peru, Philippines, Poland, Portugal, Republic of Korea, Republic of Moldova, Romania, Russian Federation, Rwanda, San Marino, São Tomé and Príncipe, Senegal, Serbia, Seychelles, Sierra Leone, Slovakia, Slovenia, Solomon Islands, Somalia, South Africa, Spain, Sri Lanka, St. Vincent and the Grenadines, Sudan, Suriname, Swaziland, Sweden, Switzerland, Syrian Arab Republic, Tajikistan, Thailand, the former Yugoslav Republic of Macedonia, Timor-Leste, Togo, Trinidad and Tobago, Tunisia, Turkey, Turkmenistan, Uganda, Ukraine, United Kingdom of Great Britain and Northern Ireland, United Republic of Tanzania, United States of America, Uruguay, Uzbekistan, Venezuela (Bolivarian Republic of), Viet Nam, Yemen, Zambia, and Zimbabwe

Despite this impressive number of states endorsing the covenant, quite a few either did not sign it or did not reinforce these principles in their national constitutions. For example, Saudi Arabia's constitution, adopted by royal decree of King Fahd in March 1992, includes no statement of equality related to gender, race, or ethnicity. Article 26 of Saudi Arabia's constitution declares, "The state protects human rights in accordance with the Islamic Shari'ah" (whose principles are different from those of the UN Declaration of Human Rights) (Constitution of the Kingdom Saudi Arabia, n.d.). It is important to note that the covenants were originally conceived as multilateral conventions, which means that they are legally binding on only those states that have accepted them by ratification or accession. However, the precedent set by *Filártiga v. Peña-Irala* (1980)[3] indicates that they are currently recognized as *law of nations,* a term that indicates an acceptance of international standards for judging human rights abuses, even in those states that have not accepted the covenants by ratification or accession.

Additional conventions relevant to workforce diversity include the International Convention on the Elimination of All Forms of Racial Discrimination, adopted in 1965; the Convention on the Elimination of All Forms of Discrimination Against Women, adopted in 1979; and the International Convention on the Protection of the Rights of All Migrant Workers and Members of Their Families, adopted in 1990.

Implementation

Having antidiscrimination legislation is an important first step, but to make a real difference in people's lives the laws must be implemented and enforced. Many countries around the world do not have adequate legislation; others have appropriate legislation but limited enforcement. In Australia, for example, current legislation has, to some degree, changed employers' views regarding discrimination in the workplace, but the legislation's impact on their actual practices is not very significant. Australian employers either do not fully understand the scope of the legislation or find ways to avoid its implementation (Bennington & Wein, 2000).

Often the obstacles for implementation are traditions and long-existing cultural practices that are discriminatory (for an example, see Box 2.2). One has only to examine the numerous reports of the UN Committee on Elimination of Racial Discrimination or those of the Committee on Elimination of Discrimination Against Women to realize that inadequate legislation and noncompliance are widespread. The following are a few informative examples:[4]

- The Committee on Elimination of Discrimination Against Women expressed concern over Russia's list of 456 occupations and 38 branches of industry that are banned for women because Russian authorities consider them "too arduous, dangerous or harmful to women's health, above all their reproductive health." The committee called on Russia to amend its labor code to include women in these occupations and industries, but also to promote and encourage the entry of women into these jobs by improving working conditions if they are said to be unsafe for women (The Committee on Elimination of Discrimination Against Women, March 2016).

- The Committee on Elimination of Discrimination Against Women published findings and recommendations following an extensive examination of Japan, Iceland, Sweden, Mongolia, the Czech Republic, Vanuatu, and Tanzania. For example, one of the recommendations for the Czech Republic party was to strengthen efforts to address gender stereotypes that perpetuate against women (March 2016). This includes adopting legislation to ensure prompt and effective action to violating any gender discriminatory rules and to raise awareness and provide education initiatives to both men and women, including employers.

- The Committee on Elimination of Racial Discrimination in its March 2002 meeting expressed concern over the difficulties experienced by Roma (an ethnic minority group popularly referred to as "Gypsies") in Lithuania in "enjoying their fundamental rights in the field of housing, health, employment and education."

- The Committee on Elimination of Discrimination Against Women expressed concern over women's rights in Nigeria (July 1998). The committee noted, "Although education and training promoted equality between men and women, certain cultural and traditional practices and beliefs remained obstacles to women's full enjoyment of rights . . . including in the areas of . . . women's labour."

- The Committee on Elimination of Racial Discrimination reviewed the situation in Nepal (October 1999), noting that although the caste system in Nepal has been abolished by law, nevertheless this system still functions and appears embedded in parts of Nepalese culture.

Box 2.2
EQUAL EMPLOYMENT LEGISLATION AND *DE FACTO* DISCRIMINATION

Case Example: Belgium

People of foreign background and their descendants, the "new Belgians," make up about 25% of Belgium's total population. Many of them (or their ancestors) were immigrants who came to Belgium immediately after World War II when workers were needed to fill labor shortages in the coal, iron, and steel industries. Workers were recruited from Italy, Spain, Greece, Morocco, and Turkey. The current population groups are the original workers, their descendants, and family members who were reunited with them (Smeesters, Arrijn, Feld, & Nayer, 2000). More recently, immigrants are coming from neighboring countries (e.g., Germany, France, and the Netherlands), but also countries in the Middle East, such as Iran and Morocco (Migration Policy Institute, 2012). There has been a rise of asylum seekers in Belgium over the last 3 decades, with the instability of countries like Iran and the former Yugoslavia causing people to migrate to countries like Belgium, which is considered relatively more stable and secure (despite terrorist threats and attacks like the March 22, 2016, bombings at the Brussels airport and metro station). Although Belgium has adequate legislation with respect to racial and ethnic discrimination, the UN Committee on the Elimination of Racial Discrimination (CERD) in its March 2002 meeting expressed concern about the increasing influence of racist and xenophobic political parties and "the difficult access of ethnic minorities to housing and employment."[5]

To address some of the UN CERD's recommendations, Belgian authorities considered awareness-raising training and initiatives as the best way to tackle discrimination. For example, specialized, compulsory training has been given to future juvenile court judges since 2007, and has proved to be the most effective way of raising their awareness of the various aspects of discrimination (UN Committee on the Elimination of Racial Discrimination, 2009). Yet concern over Belgium's (and other European nations') rise of the far-right and the xenophobic and Islamophobic trends persists, particularly after the terrorist attacks in Paris (2015) and in Brussels (2016), and the movements of refugees into many European cities (Shuster, 2016b).

An elaborate, classically designed study undertaken by the International Labour Organization (ILO) in the 1990s[6] provided some case examples that documented discrimination in employment in Belgium. The researchers carefully selected testers who posed as job applicants. The testers were university students who were matched on major job-related characteristics with one difference: One of the testers was of Belgian origin and the other of Moroccan origin. It is important to note that 40% of the total immigrant populations come from neighboring countries such as Italy, France, and the Netherlands, while Moroccan nationals make up 8% of all foreigners in Belgium. The Moroccan population is one of the largest groups of non–European Union (EU) immigrants in Belgium. The researchers report that the number of discriminatory cases amounted to 212 of 637 tests, constituting a discrimination rate of 33%. That is, in one third of the tests, the applicant of Belgian origin had a better chance of getting the job. The following example demonstrates the types of covert discrimination experienced by the testers.

(Continued)

(Continued)

Vacancy for a sales assistant in a fried-food outlet

Applicant of Belgian origin (Telephone)

The prospective employer inquired about the applicant's work experience and motivation, and then came the question of languages:

Employer: Do you speak German?

Applicant: Well, just a little—numbers . . .

Employer: But you really don't speak it? I'm sure you'll learn quickly. Come and see me tomorrow.

Applicant of Moroccan origin (Telephone)

The prospective employer started off by asking the applicant if he spoke German:

Applicant: I can count.

Employer: That's not enough, you know. You are not suitable.[7]

A similar field experiment was conducted in the United States, Germany, and the Netherlands to examine the effects of perceived race and ethnicity on the decision of employers to call job applicants for interviews (Bertrand & Mullainathan, 2004; Blommaert, Coenders, & van Tubergen, 2014; Kaas & Manger, 2012). The researchers of the U.S. study titled "Are Emily and Greg More Employable Than Lakisha and Jamal?" sent fictitious résumés to help-wanted ads in Boston and Chicago newspapers. To manipulate the applicant's perceived race, résumés were randomly assigned African American or White-sounding names. The résumés with the White-sounding names received 50% more callbacks for interviews, and the racial gap was uniform across occupation, industry, and employer size (Bertrand & Mullainathan, 2004). The German-based researchers found that a German-sounding name on a job application raised the average probability of a callback by about 14% compared to a Turkish-sounding name in a sample of 528 advertisements for student internships. The odds are even higher—24% increase in callbacks for a German-sounding name—for applications sent to smaller firms (Kaas & Manger, 2012).

Diversity-Related Employment Legislation

Most democratic and many nondemocratic countries today ban job discrimination that is related to gender, race, and ethnicity. Some go further to forbid discrimination based on other characteristics like age, caste, social class, sexual orientation, and disability. In fact, this trend is so widespread that a growing number of insurance carriers are now offering employment practices liability insurance specific to foreign countries' labor laws (Maatman, 2000; Talesh, 2015; Zweifel & Eisen, 2012).[8]

A number of countries were assessed primarily using the ILO's database[9] to determine the extent to which countries worldwide offered antidiscrimination or equal rights legislation that is applicable to employment and work (see Appendix 2.2: Global Antidiscrimination and Equal Rights Legislation Checklist of Protections Offered by a Select Number of Countries). The most popular forms[10] of antidiscrimination and equal rights legislation included protections based on gender or sex, equal remuneration, race, ethnicity, or country of origin, religious beliefs, physical disability, and sexual orientation, respectively. More than 88% of the countries reviewed provided at least one of these protections. Other categories of protections offered in some countries included the following:

- HIV status (Philippines, South Africa, and Zimbabwe) or health status (Cyprus)

- Marital status (Australia, Canada, Guyana, Ireland, Malawi, the Netherlands, Trinidad and Tobago, United Kingdom, and Zambia)

- Pregnancy (Australia, Iceland, Israel, South Africa, and United States)

- Aboriginal status (Canada)

- Political affiliation (Australia, Denmark, Malawi, the Netherlands, Northern Ireland, Zambia, and Zimbabwe)

- Family status (Canada, Malawi, and South Africa)

The following are some examples of legislation on specific issues around the world.

Broad-Based Antidiscrimination Legislation

In the United States, civil rights legislation, from the 1960s and later, outlawed job discrimination on the basis of sex, race, color, religion, pregnancy, national origin, age, and disability (Equal Pay Act of 1963, the Civil Rights Act of 1964, the Rehabilitation Act of 1973, Vietnam Era Veterans' Readjustment Assistance Act of 1974, Pregnancy Discrimination Act of 1978, Age Discrimination in Employment Act of 1967 [ADEA] and its amendments of 1978, Americans With Disabilities Act of 1990 [ADA], the Civil Rights Act of 1991, and the Lilly Ledbetter Fair Pay Act of 2009). Canada's labor legislation is similar to that of the United States in the areas of employment discrimination and employment equity (Block, 2007; Block & Roberts, 2000). Although the United States and Canada provide similar antidiscrimination protections, several differences exist. For example, Canadian laws extend to protect employees based on political beliefs and membership in organizations. The United States does not provide such protections for its employees except for membership in a union. Another difference is that the United States offers more extensive provisions to accommodate people with disabilities in employment, which is not as pervasive throughout Canadian jurisdictions (Block & Roberts, 2000).

Box 2.3
AFFIRMATIVE ACTION IN HIGHER EDUCATION: JUSTICE SCALIA'S CONTROVERSIAL COMMENTS AND BRAZIL'S UNIVERSITIES' QUOTAS

Abigail Fisher, a White woman from Texas, sued the University of Texas, arguing she was denied admission based on her race. Her case reached the U.S. Supreme Court because it touched on fundamental principles of affirmative action policies. In December 2015, during oral arguments in *Fisher v. University of Texas*, U.S. Supreme Court justice Antonin Scalia made some controversial remarks about African American students in elite colleges. According to the transcript, Justice Scalia said:

(Continued)

(Continued)

There are those who contend that it does not benefit African-Americans to get them into the University of Texas where they do not do well, as opposed to having them go to a less-advanced school, a less—a slower-track school where they do well. One of the briefs pointed out that most of the black scientists in this country don't come from schools like the University of Texas.

The justice went on:

Most of the black scientists in this country don't come from schools like the University of Texas. They come from lesser schools where they do not feel that they're being pushed ahead in classes that are too fast for them. ("Supreme Court," 2015)

These comments, which seem to suggest that African Americans should attend universities that are "less advanced" or "slower track," caused an uproar among lawmakers as well as minority groups and organizations.

Some believe that Scalia was referring to the "mismatch" theory popular among some critics of affirmative action. This theory challenges affirmative action in higher education by suggesting that minority students are harmed by policies, like affirmative action, that allow them to attend an elite school for which they may lack adequate academic preparation (Sander & Taylor, 2012). Yet critics of the theory contend that there is little to no evidence proving that mismatch has any effect on the educational outcomes of minority and nonminority populations, and that research provides mixed outcomes at best (Arcidiacono, Aucejo, & Hotz, 2013; Chingos, 2013; Kidder & Lempert, 2015).

Maatman (2015) referred to Justice Scalia's comments in the context of racial segregation and the civil rights movement of the early 1960s, claiming that forms of racism and segregation still exist today. During the early years, it was suggested that African Americans would do better if they went to "less advanced" or "lower quality" schools. For example, in *Stell v. Savannah–Chatham County Board of Education* (1963), lawyers working on the case opined there was scientific evidence demonstrating "differences in specific capabilities, learning progress rates, mental maturity, and capacity for education in general between Whites and African Americans," known today as "scientific racism."

While this is an example of the ongoing affirmative action debate at universities in the United States, similar challenges are going on in other parts of the world. In Brazil, there has been an ongoing debate about affirmative action policies, including university quotas aimed at recruiting Brazil's Black population. In 2003, the public University of the State of Rio de Janeiro (UERJ) reserved 40% of its admissions for people who declared themselves as "negro" or "pardo" (Kent & Wade, 2015). The measure triggered strong opposition, including pushback from the university community. It was reported that students were encouraged to apply for a racial quota (regardless of their race, hair, or skin color), taking into consideration that as Brazilians, they were likely to have ancestors that were Black. In some cases, these slots were filled by White students who self-identified as having a grandparent or other family member of Black descent. During the admission selection process, university staff would at times request a picture or conduct an in-person interview with the applicant, leading some applicants to have their applications rejected based on their appearance (Kent & Wade, 2015).

Legislation banning discrimination against women, immigrants, and minorities in the labor force exists in most European countries, though often in weaker forms when compared with the U.S. laws. All EU member states, except one, have constitutional provisions outlawing various forms of discrimination. The United Kingdom does not have a written constitution, but its general body of laws prohibits discrimination. As far as ordinary legislation is concerned, all EU member states' legal systems have regulations governing equal treatment and nondiscrimination in many facets of the employment relationship. Examples include access to employment, remuneration, and fair working conditions during employment

(European Union Agency for Fundamental Rights, 2014; European Union Agency for Fundamental Rights & the European Court of Human Rights, 2011). In addition to the two directives—Racial Equality Directive and Employment Framework Directive—the European Commission adopted in July 2008 a communication that presents a comprehensive approach for action against discrimination and for promoting equal opportunities (European Commission, 2016). The EU's fight against discrimination is based on taking actions to (a) improve knowledge of discrimination by raising awareness among populations regarding their rights and obligations; (b) support intermediary actors such as NGOs, social partners, and equality bodies to combat discrimination; (c) support development of equality policies at the national level and encourage exchange of good practices among EU countries; (d) achieve real change in the area of antidiscrimination through antidiscrimination training activities; and (e) push for business-oriented diversity management as part of a strategic response to a more diversified society (European Commission, 2016). The EU Council of Ministers' adoption of the directives on equal treatment of people regardless of their race and ethnic background in the labor force has signaled a trend of strengthening national legislation against racial and ethnic discrimination in employment. Some of the most advanced employment discrimination legislation in the European Union is that of the United Kingdom. It prohibits race, gender, and disability discrimination (Sex Discrimination Act of 1975, Race Relations Act of 1976, Disability Discrimination Act of 2006, Equality Act [Sexual Orientation] of 2007). It is important to note that there are no statutory limits on compensation awards for employment discrimination in the United Kingdom.[11]

A similarly long list of diversity characteristics is included in Fiji's legislation. Fiji, in its 1997 Amendment Act, denies unfair discrimination on the basis of "actual or supposed personal characteristics or circumstances, including race, ethnic origin, colour, place of origin, gender, sexual orientation, birth, primary language, economic status, age or disability, or opinions or beliefs" (Fiji Islands Constitution Amendment Act of 1997, n.d.).

Race—South Africa

South Africa's antidiscrimination legislation, Promotion of Equality and Prevention of Unfair Discrimination Act, 2000, is relatively new and broad (NATLEX, n.d.; Sheppard, 2012; Twyman, 2002). After a long rule by a tiny minority (White Afrikaners constitute only 13% of the population), the repressive apartheid regime was abolished in 1994, and the majority of the population (76% Blacks, 8.5% "Coloureds," and 2.6% Asians) were finally able to share the power in a democratic process. The new constitution, adopted in 1996, declares that the country belongs to all who live in it "united in our diversity." Chapter 2, section 9, reads as follows:

> (3) The State may not unfairly discriminate directly or indirectly against anyone on one or more grounds, including race, gender, sex, pregnancy, marital status, ethnic or social origin, colour, sexual orientation, age, disability, religion, conscience, belief, culture, language and birth.

There are two interesting elements of note about this declaration. First, the diversity list is far more inclusive than those of many other nations. Second, only "unfair discrimination" is banned, implying that it is possible to "fairly discriminate" and paving the way for affirmative action (discussed in the next chapter) (Constitution of the Republic of South Africa, 1996).

Gender—Japan

In Japan's traditional society, discrimination against women was widespread and, until 1999, its laws were not as restrictive as those of other developed countries. The first law in the country's history, introduced on July 1, 1972, to address gender discrimination in the workplace, was the "law respecting the improvement of the welfare of women workers, including the guarantee of equal opportunity and treatment between men and women in employment" (Law No. 113). Other ordinances regarding the implementation of the law were enacted in 1986, and the law was amended through Law No. 107 in June 1995.

Though it was hailed as breakthrough legislation, it was so vague that employers were able to continue their discriminatory practices. Without legal repercussions, the law required only that employers "do their best" to rectify and curtail any gender-based discrimination. Job advertisements in newspapers continued to post "male only" jobs, and women college graduates continued to encounter difficulties obtaining jobs with salaries and benefits commensurate with or equal to those of their male counterparts. Additionally, the law included "protective" articles, such as restricting women labor at night. The following case illustrates the issue:

In 1995, a student from India received a scholarship to study dental technology in Tokyo. Upon graduating from the program 3 years later, she looked for jobs in her field. Although she encountered no discrimination from employers because of her foreign origin, she was barred, as a woman, from applying for positions that required nighttime work.[12]

A 1996 landmark ruling on gender discrimination was a part of the impetus to change Japan's gender-related legislation. The case involved a group of women employees of the Shiba Shinyo Kinko Bank who sued over unequal wages and denials of promotions. The courts awarded the 13 plaintiffs 340 million yen (approximately $3 million). On April 1, 1999, a new piece of legislation, the Basic Law for a Gender-Equal Society, was introduced that rectifies the limitations of the previous law. Whereas the previous law required employers only to "do their best," the new law gave specific guidelines, such as (a) prohibiting discriminatory advertisements in the hiring process, (b) forbidding asking certain types of interview questions only to members of one gender (such as asking a woman if she plans to leave her job once she marries or has children), and (c) making it easier to start a mediation process (it can be initiated unilaterally, rather than bilaterally). The law also repealed some of the "protective" provisions that were included in the previous law, such as restricting nighttime labor for women.[13] In 2005, a new government post, the Minister of State for Gender Equality and Social Affairs, was created to advance issues of women's equality (Tompkins, 2011). Additionally, the 1986 Equal Employment Opportunity Law was revised in 2006 to encourage companies to eliminate existing gender gaps and discrimination in their workforce. In 2008, the headquarters for the Promotion of Gender Equality formulated the Program for the Acceleration of Women's Social Participation, which helps women achieve work–life balance, capacity-building, and awareness-raising to boost their participation in all fields. To spur fair treatment of nonregular women workers, the Act on Improvement, etc. of Employment Management for Part-Time Workers was revised and has been in effect since 2008 (United Nations General Assembly, 2009). However, despite the prolific equality legislation in Japan over the past couple of decades, progress in gender equality remains extremely slow compared to other industrialized countries. Between 1985 and 2008, the proportion of female full-time employees fell from 68.1% to 46.5%, which suggests that 53.5% of women in the workforce are part-time or contract workers, compared to only 19.1% of men (Blair, 2010). Another report suggests that about 55% of women are participating in the global workforce, with percentages much lower in countries like Japan. According to the most recent *No Ceilings* report (2015), the benefits of expanding women's economic opportunities in today's workforce are very clear. By expanding opportunities for women, the economy—including the gross domestic product (GDP)—grows, while poverty decreases. It is estimated that closing the gender gap in today's workforce will lead to average GDP gains of 12% by 2030 in many countries around the world (and as much as 20% in Japan).

Equal Remuneration—United States

Equal remuneration legislation requiring work organizations to pay women (and men in some countries like Norway) equally for their work was by far the most common form of antidiscrimination or equal rights legislation throughout the world. Taking equal remuneration legislation into account, in addition to anti–sexual harassment and equal rights legislation, more than 75% of the countries reviewed offer some form of protection based on gender. It is interesting to note that the first major legislation signed by President Obama, the Lilly Ledbetter Fair Pay Act, was aimed at closing a loophole in the U.S. legislation related to equal pay for equal work, making it easier to sue for wage discrimination. Lilly Ledbetter worked for 19 years at a Goodyear plant in Alabama and sued after she found that she was paid less than her male counterparts. The battle reached the Supreme Court, which ruled against her in a 5–4 decision. The high court's decision was based on the principle that a person must file a claim of discrimination within 180 days of a company's initial decision to pay a worker less than it pays another worker doing the same job. Ledbetter, who discovered this discrimination only after 19 years of working for the company, could not have possibly sued within this time frame. Under the new bill, every new discriminatory paycheck would extend the statute of limitations. President Obama said the bill "is by no means a women's issue, it is a family issue" (S. Davis, 2009; S. 181: Lilly Ledbetter Fair Pay Act of 2009).

In most countries, a woman cannot claim she has been discriminated against if she cannot fulfill reasonable physical requirements associated with performing a job, and this can often affect her level of compensation. For example, in the United States, a woman applied for a job as a prison guard and was turned down because she did not meet the minimum height and weight requirements. She brought a class action lawsuit under Title VII of the Civil Rights Act of 1964 alleging that she had been denied employment because of her sex, which is in violation of federal law. The U.S. Supreme Court affirmed a lower court's decision that the minimum weight and height requirement was reasonable and therefore not discriminatory (*Dothard v. Rawlinson*, 1977).[14] However, the Civil Rights Act of 1991 now provides that a practice that is seemingly neutral (such as setting height and weight limits) but has discriminatory impact (in this case, excluding women) violates the law. For example, setting a high school education as the employment requirement for custodial work is neutral on its face but can have a discriminatory impact on individuals who had limited access to education, and therefore would be unlawful under the Civil Rights Act of 1991.[15] More recently, the technology firm Microsoft was hit with a class action lawsuit regarding gender discrimination. A female employee was passed over multiple times for promotions, while her male counterparts, who were less qualified, were promoted. It was also found that there was a lack of diversity in Microsoft's employees, who were about 76% male. More significant, the executive leadership of Microsoft was 88% male (*Moussouris v. Microsoft Corporation*, 2015).

It is important to note that although in the majority of cases of gender discrimination women constitute the group that needs protection, the laws in most countries can be applied for men as well because they prohibit discrimination regardless of gender. For example, a 1982 U.S. ruling determined that a state university for women (Mississippi University for Women) could not constitutionally prohibit male students from enrolling for credit in its nursing school (*Mississippi University for Women v. Hogan*, 1982). Another example is the 2009 class action lawsuit on sex discrimination at Lawry's Restaurants, Inc. The company was required to pay over $1 million in fines for discriminating against males by only hiring women for server positions (Equal Employment Opportunity Commission, 2009).

Sexual Orientation—International

Much less common in international legislation is protection based on sexual orientation. A cross-referenced search of the UN ILO's database, NATLEX, and research conducted by the International Gay and Lesbian Human Rights Commission (IGLHRC)[16] shows that over 25 countries, such as Australia, Canada, Denmark, Germany, Ireland, Israel, the Netherlands, South Africa, Sweden, and the United States, offer such protections. The map illustrates the countries worldwide that provide antidiscrimination legislation based on sexual orientation (see Figure 2.2 for the map and Table 2.1 for a listing of sexual orientation legislation by country).

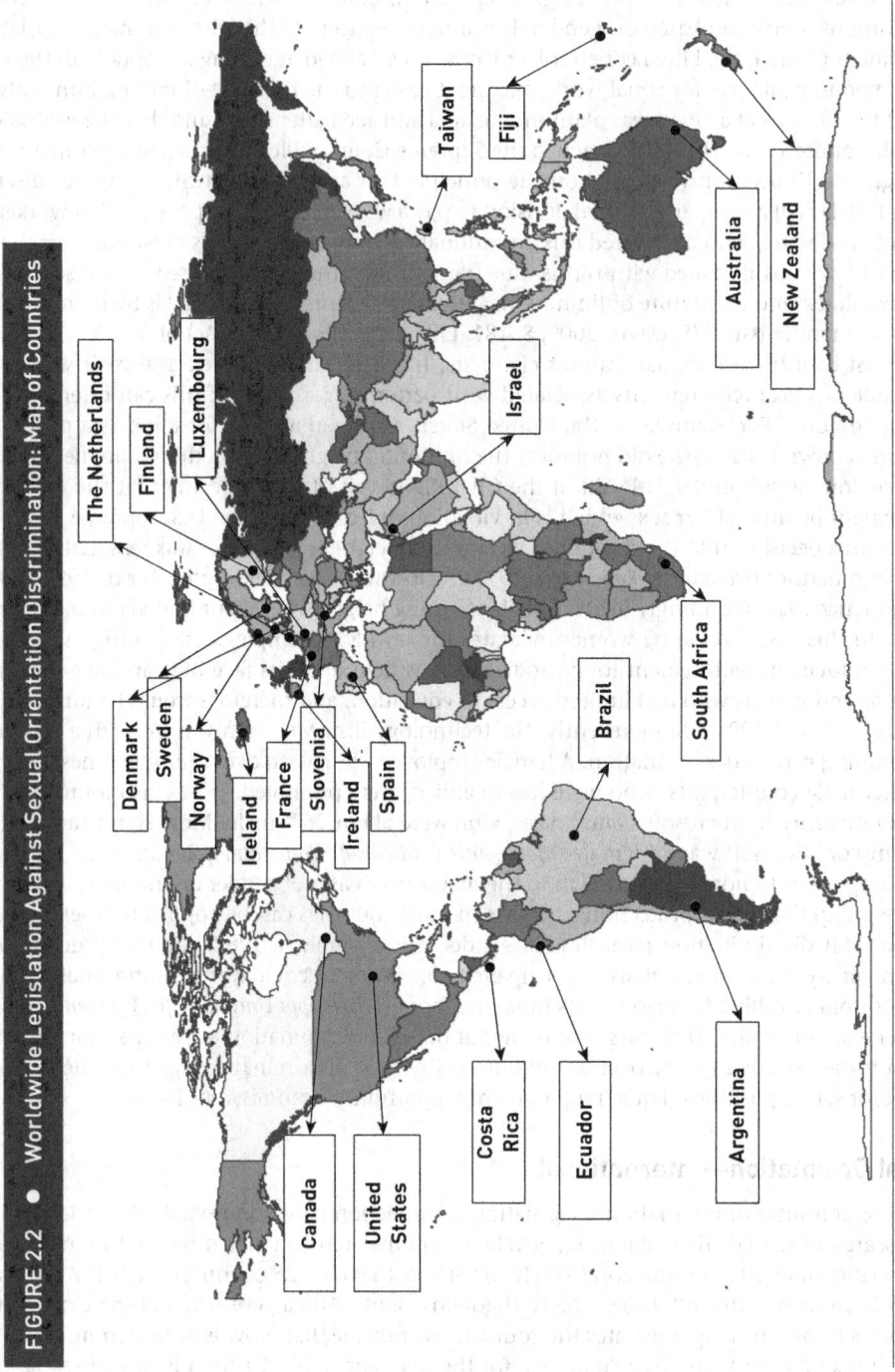

FIGURE 2.2 ● Worldwide Legislation Against Sexual Orientation Discrimination: Map of Countries

Taiwan

Fiji

Australia

New Zealand

Israel

The Netherlands

Finland

Luxembourg

Denmark

Sweden

Norway

Iceland

France

Slovenia

Ireland

Spain

Brazil

South Africa

Costa Rica

Ecuador

Argentina

Canada

United States

Sources: NATLEX, International Labour Organization (n.d.) International Gay and Lesbian Human Rights Commission [IGLHRC] (1999)

TABLE 2.1 • **Worldwide Legislation Against Sexual Orientation Discrimination: Listing by Country (Partial List)**

Country	Name of Legislation
Argentina	• Gender Identity and Health Comprehensive Care for Trans People Act (2012) • The Right to Gender Identity of People Act (2012)
Australia	• Equal Superannuation Entitlements for Same Sex Couples (2003), No. 13 • Equal Opportunity Act (Gender Identity and Sexual Orientation) (2000), No. 52 • State of Tasmania–Anti-Discrimination Act (1998) • Northern Territory–Anti-Discrimination Act (1996) • State of Victoria–Equal Opportunity Act (1995) • Capital Territory–Discrimination Act (1991) • State of Queensland–Anti-Discrimination Act (1991) • State of South Australia–Equal Opportunity Act (1984) • New South Wales–Anti-Discrimination Act (1977, 1998)
Austria	• Federal Act to Amend the Equal Treatment Act on Equal Treatment Commission and the Ombudsman (2008)
Brazil	• State of Mato–Constitution Article 10.3 (1989) • State of Sergipe–Constitution Article 3.2 (1989)
Canada	• The Canada Human Rights Act (1996) • Canada (British Columbia) Human Rights Act (1984) • Canadian Charter of Rights and Freedoms, Section 15(1) (1982) • New Brunswick Human Rights Code [Human Rights Code. 1971, c.8, s.1; 1985, c.30, s.3]a 3(1)
Costa Rica	• Law No 7771, Article 48 (1998)
Denmark	• Act No. 459 on Prohibition Against Discrimination in Respect of Employment (1996) • The Penal Code (1987), Act 626, Article 266
Ecuador	• Constitution (1998), Article 23
Estonia	• Equality of Opportunity and Treatment Act (2008)
Fiji	• Constitution, Section 38(2) of the Bill of Rights (1998)
Finland	• Act on Equality Between Women and Men (2005) • Non-Discrimination Act (2004) • Constitution (1998), Section 5 • Penal Code (1995), Chapter 47, Section 3 • The Penal Code (1995), Section 9

(Continued)

TABLE 2.1 ● (Continued)

Country	Name of Legislation
France	• The Code of Labor Law (1986, 1990) • The French Penal Code (1985)
Iceland	• The Icelandic Penal Code (1996)
Ireland	• Equal Status Act (2000) • Employment Equality Act (1998) • The Health Insurance Act (1994) • The Unfair Dismissals (Amendment) Act (1993) • Prohibition of Incitement to Hatred Act (1989)
Israel	• Equal Opportunities in Employment (1992)
Luxembourg	• Penal Code, Articles 454–457 (1997)
Netherlands	• The General Equal Treatment Act (1994) • Penal Code (1992), Articles 137c, d, e, and f; Article 429 quarter • 1992 Constitution, Article 1 DC (1983)
New Zealand	• Human Rights Amendment Act (2001) • Human Rights Act, Section 21 (1993)
Norway	• Discrimination and Accessibility Act (2009) • Anti-Discrimination Act (2005), Section 17 • Work Environment Law (clause added in 1998) • Penal Code, Paragraph 135a (1981) • Gender Equality Act (1978)
Slovenia	• Act 27 on Equality of Educational Opportunities (2007) • Law About Work Relations, Article 6 (1998) • Penal Code (1996), Article 141
South Africa	• Employment Equity Act 5 (1998) • Constitution (1996), Bill of Rights and Equality Clause (Section 9) • Constitution of the Republic of South Africa (Act No. 108 of 1996)
Spain	• Penal Code (1995), Article 22

Country	Name of Legislation
Sweden	• Anti-Discrimination Act (2009) • Discrimination Act (2008) • Ordinance No. 635 of 2008 (to amend ordinance [2007:1036] respecting the instructions of the Ombudsman Against Discrimination on the grounds of sexual orientation) • Ordinance No. 1036 of 2007 with instructions for the Office of the Ombudsman Against Discrimination on the grounds of sexual orientation • Ordinance No. 1408 (2006) (to amend Ordinance No. 170 of 1999) • Ordinance No. 146 (2006) (to amend Ordinance No. 170 of 1999) • Act No. 479 of 2005 (to amend the Prohibition of Discrimination in Working Life because of Sexual Orientation Act No. 133 of 1999) • Act No. 480 of 2005 (to amend Act No. 307 of 2003 to prohibit discrimination) • Act No. 453 of 2005 (to amend Act No. 307 of 2003 to prohibit discrimination) • Act No. 1089 of 2004 (to amend Act No. 307 of 2003 to prohibit discrimination) • Act No. 310 of 2003 (to amend the Prohibition of Discrimination in Working Life Because of Sexual Orientation Act No. 133 of 1999) • The Prohibition of Discrimination Act (No. 307 of 2003) • Prohibition of Discrimination in Working Life Because of Sexual Orientation Act No. 133 of 1999 • Ordinance No. 319 (2003) (to amend Ordinance No. 170 of 1999) • Penal Code (1987), Chapter 16, Paragraph 9
Taiwan	• Act of Gender Equality in Employment (2002), Chapter 2 • Employment Services Act (1992)
United Kingdom	• The Equality Act (Sexual Orientation) Regulations 2007, No. 1263 • The Equality Act of 2006
United States	• Equal Employment Opportunity in the Federal Government (1998) (Executive Order 11478) • Executive Order 13087 (1998) (to amend Executive Order 1147) • Don't Ask, Don't Tell Repeal Act of 2010[b] • States' civil rights laws (20 states plus the District of Columbia offer such protections: California; Colorado; Connecticut; Delaware; Hawaii; Illinois; Iowa; Maine; Maryland; Massachusetts; Minnesota; Nevada; New Hampshire; New Jersey; New Mexico; New York; Oregon; Rhode Island; Vermont; Washington, DC; and Wisconsin)[c]

Sources: NATLEX, International Labour Organization (n.d.)International Gay and Lesbian Human Rights Commission [IGLHRC] 2012; Council of Labor Affairs. Executive Yuan Taiwan R.O.C. 2012

Notes:

[a]The New Brunswick Human Rights Code can be found on the New Brunswick Department of Justice website (www.gnb.ca/acts/acts/h-11.htm). This legislation was retrieved August 11, 2002.

[b]Geidner (2010).

[c]National Gay and Lesbian Task Force (2012).

Gender Identity–U.S. and International

In the United States, there is a growing public debate about protecting the rights of transgender people in different contexts. On the one hand, there is more legislation making it illegal to discriminate against people because of their gender identity in public places, with 17 states, including Washington, D.C., having such laws on the books. On the other hand, several states have legislation banning the use of bathrooms that correspond to the individual's gender identity. The use of public bathrooms often presents a challenge for the transgender population, because they are more likely to face harassment and abuse from others when trying to use the gender-specific bathrooms that correspond to their own identity (Pelleschi, 2016). In Virginia, a law would require school boards to create policies that would allow students in public schools to use only the bathrooms that align with their gender at birth. Students who violate this policy could face a fine (House Bill No. 663, 2016). In North Carolina, a bill was passed blocking local governments from providing antidiscrimination laws that grant protection to the gay and transgender community within the state. Opponents to antidiscrimination laws argue that such antidiscrimination laws would make bathrooms unsafe for women and children ("North Carolina," 2016).

IBM, a global innovation and technology company, was one of the first institutions to provide diversity and inclusion policies for its lesbian, gay, bisexual, and transgender (LGBT) employees. Its initiatives are focused not only on providing a sense of value, but also empowering LGBT employees to engage with their clients and contribute to their full potential in the workplace. IBM is also one of the founding partners of Pride in Diversity, Australia's first and only not-for-profit workplace program designed to provide inclusion support to the LGBT employees in Australia's workplace (IBM, 2016).

Anti–Sexual Harassment Legislation—International

Sexual harassment is a widespread and underreported form of gender-based discrimination and deserves special attention. It is aimed primarily at women, although men suffer from it too. Sexual harassment often goes unreported for two reasons: First, many women are afraid of losing their jobs and hence their livelihood. This is particularly true when they are in an economically or immigration-related vulnerable situation; for example, they are single mothers, sole breadwinners, and immigrants who are not familiar with the host country's language and legislation, or they are illegal immigrants who are afraid of being deported. Second, in many cultures, reporting sexual harassment victimizes the woman a second time. She is seen as having brought shame on herself and her family, as she is blamed for being promiscuous or sexually provocative. As a result of high-profile lawsuits and pressure from grassroots women's organizations, there is a growing awareness of women's rights, and additional efforts toward creating work environments that are free of sexual pressure are being made. Around the world, more and more countries are banning sexual harassment in the workplace.

The legal definitions of sexual harassment and the protections provided under the law vary greatly from one country to the next. Those definitions are important because when they are broad and vague, they leave more room for interpretation by the courts, and as a result, it is often more difficult to prosecute perpetrators under such laws. Examples of broad definitions include Nepal's civil code on sexual harassment, which applies to women only and states that sexual harassment is "any male touching the body parts of a woman (other than his wife) with a sexual intention." Under Malaysia's Code of Practice on the Prevention and Eradication of Sexual Harassment in the Workplace, sexual harassment means any unwanted conduct of a sexual nature having the effect of verbal, nonverbal, visual, psychological, or physical harassment that (a) might, on reasonable grounds, be perceived by the recipient as placing a condition of a sexual nature on her or his employment, or (b) might, on reasonable grounds, be perceived by the recipient as an offense or humiliation, or a threat to her or his well-being, even with no direct link to her or his employment. Hong Kong's Sexual Discrimination Ordinance defines sexual harassment as any unwanted or uninvited sexual behavior that a reasonable person regards as offensive, humiliating, or intimidating, including unwelcome sexual advances or unwelcome requests for sexual favors.

South Korea's laws provide a more detailed definition. According to the Sexual Equality Employment Act and the Gender Discrimination Prevention and Relief Act, sexual harassment at work includes actions taken by a business owner, supervisor, or coworker that cause sexual humiliation to another worker through words or actions or creates an uncomfortable work environment. These actions may be in conjunction with job requirements or using the perpetrator's position in a way that creates the impression that if the victim will not yield to the sexual demands, the behavior will result in loss of a job or a disadvantage at work. These definitions relate only to direct actions by a supervisor or a coworker. They do not include situations in which the work environment itself constitutes sexual harassment, such as the use of profane language by supervisors and coworkers and posting sexually explicit posters in the workplace. Other definitions are more specific and include both direct sexual harassment and indirect. The latter refers to an oppressive work environment. The Equal Employment Opportunity Commission (EEOC) in the United States defines sexual harassment as unwanted sexual advances in the workplace that include requests for sexual favors and other verbal or physical contact of a sexual nature when these advances are made either explicitly or implicitly a condition for getting a job, keeping a job, or getting a promotion. An important evolution of the law now requires that the judge or jury see harassment not through the eyes of a reasonable person but through the eyes of a reasonable *victim*. For example, what a man may not consider harassment may be considered so by a woman. Furthermore, a work environment that is offensive, intimidating, or hostile also constitutes sexual harassment.[17] India's Supreme Court guidelines are more specific and include such unwelcome sexually determined behavior (whether directly or by implication) as (a) physical contact and advances; (b) a demand or request for sexual favors; (c) sexually colored remarks; (d) showing pornography; and (e) any other unwelcome physical, verbal, or nonverbal conduct of a sexual nature.

Similarly, the scope of protections against sexual harassment varies greatly among countries. Some countries, such as the United States, the United Kingdom, and Hong Kong, provide a relatively wide scope of protections against sexual harassment in the workplace, whereas others provide limited (e.g., Malaysia) or no protections at all (e.g., Pakistan). The European community has moved toward providing a strong protection against sexual harassment in recent years. The directive on the equal treatment of persons in the labor market, adopted by the EU Council of Ministers on June 7, 2000, amended October 5, 2002, calls for all EU members to adopt antiharassment programs, to set up national bodies and civil remedies to ensure their enforcement, and to encourage employers to take measures to combat all forms of sexual discrimination and sexual harassment in the workplace.

A similar trend has taken place in Japan and Venezuela. In 1997, the Japanese Ministry of Labor issued recommendations that are modeled after the guidelines prohibiting sexual harassment of the U.S. EEOC. At about the same time, Japan's Equal Employment Opportunity Act was amended, requiring Japanese employers to establish company policies and internal complaint procedures on sexual harassment. Venezuela has enacted its sexual harassment law (January 1, 1999) as part of the Law on Violence Against Women and Family. The law establishes sexual harassment as a crime that is punishable by a prison term of 3 to 12 months, and the offender must pay the victim double the amount of economic damages caused by the harassment, such as lack of access to jobs or promotions (Maatman, 2000).[18]

A survey conducted by the CAW (Committee on Asian Women) examined the legal provision for protection and prevention of sexual harassment at the workplace among a select number of Asian countries.[19] The findings indicate that the legislative situation in Southeast Asia is mixed. Although there are clear legal provisions laid down for the protection and prevention of sexual harassment in places like Hong Kong and South Korea, such provisions are nonexistent in countries like Pakistan. Somewhere between are countries like Malaysia, which has a code of practice rather than legal provisions for employers to establish in-house mechanisms to combat sexual harassment. For a comparison of sexual harassment laws among 11 Asian countries, see Table 2.2.

TABLE 2.2 ● Comparison of the Legal Provision for Protection Against Sexual Harassment at the Workplace Among Selected Asian Countries

Country/Name of Legislation	Questions Addressed Regarding Sexual Harassment in the Workplace						
	(1) Do legal protections against sexual harassment in the workplace exist? (2) Is there separate legislation or some section/clause of other labor laws? (3) How are victims protected? Are there specific rights defined in the law? (4) Are there any sections in the law on prevention of sexual harassment at the workplace? (5) Do administrative structures exist to facilitate the implementation of the law? (6) Is sexual harassment considered a criminal offense? (7) What is the minimum and maximum punishment permissible by law?						
	1	2	3	4	5	6	7
HONG KONG—Sex Discrimination Ordinance (Amendment) Bill of 2014	Yes	Separate legislation	They may lodge complaint in writing to the commission. The commission will then investigate the complaint and encourage conciliation between the parties in the dispute. If the complaint cannot be resolved, the commission may also provide assistance in court proceedings should the victim decide to take his/her case to court.	Yes	Yes**	Yes***	To be determined by the court
INDIA—Sexual Harassment of Women in the Workplace (Prevention Prohibition, and Redressal Act of 2013) (drafted based on multiple national and international standards and legislation)	Yes	Some clause or section of other laws	Superior guidelines refer only to the responsibility of the employers.	Yes, the law specifies guidelines to ensure protection from sexual harassment	No	Yes***	Subjected to a penalty of up to 50,000 Indian National Rupee (INR)

Country/Name of Legislation	Questions Addressed Regarding Sexual Harassment in the Workplace						
INDONESIA— Guidelines on the Prevention of Sexual Harassment (Better Work Indonesia)	Yes	Some clause or section of other laws	Guidelines refer to the responsibility of the employer.	Yes, a specified list of guidelines	No	Yes***	Depends on the offense and the employer's discretion (from a written warning to termination)
ISRAEL— Prevention of Sexual Harassment Law, 5758-1998	Yes	A section of the Sexual Harassment Law refers to sexual harassment in the workplace	Victim's protection specified (e.g., concealing the victim's identity, no disclosure of past sexual experiences, etc.).	Yes, the law specifies steps employers must take to prevent sexual harassment and address complaints efficiently	Yes	Yes	Subjected to a penalty of up to 50,000 Israeli new shekels (INS), but the courts can award higher sums with proof of damages
JAPAN— Equal Employment Opportunity Law of 1997	Yes	Some clause or section of other laws	The law refers only to the responsibility of the employers.	No	No	No	Not stipulated
MALAYSIA—The Penal Code, Section 509	Yes	Some clause or section of other laws	Whoever intended to insult the modesty of any woman, utters any words, makes any sound or gesture, or exhibits any object, intending that such word or sound shall be heard or such gesture or object shall be seen by such woman, shall be punished.	Yes	Yes	Yes	Violators will be punished with imprisonment for 5 years or with fine, or with both
NEPAL— The Civil Code	Yes	Some clause or section of other laws	Under general law provision, they can lodge complaint with the court or appropriate authority.	No	No	Yes***	Minimum: 1 rupee fine and 1 day in jail Maximum: 500 rupees fine and 1 year in jail

(Continued)

TABLE 2.2 ● (Continued)

Country/Name of Legislation	Questions Addressed Regarding Sexual Harassment in the Workplace					
REPUBLIC OF KOREA— Equal Employment and Support for Work–Family Reconciliation Act	Yes	Some clause or section of other laws	When the sexual harassment occurs within the workplace, the employer should punish the sexual harasser right away or address the issue accordingly. And the employer cannot fire or give disadvantages to the person who is sexually harassed or who says that he/she is sexually harassed.	Yes	Yes*	No	The fine imposed as follows: (a) Maximum 10 million won (South Korea currency) if the employer committed sexual harassment; (b) maximum 5 million won when the employer neglected the sexual harassment case or didn't address it appropriately; (c) maximum 3 million won when the employer did not conduct preventive trainings for sexual harassment
SRI LANKA— Article 12 (1) and (2) of the constitution and criminal law	Yes	Some clause or section of other laws	No response	No	No	Yes	Minimum: 3 years Maximum: 10 years
TAIWAN— Sexual Harassment Prevention Law	Yes	Separate legislation	Government agencies, companies, and schools are required to set up committees and rules on sexual harassment and channels for reporting violations.	Yes	Yes	Yes	(a) The fine imposed on violators is from minimum NTD 10,000 to maximum NTD 100,000; (b) the maximum punishment for the harasser is 2 years in jail or a fine of NTD 100,000
THAILAND— The Labour Protection Law	Yes	Some clause or section of other laws	The law is silent as to what activity would constitute sexual harassment.	No	No	No	Violator may result in a fine not exceeding Baht 20,000 (approximately US $500).

Sources: Based on Better Work Indonesia (2013); Committee for Asian Women (2000) cross-referenced with ILO's NATLEX database; Council of Labor Affairs, Executive Yuan Taiwan R.O.C. (2012); Government of India (2015); Hong Kong Legal Information Institute (n.d.); Malaysian Labour Law: Regulation of Employment (n.d.); Ministry of Labor in Korea (n.d.); Patel (2005); Regev (2007); "Sri Lanka" (2007); "Vishaka Guidelines Against Sexual Harassment in the Workplace" (2009).

Notes:

* The Presidential Commission on Women Affairs, Employment Equality Committee in Labour Ministry.

** The Equal Opportunities Commission (EOC).

*** Depending on the nature of the offense committed.

Practical Implications

The moral principles of just treatment of members of diverse groups—outlined in the UN Universal Declaration of Human Rights and in the various state constitutions and legislation—have some practical implications for individual workers, for groups of workers, for work organizations, and for societies. Employees who are treated unfairly are less productive, less satisfied, and less loyal to their organizations. These issues will be dealt with in the next several chapters. Relevant to this chapter is the fact that these workers are more likely to initiate lawsuits against the offending work organization. The lawsuits can carry hefty financial repercussions for the organizations. As the noted sociologist émile Durkheim predicted more than a century ago, a society that loses its organic solidarity—an internal compass for what is right and wrong—must turn to the courts for relief (Durkheim, 1893/2014). The following four examples illustrate the financial implications of discriminatory behavior in the workplace.

In one of Japan's largest sexual harassment lawsuits, the governor of the Osaka region was ordered to pay the equivalent of $107,000 to a 21-year-old university student who worked on his election campaign. The governor, Knock Yokoyama, was found guilty by Osaka's district court judge Keisuke Hayashi, who determined that in addition to sexually harassing the campaign worker (he was accused of groping her for half an hour aboard a campaign bus), the governor also tried to silence and intimidate her by offering her a gift, making false statements about her to prosecutors, and defaming her publicly. (Tolbert, 1999)

A similar example from the U.S. context pertains to racial discrimination.

A federal appeals court in San Francisco upheld a $1 million punitive damage verdict awarded to a Black man subjected to repeated harassment on the job, including numerous racial slurs by coworkers. Although management tried to characterize the racial slurs as "jokes," the court did not accept their contention. Judge Margaret McKeown wrote for a unanimous panel of three judges of the U.S. 9th Circuit Court of Appeals, "This case should serve as a reminder to employers of their obligation to keep their workplaces free of discriminatory harassment." This award is one of the largest ever in a racial harassment case based solely on offensive language. ("Award Over Racism Upheld," 2001)

In 2013, Wet Seal, a popular teen clothing store, paid $75 million to settle a racial discrimination case that accused the company of denying equal pay and promotions to Black employees. In some cases, the company was charged with discriminating against Black employees by removing them from their leadership positions and hiring Whites to fill their place (Hsu, 2013). It was alleged that top executives of the company directed senior managers to get rid of African American store managers for the sake of its "brand image." In total, over 20 charges were filed by current and former employees of Wet Seal, including a regional Wet Seal manager who was fired for hiring a Black woman to manage one of its branch locations. (NAACP, 2012)

In March 2015, Patterson-UTI, an oil and gas drilling company in Texas, was in a lawsuit pertaining to alleged discrimination, harassment, and retaliation against racial minorities across the country. According to the complaint filed by the EEOC, Patterson-UTI had engaged in similar patterns or practices that include "hostile work environment harassment, disparate treatment discrimination and retaliation against Hispanic, Latino, Black, American Indian, Asian, Pacific Islander and other minority workers in its facilities in Colorado and other states." Patterson-UTI agreed to settle for $12.26 million. (*EEOC v. Patterson-UTI Drilling Co.*, 2015)

These examples demonstrate the costly consequences of noncompliance with legislation pertaining to diversity discrimination in the workplace. There is an additional dimension to international legislation that pertains to multinational corporations. These corporations often operate in host countries whose cultural framework and legislation are very different from those of the country where the company is headquartered. When a company sends its employees overseas, this question is often asked: Do the laws of the country of origin apply or those of the host country? This question is relevant to occupational safety laws, environmental pollution laws, as well as to discrimination and equal opportunities. In the past, the courts have stated that the relevant law was that of the host country.[20] The following case illustrates the implications for employment discrimination.

In 1979, Arabian American Oil Company (Aramco), a Delaware corporation, hired Mr. Boureslan, a naturalized U.S. citizen born in Lebanon, as a cost engineer in Houston. A year later he was transferred, at his request, to work for Aramco in Saudi Arabia. Boureslan remained with Aramco in Saudi Arabia until he was discharged in 1984. After filing a charge of discrimination with the Equal Employment Opportunity Commission (EEOC), he instituted a suit in the United States District Court for the Southern District of Texas against Aramco and Arabian American Oil Company. He sought relief under Title VII of the Civil Rights Act of 1964 on the ground that he was harassed and ultimately discharged by the respondents on account of his race, religion, and national origin. In dismissing this claim, the court ruled that it lacked jurisdiction because Title VII's protections do not extend to U.S. citizens employed abroad by American employers. The Court of Appeals affirmed this decision. (*Equal Employment Opportunity Commission v. Arabian American Oil Co. et al.*, 1991)

Since then, however, new developments included in the U.S. EEOC manual prohibit discrimination by an American employer even when the employer is operating abroad. Furthermore, the EEOC manual also prohibits discrimination by a foreign employer that is controlled by an American employer (i.e., financial control, common ownership, common management).

Summary and Conclusion

This chapter examines global legislation related to equity and fairness in employment. In democratic countries, the laws represent a value system shared by the people. To identify such a shared value system globally, one has to search for a global representative body that can specify a similarly shared value system for all human beings. The United Nations, with all its faults (most governments represented are not democratic), is the closest to such a representative body. The Universal Declaration of Human Rights, adopted in 1948 by the UN General Assembly, stands on two philosophical principles: (a) the right to liberty and equality is the birthright of every human being and cannot be alienated; (b) human beings, as distinguished from other creatures, are rational and moral and therefore entitled to certain rights and freedoms. The International Bill of Human Rights provides the universal moral basis for nondiscrimination in employment because it forbids "distinction of any kind, such as race, colour, sex, language, religion, political or other opinion, national or social origin, property, birth or other status."

Some countries, such as the United States, Canada, and many members of the European Union, have broad-based antidiscrimination legislation that outlaws discrimination based on a wide array of characteristics such as gender, race, ethnicity or country of origin, religious beliefs, physical disability, and sexual orientation. South Africa's relatively recent legislation (the apartheid regime was abolished in 1994) provides a very broad protection from discrimination, listing a wide array of characteristics including "race, gender, sex, pregnancy, marital status, ethnic or social origin, colour, sexual orientation, age, disability, religion, conscience, belief, culture, language and birth."

Noncompliance with these laws may have severe consequences. Employees who are treated justly by their employers are more likely to be more productive and more loyal. Antidiscrimination diversity legislation has the potential to deter discriminatory employment practices because of its potential costly consequences. It is important to note that, depending on each country's cultural climate and court system, the success of such lawsuits, or even the likelihood that a victim of such action will press charges, greatly varies. Therefore, to avoid penalties and lawsuits and to reap the rewards of compliance, managers today must understand the legislative- and business-related social policies of the countries where they are doing business.

Appendix 2.1. Universal Declaration of Human Rights

Universal Declaration of Human Rights

Adopted and Proclaimed by General Assembly Resolution 217 A (III) of 10 December 1948

On December 10, 1948, the General Assembly of the United Nations adopted and proclaimed the Universal Declaration of Human Rights, the full text of which appears in the following pages. Following this historic act, the assembly called on all member countries to publicize the text of the declaration and "to cause it to be disseminated, displayed, read and expounded principally in schools and other educational institutions, without distinction based on the political status of countries or territories."

Preamble

Whereas recognition of the inherent dignity and of the equal and inalienable rights of all members of the human family is the foundation of freedom, justice and peace in the world,

Whereas disregard and contempt for human rights have resulted in barbarous acts which have outraged the conscience of mankind, and the advent of a world in which human beings shall enjoy freedom of speech and belief and freedom from fear and want has been proclaimed as the highest aspiration of the common people,

Whereas it is essential, if man is not to be compelled to have recourse, as a last resort, to rebellion against tyranny and oppression, that human rights should be protected by the rule of law,

Whereas it is essential to promote the development of friendly relations between nations,

Whereas the peoples of the United Nations have in the Charter reaffirmed their faith in fundamental human rights, in the dignity and worth of the human person and in the equal rights of men and women and have determined to promote social progress and better standards of life in larger freedom,

Whereas Member States have pledged themselves to achieve, in co-operation with the United Nations, the promotion of universal respect for and observance of human rights and fundamental freedoms,

Whereas a common understanding of these rights and freedoms is of the greatest importance for the full realization of this pledge,

Now, Therefore THE GENERAL ASSEMBLY proclaims THIS UNIVERSAL DECLARATION OF HUMAN RIGHTS as a common standard of achievement for all peoples and all nations, to the end that every individual and every organ of society, keeping this Declaration constantly in mind, shall strive by teaching and education to promote respect for these rights and freedoms and by progressive measures, national and international, to secure their universal and effective recognition and observance, both among the peoples of Member States themselves and among the peoples of territories under their jurisdiction.

Article 1
All human beings are born free and equal in dignity and rights. They are endowed with reason and conscience and should act towards one another in a spirit of brotherhood.

Article 2
Everyone is entitled to all the rights and freedoms set forth in this Declaration, without distinction of any kind, such as race, colour, sex, language, religion, political or other opinion, national or social origin, property, birth or other status. Furthermore, no distinction shall be made on the basis of the political, jurisdictional or international status of the country or territory to which a person belongs, whether it be independent, trust, non-self-governing or under any other limitation of sovereignty.

Article 3
Everyone has the right to life, liberty and security of person.

Article 4
No one shall be held in slavery or servitude; slavery and the slave trade shall be prohibited in all their forms.

Article 5
No one shall be subjected to torture or to cruel, inhuman or degrading treatment or punishment.

Article 6
Everyone has the right to recognition everywhere as a person before the law.

Article 7
All are equal before the law and are entitled without any discrimination to equal protection of the law. All are entitled to equal protection against any discrimination in violation of this Declaration and against any incitement to such discrimination.

Article 8
Everyone has the right to an effective remedy by the competent national tribunals for acts violating the fundamental rights granted him by the constitution or by law.

Article 9
No one shall be subjected to arbitrary arrest, detention or exile.

Article 10
Everyone is entitled in full equality to a fair and public hearing by an independent and impartial tribunal, in the determination of his rights and obligations and of any criminal charge against him.

Article 11

(1) Everyone charged with a penal offence has the right to be presumed innocent until proved guilty according to law in a public trial at which he has had all the guarantees necessary for his defence.

(2) No one shall be held guilty of any penal offence on account of any act or omission which did not constitute a penal offence, under national or international law, at the time when it was committed. Nor shall a heavier penalty be imposed than the one that was applicable at the time the penal offence was committed.

Article 12

No one shall be subjected to arbitrary interference with his privacy, family, home or correspondence, nor to attacks upon his honour and reputation. Everyone has the right to the protection of the law against such interference or attacks.

Article 13

(1) Everyone has the right to freedom of movement and residence within the borders of each state.

(2) Everyone has the right to leave any country, including his own, and to return to his country.

Article 14

(1) Everyone has the right to seek and to enjoy in other countries asylum from persecution.

(2) This right may not be invoked in the case of prosecutions genuinely arising from non-political crimes or from acts contrary to the purposes and principles of the United Nations.

Article 15

(1) Everyone has the right to a nationality.

(2) No one shall be arbitrarily deprived of his nationality nor denied the right to change his nationality.

Article 16

(1) Men and women of full age, without any limitation due to race, nationality or religion, have the right to marry and to found a family. They are entitled to equal rights as to marriage, during marriage and at its dissolution.

(2) Marriage shall be entered into only with the free and full consent of the intending spouses.

(3) The family is the natural and fundamental group unit of society and is entitled to protection by society and the State.

Article 17

(1) Everyone has the right to own property alone as well as in association with others.

(2) No one shall be arbitrarily deprived of his property.

Article 18

Everyone has the right to freedom of thought, conscience and religion; this right includes freedom to change his religion or belief, and freedom, either alone or in community with others and in public or private, to manifest his religion or belief in teaching, practice, worship and observance.

Article 19

Everyone has the right to freedom of opinion and expression; this right includes freedom to hold opinions without interference and to seek, receive and impart information and ideas through any media and regardless of frontiers.

Article 20

(1) Everyone has the right to freedom of peaceful assembly and association.

(2) No one may be compelled to belong to an association.

Article 21

(1) Everyone has the right to take part in the government of his country, directly or through freely chosen representatives.

(2) Everyone has the right of equal access to public service in his country.

(3) The will of the people shall be the basis of the authority of government; this will shall be expressed in periodic and genuine elections which shall be by universal and equal suffrage and shall be held by secret vote or by equivalent free voting procedures.

Article 22

Everyone, as a member of society, has the right to social security and is entitled to realization, through national effort and international co-operation and in accordance with the organization and resources of each State, of the economic, social and cultural rights indispensable for his dignity and the free development of his personality.

Article 23

(1) Everyone has the right to work, to free choice of employment, to just and favourable conditions of work and to protection against unemployment.

(2) Everyone, without any discrimination, has the right to equal pay for equal work.

(3) Everyone who works has the right to just and favourable remuneration ensuring for himself and his family an existence worthy of human dignity, and supplemented, if necessary, by other means of social protection.

(4) Everyone has the right to form and to join trade unions for the protection of his interests.

Article 24

Everyone has the right to rest and leisure, including reasonable limitation of working hours and periodic holidays with pay.

Article 25

(1) Everyone has the right to a standard of living adequate for the health and well-being of himself and of his family, including food, clothing, housing and medical care and necessary social services,

and the right to security in the event of unemployment, sickness, disability, widowhood, old age or other lack of livelihood in circumstances beyond his control.

(2) Motherhood and childhood are entitled to special care and assistance. All children, whether born in or out of wedlock, shall enjoy the same social protection.

Article 26

(1) Everyone has the right to education. Education shall be free, at least in the elementary and fundamental stages. Elementary education shall be compulsory. Technical and professional education shall be made generally available and higher education shall be equally accessible to all on the basis of merit.

(2) Education shall be directed to the full development of the human personality and to the strengthening of respect for human rights and fundamental freedoms. It shall promote understanding, tolerance and friendship among all nations, racial or religious groups, and shall further the activities of the United Nations for the maintenance of peace.

(3) Parents have a prior right to choose the kind of education that shall be given to their children.

Article 27

(1) Everyone has the right freely to participate in the cultural life of the community, to enjoy the arts and to share in scientific advancement and its benefits.

(2) Everyone has the right to the protection of the moral and material interests resulting from any scientific, literary or artistic production of which he is the author.

Article 28

Everyone is entitled to a social and international order in which the rights and freedoms set forth in this Declaration can be fully realized.

Article 29

(1) Everyone has duties to the community in which alone the free and full development of his personality is possible.

(2) In the exercise of his rights and freedoms, everyone shall be subject only to such limitations as are determined by law solely for the purpose of securing due recognition and respect for the rights and freedoms of others and of meeting the just requirements of morality, public order and the general welfare in a democratic society.

(3) These rights and freedoms may in no case be exercised contrary to the purposes and principles of the United Nations.

Article 30

Nothing in this Declaration may be interpreted as implying for any State, group or person any right to engage in any activity or to perform any act aimed at the destruction of any of the rights and freedoms set forth herein.

Source: "Universal Declaration of Human Rights"; Hundred and eighty-third plenary meeting; Resolution 217(A) (III) of the United Nations General Assembly, December 10, 1948; The Office of the High Commissioner for Human Rights. http://www.ohchr.org/EN/UDHR/Pages/Introduction.aspx

Appendix 2.2. Global Antidiscrimination and Equal Rights Legislation Checklist of Protections Offered by a Select Number of Countries

Universal Declaration of Human Rights (10 December 1948)

	Race/Ethnic Origin/Country of Origin	Religion/Religious Beliefs	Gender/Sex	Equal Remuneration (pay)	Sexual Harassment	Physical Disability	Mental Disability	Age	Sexual Orientation	Other	Total Number of Protections Offered per Country
AUSTRALIA	✓	✓	✓	✓	✓	✓	✓	✓	✓	A, B, C, D, F	14
AUSTRIA	✓	✓	✓	✓	✓	✓	✓	✓	✓	B, C, J	12
BELARUS – RUSSIAN FEDERATION		✓				✓	✓			J, G, L	6
BELIZE	✓	✓	✓			✓				C, J	6
CANADA	✓	✓	✓	✓	✓	✓	✓	✓	✓	B, E, G, H, I, J	15
CHINA			✓	✓	✓					A, B, C, J	7
HONG KONG	✓		✓	✓	✓	✓	✓			B, C, G, J	10
CONGO			✓	✓						A, K	3
CYPRUS	✓	✓	✓	✓					✓	F, J, L, N	10
CZECH REPUBLIC	✓	✓	✓	✓						C, F, G, J, M, N	10
DENMARK	✓	✓	✓	✓		✓	✓	✓	✓	C, F, J, L, M	14

	Race/ Ethnic Origin/ Country of Origin	Religion/ Religious Beliefs	Gender/ Sex	Equal Remuneration (pay)	Sexual Harassment	Physical Disability	Mental Disability	Age	Sexual Orientation	Other	Total Number of Protections Offered per Country
EGYPT	✓	✓	✓			✓	✓		✓	L	7
FIJI	✓	✓	✓		✓				✓	A	6
FINLAND	✓	✓	✓	✓	✓	✓	✓	✓	✓	D, G, J, L, M, N	15
GERMANY	✓	✓	✓			✓	✓	✓	✓	C, J, L	10
GUYANA	✓	✓	✓	✓	✓	✓	✓	✓		B, C, F, J	12
HUNGARY	✓	✓	✓			✓	✓	✓		D, F, G, J	9
ICELAND	✓	✓	✓	✓	✓	✓	✓		✓	C, J	10
INDIA			✓	✓						C, G	4
INDONESIA	✓					✓	✓			A, C, K	6
IRAQ				✓							1
IRELAND	✓	✓	✓	✓	✓	✓	✓	✓	✓	B, J	11
ISRAEL	✓	✓	✓	✓		✓	✓	✓	✓	B, C, J	11
JAMAICA	✓	✓	✓			✓	✓	✓		A, F	6
JAPAN		✓	✓		✓	✓	✓	✓		C, G, J	9
KOREA	✓	✓	✓		✓	✓	✓	✓		B, D, J	10
LITHUANIA	✓	✓	✓	✓	✓	✓	✓	✓	✓	C	10
MALAWI	✓	✓	✓			✓	✓	✓	✓	J	8

(Continued)

[Continued]

Country	Race/ Ethnic Origin/ Country of Origin	Religion/ Religious Beliefs	Gender/ Sex	Equal Remuneration (pay)	Sexual Harassment	Physical Disability	Mental Disability	Age	Sexual Orientation	Other	Total Number of Protections Offered per Country
MALTA	✓	✓	✓	✓	✓	✓			✓	B, F, J, N	11
NAMIBIA	✓	✓	✓		✓	✓				B, D, G	7
THE NETHERLANDS	✓	✓	✓	✓	✓	✓	✓	✓	✓	B, C, D, F, J	14
NEW ZEALAND	✓		✓	✓	✓	✓	✓	✓	✓	A, J, K, L	12
NIGERIA	✓	✓	✓							K	4
NORWAY	✓	✓	✓	✓	✓	✓			✓	C, J	9
PHILIPPINES			✓		✓	✓	✓			A, J	6
POLAND			✓		✓	✓	✓			J	5
REPUBLIC OF SOUTH AFRICA	✓	✓	✓		✓	✓	✓	✓	✓	A, B, C, D, F, J	14
RUSSIAN FEDERATION	✓					✓	✓	✓		A, C, F, J, K, M	10
SAINT LUCIA				✓	✓					C, M	4
SAINT VINCENT AND GRENADINES	✓			✓	✓		✓	✓			5
SAUDI ARABIA	✓				✓		✓				3

	Race/ Ethnic Origin/ Country of Origin	Religion/ Religious Beliefs	Gender/ Sex	Equal Remuneration (pay)	Sexual Harassment	Physical Disability	Mental Disability	Age	Sexual Orientation	Other	Total Number of Protections Offered per Country
SWEDEN	✓		✓	✓	✓	✓	✓	✓	✓	C, J, M	11
THAILAND				✓		✓	✓	✓			4
TRINIDAD AND TOBAGO	✓		✓	✓			✓			B	5
TUNISIA	✓		✓	✓		✓					3
UKRAINE	✓		✓	✓		✓	✓			A, J	6
UNITED KINGDOM	✓	✓	✓	✓	✓	✓	✓	✓	✓	B, C, J	12
ANGUILLA (U.K.)	✓			✓							2
BERMUDA (U.K.)											0
FALKLAND ISLANDS (MALVINAS) (U.K.)				✓					✓		2
GIBRALTAR (U.K.)				✓	✓						2
ST. HELENA (U.K.)				✓					✓		2
NORTHERN IRELAND (U.K.)	✓	✓	✓	✓	✓	✓		✓	✓	B, C, D, F	11

[Continued]

47

[Continued]

Country	Race/ Ethnic Origin/ Country of Origin	Religion/ Religious Beliefs	Gender/ Sex	Equal Remuneration (pay)	Sexual Harassment	Physical Disability	Mental Disability	Age	Sexual Orientation	Other	Total Number of Protections Offered per Country
UNITED STATES OF AMERICA	✓	✓	✓	✓	✓	✓	✓	✓	✓b	C, D	11
VANUATU			✓			✓					2
ZAMBIA	✓	✓	✓			✓				B, F	6
ZIMBABWE	✓		✓		✓	✓				A, F	6
TOTALS	41 (71%)	33 (57%)	49 (86%)	30 (53%)	31 (54%)	42 (74%)	29 (51%)	21 (37%)	24 (42%)		

✓ protection offered

Sources: Bureau of Democracy, Human Rights and Labor (n.d.); NATLEX, International Labour Organization (n.d.).

Notes: Other categories defined:

A = HIV status
B = marital status
C = pregnancy
D = affirmative action legislation
E = aboriginal
F = political affiliation
G = visible minorities
H = ancestry
I = source of income
J = family status
K = nondiscrimination—not elsewhere specified
L = general equal rights statement—not elsewhere specified
M = health status
N = language

Note: The specific legislation offering protections based on sexual orientation is from the ILO's database NATLEX and the IGLHRC. Twenty states plus the District of Columbia offer such protections. The states include California; Colorado; Connecticut; Delaware; Hawaii; Illinois; Iowa; Maine; Maryland; Massachusetts; Minnesota; Nevada; New Hampshire; New Jersey; New Mexico; New York; Oregon; Rhode Island; Vermont; Washington, DC; and Wisconsin.

Notes

1. The International Bill of Human Rights can be obtained directly from the United Nations and can also be accessed from the UN official website (www.un.org/Overview/rights.html). This section is based, in part, on UN Fact Sheet No. 2 (Rev 1): The International Bill of Human Rights. It can also be found at the UN official website (http://unhchr.ch/html).

2. Although the UN Universal Declaration of Human Rights was initially drafted as a *secondary authority* (a legal term indicating that it is an ideal notion rather than enforceable law), it has become customary international law as a result of its long existence and acquiescence by a majority of countries. A case in point is a lawsuit brought in a U.S. court by a Mexican family against a Mexican official for acts of torture committed in Mexico against their son. The judge accepted their claims based on the UN Declaration of Human Rights. See *Filártiga v. Peña-Irala,* 630 F.2d 876 (U.S. Court of Appeals, Second Circuit, 1980).

3. Please refer to the previous note.

4. These examples are taken from the committee's protocols. They can also be found on the official website of the Office of United Nations High Commissioner for Human Rights (http://www2.ohchr.org/english/bodies/cerd/).

5. See the complete protocol of the UN Committee on the Elimination of Racial Discrimination, March 2002 (an electronic copy is available at http://www2.ohchr.org/english/bodies/cerd/).

6. For the complete study, conducted in several EU countries, see Zegers de Beijl (1999).

7. Smeesters et al. (2000), p. 46.

8. For a discussion of implications of antidiscrimination laws to insurance claims, see Maatman (2000), pp. 34–35.

9. The UN ILO has created a database, called NATLEX, that references over 55,000 national laws related to employment, social security, and related human rights. NATLEX is available to researchers and to the public (in English, French, or Spanish) through its publications and through its website (www.ilo.org/dyn/natlex/natlex_browse.home).

10. Over 20% of the countries reviewed had to have legislation in the appropriate category to be considered a most popular form of antidiscrimination legislation.

11. The United States is the only country that allows punitive damages awards. Punitive damages entail a sum of money designed to punish the defendants and to deter others from repeating the offense. Typically, punitive damages against large corporations range in millions of dollars.

12. This is based on a personal interview—July 2002. Per the interviewee's request, her name is kept confidential.

13. In the United States, the laws allow for "fair discrimination" in gender-related employment, when the discrimination is based on gender differences in physical abilities (e.g., *Dothard v. Rawlinson,* 433 U.S. 321 [1977]).

14. It is interesting to note that while the suit was pending, the Alabama Board of Corrections adopted a regulation that created male-only and female-only positions in the prison system. The effect was to exclude women from 75%

(Continued)

(Continued)

of the jobs in the system. The plaintiff amended her suit to include a claim that the regulation violated federal law. The three-judge panel held that both the statute and regulation violated Title VII. The court held that the applicant had shown the statute had a discriminatory effect, and the director had failed to show the challenged requirements were job-related. The court held, however, that the regulation fell within the narrow exception for bona fide occupational qualifications because most of the jobs in Alabama's atypical, unclassified system were just too dangerous for women. The Supreme Court affirmed the district court's decision with respect to the statute setting minimum height and weight requirements but reversed the district court's decision with respect to the regulation, which created male- and female-only positions.

15. The *Griggs v. Duke Power Company* (1970) case (which preceded *Dothard v. Rawlinson,* 1977) determined that the Duke Power Company's intradepartmental transfer policy requiring a high school education and the achievement of minimum scores on two separate aptitude tests violated Title VII of the Civil Rights Act of 1964. Specifically, the U.S. Supreme Court concluded that neither the high school graduation requirement nor the two aptitude tests were directed or intended to measure an employee's ability to learn or perform a particular job or category of jobs within the company. The Court concluded that the subtle, illegal purpose of these requirements was to safeguard Duke's long-standing policy of giving job preferences to its White employees and was discriminatory against its African American employees. In fact, the Court determined that not only overt discrimination is illegal but also that practices that are fair in form but discriminatory in practice are against the law. This theory of the law, the "disparate-impact" theory, was chipped away in the *Dothard v. Rawlinson* (1977) decision and was almost eliminated in *Wards Cove Packing Co., Inc. v. Atonio* (1989). The latter decision was so extreme that it motivated Congress to amend Title VII of the Civil Rights Act of 1964. In essence, the theory of discriminatory impact is now the law of the land.
16. The IGLHRC is a nonprofit, nongovernmental organization (NGO) based in the United States. IGLHRC's commitment is to individual and community human rights as well as eliminating discrimination or abuse based on sexual orientation, gender identity, or HIV status. For more information on IGLHRC, visit its website (www.iglhrc.org/).
17. *Mississippi University for Women v. Hogan,* 458 U.S. 718 (1982).
18. Interestingly, this seems to be based on a logic that is similar to the punitive damages awards granted in the United States (see note 11).
19. Established in 1992, CAW is a grassroots organization with 28 chapters in 13 Asian countries working actively to raise awareness of women workers rights in Asian countries. A more detailed description of the survey was published in the *Asian Women Workers Newsletter.* An electronic copy is available at http://cawinfo.net/
20. The U.S. Congress, in some cases, has specifically indicated that particular legislation is extraterritorial. That is, Congress has the authority to enforce its laws beyond the territorial boundaries of the United States. cf. *Foley Bros., Inc. v. Filardo,* 336 U.S. 281, 284–285 (1949); *Benz v. Compania Naviera Hidalgo, S. A.,* 353 U.S. 138, 147 (1957).

3

Discrimination, Equality, and Fairness in Employment

Social Policies and Affirmative/ Positive Action Programs

> The inequality of rights has no other source than the law of the strongest. Was there ever any domination that did not appear natural to those who professed it? We ought not to ordain that to be born a girl instead of a boy, any more than to be born black instead of white, shall dictate a person's position through life.

—John Stuart Mill (1806–1873), English philosopher and influential liberal thinker of the 19th century

The International Bill of Human Rights, as well as the various national laws described in the previous chapter, is aimed at banning discrimination and assuring equal opportunities to people regardless of their gender, race, ethnicity, age, disability, or other characteristics that are not relevant to their job-related skills. These laws are *negative* in that they prohibit discrimination in employment. In the past several decades, a new category of protections has emerged—social policies that are *positive* in that they aim to change the rules and provide advantages to groups that have traditionally suffered discrimination. These social policies go beyond assuring equal rights to correct past wrongs. They are grouped under titles such as "positive action" in Europe (e.g., United Kingdom Equality Act of 2010; Archibong & Sharps, 2011; Caruso, 2003; Kennedy-Dubourdieu, 2007) or "affirmative action" in the United States (e.g., United States Executive Order 11246, 1965; Leiter & Leiter, 2011; Libertella, Sora, & Natale, 2007). Other countries that have later adopted similar policies have used one or the other of these terms (see, for example, Alon, 2015; Moses, 2010; Sowell, 2004; Sunstein, 1999; White, 2001). This chapter begins with a discussion of different types of discrimination to provide the context for these policies and then turns to the specific policies in various countries whose aim is to actively promote equality and fairness in employment. It concludes with the public and political debate over these policies and the challenges they pose for business practices.

Discrimination and Equality in Employment

Originally morally neutral in its meaning, the word *discrimination* has acquired a negative value, particularly in the context of employment. The dictionary, for example, reflects this duality by providing both meanings. The first two definitions (1 and 2) are morally neutral, and the second definition (3) is morally negative: "Discrimination: (1) the act of discriminating; (2) the quality or power of finely distinguishing; (3) the act, practice, or an instance of discriminating categorically rather than individually" (*Merriam-Webster's Collegiate Dictionary,* 2002). The UN International Labour Organization (ILO) defines discrimination as "any distinction, exclusion or preference made on the basis of race, colour, sex, religion, political opinion, national extraction or social origin, which has the effect of nullifying or impairing equality of opportunity or treatment in employment or occupation" (United Nations Discrimination [Employment and Occupation] Convention, 1958). For the purposes of the current discussion on discrimination in employment we define the following:

> Discrimination in employment occurs when (a) individuals, institutions, or governments treat people differently because of personal characteristics like race, gender, or sexual orientation rather than their ability to perform their jobs and (b) these actions have a negative impact on access to jobs, promotions, or compensation. (Mor Barak, 2005)

There are several classifications of discriminatory acts that can help us in understanding the way discrimination is manifested in the workplace (Velasquez, 2011). First, discrimination can be *overt* or *covert.* Overt discrimination occurs as a result of an explicit policy or law that generates unequal treatment; covert discrimination is the result of an implicit side effect of another policy or decision. Second, discrimination can be *individual* or *institutional.* It is individual when a single manager or a coworker in conjunction with his or her individual prejudice performs the action or actions; it is institutional when it is performed as part of the organization's common practices or policies. Finally, discrimination can be characterized by the motivation behind it and can be either *intentional* or *unintentional.*[1] The following examples may help demonstrate these distinctions.

The first example comes from the July 1943 issue of *Mass Transportation* (see Box 3.1). Male supervisors of women in the workforce wrote these "Eleven Tips on Getting More Efficiency Out of Women Employees" during World War II. It is clearly prejudicial: "Numerous properties say that women make excellent workers when they have their jobs cut out for them, but that they lack initiative in finding work themselves," and derogatory: "You have to make some allowances for feminine psychology. A girl has more confidence and is more efficient if she can keep her hair tidied, apply fresh lipstick and wash her hands several times a day." Though it seems laughable today, the "advice" given to managers in this piece was considered serious and meant to be helpful.

The discrimination in this example is overt. Clearly, the authors were not aware there was anything wrong with their attitude and didn't make any attempt to hide their prejudice; it is institutionalized—this is not an act of a single manager but instructions given to all managers; and it is intentional. The intent of the authors was to treat women differently because women were perceived to possess inferior characteristics.

Box 3.1

DISCRIMINATION CATEGORIZATION: MANAGEMENT ADVICE IN 1943

The following is an excerpt from the July 1943 issue of *Mass Transportation.* This was written for male supervisors of women in the workforce during World War II:

Eleven Tips on Getting More Efficiency Out of Women Employees

There's no longer any question whether transit companies should hire women for jobs formerly held by men. The draft and manpower shortage has settled that point. The important things now are to select the most efficient women available and how to use them to the best advantage.

Here are eleven helpful tips on the subject from Western Properties:

1. Pick young married women. They usually have more of a sense of responsibility than their unmarried sisters, they're less likely to be flirtatious, they need the work or they wouldn't be doing it, they still have the pep and interest to work hard and to deal with the public efficiently.

2. When you have to use older women, try to get ones who have worked outside the home at some time in their lives. Older women who have never contacted the public have a hard time adapting themselves and are inclined to be cantankerous and fussy. It's always well to impress upon older women the importance of friendliness and courtesy.

3. General experience indicates that "husky" girls—those who are just a little on the heavy side—are more even-tempered and efficient than their under-weight sisters.

4. Retain a physician to give each woman you hire a special physical examination—one covering female conditions. This step not only protects the property against the possibilities of lawsuit, but reveals whether the employee-to-be has any female weaknesses which would make her mentally or physically unfit for the job.

5. Stress at the outset the importance of time—the fact that a minute or two lost here and there makes serious inroads on schedules. Until this point is gotten across, service is likely to be slowed up.

6. Give the female employee a definite day-long schedule of duties so that they'll keep busy without bothering the management for instructions every few minutes. Numerous properties say that women make excellent workers when they have their jobs cut out for them, but that they lack initiative in finding work themselves.

7. Whenever possible, let the inside employee change from one job to another at some time during the day. Women are inclined to be less nervous and happier with change.

8. Give every girl an adequate number of rest periods during the day. You have to make some allowances for feminine psychology. A girl has more confidence and is more efficient if she can keep her hair tidied, apply fresh lipstick and wash her hands several times a day.

9. Be tactful when issuing instructions or in making criticisms. Women are often sensitive; they can't shrug off harsh words the way men do. Never ridicule [a] woman—it breaks her spirit and cuts off her efficiency.

10. Be reasonably considerate about using strong language around women. Even though a girl's husband or father may swear vociferously, she'll grow to dislike a place of business where she hears too much of this.

11. Get enough size variety in operator's uniforms so that each girl can have a proper fit. This point can't be stressed too much in keeping women happy.

Source: July 1943 issue of *Mass Transportation*

Additional examples (see Box 3.2 and Box 3.3) are more recent and come from the experiences of an Arab Muslim in an auto appliances company and of African American employees in the U.S.-based Xerox Company.

Box 3.2

DISCRIMINATION CATEGORIZATION: HARASSMENT OF ARAB MUSLIM AT AN AUTO APPLIANCES COMPANY

The Equal Employment Opportunity Commission (EEOC) found that an Arab and Muslim mechanic at National Tire and Battery (NTB) company suffered from harassment because of their religion and national origin. The harassment charges included managers and co-workers calling the worker "Taliban," "al Qaeda," "bin Laden," and "terrorist," and even accusing him of making bombs. It was also alleged that the Defendant, National Tire and Battery, were aware of the harassment and, at times, witnessed some of the offensive comments but failed to take corrective measures. The case was resolved by the Chicago District Office in October 2015 and the Defendants were ordered to pay $22,500 in fees and undergo injunction relief, including training of managers on EEO laws (EEOC, 2016).

Besides the monetary payment to the former NTB employee, the 2-year consent decree prohibited NTB and its employees from harassing fellow workers because of religion or national origin, and from retaliating against employees who complain about harassment. Also, NTB must train managers on how to respond to harassment complaints; submit periodic reports to the EEOC about religious and national origin harassment complaints; and post notices at Orland Park and Matteson regarding the outcome of the lawsuit.

"When employers learn of harassment, the law requires that they take prompt and effective action to stop it," said John C. Hendrickson, regional attorney of EEOC's Chicago District Office, which is responsible for litigation in Wisconsin, Illinois, Minnesota, Iowa, North Dakota, and South Dakota. "Unfortunately, that did not happen here. But we are pleased that NTB agreed to an early resolution of this case that provides for fair compensation to the employee who was harassed and implements measures that will help prevent others from suffering similar misconduct in the future" (EEOC, 2015).

In response, the company stated, "NTB Tire & Auto Service Centers is committed to the safety and well-being of our customers and associates. Harassment and misconduct have no place in our workplace" (*Tire Business*, 2015).

Sources: Comer, K. (2002, August 8). Black employees to file discrimination lawsuit against Xerox. The Associated Press State & Local Wire. Retrieved August 14, 2002, from http://web.lexis-nexis.com/universe/printdoc

The findings about the Xerox work environment actions can be characterized as discrimination that is (a) covert—this was not a stated policy of the organization (in fact, based on the company's statement, these actions seem to go against its stated policy); (b) institutionalized—these actions were not done by a single individual nor as an isolated incident but were widespread enough throughout the organization to constitute an unofficial subculture; and (c) intentional—the systematic discrimination placed the Black employees at a disadvantage.

Box 3.3

DISCRIMINATION CATEGORIZATION: BLACK EMPLOYEES FILE A DISCRIMINATION LAWSUIT AGAINST XEROX

Black sales representatives at Xerox, an American and global corporation that sells business services and document technology products, filed a class action lawsuit contending that they suffered from racial discrimination by being routinely excluded from opportunities that would have allowed them to earn higher commissions and to advance. The lawsuit, filed in 2001 in federal court in Brooklyn, was approved class action status in 2004 and settled in 2008.

The workers said they were assigned to less profitable territories than White coworkers or were assigned to territories based on their race. They also contend they were passed over for more lucrative territories, promotions, and were denied commissions they had earned.

The lawsuit cited Frank Warren, a plaintiff in the suit, who was assigned a territory in the New York borough of the Bronx that required a car. When he notified Xerox that the territory would be a hardship because he did not have a car, he allegedly was told by a vice president–general manager that he was assigned to the Bronx because "Blacks and the Bronx go hand in hand."

In the case settlement in 2008 Xerox agreed to pay $12 million to 1,100 former and current employees including legal fees. The company also agreed to establish a task force of Xerox employees to ensure that Black sales representatives are compensated in a nondiscriminatory manner by assessing how sales territories are assigned and other issues.

Xerox denied it engaged in policies or practices of unlawful discrimination or retaliation or other unlawful conduct. "However, Xerox believes it is in the best interest of its shareholders and employees to settle the lawsuit, bringing to an end the protracted and costly litigation," the company said in a statement (Singer, 2008).

Source: Harvey, C. (2012). Contextualised equality and the politics of legal mobilization: Affirmative action in Northern Ireland. Social & Legal Studies, 21, 23–50; Rea, D., & Eastwood, J. (1992). Legislating for Northern Ireland's fair employment problem. International Journal of Manpower, 13(6–7), 31–39; Osborne, B. (2005). Fair employment in Northern Ireland: A generation on. Belfast: Blackstaff Press.

Theoretical Perspectives of Discrimination and Affirmative Action

Affirmative or positive action policies originated from the notion that discrimination against whole groups that has been persistent, institutionalized, and long term cannot be remedied simply by banning such actions. Although antidiscrimination legislation is essential, these policies emerged out of the recognition that such legislation may not be enough to create a work environment that provides equality of opportunities for all and may actually cement past inequalities.

Affirmative or positive action policies have two goals: (a) righting past wrongs—compensating groups that have been disadvantaged in the past with better opportunities in the present—and (b) achieving social goals of increasing the representation of traditionally disadvantaged groups in more lucrative jobs as well as management and leadership positions. The rationale behind these policies is that they redress past discrimination by giving preference in hiring and promotion to members of groups that have suffered discrimination in the past. Considering that for a long time these groups have had limited access to education, high-paying and prestigious jobs, networks of influence, and promotion opportunities, they may continue to be deprived of these opportunities if not given such advantages until a more balanced representation can be achieved.

There are several theoretical paths explaining discrimination in employment and the need, or lack thereof, for affirmative action policies. "Neoclassical" economists assume that, in a competitive market, the "taste" for discrimination cannot be indulged because it would be too costly for employers (Becker, 1971; Figart, 2005; Fleury, 2012; Flinn, 2015). Employers would lose their competitive advantage if they do not utilize the wide range of skills and talents offered by women, members of minority groups, older adults, sexual minorities, and people with disabilities. If employers continue to discriminate against these groups, their productivity will be reduced, ultimately resulting in reduced income for employers. Strictly following this logic, there is no need for any policies that encourage employers to give equal opportunities to all because it is in their own economic best interest. The problem with this logic is that it assumes that discrimination is simply a taste, disregarding the fact that this behavior is embedded in deeply engrained prejudicial perceptions that color people's evaluation of other people's skills, abilities, and talents. In other words, if one is prejudiced, say, against older people, he or she will make a series of inaccurate and often prejudicial assumptions (they are slow, inaccurate in their work, lacking in technical skills, etc.). Operating from a mindset that affects perception of reality, an employer is not likely to objectively determine the prospective employee's real qualifications—for example, a woman's ability to manage an engineering team—and is less likely to hire her for a management job (Arrow, 1973, 1998). Decisions that are propelled by prejudices tend also to perpetuate them: The employer may never realize the potential economic loss for his or her business enterprise by not hiring that woman (e.g., her unique talents). It has been suggested, therefore, that the economic process cannot be insulated from stereotypes held by employers and affecting their judgment (Bennington & Wein, 2000; Drydakis & Vlassis, 2010; Kaas & Manger, 2012). Nevertheless, neoclassical economists generally argue for deregulating the labor market and removing legal and policy restrictions to allow employers to use pure economic principles in their employment decisions.

At the other end of the theoretical spectrum is the "equal opportunities" school, which considers institutional and cultural factors as the cause of discrimination (McDonald & Potton, 1997; Roemer, 2002; Sterba, 2011). Groups that have traditionally been discriminated against suffer from three types of interconnected barriers that may perpetuate the discrimination against them. The first is stereotyping, which excludes them from lucrative and desirable jobs; the second is exclusion from positions of authority, which perpetuates their image of being incapable of doing certain jobs; and the third is lack of role models and mentors within their groups who are in positions of power and influence and who can assist them in obtaining and retaining desirable jobs.

Unlike the neoclassical economists, who believe that distributive justice will resolve on its own due to the forces of the market economy, equal opportunities theorists believe that the forces that have originally led to discrimination will also work to preserve it. For example, in the past—and to a somewhat lesser degree today—the dominant stereotype of women was that they could not handle the pressure of top management, and such positions were entirely outside their reach (the infamous "glass ceiling"). As a result, for a long time there was no evidence to disprove this stereotype, and discrimination was perpetuated. Furthermore, because many positions are obtained through networking and many promotions are attained through mentorship and role modeling, there were no women available to support and mentor other women in their quest for management jobs.

The main argument of the equal opportunities school of thought is that ending discrimination does not create equal opportunities because women, Blacks, people with disabilities, and other groups that have been discriminated against do not have the same resources available to them as members of the dominant groups. The main argument against this school of thought is that preferential hiring is another form of discrimination.

Social Policies and Affirmative/Positive Action Programs

In contrast to the passive nondiscrimination dictated by the equal employment legislation described in the previous chapter, affirmative or positive action means that employers must act directly and aggressively to remove all barriers that prevent women and members of minority groups from having equal access to education, employment, and political processes. Although these policies do not equal quotas (Code of Federal Regulations, title 41, sec 60–2.16, 2014), some affirmative action plans may include quotas if courts find purposeful systemic discrimination in specific areas (Heath, 2014; Tomei, 2003).

Legal Arrangements for Affirmative and Positive Action Policies

Despite the public debate about these programs and the challenges presented in several judicial systems, governments around the world continue to legislate for affirmative or positive action in employment in favor of designated groups (ILO, 2014). These programs operate under different legal arrangements. A review of select countries using the ILO's NATLEX database revealed information about 18 countries that currently have affirmative action policies. (Please note that the list is illustrative, not exhaustive; see Table 3.1.)

Specifically, countries such as South Africa, Namibia, India, the United States, and the European Union (EU) all have differing ways of operating and implementing affirmative action programs:

- South Africa and Namibia have both adopted legislation requiring employment equity through means that include affirmative action—the Employment Equity Act No. 55 of 1998 in South Africa and the Affirmative Action (Employment) Act No. 6 of 2007 in Namibia.[2]

- In South Africa, the 1998 Employment Equity Act specifies a commitment to implement affirmative action measures in order to ensure equitable representation by "designated groups" in all occupational categories and levels of the public workforce.

- The European Community passed the Equal Treatment Directive in 1976,[3] but it was limited to equal pay and equal treatment and applied only to gender and not to race or any other groups. In 1984, a council positive action recommendation was issued that suggested parallel action be taken by governments to include industry and other bodies concerned in order to counteract prejudicial effects on employment.[4] Following the 1984 council recommendation, several European Community members initiated positive action legislation and policies (specific examples are included in the next section). Article 13 of the Amsterdam Treaty declared the principle of equal treatment for the EU's increasingly multiethnic community and the need to fight against racism and xenophobia. Adopted in June 2000, the European Council Directive (2000/43/EC)[5] "implementing the principle of equal treatment between persons irrespective of racial or ethnic origin" was amended in 2006 (2006/54/EC) to include protection against gender discrimination placing far-reaching and specific demands on member states. It included the requirement to inform the commission of measures taken by member states to implement the directive. It also stressed the need to promote "conditions for a socially inclusive labour market" in order to achieve the objectives of the EC Treaty.

- The United States has a relatively long experience with affirmative action programs. The term *affirmative action* first appeared in President John F. Kennedy's Executive Order 10925 of 1961. It reappeared 4 years later in 1965 when President Lyndon B. Johnson signed Executive Order 11246 requiring "employers doing business with the federal government to develop affirmative action plans to assure equal employment opportunities in their employment practices."

TABLE 3.1 ● Affirmative Action Legislation Worldwide (Select Countries)

Country/Legislation (Targeted Groups)

AUSTRALIA—Affirmative Action Equal Opportunity for Women in the Workplace Amendment Act of 2012 (No. 179 of 2012)

Private employers with 100 or more employees and higher education institutions are required to create affirmative action programs. (*women*)

AUSTRIA—Employment of Persons With Disabilities Act (No. 22/1970)

Requires organizations employing 25 or more employees to have at least one disabled person employed per every 25 employees. (*persons with disabilities*)

CANADA—Employment Equity Act (1995)

Employers are required to identify and eliminate employment barriers against persons in designated groups. As a part of that, employers are required to institute policies that ensure that designated groups are represented in the workforce. (*women, aboriginal peoples, persons with disabilities, and members of visible minorities*)

COLOMBIA—Law of Quotas No. 581 (2000)

The law promotes the participation of women in the public sector within positions that carry decision-making power in the Colombian government. It requires that at a minimum, 30% of the highest decision-making positions in the public sector at the National Department District and municipal levels be filled by women. (*women*)

COSTA RICA—Electoral Code Law No. 7653 (1996)

The law guarantees the representation and participation of women in politics within Costa Rica as a method to eliminate discrimination in the public and political life of women. The law requires that women be allowed to be participants in any organization that is subject to public elections and to partake in the formulation and implementation of governmental policies. Furthermore, the law requires that all political parties ensure that at least 40% of all political positions subject to the popular vote be filled by women. (*women*)

ETHIOPIA—The Constitution of the Federal Democratic Republic of Ethiopia (1994)

Employers are required to promote the rights of women through remedial and affirmative measures that promote their well-being, including maternity leave with full pay. (*women*)

TABLE 3.1 ● (Continued)

Country/Legislation (Targeted Groups)
FINLAND—Act Respecting Equality Between Women and Men (1986)
Public authorities are required to actively promote gender equality by removing obstacles through training and education, as well as by placing men and women in work positions and creating equality in working conditions. *[gender]*
FRANCE—Law in Favour of Disabled Workers 1987 (Act 87-517) (1987)
Public and private establishments or enterprises with 20 or more employees are obliged to employ workers with disabilities at a level of 6% of the total number of staff employed. *[persons with disabilities]*
HUNGARY—Provisions Respecting Gender Participation in Governmental Councils, Administrations, Delegations, etc.—Implementation and Reporting Methods (No. 110 of 1996)
Requires a minimum of 40% representation of men and women in all public committees that are made up of at least four members. In committees with two or three members both genders must be represented. *[gender]*
INDIA—The Persons With Disabilities (Equal Opportunities, Protection of Rights and Full Participation) Act (1995) (No. 1 of 1996)
Creates affirmative action plans, programs that provide education and training for disabled children, and an employment exchange for persons with disabilities. Requires that every appropriate government appoint a percentage of vacancies of not less than 3% for persons or class of persons with disability. *[persons with disabilities]*
IRELAND—Employment Equality Act (No. 21 of 1998)
Prohibits discrimination in the workplace. Sets forth explicit provisions regarding gender equality and matters related to sexual harassment. *[gender, marital status, religion, sexual orientation, race, disability, and age]*
KENYA—The Employment Act (2007)
Allows employers to make use of affirmative action measure in order to eliminate discrimination and promote equality in the workplace. *[not specified]*

(Continued)

Country/Legislation (Targeted Groups)

NAMIBIA—Affirmative Action (Employment) Amendment Act, 2007 (No. 6 of 2007)

Requires that employers create affirmative action programs to promote employment and give preferential treatment (providing employment and removing employment barriers) to individuals in designated groups. Establishes an Employment Equity Commission. *[women, persons with disabilities, and disadvantaged ethnic groups]*

NORWAY—Public Limited Companies Act, 2003

Requires the boards of public limited companies to have each sex make up at least 40% of the representatives on the board. *[gender]*

SOUTH AFRICA— Employment Equity (Amendment) Act (1998) (Act No. 47 of 2013)

Employers (50+ employees), employers with more than a specified annual turnover, and the state are required to take affirmative action measures for designated groups as well as develop an employment equity plan. Establishes a Commission for Employment Equity. The amendment of 2013 provides additional provisions on sexual harassment in the workplace and wage discrimination. *(Black people, women, and persons with disabilities)*

SWEDEN—Equal Opportunities (Amendment) Act (1991) (Act No. 476 of 2005)

Employers are mandated to promote equal representation of both sexes in the workplace. This is to be accomplished through training and recruitment policies and by giving preference to applicants of the underrepresented sex. Employers with more than 10 employees are required to create an annual plan of action outlining positive measures to promote equal opportunity. The amendment of 2005 adds provisions regarding discrimination against job seekers or employees and prohibition of sexual harassment. *[gender]*

UNITED STATES—Executive Order 11246 (1965) and Affirmative Action Programs Rule (41 CFR Part 60) (1970)

Employers who conduct business with the federal government are required to develop affirmative action plans. *[race, color, religion, sex, national origin]*

VIETNAM—The Labour Code Act of 2012

Employers are required to provide gender equality and measures to promote gender equality when recruiting and training employees or future employees. Employers must ensure the wage is paid equally without gender-based discrimination . . . [G]ive consideration to designated groups in the recruitment process as well as to give group members priority in employment (when more than one qualified applicant): war veterans, sick war veterans, or members of their families. *[persons with disabilities, gender]*

Source: International Labor Organization (2014).

Principles of Affirmative Action and Positive Action Programs

Programs to actively encourage a more representative workforce, as well as the incentives governments give to comply with such requirements, vary greatly from one country to the next. There are, however, several principles that are common to all such programs (Alon, 2015; Velasquez, 2011; Yang, D'Souza, Bapat, & Colarelli, 2006). Typically, affirmative/positive action programs:

- Are intervention measures

- Cut across, and attempt to influence, the operation of free-market mechanisms

- Aim to actively reverse past discrimination against specific groups

- Are intended as temporary actions, which will be withdrawn once the situation is rectified

The following discussion covers the three elements of these essential programs: (a) their specific goals and target population; (b) policies and activities covered by those programs; and (c) enforcement, incentives, and sanctions.

Specific Goals and Target Population

In general, the goals of these programs are to provide better opportunities to population groups that have been discriminated against in the past and to increase their representation in public service jobs and in management and leadership positions. In the United States, for example, the goal of affirmative action programs is to compensate for past discrimination and to correct current discrimination by ensuring equal employment to members of minority groups and women. Similarly, the goal of positive action programs in Europe is to compensate population groups that have been discriminated against in the past by providing them with a competitive advantage in the present (Caruso, 2003; Waddington & Bell, 2011).

The South African affirmative action measures were implemented in order to ensure equitable representation by "designated groups" in all occupational categories and levels of the workforce. "Designated groups" are defined as Black people (Africans, "Coloureds," and Indians), women, and people with disabilities (Employment Equity Act, No. 5, 1998). It is important to note that although preferential treatment is meant only for "suitably qualified people," the definition of such suitability is very broad and may be a product of formal qualifications, prior learning, relevant experience, or "capacity to acquire, within reasonable time, the ability to do the job."

India, the world's largest democracy, has long been struggling with hierarchical social structures in the form of its traditional caste system (Deshpande, 2007; Moffatt, 2015; Sowell, 2004; Zacharias & Vakulabharanam, 2011). The 1998 Employment Equity Act specifies a commitment to implement affirmative action measures in order to ensure equitable representation by "designated groups" in all occupational categories and levels of the workforce. In an effort to make its society more equitable, India employs "reservations"—a system of quotas in the public service system, set aside for minorities. The target populations for preferential treatment include three groups: (a) the Scheduled Castes (about 16% of the population), (b) the Scheduled Tribes (about 8% of the population), and (c) the Socially and Educationally Backward Classes (also called "Other Backward Classes" and constituting about 52% of the population). These quotas have been controversial in India, leading to protests from groups who believe they do not benefit from the quotas (Heath, 2014).

When examining affirmative or positive action policies from an international perspective, it is clear that each country's specific historical and cultural background dictates the nature of its policies. Two interesting examples illustrate this issue: The first example comes from India and South Africa. What distinguishes the affirmative action programs in both India and South Africa from most other national programs is that the target populations are not minorities but practically constitute a majority of the population. The second example comes from Norway. Although in most countries women are the focus of any gender-related affirmative action, in July 1998, Norway enacted Ordinance (No. 622 of 1998) Respecting Special Treatment of Men. This legislation creates special provisions for men in certain occupations, like child care and education, in which they are not well represented (Hodges-Aeberhard, 1999; ILO 2014; Teigen, 2011).

Policies and Activities

Affirmative or positive action policies and programs are designed to increase the number of qualified applicants from designated groups (depending on each country's definition of these groups) in the workforce. They usually employ two main strategies:

The first strategy involves *placing requirements on the composition of the public workforce.* This is done through specifying recruitment and promotion strategies for actual increase in representation of the designated groups (popularly referred to as quotas). India's "reservations" policy, which applies to public positions only and not to private employers, is a prime example of this approach. Under India's reservations policy, the federal government has set aside a quota of federal and state government positions to improve the representation of designated groups that were discriminated against in the past (Boston & Nair-Reichert, 2003; Jensenius, 2015; Sunstein, 1999). The quotas are designed to reflect these groups' representation in the population (indicated earlier) and include 15% for the Scheduled Castes and 7.5% for the Scheduled Tribes. No specific quota was set aside for the Other Backward Classes, though a 1963 India supreme court ruling indicated that all reservations together should not exceed 50% of the positions. The responsibility for implementing affirmative action in India belongs to *designated employers,* a term that includes all municipalities and most government organizations and larger organizations (defined either by the financial scope of their business or as having more than 50 employees). Each employer is required to conduct analyses of the employment barriers standing in the way of inclusion and promotion of the designated groups, prepare an employment equity plan, and report annually to the director general of the Department of Labor on the progress made in the implementation of such a plan. The employment equity plan has to state the objectives to be achieved each year, the affirmative action measures with timetables and strategies to be implemented to accomplish them, as well as procedures to accomplish the plan.

The second strategy involves *encouraging private businesses to actively recruit and promote* employees from the designated groups. Governments achieve this goal by providing businesses with incentives, like better access to government contracts. In the United States, for example, employers who initiate plans to ensure equal employment by actively recruiting minorities and women are given preferential access to government contracts. Similar public policies in some European countries, such as the United Kingdom's positive action, originate from the same ideology—compensating population groups that have been discriminated against in the past by providing them with a competitive advantage in the present (other things being equal). In Belgium, for example, following the European Community recommendation, a royal decree was passed that made provisions for the signing of an accord between the government and individual employers. The positive action programs were piloted with Belgacom—formerly RTT, the national television company—and since then there have been more than 50 conventions signed with private-sector employers. In each case, assistance has been given from a team of state-funded experts operating within a common set of positive action guidelines. In Italy, there are more trade unionists than in any other country in the EU (Fulton, 2015). Trade unions in Italy have introduced positive action into collective bargaining, and today many employment contracts contain positive action clauses (Chater & Chater, 1992; Kirton & Greene, 2002; Martinez Lucio & Perrett, 2009).

An interesting example of positive action through legislation aimed at reducing religious discrimination is Northern Ireland's Fair Employment Act of 1989, which was amended in 1998 (see Box 3.4). The goal of that legislation was to make the workforce representation of the two religious communities, Protestants and Roman Catholics, equal to their proportions in the population at large. This goal was attempted by granting far-reaching enforcement powers to the Fair Employment Commission. Despite this forward-thinking legislation, it is clear that inequalities in employment are rooted in the complexities of the histories, identities, and cultures of the two communities and are not easily eradicated via legislation (Harvey, 2012; Lucas & Jarman, 2016; Muttarak, Hamill, Heath, & McCrudden, 2013; Rea & Eastwood, 1992).

Box 3.4

EQUAL EMPLOYMENT LEGISLATION AND RELIGIOUS DISCRIMINATION: THE CASE OF NORTHERN IRELAND

Roman Catholics in Northern Ireland have suffered severe disadvantages in the labor market for a long time. Until 1989, Section 5 of the Government of Ireland Act 1920 was the only legal protection against religious discrimination for the citizens of Northern Ireland. It stated that the Northern Ireland parliament was prohibited from making any law that would "give preference, privilege or advantage or impose any disability or disadvantage on account of religious belief or ecclesiastical status." Following Northern Ireland's civil rights movement of the 1960s and the surge in civil disorder, the governor of Northern Ireland appointed a commission headed by Lord Cameron to investigate the allegations of religious and political discrimination. The commission's 1969 report confirmed that injustices in the areas of housing and public employment led to the surge of civil unrest. Several declarations followed, with the eventual result of the 1976 Fair Employment (North Ireland) Act that outlawed job discrimination on the grounds of religion and political opinion in both public and private employment. A decade later, however, it became clear to the government that the 1976 act was having a minimal impact on Catholic disadvantages in employment.

Interestingly, strong pressure to change this situation came from a group of Irish American lobbyists who urged U.S. companies with investments in Northern Ireland to increase the numbers of Roman Catholics in their workforces. Articulating their position, the group drew the "MacBride Principles," named after one of the original signatories and modeled after the Sullivan Principles that were developed earlier to guide companies operating in South Africa.

These actions, in addition to reports on the status of employment discrimination, convinced the government of the need to introduce new legislation. The eventual outcome was the Fair Employment (Northern Ireland) Act 1989. The aim of the new legislation was to ensure that the proportions of the two religious communities in employment would be equal to their proportions in the population at large.

(Continued)

(Continued)

The 1989 law provides for close auditing of employers' practices in achieving employment equality. It arms the Fair Employment Commission with additional powers and resources. Specifically, it requires all employers of more than 10 people to monitor the religious composition of their workforce and to provide an annual report to the commission. Employers are also required to provide 3-year reviews of their recruitment, training, and promotion practices and policies. The penalties include not only fines for discrimination and failure to register and monitor but also exclusion from competing for government contracts and denial of any government grants. In 1998, the law was amended to include the monitoring of religious composition of part-time staff. Including part-time employers allowed the commission to get a better sense of the entire workforce. The 1998 amendment to the act also outlawed any discrimination based on religion or politics in the provision of food, facilities, and services; however, it still kept the essential elements of the 1989 law (Northern Ireland Assembly, 2012).

The strong fair employment legislation in Ireland over the past few decades has played its part, and there has been substantial improvement in the employment representation, most markedly in the public sector but not confined to it. Catholics are now well represented in managerial, professional, and senior administrative posts. There are some areas of underrepresentation, such as local government and security, but the overall picture is a positive one. Catholics are still more likely than Protestants to be unemployed. There are emerging areas of Protestant underrepresentation in the public sector, most notably in health and education. This is evident at many levels, including professional and managerial.

There has been a considerable increase in the numbers of people who work in integrated workplaces. At a time when public housing, for example, is virtually completely segregated, this represents another positive trend in the assessment of the implementation of the legislation. Evidence now suggests that unlike a generation ago, when a person's religious affiliation determined social mobility, now it is mainly education that is the determinant factor. Evidence also suggests that affirmative action agreements between the Equality Commission and employers have helped redress both Catholic and Protestant underrepresentation as a vital part of the process of change.

Despite this far-reaching legislation, it is clear that religious animosity still exists and that, despite the remarkable progress, segregation by religion in employment situations remains a challenge in Northern Ireland.

Sources: Barnes, R. (2009). Justices Rule for White Firemen In Bias Lawsuit, Washington Post, June 30. Retrieved July 24, 2009, from http://www.washingtonpost.com/wp-dyn/ content/article/2009/06/29/AR2009062901608.html; Ricci v. DeStefano (2009); Savage, C. (2009, June 10). Videos shed new light on Sotomayor's positions. New York Times. Retrieved on http://www.nytimes.com/2009/06/11/us/politics/ 11judge.html?_r=1; Scandal lets malaysia prove its mettle. (2002, October 16). The New York Times, p. W1. [An exerpt of the article can be found at http://query.nytimes.com/gst/abstract .html?res=FB0C12F6345E0 C758DDDA90994DA404482]

Enforcement, Incentives, and Sanctions

Some countries institute an official body that is responsible for evaluating compliance and enforcing the policies through sanctions or incentives. Sanctions include primarily monetary fines for organizations that do not comply with the policy. In South Africa, for example, the director general of the Department of Labour, who receives the employers' progress reports, has the power to make compliance demands on the designated employers. A Commission for Employment Equity, with a chair and eight members, is appointed by the minister of labor to render advice on these matters. Penalties can range from 500,000 to 900,000 rand (roughly $40,912–$73,641).[6]

As a further example, Australia's Affirmative Action (Equal Opportunity for Women in the Workplace) Act of 1999, which was amended in 2012, requires that organizations with more than 100 employees have an affirmative action program in place. Even though the legislation was enacted in 1986, some employers did not respond to it until the 1990s. Additionally, many organizations are not covered within the act (less than 44% of those in the private sector are covered), and many women are excluded if they work part-time, have temporary jobs, or are in the category of low-paid employees. As a part of Australia's Affirmative Action Act, organizations are required to evaluate their employment statistics and human resource (HR) practices, and to consult with women employee groups and with trade unions to develop an individualized affirmative action program. Organizations are also required to submit their reports and subsequent plans to the Affirmative Action Agency. Despite these aspects of the act, the penalties for not complying with the requirement are limited and rarely enforced (Konrad & Hartmann, 2001; Leiter & Leiter, 2011; Strachan & Jamieson, 1999).

The Public Debate Over Affirmative and Positive Action Policies

The public debate over positive/affirmative action policies has focused on social justice and economic principles. Proponents of these policies claim three main arguments: The first is compensatory justice—past injustices need to be undone and compensation should be given to those who were disadvantaged as a result of discriminatory traditions or intentional policies; the second is distributive justice—the social goods and wealth of a country should be distributed equally; and the third is social utility—everyone in a society has something important to contribute, and the common good is best served by everyone's participation in the economic and social system. Opponents of these policies present arguments that can also be classified into three groups: First, reverse discrimination is another form of unfair practices that perpetuate discrimination, although it is now practiced on a different group; second, preferential policies go against the principles of individualism and interfere with the forces of a free-market economy; and third, preferential practices may result in poor services and products because incompetent or unsuitable people may be appointed to jobs.[7] Some claim that affirmative action policies ultimately hurt the minorities they were designed to assist in the first place. Opponents of affirmative action posit that preferential treatment of minority groups engenders resentment among other groups and perpetuates stereotypes about the groups that undermine the minority group as a whole (Cohen & Sterba, 2003; Hull, 2015; Sterba, 2011). Furthermore, even among proponents of strong social policies, there is uneasiness with policies that may amount to "quotas" and outright reverse discrimination because they undermine the real achievements of members of underrepresented groups and perpetuate the notion that members of these groups intrinsically lack the characteristics for success in employment and will always need special assistance.[8] The controversy around affirmative and positive action is reflected in the numerous challenges it has faced in courtrooms throughout the world. It is interesting to note that despite the diversity of countries and jurisdictions, courts have generally supported the concept as an acceptable tool in the struggle to eliminate discrimination in employment.[9]

Affirmative or positive action programs have been challenged in the courts, mostly on grounds that they contradict a specific country's equal rights assurances under its constitution or legislation. South Africa's constitution presents a very interesting way of solving this dilemma. In banning unfair discrimination (see page 29), South Africa's constitution implies that fair discrimination is permissible. Chapter 10 of the constitution states that public administration must be broadly representative of the South African people. It further notes that although objectivity and fairness must be applied, an important goal is redressing the imbalances of the past and achieving broad representation. The South African constitution, unlike that of the United States, for example, sanctions affirmative action.[10]

Affirmative action policies were challenged in the U.S. courts repeatedly over the years when the courts were asked to reconcile these preferential policies with the equality principle stated in the Fifth and Fourteenth Amendments to the U.S. Constitution. Early Supreme Court decisions affirm these policies, but from the 1980s on, as the Supreme Court's composition became more conservative, the Court's decisions were less and less supportive. For example, in 1989 the Court ruled in favor of the J. A. Croson Company, a nonminority-owned construction firm that sued the city of Richmond, Virginia, claiming that its policy of setting aside at least 30% of the dollar amount of contracts to minority business enterprises was discriminatory. The Court found that because the city had failed to demonstrate the need for remedial action in the awarding of its public construction contracts, its treatment of its citizens on a racial basis violated the Constitution's Equal Protection Clause (*Richmond v. J. A. Croson Co.*, 1989). Questions about the constitutionality of race-based set-aside policies emerged again in the *Adarand Constructors v. Peña* case, which came before the U.S. Supreme Court in 1995. The U.S. Department of Transportation awarded a highway construction contract in the state of Colorado to the Mountain Gravel and Construction Company. The contractor then sought bids for subcontracting. Although the lowest bid was posted by Adarand Constructors, the contract was given to Gonzales Construction because of the latter company's composition of a large proportion of workers considered from disadvantaged backgrounds. The Supreme Court found that awarding the contract to Gonzales Construction based purely on the racial composition of the company was in violation of the Fifth Amendment's Due Process Clause (*Adarand Constructors v. Peña*, 1995). (See Box 3.5 for the Supreme Court's ruling in favor of White firefighters.)

Box 3.5

MAKING THE CASE AGAINST AND FOR AFFIRMATIVE ACTION: THE U.S. SUPREME COURT'S RULING IN FAVOR OF WHITE FIREFIGHTERS AND THE FIRST LATINA SUPREME COURT JUSTICE

Eighteen White firefighters, including one Hispanic, sued the City of New Haven claiming racial discrimination. The case stemmed from a lieutenants' promotion examination administered to New Haven, Connecticut, firefighters in 2003. After no African American firefighters ranked high enough to be promoted to the rank of lieutenant, the city's Civil Service Board threw out the results and decided not to make any immediate promotions. The city claimed that it was simply trying to avoid being sued by the Black firefighters who argued that the test was unfairly skewed. A district judge sided with the city and tossed the suit out before trial. A year later, a three-judge Second Circuit panel backed that decision.

The U.S. Supreme Court agreed to hear the case in 2009 and in a dramatic ruling declared that the White firefighters were unfairly denied promotion because of their race, making this a reverse discrimination case. The Supreme Court's decision was closely split in a 5–4 ruling along conservative-liberal lines.

Writing for the majority opinion, Justice Anthony Kennedy noted, "Whatever the City's ultimate aim—however well intentioned or benevolent it might have seemed—the City made its employment decision because of race. The City rejected the test results solely because the higher scoring candidates were white."

For the dissenting justices, Justice Ruth Bader Ginsburg wrote that the majority's opinion "ignores substantial evidence of multiple flaws in the tests New Haven used. The Court similarly fails to acknowledge the better tests used in other cities, which have yielded less racially skewed outcomes." She expressed the justices' concern that the city of New Haven, with almost 60% minority, would be "served by a fire department in which members of racial and ethnic minority are rarely seen in command decisions" (Barnes, 2009; *Ricci v. DeStefano*, 2009).

There is an interesting caveat to this Supreme Court ruling—on the three-judge Second Circuit panel that ruled in favor of the city of New Haven was Judge Sonia Sotomayor, the first woman of Latin descent to be nominated and confirmed to the U.S. Supreme Court. The Supreme Court's decision came only weeks before the congressional confirmation hearings for Judge Sotomayor, and it was used by Sotomayor's opponents to support their criticism of her as an "activist judge" who endorses reverse discrimination. On several occasions during her judicial career, Sotomayor declared that she was "a perfect affirmative action baby." Recounting her modest upbringing (the daughter of parents who moved from Puerto Rico to the Bronx, her father died when she was only 9 years old, and her mother raised Sonia and her brother as a single mother, barely making ends meet), Sotomayor has credited affirmative action programs with her admission to both Princeton and Yale.

She once said "affirmative action got me into Princeton," noting that her scores on standardized entrance examinations were lower than those of her classmates and that those test scores were overlooked by the admissions committees at Princeton and Yale because she was Hispanic and grew up in poor circumstances. "With my academic achievement in high school, I was accepted rather readily at Princeton and equally as fast at Yale, but my test scores were not comparable to that of my classmates," she said. "And that's been shown by statistics, there are reasons for that. There are cultural biases built into testing, and that was one of the motivations for the concept of affirmative action to try to balance out those effects." However, she did graduate summa cum laude from Princeton and was the editor of Yale's law journal. Her comments came in the context of explaining why she thought it was "critical that we promote diversity" by appointing more women and members of minorities as judges.

Sources: Barnes (2009); *Ricci v. DeStefano* (2009); Savage (2009); "Sotomayor Found Her 'Competitive Spirit'" (2013).

The fate of affirmative action policies in the United States took a very interesting turn in the mid-1990s. In November 1996, the California voters approved Proposition 209, which amended the state's constitution, and stated:

Neither the State of California nor any of its political subdivisions shall use race, sex, color, ethnicity or national origin as a criterion for either discriminating against, or granting preferential treatment to, any individual or group in the operation of the state's system of public employment, public education, or public contracting.[11]

Proposition 209 was unsuccessfully challenged in the courts (it was upheld in the Ninth Circuit Court of Appeals, and the Supreme Court turned down a request to hear the case in November 1997, practically voiding all affirmative action initiatives). The state of Washington followed suit by passing a similar resolution in 1998, and other states have contemplated similar measures. President Bill Clinton was known to have phrased the slogan "Don't end, amend!" about affirmative action programs, but under his presidency no new initiatives were generated to institute such amendments. Therefore, unlike the state of affairs in South Africa, the tension between affirmative action and the equality principles in the U.S. Constitution has remained a contentious issue.

The heated debate over affirmative action was centered at the University of Michigan's Ann Arbor campus in the early 2000s when two lawsuits were brought against the university due to its use of affirmative action policies in its admissions process (Perry, 2007). The first suit was brought by Jennifer Gratz, a high school student who claimed to have been rejected for undergraduate admissions due to reverse discrimination (*Gratz v. Bollinger,* 2003). The second suit was brought by Barbara Grutter, a Caucasian woman who was rejected from the University of Michigan's law school. Grutter claimed that her application was rejected due to reverse discrimination (*Grutter v. Bollinger,* 2003). Both cases were brought before the U.S. Supreme Court, and a decision was rendered on both in 2003. The Supreme Court ruled that the use of affirmative action in the undergraduate admissions process at the University of Michigan was unconstitutional, as the process being utilized for admission was thought to resemble quotas too closely. The Court, however, ruled that the use of affirmative action in the process of admission at the University of Michigan's law school was in fact constitutional, as it did not make use of any quotas but rather used an individualized and holistic view of applicants to make admissions decisions.

The election of the first African American president, appointment of the first Latina Supreme Court justice, and granting of similar high-profile leadership positions to members of underrepresented racial and ethnic groups gave rise to renewed demands for dismantling affirmative action policies. The central claim is that these policies are not only unnecessary but they are unfair to those who are not beneficiaries. In February 2012, the Supreme Court agreed to hear a potentially landmark case that could end or markedly change affirmative action policies in higher education. In *Fisher v. the University of Texas* (2012), Abigail Noel Fisher, a White applicant, claimed she was denied admission to the undergraduate program at the University of Texas at Austin in 2008 solely because of her race (Gutiérrez, 2013). The lawsuit states that the University of Texas engaged in "blatant racial balancing" to ensure a diverse class of entering students. Since the University of Texas revised its admissions policies following the 2003 *Grutter v. Bollinger* case, the number of African Americans graduating has nearly doubled, and the number of Latino graduates has increased by almost 50%. Any decision of the Supreme Court will apply nationwide and will affect admissions policies to universities throughout the United States (Winkler, 2012). The continuing public and legal debate demonstrates that affirmative action policies remain controversial and that whether they remain intact, are modified, or are dismantled altogether, the implications for individuals' lives are very real.

The debate over affirmative/positive action programs has reverberated throughout the world, with some countries implementing new affirmative action policies while others roll them back. In Malaysia, for example, the affirmative action policies enacted after the 1969 race riots between the majority Malays and the minority ethnic-Chinese Malays have come under attack in recent years for slowing down the economic development of the country. The original goal was to help Malays catch up economically with ethnic-Chinese Malays, who make up around a fourth of the country's 27 million people but who control a disproportionately large share of businesses and trade. The hope was that private Malay entrepreneurs would eventually emerge to take control. Thus far, however, relatively few Malay entrepreneurs have capitalized on the race-based initiatives. In the meantime, some economists in Malaysia say that those same programs now threaten to undermine Malaysia's fortunes by making it tough for some non-Malay entrepreneurs to go up against competitors in countries such as China, Vietnam, and Singapore. Since taking office in April 2009, Prime Minister Najib Razak, a Malay, has moved to attract more foreign investors. He recently issued new rules allowing foreign investors to enter selected service, financial, and legal businesses without having to give up equity to local ethnic-Malay partners. "The world is changing quickly and we must be ready to change with it or risk being left behind," Mr. Najib told an investment conference on June 30, 2009. But he stressed in an interview that "we mustn't lose sight of the overall objective of a more equitable and just society" (Hookway, 2009). Some countries have even considered eliminating affirmative action policies altogether. On October 18, 2005, the Constitutional Court of the Slovak Republic determined that the provision of the *antidiskriminaèný zákon* (Antidiscrimination Act) regarding the positive (affirmative) action principle was unconstitutional. Two years earlier, in 2003, the Slovak government adopted specific measures containing programs of positive actions toward, and in favor of, the Roma population (a minority group, also known as "gypsies") that has suffered widespread discrimination. The court argued that

> The Constitution prohibits both positive and negative discrimination for the reasons stated in this provision, i.e., having regard to sex, race, colour, language, belief and religion, political affiliation or other conviction, national or social origin, nationality or ethnic origin, property, descent or any other status.

Therefore, the court declared that adoption of specific compensatory measures, although generally recognized as legislative techniques for the prevention of disadvantages pertinent to racial or ethnic origin, was incompatible with the country's constitution and had to be dismantled (Buzinger, 2007; ILO, 2007).

Summary and Conclusion

> And while the law [of competition] may be sometimes hard for the individual, it is best for the race, because it ensures the survival of the fittest in every department.
> —Andrew Carnegie, *The Gospel of Wealth*, 1889

Global affirmative or positive action programs aim to change rules and provide advantages to groups that have traditionally suffered discrimination. They stand in contrast to the laws reviewed in the previous chapter because they encourage positive action (equal and even favorable treatment of certain groups) rather than prohibit negative treatment (discrimination) in employment. These types of policies go beyond ensuring equal rights to correct past wrongs. Several principles of affirmative or positive action programs are common to all countries, although the program can vary greatly from one country to the next. Typically, affirmative or positive action programs provide measures for interventions, cut across and attempt to influence the operation of free-market mechanisms, aim to actively reverse past discrimination against specific groups, and offer temporary actions.

There are those who claim that business enterprises should not be burdened with concerns for people and society but be able to pursue single-mindedly their financial interests. It is argued that in a perfectly competitive free market, the pursuit of profit will by itself ensure that the members of society are served in the most socially beneficial way.[12] On the other hand, businesses operate in a social context, and they need to be ethical and abide by the rules of the host country. Understanding the legislation and social policies of the host country is important because it provides businesses with important knowledge of the value context in a specific country. From a practical perspective, businesses need to understand the legal context in order to practice legally and avoid lawsuits.

Although the legislation and public policies described in this chapter have been conceived with the good intentions of providing diverse groups with better opportunities, they have generated some unintended consequences that are not always positive for individuals and for the well-being of the nations. For example, affirmative action practices in South Africa have caused many Afrikaners (Whites) to leave the country. With not enough well-trained Black people to replace them, this "White flight" has had a negative impact on the South African economy. Another unintended side effect of these programs is the rush for people to classify themselves as members of a disadvantaged group in order to reap the benefits of preferential treatment (e.g., groups in India who want to be classified as Backward). The backlash against these policies includes a call to dismantle the programs—a call that has been successful in some instances (e.g., California; see previous section).

Proponents of affirmative action programs are concerned that the recent trend to eliminate these programs may cause a sweeping reversal of the policies that will result in erosion of their achievements. They fear that without the sanctions and incentives of these programs, companies may no longer be proactive in recruiting and retaining women and minority workers, and the representation of these groups in the workforce will decrease. On the other hand, opponents believe that the combined effect of the legislation and public policies has already made enough of a difference and that there is no need to continue with those programs. Their main concern is that if the programs drag on long enough, they will become an entitlement rather than a measure to remedy past inequalities. Both sides agree, however, that some form of time limit needs to be set on these programs. In the long run, the hope is that the impact of these programs—along with the existence of strong antidiscrimination—will result in a more egalitarian workplace that accurately represents the general population of each nation.

Notes

1. For a detailed discussion of discrimination categorizations, see Velasquez (2011), pp. 319–341.

2. The full text of these acts is available in the ILO's national labor law database (NATLEX): http://natlex.ilo.org

3. Equal Treatment Directive 76/207/EEC, 1976. Articles 1(2) and (3) state, "This Directive shall be without prejudice to provisions concerning the protection of women particularly as regards to pregnancy and maternity and this directive shall be without prejudice to measures that promote equal opportunity for men and women. In particular by removing existing inequalities which affect women's opportunities in areas referred to in

article 1(1) i.e., access to employment including promotion and to vocational training and as regards working conditions and social security."

4. The Council Positive Action Recommendation 84/635/EEC, December 1984.

5. Council Directive 2000/43/EC of June 29, 2000, Race Relations (Amendment) Act 2000 and the EC Article 13 Race Directive.

6. Exchange rate as of June 2015, as quoted at www.oanda.com/convert/classic

7. For a discussion of the pros and cons of affirmative actions, see Tummala (1999), pp. 495–508, and Hodges-Aeberhard (1999), pp. 247–272.

8. See, for example, a discussion of quotas for religious groups in Ireland in Rea and Eastwood (1992), pp. 31–39.

9. For a thorough review of court cases in the United States, South Africa, and the European Court of Justice, see Hodges-Aeberhard (1999), pp. 247–272.

10. For a detailed discussion of South Africa's legislation and examples of court cases, see Hodges-Aeberhard (1999), pp. 247–272, and Tummala (1999), pp. 495–508.

11. State of California Constitution, Article I, section 31.

12. For a discussion of the objections for enforcing corporate ethical standards, see Velasquez (2011), pp. 23–26.

Websites

NATLEX Australia: http://www.ilo.org/dyn/natlex/natlex4.detail?p_lang=en&p_isn=2947&p_country=AUS

NATLEX Austria: http://www.ilo.org/dyn/natlex/natlex4.detail?p_lang=en&p_isn=42258&p_country=AUT

NATLEX Canada: http://www.ilo.org/dyn/natlex/natlex4.detail?p_lang=en&p_isn=43272&p_country=CAN

NATLEX India: http://www.ilo.org/dyn/natlex/natlex4.detail?p_lang=en&p_isn=51207&p_country=IND

NATLEX Ireland: http://www.ilo.org/dyn/natlex/natlex4.detail?p_lang=en&p_isn=53838&p_country=IRL

NATLEX Namibia: http://www.ilo.org/dyn/natlex/natlex4.detail?p_lang=en&p_isn=82563&p_country=NAM

NATLEX South Africa: http://www.ilo.org/dyn/natlex/natlex4.detail?p_lang=en&p_isn=90682&p_country=ZAF

NATLEX Sweden: http://www.ilo.org/dyn/natlex/natlex4.detail?p_lang=en&p_isn=70960&p_country=SWE

(Continued)

(Continued)

NATLEX Vietnam: http://www.ilo.org/dyn/natlex/docs/MONOGRAPH/91650/114939/F224084256/VNM91650.pdf

United Kingdom Equality Act of 2010: Retrieved June 21, 2015, from http://www.legislation.gov.uk/ukpga/2010/15/section/158

United States Executive Order 11246, 1965: Retrieved June 21, 2015, from http://www.legislation.gov.uk/ukpga/2010/15/section/158

4

Global Demographic Trends

Impact on Workforce Diversity

MARTHA FARNSWORTH RICHE
AND MICHÀLLE E. MOR BARAK

No more shall there be in it an infant that lives but a few days, or an old person who does not live out a lifetime; for one who dies at a hundred years will be considered a youth, and one who falls short of a hundred will be considered accursed.

—Isaiah 65:20 (NRSV)

Global demographic trends echo this ancient prophecy, as more-developed countries are undergoing an unprecedented demographic transition, one that calls into question traditional assumptions about the characteristics of the working-age population. First, in countries where more adults survive to live a full working life on the one hand and have fewer children on the other, working-age populations, as traditionally defined, are aging. Second, as the economic premium for advanced education rises, increasing numbers of young people enter the workforce later than the traditional ages. Third, as the amount of time people live past the traditional ages for leaving the labor force lengthens, people are working longer, especially in countries that lack retirement security. To put these trends in context, some demographers have estimated that the average baby girl born in the United States, France, or many of the most economically developed countries has a longer life expectancy, as much as 100 years (see, for example, Gielen, 2016; Vaupel et al., 1998). With similar improvements projected for most developed countries, along with relatively smaller cohorts of young workers, many are questioning whether their economies can afford to lose workers to retirement at the traditional ages, let alone afford to fund them to do so. These trends increase age diversity in the workforce of more-developed countries.

At the same time, the working-age population in the least-developed countries is growing rapidly and in the traditional pattern—among youth. This growth is particularly pronounced because here, as worldwide, more children than ever before are living to adulthood and to have children of their own. Though fertility rates have fallen in these countries, they are generally higher than elsewhere, so births continue to drive population growth.

Thus, as economic integration and societal globalization diversify the world's workforce in new ways, global demographic trends amplify this development. On the one hand, the working-age population is surging in the least-developed countries. Their rapidly growing numbers of young people will continue to increase the supply of new workers in the developing world as their children, born and yet to be born, eventually reach working age. On the other hand, the world's more-developed countries are experiencing slowing rates of population growth, even population declines. Their static or declining numbers of young people, combined with improved health in mid- and later life, are tilting their working-age populations toward mature age groups.

Meanwhile, global economic integration, based in part on differences in labor costs, has amplified the role of migration in balancing labor demand and supply. As in the past, workers continue to migrate to find employers; with global integration, however, employers can also migrate to find workers. As a result, people from diverse backgrounds, with diverse human capital and diverse expectations, are increasingly encountering one another in the workplace. This diversity is accentuated by changes within national populations that are increasing the proportion of the workforce that is made up of nontraditional native-born workers—particularly women but also older people, people with disabilities, and people with nontraditional sexual orientations.

This chapter provides an overview of global demographic trends that contribute to increasing workforce diversity throughout the world. We begin with international population trends—trends in the working-age population in different regions and migration trends across borders. We then describe some national population trends specifically related to gender, age, disability, and sexual orientation that contribute to increased diversity in the workplace.

International Population Trends

The world's population, virtually static throughout most of history, has grown to unprecedented size over the past 2 centuries, largely due to advances in health care that developed in the industrialized world, then spread to the developing world (see Figure 4.1). At the beginning of the 20th century, the world had 1.7 billion people. By 1960, after health advances had become widespread in the industrialized countries but before they became common in the developing countries, the world had 3 billion people. Then various aid programs took the new advances around the world, and its population surged past 6 billion by the century's end. It was 7.2 billion in 2014, and is slated to surpass 8 billion by 2025 and reach 9.5 billion in 2050 (Population Reference Bureau, 2016; United Nations, 2015b). This growth reflects the advances in curing infectious childhood diseases, sanitation, and public health that now permit children in most countries to live to adulthood and to have healthy children of their own.

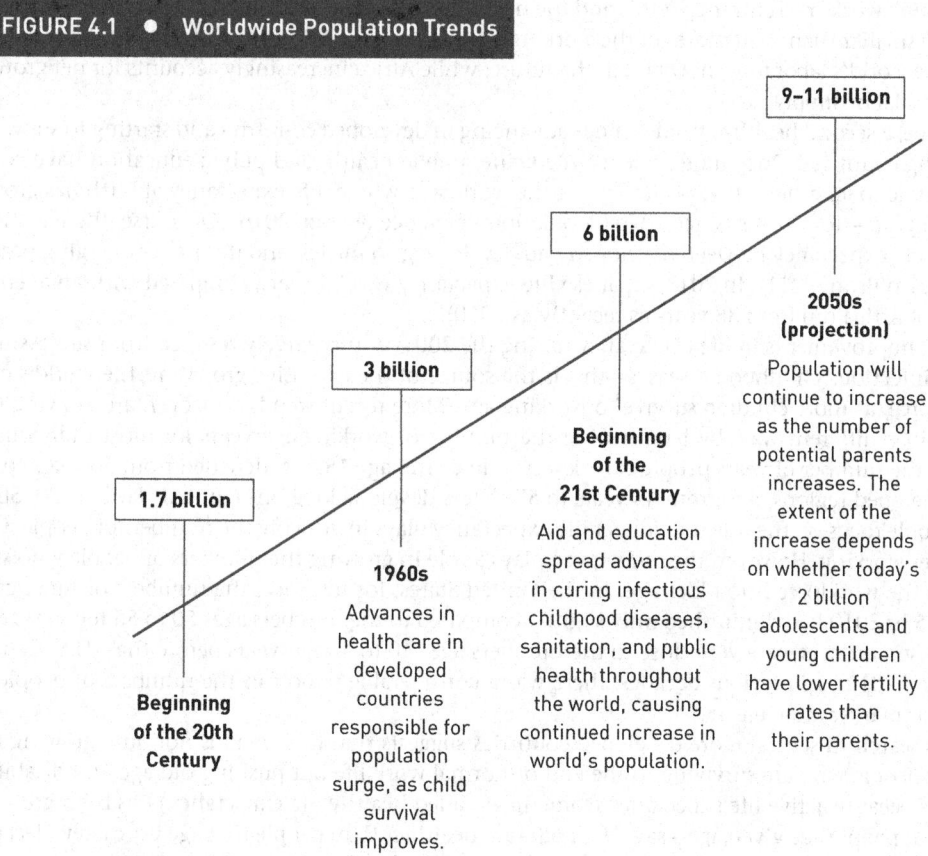

FIGURE 4.1 ● Worldwide Population Trends

9–11 billion

6 billion

3 billion

1.7 billion

**2050s
(projection)**

Population will
continue to increase
as the number of
potential parents
increases. The
extent of the
increase depends
on whether today's
2 billion
adolescents and
young children
have lower fertility
rates than
their parents.

**Beginning
of the
21st Century**

Aid and education
spread advances
in curing infectious
childhood diseases,
sanitation, and public
health throughout
the world, causing
continued increase in
world's population.

1960s

Advances in
health care in
developed
countries
responsible for
population
surge, as child
survival
improves.

**Beginning
of the 20th
Century**

At the beginning of the 21st century, the world had about 1 billion adolescents and 1 billion more young children: the parents of the next generations of workers. These are the people who will grow the world population to 9.5 billion as they have their own children, if fertility rates continue to decline at their current pace (United Nations, 2015b). If rates do not decline, the United Nations (UN) sees the world's population growing more than a billion more, reaching nearly 11 billion in total in 2050. Thus, the childbearing decisions of today's young people will determine how large the world's population becomes, as well as the size, composition, and locus of the workforce of the future.

The developing world already has unprecedented numbers of young people, many of whom would have died at young ages before the public health advances of the last half-century. From an employment perspective, the primary challenge is absorbing the 3 billion people who doubled the world's population during the last 40 years of the 20th century. Age 54 or under in 2015, the members of the workforce of the next 2 decades are working, looking for work, or searching for the education that will help them when they reach working age. What global demographic trends might affect diversity in workplaces?

Populations are growing at different rates around the world, changing the composition of its population. More than 60% of the world's working-age population, ages 15–59, was in Asia in 2015, compared with less than 5% in North America.[1] Africa had 14%, whereas Latin America (including the Caribbean) had 9% and Europe 10% (United Nations, 2015b). Looking at the population under age 15 in 2015, the source of young workforce entrants in this and the next decade, Africa had 25%, while the shares of other regions were smaller than their shares of the working-age population. Asia clearly represents the center of gravity of the world's labor force now and in the future, while Africa increasingly accounts for net growth in the world's labor supply.

Meanwhile, a second health-related trend is advancing in developed countries and starting to show up in developing countries. Once more, science/medicine, public health, and public education have combined, this time to lengthen life expectancy. For the world as a whole, life expectancy at birth has grown by nearly 15 years—to 71—just since 1970 (Population Reference Bureau, 2016). Of course, there is still a wide gap in life expectancy between developed and developing countries, and it is not converging neatly or rapidly (C. Wilson, 2011). In 2013, Japanese life expectancy was 83 years, compared with an average of 59 in all of Africa (up from 38 years as recently as 1950).

The great improvements in life expectancy during the 20th century largely resulted from successfully combating infectious childhood diseases—this is the source of the explosive growth in the world's current labor force, as more children survive to working age. More recent trends, however, are growing the labor force in a different way, by lengthening the number of working-age years for most individuals. Since 1950, the number of years people can expect to live after age 15 has increased from 56 years to 63 in more-developed regions, and from 43 years to 57 in less-developed regions (United Nations, 2015b).

Some people focus on the role that longer life expectancy plays in growing the numbers of people who are no longer working. However, the same trend plays a role in growing the numbers of people who stay involved in the workforce into older age. In the United States, for instance, the numbers of Americans ages 60 to 65 in 2010 had diminished only slightly compared to the numbers ages 50 to 55 ten years earlier, and those numbers were very close to the numbers ages 40 to 45 ten years before that (U.S. Census Bureau, 2001, 2012). In previous decades, there was a considerable fall-off in the numbers of people at each ten-year marker after age 45.

Recent research in several more-developed countries suggests that this trend is not only growing the numbers of people who are surviving to the end of normal work life but pushing old age and disability back. This is because active life expectancy (sometimes called healthy life expectancy) has been growing too, such that people at a given age—say, 60 or 65—are healthier than people that age were a few decades earlier in terms of their activity levels (Manton, Corder, & Stallard, 1997; Manton, Gu, & Lowrimore, 2008). They also have higher educational attainment, which is directly correlated to better health in old age. The result is that "old age" is occurring at older ages for many, and the ability to work, if necessary, is commensurately extended.

This is good news for individuals, though it contains new challenges for employers and societies. Perhaps the most important challenge is that for the first time in history, a country whose fertility rate is around replacement level (2.1 children, to replace both parents in the population) is beginning to experience roughly equal numbers of people in each living generation, except the very oldest. The age composition of the U.S. population is a good example of this change (see Figure 4.2).[2] As recently as 1970, the U.S. age picture represented the classic "population pyramid," in which each younger generation outnumbered the next older generation. In a revolutionary change, the U.S. population pyramid is turning into a "population pillar," with roughly equal-sized generations into older ages.

Meanwhile, the contrast between less-developed countries, which manifest the classic youth-dominated population picture, and developed countries is stark. This is because developed countries whose fertility rates have been below replacement level for a considerable time are looking at a population that contains considerably more older people than younger ones. This is particularly so in Europe, whose overall population is projected to decline slightly between 2000 and 2050 (United Nations, 2015b). This slight absolute decline masks a stunning reversal of the relative shares of the older and younger populations. The numbers of Europeans under age 15 are projected to decline by 15% by 2050, while the

FIGURE 4.2 • Historic and Projected Age Composition, 1970 and 2050

From Pyramids to Pillars, United States

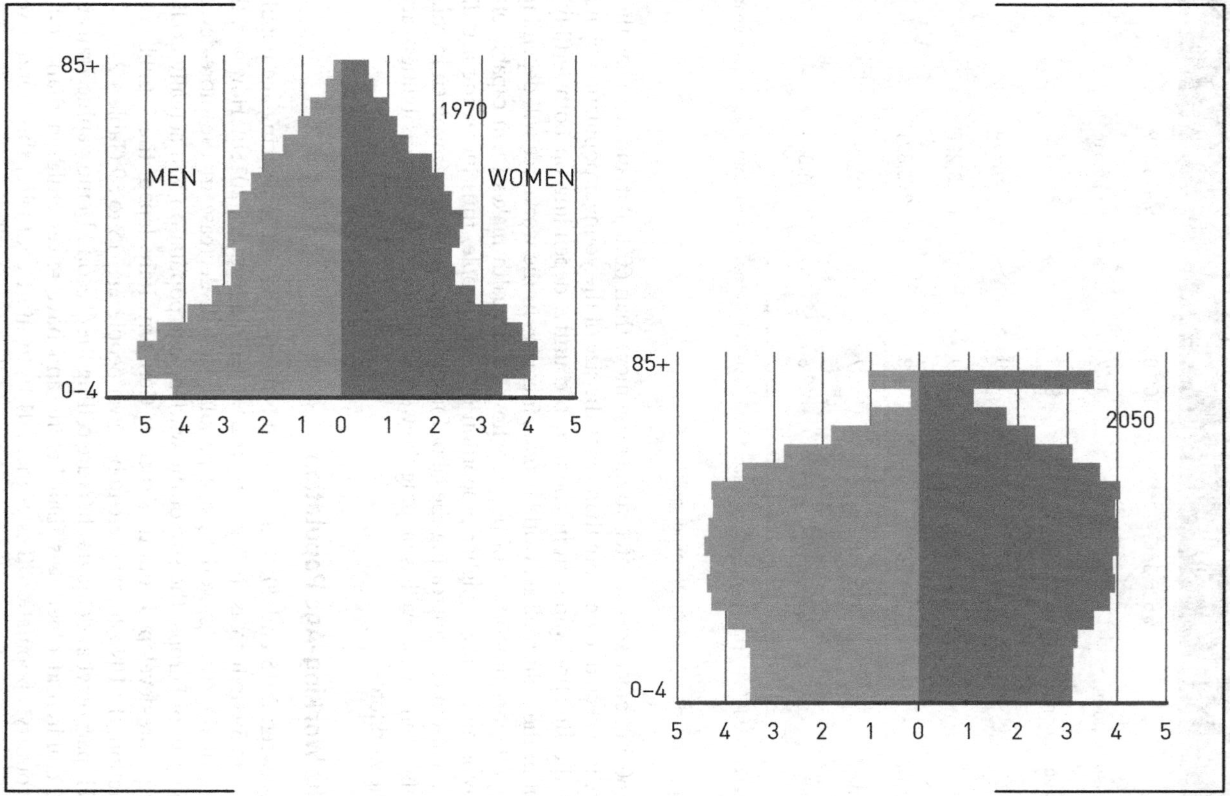

Source: U.S. Census Bureau

TABLE 4.1 • Population Ages 15–59 (in 1,000s)				
	2015	Percentage of world	2050	Percentage of world
World	4,525,366	100.0	5,496,139	100.0
More-developed regions	753,749	16.7	675,816	12.3
Less-developed regions	2,771,616	83.3	4,820,323	87.7
Europe	450,891	10.0	361,956	6.6
Africa	628,777	13.9	1,410,238	25.7
North America	217,233	4.8	243,821	4.4
LA/Caribbean	395,048	8.7	448,294	8.2
Asia/Oceania	2,833,417	62.6	3,031,830	55.2

Source: United Nations. (2011). World population prospects (2010 Revision). Retrieved from http://esa.un.org/unpd/wpp/Excel-Data/population.htm

Note: Percentages do not add to 100% due to rounding.

numbers age 60 and older are expected to increase more than 60%. Put another way, the older population in Europe is expected to be more than twice the size of the younger population by mid-century.

Of course, the situation varies from country to country, depending on both fertility rates and net migration. But in the industrialized world overall, increases in the workforce will depend more than ever on employing a higher proportion of people whose good health makes them capable of working. This essentially means employing a higher proportion of older people, thus increasing age diversity within the workforce. It also means increasing the labor force participation rates of women in countries where it has traditionally been low, as well as tapping the work skills of people with disabilities—again, increasing diversity in the workforce.

Trends in the Working-Age Population

Worldwide, between 2015 and 2050, the United Nations expects the working-age population, defined here as ages 15 to 59, to increase by more than 20% (United Nations, 2015b). However, the UN expects that the share of the world's working-age population will decrease in the more-developed regions; indeed, in the case of Europe, the size of the working-age population will actually decline (Table 4.1). Specifically, in more-developed countries such as Germany, Italy, Japan, the Republic of Korea, or the Russian Federation, the UN expects there to be fewer people ages 15 to 59 (Table 4.2).

This trend is part of what demographers are calling the "Second Demographic Transition," in which women have children at older ages than before, and have fewer children than would be required to replace a country's population (Lestaeghe, 2010). In most countries, this trend is related to more women participating in the workforce. Indeed, declines in fertility are particularly pronounced in countries where policies and practices have not adapted to the increasing presence of women in the workforce. Fertility rates are somewhat higher in countries like France that have made it easier for

TABLE 4.2 • Population Ages 15–59, Selected Countries (in 1,000s)				
	2015	Percentage of world	2050	Percentage of world
World	4,525,366	100.0	5,496,139	100.0
France	37,097	0.8	38,087	0.7
Germany	48,795	1.1	34,685	0.6
Italy	35,646	0.8	28,443	0.5
Japan	68,413	1.5	48,547	0.9
Republic of Korea	33,525	0.7	23,917	0.4
Russian Federation	90,662	2.0	65,823	1.2
United Kingdom	37,586	0.8	38,499	0.7
United States	195,171	4.3	219,861	4.0

Source: United Nations. (2011). World population prospects (2010 Revision). Retrieved from http://esa.un.org/unpd/wpp/Excel-Data/population.htm

Note: Percentages do not add to 100% due to rounding.

women to combine child-rearing and work, though fertility in those countries is still slightly below replacement level (Myrskla, Goldstein, & Cheng, 2013).

Even if fertility rates increase in countries where they are very low, the current deficit in young people cannot be replaced except by immigration. More-developed countries that accept relatively high levels of immigration, such as the United States, will have more people in those ages, though not enough to keep up with the pace of rapid population growth throughout the developing world as today's "youth explosion" enters the working ages.

Given these contrasting growth rates, today's more-developed countries can expect their share of the world's working-age population to drop from over 17% to 12% by 2050 (Table 4.1). In contrast, working-age populations will continue to swell in less-developed regions, as the substantial youth bulges produced by high fertility rates in earlier decades reach working age.

In most countries, people have become accustomed to having children survive, and fertility rates have declined. So over the next 2 decades, this bulge should be absorbed virtually everywhere except in Africa, which may contain 40% of the world's children in 2050 (United Nations, 2015b). Consequently, Africa may be the last frontier of "excess" labor available for low-wage competition in its home countries.

The impact of the HIV/AIDS pandemic on population growth has injected some uncertainty into this overall picture. This impact is difficult to estimate, given the lack of reliable statistics about its prevalence in most countries. Estimates from the U.S. Census Bureau have suggested that although deaths from AIDS have dampened population growth rates in Africa, fertility is so high there that populations will continue to grow in most though not all countries (Stanecki, 2002). Population growth will also be dampened slightly in Asian countries such as Burma, Cambodia, and Thailand (Stanecki, 2002).

Probably the most significant effect of HIV/AIDS on workforce diversity will not be on the numbers of workers but on the age structure of the workforce, particularly in countries where the pandemic was severe. As people tend to contract AIDS relatively young, an estimated median survival rate of around 10 years means that the effect is felt among men in their 40s and women in their 30s. This dynamic works against the worldwide trend toward longer life expectancy, and thus to increasing shares of older workers (C. Wilson, 2011).

Migration Trends

Migration is the other element in population change, in addition to births and deaths. One aspect of the new demographic transition is the important role of migration in offsetting, fully or partially, population declines caused by unprecedented low rates of fertility (Coale & Zelnik, 2015; Lestaeghe, 2010), with obvious effects on diversity. UN demographers have calculated how many migrants it could take to keep the working-age population the same size in various industrial countries over the first half of this century (United Nations, 2000a). Given the relatively lower numbers of children being born there, they calculated that Europe as a whole would need to receive a net 3.2 million migrants a year to keep its working-age population from declining. In contrast, the United States continues to have enough births to keep its working-age population constant, so immigration serves to grow that population.

Recent decades have seen major changes in the size, direction, and complexity of international migration, most notably in the growth of migration from developing to developed regions. The global stock of international migration is estimated to have increased from 154 million in 1990 to 232 million in 2013 (United Nations, 2015b). Although these annual migration flows may be small relative to the size of the world population, social and cultural differences tend to make migrants particularly visible, particularly those who come from the global South to the global North. Now, new poles of economic growth are emerging in the global South and are expected to stimulate new migratory flows, this time from South to South. Both flows are controversial because of their impact on diversity, as well as on the economic prospects of native-born populations in the receiving countries.

Migration data are generally imperfect for workforce analysis because they are typically derived from records kept by countries as they "control" their borders (i.e., monitor and record entries) (Zlotnick, 1994). Tourists often become workers, as do students who stay beyond their schooling. Others enter by avoiding border controls altogether, while some countries, notably members of the European Union, have modified and even abolished such controls for member nations. At the same time, countries are much less likely to monitor and record exits.[3] Thus, the extent of return migration, particularly circular migration, is widely ignored, even though migration experts consider it of prime importance for analyzing employment trends. The migration of workers from Eastern to Western Europe during the early part of the 21st century, and then their return home in the global economic crisis that began in 2007, is a notable example. This and other evidence suggests that globalization allows many international migrants to reinvent long-standing patterns of seasonal and temporary movement for work rather than choosing permanent settlement in a new country. However, this aspect of the global labor force is largely unmeasured.[4]

In terms of diversity, the important trend is the change in the direction of migration flows since the 1960s. Migration flows from less-developed countries—to both developed and developing countries alike—have replaced the flows of Europeans in the opposite direction. Essentially, population stabilization or decline in Europe has replaced several centuries of European population explosion, which fueled European colonization of most of the rest of the world (Chesnais, 2000). In the meantime, population has exploded in the developing world. In search of work and livelihood, many leave their home countries for the developed countries (see, for example, Box 4.1). Certain migrants' need to find work sometimes meets demands in the host countries for their specific skills. For example, women from the Philippines have found a large international demand for their services as caregivers to children and the elderly (see, for example, Box 4.2). More generally, slow population growth in most developed countries and rapid growth in developing countries has been causing the foreign-born share of the population in developed countries as a whole to rise (see Figure 4.3 and Table 4.3).

FIGURE 4.3 ● International Demographic Trends

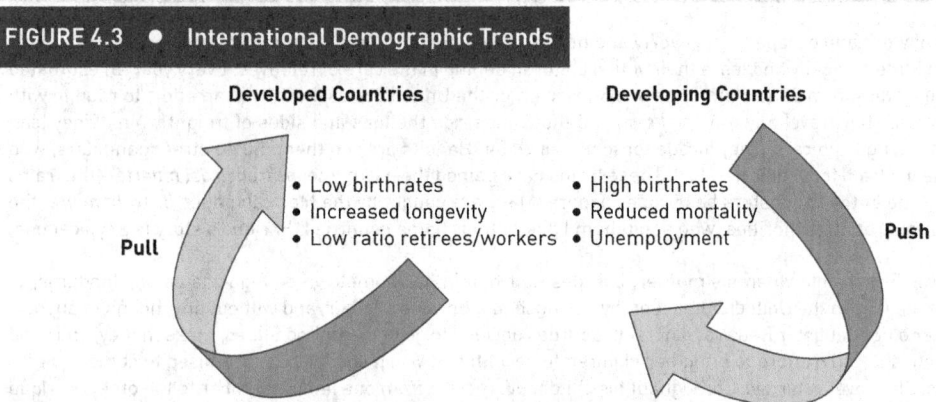

Developed Countries	Developing Countries
• Low birthrates	• High birthrates
• Increased longevity	• Reduced mortality
• Low ratio retirees/workers	• Unemployment

Pull   Push

Both push and pull factors are working toward the same outcome:
a more diverse global workforce.

TABLE 4.3 ● The Foreign-Born Share of the Population of More-Developed Regions and Selected Countries

	1990	2000	2010	2013
World	2.9	2.8	3.2	3.2
More-developed regions	7.2	8.7	10.5	10.8
Europe	6.8	7.7	9.3	9.8
* Sweden	9.2	11.3	14.8	15.9
* Ireland	6.5	10.1	12.7	15.9
* United Kingdom	6.4	8.0	11.3	12.4
* Germany	7.4	10.8	11.7	11.9
* Austria	10.3	12.4	15.2	15.7
Northern America	9.8	12.8	14.8	14.9
* United States	9.1	12.2	14.2	14.3

Source: United Nations. (2011). World population prospects (2010 Revision). Retrieved from http://esa.un.org/unpd/wpp/Excel-Data/population.htm

Box 4.1

THE WOMEN WHO LEAVE, THE CHILDREN WHO FOLLOW: ENRIQUE'S STORY

In search of work and escape from poverty and hunger, many mothers from Central America and Mexico enter the United States illegally and leave their young children behind in the care of relatives. Every year an estimated 48,000 youngsters from Central America and Mexico enter the United States illegally in an effort to reunite with their mothers. They travel any way they can, and thousands ride the tops and sides of freight trains. They leap on and off rolling train cars. They forage for food and water. Bandits prey on them. So do street gangsters, who have made the train tops their new turf. These trains have gained the nickname *los trenes del muerte*—the trains of death. None of the youngsters has proper papers. Many are caught by the Mexican police or by *la migra*, the Mexican immigration authorities, who send them back to their home countries. Enrique's story is a typical one.

Enrique was 5 years old when his mother, Lourdes, left him in her hometown of Tegucigalpa, in Honduras, to immigrate illegally to the United States. Left by her husband, Enrique's father, and without any means to support her son, her older daughter Belky, and herself, Lourdes decided to go to the United States, make money, and send it home until she could afford to bring her children to be with her. When she left, she promised to come back for them soon. She never returned. Throughout his childhood, moving from one family member to the other, Enrique dreamed of reuniting with his mother. At age 17, after six failed attempts to travel to the United States illegally, he was finally reunited with his mother in North Carolina. A few months later he learned that Maria Isabel, the girlfriend he left back in Honduras, had given birth to their daughter. Enrique sent money to bring Maria Isabel to the United States. In a sad twist of fate, both Enrique and Maria Isabel decided to leave the baby behind with Maria Isabel's mother until they had enough money to send for her.

Shortly after arriving in the United States, Maria Isabel and Enrique were able to come up with $5,000 to pay a smuggler to bring their daughter, Jasmine, to the United States. A decade later, the young man (now in his late 20s) is living in the United States with Maria Isabel and his mother, Lourdes, in Florida. Since arriving in the United States, Enrique has struggled with unemployment and drug use, some of which he picked up when living in Honduras. Today, children continue to leave Honduras and head for the United States. According to Enrique's aunt, approximately 50% of neighborhood children leave with a smuggler, about 20% with a parent, and an estimated 30% go alone to the United States, just like Enrique did (Nazario, 2002, 2007, 2014).

And it is becoming more diverse. In 2013, China became the top sending country for immigrants to the United States, replacing Mexico, the longtime leader (Jensen, 2015). During the first decade of the 21st century, immigration from China increased while immigration from Mexico declined, particularly after the financial crisis of 2007 caused a major recession in the United States. However, as recently as 1970, people born in Italy, Germany, and the United Kingdom, as well as in Canada, each outnumbered the Mexican-born in the U.S. population at the beginning of the 21st century (Organisation for Economic Co-operation and Development [OECD], 2000). Today's large immigrant groups in the United States include people from India, the Philippines, Korea, and Japan, validating Chesnais's perception that that the United States "is no longer primarily a European country" (2000).

In the meantime, countries that not so long ago sent immigrants to settlement countries like the United States are now receiving immigrants themselves. Sweden, once a major contributor to the U.S. population, is a good example. Migration into Sweden turned positive (i.e., more people entered than left) during the 1960s (Council of Europe, 2000). Now there are more Swedes who were born in Iran than

Box 4.2

THE PRICE OF MIGRATION FOR WOMEN FROM THE PHILIPPINES

Bea, a 26-year-old woman, had been living in Denmark since she migrated there from the Philippines. Bea became pregnant and was scared to go to the doctor because she had no documentation and feared she would be deported. She continued to work as a cleaner and did not seek any medical care. When she went into labor, she did not go to the hospital until the pain became unbearable. Her boyfriend and friends later took her to the hospital, where she had to have an emergency caesarean section. Tragically, the baby later died. She was in the hospital for 2 weeks. During that period, every time a doctor or a nurse would come into the room they would tell her that she was in the country illegally and they would have to report her to the police. A short time later, the police came to the hospital and told her she had to leave the country. She pleaded with the police because she did not want to go back to the Philippines, but they told her that she had no choice. Bea often wondered if the baby's death could have been prevented if she had received medical care during her pregnancy (Women and Global Migration Working Group, 2016).

Filipina women have found a large international demand for their services as caregivers to children and to the elderly. However, their experiences vary widely depending on the destination country. Filipinas work as caregivers most commonly in Saudi Arabia, Hong Kong, Japan, the United Arab Emirates, and Taiwan (Kang & Tran, 2003). Other countries such as the United States also employ a large number of Filipinas. However, most of the women live and work illegally in these countries, making it difficult to accurately estimate their numbers. Canada has been a popular destination since the introduction of Canada's Live-in Caregiver Program under which foreign workers have an opportunity to incorporate into the social structure and can live comfortably, have a chance to bring their families to Canada after 2 years, and be eligible to apply for citizenship (Baga-Reyes, 2003; Cristaldi & Darden, 2011; Fudge, 2011).

However, most countries' policies are not as generous as Canada's. For example, Taiwan, which is now the fifth most popular destination for Filipina women, has significantly less desirable economic conditions. Taiwan has set a minimum monthly wage of $TND 15,840 (Taiwanese new dollars; US$480), for a 40-hour workweek. However, after factoring in the cost of mandatory payments for food, accommodations, and monthly broker fees, the women are left with $TND 10,040 to $TND 11,840 (US$304 to US$359). Furthermore, in order to obtain a job in Taiwan, most of the women had to pay a broker's placement fee. That fee can be as high as $TND 100,000, which is usually borrowed from the broker and paid later from the woman's wages (Kang & Tran, 2003). With all of the fees associated with the legal work opportunities in Taiwan, it is little wonder that many of the women head to countries such as the United States to work illegally for wages as little as $3 per hour, with no pay for overtime.

in Norway, more born in Iraq than in Germany, and more born in Turkey or Chile than in the United States or the United Kingdom (United Nations, 2015b).

Because of its impact on diversity, people are largely aware that population movement from the Southern Hemisphere to the Northern one has become an important driver of global migration. They are less likely to be aware that what is called "free movement" migration, mostly between the member states of the European Union, is equally important—in 2012, for the first time ever, "such movements within Europe matched legal permanent migration from outside Europe" (Organisation for Economic Co-Operation and Development, 2014). Diversity produced by "free movement" migration is less problematic from a cultural and racial standpoint, but it still requires making adjustments in the workplace. Meanwhile, as the role of migration in increasing diversity in developed countries gains attention, it continues to be important in developing countries. The difference is that migration-produced diversity in the latter countries tends to involve people from within the region, who may be less "different."

This process continues to evolve, as countries that have been supplying migrants develop, economically, relative to the countries that have been traditional destinations for their unemployed or underemployed workers. For instance, migration to the United States from Mexico slowed so much starting in 2005 that it ceased to exceed return migration. As a result, net migration from Mexico was essentially zero between 2005 and 2010, for the first time in several decades (Passel, Cohn, & Gonzalez-Barrera, 2012). In part, this slowdown could be attributed to poor economic conditions in the United States, but in part it reflected decreasing birthrates and expanding opportunities in Mexico (Cave, 2011). In addition, heightened border enforcement and increased deportations by the U.S. authorities contributed to this trend (Passel et al., 2012).

Finally, refugees have become an unprecedented part of migration flows, in numbers not seen since World War II. According to the United Nations High Commissioner for Refugees (UNHCR), at the end of 2013 the world counted 51.2 million displaced people—and this number rose to 59.5 million in 2014 (Edwards, 2014). The bulk of these refugees remain in the global south, but large and increasing numbers seek a better life in more-developed countries (United Nations, 2015b). These numbers are so large they are overwhelming the systems designed to process and measure them.

Successful claims for asylum are measurable, although they far understate the increase in demand, and can illustrate the larger trends. Such claims rose by 20% in 2013: Germany received the largest number of asylum claims, followed by the United States, Sweden (with the largest number of claims relative to its population), France, and Turkey (OECD, 2015). Syrians fleeing their civil war make up the largest single group of asylum seekers, followed by refugees from conflict and economic failure in parts of Africa, particularly Eritrea and Somalia. In short, today's refugees present a diversity challenge to the countries in which they would like to settle.

National Trends

Diversity in the workplace is a growing concern in many countries, and this concern extends well beyond the ramifications of international population trends. Simply put, shifts in the nature and location of economic activity are combining with social and demographic trends to increase the role of nontraditional workers, particularly women, in the paid workforce in all but the least-developed countries. At the same time, international support for human rights—reinforced by messages delivered through global communications and entertainment networks—is blurring traditional patterns of workplace discrimination on the basis of religion; social class; caste, race, or ethnic origin; disability; or sexual orientation, as well as age and gender.

Gender Diversity

Increasing numbers and shares of women in the workplace may be the most important component of diversity at the national level in most of the world, not only because of their strengthened presence but also because their changing roles have a simultaneous effect at home and work. Historically, only a small proportion of women could afford to remain outside the labor force, no matter what their family responsibilities, but they tended to work as unpaid family labor, particularly in agriculture or the informal economy. This is still the case for women in some countries, notably in sub-Saharan Africa. However, women's share of the paid labor force has become large, particularly in economies where higher educational attainments are allied with higher earning prospects in the formal economy. Thus, a country's scale of development is a major determinant of women's presence in the workplace (International Labour Organization, 2011).

Globally, a large increase in women's labor force participation in recent decades took place during the 1980s and 1990s. This trend is well illustrated by its evolution in Latin America. In 1980, little more than one quarter of the measured workforce was female in Central and South America; by 1997, women made up one third of the workforce in Central America and nearly two-fifths in South America (United Nations, 2000a). Women's share of the workforce also grew significantly in the more-developed regions during those two decades. More recently, in many regions where women have traditionally been discouraged from working outside the home, they have increased their share of the measured labor force, although it remains relatively small (Table 4.4).[5]

Whether women's participation rates are high or low, the gap between women's and men's rates is narrowing in most regions (Table 4.4). This results from two intersecting trends: increased rates of participation for women and decreased rates for men, especially where pension schemes have encouraged early retirement. Changes in the age composition of the working-age population also may change women's share of the labor force. For instance, the share of women in the labor force may increase even more in countries where populations are aging, as women tend to live longer than men. Many women need to support themselves in the absence of a husband; others seek paid activity outside a home that no longer contains children. In either circumstance, where women's educational attainment equals men's (or exceeds it), employers in most countries can expect challenges to practices that favor men at all levels of the workforce, including supervisory or executive positions.

TABLE 4.4 ● Labor Force Participation Rates

	2000		2013 (preliminary)	
	women	men	women	men
North Africa	21.6	74.8	24.0	74.5
Sub-Saharan Africa	63.2	77.3	65.1	76.6
Latin America and Caribbean	48.0	80.7	53.6	79.5
East Asia	69.4	82.6	63.3	77.9
Southeast Asia and the Pacific	58.5	82.7	59.2	82.0
South Asia	34.7	83.2	30.5	80.7
Middle East	16.3	74.3	18.9	75.0
Developed economies and the European Union	51.8	70.2	52.9	67.4
Central and Southeastern Europe (non-EU) and CIS	49.1	69.2	50.3	70.7
WORLD	51.9	78.7	50.3	76.6

Source: Organization for Economic Co-operation and Development (OECD), 2009 (Table A.2.3.). *Organization for Economic Co-operation and Development (OECD), (2011) , Table A.2.3.

Note: The 2007–2008 financial crisis affected labor force participation trends, but the effect was uneven across regions. The ILO notes that "the drop in participation rates has been particularly pronounced in East and South Asia, where many women have left the labour market."

In sum, women have been more active economically in most regions, especially in regions where they had been relatively less active a quarter century ago. As a result, women's economic activity rates are increasingly similar around the world, except in countries—primarily in the Middle East and North Africa—where society invests less in girls' education and constrains women's roles outside the home.

Women's increased participation in the labor force is the product of several social and economic changes. In most countries, large numbers of women have achieved control over their fertility, thus expanding their opportunities for education and employment. As a result, both advocates and policy-makers are addressing employment-related barriers such as negative attitudes toward employed women and unfavorable public policies regarding family and childcare, part-time employment, maternity benefits, and parental and maternal leave. Meanwhile, both economic growth and expansion of services and other sectors that tend to employ large numbers of women contribute to their increased employment.

Indeed, global economic development policy now makes fostering women's employment opportunities a priority in developing countries. World Bank economists have concluded that countries that limit women's employment lose as much as a percentage point of potential annual growth through inefficient allocation of productive resources (Cuberes & Teignier-Baqué, 2011; World Bank, 2001). Low investment in female education is also costly to poor countries. One influential study estimated that decreasing the already low gender gap in school enrollment in East Asia boosted its annual economic growth rate by 0.5% to 0.9% over South Asia, the Middle East, and sub-Saharan Africa between 1960 and 1992 (Klasen, 1999). Another study estimated that in developing countries, closing the joblessness gap between girls and boys yields an increase in gross domestic product of up to 1.2% in a single year (Chaaban & Cunningham, 2008).

In addition to the economic benefits of turning dependents into producers, researchers have shown that women's paid employment increases human capital investment in children and thus in the future labor force.[6] Women who have other choices for their lives also tend to limit their childbearing, bringing fertility rates down so that the future labor force is of a size that the national economy can more readily absorb. This important development ensures that diversity issues regarding gender in the workplace will be increasingly salient in most countries, not just the more-developed ones.

Both demographic and social changes are altering the pattern of economic activity over women's lives, creating new challenges for diversity management. Until recent decades, women in industrialized countries typically entered the labor force as soon as they completed their formal education, leaving within a few years to bear and raise children. Now, with secondary and higher education more common, participation rates are high for women in their 30s and 40s. Higher education simply makes it more costly for women to leave the labor force, as more education qualifies them for better-paying jobs and for jobs that provide advancement. This change has been most visible in Europe and North America, where patterns of economic activity for women have come to resemble patterns for men.

In these countries as well, relatively low levels of fertility mean that women whose children are grown are an increasingly important part of the labor force. In the United States, for instance, participation rates rose for older women as the well-educated baby boomers aged, and in 2008, the female workforce became roughly evenly divided between women under age 45 (generally considered the boundary between women's fertile and nonfertile years) and over it (U.S. Bureau of Labor Statistics, 2009). With two children or fewer and an increasing life expectancy, women in the more industrialized countries are spending a much smaller share of their adult life in parenting.[7] Thus, in their 40s, most women effectively complete their conventional, gender-based responsibilities in the home. Seeing the prospect of extended work lives after their children have grown, younger women may be less willing to accept inferior access to skill development during the early years of their careers.

Trends in Latin America and the Caribbean parallel women's participation trends in the more-developed regions, but here women's participation rates have increased even more in the past decade. In Africa, where agriculture remains the primary industry, women have generally been economically active throughout their lives, including their childbearing years, and little has changed. Indeed, in a few African countries, women's participation rates have been slightly higher than men's (International Labour Office, 2014). Asia is much more heterogeneous, and economic activity rates differ widely among countries (International Labour Office, 2014). However, outside of countries where women face educational, cultural, and institutional barriers, women are increasingly in the paid labor force during their childbearing and child-rearing years, making employer work-family policies an important aspect of diversity management around the world.

Age Diversity

Demographic change is increasing diversity in national workforces in yet another way, as longer life expectancies expand the population of older people. Few people realize the important contribution of mortality improvement to population growth. Yet throughout the 20th century, for instance, mortality improvement added more people to the U.S. population than did the significant amount of immigration the country experienced. Current U.S. population growth derives as much if not more from "postponed" deaths as from immigration.

Populations in all regions of the world, not just the more-developed ones, are growing older, meaning that growth rates are higher among people who are at older ages than younger ones. In more-developed countries, migration patterns slightly mitigated the effects on population aging of reduced fertility and improved mortality between 2005 and 2010.[8] In less-developed countries over the same period, the population aged slightly faster. Aging is occurring more rapidly in these countries largely because the growth rate in births has declined more rapidly, and is heavily concentrated in recent decades (Preston & Stokes, 2012).

In developing countries, most women and men who survive into old age must remain in the labor force. In developed countries, economic activity at older ages decreased in recent decades, mainly due to pension schemes that tended to allow or even encourage early retirement. The shift of employment away from agriculture has also had an effect, as older people traditionally found useful work on family farms. However, in many countries this downward trend is now slowing or even reversing as workers consider how to fund a lengthening postemployment life, and governments worry about the sustainability of pension systems.

Developed or developing, most countries can expect to see larger numbers of older people in the workforce simply because improvements in mortality continue to increase the proportion of the working-age population that lives to the end of the normal work life, however that is defined. At the same time, the workforce contains a smaller proportion of young people, even in countries that still have high fertility rates, because more of them are extending their education. These two shifts have the general effect of making the workforce more diverse in terms of workers' ages.

In the United Kingdom, for example, the working-age population in 2015 (defined here as age 15 to 64 to make age 40 the midpoint) is estimated to contain slightly more people age 40 and older as under age 40. Japan's working-age population is even larger at older ages. In South Korea, fully 56% of the working-age population has been estimated to be age 40 or older in 2015. In contrast, only 30% are estimated to be 40 or older in Pakistan, where high fertility rates continue to grow the youth population (United Nations, 2015b).

In countries that are experiencing workforce aging, some age-related diversity issues are obvious, such as those related to pay and benefits. For instance, rewarding workers for years they've spent on the job can produce disruptive inequities in the absence of visible skill differences. Or skewing benefits to people who are raising children can cause trouble with those whose later life needs are quite different.

Other issues are less obvious. In cultures where older people are accustomed to higher status at work, larger numbers of older people mean that not all can be included among the relatively smaller numbers in the upper ranks of the workforce, even if employers are willing to delay promoting younger people and younger employees are willing to go along.[9] Family issues are also changing for workers in all parts of the life cycle. For instance, smaller families and longer work lives often mean that working men or women at any age may need to care for family members, as there are fewer people available at home. As longer life expectancy does not ensure longer marital life expectancy, workers may acquire and lose family members through marriage and divorce as well as births and deaths, further diversifying the set of work-family issues.

Box 4.3
"REVERSE MENTORSHIP"—MILLENNIALS AND BOOMERS IN TODAY'S WORKFORCE

In the past, more experienced and older workers would mentor less experienced and younger workers. Yet, given the fast pace of technological advancements in today's workplace, more employees and employers are recognizing that there is a lot to be learned from younger generations. A new corporate trend, "reverse mentorship," is making its way to provide this exact opportunity. Reverse mentorship allows the older generations to get in touch with the future by learning from the millennials, who may look at things differently and understand the importance and connections to technology in today's world ("Reverse Mentoring," 2011). At Google, for example, a company with a large proportion of employees under the age of 30, older workers have come together to create an employee support group called Greyglers. This support group provides opportunities for Google staff to learn from their peers of all ages, and to gather insight from different generations that will inform programs and policies ("The Millennial Beard," 2015). Yet some criticize Google, a company with a median employee age of 29, for having a climate that discriminates against older workers (one lawsuit by a former technology manager was settled out of court and another is still pending) (Russon, 2015; Swift, 2010; Thibodeau, 2015).

Members of the millennial generation, those born between 1981 and 1996 (according to the Pew Research Center, 2016), have been entering the workforce in increasing numbers. Concurrently, members of the baby boomer generation are still active, and many plan to continue their involvement in the workplace beyond the traditional retirement age (out of financial necessity or because they wish to continue being productive). Today's millennials are one of the largest generational cohorts since the baby boomers (Wiedmer, 2015) and bring different viewpoints and perspectives to the workplace (Tiwari, 2016). Although it is difficult to generalize about a large and very diverse cohort, there are some characteristics that are more typical of this generation (Tulgan, 2016). The millennial population is known to be more immersed in technology (e.g., social media, Internet, smart phones, computers) than any other generation and tend to use these platforms for social, educational, and work purposes. For example, technology enhancements play a role in the way millennials in leadership positions communicate with staff or approach work-related problems (Rikleen, 2015). Although technology provides new and innovative ways to address work productivity and efficiency, it forces everyone in the workplace to be "digitally literate" and requires employees to stay well-informed with constantly evolving technology (Rikleen, 2015).

The engagement and transition from baby boomers to millennials in the workplace has created work-engagement challenges for management (Riley, 2015). At the same time that some members of the baby boomer generation are planning for retirement, many are still active in the workplace, and many are managing or being managed by members of the millennial generation. Taking into consideration the diversity within each cohort, researchers have identified some characteristics that are more typical to the baby boomer on the one hand and the millennial on the other. Some studies suggest that millennials are academic- and achievement-oriented, rule followers, and community-oriented, while others suggest that millennials are dependent on support from others, self-centered, entitled, and even lazy and disloyal (Rikleen, 2015). Research on the baby boomer generation suggests that they are independent, focused on competitive and goal-oriented work, and often believe in a hierarchal work structure and rankings. This generation is often well-established in their careers and holding positions that allow them to have power, responsibility, and authority in the workplace (Wiedmer, 2015).

Intergenerational challenges are not unique to specific countries, and companies that operate globally are facing similar challenges in different contexts, though the challenges might be different. For example, at a time when the workforce in much of the world's developed countries is aging, India's population is getting younger, requiring organizations to consider ways to connect with each generational cohort in order to keep high rates of engagement, productivity, and attrition (Tiwari, 2016).

An interested perspective can be gleaned from a survey administered in 2015 by Deloitte, an international consulting firm, to nearly 7,700 millennials representing 29 countries. The purpose of this survey was to obtain a better understanding of the millennial generation, including their values and drivers for job satisfaction. The findings from this survey indicated that 44% of millennials will leave their job in the next 2 years, and 71% of those who are likely to leave will do so because they are unhappy with the leadership training and skills (or lack thereof) that are provided by their employer.

Employees who reported high levels of employee satisfaction were more likely to indicate that their employer provided open and free-flowing communication, a supportive work culture, a strong vision and sense of purpose beyond financial opportunities and success, a sense of encouragement among all employees, a strong commitment to equality and inclusiveness, and finally, support and understanding of the goals and motivations of younger, emerging employees. When it came to senior leadership opportunities, 50% of male and 48% of female respondents said they felt like they were "being overlooked for potential leadership positions" (Deloitte, 2015). Although the findings indicated a general lack of leadership consideration for the millennial generation, men (21%) were more likely than women (16%) to say that they lead a department or are members of the senior management team (Deloitte, 2015).

Learning how to recognize and understand generational and cohort differences can help employers and their staff learn ways to manage the workforce more effectively and create a diverse and productive work space. Tiwari (2016) recommends leveraging the strengths of each generation to create diverse and comprehensive teams of employees, while also guiding internal policies, program development, and strategies to increase attraction and retention with all generations in the workplaces. One way an organization can work to address multigenerational diversity is through employee resource groups. For example, Johnson & Johnson, a global science and research-based company headquartered in the United States, has an employee resource group for millennials (Rikleen, 2015). The group's vision is to provide educational awareness regarding the culture and characteristics of millennials, to identify opportunities to empower and support millennials through professional growth, and to establish relationships with millennials and other employees to foster a deeper and more informative understanding of this generation. While the employee resource group is titled Millennials, it is open to all generations, "cultivating knowledge sharing among generations" (Rikleen, 2015).

Racial and Ethnic Diversity

Diversity most often refers to the inclusion of racial and ethnic groups who have historically been allotted a subservient status in the national workplace. This aspect of diversity interacts with issues of labor supply around the world. Given the differences in population aging, migration from the global South to the global North would seem a commonsensical solution to such issues: "The bottom-heavy population pyramids of Africa and the top-heavy pyramids of Europe fit together hand in glove. However, integrating the two over the next twenty-five years would require immigrant flows from Africa to Europe that are more than ten times higher than current levels" (Bloom, Canning, & Lubet, 2015).

To some extent, such replacement migration is occurring (Wilson, Sobotka, Williamson, & Boyle, 2013). Part of this "replacement" occurs because immigrants who arrived as children grow up to have children of their own. Wilson et al. (2013) found that in many European countries, cohorts of women born during periods of "subreplacement" fertility actually reached the size corresponding to population replacement by the time they reached their fertile years. In this sense, immigration of children swells subsequent cohorts of parents. The other part of replacement fertility consists of immigration of adults.[10]

Both kinds of migration increase racial and ethnic diversity within a country. Concerns about such diversity join anti-immigrant sentiments based on culture or fear of job loss to produce calls to reduce or even halt immigration. However, in many countries, "different" racial and ethnic populations are growing even without continuing immigration because their fertility rates are high relative to the historically favored population.[11] (Higher fertility is generally associated with lower socioeconomic status.) In this sense, racial and ethnic diversity is "baked in," and not subject to being halted by policy changes. As a result, growth in numbers is combining with attitude change to promote attention to issues of inclusion, particularly in the workplace.

Around the world, the latter part of the 20th century saw a widespread change of attitude toward historically excluded populations—from discrimination and exploitation to tolerance and even inclusion. Granted, neither this change nor concomitant changes in policies and behavior have occurred rapidly or uniformly. Still, civil and human rights movements continue to work toward equalizing educational and employment opportunities across racial and ethnic lines. In the context of an integrated world economy, this advocacy increases the demand on employers to introduce and manage harmonious human relations policies in the workplace.

In the past few decades, immigration and differential fertility trends have made racial and ethnic diversity in the workforce a particularly important issue in many industrialized countries. For example, U.S. economist William Darity Jr. has asserted that "Germany's Turkish and other immigrant workers, France and the UK's African, Middle Eastern and South Asian workers, Japan's Korean workers, and Canada's non-White workers are in the same position as minority workers in the United States" (Darity, 1999, p. 81). However, many national workforces have long featured one or more varieties of excluded groups: castes and tribal groups in India, Blacks and "Coloureds" in South Africa, and Catholics in Northern Ireland are examples.

Box 4.4
ETHNIC DIVERSITY IN MALAYSIA

With a political majority of native-born Malays, or *bumiputra*, Malaysia made a commitment to use economic development to narrow the income gap with the ethnic-Chinese Malays via a set of affirmative action policies. These policies have had some success in reducing the income gap, partly because of programs to increase company ownership among native Malays. Thanks to substantial economic growth, even the Chinese-origin Malaysians have done well, with only foreign owners losing from this diversity program (Darity & Deshpande, 2000; Gomez, 2009).

However, programs to close the income gap among workers have been constrained by lower levels of education, especially English language education, among Malays of rural origin (Lee, 2012). Meanwhile, the government has acknowledged that the policies, although successful in creating a Malay middle class, have also created a culture of entitlement (Arnold, 2002) and marginalization of non-Malay groups (Daniels, 2010). Reporting the fallout from a corporate scandal, the *New York Times* quoted local executives as saying that "too often . . . managers win promotions because of their ethnic background and connections rather than their ability" (Arnold, 2002). And those who prove competent are reportedly rewarded with more responsibility until it eventually overwhelms or even corrupts them.

The growing importance of the market in many countries is making private workplaces a particular focus of diversity concern because governments have tended to focus inclusion efforts on public education, government jobs, and political representation. Until very recently, the private sector had not introduced affirmative action initiatives in its organizations (Klarsfeld, Booysen, Ng, Roper, & Tatli, 2014). For instance, India made a commitment in its constitution to address the sustained social and economic backwardness of its tribal groups and the groups at the bottom of its caste system. However, these groups are still vastly underrepresented among middle- and higher-income groups. In large part, this is due to the recent liberalization and privatization of much of the economy, which has both created funding problems for public education and constrained the growth of government employment (Darity & Deshpande, 2000; Klarsfeld et al., 2014). These trends limit the impact of government efforts, turning reformers' attention toward the private sector.

In some countries, the excluded group may actually be more numerous, as in Malaysia, where native Malays outnumber people of Chinese origin and thus dominate the government (see Box 4.4). Or they may be equally numerous, as in Ghana, where citizens of East Indian and African origins each have their own political party and the electoral cycle determines which one can influence the workplace (Darity & Deshpande, 2000). So diversity issues in the workplace are not necessarily a question of numbers; nor are they a question of degree of economic development. According to Darity and Deshpande, "The universal persistence of racial and ethnic discrimination in labor markets in countries at all levels of development is a striking stylized fact of the modern world in the presence or absence of programs of redress for groups with inferior status" (p. 81).

Even when outright discrimination on the basis of group membership does not exist, educational differences tend to build a concrete barrier between workers of different racial and ethnic origins. Though individuals from minority populations may not have been deliberately excluded from the educational system, their relative poverty has generally hindered them from taking full advantage of it. Consequently, a country's efforts to overcome educational disparities generally herald efforts to improve representation in the workforce, particularly at higher levels. However, employers may need to undertake leadership if educational efforts are lagging workplace needs and workplace inequalities are hampering their ability to maximize workforce productivity.

Ability and Disability Diversity

An estimated 15% of the world's population, 1 billion people, have physical disabilities, and about 80% of them are of working age (International Labour Organization, 2014). Global data on employment are truly sparse in relation to people with disabilities, although it is evident that compared to persons without disabilities, they experience higher rates of unemployment and economic inactivity. Some countries gather data on such employment through their census, but they tend to be unreliable (census methods are designed to count people, not collect information about their characteristics). Disability data reported as part of a program, rather than self-reported, tend to be more reliable—but that presupposes the existence of programs. Most existing programs produce data on work-related disabilities and compensation for them, not on people who can't get work because they have disabilities. Meanwhile, modern medicine is doing a better job of saving people's lives and may thus be indirectly growing the numbers of those with physical disabilities who not only survive longer but are also employable.

Developed countries generally provide benefits to people who have had disabilities from childhood. In some countries, these benefits are constructed in such a way as to discourage people with disabilities from finding paid employment because they would lose allowances that help them cope with costs they incur as a result of their disability. In other countries, this disincentive does not exist (International Labour Office, 2000). However, it is probably safe to say that in no case are these benefits sufficiently lavish to substitute for paid employment. In developing countries, according to the International Labour Organization (ILO), people who "have disabilities which prevent them from supporting themselves are usually unable to receive any benefit, except, possibly, social security where it exists"—and where it exists, it usually excludes most low-income earners, whether self-employed or wage earners, in or out of the formal economy (International Labour Office, 2000).

Thus, people with disabilities have a strong interest in removing barriers to potential employment. In countries with little or no population growth, people with disabilities can swell the labor supply. And, if for no other reason, longer life expectancies are likely to make governments less willing to provide lifetime support, however parsimonious, to people who incurred their disabilities as adults. These and other factors suggest that people with disabilities are likely to be a factor in increasing workforce diversity.

Sexual Orientation Diversity

The civil rights movement has fostered a continued striving for fairness toward all population groups in the workplace, including people with nontraditional sexual orientations. However, this type of diversity is less likely to be protected by law than other types. For instance, in the United States, there is no federal law prohibiting discrimination in the workplace based on sexual orientation or gender identity, and only a minority of the 50 states have such laws. "Now that gay Americans have gained the right to serve in the military and to marry, the workplace remains one of the last battlegrounds for gay rights advocates" (Stewart, 2015). Absent legal direction, the motivation for acknowledging such diversity seems to be recruiting and retaining talented employees.

Similar to disability, global data on sexual orientation are hard to come by, and information on sexual orientation that is collected through census data tends to be less reliable than data on less-controversial topics. Absent data, sheer population growth probably means that the number of people with nontraditional sexual orientations is growing. Moreover, other trends suggest that these groups may be growing relative to populations as a whole. Public opinion polls report that younger people in developed countries are becoming more accepting of an array of sexual orientations; thus, more people may be willing to acknowledge their membership in these population groups. Indeed, in recent years the attitude shift in more-developed countries has been profound. In the United States, for example, the armed forces have revised their prohibition against self-acknowledged homosexuality, and are reviewing their stance against the service of transgender people.

Countries where labor is in short supply are likely to address barriers to full employment of all working-age adults, including those with nontraditional sexual orientations. This is all the more likely in that today's smaller families provide less economic shelter for people unwilling to confront hostility in the workplace. Thus, diversity in sexual orientation or identity is likely to surface in many workplaces.

Gender Identity Diversity

Most recently, there has been a lot of controversy around gender identity in the United States and other countries. In the United States, for example, U.S. Olympian Bruce Jenner came out in a very public way as a transgender woman. "My brain is more female than male . . . it's hard for people to understand that, but that's what my soul is," said Jenner in an interview with Diane Sawyer in 2015 ("Bruce Jenner," 2015). According to the Williams Institute in California (2016), the lives of nearly 300,000 transgender youth and adults (over age 13) are negatively affected by state legislation in the following 15 states: Hawaii, Illinois, Indiana, Kentucky, Massachusetts, Mississippi, Missouri, Oklahoma, South Carolina, South Dakota, Tennessee, Virginia, Washington, Wisconsin, and Wyoming. For example, House Bill 4474 in Illinois would require students to use public restrooms in school according to the sex they were assigned at birth, not the one corresponding to the gender with which they identify. In order to use a single-occupancy facility at the school, they would need a parental consent form (Herman, Mallory, & Wilson, 2016). On the other hand, some states institute legislation that protect transgender people, such as House Bill 2181 in Hawaii that prohibits individuals and employers from discriminating against transgender people based on their own personal religious or moral values and beliefs.

Past policies that have decriminalized behaviors related to sexual orientation (such as previously, in England, Wales, and Canada) did not lead to similar reforms in legislation and public policies related to gender identity. According to Lennox and Waiters (2013), the main reason for the limited advancements in protection of transgender people was the absence of definitions of gender identity in the International Human Rights Law. This void, in turn, placed limits on the ability of legislators to provide adequate legislation and to increase awareness through advocacy for the transgender population.

In 2006, a group of distinguished international human rights experts from 25 countries met in Yogyakarta, Indonesia, to put together a set of principles, referred to as the Yogyakarta Principles, relating to sexual orientation and gender identity. These principles provide a universal framework to address a broad range of human rights standards, their connection to issues of sexual orientation and gender identity, and detailed recommendations to promote and protect human rights (Lennox & Waiters, 2013; Yogyakarta Principles, 2006).

Summary and Conclusion

Broad demographic trends spell more diversity in the global workplace as the world adapts to a new age in which most children survive to adulthood and most adults survive to old age. In more-developed countries, the biggest impetus for workforce diversity will come from population stabilization and population aging. Countries will choose between growing the labor force through immigrants or through employing more nontraditional workers. Either choice will increase diversity in the workplace. In less-developed countries, diversity will come from population growth—foreign employers will continue to tap an underemployed and presumably less demanding workforce, and governments will seek new forms of employment to provide jobs for their growing numbers, while emigration continues to be an attractive alternative.

These trends interact, sometimes reinforcing, sometimes counteracting one another in relation to workforce diversity. Age diversity is a particular example, as older workers have been accustomed to excluding "different" others from the workplace, and may have difficulty accepting them. To the extent that younger workers have grown up in an environment of inclusion, such as attending school with members of the opposite sex or people from different religious or ethnic backgrounds, diversity is much less problematic. One implication is greater difficulty adjusting to differences among workers in established industries and businesses, compared to newer ones.

Aside from these demographic dynamics, widespread improvement in education over the last century has created a more highly educated and thus more aspiring workforce around the world. In the more-developed world, working-age people are knowledgeable about their rights and about how to make sure they are observed. In the developing world, awareness of individual and group rights is one more lesson being learned from the advanced economies. This trend alone is probably sufficient to ensure that issues related to diversity will touch more and more workplaces in the years to come.

Notes

1. The quantitative comparisons made in this chapter use varying time periods and age groups. This is unavoidable given the relative paucity of comparable international data. Indeed, only recent initiatives on the part of international agencies and research institutions make such comparisons possible at all.

2. The factors that slightly distort the lower half of this "pyramid"—the small depression and the large baby boom generations—are not unique to the United States.

3. Zlotnick (1996) offers a concise summary of the problems in accounting for migration flows, including problems of classification and problems of comparability. As she points out, migration is politically sensitive along a variety of dimensions, and countries often prefer not to know the realities.

4. Sociologist Saskia Sassen has written extensively of the ways in which globalization calls for new ways of thinking about migration, especially in a workforce context. For instance, circular migration is common, in which people prefer to work in one country to earn higher wages but to maintain their personal, cultural, and political interests by returning home on a regular basis. This migration can be temporary, just to earn a certain amount of money or acquire a certain amount of experience, knowledge, or credentials. It can be also be recurring, whether seasonally or simple commuting. See Sassen (1999) for an introduction to these and related issues.

5. Women's work for household consumption is not included in labor force statistics, and their unpaid labor for family enterprises, including farms, also tends to be overlooked, although their products are sold or traded. Underreporting is particularly common in countries where the culture frowns on women's economic participation (Bloom & Brender, 1993). Moreover, in less-developed countries, the bulk of women working for pay are in the informal sector (where street vending is a typical activity). This sector also poses problems for measurement.

6. World Bank and other researchers have traced how poor people in developing countries spent additional income and found that women were more likely than men to spend it on food, clothing, medical care, and education for their children (World Bank, 2001).

7. King (1999) calculated that in the United States, men and women each

spend, on average, an estimated 35% of the years between ages 20 and 69 raising children.

8. Preston and Stokes (2012) estimate that improvements in survivorship contributed the largest amount, 82%, to population aging in more-developed countries between 2005 and 2010, while declines in the growth rate of births contributed 23%. Migration patterns thus contributed about 5% to limiting population aging.

9. At an international meeting of experts on aging populations in the late 1990s, one author heard representatives from Japan and China reject the possibility of extending the work life because, they said, "How can we promote young men if older ones don't leave?"

10. A few countries in Eastern and Southeastern Europe are experiencing low fertility coupled with immigration. (Wilson et al., 2013). These countries are facing substantial population decline; they are also countries in which diversity is quite different from the experience of their neighbors.

11. Data are not readily available to make comparisons across national boundaries, in large part because the definition of excluded populations varies so much. Generally, population groups are excluded on the basis of caste, religion, language, race, or national origin.

5

Socioeconomic Transitions

The New Realities
of the Global Workforce

MARTHA FARNSWORTH RICHE
AND MICHÀLLE E. MOR BARAK

There is no difference among classes of people. All the world is of divine origin.

—*The Mahabharata*, ancient Sanskrit epic

National states currently face a new set of economic conditions that push toward the neutralization of borders and diminish, or at least alter, state sovereignty and unilateral state action. Further, . . . *the emerging human rights regime makes the individual regardless of nationality, a possessor of rights.*

—Saskia Sassen, *Guests and Aliens*, 1999

C hanges in the global division of labor are blurring traditional geographic and corporate boundaries. At the same time, a growing concern for human rights in countries around the world calls for the inclusion of previously excluded people in mainstream economic activities. Whether national or international, the merger of people with different cultures and characteristics in the workplace is an increasingly salient management concern. This chapter examines the economic and social forces that create a more diverse workforce worldwide. We examine trends in worker migration, occupational needs, and educational attainment and their implications for increased diversity in global workplaces.

Flows of employers as well as workers are an important feature of the integration of the global economy. This is due in large part to imbalances in labor demand and supply (as described earlier in Chapter 4, Global Demographic Trends). Migration of working-age people has traditionally contributed to resolving such imbalances (Sassen, 1999), and it is still a solution for many in developing countries, whether they are highly skilled or simply seeking a livelihood. However, the numbers now entering working age in the developing countries are far larger than those willing to leave their homeland, with the latter already exceeding the numbers that better-off nations seem willing to absorb. Instead, globalization is allowing these countries to export many of their employers, particularly those in labor-intensive industries that make a product that is transportable.

In strictly economic terms, it makes sense to move such jobs to people who find them superior to their local alternatives. Even when these jobs stay put, they often fall to immigrants because native-born workers demand wages that could price the products out of the international market. Kabeer (2000) illustrates both situations in her study of Bangladeshi apparel workers in England and Bangladesh. In the English context, the immigrant workers see themselves as exploited, whereas in Bangladesh, the workers find the same jobs a significant improvement over alternatives. In short, the context matters: Jobs that are low paying and low status in an industrialized country can be exported as higher paying and higher status to developing countries.

Either way, migration of workers or migration of employers, the resulting encounter of people from different places with different cultures and capabilities, is an important source of workplace diversity. This is particularly so because societies tend to racialize immigrants, describing them as "aliens" when they arrive, "minorities" if they settle. Describing long-settled populations, including many born in the new country, Sassen (1999) remarks, "In France they are referred to as immigrés even when they have become French" (p. 143). Similarly, Zinn (1994) comments on the euphemism used in Italy to refer to immigrants from developing countries: "Consider that the Italian euphemism for the immigrants from developing countries is *immigrati extracomunitari*—that is, non-EEC immigrants. As a U.S. citizen, I am technically an *extracommunitare*, too, though in fact no one would really consider me as one" (p. 54). In the Netherlands, Sweden, and Belgium, most immigrants are described as "minorities," and in Britain as "ethnic minorities," although the United Kingdom has its own British ethnic minorities—Scottish, Welsh, and Irish (Sassen, 1999).

A significant foreign presence in industrial-country workforces is not new. Historical studies such as Sassen's document a large role for foreign workers in Western European countries before modern times, and other large industrial economies had their birth in traditional immigrant-receiving countries such as the United States and Canada. More recently, some European countries made up for population losses during World War II by recruiting workers from abroad. However, migration is dynamic, and the origins of immigrant workers can become more diverse over time.

The history of immigration in France, for example, reveals that the makeup of immigrants has been transformed in recent years. Most of the workers who immigrated in search of work post–World War II were Poles, Belgians, or Swiss, who were in essence Europeans with physical characteristics not much different from those of the French. In recent decades, however, many worker immigrants have been Africans and Asians (Alba & Silberman, 2002). Germany offers another example; it developed a "guest worker" recruitment strategy in pursuit of economic development. Thousands of workers were brought in from countries such as Turkey, Yugoslavia, and Italy to work on German assembly lines with the mutual expectation that the situation would be temporary (Martin, 1994). As Zlotnick (1994) points out, after World War II, "the scale of the population inflows experienced by the main labor-importing countries of Europe was large" (p. 366). Although outflows were also large, as migration to the United States and other immigrant-receiving countries continued, the general assumption in these countries that foreign workers would leave when no longer needed was flawed. Unlike recent "return" migrants from within the European Union (EU), large numbers of foreign workers came with their families and stayed, constituting an important source of today's workforce diversity.

Differences in national population growth rates are likely to make the issue of workforce diversity increasingly salient in Europe in particular. The shrinking share of young and new native workforce entrants described earlier should increase the proportion of foreign-born workers and their descendants, even if immigration flows lessen.

Elsewhere, although affected by the severe global economic contraction that began in 2007, other developed economies, including oil-producing countries in the Middle East, attract large numbers of foreign migrants, largely from developing countries. From about the mid-1970s, the rapid depletion of the supply of native-born workers caused fast-growing economies in the Gulf region to cast their recruitment net eastward to South and East Asian countries. Almost concurrently, the major labor exporters in the Arab region (such as Jordan and the Yemen Arab Republic) also became labor importers because they had to fill vacancies created by the departure of their workers for employment in oil-exporting countries (Athukorala, 1986). In countries like Dubai and Kuwait, the workforce grew rapidly and changed in composition as a result of work-related migration. For instance, in 2000, 81% of all employed people in Kuwait were international migrants (International Labor Organization, 2012).

Although rapid population growth, per se, is not correlated with growth in the rate of emigration, simple population growth means that the same relative flows contain more people. Moreover, there is an association between development and emigration. Improving economic conditions in poor countries give more of their people the resources to take advantage of superior opportunities in countries with relative labor shortages (Commission for the Study of International Migration and Cooperative Economic Development, 1990). Even when these opportunities mean relatively menial jobs that natives often no longer wish to do, the relatively higher wage scale makes migration attractive. After all, a menial job today can provide the seed money for a small business tomorrow or serve as the first step on an attractive career ladder. In short, population trends are making culturally based workforce diversity a fact of life for developed countries around the world.

Worker Migration

Managing diversity that arises from immigration has certain predictable aspects, if only because worker migrations tend to be geographically patterned. International migrants tend to head for countries with which they share either an historic relationship or geographic propinquity. For instance, European Union countries that have traditionally been immigrant receivers have long-standing relations with countries in their former colonial empires. The Irish were still the largest share of foreign-born workers in the United Kingdom in 2002, even though their numbers were fewer than they had been (presumably reflecting improved economic conditions at home). Similarly, North Africans were by far the largest share of foreign-born workers in France in 2000, followed by workers from neighboring Mediterranean countries (International Labor Organization, 2012). Meanwhile, the proportion of foreign or foreign-born workers has grown in European countries that are primary destinations for people from neighboring countries in Eastern Europe. For instance, the numbers of foreign-born workers in Austria more than doubled, from 150,900 in 1988 to 384,663 in 2005 (International Labor Organization, 2012).

Overall, cross-border mobility within the EU is relatively low, as evidenced by the general reluctance of most people to migrate for work given alternative, albeit less attractive, opportunities at home. In the mid-1990s, when movement within the Union became easier while earnings differences remained significant, only 5 million EU natives were working in an EU country that was not their country of citizenship (Sassen, 1999). Despite the existence of labor shortages in some places and job shortages in others, workers' mobility within EU member states averaged only 1% each year between 2000 and 2005 (European Commission, 2008). The widespread economic crisis that began in 2008 saw the return of many such migrants to their home country, but within a few years these flows saw a modest rebound (Organisation for Economic Co-Operation and Development [OECD], 2014).

In a sense, intra-EU worker migration mitigates the diversity challenge because it replicates past flows that were geographically patterned by shared language, culture, or history. For instance, the Irish have historically chosen the United Kingdom over other European destinations; the Italians, Spanish, and Portuguese have tended to choose France; and the Finns chose Sweden. Many of these migrants took advantage of improved conditions to return home, but others settled permanently in the host country. To the extent that they did not fully assimilate with the native population, they and their descendants represented the first wave of diversity concerns.

However, more foreign-born EU workers come from non-EU countries than from within the Community (European Commission, 2008; OECD, 2014). In 2013, the OECD reported that some 55 million workers in its countries were foreign-born (OECD, 2013). In the first decade of the 21st century alone, the OECD countries added 16 million international migrant workers, representing about 70% of overall employment growth. In that decade, the number of international migrants from Asia and Latin America and the Caribbean grew by 44% and 36%, respectively. However, the African migrant community grew more than any other community: 53%.

These migrants represent a second wave of diversity concerns—culturally distant, albeit with a partially shared past. Foreign residents in the United Kingdom tend to be from former colonies in Asia or Africa, as well as the United States (International Labor Office, 2012). Similarly, the Netherlands absorbed large waves of immigrants from its former colony Suriname in response to political problems tied to Suriname's transition to independence (Dew, 1994). Turk and Yugoslav immigrants tend to be found in Germany, North African ones in France. Spain demonstrates the importance of both colonial relationships and geographic propinquity. In 2006, more than 266,000 Ecuadorians were working in Spain; the next largest group was from Morocco (250,000) (OECD, 2009).

For all these reasons, the origins of workforce diversity in EU countries have tended to be relatively predictable. Countries with vibrant economies tend to attract immigrants from their former colonies and/or their relatively impoverished neighbors, augmented by workers recruited from such traditional labor-exporting regions as Turkey and North Africa. Although mature migration flows tend to diversify their destinations, new flows, such as those now coming from parts of Asia or Africa, tend to be concentrated along historically traditional lines.

Immigration is beginning to diversify workplaces in some Eastern European economies, including countries that have joined an expanded EU. In the first years after the changeover from Communism, immigrants tended to be expatriates returning home, but law and policy changes regarding long-term residency have fostered an intensified immigrant inflow, notably in the Czech Republic and also in Poland and Hungary (OECD, 2009). By and large, inflows come from neighboring countries, but there has also been a significant inflow of highly qualified employees from EU countries to manage subsidiaries set up in Central and Eastern Europe (OECD, 2000).

Overall, increasing variety in both the sources and the destinations of worker migrants is making workforce diversity salient in developing countries, too. The United Nations has estimated that between 2005 and 2010, for the first time the growth rate of the migrant stock (meaning all migrants, not just workers) for less-developed regions surpassed the rate for more-developed regions (United Nations, 2011a). By 2013, some 82.3 million international migrants who were born in the global South resided in the global South, slightly exceeding the number of international migrants born in the global South who were living in the global North (81.9 million) (OECD, 2013).

Although data in these countries are sparse, they suggest that these migrants tend to stay within their regions—African migrants tend to go to other countries in Africa, Asian migrants to other countries in Asia. Oil-rich, labor-poor countries in the Middle East have been the most notable recipients of worker migrants, especially from a wide range of Asian countries. Indeed, Saudi Arabia and the United Arab Emirates are among the top 10 migrant host countries worldwide (OECD, 2013). However, the growing numbers of emigrants from East and Southeast Asia have been seeking a greater variety of destinations—including the Philippines, the Republic of Korea, Japan, the United States, and Thailand (Zlotnick, 1994). Hostile reactions by close neighbors—as when Malaysia expelled thousands of illegal Indonesian workers in 2002—if repeated, also make distant migration destinations more attractive.

The Gulf States are a potentially interesting laboratory for studying workplace diversity because they combine both aspects of international worker migration—very low and very high skill levels—with ethnic and cultural differences. Oil exploitation in these countries involves large numbers of low-wage, dirty, and dangerous jobs, as well as many highly skilled construction and management jobs. Meanwhile, the resulting oil riches until recently created enough pleasant, largely public-sector jobs to employ the native-born workforce. It will be interesting to follow developments in states such as Saudi Arabia as ever larger numbers of native-born youth outstrip the ability of the public sector to absorb them, thus forcing diversity in the private-sector workplace.

Central America (particularly Mexico) and the Caribbean have been a major source of worker migrants, particularly to the United States. Mexico has been by far the largest source of foreign-born labor in the United States in recent decades (OECD, 2014). Joining with large new flows of migrants from Asia, particularly from Korea, China, India, and Vietnam, these immigrants have increased concerns about workforce diversity throughout North America. Overall, however, this region is considerably more favorable to immigrants than is Europe, where the effect of immigration on more homogeneous workforces and societies has become an important political issue.

Meanwhile, deteriorating economic conditions that began with the financial crisis of 2007–2008 caused many economic migrants to return home. Return migration is generally not measured, but reportedly many Eastern Europeans left the Western European Union countries where they had been working before the crisis; and the United States/Mexico migrant flows have evened out (Passel, Cohn, & Gonzalez-Barrera, 2012). Individual examples of return migration are also prominent, such as successful Indian or Chinese migrants returning to their home countries to take advantage of new opportunities to invest and grow businesses. As part of a program to draw in Chinese who have studied or worked abroad, "China is offering bonuses equivalent to about $158,000 to experienced university professors and researchers, particularly in the sciences and technology, who return to teach" (Partnership for a New American Economy, 2012). This report also describes how other countries are recruiting their natives with key skills from the United States. Return migration in general, and targeted recruiting of natives working abroad, may seem to counter cultural diversity, since the targets are people with similar ethnicity and nativity. However, the cultural differences that the returnees bring with them may not be inconsequential in the workplace.

Occupational Diversity

The occupational patterning of migrants is also predictable in broad categories, if both sides of the migration equation are considered. On the one hand, migrant workers move primarily in search of economic opportunities. On the other hand, their opportunities and their place in the workforce are determined by the evolution of the receiving economy, as well as by the capabilities migrants possess relative to workers in the host country.

Analyses that focus on the global division of labor highlight the role of migration in filling low-pay, low-status jobs in the service sectors of developed countries. The resulting workplace diversity is one in which the workers are different from both the employers and the customers, each calling for specialized diversity management. However, in countries where immigrants make up a particularly large share of the labor force, they are dispersed more widely across the occupational and industry spectrum. One clear trend in the industrial countries that are members of the Organisation for Economic Co-operation and Development (OECD) is toward dispersion across industrial sectors; another is an increasing share of temporary and highly skilled workers in the total flows (OECD, 2010, 2013). Both trends contribute to broader-based workplace diversity.

A long and rich literature explores the diversity of contributions that immigrant workers have made, including fulfilling seasonal demands, making up for shortages of appropriate native workers, or supplying special skills.[1] Currently, two trends dominate the role of immigrant workers in national economies, with different effects on workplace diversity.

First, advanced economies that reward and subsidize high educational attainment are increasingly experiencing a need for workers to perform unskilled tasks, particularly the service tasks that national economies cannot export. These jobs attract people from countries where well-paying jobs are few and wages generally low. In addition to making more money than they could at home, migrants also gain access to a wider array of opportunities—for their children as well as themselves.

For example, South Korea, a traditionally homogeneous society, created a migrant worker program in order to fill jobs that can be described with the "three Ds"—Difficult, Dirty, and Dangerous—because of native South Koreans' aversion to these jobs as the country began to prosper in the 1980s (Seol, 1999). Similarly, during Nigeria's period of relative economic buoyancy in the 1970s, many of its neighbors, particularly Ghana, but also Burkina Faso, Togo, Benin, and Niger, suffered their worst setbacks. Large numbers of workers from those countries flocked to Nigeria in search of jobs and a better standard of living. There were professionals like doctors, lawyers, engineers, architects, university lecturers, teachers, and nurses; there were middle-level skilled workers such as technicians and artisans for the building industry; and there were thousands of unskilled laborers to fill the gaps shunned by Nigerians, such as domestic workers, construction laborers, conservancy workers, casual dockworkers, and hawkers for the food and beverage industry. Many of these were undocumented or in an irregular situation regarding entry, stay, or employment (Frempomaa, 1986).

As Sassen (1988) has pointed out, the concentration of immigrant labor in service jobs in developed countries is essentially the counterpart of the export of low-wage manufacturing jobs to developing countries. In both cases, economic integration makes labor specialization into a global rather than national phenomenon. Such migration increases the overall diversity of the workforce in the receiving country but not necessarily the diversity of its workplaces.

Agriculture is a common example of substituting foreign workers for native-born workers. The OECD found that during the late 1990s, overall employment in agriculture decreased in several European countries while the number of foreign farm workers increased. In contrast, both overall employment and the numbers of foreign workers increased in the services sector in most of these same countries (OECD, 2000, 2010). The economic cycle affects all such arrangements as foreigners' employment fluctuates more markedly than total employment, and the 2007–2008 financial crisis had a predictably severe impact, particularly on migrant men employed in the construction and manufacturing sectors (OECD, 2013). Thus, workplace diversity varies across economic sectors and economic conditions.

Second, highly skilled people from developing countries often migrate in search of better opportunities than their home economies can offer. India is a notable example of a country whose educational system has outstripped its economic development. Emigration is easier for the highly skilled because they are more likely to have information about employment opportunities, including personal connections or experiences, as well as the resources to invest in migration.

Meanwhile, receiving countries often have special programs to facilitate skilled migration, especially for temporary workers. For example, the United States saw a dramatic increase in H1B visas during the high-tech industry boom of the late 1990s. These visas allow high-tech employers to import electrical engineers and computer programmers from places such as India and China for up to 6 years. However, the number of visas available (65,000, with another 20,000 for people holding an advanced degree) is far below the demand for them—the U.S. Department of Homeland Security had received nearly 233,000 applications for the 2015 program by the time it stopped taking applications (U.S. Department of Homeland Security, 2015).

Although there is no indication that the natural human reluctance to leave home and family is any less pronounced among the highly skilled, in some countries policy failures by governments have encouraged large numbers of skilled people to emigrate. Scientists, especially doctors, university professors, and other professionals, have trouble finding work if a country's educational system has produced more than the country can employ. This is particularly true in countries with policies that depress capital formation and thus the demand for skilled labor (World Bank, 1995). In any case, this migration spreads workforce diversity to a variety of workplaces in receiving countries. Yet because they lack political rights enjoyed by citizens and are unable to vote, organize politically, and bring pressure to bear on government, they can work under terms unacceptable to nationals. In some countries, they are also vulnerable to expulsion if they become too assertive (Cholewinski, 1997; Guerin-Gonzales & Strikwerda, 1993).

Whether high- or low-skilled, large numbers of migrants work abroad for a limited period and then return home. In some cases, they may have earned enough money to better their situation at home; in others, the sending economy may have created new opportunities. Ireland used to be an example of the former; then, until the financial crisis of 2007–2008 at least, it became a good example of the latter. Similarly, widespread prosperity in the EU also turned Italy, Spain, Greece, and Portugal from net exporters of workers to net importers, up to the 2007–2008 financial crisis.

The response to that crisis provides evidence that workers from both high- and low-skill segments are now part of a cross-border and even global labor market. In addition to return of previous migrants, temporary labor migration was one of the first migration channels to be affected by the economic downturn (OECD, 2010). This change was due in part to policy changes in affected countries that largely affected unskilled workers, such as refusal to renew temporary work permits and provision of assistance in returning home. In addition, some countries tightened their policies on family reunification and naturalization, like language and civics tests that directly address the issue of differences with the native population (OECD, 2010).

Immigrant workers do not just have the choice of staying or returning home, but of doing both. When travel was costly and difficult, migrants settled in the new country for good, or at least until retirement, and stayed there even in the face of negative labor market developments. Now, low-cost transportation and communication technology make it possible for workers to call two places "home."[2] Rather than settle permanently in a new country, even in favorable economic conditions, many worker migrants prefer to maintain their residence in their country of origin if they are allowed to circulate freely.[3] Managing diversity that results from this circular migration may require different tools and policies than managing diversity that represents permanent settlement.

Migration of Employers

In contrast to the previous period of economic globalization (1850 to 1914), when massive emigration of working-age people helped to resolve national imbalances between labor supply and labor demand, the current period of globalization has also featured mass migration of employers.[4] Essentially, in a liberalized trade environment, transnational corporations export capital to reduce their labor costs and, indirectly, create new markets for their products (see Box 5.1). The resulting workplace can feature a cross-cultural confrontation of foreign management and domestic labor, sometimes complicated by in-migration of skilled personnel from still other countries.

Box 5.1
OUTSOURCING: EXPERIENCES OF DISPLACED WORKERS AND THOSE WHO RECEIVE THEIR JOBS

In 2015, some 250 employees lost their jobs when their employer, The Walt Disney Company, outsourced their positions to highly skilled technical workers from a firm based in India. Yet, after receiving their pink slips, many employees were required to train their replacements to do the jobs they were once doing. One of the employees said, "I just couldn't believe they could fly people in to sit at our desks and take over our jobs exactly . . . it was humiliating to train somebody else to take over your job. I still can't grasp it" (Preston, 2015).

The outsourcing trend is expected to continue. Forrester Research predicts that 3.3 million service jobs in the United States will be outsourced overseas by 2015 (Cook, 2004). Most of those jobs have been going to India,

(Continued)

(Continued)

where large centers are being built to write software, manage technical support, and provide customer service and other activities for U.S. corporations. The practice came under scrutiny in the United States when the media reported that laid-off employees who encountered problems in receiving public assistance in the form of food stamps were calling a customer service center that was located in India. The irony was not lost on public officials, who ordered the subcontractor to relocate the food stamp customer service center back to the United States (MacPherson, 2004).

The reason for the outsourcing is obvious: cost savings. For example, Indian computer programmers earn about $12,500 annually, which is one sixth the average of U.S. programmers (Drajem, 2004). Sherry Toly, spokesperson for Watchmark-Comnitel, summed up the company's decision to outsource positions to India. "The situation was to close our doors or look at ways to reduce our operations so we can stay in business during a very, very difficult time" (Cook, 2004).

What does outsourcing mean to the workers in India? Some think that at such relatively low wages, the workers in India are living close to poverty, or worse. In fact, for college-educated young people in India, a job at a call center is considered a plum position ("The Good Life," 2003). Though the work may involve long hours on the phone or at a computer terminal and working around the clock, the pay is good relative to other jobs in India, and the work environment is typically pleasant. These jobs are highly desired by young educated people because of the scarcity of jobs in India, and often thousands of job seekers show up for job interviews when a new center opens up. Not every employer who has outsourced work is happy with the results. Wesley Bertch of Life Time Fitness had an Indian company write software for his company. He was initially drawn by the rate of $6 per hour, compared with $60 per hour for U.S. programmers. However, after receiving software filled with bugs, and then being charged to fix the errors, Bertch regretted his decision. Bertch has joined a growing number of businesses, such as Lehman Brothers, Capital One, and Dell Computers, that have reversed their outsourcing decisions and returned positions to the United States (Stone, 2004).

Foreign direct investment (FDI)—the net amount of investment by nonresidents in enterprises in which nonresidents exercise significant management control—is an imperfect but nonetheless useful measure of this change because it is directly tied to production.[5] Foreign direct investment dropped sharply with the 2007–2008 financial crisis, according to the United Nations Conference on Trade and Development (UNCTAD). It recovered in 2012 but dropped below its peak again in 2014, "influenced mainly by the fragility of the global economy, policy uncertainty for investors and elevated geopolitical risks." However, UNCTAD projects that FDI will continue to rise (United Nations, 2015a).

Developing economies, particularly in Asia, absorb over half of those flows, reaching a historically high level of $681 billion in 2014, even while the overall level of FDI decreased. In addition, outflows from developing economies continue to grow, and in 2014 accounted for over 30% of the global total; UNCTAD points out that developing Asia now invests abroad more than any other region. In short, both the sources and the destinations of transnational investment have become more diverse. For example, in 2014, "Nine of the 20 largest investor countries were from developing or transition economies" (United Nations, 2015a).

Foreign direct investments span virtually all countries and economic activities, creating various forms of workplace diversity. Sometimes the diversity impact is restricted to cultural differences in the executive suite, as in the failed merger/acquisition of the U.S. car producer Chrysler and the German producer Daimler-Benz. (After undergoing bankruptcy and a government bailout, Chrysler was subsequently acquired by the Italian Automaker Fiat.) At other times, FDI pits managers from one country against workers in another, as exemplified by trade union and gender-based challenges to Japanese car executives in the early days of their investment in U.S. plants. The evolution of the Mitsubishi plant in Normal, Illinois, is a prime example. It was one of the most automated yet least productive plants in the industry. It was also known for the abusive, humiliating—and illegal—way female workers were treated. Remarkably, the plant became a model of workplace reform, thanks to training, a zero-tolerance policy on discrimination and sexual harassment, and a mission statement that puts respect for others ahead of even vehicle quality.

Japanese management had been thinking of closing the plant due to the negative attention it was receiving. In 1998, Mitsubishi agreed to pay $34 million to settle a sexual harassment lawsuit brought by the Equal Employment Opportunity Commission on behalf of 500 female workers at the plant. The high-profile case dragged on for 3 years, sapping worker morale already depleted by a distant relationship between American workers and Japanese managers. The lawsuit told a story of a bleak workplace: sexual graffiti written on fenders about to pass female line workers, pornographic pictures taped on walls, male workers taunting women with wrenches and air compressors, and women who complained of being fired or passed over for advancement. Then in 2001, while the American plant manager and his team were working on changing the plant's culture regarding attitudes toward women, Mitsubishi agreed to pay a multimillion-dollar settlement to African American and Hispanic workers who were claiming racial and job discrimination. To the extent that strengthening the capacity for innovation is behind many of these joint ventures, managing workplace diversity can involve managing differences among employees who are relative equals in terms of workplace status but cause unacceptable breaches in human rights.

These examples come from the experience of FDI between developed economies. However, the growing share of direct foreign investment going to developing countries has received more attention, in part because the diversity implications can be encouraging on the one hand, but troubling on the other. Essentially, declining transportation and telecommunications costs have combined with trade liberalization, capital mobility, and globalizing markets to integrate economic activity around the world (Perraton, Goldblatt, Held, & McGrew, 2000). These cost declines have combined with trends in labor supply to shift much manufacturing for the world market to several developing countries (Bloom & Brender, 1993). Indeed, the global slowdown that followed the peaking of global GDP in 2000 intensified competitive pressure on transnational corporations, thus accentuating the value of lower-cost locations—a trend reinforced by the subsequent, more severe global downturn in 2007–2008.

Just as worker migration is a dynamic process, leading to constant change in supplying and receiving countries, so too is employer migration, as the role of labor cost shifts the overall business equation, and relative wages shift too. Currently, as technology advances, it is making low wages less critical in the overall price of goods produced, and many global employers are rethinking their location. For example, rising labor costs in China have caused some multinational employers to return production to developed countries, or to put an additional production base in a lower-cost country ("A Third Industrial Revolution," 2012). They have also caused Chinese and other South-based firms to invest in developed countries, such as the United States, where lagging wages, relative to rising ones at home, add to the attraction of being closer to U.S. markets (Tabuchi, 2015). Such shifts can also be challenging from a diversity perspective. At one new Chinese-owned textile mill in South Carolina, the Chinese trainer was shocked by the occasional tardiness of American workers, and their lower rates of productivity compared with workers in China (Tabuchi, 2015).

Another new trend is the intensification of FDI flows among developing countries in the global South, now accounting for a third of global flows (United Nations, 2015a). UNCTAD reports, "The largest outward investing economies include Brazil, China, Hong Kong (China), India, the Republic of Korea, Malaysia, Mexico, Singapore, South Africa and Taiwan Province of China." These countries tend to invest in economies that are in their immediate region, or where they have a significant presence due to population diasporas. Such familiarity may ease diversity challenges. That is less likely for investments motivated by efficiency-seeking reasons (for example, multinational enterprises from the Republic of Korea investing in East and Southeast Asia) or for those motivated by access to potentially large markets, as in South Asia. Similarly, the geography of natural resources determines FDI in extractive industries, as seen in the high bilateral FDI intensities between China and a number of African countries. In these cases, cultural differences are more likely to come into play.

In addition to employing large and growing underemployed workforces, foreign direct investment can support the development of the host economy by increasing access to technology, improving workforce quality, or enhancing export potential. Concerns arise when the investment exploits and abuses the country, particularly its natural and human resources. For example, in 1984 in Bhopal, India, because of low safety standards, an explosion at the U.S.-based Union Carbide chemical plant released a deadly gas that formed a cloud over a large populated area, resulting in an environmental disaster and the immediate deaths of an estimated 2,500 people (see Box 5.2). In other instances, export-oriented manufacturers may "slice the value chain" to remove labor-intensive, low-skill processes to countries with large numbers of people willing to work for low wages. Although in some cases these workers may improve their income, or acquire new skills, in other cases, workers may be exploited and even abused, as documented by organizations advocating the institution and implementation of minimum labor standards.[6]

Box 5.2

THE BHOPAL DISASTER: ECONOMIC EXPLOITATION AND HUMAN TRAGEDY

In the early morning hours of December 3, 1984, the U.S.-based Union Carbide Corporation's chemical plant in Bhopal, India, exploded, killing thousands and creating the worst industrial disaster the world has yet seen. The Bhopal gas-leak disaster has raised a number of complex legal, ethical, economic, technological, sociopolitical, and ecological questions and issues (Ansell & Tinsley, 2011; Broughton, 2005; Dias, 1997; Sharma, 2015; Van Voris & Hurtado, 2012). More than 10,000 people were killed (a few thousand immediately and many more later as a result of injuries and diseases), and estimates put the numbers of people injured or disabled as a result of the explosion at about 2 million. Whole communities were displaced and impoverished. Immediately following the disaster, the government of India put together plans to build a "gas relief" system, a set of hospitals where those who were exposed to gas could get free treatment; however, by the time the hospitals were built in the late 1990s, over a decade had past and it was too late for those who needed treatment the most (Hanna, 2015). The Supreme Court of India reached settlement in 1989 (the original claim of US$3 billion was settled for only US$470 million—a settlement many jurists and human rights activists considered grossly unfair). Justice P. N. Bhagwati noted, "The Court order places the value of Indian life at a ridiculously low figure because, after all, we are browns and blacks and not favored whites!"

Union Carbide initially blamed the Bhopal accident on Sikh terrorists. Later, the company blamed it on disgruntled employees who tried to sabotage the plant. However, most experts agree that the accident resulted from Union Carbide's use of inferior safety standards at the Indian plant, compared with those found in the United States. One example of the differences in standards is the leak-detection system that was used. At Union Carbide's Virginia plant, a computerized system was installed that kept track of pressures, temperatures, and chemical levels, indicating where a leak was occurring. At the Bhopal plant, gas leaks were detected by human sight or smell (Bhargava, 1986). The Bhopal disaster was followed by years of litigations with efforts to hold Union Carbide and its top management responsible for the magnitude of the disaster and its aftermath. For example, Union Carbide estimated that 3,800 people were killed by the leak, but a study by Amnesty International showed that 7,000 people died within days of the leak and another 15,000 died later from exposure to the gas. Residents living near the plant claimed, through their representatives in the courts, negligence on the part of Union Carbide, and sought punitive and compensatory damages as well as medical monitoring due to sustained injuries from exposure to soil and drinking water polluted by hazardous waste. More than a quarter of a century later, the case still reverberated through the U.S. court systems with the 2012 decision by a U.S. district judge in Manhattan, New York, John Keenan, who ruled that the company and its CEO at the time were not liable for environmental remediation or pollution-related claims made by residents near the plant (*Sahu v. Union Carbide*, 2009; Van Voris & Hurtado, 2012).

Implications for Diversity of Gender, Disability, and Sexual Orientation

Migration of both people and employers not only puts people from different countries into the same workplace, it also imports their cultural dispositions regarding other forms of diversity. Racial, ethnic, and religious diversity are almost a given in most situations involving cross-national origins. Age diversity can also be an issue because migrants tend to be young; and so can disability, because migrants tend to come from countries where there are not enough jobs to go around and investing in the disabled can be considered a "luxury." Probably the most sensitive and least discussed form of diversity relates to sexual orientation. Cultural taboos can bring a strongly disruptive element into workplaces where law and custom join to protect a range of choices.

Gender diversity is a major issue in most immigrant-receiving countries, though in some areas such as the Gulf States, women typically work in separate occupational and physical environments. A notable concern is the widespread employment of young women in export-manufacturing zones, reportedly because their culture and traditions make them malleable and easy to exploit (Elson, 1999). Southeast Asian girls, exploited economically and physically by older men from wealthier Asian countries, are probably the most negative image of today's workplace diversity. The divergence between culturally conservative and culturally progressive economies on issues such as gay rights, including same-sex marriage, is also likely to emerge as a workplace issue. On the other hand, migration of employers, employees, information, and technology between countries can increase workers' awareness of their rights in the workplace (see Box 5.3).

Box 5.3

SEXUAL HARASSMENT AND THE HIGH-TECH INDUSTRY

The United States and India are closely bound in the global computer software industry, and several Indian software exporters have affiliates in the United States, including the largest: Infosys Technologies Limited. The U.S.-based company's highest-paid employee, the head of global sales and marketing, resigned in 2002 after his executive assistant sued him and the company for sexual harassment (Arnold, 2002). According to the newspaper account, "The lawsuit . . . sent Indian software companies scurrying to make sure their policies comply with United States law." A woman consultant for a software company who has the opportunity to train abroad, says that the job often comes with its drawbacks: "unwelcome behaviour from some male colleagues" ("Indian Firms Take Little Notice," 2013). With industries continuing to expand to other countries, many of which have different human rights policies, such as the sexual harassment debate between the United States and India, this issue continues to grow.

Although Indian laws defined sexual harassment in the workplace in 1997, human resource specialists there said the issue had been largely ignored, in part because in India, women feared the stigma attached to reporting. However, in this industry large numbers of Indians work in overseas offices and at customer sites, making multicultural interaction more frequent and more fraught.

After the litigation at Infosys, one large firm undertook an audit, put its reworked policy on its intranet, and increased cross-cultural sensitivity training for its employees. Another firm with multiple overseas offices undertook a worldwide review of its employee conduct policy, which had been culture- and country-specific. As one executive put it, "We are sensitizing our managers in issues like gender discrimination, noncompetitive behavior, and age discrimination." And the Infosys chief executive concluded, "Multicultural interaction is becoming a very important part of our work environment." These examples point out the multiple aspects of diversity in the workplace. Managing all these forms of diversity in an increasingly cross-national workplace requires an understanding of cultural differences. Where migrant workers are involved, employers need to effectively communicate the host country's workplace norms. Where migrant employers are involved, managers may have to address multiple constituencies, at home as well as in the host country.

Educational Trends and Workforce Diversity

The other important demographic element that has broad implications for diversity in the global workforce is the rising level of educational attainment around the world. The relative educational level of a country's labor force is becoming particularly important, given the increasing role of advanced technology, and countries are attempting to respond to this need.

In the developed regions, secondary education has become virtually universal, and the less-developed regions are catching up. In 2013, fully 75% of the relevant age group in these regions was enrolled at the secondary level, up from 63% a decade earlier (United Nations Educational, Scientific, and Cultural Organization [UNESCO], 2015). Even in laggard regions, gross enrollment ratios are improving. In 2013, gross enrollment at the secondary level was 66% in South and West Asia, up from 50% in 2004; in sub-Saharan Africa, it advanced from 31% to 43%. In these countries, girls are much less likely to be enrolled than boys—this accounts in part for the low enrollment rates relative to other developing countries.

Enrollment in higher education is also increasing around the world, although developed countries still maintain a substantial advantage. At higher levels of education, such as the bachelor's level, women are nearly as well represented as men—indeed, in some countries, they are better represented (UNESCO, 2015). Thus, in terms of workplace diversity, even in countries where most women have much less education than men, the expectations of educated women workers may not be so different from women workers in other parts of the world, albeit quite different from other women in their country, particularly the rural poor.

In a few places around the world, such as the Barefoot College in Tilonia, India, innovative educational initiatives are helping the rural poor in developing countries to improve their lives through educational attainment (see Box 5.4).

These trends are diversifying the educational attainment of immigrants, and complicating diversity challenges in many workplaces. In the United States, for example, immigrants have a U-shaped pattern of educational attainment: Immigrants from Mexico and Central America tend to have less education than the average American, while immigrants from Asia tend to have more. A large survey taken around the time of the recent financial crisis (2006–2008) found that among noncitizens ages 25–29, nearly half the ones from countries in the Americas lacked a secondary education, while nearly 94% from India or Pakistan, and 82% from China, Hong Kong, or Taiwan, had postsecondary education (U.S. Census Bureau, 2010). Consequently, some low-wage American workplaces are dominated by poorly educated immigrants and are not diverse at all, while other workplaces, often with high wages, are extremely diverse.

In developed countries in general, highly educated immigrants have lower employment rates than similarly educated natives; this may reflect language and/or credentials differences. But in some of these countries, though not all, immigrants with low educational attainment have higher employment rates than similarly educated natives. According to the OECD (2011), this "may reflect the strong demand for workers in low-skilled jobs which are no longer taken up by the in-coming cohorts of native-born workers."

Box 5.4

BAREFOOT COLLEGE: EDUCATING THE RURAL POOR

Urban engineers in India said it was technically impossible to build hand water pumps in Ladakh, a remote Indian region in the Himalayas at an elevation of 15,000 feet. However, a group of mostly illiterate drillers proved the engineers wrong. Not only did they install the pumps, but they also managed to get them to work throughout the winter when temperatures drop to –50 deg C (–58 deg F). Now, over 50,000 people benefit from the use of these hand pumps ("Tyler Prize for Environmental Achievement," 2009). These illiterate drillers are a small sampling of the people who have benefited from Bunker Roy's Barefoot College.

Founded in 1972, Barefoot College was designed to alleviate the suffering of the rural poor in India. The school is located in Tilonia, a village of 2,000 people in Rajasthan, one of India's largest and poorest states, where over 45% of men and 80% of women are illiterate. Additionally, more than half of the children between the ages of 6 and 14 do not attend school ("Barefoot College," 2003).

"We believe that paper-qualified, urban-trained experts and professionals can easily be replaced by people from the village," says Mr. Roy. "People in Tilonia do not need knowledge; they need confidence and assurance that the skills they already have are enough to improve their quality of life" ("Barefoot College," 2003). Barefoot College has helped students learn to be effective teachers, doctors, health care workers, solar engineers, hand pump mechanics, designers, accountants, and communicators ("Barefoot College," 2003). The end result is that the school has helped create jobs for nearly 7,000 people, including women and youths (United Nations Environment Programme, 2004). The benefits of Barefoot College do not end with the creation of jobs. It is also educating the next generation with its night schools. Over 150 schools were created to meet the needs of children who cannot go to school during the day, typically because they are too busy grazing sheep and goats. Therefore, the classes are offered at night and taught by local residents who have been trained at Barefoot College.

Contrary to typical trends in developing countries, the night schools have attracted more girls than boys, thanks to the advanced lighting system they use. The lighting increases the school's safety, which increases the likelihood that parents will send their girls to school. "Sixty percent of children don't go to school, because they have to look after animals—sheep, goats—domestic chores . . . because of night schools of Tilonia, over 75,000 children have gone through these night schools" (Roy, 2011). Barefoot College has earned awards from such prestigious organizations as the United Nations. Its accomplishments span an array of areas, including the environment (for powering the schools with solar electricity); children's parliament (which manages the night schools); and promoting volunteerism, social entrepreneurship, and education. If imitation is the best form of compliment, then Bunker Roy and Barefoot College have received that honor as well. The model has been adopted in 17 states across India and replicated in 15 countries in Africa, Asia, and South America. Gradually, Barefoot College is turning rural women into engineers. A more recent initiative on solar engineering has trained over 70 women to become Barefoot solar engineers (which they refer to, themselves, as "solar mommas"). These are women, many who are semiliterate or illiterate, who have learned to become experts when it comes to solar engineering. Barefoot College launched the solar training initiative program, in partnership with UNWomen, to teach women how to distribute, install, and maintain solar energy in households ("Barefoot College," 2015).

Taken together with population growth, educational improvements in the developing world are changing the comparative advantage of different populations in the global workforce, and contributing to the location decisions of employers. Essentially, "In the same way that the MDRs [more-developed regions] will have a lower and lower share of the world's population than the LDRs [less-developed regions] in the future, the human capital of the planet will be concentrated increasingly in today's LDRs" (Goujon & Lutz, 2004, pp. 136–137). Although the developed countries continue to have the world's best-educated populations, their lower rates of population growth are decreasing their share of the world's educated working-age people. China alone has more working-age people in all educational categories than Europe and North America (Goujon & Lutz, 2004), and it is gradually moving to superiority at higher levels of education. Thus, because of its large population, it will have large numbers of better educated people in 2030 than, say, Europe and North America, although a larger *share* of the population in those regions will be better educated. Even if the pace of educational improvement in the developing countries falters, simple population growth will give these countries a majority of people ages 20–65 with a higher education by 2030, according to estimates from the International Institute for Applied Systems Analysis (IIASA) (Goujon & Lutz, 2004).

The same combination of population and educational trends is also growing in the less educated or unskilled population in developing countries, particularly in South Asia and sub-Saharan Africa, where investment in education has lagged. The numbers of adults with no education at all will continue to grow in sub-Saharan Africa and the Middle East over the next 3 decades, according to the IIASA estimates (Lutz & Goujon, 2001). The numbers with a primary education will grow substantially in all developing regions (except China and Central Asia, where growth will be most intense among working-age people with a secondary education).

Thus, from a labor supply standpoint, the world's working-age population at all educational levels is shifting from the developed to the developing world. Other things being equal, the extent to which these economies absorb these workers productively will influence how many of them migrate in search of employment or how many transnational employers move to the developing world to find employees. Either outcome will increase diversity in workplaces around the world.

This broad-based improvement in the educational level of the global workforce also suggests an improved context for managing and implementing inclusive workforce policies. Ignorance is generally related to intransigence regarding interpersonal differences; education, to greater acceptance of those differences. Surveys suggest that contemporary young people are more tolerant than their elders regarding many kinds of diversity, if only because global information and entertainment networks have increased their shared knowledge.

Summary and Conclusion

Workforces are becoming increasingly diverse, due largely to the interaction of demographic trends and economic evolution and to the international human rights movement. These trends should continue to promote diversity in the global workplace although the social tensions they engender, along with broader economic or political failures, may occasionally set them back in the short term. By and large, though, managing workforce diversity effectively will be necessary in a globalizing world, and will also benefit national economies as well as national and international employers.

For instance, countries can enhance their economic success via their ability to welcome workers from other countries. This is especially true for countries that are experiencing tight labor markets, either because economic growth is outpacing labor force growth or a particular sector needs staffing up. Ireland in the early 21st century provides a useful example, as the government helped create a comparative advantage for transnational firms' sales and support call centers. In response, some companies concentrated their European operations under one Irish roof, bringing in natives from all over Europe to help their compatriots with their purchases—in their own language—when they dialed a toll-free number from home. Where public policy deliberately creates diversity, managing it requires attention from both government and society, including help when economic conditions change (as they did in Ireland with the subsequent financial crisis) and foreign workers need or want to return home.

The globalization of information and entertainment, hastened by the Internet, is reaching virtually everywhere and, in the process, promoting more encounters among diverse people. Young people are more inclined to use these communications channels and thus to take these encounters for granted, fostering a greater acceptance of diversity. As diversity becomes more widespread, they may become impatient with elders who display the old reticence, or old patterns of discrimination.

At the same time, traditionalists may find it difficult to change long-held attitudes and beliefs. This is more likely to the extent that these attitudes are rooted in religion, which so many cite to explain their reluctance to accept workers who have diverse sexual orientations. And both governments and employers can be daunted by the financial costs of accommodating worker diversity, such as retooling the workplace to meet the needs of persons with different physical abilities.

Thus, part of the challenge of managing workforce diversity is managing the diversity of people's preconceived notions about those outside their own mainstream culture, especially those notions acquired when social norms and economic needs were different. In that sense, the demographics of diversity include managing the demographics of past attitudes as well as future workforce trends.

Notes

1. Sassen (1999) provides a good historical overview from the European perspective.

2. This choice is facilitated by the growing acceptance of dual nationality.

3. Sassen (1999) offers the examples of Polish women working as cleaners in Germany and Africans working in Italy. Street peddlers, selling objects made at home, are a common example; so is the growing number of computer-related technicians.

4. Williamson (1998) offers an insightful comparison of the current and early period of globalization, along with an instructive account of the earlier antiglobalization backlash.

5. For instance, FDI measures understate the growth of transnational corporations, which finance much of their growth internally or from capital markets (Perraton et al., 2000).

6. Kabeer (2000) provides an example of the difficulty of making this distinction. She found that work in an apparel factory was socially as well as financially empowering for Bangladeshi women, who are normally tightly controlled by family members. A particularly interesting insight came from the women who told her that being locked into the factory was a form of maintaining their *purdah* (seclusion) and thus a necessary condition for them to be able to work. This stands in sharp contrast to the Western activists who use such conditions as "proof" of exploitation.

Social Psychological Perspectives of Workforce Diversity

PART II

6

Defining Diversity in a Global Context

Prejudice and Discrimination

Bury me standing; I've been
on my knees all my life.

—Isabel Fonseca, *Bury Me Standing: The Gypsies and their Journey*, 1996.

This saying from Romany, the language of the Rom (or Roma) people, refers to the centuries-long discrimination suffered by this persecuted minority in Europe. The Rom are descendants of a wandering people who appeared in Europe in the 13th or 14th century, most likely a lost caste from India that was expelled or voluntarily left. Europeans originally thought that they came from Egypt, and hence they came to be called "Gypsies."

In recent years, there has been a tendency to downplay the adverse implications of diversity. A few years ago, I observed a diversity seminar in the Southern Californian branch of an international high-tech company. The trainer, with elaborated enthusiasm, exclaimed, "Isn't it wonderful—we are *all* diverse! *Each one of us* is different from the other." She went on to lead an exercise in which participants were asked to identify the qualities that make them "diverse." Those qualities included salient individual characteristics such as race, gender, age, sexual orientation, and disability but also included less significant attributes such as the high school they attended, their hair color, and taste in clothing and foods. The trainer was clearly trying to help the participants develop empathy for people who are different from the mainstream in American society through identifying the qualities that make all people different. Her approach, however, represents a common confusion between benign differences and differences that have practical or even detrimental consequences in people's lives.

It is important to note that there is a fundamental difference between attributes that make a person a unique human being and those that—based on group membership rather than individual characteristics—yield *negative or positive consequences*. For example, growing up in rural China would create barriers to employment, whereas growing up in urban China could give a job seeker a significant advantage in the job market; being a man in Japan would be associated with more and better job opportunities than being a woman; and belonging to the lower castes in India would be a disadvantage in the workplace as compared with belonging to the upper castes.

Keep in mind that workforce diversity *is not* about the anthropological differences between people that "make them special" (using the terminology of that diversity trainer); diversity *is* about belonging to groups that are visibly or invisibly different from whatever is considered "mainstream" in society. In short, it is about being susceptible to employment consequences as a result of one's association within or outside certain social groups.

The interpersonal characteristics that create those group identities may be different in various parts of the world. Regional differences, for example, may be benign in some areas but consequential in others. If you grew up in Northern California, your high school experiences might have been different from those of someone who grew up 500 miles to the south in Southern California, though you would not be treated differently in the workplace. However, if you grew up in southern Italy and applied for a job in northern Italy, a distance of about 400 miles, you might suffer negative consequences because employers might consider you less educated and less hardworking than your northern counterparts. This is due to the traditional differences and sharp socioeconomic and educational disparities between Northern and Southern macro areas in Italy (Capuano, 2011; Verdicchio, 1999).

China is another country where significant regional differences have major implications for employment. A few years ago, I was invited to lecture at several universities in Beijing. During my presentation at People's University, a student complained about the difficulties that she and her women colleagues would encounter in finding suitable jobs upon graduation. She noted the interaction between regional affiliation and gender in creating unspoken employment-determinant diversity categories in China: "There are four groups of job seekers in China in descending order of advantage: urban men, urban women, rural men, and rural women." Her statement demonstrates that gender and region (urban versus rural) are important diversity characteristics in China's cultural context. Similarly, caste is a salient diversity category in India, and it influences the workplace even in the face of diversity management activities. Donnelly (2015) conducted a qualitative examination of diversity and inclusion management in information technology (IT) services in multinational organizations located in India. In this study, Donnelly (2015) conducted semistructured interviews with 14 top-level human resource management specialists/CEOs at 11 different firms and one IT industry specialist. In addition to exploring diversity categories such as age, gender, and ethnicity, Donnelly (2015) collected interview and documentary data about social class diversity. Interviewees explained that even though diversity management activities were in place (e.g., trainings and celebrations), "staff and management often referred to so-called castes and so effectively recognized and reinforced the legitimacy of these distinctions by religion, ethnicity, social class, and region/state" (p. 211). This example illustrates how strong and salient diversity categories, such as castes, can permeate the workplace, even in the presence of formal diversity and inclusion initiatives.

Geographic region, gender, race, ethnicity, or other distinguishable characteristics may thus define a person as belonging to a more- or less-favored group and can have either beneficial or detrimental consequences for one's job prospects. What are the positive or negative consequences of belonging to a more- or less-favored group? This chapter examines several concepts that are often used to express psychological processes and actual behaviors involved in intergroup relations that lead to the dominance or advantage of one group over another in society. As a first step, we need to understand how *group distinction categories*—what we commonly call diversity—are being defined around the world.

Workforce Diversity Defined

In the summer of 2001, I was fortunate to receive a grant from the Rockefeller Foundation to organize an international colloquium on global perspectives of workforce diversity. With the magnificent backdrop of Lake Como and the Swiss Alps, the 18 distinguished scholars from 14 different countries met at the foundation's Villa Serbelloni in Bellagio. As the meetings got under way, it quickly became clear that the concept of workforce diversity did not travel well across cultural and national boundaries. The representative from China and the representative from Mexico both noted that if the term *workforce diversity* were to be translated into their respective national languages, it would not make sense. They indicated that the term *diversity* itself is usually used to describe the varieties in fauna and flora[2] and does not yet have the human resource (HR) connotation it has acquired in other parts of the world. The discussions at the Bellagio conference illustrate the challenge of generating terms that will have common meanings across national boundaries and facilitate effective communication aimed at solving problems of intergroup relations in the workplace. Although the U.S. HR connotation of the word *diversity* is gradually catching on in many parts of the world (the European Union [EU], South Africa, and India are some examples), the specific definitions may be different. A discussion of these definitions is, therefore, warranted.

As noted in the earlier chapters, the globalizing economy with its trends of immigration and worker migration makes workforce diversity an increasingly common phenomenon in many countries around the world. Europe's societies are becoming heterogeneous, and even traditionally homogeneous societies such as Korea and Japan are seeing greater diversity, primarily in their major cities. In recent years, research and scholarly work on diversity have been generated in parts of the world other than the United States. Consequently, there is a growing need for a broader and more inclusive definition of diversity that will allow both scientists and practitioners to communicate clearly across cultural and national boundaries. Philomena Essed (1996, 2002; Essed & Trienekens, 2008) notes the difficulties posed by the use of the concept of diversity in her home country, the Netherlands, as well as the broader European perspective. Essed and Trienekens (2008) identify two Dutch terms that are relevant to understanding discrimination and exclusion: *allochtoon* and *autochtoon*, and state that "The mutually exclusive categories of autochtoon and allochtoon set apart 'US' from 'THEM'; the real Dutch (autochtoon) from the not-quite-Dutch (allochtoon)" (p. 57). The formal definition of *allochtoon* as used by the Dutch government in legislation, the authors note, includes residents born elsewhere, as well as their children, even when born in the Netherlands and even when one parent was born in the Netherlands as well. However, in its everyday use, allochtoon would typically refer to foreign-born as well as Dutch citizens who have darker skin tones, while autochtoon would be applied to Dutch citizens as well as foreign-born individuals with White skin tones. Therefore, being European is not a single category that includes diverse people within it; rather, there is a distinction between "real" Dutch and "not quite" Dutch, as well as "real" Europeans and "aspiring to be" Europeans. Thus, Essed and Trienekens (2008) claim, "In practice, allochtoon captures the mix of racial thinking and cultural hierarchies" (p. 57).

Essed and other authors note the different connotations the diversity concept has in Europe. Point and Singh (2003) identified how the definition of diversity and its dimensions vary across Europe through an examination of diversity statements on 241 top companies' websites in eight European countries (Finland, France, Germany, the Netherlands, Norway, Sweden, Switzerland, and the United Kingdom). With respect to identifying the dimensions of diversity, gender was the most cited dimension, appearing on 83 websites followed by culture on 79 websites. The multiracial, multicultural, and multiethnic meanings of diversity are dominant in online statements, especially in German companies. Diversity statements on the websites of UK companies feature race and ethnicity rather than culture, while French and German companies have statements about the broader notion of culture. "Cultural diversity" for the French includes both cultural expression and cultural differences. The United Kingdom was the only country with online statements that reported almost all the identified dimensions, while French companies disclosed the least information about diversity dimensions. Swiss and Norwegian online statements often mentioned workforce diversity without providing any specific dimension, whereas Finnish companies tended to provide a precise definition of diversity.

Jonsen, Maznevski, and Schneider (2011) in a review of research related to diversity indicate that the definitions of diversity as well as the field as a whole have been dominated by U.S.-centric research, and conclude that "the diversity field itself is not very diverse" (p. 35). Examining diversity management from an Australian perspective, Kramar (2012) echoed the same sentiments and indicated that originally the term diversity was used in the context of natural systems, referring to the variety of all living things, and has only acquired the workforce connotation in the 1980s and 1990s in the U.S.-based research. The literature presents a plethora of definitions, and there is some confusion about the nature of diversity: Is diversity about demographic categories, different identities, various life perspectives, life conditions, or all of the above (Essed & de Graaff, 2002)? Because of these varying definitions and country-specific cultural contexts, there are different connotations to the term *diversity*. In the Netherlands, for example, "when you say 'diversity,' the Dutch ear will hear 'ethnic difference'" (Essed & de Graaff, 2002), and the word diversity is often used interchangeably with the word immigrants, as well (Glastra, Meerman, Schedler, & De Vries, 2000). Another example is Denmark, originally a fairly homogeneous society with a strong emphasis on social equality, and vastly different from the United States, with its heterogeneous social composition and market economy, where the concept of diversity management has been transformed to *mangfoldighedsledelse*—literally, "plurality leadership" (Boxenbaum, Gjuvsland, & Leon, 2011). The following excerpt from an article by Helen Bloom (2002) further illustrates this point:

> To U.S. corporations, *diversity* is mainly about race, ethnicity, gender, religion, physical disability, age, and sexual orientation. To Europeans, *diversity* is about national cultures and languages—and it is a reality with which they have always lived. So when Americans tell Europeans to establish a diversity policy, their reaction is, "We already have diversity! It is not something we must invent or control. It's there by definition."
>
> Many Europeans don't even understand what Americans mean by *diversity*. In many European languages, the closest word to it emphasizes differences and implies categorization, partition, and separation. To them, then, the term means the reverse of the inclusion principles underlying U.S. diversity policies. In addition, European managers now connect the term with U.S. social and legal issues, and react against it: "If this is American stuff, I don't want to know it. Americans have unique problems. We want to do our own thing." For Europeans, that means finding ways to overcome linguistic and national differences in order to forge pan-European business strategies. (p. 48) [italics added]

A review of the business, organization, and HR literature produced three types of definitions of diversity: (a) narrow category–based definitions (e.g., gender, racial, or ethnic differences); (b) broad category–based definitions (e.g., a long list of categories, including marital status and education); and (c) definitions based on a conceptual rule (e.g., variety of perspectives, differences in perceptions and actions). The following sections explain this typology, and Table 6.1 provides examples for each of the definition categories.

TABLE 6.1 ● A Typology of Diversity Definitions

Source	Definition of Diversity	Narrow Category-Based	Broad Category-Based	Based on a Conceptual Rule
Acquavita, Pittman, Gibbons, & Castellanos-Brown (2009)	Diversity is often viewed as differences in race, ethnicity, gender, and sexual orientation.	✓		
	Personal diversity characteristics, however, encompass multiple dimensions, including age, educational status, religion, and job tenure.		✓	
	Organizational diversity characteristics include the composition of the organization and organizational practices.			✓
Buengeler & Den Hartog (2015)	Use Van Knippenberg et al.'s definition of differences between individuals on any attribute that lead to the perception that another person is different from self in the context of national diversity, which is associated with both "surface-level" (e.g., language and physical features) and "deep-level" individual differences (e.g., beliefs and values).			✓
Childs (2005)	In addition to race, gender, and physical disabilities, it includes human differences such as culture, lifestyle, age, religion, economic status, sexual orientation, gender identity and expression, marital status, thought, and geography.		✓	
Cox (1994)	Cultural diversity means the representation, in one social system, of people with distinctly different group affiliations of cultural significance.			✓
Cox (2001)	Diversity is the variation of social and cultural identities among people existing together in a defined employment or market setting.			✓
Diller (2010)	Cultural diversity refers to the array of differences among groups of people with definable and unique cultural backgrounds.			✓
DiTomaso, Post, & Parks-Yancy (2007)	Workforce diversity refers to the composition of work units (work group, organization, occupation, establishment or firm) in terms of the cultural or demographic characteristics that are salient and symbolically meaningful in the relationships among group members.			✓
The Diversity Task Force (2001)	Diversity includes all characteristics and experiences that define each of us as individuals.			✓

Source	Definition of Diversity	Narrow Category-Based	Broad Category-Based	Based on a Conceptual Rule
Dobbs (1996)	Broadly defined, diversity may refer to any perceived difference among people: age, functional specialty, profession, sexual preference, geographic origin, lifestyle, tenure with the organization, or position.		✓	
Fleury (1999)	We define diversity as a mixture of people with different group identities within the same social system.			✓
Glastra, Meerman, Schedler, & De Vries (2000)	The notion of diversity is predominantly used to refer to the variety of individuals and groups with whom work organizations are confronted in their labor markets, among their consumers and their employees.			✓
Gorman (2000)	Diversity should be understood as the varied perspectives and approaches members of different identity groups bring to the workplace.			✓
Grant & Kleiner (1997)	In the workplace today not only does diversity imply difference in people based on their identification with various groups but it is also a process of acknowledging differences through actions.			✓
Harrison & Klein (2007)	We use the term *diversity* to describe the distribution of differences among the members of a unit with respect to a common attribute, X, such as tenure, ethnicity, conscientiousness, task attitude, or pay. Diversity is a unit-level, compositional construct. . . . Diversity is also attribute-specific. A unit is not diverse per se. Rather, it is diverse with respect to one or more specific attributes of its members.			✓
Harrison & Sin (2006)	Diversity is the collective amount of differences among members within a social unit.			✓
Hartenian & Gudmundson (2000)	Workforce diversity was defined, therefore, as the percentage of Asians, Blacks, and Hispanics employed by the firm. [Defined for the purposes of a research study. Authors note diversity is more inclusive.]	✓		
International Labour Organization (ILO) (2005)	A workforce at enterprise level that includes workers from different national, ethnic, cultural or language backgrounds, workers with physical or mental handicaps, etc.		✓	

[Continued]

TABLE 6.1 ● (Continued)

Source	Definition of Diversity	Narrow Category-Based	Broad Category-Based	Based on a Conceptual Rule
Jackson & Joshi (2011)	The term diversity is now widely used by scholars to refer to the composition of social units. . . . It is useful to differentiating among various types of diversity, because different types of diversity may have different consequences. Relations-oriented diversity refers to the distribution of attributes that are instrumental in shaping interpersonal relationships. Age, gender, and personality characteristics are examples of relations-oriented diversity. Task-oriented diversity refers to the distribution of attributes that are potentially relevant to the team's work. Organizational tenure, formal credentials and titles, and cognitive abilities are examples of task-oriented diversity. . . . Readily detected diversity refers to differences among team members on attributes such as gender, age, nationality—attributes that are easily discerned. Underlying diversity refers to differences among team members on attributes that generally become known only through interaction, such as personality, attitudes, and skills.			
Jimenez-Cook & Kleiner (2005)	Since the inception of the concept of diversity, it has evolved to take into consideration not only ethnicity, race, and religion but also age, socioeconomic class, spiritual belief, disability, marital status, gender, sexual orientation, and more. . . . Organizations need to be influenced by and consider the needs of individuals with different learning styles, cultures, and life experiences.			
Joshi & Roh (2009)	We define diversity as an aggregate team-level construct that represents differences among members of an interdependent work group with respect to a specific personal attribute.			✓
Kossek & Lobel (1996b)	Diversity includes differences derived not only from ethnicity and gender but also based on differences in function, nationality, language, ability, religion, lifestyle, or tenure.		✓	

Source	Definition of Diversity	Narrow Category-Based	Broad Category-Based	Based on a Conceptual Rule
Kreitz (2008)	Both cognitive and demographic diversity can be indicative of variety—i.e., differences regarding task-relevant resources such as knowledge, experience, and perspectives that reflect a potential for improved team performance.			✓
Lai & Kleiner (2001)	Diversity is not only formed by sex but also by race, color, religion, and national origin.	✓		
Lau & Murnighan (1998)	We limit our consideration of diversity to demographic differences, focusing particularly on age, sex, race, and job tenure or status.	✓		
Mitchell et al. (2015)	Diversity is conceptualized in terms of heterogeneity in professional composition—the number of different professional backgrounds represented in a group or team.	✓		
Moore (1999)	[Diversity] is used as a criterion to segregate people into certain jobs and certain organizational levels, and it has to do with invisible as well as visible characteristics. . . . Generally though, strong indicators of diversity tend to include such dimensions as gender, skin color, age, cultural background, accent, and levels of physical ability. Weaker dimensions include other physical characteristics such as height and eye color.		✓	
Muller & Parham (1998)	Workforce diversity is understood as the presence in organizations of men and women from different cultural and racioethnic backgrounds, sexual orientations, physical abilities, and age.	✓		
Nishii (2013)	This study focuses on gender diversity as a type of demographic diversity. Gender diversity was calculated using Blau's (1977) index. Racial, age, educational, and tenure diversity were also included in the model as control variables.	✓		

(Continued)

TABLE 6.1 ● (Continued)

Source	Definition of Diversity	Narrow Category-Based	Broad Category-Based	Based on a Conceptual Rule
Nixon & West (2000)	[Multicultural diversity] includes such differences as age, economic status, education, family type, gender, personality type, race, religion, geographic origin, and sexual orientation. In addition, by defining diversity broadly as being everything that makes us different from others, including communication styles and work styles, all employees can "buy into" the value of building a culture that supports diversity.		✓	✓
Ocholla (2002)	Diversity is based on recognition of harmony in differences and emphasis on similarities in differences. This approach provides the patience and tolerance for recognizing, knowing, experiencing, embracing, benefiting, and fulfilling each other as well as accommodating the unique social differences and quite often transforming them into similarities for the benefit of the majority. Current social relations, created largely through urbanization and globalization, assume that people increasingly appreciate each other's culture, cuisine, attire, religion, language, sports, music, art, interests, tastes and values.			✓
Olsen & Martins (2012)	Diversity refers to differences among members of a group or organization on any characteristic.			✓
Parham & Muller (2008)	The definition of diversity has shifted from a group level phenomenon in which disparate treatment occurs to an exploration of individual differences.			✓
Prasad, Pringle, & Konrad (2006)	Workplace diversity is a more relevant concept if it focuses on those differences that have been systematically discriminated against, irrespective of whether or not they receive legal protection. . . . Diversity is also about respecting and valuing differences, whether they are gender-, race-, or ethnic-based differences in lifestyles, appearance, linguistic proficiency, communication, and decision-making styles, etc.		✓	✓
Qin, Smyrnois, & Deng (2012)	Diversity is referred to as the distribution of any attribute that people use to tell themselves that another person is different.			✓

Source	Definition of Diversity	Narrow Category–Based	Broad Category–Based	Based on a Conceptual Rule
Roberge & Dick (2010)	Diversity is defined at different conceptual levels—individual and group levels. Diversity adopting an individual focus refers to the perceived differences from the self and addresses questions such as "Who am I, as individual?" or "Who am I, as a group member?" Diversity adopting a group focus addresses questions of group identities such as "Who are we, as members of different groups?"			✓
Roberson (2006) Also used by Boekhorst (2015)	Diversity describes heterogeneity in group or organizational demographic composition. Diversity focuses primarily on differences and the demographic composition of groups or organizations.		✓	
Saz-Carranza & Ospina (2011)	Diversity refers to variability in structural and institutional traits within and across organizations not only with respect to demographics and cultures but also to other features of interest that are comparable within fields and populations of organizations.			✓
Shackelford (2003)	The new definition of diversity includes the traditional categories of race and gender. In addition, it includes people with disabilities, gays and lesbians, and other nontraditional categories. One of the most interesting categories being used by some employers is "diversity of thought"—which they say can be obtained by hiring individuals with different degrees, college affiliations, education or social economic backgrounds from their current employees.		✓	
Shen et al. (2009) Also used by Donnelly (2015)	Workforce diversity is discussed in terms of visible and invisible differences including age, marital status, social status, disability, sexual orientation, religion, personality, ethnicity and culture. A diverse workforce is described as having a variety of beliefs, values, and worldviews. The authors note that the salience of different diversity issues (and presumably, categories) is country dependent.		✓	
Svehla (1994)	Workforce diversity encompasses a mosaic of races, ethnic and religious backgrounds, sexual orientation, personality orientations, family situations, ages, and physical abilities. Workforce diversity can also refer to diverse functions within an organization.		✓	

(Continued)

TABLE 6.1 ● (Continued)

Source	Definition of Diversity	Narrow Category–Based	Broad Category–Based	Based on a Conceptual Rule
Theodorakopoulos & Budhwar (2015)	In a review of key themes in the diversity and inclusion management field, the authors focus on six dimensions of diversity: ethnicity and race, culture, gender, age, disability, and sexual orientation.		✓	
Thomas (1991)	Diversity includes everyone; it is not something that is defined by race or gender. It extends to age, personal and corporate background, education, function, and personality. It includes lifestyle, sexual preference, geographic origin, tenure with the organization, exempt or nonexempt status, and management or nonmanagement.		✓	
Thomas (2005)	Diversity is the differences and similarities that exist among the elements of a specific mixture. It does not refer solely to differentiating characteristics, nor to characteristics that are easily observable. Diversity is both dynamic and interactive. It cannot be predicted by external appearances.			✓
Unzueta & Binning (2012)	Diversity can be defined as consisting of at least two distinct dimensions of diversity: (a) the numerical representation of underrepresented minorities in an organization, and (b) the hierarchical representation of underrepresented minorities at specific levels of the organization's hierarchy. Numerical representation refers to the percentage of traditionally underrepresented minorities in a particular organization. Hierarchical representation refers not to how many minorities an organization employs but rather to where in an organization's structure are such individuals represented.			✓
Van Knippenberg & Schippers (2007)	Diversity is a characteristic of social grouping that reflects the degree to which objective or subjective differences exist between group members.			✓
Van Knippenberg et al. (2004)	Diversity is conceptualized as "differences between individuals on any attribute that may lead to the perception that another person is different from [the] self."			✓

Narrow Category–Based Diversity Definitions

The concept of workforce diversity originated in the U.S.-based organizational literature because, having defined itself early as a country of immigrants, the United States had to contend with diversity from its inception (Kurowski, 2002; Wallulis, 2012). Therefore, some of the initial definitions of diversity were anchored in the U.S. experience and its mixed racial/ethnic, census-based categories of diversity, such as Caucasians (or Whites), African Americans (or Blacks), Hispanics (or Latinos), Asian Americans, and Native Americans. The narrow category–based diversity definitions are determined by discrimination legislation and include gender, racial and ethnic groups, national origin, disability, and age.[3] These U.S.-based definitions are not often transferable to other cultures or applicable in other countries[4] (Ferner, Almond, & Colling, 2005). As an illustration, Sheila Walker (2002) discusses the complexity of economic differences in distinguishing racial or ethnic differences in Brazil as compared with the United States. She states,

> The idea that wealth or any other variable can somehow rescind one's most significant racial origin, i.e., those that determine into which of the only two available categories one falls, is a foreign concept in the United States. In contrast, a Brazilian anecdote tells of a poor Afro-Brazilian who laments to a very affluent Afro-Brazilian about how hard life is in Brazil if one is black. The rich man's response is "I know. I used to be black." . . . Consequently, in Brazil, being black, or for that matter being white for the economically unfortunate, just may be a transitory state. . . . Even with respect to appearance, the lines drawn at the limits of the shared categories of black and white are in different places in Brazil and the United States. Many "white" Brazilians would be considered black in the United States by both appearance and ancestry. (p. 19)

Researchers and practitioners in other parts of the world also encounter difficulties when applying the U.S.-based, narrowly defined concept of diversity. For example, with its increasingly multicultural population (Maoris are now 14.5%, Pacific Islanders are 4.8%, and Asians are 5.5% of the population), New Zealand is coping with workplace diversity issues that are similar to those of other developed countries. Women are making up almost half (48.3%) of the workforce, the proportion of older workers is larger, and ethnic diversity has become much more salient in the population and in the workforce (New Zealand Ministry of Social Development, 2009) due to accelerated immigration from East Asia, India, Africa, and the Middle East, and there are significant differences among New Zealand's major ethnic groups in birthrates (Houkamau & Boxall, 2011). By 2026, the Maori population is projected to increase by an average of 1.3% a year, the Pacific Island population by 2.4% a year, and the Asian population by 3.4% a year, while the European or *Pakeha* population is projected to increase by only 0.4% a year. On this trajectory, the European group will comprise 69.5% of the population by 2026, down from 76.8% in 2006 (Statistics New Zealand, n.d.). However, Jones, Pringle, and Shepherd (2000) note that the U.S.-based notion and specific categories of diversity may not be applicable to New Zealand because it is "ethnocentric and culturally limited" (p. 378). Even when attempting to use narrow categories that will be applicable to each country based on its antidiscrimination legislation, such as religion in Ireland or castes in India, the result may be too limiting, and the definition may need to be updated periodically as laws evolve and change.

Broad Category–Based Diversity Definitions

Over the years, as more scholars and practitioners became interested in the study of diversity, the definition of the term has expanded to include differences in race, gender, ethnicity, age, cultural background, social class, disability, and sexual orientation. An expanded definition of diversity may also include such variables as marital status and education as well as skills and years in the organization (e.g., Acquavita, Pittman, Gibbons, & Castellanos-Brown, 2009; Carrell, Mann, & Sigler, 2006; Donnelly, 2015; Harrison & Sin, 2006; Jackson & Joshi, 2011; Jimenez-Cook & Kleiner, 2005; Joplin & Daus, 1997; Kearney, Gerbert, & Voelpel, 2009; Point & Singh, 2003; Shen, Chanda, D'Netto, & Monga, 2009; Thomas, 1991). A common typology for this expanded definition provides a useful distinction between two types—visible and invisible:

- Visible diversity refers to characteristics that are observable or readily detectable attributes such as race, gender, or physical disability. Simply put, these are the characteristics you would notice of people walking down the hall, even if you knew nothing else about them.

- Invisible diversity refers to underlying attributes such as religion, education, and tenure with the organization. To be aware of a person's invisible diversity, you would need additional information from other sources (Cummings, Zhou, & Oldham, 1993; Jackson & Joshi, 2011; Jackson, Joshi, & Erhardt, 2003; Jackson, May, & Whitney, 1995; Jonsen et al., 2011; Kreitz, 2008; Tsui, Egan, & O'Reilly, 1992; Tsui, Porter, & Egan, 2002; Van Knippenberg & Schippers, 2007).

This distinction is important and has practical relevance. It is easier to form or harbor prejudices, biases, and stereotypes and to discriminate against people whose diversity characteristics belong to the first category of visible and readily detectable attributes. Invisible differences should not, however, be omitted from discussions of diversity. Individuals who are different from the organizational mainstream on those invisible characteristics can also experience discrimination and, as a result, have their work potential compromised. A case in point is sexual orientation, which can be invisible if a person chooses to keep it confidential but which can trigger prejudice and discrimination if the information gets out. Although the first category refers only to observable characteristics, one of the major reasons why diversity of any type creates difficulty for groups is attributable to complex and often implicit differences in perspective, assumptions, and causal beliefs with which the observable differences are assumed to be correlated (Milliken & Martins, 1996). These categories, therefore, are not necessarily mutually exclusive (Chatman & Flynn, 2001) because often a visible characteristic such as ethnicity may be associated with a less visible one such as socioeconomic status. Diversity, then, often becomes the interaction of visible and invisible dimensions, the former leading to unproven assumptions about internal qualities. For example, Black South Africans are more likely to belong to the lower socioeconomic group than White South Africans. Disability status is another diversity category comprised of visible dimensions that can trigger negative assumptions about internal qualities. Lengnick-Hall, Gaunt, and Kulkarni (2008) interviewed 38 corporate executives in eight U.S. states and asked employers why they do not hire people with disabilities. Employer concerns include assumptions, often stemming from stereotypical views, that people with disabilities may lack necessary job qualifications, be less productive, have more safety accidents than nondisabled employees, sue employers for discrimination, and hurt coworker morale (Lengnick-Hall et al., 2008).

Another example for the complexity of diversity attributes in generating both positive and negative outcomes is presented by a study of diversity among the members of river basin councils in Brazil (Bell, Engle, & Lemos, 2011). The authors of the study examined a mix of visible and invisible characteristics among council members, including age, income, education, and worldview. They found that, on the one hand, the more diversity in organizations and sectors represented on a council, the more council members participated in council activities and perceived decision making to be democratic. On the other hand, diversity in worldviews and in what members perceive to be the most pressing problems facing the basin was negatively associated with measures of participation and generally led to poorer outcomes for the council. This research demonstrates the complexity of the diversity construct and the importance of clearly defining diversity characteristics, particularly if we are interested in making viable connections between diversity attributes and specific outcomes. Considering the limitations of the broad-based definitions of diversity, Cooke (1999) notes, "The list [of diversity characteristics] has now grown so long that we may wonder how we will ever be able to create a workplace that is sensitive to the needs of all, and is still productive" (p. 6).

Definitions Based on a Conceptual Rule

In contrast to actually listing the common categories of diversity (e.g., age, gender, or race), there are some definitions that provide a conceptual articulation of diversity (e.g., Buengeler & Den Hartog, 2015; Cox, 2001; DiTomaso, Post, & Parks-Yancy, 2007; Joshi & Roh, 2009; Kreitz, 2008; Unzueta & Binning, 2012; Van Knippenberg & Schippers, 2007; Van Knippenberg, De Dreu, & Homan, 2004). For example, Linda Larkey (1996), one of the first to use a conceptual rule, defined diversity as (a) differences in worldviews or subjective culture, resulting in potential behavioral differences among cultural groups; and (b) differences in identity among group members in relation to other groups.

The basic assumption is that members of a given culture are likely to share a set of symbols, values, and norms that are at the root of their common worldviews and behaviors (Baugh, 1983; Collier & Thomas, 1988; Hirst, van Dick, & van Knippenberg, 2009; Triandis, 2003). These shared views and behaviors, in turn, create a sense of belonging among group members with respect to other groups (Ashforth & Mael, 1989; Ellemers & Haslam, 2012; Giles & Coupland, 1991; Giles & Johnson, 1986; Konrad, 2003; Triandis, 2003). This group identity, therefore, although providing a sense of belonging among the group members, also fosters a perception of not belonging or exclusion from other groups. This is relevant to understanding perceptions and behaviors, such as prejudice and discrimination, toward members of other groups, regardless of whether they represent majority or minority views.

Several theorists and researchers have advocated a move away from contrasting disadvantaged and privileged groups with regard to diversity, suggesting instead an individualized approach. Roosevelt Thomas (1991) articulates this conceptual framework in his book *Beyond Race and Gender:*

> Diversity includes everyone; it is not something that is defined by race or gender. It extends to age, personal and corporate background, education, function and personality. It includes lifestyle, sexual preference, geographic origin, tenure with the organizations. . . and management or nonmanagement. (p. 10)

Diversity trainers such as the one cited at the beginning of this chapter have readily embraced this approach. Many diversity trainers, as well as HR managers, find this broad definition appealing because it allows them to pull everyone in the organization under the "diversity umbrella," thus avoiding the controversial process of identifying groups with or without power, those who are discriminating, and those who are discriminated against. This politically acceptable approach also allows them to avoid alienating the powerful members of the majority groups who, in most organizations, are at the top of the management pyramid and who make decisions about organizational processes, including what kind of diversity training employees will receive. The very characteristic of this definition—including all differences under the diversity concept—that some find so appealing is also the limitation of this definition. By including all types of individual differences as "diversity," this definition suggests that *all* differences are equal and, therefore, trivializes those differences. The main criticism is that such expanded definitions reduce diversity to benign differences among people, thereby diluting the serious consequences of prejudice, discrimination, and lack of power that were clearly associated with the original set of diversity characteristics (Linnehan & Konrad, 1999). For example, the oppression and discrimination suffered by Black people in the United States or in South Africa can hardly be equated with the different treatment employees receive due to their tenure in an organization or their management position within a company. Furthermore, when diversity is very broadly and ambiguously defined, people can read into it content that suits their own worldviews. In a study of the relationship between worldviews of social dominance and diversity perceptions, Unzueta, Knowles, and Ho (2012) demonstrate that under conditions of ambiguous information, individuals with anti-egalitarian racial worldviews broadened their definition of diversity to include occupational (nonracial) heterogeneity when an organization's racial heterogeneity was low. By contrast, individuals with egalitarian worldviews broadened their construal of diversity to include occupational heterogeneity when an organization's racial heterogeneity was high. These findings suggest that when diversity is not clearly defined, individuals with different perspectives can interpret the concept in very different ways to fit their own worldviews.

Toward a Global Definition of Diversity

As a backlash to the all-inclusive definitions of diversity, some scholars, as previously noted, argue that such broad diversity categories dilute the real meaning of diversity. They advocate focusing only on the distinction categories that have been most persistent over the years and that have had the most serious impact on employment as a barometer of other societal consequences (Essed, 2002; Healey, 2009; Linnehan & Konrad, 1999; Linnehan, Konrad, Reitman, Greenhalgh, & London, 2003; Nkomo, 2001). They specifically identify race, gender, and social class as the fundamental diversity categories (Essed, 2002; Zanoni, Janssens, Benschop, & Nkomo, 2010). For example, Nkomo (2001) asserts that the expanded definition of diversity "overlooks the role of conflict, power, dominance, and the history of how organizations are fundamentally structured by race, gender, and class" (p. 9). Nkomo (2001) continues, "Race, gender and class create and maintain the most fundamental divisions in organizations. Diversity work must be about ending the domination of these systems of oppression" (p. 23). Holvino (2010) argues that it is not enough to examine race, gender, and class separately but that organizational research needs to focus on the intersections of race, gender, and class as simultaneous processes of identity. As another example, Linnehan and Konrad (1999) declare that broad-based definitions of diversity diminish the emphasis on intergroup inequality and sensitive historical and institutional problems related to stereotyping, prejudice, discrimination, and disadvantage. Similarly, Essed (1996, 2002) focuses on experiences of nondominant groups of gender, ethnicity, and culture in her work.

Against the backdrop of the broad definitions, on the one hand, and the narrow ones, on the other, generating a definition of workforce diversity that will be relevant in different countries and applicable in various cultural and national contexts proves to be a challenge. Trying to name specific diversity categories that can be relevant across cultures and nations is a futile effort. For example, the distinction between Catholics and Protestants that is central to diversity in Ireland is irrelevant in predominantly Muslim countries such as Pakistan; the distinction between various castes used in India is irrelevant in Belgium; and the racial distinction utilized in South Africa is irrelevant in China. Generating terminology that will be applicable across cultural and national boundaries is, therefore, essential.

There are some general distinction categories that do seem to cut across many (though not all) national and local cultures. These include gender, race, ethnicity, age, sexual orientation, and disability. However, there are two problems in utilizing some of these distinction categories to define diversity:

1. Some of the distinction categories may have either a positive or negative impact on employment and job prospects in different countries. For example, in Western nations, younger employees are considered more desirable because they are perceived to have new ideas, better technological skills,

and a more dynamic and flexible attitude. In Eastern and more traditional societies like China, the old are revered and believed to possess desirable qualities of wisdom and experience. Therefore, although age discrimination may be relevant in both types of societies, its impact might be very different.

2. These distinction categories are not exhaustive of the domain. Many countries utilize diversity categories that are not included on this list. For example, religious affiliation in Ireland, regional location (rural versus urban) in China, and castes in India are powerful diversity categories that are not included in the list. A more recent example is HIV status, which has been identified as a distinct diversity category in both South Africa and Zimbabwe based on the terms used in these countries' antidiscrimination legislation. (For a discussion of antidiscrimination legislation, refer to Chapter 2 of this book.) Similarly, involvement in a lesbian or gay male relationship is punishable by death in some countries, although in others it is tolerated or even embraced (Amnesty International, 2012).[5] These laws have direct bearings on how gays and lesbians are treated in the workplace and the freedom or lack thereof that they have to express their sexual orientation in everyday life, including the workplace.

The logical solution to the problem of finding a global definition for diversity that can be relevant in different cultural and national contexts is to define diversity by (a) the *process* of generating distinction categories—groups with a perceived common denominator in a specific national or cultural context, and (b) the *consequences* of belonging to these groups—the potential harmful or beneficial impact on employment and job prospects.

Therefore, the definition of workforce diversity—*in the global context*—utilized in this book is as follows:

> Workforce diversity refers to the division of the workforce into distinction categories that (a) have a perceived commonality within a given cultural or national context, and that (b) impact potentially harmful or beneficial employment outcomes such as job opportunities, treatment in the workplace, and promotion prospects—irrespective of job-related skills and qualifications.

This definition addresses the limitations encountered in applying some of the previous definitions to the global context. First, it provides a broad umbrella that includes any distinction categories that may be relevant to specific cultural or national environments without prespecifying the categories and without limiting the content of the domain. This approach does not list the distinction categories and therefore does not limit them to specific categories (e.g., to only gender, race, and ethnicity), thus allowing the inclusion of categories that may be relevant in some cultural contexts and not in others (e.g., regional differences or HIV status). It therefore overcomes the limitations of the narrow definitions of diversity because it is sufficiently broad to be relevant in various cultural and national contexts. Second, this definition emphasizes the importance of the consequences of the distinction categories and thereby overcomes the limitation of the broad definitions that include benign and inconsequential characteristics in their diversity categories. This second advantage is also a limitation because the use of consequences of diversity as part of the definition makes it difficult to use them as outcome variables in diversity research.

The debate around diversity and inclusion definitions continues, and in 2015, *The International Journal of Human Resource Management* published a special issue called "A Global Perspective on Diversity and Inclusion in Work Organizations." In that issue, Farndale, Biron, Briscoe, and Raghuram, (2015) identify three challenges related to the study of diversity and inclusion in a global context, two of which pertain to definitions. One challenge the authors discuss is the need for more context-specific definitions of diversity and inclusion, and they call for more single-country studies that use the country context to explain diversity and inclusion themes (Farndale et al., 2015). An example of a study that addresses this challenge is an article by Tang et al. (2015), which explores the concept of inclusion in the Chinese context. Findings illustrated that although there is some overlap with Western conceptualizations of inclusion, there were also some Chinese-specific considerations for understanding the meaning of workplace inclusion, such as a tolerance dimension (i.e., tolerating employees' mistakes). The second challenge Farndale et al. (2015) identify is the need to include globally relevant dimensions in diversity and inclusion definitions. Addressing this issue requires multiple country studies, a greater effort to include diverse perspectives (e.g., expatriates, migrants, refugees, and exiles), and consideration of diversity in values (Farndale et al., 2015).

What are the adverse consequences of the diversity distinction categories? *Stereotypes, prejudice, discrimination, oppression,* and *exclusion* are terms used to describe attitudes and behaviors that often affect the distribution of resources and privileges in society that are based on group membership rather than on employment-related characteristics such as level of education, commitment, and job-related skills. Donald M. Taylor and Fathali M. Moghaddam (1994) define stereotypes, attributes, and discrimination as "mechanisms by which advantaged and disadvantaged group members perceive and interpret interactions that appear to be based on their category membership rather than on their individual characteristics" (p. 159). At the basis of both intergroup attitudes and behaviors are the diversity or group-affiliation categories used to make the distinction between the advantaged and the disadvantaged in each society. Now that we have defined diversity in the global context, we are ready to examine the attitudes and behaviors that are associated with these distinction categories.

Stereotypes and Prejudice

Each one of us holds stereotypical views of groups other than our own, and sometimes about our own group as well. Examples of stereotypes include, "The French have gourmet tastes"; "Italians are great lovers"; "the Chinese are hardworking"; "women are emotional and men are rational." These stereotypes serve a very practical function. Rather than starting with no information when we encounter a person from another group, we begin with a framework that gives us a sense of confidence that we know something about the other person. These impressions have been formed by a combination of social, cultural, and political influences that include previous chance encounters with people of that group, popular media images, cultural norms of tolerance, partial truths that we have picked from various other sources, as well as contextual variables that are influenced by current events (Bar-Tal, 1997; Bar-Tal & Labin, 2001; Doki, 2012; Posthuma & Campion, 2009). For example, Doki (2012) examines cultural stereotypes as they come to bear on intermarriages between two distinct groups in Nigeria—members of the Tiv and the Igede ethnic tribes—residing in the Benue State within the central region of the country. The author notes several stereotypes that members of each group hold about the other tribe, such as that the Tiv people do not treat women with respect or that the Igede tribe members are only good as servants either on the farm or in the house. Though the historic roots as well as the present realities of these stereotypes are easily disputable, as the author eloquently demonstrates, these stereotypes are still strong enough to prevent or minimize the number of such intermarriages among the two tribes. These perceptions are often inaccurate when applied to an individual member of a group, as well as to the group as a whole. Yet these perceptions and categorizations often steer expectations of an individual or group and serve to justify actions that may turn out to be harmful or immoral (Tavris & Aronson, 2007). For example, the myth of the "model minority," as applied to Asian Americans in the United States, refers to an overachieving, supersuccessful ethnic group without significant problems (Lee et al., 2009; "What 'Model Minority,'" 1998). This notion misrepresents the complex and diverse experiences of Asian Americans by "glossing over huge differences within a group of people who come from more than two dozen countries and include Asian Indian professionals and Vietnamese peasants" (Kamen, 1992, p. A1). As a result, the social and mental health needs of Asian Americans may be overlooked, and those who do not fit this model may be subjected to racial hostility and stress in the workplace and in the community (Lee et al., 2009). Unlike the supposedly positive stereotypes of Asian Americans as a model minority, most age-related stereotypes ascribe negative characteristics to older workers. A systematic review of the literature reveals that the prevailing stereotypes of older workers are that they are less motivated, have lower ability, and are less productive (Posthuma & Campion, 2009). Research findings, however, indicate that employee age is less important to job performance than individual skill and health. In other words, these stereotypes overlook individual differences within older workers that are generally greater than the differences between different age groups.

The dilemmas associated with identity-based stereotypes are fiercely declared by Ziauddin Sardar (2001), a Muslim living in England (see Box 6.1). This example also echoes the importance of intersectionality that is discussed in Chapter 7—each one of us carries multiple and complex identities that interact such that every individual experiences bias in different contexts in a unique way depending on the identity or identities that are most salient in each particular context (Crenshaw, 1989; McBride, Hebson, & Holgate, 2015).

Box 6.1

ZIAUDDIN SARDAR STATEMENT ON HIS IDENTITY AND SUBSEQUENT STEREOTYPES

When people ask me where I am from, my standard reply is "Hackney." I wasn't actually born in Hackney, but I grew up in the borough. Hackney shaped my formative years and provides me with my childhood memories. It is home; and that's where I am from.

This is a difficult thing for most White people to grasp. They look at me and exclaim: "Surely, you're Asian." However, there is no such thing as an Asian. Asia is not a race or identity: it is a continent. Even in Asia, where more than half of the world's population lives, no one calls him or herself "Asian." If you are not Chinese or Malaysian, then you are an Afghan or a Punjabi. Moreover, the meaning of the term changes from place to place. In the United States, the Asian label is attached to Koreans, Filipinos and Chinese. In Britain, we do not use the term Asian to describe our substantial communities of Turks, Iranians or Indonesians, even though these countries are in Asia.

. . . There are others who look at me and say: "Oh, you're Indian." Sixty years ago, before the emergence of Pakistan and Bangladesh, this would have been a passable description. But today "Indian" has become almost as meaningless as "Asian," largely because the two terms have coalesced. They are lazy references to people of Indian subcontinental lineage. But for Pakistanis, Bangladeshis, Sri Lankans, and Nepalese, the label is offensive. By lumping these diverse communities into a single category, we make them invisible.

. . . When I really want to tell people who I am, I say I am a Muslim. Their reaction is an unbelieving stare—betraying complete incomprehension. This is because, first, at a time when no one actually believes in anything, people who express a religious identity—Muslims or Catholics or Orthodox Jews—appear to be totally out of sync. Second, although "Asian" and "Indian" suggest amorphous yet containable differences, "Muslim" describes a specific and volatile difference. Muslims are not simply a brand of believers: they are rampant, dangerous, and impenetrably different believers.

(Continued)

(Continued)

. . . In certain circles, saying you are a Muslim almost amounts to a declaration of war. Among feminists, for instance, I am automatically a chauvinist who forces his wife to walk several paces behind him. At secular intellectual gatherings, I am dogmatic and irrational even before I open my mouth. For some people, my name alone suggests that I must be a supporter of military dictators and terrorists.

Source: Sardar, Z. (2001, July 30). More hackney than bollywood. *New Statesman*, 14, 14 -16. © All rights reserved. New Statesman Ltd. 2009.

Often confused, stereotyping and prejudice are distinct concepts, and their definitions differ:

A stereotype is a standardized, oversimplified mental picture that is held in common by members of a group.[6]

A prejudice is derived from the verb *to prejudge* and refers to a preconceived judgment or opinion held by members of a group.[7] Most commonly, a prejudice is perceived as an irrational attitude of hostility directed against an individual, a group, a race, or their supposed characteristics.

Both concepts have long been important building blocks in most theories that deal with intergroup relations, as we shall see in the next chapter. Willard Enteman (1996) describes the original meaning of the word *stereotype* as follows:

While the origin of the word "stereotype" has been almost entirely lost in the dim recesses of linguistic history, it is most closely associated with journalism as a trade. The older print people among us will remember that the original stereotype was called a flong, which was a printing plate that facilitated reproduction of the same material. The typesetter could avoid recasting type by using the stereotype. Thus, a stereotype imposes a rigid mold on the subject and encourages repeated mechanical usage.

. . . The purposes of the stereotype are the same as in the print history. They are grounded in laziness. In standard economics, efficiency is another term for laziness. The person who substitutes a stereotype for careful analysis simply does not want to work harder than necessary to achieve a superficially acceptable result. (p. 9)

The stereotype concept was originally developed with respect to ethnic groups and has been perceived as morally wrong. Its early definitions reflect this focus. For example, Jack Brigham (1971) defined a stereotype as "a generalization made about an ethnic group, concerning a trait attribution, which is considered to be unjustified by an observer" (p. 29). Stereotypes were originally considered undesirable because they were thought to be either (a) the result of an inferior cognitive process—that is, a process that utilizes overgeneralization or oversimplification—or (b) morally wrong because they categorized people who had no desire to be categorized (Corrigan, 2004; Taylor & Moghaddam, 1994). For an example of a persistent stereotype of the Roma people (also called "Gypsies") over the ages, please see Box 6.3. Steele (2011) notes that there is a level of predictability in stereotypes in a particular society that most members of that society would be aware of, and "that means that whenever we're in a situation where a bad stereotype about one of our own identities could be applied to us—such as those about being old, poor, rich, or female—we know it" (p. 5). As a result, individuals know from an early stage of their lives that anything they do that fits the stereotypes common in society about one of their identities could be taken as confirming that stereotype. This threat follows members of the group into any situation where it might be relevant for the stereotype to be applied like a balloon over their head and can be very hard to shake (Steele, 2011).

Box 6.2

THE FEAR OF BEING JUDGED: HOW STEREOTYPES OUTSIDE OF THE WORKPLACE AFFECT BEHAVIOR INSIDE THE WORKPLACE

You are in the lobby filling out some basic paperwork before you step into a job interview you have been waiting months to do. For a split second you linger on the gender category checkbox before quickly finishing the remaining questions. As the hiring manager calls your name, you suddenly realize that you are more anxious than you thought you were. What if they don't think women can be good leaders? What if they think I'm too passive for this job? Too emotional? Unable to manage the budget effectively? As the interview begins, you have difficulty clearing your mind of these distracting thoughts. . . .

Stereotype threat affects individuals who are in an identity group that is associated with widely known, negative stereotypes. Stereotype threat is self-evaluative and describes the fear of being judged by others and unintentionally confirming these well-known stereotypes (Steele & Aronson, 1995). Research across a variety of disciplines shows that stereotype threat can hurt performance (Aramovich, 2014; Flore & Wicherts, 2015; Huber, Seitchik, Brown, Sternad, & Harkins, 2015; John-Henderson, Rheinschmidt, & Mendoza-Denton, 2015; Roberson & Kim, 2014; Schmader & Hall, 2014). For stereotype threat to disrupt performance, a person doesn't even have to believe the stereotype to be true—he or she simply has to know of the stereotype, and the task has to be explicitly framed as indicative of ability (Steele & Aronson, 1995). One example is presenting a math test as reflective of intellectual ability.

The presence of stereotype threat can negatively affect performance in the workplace—especially with tasks that are difficult or complex (Kray, Galinsky, & Thompson, 2002; Roberson & Kulik, 2007; Roberson, Deitch, Brief, & Block, 2003). As Roberson and Kulik (2007) note, "The potential for stereotype threat exists any time employees' beliefs about the particular traits needed for good job performance are linked to stereotypes about groups" (p. 30). Von Hippel, Issa, Ma, and Stokes (2011) conducted three studies to examine the effects of stereotype threat on working women. The first study focused on social comparisons to men, stereotype threat, and separation with the female identity. As the authors note, social comparisons to men are not unlikely as men typically have higher salaries, receive promotions more quickly, and are given more visible projects and responsibilities. Study 1 results indicate that women who compare themselves to men experience more stereotype threat and that these feelings are related to separation between their gender and worker identities. This identity separation can have negative mental health consequences for women. In contrast, social comparison with other women showed no such effects. The second study examined the relationship between stereotype threat and career aspirations. Similar to Study 1, women who compared themselves to men experienced more stereotype threat, which was related to lower expressed confidence that they would reach their career goals. Again, comparisons with other women did not show these effects. The third study examined relationships among stereotype threat, job satisfaction, and intention to quit. Linking the studies together, these findings suggest that among working women, stereotype threat is negatively related to job satisfaction and positively related to intention to quit through the pathways of identity separation and negative perceived likelihood of attaining career goals.

Stereotype threat helps explain how stereotypes outside of the workplace coupled with conditions inside the workplace (salience of stereotypes and framing of tasks) can influence employee performance. Furthermore, stereotype threat is an important consideration for diversity and inclusion initiatives (Roberson & Kim, 2014). Schmader and Hall (2014), in an article examining diversity training in the workplace, described three ways that diversity training can mitigate stereotype threat in work environments: Diversity training signals that the organization values underrepresented and marginalized groups, helps to establish positive norms, and can even change previously held

(Continued)

(Continued)

stereotypes. However, Schmader and Hall (2014) note that diversity training has to be delivered in a specific way if stereotype threats are to be reduced. More specifically, the training must frame diversity as an organizational goal, include discussion of implicit biases (rather than focusing on explicit discrimination), and encourage a shared commitment to workplace inclusion.

Zegers de Beijl, R. (Ed.). (1999). Documenting discrimination against migrant workers in the labour market. Geneva: International Labour Office; Smeesters, B., Arrijn, P., Feld, S., & Nayer, A. (2000). The occurrence of discrimination in Belgium. In R. Zegers de Beijl (Ed.), Documenting discrimination against migrant workers in the labour market. Geneva: International Labour Office; Michelangelo Merisi da Caravaggio, The Fortune Teller. 1594. Painting. Oil on Canvas. Capitolini Museum. Retrieved from http://en.wikipedia.org/wiki/File:The_Fortune_Teller-Caravaggio_(Rome).jpg

Early studies (e.g., Katz & Braly, 1935) presented research participants with an ethnic group label and asked them to check off or rate the extent to which each of a long list of trait adjectives best described the ethnic group.

Box 6.3

THE NOBLEMAN AND THE FORTUNE TELLER: ART AND STEREOTYPES IN RENAISSANCE ITALY

In the Capitolini Museum in Rome, a painting by the famous Italian Baroque artist Michelangelo Merisi da Caravaggio is displayed prominently. The painting, named *The Fortune Teller* and dated 1594, depicts a wealthy young man having his palm read by a seemingly innocent Gypsy girl (identifiable by her unique attire). Naively trusting and apparently easily distracted by the young girl, the boy flirtatiously gazes into the Gypsy girl's eyes. Close inspection of the painting (supported by contemporary sources) reveals what the young man has failed to notice: The girl slips the ring off his finger while she gently strokes his hand. The painting so impressed Cardinal del Monte, Caravaggio's first important patron, that around 1595 he commissioned another version from Caravaggio for himself, and that second version of *The Fortune Teller* is currently in the Louvre museum in Paris.

From an artistic perspective, this painting provided a break from the typical techniques and subjects of the time. Caravaggio was said to handpick the Gypsy girl on the street to prove that he did not need to copy works of the masters from antiquity, which was a common practice among artists of his period. The painting was innovative not only in its technique and color palate (warm golden colors that provide a serene atmosphere) but also in the selection of the subject: Rather than depicting a biblical didactic theme, the painting represents a real-life scene (Christiansen, 1994).

It is the latter that is relevant to our discussion here. The painting demonstrates the persistence of stereotypes during the ages. For more than a thousand years, the Roma people (also called Gypsies, but including several groups who identify themselves as Travellers, Manouches, Ashkali, and Sinti) have been an integral part of European civilization. With an estimated population of 10 to 12 million in Europe (approximately 6 million of whom live in the EU), Roma people are the biggest ethnic minority in Europe. Most Roma are EU citizens. Many face prejudice, intolerance, discrimination, and social exclusion in their daily lives (Fonseca, 1996). They are marginalized and live in very poor socioeconomic conditions.

Recognizing that European institutions and EU countries "have a joint responsibility to improve the social inclusion and integration of Roma," the European Commission for Justice adopted a Communication on an EU Framework for National Roma Integration Strategies by 2020, which includes initiatives such as providing access to employment, improving access to housing and essential services, and reducing the gap in health status between the Roma and the rest of the population (European Commission for Justice, 2011). In response to the EU framework, member states developed national Roma strategies, but there were also some controversial actions related to the Roma. In 2010, for example, French president Nicolas Sarkozy ordered the dismantling of more than 100 camps set up by Roma of eastern origin (Bulgaria and Romania), and the French government announced the deportation of 700 Roma people. They were offered €300 per adult and €100 per child as "aid for a humanitarian return." French authorities claimed that they were acting in accordance with EU

law by repatriating Roma who had been in France for more than 3 months without work. They also said that most of the repatriations were voluntary. The operation was criticized by human rights organizations and also by President Sarkozy's opponents, who accused him of using the issue to boost his flagging support ("The Islamic Veil," 2010). In the meantime, the EU Commission for Justice continued to push for integration and inclusion policies. On May 21, 2012, the commission provided a report assessing national efforts of EU members to integrate the Roma people and published its conclusion in the communication "National Roma Integration Strategies: A First Step in the Implementation of the EU Framework" (European Commission for Justice, 2012).

The Fortune Teller exemplifies not only the long-lasting value of a remarkable work of art through the ages but also the enduring power of stereotypes against a group of people for many centuries.

Several studies demonstrate both positive and negative stereotyping of various groups in different societies (e.g., Bergsieker, Leslie, Constantine, & Fiske, 2012; Burkley & Blanton, 2009; Levy & Leifheit-Limson, 2009). In one study conducted in South Africa, 265 students completed a questionnaire that attempted to measure ethnic group identification and particular interracial attitudes. Significant indications of racist stereotypes were found in all racial groups, with a strong positive bias toward participants' own racial groups and a negative bias toward other racial groups (Slabbert, 2001). Another study examined stereotypes of older workers in New Zealand. The participants—including 2,137 members of New Zealand's largest union and 1,012 employers who belong to New Zealand Employers' Federation—were asked to indicate whether they agree or disagree with a series of statements under the term *views of the older worker*. The results indicate that the negative stereotypes held by both groups were "adaptability factors," such as resistance to change and problems with technology, particularly computer technology. The positive stereotypes also related to "adaptability factors," but in this case they were reliability, loyalty, and job commitment (McGregor & Gray, 2002). Littrell and Nkomo (2005) noted that gender stereotypes are the psychological characteristics differentially associated with women and men across many cultural groups. During an 8-year study, the authors found that Black women, having entered careers traditionally dominated by White men, have been subjected to a particular form of sexism shaped by racism and racial stereotyping (Nkomo, 2001). Moreover, gender stereotypes affect perceptions of leaders and managers (Littrell & Nkomo, 2005). Serving as the first woman editor of a major newspaper in New Zealand in the mid-1980s, Judy McGregor (2006) examined New Zealand women's representation at the governance level and in the media. She found little progress of women to top newspaper editorships or broadcasting executive positions. She also discovered that their status was still low because of the so-called "feminization" of the media in the past 30 years.

Another example of gender stereotyping and discrimination in the workplace is the U.S. case of *Price Waterhouse v. Hopkins*. The woman at the center of the case, Ann Branigar Hopkins, was denied a promotion to partner in the accounting firm because her interpersonal skills were considered too abrasive although the partners strongly praised her skills and abilities to secure major contracts. Her partnership was initially delayed for 1 year. In that period, she was told that she could improve her chances "by walking, talking, and dressing more femininely." In the following year, she was again denied partnership. Hopkins then quit and took action against the firm. She filed a lawsuit charging gender discrimination under Title VII of the Civil Rights Act of 1964. After bouts in the federal courts, in a landmark decision, Hopkins eventually won and was awarded partner (Coleman, 2012; Hopkins, 2006; *Hopkins v. Price Waterhouse*, 1985; *Hopkins v. Price Waterhouse*, 1987; *Price Waterhouse v. Hopkins*, 1989).[8]

Box 6.4

"YOU SPEAK ENGLISH REALLY WELL": THE INSIDIOUS NATURE OF MICROAGGRESSIONS

"You have a very unique look."

"I like you. You're cool. But some others, you know, why do they have to shove it in our face?"

"All of the 'independent women' I knew eventually settled down and got married. Your instinct will kick in soon."

"But you don't look Jewish!"

"Are you sure you are old enough to work here?"

"Oh, that's why you don't have an accent. You're part White."

"Your hair is so cute! What are you mixed with?"

"No offense, but you're more of a mother hen than a team leader."

"Sometimes I forget that you're Black."

"Really? You've never been out of the country? You were born here?"

"Don't go getting too independent. Men don't like that."

"If everybody would just stop making everything about race, you would realize that everything is actually ok."

"Oh, you are so exotic."

"Oh great, we are getting a woman employee. Now we have to make sure that our conversations are work-friendly."

These statements were posted on a microaggressions blog whose goal is to make "visible the ways in which social difference is produced and policed" through everyday comments (Microaggressions website, n.d.). Microaggressions were originally defined as "brief and commonplace daily verbal, behavioral, or environmental indignities, whether intentional or unintentional, that communicate hostile, derogatory, or negative racial slights and insults toward people of color" (Sue et al., 2007). Microaggressions can be directed toward members of any disadvantaged or minority group. In addition to race and ethnicity, microaggressions are studied in areas such as gender, sexual orientation, disability, mental health status, and religion (Basford, Offermann, & Behrend, 2014; Bostwick & Hequembourg, 2014; Gonzales, Davidoff, Nadal, & Yanos, 2014; Nadal, 2012; Sue, 2010; Yearwood, 2013). In a recent study, Nadal et al. (2015) qualitatively examined the intersection of microaggressions related to race, ethnicity, gender, sexuality, and religion. These researchers identified themes related to the intersection of identities, highlighting the ways in which the combination of different identities affects one's experience with microaggressions. Intersectional themes from this study include exoticization of women of color, gender-based stereotypes for lesbians and gay men, invisibility and desexualization of Asian men, and assumptions of inferiority or criminality of men of color (Nadal et al., 2015).

Microaggressions are brief, subtle, and often "lie beneath visibility or consciousness" (Nadal et al., 2015; Sue, 2010). Microaggressions have been studied in the context of clinical practice, university campus climate, classroom dialogues on race, and mental health outcomes (Constantine, 2007; Sue et al., 2007, 2009; Torres, Driscoll, & Burrow, 2010; Yosso, Smith, Ceja, & Solórzano 2009). Recent studies have also examined microaggressions in the workplace (Basford et al., 2014; Offerman et al., 2013, 2014; Shenoy-Packer, 2015). For example, Shenoy-Packer (2015) qualitatively examined how immigrant professionals (IPs) experience microaggressions and identified the critical sensemaking strategies they use to cope. Findings suggest that immigrant professionals faced microaggressions through sarcasm, stereotypes, and skepticism. As one participant expressed, "sometimes being in a business setting and they detect an accent, it goes right into, where you're from, how long have you been here, why did you move here? It always gets personal but it shouldn't. When you're in a business setting you want it to stay all business but that never happens. I mean I'm the same as my American coworker. Sometimes it bothers me" (Shenoy-Packer, 2015). In this study, immigrant professionals used three types of sensemaking strategies in response to microaggressions: rationalizing, creating alternate selves, and taking ownership or blaming oneself. As these findings illustrate, managers committed to an inclusive workplace must be aware of the hidden, yet damaging, effects of microaggressions in the workplace.

A growing body of research puts less emphasis on the negative aspects of stereotyping and views stereotyping as a basic cognitive process that is not necessarily bad and not necessarily informed by prejudice (Blair, 2002; Devine, 2001; Gocłowska, Crisp, & Labuschagne, 2012; Greenwald & Banaji, 1995; Judd, Blair, & Chapleau, 2004; Levy, 1999; Lowery, Hardin, & Sinclair, 2001; van den Bos & Stapel, 2012; Yarhouse, 2000). The emphasis in those works is on associations between daily events that result in the creation of stereotypes. Thus, a group may become associated with a particular characteristic not as a function of explicit prejudice but out of a basic cognitive process (Taylor & Moghaddam, 1994). For example, in the early 1990s, media reports included several incidents of Korean immigrants in Los Angeles who physically defended their shops against robbers.[9] A stereotype of Korean immigrants as store owners was reinforced, and perhaps another stereotype of Korean immigrants as fierce fighters may have emerged. However, sometimes a stereotype of a group may be generated based on popular media images from one country and be inappropriately applied for the same group in another country (Van Dijk, 2007). For example, beliefs about Muslim women suggesting that they are veiled and often sheltered are based on popular images from the Middle East, which are globally applied. In an analysis of Muslim women's images in the Canadian media, Diane Watt (2012) notes that "representations of covered women as oppressed, exotic, and threatening are widespread, especially in the news media." Actually, in a U.S.-based study by Jen'nan Ghazal Read (2002), Muslim women were well educated, held progressive gender views, and were represented in the labor force. Fauzia Ahmad (2012) similarly presents a critique of popular representations of "arranged marriages" for Muslim women and argues that the British matrimonial practices for Muslim women have shifted from parentally arranged matches to a highly individualized and commercialized process.

The concept of prejudice refers to people's attitudes toward members of other groups—expecting certain behaviors from them that are mostly pejorative. Gordon W. Allport (1954/1979) in his seminal book *The Nature of Prejudice* defined prejudice as "an antipathy based on faulty and inflexible generalizations. It may be felt or expressed. It may be directed toward a group as a whole or toward an individual because he is a member of that group" (p. 9). The word prejudice, derived from the Latin noun *praejudicium,* means to prejudge. Although it is possible to have positive prejudice as well—that is, to think well about others without sufficient justification (e.g., reverence for the wisdom of the elderly)—the word prejudice has acquired a negative connotation. The two important elements in understanding prejudice are that it involves passing judgment on the other without sufficient warrant, and that it involves negative feelings (Allport, 1954/1979; Ponterotto, Utsey, & Pedersen, 2006). Prejudice is a schema of negative evaluations and characteristics that are attributed to groups perceived as racially and culturally different (Van Dijk, 1987, 2006). Philomena Essed (1995) emphasizes the ideological basis of prejudice, noting, "The negative evaluations are generalizations based on insufficient or biased representations that are constituent elements of an ideology rationalizing and reinforcing existing systems of racial and ethnic inequality" (p. 45). For example, in a study of interethnic perceptions, Gilbert, Carr-Ruffino, Ivancevich, and Lownes-Jackson (2003) found that African American men were more likely viewed as incompetent and not as courtly and mannerly as African American women and Asian American women and men. This was despite having similar job-related qualifications and history.

Geert Hofstede makes a distinction between two kinds of stereotypes. The first are *heterostereotypes*—perceptions about members of the other group—and the second are *autostereotypes*—perceptions about one's own groups (Hofstede et al., 2010, pp. 388–389). It stands to reason that people will incorporate generally positive and favorable characteristics into their autostereotypes and generally negative and unfavorable characteristics into the way they perceive groups other than their own, their heterostereotypes. For example, the 2003 Iraq conflict brought to the surface negative stereotypes of allied nations that took different positions on the war. The French saw the Americans as arrogant and as bullies, and the Americans saw the French as naïve and greedy.

A similar process occurs with respect to prejudice. Negative attributes are associated with members of other groups, or *out-groups,* and positive characteristics are associated with members of one's own group, or *in-group.* In a classic study by Howard and Rothbart (1980), subjects were randomly assigned to one of two different groups in which they did not know anyone. They were then presented with a mix of positive and negative information about their group (the in-group) and the other group (the out-group). Subjects had more favorable expectations about in-group members and more negative expectations about out-group members, even though they did not personally know the members of either group. In addition, people tend to perceive their in-group as heterogeneous, whereas the out-group is seen as mostly homogeneous. Taylor and Moghaddam (1994) note that popular statements such as "I can't tell one from the other" and "They all look the same to me" reflect this perception of the out-groups as more homogeneous than the in-group, which is part of the stereotyping process (p. 163). Regardless of which group is considered the majority and which is viewed as the minority in a particular cultural or national context, people perceive more variability in the characteristics of their own group than in the characteristics of out-groups. For example, in the old Hollywood western movies of the 1940s and 1950s, Chinese men were typically cooks, whereas White men could be cowboys, sheriffs, town mayors, and even horse thieves and villains.

In an effort to understand diversity, research has been conducted in recent years that examined various characteristics of the workforce and the attributes of specific groups. Some generalizations that have come out of this literature have been used in diversity trainings designed to help employees become more sensitive to prejudice and discrimination. These applications, however, are not always helpful or productive. For example, a U.S.-based training program taught managers preparing for assignments in China that if a subordinate does not look into his or her supervisor's eyes during a conversation, it is a sign of respect. What the trainees did not realize was that this may not always be the case. One manager who was later posted in the company's branch in Beijing reported that it took him a while to realize that one of his direct subordinates was averting his eyes not out of respect but because of resentment; that employee had a good reason for resenting the new American manager—he was demoted from his job to make room for the U.S. manager's position.

Sometimes generalizations about certain ethnic groups used in diversity training can actually backfire, as in the case of diversity training conducted at the Lucky Stores chain in 1988. The diversity workshops were designed to help participants identify gender- and ethnic-based stereotypes. In an interesting twist, one of the company's representatives took notes that detailed comments such as "Black females are aggressive" and "women cry more." An employee of the company found the notes and attributed the content to the lack of promotions for women and ethnic minorities in the company. Employees then sued the company for discrimination, and the notes from the workshop were entered into evidence. The employer was found guilty (Caudron, 1993).

It is important to remember that although it is legitimate to categorize groups and to study their common traits, behaviors, and beliefs, applying that information to specific individuals may be misleading and may constitute stereotyping. Greet Hofstede (1997) refers to this very point, stating, "Stereotyping occurs when assumptions about the collective properties of a group are applied to a particular individual from that group" (p. 253). Individual behavior, although to some degree a product of the cultural group, is also highly influenced by the family of origin and, of course, the unique individual's characteristics. For this reason, research indicating associations between personality and culture should be interpreted as statistical, not absolute, and there is no justification for using characteristics of national culture as stereotypes for individuals from these nations (Hofstede et al., 2010). In order to avoid the negative aspects of stereotyping, all of these elements should be taken into consideration when viewing an individual whose culture is different from one's own (see Figure 6.1).

FIGURE 6.1 • A Framework for Viewing Individuals Whose Culture Is Different From One's Own

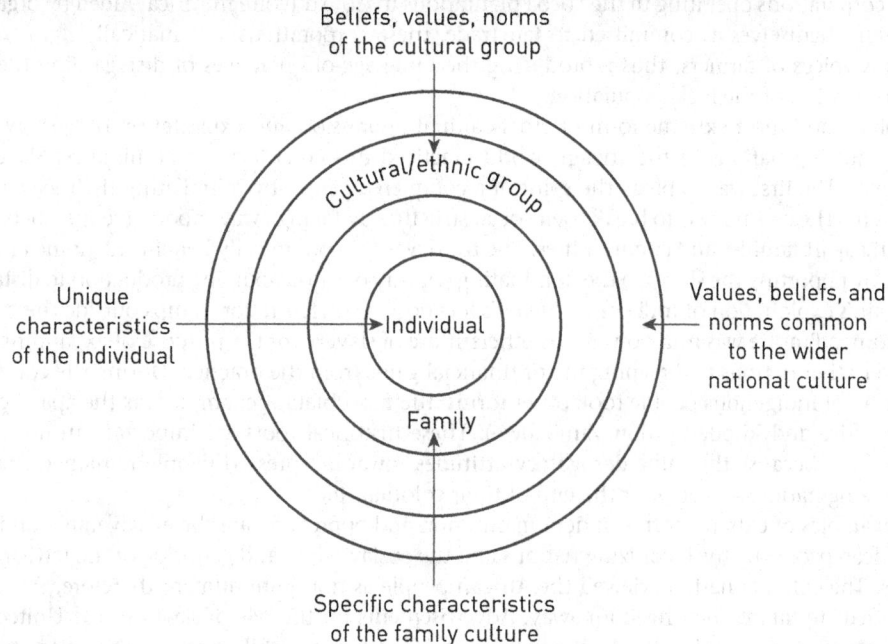

Beliefs, values, norms of the cultural group

Cultural/ethnic group

Unique characteristics of the individual

Individual

Values, beliefs, and norms common to the wider national culture

Family

Specific characteristics of the family culture

When encountering a member from another group, rather than rely on the oversimplified mental picture provided by a stereotype, one should recognize that the person's attitudes and behaviors are the result of the interaction among the person's unique individual characteristics, the family environment, and the values and norms that are common to his or her cultural group. The use of stereotypes and prejudices is an unfortunate, abbreviated way of sizing someone up. It is much easier than making the effort required to actually know the other person.

Dehumanization and Oppression

Stereotypes and prejudices also make it easier to relate to the other person as not only different but inferior and as such not worthy of equal rights and treatment. The most extreme psychological mechanism in viewing members of other groups as inferior is *dehumanization,* and its behavioral manifestation is oppression. Thus, at the root of oppression is a systematic process of dehumanization of the target people. Oppression is the unjust or cruel exercise of authority or power—most often used by one group to dominate another. A developed society governed by rules of law needs a rational justification for practicing any form of domination. The psychological process involved in this justification includes relating to out-group members as less human, inferior, or fundamentally different in ways that make them undeserving of equal treatment. This logic has often been used in the past to justify oppression as a method for bringing enlightenment to "primitive" nations. A prime example is "the White man's burden" logic that was used to justify colonialism as an "obligation" of the European nations to bring enlightenment to the rest of the world (Moreton-Robinson, 2011). A remnant of this colonialism ideology is the paternalistic approach toward minorities of color in Europe. Philomena Essed (1991, p. 16) describes the manifestation of this ideology in the Netherlands under the title "the Dutch burden," indicating that this paternalism was motivated by "good intentions" to "help" Blacks cope with "modern" Dutch society. Athreya (2011) provides a specific example of an extension of this ideology in the current practices of several large multinational corporations operating in the cocoa plantations in Côte d'Ivoire in Africa. Aided by organizations that present themselves as committed to fair trade, these corporations systematically ignore or silence indigenous voices of farmers, thus reproducing the same age-old practices of disregarding the right for self-determination of the local population.

The oldest and most extreme form of cross-cultural oppression and exploitation of work was slavery. Many conquering nations in the ancient world practiced this cruel form of dominance. Slavery served several goals: The first was to break the spirit of a conquered people by humiliating their leaders through enslavement. The second was to break their social structure by taking away productive members of society and tearing apart families and communities. The third was to economically benefit the homeland through free labor by importing the slaves to the dominating country or by outsourcing production to distant shores (e.g., Britain's exploitation of India or Germany's location of concentration camps outside the homeland).

The Roman Empire was infamous for its efficient use of slavery for the purpose of expanding its dominance over other nations and reaping major financial gains from the practice. During the colonial years, exploitation of indigenous people took other forms; the most blatant example was the apartheid regime in South Africa and Rhodesia (now Zimbabwe). These historical roots are important in understanding discrimination because the same derogatory attitudes toward oppressed people remained ingrained in the colonizing nations—even after the end of their colonial rule.

Two examples of extreme forms of dehumanization and oppression are the enslavement and genocide of the African people by the colonizing nations and the enslavement and genocide of the Jewish people by the Nazis. The colonial nations viewed the African people as not quite human; therefore, the oppressors felt "justified" in taking their freedom away. Advertisements for the sale of slaves in the United States in the 18th century, proclaiming the work qualities of African slaves while depicting them in stereotypical straw skirts, provide an example of the way this cruel and efficient industry created an image of the slaves as subhumans.

Similarly, the Nazis viewed the Jews as an inferior race and used their racist theory to justify the enslavement and genocide of the Jewish people. In 2000, the German foundation Remembrance, Responsibility, and Future was established by German law to provide $5 billion in funds to former slaves and forced laborers during World War II. Slavery and oppression were justified by cultural ideologies of racial superiority such as those of colonial Europe and of the Nazis. These cultural ideologies that are at the base of racism, sexism, ageism, ethnocentrism, and all the other "isms" characterize the dominant race, gender, or specific ethnic group as being inherently superior to the other groups, simply because of their birthrights (e.g., race, gender, or ethnic origins) (Fernandez, 1991, p. 35).

Although there is no comparison between the harm done to a person who is enslaved and the harm done to someone who is discriminated against in the workplace, the psychological process at the root of these practices resides on a continuum. This discussion of oppression and dehumanization provides the basis for understanding the employment-related discrimination described in the next section.

Employment-Related Discrimination

Though originally morally neutral in its meaning, the word *discrimination* has acquired a negative value, particularly in the context of employment. Discrimination in employment occurs when (a) individuals, institutions, or governments treat people differently because of personal characteristics such as race, gender, or sexual orientation rather than their ability to perform their job; and (b) these actions have a negative impact on access to jobs, promotions, or compensation. The UN International Labour Organization (ILO) Discrimination Convention of 1958 (No. 111) defines discrimination as,

> Any distinction, exclusion or preference . . . which has the effect of nullifying or impairing equality of opportunity or treatment in employment or occupation as may be determined. In this convention the grounds for non-discrimination include race, colour, sex, religion, political opinion, national extraction or social origin. (Zegers de Beijl, 2000, p. 10)

Analyzing the evolution of workplace-based discrimination in international law, Sheppard (2012) describes the process of expanding the discrimination paradigm to include principles of inequality at work. While banning discrimination was initially understood as a fairly limited legal principle that would ensure equal treatment for individuals with similar work qualifications and situations, it evolved to include group-based patterns of inequality at work. The author notes that manifestations of group-based disparities—in terms of gender, race, national or ethnic origin, disability, social origin, political belief, religion, and sexual orientation—are relevant to understanding systemic processes of discrimination. Attending to the inequities experienced by the most economically disadvantaged and marginalized groups in society makes a significant contribution to greater equality at work for all. As we enlarge our understanding of discrimination to embrace the systemic and structural dimensions of group-based inequalities, antidiscrimination law converges with other domains of international labor law and contributes to both the empowerment of workers. This resulting convergence between antidiscrimination law and legal initiatives to reduce class-based socioeconomic inequality and poverty ultimately benefits society as a whole.

Around the world, gender has been one of the most commonly used criteria for discrimination in the workplace. Although not as crude as robbing the others of their human qualities—as in the racist ideologies—the logic used to justify women's discrimination has relied on perceptions of a difference in their "destiny" in life, often citing religious justification. Consider the following statement: "The paramount mission and destiny of women are to fulfill the noble and benign offices of wife and mother. This is the law of the creator" (Joseph P. Bradley, U.S. Supreme Court justice, 1873).

Justice Bradley made this statement when, in 1873, the Supreme Court threw out a case by a woman who could not become a lawyer simply because of her gender.[10] A hundred years later, the prime minister of Japan made a similar statement: "First of all, I want women, as mothers, to become 100 percent wonderful mothers. Then I want them to become good wives. And I want them to become ladies capable of making contributions for society also" (Yasuhiro Nakasone, prime minister of Japan, 1984).[11]

Members of ethnic and national minorities have also been frequent victims of discrimination. A multinational study conducted by the UN's ILO found that discrimination against migrant and ethnic minority job applicants was widespread (Zegers de Beijl, 2000) (see Box 6.5). The average discrimination rates in the countries studied were around 35%. A particularly interesting facet of this study is that it was able to pinpoint the stage during which discrimination had occurred. Most of the direct discriminatory rejections occurred in all the countries in the first stage of the application process, resulting in these applicants being denied the opportunity to present their credentials. In other words, the discrimination occurred as soon as the applicants introduced themselves using foreign names that were not typical of their new country of residence.

Box 6.5

DOCUMENTING EMPLOYMENT DISCRIMINATION AGAINST MIGRANT WORKERS

In order to document the process of discrimination, the UN ILO initiated a classic multinational "situation testing" study, using research methodology that preserves the real-life quality of observations in a systematic and objective way (Zegers de Beijl, 2000). The process involved two testers, one belonging to the majority group in the country, the other to a minority group, who applied to the same position and interacted with the employer or manager who had the authority to make the hiring decision. The applicants were matched on criteria that concern an employer recruiting for a job, including age, educational background, and work experience. The main difference between the testers was their racial or ethnic background. Because the study used a highly controlled protocol, the results in actual hiring rates were attributable to the difference in race, ethnicity, or nationality backgrounds of the applicants. The study was applied in four European countries: Germany, the Netherlands, Belgium, and Spain. The results indicated that on average, migrants were discriminated against in one in three application procedures. Discrimination occurred in all three stages of employment—the initial inquiry, the job interview, and the actual offer of the job.

a. *Discrimination during the inquiry stage.* Discrimination was at its most flagrant during this stage. Migrants were often simply told that the vacancy had already been filled whereas the national applicant was invited for an interview. In some cases, the migrant applicant was told straight away that foreigners were not wanted.

b. *Discrimination during the job interview.* During this stage, there were a considerable number of cases in which the migrant candidate was asked for more qualifications than the native candidate or queried about residence status and work permit whereas the other candidate was not.

c. *Discrimination in the job offer.* During this stage, even when the migrant candidate was offered a job, the terms and conditions of employment tended to be inferior to those offered to the national applicant. In other words, migrant workers were treated as though they were undocumented foreigners (even though they were not) who could be easily exploited.

Vacancy for a Photographic Model

The following is an example of a discriminatory exchange that occurred in the inquiry stage in the German sample: The Turkish applicant called first and, after having introduced himself, was asked to give his height. When he stated that he was 1.82 meters, he was turned down for being too short; he was told that the minimum height requirement (not mentioned in the job advertisement) was 1.85 meters. Then, the German applicant telephoned. After giving his height (1.84 m), he was invited for an interview. When he then asked whether 1.84 meters would still be all right, he was given a reply in the affirmative.

Source: Zegers de Beijl (2000).

Religion can be another source of employment discrimination. A Muslim-American woman, Samantha Elauf, filed a lawsuit against the clothing retailer Abercrombie and Fitch citing discrimination at a job interview in 2008 because she was wearing a *hijab* that supposedly violated the company's "look policy" for sales staff members ("US Muslim in Abercrombie," 2015). A compelling aspect of this discrimination case is the fact that a hiring manager at the Tulsa, Oklahoma, store admitted to giving Elauf a lower score when learning that wearing a hijab violated Abercrombie and Fitch policy ("A Muslim Woman Beat Abercrombie," 2015). In June 2015, the U.S. Supreme Court ruled, 8–1, that Abercrombie and Fitch violated the 1964 Civil Rights Act. The company has since reversed its policy on headscarves ("US Muslim in Abercrombie," 2015).

There has also been recent progress in the area of employment discrimination based on sexual orientation. In July 2015, the Equal Employment Opportunity Commission (EEOC) ruled that discrimination based on sexual orientation also violates the Civil Rights Act of 1964 (Freedom to Work, 2015). This decision followed several years of data tracking by the EEOC. The EEOC received 643 allegations of discrimination related to sexual orientation in 2013, 918 in 2014, and 505 in the first two quarters of 2015 (EEOC, n.d.). This issue extends beyond the United States. According to a recent Catalyst report using a European sample, 47% of individuals who identify as LGB reported discrimination and harassment based on their sexual orientation (Catalyst, 2015). Furthermore, only 61 countries worldwide prohibit sexual orientation–based employment discrimination (ILGA, 2014).

Summary and Conclusion

Understandably, the concept of workforce diversity does not travel well across cultural and national boundaries. There is an underlying challenge in generating a term that will have common meanings across national boundaries and that will facilitate effective communications aimed at solving problems of intergroup relations in the workplace. Against the backdrop of the broad definitions on the one hand and the narrow ones on the other, generating a definition of workforce diversity that will be relevant in different countries and applicable in various cultural and national contexts proves to be a challenge. The logical solution to the dilemma of finding a global definition for diversity that can be relevant in different cultural and national contexts is my proposed two-stage definition of diversity (Mor Barak, 2005): (a) the process of generating distinction categories—groups with a perceived common denominator in a specific national or cultural context, and (b) the consequences of belonging to these groups—the potential harmful or beneficial impact on employment and job prospects.

This chapter also defines and analyzes two concepts that are relevant to understanding diversity: stereotyping and prejudice. These concepts, although often confused, are distinct, and their definitions clearly differ from one another. A stereotype is a standardized, oversimplified mental picture that is held in common by members of a group. In contrast, prejudice refers to a preconceived judgment or opinion held by members of a group. Most commonly, a prejudice is perceived as an irrational attitude of hostility directed against an individual, a group, a race, or their supposed characteristics. Stereotypes and prejudices are often used to label other people unjustly, to relate to them as inferior, and to discriminate against them. Once they are labeled as inferior, it is easier to dehumanize members of other groups and to perceive them as not worthy of equal rights and treatment. In this chapter we study examples of extreme manifestations of dehumanization and oppression—specifically, slavery and genocide.

Discrimination in employment occurs when (a) individuals, institutions, or governments treat people differently because of personal characteristics such as race, gender, or sexual orientation rather than their ability to perform their jobs, and (b) when these actions have a negative impact on access to jobs, promotions, or compensation. Around the world, gender has been one of the most commonly used criteria for discrimination in the workplace. Other groups that have commonly been discriminated against are ethnic and national minorities.

This chapter presented several perspectives on diversity and suggested a definition that can be applicable to countries around the world. By-products of the adverse effects of diversity—stereotypes, prejudice, oppression, and discrimination—and their impact on the distribution of resources and privileges in society were discussed. Group membership or diversity characteristics, rather than employment-related qualifications such as level of education or job-related skills, were shown to have historically prevailed across the globe. Extreme as well as not uncommon applications of these practices were presented. The work environment is an important arena in which these mechanisms of intergroup relations are being played out. This is because of individual and group efforts to gain advantage in the competition for (real or perceived) limited resources or out of misguided, ill-informed, or blatantly malicious attitudes toward other groups. Most people derive their livelihood from their jobs, as well as personal identity and self-fulfillment. The consequences of mechanisms such as stereotypes and discrimination can be detrimental to those affected, their families, and communities.

Notes

1. Quote from Fonseca (1996, p. 306).

2. Indeed, this was the common usage of the word diversity in the United States and in Europe before the term had acquired its HR connotation. Charles Darwin's use of the term demonstrates this: "When we reflect on the vast diversity of the plants and animals which have been cultivated, and which have varied during all ages under the most different climates and treatments . . ." (Darwin, 1859/1995, p. 71).

3. For example, U.S. federal laws prohibiting discrimination include Title VII of the Civil Rights Act of 1964, which prohibits employment discrimination based on race, color, religion, sex, or national origin; the Age Discrimination in Employment Act of 1967 (ADEA), which protects individuals who are 40 years of age or older; Title I and Title V of the Americans With Disabilities Act of 1990 (ADA), which prohibits employment discrimination against qualified individuals with disabilities in

the private sector and in state and local governments; and Sections 501 and 505 of the Rehabilitation Act of 1973, which prohibits discrimination against qualified individuals with disabilities who work in the federal government.

4. These narrow category–based diversity definitions are not entirely useless in a global context. Whether out of the United States or other countries, such definitions may provide an example or inspiration to other countries even if, in their respective contexts, they are not always or immediately applicable or transferable.

5. Different cultures have different perceptions and attitudes toward homosexuality, and these views are expressed in national legislation. An extreme view of homosexual relations was expressed by President Yoweri Museveni of Uganda, who said, "Look for homosexuals, lock them up and charge them" ("Lock Up Gays," 1999). According to Amnesty International (2012), gaps in antidiscrimination legislation related to sexual orientation still persist around the world and in Africa: "Discrimination against people based on their perceived or real sexual orientation or gender identity worsened. Politicians not only failed to protect people's right not to be discriminated against, but often use statements or actions to incite discrimination and persecution based on perceived sexual orientation" (p. 7).

6. For an overview of definitions of the stereotype concept, see Taylor and Moghaddam (1994), pp. 159–166.

7. For the origins and societal perspective of prejudice, see Cox (1994), pp. 64–74.

8. Hopkins details her experiences in her book, *So Ordered: Making Partner the Hard Way* (1996).

9. One such example was a famous 1992 incident in Los Angeles when a 15-year-old girl was shot in the back of the head in Los Angeles by a Korean store owner who thought the girl was shoplifting. This incident was the result of long-standing tensions between Korean store owners and African American residents (Ford & Lee, 1991).

10. A *Time* magazine article from June 4, 1984, "Getting a Piece of the Power: Women Barred From Partnerships Can Now Go to Court," described the 1984 Supreme Court unanimous ruling that it was illegal for law firms to discriminate against women in deciding on partnership simply because of their gender (p. 63).

11. *Japan Times,* May 15, 1984, p. 2.

Vive la Différence?

Theoretical Perspectives on Diversity and Exclusion in the Workplace

I don't want to belong to any club that would accept me as a member.

—Groucho Marx, comedian and actor

Groucho Marx had a humoristic take on the sense of exclusion experienced by those who cannot belong to the inner circles of society. Why do people form a strong sense of belonging to groups? What dynamics dictate intergroup relations? How can we explain conflicts and hostilities among ethnic groups? The previous chapter reviewed major concepts describing the social psychological mechanisms that contribute to attitudes and behaviors toward diversity in the workplace. This chapter presents *orienting theories* that sensitize us to ideas that are important for understanding workplace exclusion and *explanatory theories* that address the following questions: Why do employees feel excluded in their workplace? How can experiences of exclusion influence employee attitudes, behaviors, and performance? Why are there conflicts between groups in the workplace?

Over the years of research and scholarly investigation, several theories have been generated that explain the nature of intergroup relations. This chapter begins with an examination of the concept of the inclusion-exclusion continuum and its relevance to today's diverse workforce. It explores research on organizational demography that points to the connection between diversity and exclusion and examines several social psychological theories on diversity and intergroup relations. The chapter elaborates on social identity theory, concluding with its implications for explaining diversity and exclusion in a global context.

Diversity and Exclusion: A Critical Workforce Problem

"Diversity makes business sense."

"People are our most precious commodity."

"We are gender and color blind."

"We do not discriminate, we incorporate."

These were some of the poster slogans that greeted me as I walked into the lobby of a large international high-tech company headquartered in Southern California. I was there at the invitation of the CEO to evaluate the company's diversity policies. As a first step, I interviewed employees, both men and women, from different levels in the organization and of various backgrounds. Personal disclosures by interviewees underscored the company's challenge of moving beyond its uplifting slogans to create a culture that was truly inclusive. Most White men expressed the belief that the company was "blind to ethnic and gender differences" and therefore fair in its practices. Women and members of racial/ethnic minority groups, however, reported different experiences: They primarily talked about lost job opportunities and missed promotions. The word most often used by interviewees was *exclusion*. They felt left out of social and informational networks and barred from the organization's decision-making process. One middle-aged minority manager, recalling the difficulty she had rising to her current position, told me that her promotion was initially blocked because her supervisor expressed the belief that she "did not possess the communication skills needed for a managerial job" because she came from a different culture. "That was nonsense," she said. "I am very good at what I do, but I am a woman in a man's job. I am short, my skin is dark, and I have a funny accent. The fact was that I just didn't fit in—and management's solution was to exclude me."

One of the most significant problems facing today's diverse workforce is that of exclusion—both the reality experienced by many and the perception of even greater numbers of employees that they are *not* viewed by top management as an integral part of the organization (Choi & Rainey, 2010; Hitlan, Cliffton, & DeSoto, 2006; Insch, McIntyre, & Napier, 2008; Kalev, 2009; Kanter, 1992; Mor Barak, 2011; Shore et al., 2011; Wood, 2008). The inclusion-exclusion continuum[1] is central to the discussion in this chapter and is defined here:

> The concept of inclusion-exclusion in the workplace refers to the individual's sense of being a part of the organizational system in both the formal processes, such as access to information and decision-making channels, and the informal processes, such as "water cooler" and lunch meetings where information and decisions informally take place. (Mor Barak, 2000b, 2005, 2014)

The distinction between inclusion-exclusion and organizational involvement is that the latter's focus is on organizational activities that foster the development of policies and procedures aimed at creating an environment where individuals have better access to company knowledge and information channels (Harris, 2011; Lawler, 1992, 2008). The high-involvement approach to management focuses on moving power to lower levels in the organization so that workers could participate in important decisions about how work is done and take responsibility for their performance. Interestingly, the high-involvement approach seems to be easier to install in countries that have a democratic political tradition, perhaps because it places a great emphasis on allowing workers to make decisions, giving them feedback about the effectiveness of their performance, and challenging them to develop and use their skills and abilities (Lawler, 2008). The concept of inclusion-exclusion, by contrast, is an indicator of the way employees experience and perceive their position in the organization relative to its "mainstream." Sometimes the experience of exclusion is blatant, such as when a Suriname-born Dutch project manager was not invited to a meeting of other project managers and was later told by his boss, simply, "I didn't think you needed to be there." But more often, it is subtle and unintentional. A woman who served as a CFO of a large health care company (and the only woman among the company's top management) once told me that during breaks in the company's top-management team meetings, the guys would continue the discussions on the way to, and while in, the washroom. When she finally protested being excluded from these discussions, her colleagues belittled her concerns, saying there was no need to make a fuss over such a trivial matter.

Though diversity distinction categories vary from one culture or country to the next, the common factor that seems to transcend national boundaries is the experience of exclusion, particularly in the workplace. Individuals and groups are implicitly or explicitly excluded from job opportunities, information networks, team membership, human resource (HR) investments, and the decision-making process because of their actual or perceived membership in a minority or disfavored identity group. Yet inclusion in organizational information networks and in decision-making processes has been linked to better job opportunities and career advancement in work organizations (e.g., Cunningham, 2007; O'Leary & Ickovics, 1992; Shore et al., 2011), as well as to job satisfaction (e.g., Acquavita, Pittman, Gibbons, & Castellanos-Brown, 2009; Bortree & Waters, 2008; Mor Barak & Levin, 2002), well-being (e.g., Mor Barak & Levin, 2002; Vakalahi, 2012), job performance, and organizational commitment (e.g., Cho & Mor Barak, 2008; Findler, Wind, & Mor Barak, 2007; Shore et al., 2011), all of which are related to employees' intention to leave and actual turnover (e.g., Buttner, Lowe, & Billings-Harris, 2012; Mor Barak, Levin, Nissly, & Lane, 2006). Some scholarly work, though clearly not enough, examined the interaction between diversity distinction categories, such as race/ethnicity and gender, pointing to the compounding complexity of understanding racial prejudice when entangled with sexism (Bell, 1990, 1992, 2004). Research indicates that racial and ethnic minority women commonly believe they are excluded from the organizational power structure and have the least access to organizational resources from among disfavored groups (Hall, Everett, & Hamilton-Mason, 2012; Kossek & Zonia, 1993; Mor Barak, Cherin, & Berkman, 1998; Shorter-Gooden, 2004). In addition, ethnic minority women are often required to fit into the existing culture with respect to their behavior and appearance if they want to penetrate networks of influence or be given opportunities for career development and advancement (Claringbould & Knoppers, 2007; Kamenou & Fearfull, 2006; Kamenou, Netto, & Fearfull, 2012). Employees' experience and sense of exclusion, therefore, may play a critical role in explaining both their lack of job opportunities and dissatisfaction with their jobs, respectively.

Overview of Social Psychological Theories of Diversity and Exclusion

On a global scale, a gradual shift has been taking place in research and theory development related to diversity, intergroup relations, social identity, and multiculturalism in the beginning of the 21st century. More cross-national collaborations have been taking place, creating a conversion of ideas, concepts, and theoretical formulations from different regions and national contexts around the world. Prior to that, the research and scholarly work on individual and intergroup differences in the workplace has been disjointed. Although there were similarities in areas of research (e.g., gender and intergroup relationships), they were often examined under different frameworks and with different terminology. Taylor and Moghaddam (1994) echoed a concern expressed by several authors before them (e.g., Berlyne, 1968; Kennedy, Schrier, & Rogers, 1984; Sexton & Misiak, 1984) that theory development in Europe and in North America has occurred with little mutual influence. What these authors (Taylor & Moghaddam, 1994) called the "isolationism" or "monocultural science" (p. 10)—the parallel tracks taken by theorists in these two regions—may have been the result of lack of awareness of each other's work or a general sense that theories developed in one region are not relevant to the other. Broadly speaking, social psychological theories regarding diversity, social identity, and intergroup relations have been developed primarily in two locations—North America and Western Europe. Beyond these two regions, little or no attention has been paid to issues of exclusion in the workplace.

Although North American scholars have often identified their work under the title of workforce diversity, European scholars and the few scholars from other countries who have published in this area usually identified their work under titles such as gender studies, demography of the workforce, labor migration, and guest workers. The difference has been much more than a semantic preference and seems to have stemmed from different perspectives and worldviews. North American researchers have focused on diversity of the workforce (e.g., gender, racial, and ethnic differences), which emanated from the region's historical role in absorbing immigrants and a value system rooted in equal employment opportunity, antidiscrimination, and fairness paradigms. European research has centered on immigration, worker migration, and gender work roles and the inherent social and emotional difficulties in integrating immigrants and women into each country's relatively stable social fabric and gender roles. The increased movement of individuals and groups across national boundaries has triggered debates among European countries, as well as in other regions of the world, regarding the multicultural nature of their societies (Bertossi, 2010). The global trends of immigration and worker migration, as well as legislation and social policies related to the workplace noted in the first part of this book, underscore the need to examine theories generated in different parts of the world and to engender an integrated approach to understanding workforce diversity and intergroup relations.

Theoretical Underpinnings of the Inclusion-Exclusion Construct

Imagine that today is your first day at a new job. Your morning was spent touring the building, meeting with your boss, filling out HR paperwork, and settling into your new workspace. As you review the company handbook for new employees, you notice a sentence that says: "*We value diversity. As a manager, it is your job to create and encourage an inclusive workplace.*" You will soon be meeting with your new team for the first time. Like most organizations, your team is diverse. Furthermore, you genuinely want your team members to feel included. Yet, as you consider your new team and responsibilities, you are left wondering a few things: *What do I need to be aware of to actually create an inclusive workplace? Why do people feel excluded? How does it affect outcomes that I care about as a manager? Why is there conflict among employees?* The following sections aim to shed light on the theoretical underpinnings of the inclusion-exclusion construct and present two types of theories. The first type, *orienting theories*, acts as a broad lens for thinking about—or "orienting" you—to this topic. These theories highlight the complexity of the construct and present ideas that one should be sensitive to when considering workplace exclusion. The second type, *explanatory theories*, helps explain relationships and answer questions about why exclusion and conflict exist and how they can affect outcomes in the workplace.

Orienting Theories of Diversity and Exclusion

Although many theories offer explanations of "why" and "how," orienting theories act as broad theoretical lenses that sensitize us to issues that are important for understanding a particular topic (Bengtson, 2005; Bengtson & Settersten, 2016). In this section, we discuss how critical race theory and intersectionality theory can be used to orient and familiarize us to concepts and ideas that guide our understanding of workplace exclusion (see Figure 7.1). To start, *critical race theory* provides a lens for considering the origins, experiences, and consequences of workplace exclusion. Key tenets of critical race theory are: Stereotypes are ubiquitous and racism is an everyday experience for people of color; the "White over Color hierarchy" provides both material and psychological benefits to the dominant group; race is a social construction and racial categories emerge, evolve, and are manipulated over time; racism intersects with other forms of oppression; and minority status entails a "presumed competence" to discuss race and racism in a way that individuals from a dominant group cannot (Carbado & Roithmayr, 2014; Delgado & Stefancic, 2012). Critical race theory has prompted the development of other theoretical branches, including LatCrit theory, which focuses on experiences and issues relevant to Latinos/as, Asian critical thought, critical race feminism, and Queer-Crit theory (Delgado & Stefancic, 2012; Olden, 2015). Several scholars have applied critical race theory to the field of human resource development, calling for the use of this theory to better understand power, racism, and intergroup conflict in organizations (Byrd, 2007; Rocco, Bernier, & Bowman, 2014).

Intersectionality theory is another orienting theory for understanding the exclusion construct. This theory sensitizes us to the importance of viewing the overlap between different forms of social inequality, oppression, and discrimination to create a multidimensional picture of diversity (Crenshaw, 1989; Lutz, Herrera Vivar, & Supik, 2011). The concept of intersectionality challenges the notion that social problems can be broken down into separate issues that only affect specific identity groups. According

---

FIGURE 7.1   •   Orienting and Explanatory Theories of Diversity and Exclusion

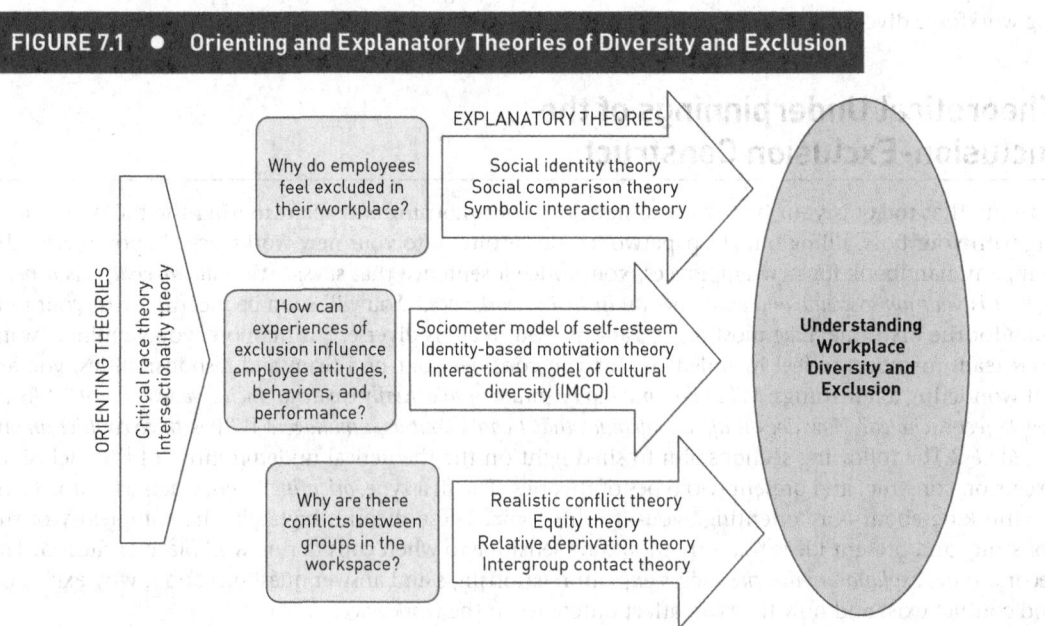

to intersectionality theory, the "single-axis framework" in which discrimination and oppression are framed in terms of discrete categories (for example, focusing only on race or gender and ignoring the overlap of these two identities) creates artificial boundaries, encourages mutually exclusive interests, and causes intergroup conflict (Cho, Crenshaw, & McCall, 2013; Crenshaw, 1989; Wells, Gill, & McDonald, 2015). Intersectionality theory promotes the idea that each person experiences bias in a unique way because we simultaneously carry multiple and complex identities and these identities interact with each other (Crenshaw, 1989; McBride, Hebson, & Holgate, 2015). In a study of gender and race intersectionality among engineering students, Ro and Loya (2015) examined learning outcomes related to core competencies in engineering programs. Results from this study showed that the influence of gender on learning outcomes differed by race and ethnicity. For example, for three of the learning outcomes—design, contextual competence, and communication skills—Black women rated themselves significantly lower than White women. There was no statistically significant difference between Black and White men. As this finding illustrates, it is the combination of identities (in this case, race and gender) that produces a particular outcome, and this experience may be unacknowledged if the two identities are examined separately.

Consider the complex set of identities that you carry with you to work or the classroom. Suppose your manager praises you in front of your whole team. Or suppose that you find out that people on your team went out for a drink after work but did not invite you. How might different situations or encounters positively or negatively highlight one or some of your identities? Intersectionality theory helps us understand that the way people experience exclusion directly reflects their multiple, overlapping identities.

Explanatory Theories of Diversity and Exclusion

Explanatory theories help answer specific questions of "why" and "how" and inform the selection of critical variables, relationships, and mechanisms that answer a particular research question (Bengtson & Settersten, 2016). In the next sections, we identify explanatory theories relevant to the study of workplace exclusion and describe how they can be used to explain three driving questions: (1) Why do employees feel excluded in their workplace? (2) How can experiences of exclusion influence employee attitudes, behaviors, and performance? (3) Why are there conflicts between groups in the workplace? (See Figure 7.1.)

Explanatory Theories Addressing Question 1:
Why Do Employees Feel Excluded in Their Workplace?

Social Identity Theory

Social identity theory is a cognitive social psychological theory that originated in Europe and gained popularity in North America and other regions of the world. It provides the connection between social structures and individual identity through the meanings people attach to their membership in identity groups such as those formed by race, ethnicity, or gender (Tajfel, 1982/2010). The core premise of this theory is that in many social situations people think of themselves and others not as unique individuals but rather as members of specific social groups (Ellemers & Haslam, 2012). The theory postulates that people tend to classify themselves into social categories that have meaning for them and that this classification shapes the way individuals interact with others from their own identity group and from other groups (Tajfel, 1978, 1982/2010; Tajfel & Turner, 1986; Turner, 1987). In essence, an important way a person defines self is through belonging to and membership in groups. As a result, people categorize others into groups and configure internal representations of them to fit the prototype of the category (Hogg, 2006; Hogg & Reid, 2006). Once others have been placed in those mental categories they are viewed as the embodiments of their identity groups and not as unique individuals (J. B. Davis, 2009).

The central proposition of the theory is that people desire to belong to groups that enjoy *distinct* and *positive* identities (Tajfel, 1978). Through *social comparisons* between the in-group and out-group, in-group members will make an effort to maintain or achieve superiority over an out-group in some dimensions (Tajfel & Turner, 1986). Therefore, those who belong to groups with higher perceived social status will accept and *include* people they consider to be like them, while *excluding* those they perceive to be different from them (Tajfel & Turner, 1986; also see Pettigrew, Allport, & Barnett, 1958). Social identity theory was originally conceptualized as a megatheory in that it can explain the universal effects of social categorization and group membership regardless of the specific type of group. It is this all-embracing orientation of social identity theory that makes it relevant for the study of diversity from an international perspective.

Origin and Significance

Originally formulated by Henri Tajfel and John Turner (1979, 1986), social identity theory was developed in an attempt to explain relations between groups from a truly social psychological perspective. The context for developing the theory is, in itself, an interesting example of intergroup relations—the intellectual relationship between North American and European social psychologists in the second half of the 20th century. Henri Tajfel was a central figure in a movement that took shape in the late 1960s to develop a distinctive European social psychology. Tajfel was a Jewish survivor of the Holocaust moved by his own experiences to explore how people who had been living together as neighbors and friends could come to see each other as enemies even when there was no rational reason to do so (Ellemers & Haslam, 2012). Unlike their North American counterparts at the time who adopted models that described people as rational and living in cohesion, European social psychologists increasingly focused on concepts that reflected the discord and conflict present in society. Moscovici (1972), for example, expressed discontent with the existing models of what he called the "social psychology of the nice person" (pp. 18–19) (e.g., "the leader is a person who understands the needs of members of his group," and "understanding the point of view of another person promotes cooperation") and called for the development of models that are realistic and reflective of change and conflict at the intergroup level. The movement's emphasis was on giving the *social* aspects of social psychology relatively greater importance by focusing on the individual within the context of broad social structures (Taylor & Moghaddam, 1994).

As a mega or grand theory, social identity has a wide appeal because it examines the connections between group membership and contextual social processes regardless of the specific type of group. It can, therefore, be applied to intergroup relationships with regard to the salient attribute of, for example, skin color, as it is manifested in South Africa or the United States, or to the saliency of language in creating a separate identity in French Canada, Wales, or Belgium (Tajfel & Turner, 1986). Over the years, social identity theory gained influence and served as an important impetus for social psychological research on intergroup relations and has inspired additional theoretical developments in Europe, North America, and, to a lesser degree, other regions of the world (Cornelissen, Haslam, & Balmer, 2007; Ellemers & Haslam, 2012; Haslam & Ellemers, 2005; Hogg, 2006; Hogg & Terry, 2000; Hornsey, 2008).

Central Concepts and Propositions

Several concepts serve as the building blocks of social identity theory and are central to its propositions. This section expands on two areas of the theory that are relevant to understanding intergroup relations: (1) social categorization and intergroup discrimination, and (2) social identity and social comparison.

(1) *Social categorization and intergroup discrimination.* Social categorization is a cognitive tool that is used to "segment, classify and order the social environment, and thus enable the individual to undertake many forms of social actions" (Tajfel & Turner, 1986, pp. 15–16). Early studies on categorization focused on nonsocial stimuli (Tajfel, 1957, 1959; Tajfel & Wilkes, 1963), indicating that we categorize objects to help us function in the physical world. For example, if we want to drive a nail to the wall and do not have a hammer, we'll look for another object in the same category of hard and heavy objects that can serve the same purpose, such as a brick or a stone. Or if we find ourselves without an umbrella on a rainy day, we would look for an object that could similarly protect us from the rain, such as a plastic bag or even a newspaper. The same principle is at work with social stimuli—categorizing people (including ourselves) into groups with a perceived common denominator helps us function in the social environment. Social categories include groups such as Europeans, women, teachers, Muslims, Blacks, gays, and managers. Although categorization of both objects and people may serve to simplify the world, people are more complex than objects in that values and norms, as well as one's own group identification, may influence social categorization and attitudes toward others. People tend to give members of their own group the benefit of the doubt in ambiguous situations that they would not give to members of other groups. In a workplace recruitment situation, for example, being fired or laid off from a previous job because of excessive absenteeism would typically count against an applicant's chances of being hired, but in a college-based experiment, both Black and White individuals gave the benefit of the doubt to members of their own group and not to members of out-groups (Chatman & Von Hippel, 2001). Similarly, people's social identification as Whites in Pettigrew and his colleagues' (1958) research, and their positive perception of their own group, made them more likely to exclude others when group identification was ambiguous (see Box 7.1 for a description of the experiment).

Box 7.1

THE BINOCULAR RESOLUTION CLASSICAL EXPERIMENTS OF RACIAL CATEGORIZATION IN SOUTH AFRICA: PRESTIGE OF GROUPS, IDENTIFICATION, AND EXCLUSION

In a classic series of experiments conducted in the middle of the 20th century, a team of researchers (Pettigrew et al., 1958) tested the link associated with in-group identification, perception of group prestige, and social categorization. Their most famous study was conducted in the highly charged racial climate of South Africa in the 1950s during apartheid.

Pettigrew and his colleagues used a stereoscope, a device that presents a picture of a different face to each eye and merges those images in order to test how individuals classify the race of facial images that combine persons from two different racial groups. The researchers utilized the perceptual phenomenon of binocular rivalry to introduce considerable uncertainty into the task of recognizing the race or ethnic group of each face. The sample included a nonrandom purposive sample of participants representing the full diversity of ethnic groups in South Africa, both men and women, and in a variety of occupations. The participants were Afrikaners, English-speaking Whites, Coloureds,[1] Indians, and Black Africans. Participants were given only 2 seconds to view the pictures and classify the race of the image in the picture. They were allowed, however, to indicate uncertainty in assigning a category.

(Continued)

(Continued)

In interpreting the results, it is important to remember the prestige and privileges that were associated with belonging to each group in South Africa during apartheid, with Whites—particularly Afrikaners—assuming they were racially superior and enjoying a privileged life, Coloureds and Indians the semi-"neutral" group in the middle, and Black Africans the most oppressed.

The Afrikaner participants were more likely to place ambiguous images in the "extreme" group, Black African, rather than the "neutral" group, Coloured or Indian, and less likely to place any ambiguous image in the "extreme" category of White. Their decisions seemed to be informed by a motivation to keep their group as "pure" as possible by adopting a strategy of overexclusion from the European group and overinclusion in the African group. This experiment demonstrates that when people classify others into social categories, (a) their self-identification with a specific category affects their classification of others, and (b) the social context and group prestige and hierarchy affect the classification process (Pettigrew et al., 1958).

¹A term used in the context of South Africa's apartheid culture to denote a person of mixed race.

Later studies replicated the findings in the United States with similar results for racial/ethnic categories relevant to that culture (Lent, 1970) and demonstrated that prejudiced individuals were more cautious in assigning racial categories in a presumed effort to preserve in-group and out-group distinctions (Blascovich, Wyer, Swart, & Kibler, 1997; Castano, Yzerbyt, Bourguignon, & Seron, 2002). In a series of studies in the Netherlands, Dotsch, Wigboldus, Langner, and Van Knippenberg (2008) examined whether prejudiced people also have more negatively stereotyped mental representations of faces of people in the out-group. Their studies examined people's attitudes toward Moroccans, a highly stigmatized immigrant group in the Netherlands. Their findings indicate that the more prejudiced people are, the more criminal-looking their prototype of Moroccan faces is. Because more prototypical exemplars are processed more fluently (Winkielman, Halberstadt, Fazendeiro, & Catty, 2006), prejudiced individuals may find it easier to categorize criminal-looking Moroccan faces as Moroccan than to categorize innocent-looking Moroccan faces as Moroccan. The authors suggest that this process may also function as a stereotype-maintaining device (Dotsch et al., 2008).

With the increased numbers of interracial and interethnic marriages in recent decades, there is a growing awareness that racial and ethnic identification often do not fall along the lines used by social institutions in the past. For example, a man born to a British immigrant from Liberia and a White British woman may see himself as both Black and White and both African and European. Others are more likely to categorize him as belonging to one race or nationality or the other, depending on his dominant features. A prominent example is U.S. president Barack Obama, the son of a U.S. mother born in Kansas and an African father born in Kenya. President Obama has roots in three continents—America, where he was born and raised; Africa, the continent of his father's ancestry; and Asia, where he spent part of his childhood with his mother and Indonesian stepfather. His multicultural heritage was touted as a strength by his supporters, who wished to highlight his openness to different life experiences, and as a weakness by his opponents, who tried to paint him as detached from the common American experience. Many issues of categorization related to President Obama's identity emerged during his presidential campaigns in ways that had never previously been experienced in the United States (or in many other countries, for that matter). In a famous incident in a town hall meeting, Obama's opponent, Senator John McCain, corrected a woman who told him she "could not trust Obama because he was an Arab" (Obama is neither an Arab nor a Muslim) (Blumiller, 2008). In a controversial cover illustration intended to mock the stereotypes, bigotry, and misconceptions surrounding Obama's background, *The New Yorker* magazine

(July 28, 2008) depicted Barack and Michelle Obama in Arab and terrorist attire, bumping fists as a U.S. flag burns in the fireplace of the White House Oval Office. On the other hand, some were asking, "Is Obama Black enough?" debating his authenticity as a Black man in America (Coates, 2007).

A Web-based survey of a probability sample at the University of Michigan in the United States asked students to categorize the people in a set of photographs as White, African American, Latino, Asian American, American Indian, Pacific Islander, or other (Harris, 2001). The researcher found a significant discrepancy between the responses of the people who were the subjects in the photographs and those by the survey participants. More specifically, individuals who self-identified with multiple races were more likely to be identified by survey participants with only one racial group. Furthermore, the categories chosen by the survey participants were related to the survey participants' own racial or ethnic category, similar to Pettigrew and his colleagues' findings. An interesting caveat is that White students who were roommates of non-White students were more attuned to the complexity of the images they saw and used more racial groups to more accurately classify the photographs.

Tajfel and his colleagues were also interested in the impact of social categorization on discrimination, and their now classic "minimal group experiments" were designed to examine that aspect of intergroup relations (for a description of these studies, see Box 7.2). The groups used in their experiments were designed to be "minimal" in that individuals were informed that their membership to the group was randomly assigned, that it was anonymous, and that criteria for social categorization were not linked to rewards, thus eliminating conditions that may be associated with realistic conflict rooted in competition for resources (Ellemers & Haslam, 2012; Tajfel, Flament, Billing, & Bundy, 1971; Taylor & Moghaddam, 1994). Their studies showed that even in a minimal group situation, in which none of the conditions associated with realistic conflict should be operating, people tended to discriminate against members of out-groups simply because they belonged to a different social category. Therefore, the mere categorization of individuals, either voluntary or assigned, is all that is necessary to create in-group favoritism and out-group discrimination.

The minimal group experiments, in their different variations over the years, are powerful demonstrations of prejudice and discrimination that can be generated even by the very minimal conditions.

(2) *Social identity and social comparison.* Identity, according to social identity theory, has two components: a personal component derived from idiosyncratic characteristics—such as personality and physical and intellectual traits—and a social component derived from salient commonalities of group memberships—such as race, sex, class, and nationality (Ashforth & Mael, 1989; Ellemers & Haslam, 2012; Tajfel, 1982/2010). Further investigation into social identity gained through work relationships expanded the application of social identity beyond the relationship between the individual and the group to gain insights from interpersonal relationships such as supervisor-subordinate and coworker-coworker (Brewer & Gardner, 1996; Sluss & Ashforth, 2007). Social identity is a perception of oneness with a group of persons (Ashforth & Mael, 1989; Cornelissen et al., 2007; Haslam & Ellemers, 2005; Hogg & Terry, 2000, 2001). Sometimes, however, this perception of oneness is the result of being categorized by the larger society as members of a particular group. For example, despite their distinct cultural heritage and complex historical relationships, individuals who emigrate from countries such as Korea, China, and Japan are "lumped" into one group known as "Asian" when they live in North America or Europe (Choi, 2001). The differences between these individuals who come from very different countries, backgrounds, and histories are forgotten—with any uniqueness misunderstood at best (Fowler, 1996). However, over the years, individuals from these countries, and particularly the second-generation immigrants, have developed a sense of identity that is tied to being Asian Americans or Asian Europeans.

Box 7.2

THE CLASSIC MINIMAL GROUP EXPERIMENTS

Tajfel and his colleagues knew that people favor members of their own group (in-group) over members of other groups (out-group). However, these investigators (e.g., Billig & Tajfel, 1973; Tajfel et al., 1971) were interested in identifying the minimal conditions necessary to produce prejudice and discrimination. They conducted a series of studies using minimal manipulations of group membership, hence the name *minimal group experiments*. The aim of these experiments was to test whether discrimination will result from minimal conditions that generate categorization.

The participants in the minimal group experiments were 64 boys of 14 to 15 years of age from a comprehensive school in Bristol, England. All the boys came from the same house and knew one another well. An early experiment (Tajfel et al., 1971) demonstrates the principles of the minimal group experiments. The experiment had two distinct parts:

1. *Establish an intergroup categorization.* The boys were brought together in a lecture theater and asked to estimate the number of dots flashed onto a screen (they were told that the experimenters were interested in the study of visual judgments). The boys were told that they tended either to overestimate or underestimate the number of dots. The experimenters pretended to mark the boys' answers, when, in fact, the boys had been randomly allocated to their groups. Also, there was no value attached to either overestimating or underestimating—both were seen as equally inaccurate.

2. *Assess the effects of this categorization on intergroup behavior.* When the boys were asked to allocate monetary rewards (on a set of matrices), overestimators consistently allocated more points to other overestimators and underestimators to other underestimators, although the identity of the others was not revealed to them.

The results demonstrate that although the groups were based on a meaningless classification and members had no contact with one another, they still showed a preference for the in-group.

The criteria for minimal groups are as follows (Schiffman & Wicklund, 1992):

1. No face-to-face interaction.

2. Personal identity of group members should not be known.

3. There should be no particular advantage to belonging to a particular group or logical reason for holding a negative attitude against the group (e.g., overestimators versus underestimators).

4. There should be no advantage or gain for the individual as a result of making a particular decision about reward allocation.

5. The strategy employed when differentiating between groups should conflict with a more "rational" strategy.

Many studies that provide still more convincing evidence of the prejudice and discrimination resulting from even an arbitrary group categorization (e.g., Bourhis, Sachdev, & Gagon, 1994; Dunham, Baron, & Carey, 2011; Li, Dogan, & Haruvy, 2011) followed in the footsteps of Tajfel and his colleagues' research. In one such experiment, Locksley, Ortiz, and Hepburn (1980) told participants they were being assigned to groups at random and actually showed them the lottery ticket that determined whether they were members of the Phi group or the Gamma group. Even with this explicitly random assignment, study participants still showed a preference for members of their own group. In a laboratory experiment simulating trading markets, the researchers created an artificial sense of group identity by using art preferences or college majors in different treatments and demonstrated that both the selection of trading partners and the determination of the price were influenced by the individuals' artificially induced group membership (Li et al., 2011). Similarly, a series of studies with random group assignments demonstrated that the mere assignment to groups was sufficient to induce intergroup bias even among 5-year-old children (Dunham et al., 2011).

Social identity involves a process of self-categorization, along with an attachment of value to the particular social category (Pettigrew, 1986). Together, these two elements (a) group categorization, and (b) value attachment and constitute social identity (Turner & Giles, 1981). Social identity is defined as the individual's knowledge that he or she belongs to a certain social group or groups, together with some emotional and value significance to him or her of the group membership (Tajfel, 1978, p. 63).

Social identity stems from the categorization of individuals, the distinctiveness and prestige of the group, the salience of out-groups, and the factors that traditionally are associated with group formation. Most important, and most relevant to the present discussion, social identification leads to activities that are congruent with the group's collective identity, that support institutions that embody their identity, and that foster stereotypical perceptions of self and others (Ashforth & Mael, 1989; Hirst, van Dick, & van Knippenberg, 2009). *Social comparison* is the process that people use to evaluate themselves by comparing their group's membership with other groups. The basic hypothesis is that pressures to positively evaluate one's own group through in-group/out-group comparisons lead social groups to attempt to differentiate themselves from each other (Tajfel, 1978; Tajfel & Turner, 1986). The aim of differentiation is to maintain or achieve superiority over an out-group on some relevant dimension.

Limitation of Social Identity Theory
in Understanding Diversity and Exclusion

One criticism of social identity theory is that it has tautological elements in its conceptualization. The first is the link between self-esteem and discrimination (self-esteem is described as the motive for discriminating against out-group members, as well as the consequence of this discrimination). The second is in defining social identity (the theory claims that when social identity is salient, individuals act as group members; yet if they don't act as group members, it is because, in that case, social identity is not salient) (Abrams, 1992; Abrams & Hogg, 1988; Taylor & Moghaddam, 1994). Another criticism lies in the theory's very broad and rather generic view of social categories. Specifically, the multifaceted nature of social identity makes it difficult to determine one specific social category that might be more salient than others (Bodenhausen, 2010). This difficulty is highlighted by intersectionality theory and the focus on race, gender, and class as major categories that are relevant to understanding the discrimination experienced by people who belong to those groups but more severely to those who belong to more than one group (Crenshaw, 1989; Lutz et al., 2011). Because the theory places all types of categorization as equal, it cannot account for the heightened significance of race, gender, and class in many cultures and nations due to their deep historical roots in both the Western world and in previously colonized countries. Finally, social identity theory conceptualizes identity primarily as self-defined. It therefore downplays the consequences of other groups defining individuals and affecting their sense of inclusion or exclusion.

Implications of Social Identity Theory to Diversity and Exclusion

Every society and every organization consists of a large number of groups, and every person represents a number of these groups when dealing with other people (Alderfer & Smith, 1982). Demographic characteristics of organizations, such as race and sex distributions, help to shape the meanings people attach to their identity group memberships at work (Ely, 1994; Ely & Roberts, 2008). As social identity theory has demonstrated, the way we perceive our social reality is significantly determined by our group memberships, such as gender and racial/ethnic affiliation. It follows that individual experiences vis-à-vis work organizations and their perceptions of organizational actions and policies will be affected by their identity group memberships. This social psychological perspective is useful to the current discussion because it indicates how identity groups shape applicant and worker experiences, perceptions, and behaviors in different employment settings. It is particularly relevant when membership in an identity group is associated with exclusion from employment opportunity and job mobility.

Tajfel and Turner (1986) conceptualize *group* as

> a collection of individuals who perceive themselves to be members of the same social category, share some emotional involvement in this common definition of themselves, and achieve some degree of social consensus about the evaluation of their group and of their membership in it.

Following from that, their definition of intergroup behavior is identical to that of Sherif (1966, p. 62): "any behavior displayed by one or more actors towards one or more others that is based on the actors' identification of themselves and others as belonging to different social categories." When a social group's status position is perceived to be low, it affects the social identity of group members. A group's *status* is the outcome of the social comparison process described earlier; it reflects the group's position on some evaluative dimensions relative to relevant comparison groups (Tajfel & Turner, 1986).

Low subjective status does not promote intergroup competition directly but rather indirectly, through its impact on members' social identity. When faced with negative or threatened social identity, individuals may utilize one of the following strategies:

- *Individual mobility.* Individuals will attempt to pass from a lower-status to a higher-status group by disassociating themselves psychologically and behaviorally from their low-status group. For example, immigrants who feel that their social identity is devalued by the host society because most of the members of their ethnic group hold low-status or menial labor jobs could choose to distance themselves from their co-ethnic peers through individual mobility (Ellemers & Haslam, 2012; Shinnar, 2008). When the opportunities for upward mobility exist, low-status group members are often willing to choose individual upward mobility over a collective action. It is based on the assumption that the society is flexible and permeable and that through talent, hard work, or luck one can move from an undesirable group to a more desirable one (Tajfel & Turner, 1986). When successful, such a strategy will lead to a personal solution but will not make a difference in the group's status. An interesting example is women's social status in India. Although women have long had access to powerful professions such as in politics and medicine, they are still perceived as incompetent and not suitable for management and leadership. Despite having a woman as prime minister (Indira Gandhi was elected and served as prime minister of India from 1966 to 1977 and again from 1980 to 1984) and despite the number of women who have risen to top management positions in Indian organizations, women are typically stereotyped as being "less intelligent, less able to meet the demands of the job, less competent and in general have to work much harder than men to get the same results" (Nath, 2000).

- *Group mobility through "social creativity."* Group members may seek positive status for the group as a whole by redefining or altering the elements of the comparative situations (Ellemers & Haslam, 2012; Shinnar, 2008). This coping mechanism is more psychological in nature compared to individual mobility and involves altering one's perceptions rather than taking direct action (Wright & Tropp, 2002). This could take place by, for example, changing the values assigned to the attributes of the group so that comparisons that were previously negative are now perceived as positive (such as the slogan used by African Americans, "Black is beautiful") (Tajfel & Turner, 1986). Social creativity includes strategies such as: (a) seeking new elements for intergroup comparisons, such as comparing oneself to an outperforming in-group member, which can be identity enhancing because it reflects positively on the group identity (Schmitt, Branscombe, Silvia, Garcia, & Spears, 2006); (b) redefining existing elements for such comparisons so that previously negative comparisons become positive; and (c) selecting an alternative referent group to which one's in-group is compared—instead of comparing one's group to the dominant majority, one may choose the referent group from other minorities. Group mobility through social creativity involves selecting new elements for intergroup comparisons leading to a more favorable evaluation. Individuals search for new, positive aspects of their group to justify the features not welcomed by other groups, or they seek features they deem superior. As another example, a sample of non-English-speaking, non-European, international university students from 32 countries was studied to determine whether their sense of belonging to an international student identity group would counterbalance their sense of exclusion within the university. The researchers found not only that the students' group identification increased but also that it positively predicted improved self-esteem for the members. This research was insightful in two ways. First, it demonstrated that being perceived by *others* as a group was all that was needed to create a new group identity, and second, it demonstrated that this new group identity gave them a more positive sense about themselves as foreign students (Schmitt, Spears, & Branscombe, 2003). This study provides support to the rejection-identification model (Branscombe, Schmitt, & Harvey, 1999) proposing that although perceived prejudice has psychological costs, those costs are suppressed by increased identification with one's minority group.

- *Social competition.* Members of a group may seek to improve their status by direct competition with the higher-status group. This coping mechanism refers to engagement in social action in order to promote change in the status quo and improve social comparisons that are unfavorable to one's own group. In the case of Mexican Americans, an example for social action to promote a more positive group identity is the Chicano movement of the 1960s. Deaux, Reid, Martin, and Bikmen (2006) found that immigrants of color who have been in the United States for more than 8 years were more likely to reject social inequality and engage in collective action to improve the conditions of their group. The assumption underlying the social competition coping mechanism is that "the nature and structure of the relations between social groups in the society is characterized by marked stratification, making it impossible or very difficult for individuals, as individuals, to divest themselves of an unsatisfactory, underprivileged, or stigmatized group membership" (Tajfel & Turner, 1986, p. 9). In this system, individuals interact with one another based on their respective group memberships and not as individuals. To achieve positive distinctiveness, they may try to reverse their position relative to the other groups. This challenge, however, may generate conflict and antagonism between the subordinate and the dominant groups, in that it involves redistribution of scarce resources and a reassignment of power. A prime example of this conflict is the use of affirmative action policies to give disadvantaged groups better opportunities and the debate over reversing those policies, particularly when the economy is down and jobs are scarce. Although it is commonly believed that the antidote to categorizations that breed exclusion is more social contact between individuals from different groups, Geert Hofstede (1997) warns that, contrary to popular belief, intercultural encounters among groups do not automatically breed mutual understanding. In fact, such contacts, unless they are prolonged and allow individuals from each group to really get to know individuals from another, usually confirm each group's previous perceptions of the other group. Isaac Olawale Albert[2] ("Nigeria—Watchdog Goes Back to School," 2002), commenting on the situation in Africa where tribal conflicts are a common occurrence, concurs:

> When "diverse peoples" meet, most especially as a result of social and geographical contacts, a culture shock is produced. It is within this framework that diversity becomes a development question that must be carefully managed. If well managed, diversity could be a major asset to society.

Social Comparison Theory and Symbolic Interaction Theory

The universal human need to be included in social systems has its roots in the way people have traditionally satisfied their basic needs. Because human beings have always depended on one another for their livelihood and needed to work together in order to get food, shelter, and clothing, social inclusion has had an important survival function through the ages and across cultures (Baumeister & Leary, 1995; Vohs & Baumeister, 2010). Festinger's (1954) social comparison theory (Corcoran, Crusius, & Mussweiler, 2011; Dijkstra, Gibbons, & Buunk, 2010; Greenberg, Ashton-James, & Ashkanasy, 2007; Guimond, 2006) and Mead's (1982) symbolic interaction theory (Appelrouth & Desfor Edles, 2007; Denzin, 2007) provide insights into the role of inclusion-exclusion experiences of individuals in social systems. The social comparison process, as delineated by Festinger, postulates that individuals have the need to evaluate themselves and to assess their relative standing within groups. For this process, individuals use their employee peer group as a referent (Goodman & Haisley, 2007; Greenberg et al., 2007; Zagenczyk, Scott, Gibney, Murrell, & Thatcher, 2010). A study of immigrant youth in Denmark illustrates the sense of exclusion that can result from the social comparison process. A study of the settlement of Iraqi women refugees in Copenhagen illustrates the sense of exclusion that can result from the social comparison process (Penderson, 2012). Utilizing extended case study analysis methodology, the author highlights the discrimination these women face as immigrants and Muslims in Danish society and, as a result, their downward "class journey" experience as part of their resettlement process.

Social comparison is "embedded deeply into the fabric of organizational life," and this process can happen through both planned activities (e.g., formal performance evaluations) and unplanned interactions in the workplace (e.g., chatting with a coworker about your pay) (Greenberg et al., 2007, p. 23). One such process that is relevant to experiences of exclusion is the use of social comparison to assess organizational justice. Comparing yourself to relevant others in your organization can influence how fair you think your workplace is in terms of outcomes such as salaries and benefits (distributive justice), procedures used to determine compensation and other benefits in the organization (procedural justice), and interpersonal relationships with others in the organization such as coworkers and supervisors (interactional justice) (Greenberg et al., 2007). Perceptions of exclusion may arise when employees compare themselves to others and feel that they are treated differently (and unfairly) because of their membership in a particular identity group. Social comparison processes may also help to explain affective workplace behavior. The "contrast effect" explains how people generally feel good when making downward comparisons (others are worse off) and bad when making upward comparisons (others are better off) (Greenberg et al., 2007; Mussweiler & Strack, 2000). Exclusionary workplaces may create negative feelings when employees perceive that they are consistently "worse off" in the organization than others because of their identity group membership.

The symbolic interaction process highlights the fact that individual interpretation and synthesis of symbols and objects in their environments drive both situational analysis and individual behavior. Mead (1982) describes this process as seeing oneself from the viewpoint of others in determining how one stands in the world. Together, these social psychological theories provide us with the concept of the interior monologue—the internal evaluation process that individuals continuously engage in with regard to their social environment. These evaluations are the chief methodology that individuals utilize to assess their position within groups and organizations and are assumed to be universal, not culture-specific.

Both processes—assessing one's own standing relative to others (social comparison) and seeing oneself from the viewpoint of others in determining how one stands in the world (symbolic interaction)—are methods we all use to deal rationally with our work environments. These theories imply that the perception of group inclusion is an important continuous process in the individual's desire to secure positive group affiliations. Perceptions of inclusion or exclusion, therefore, are a form of an ongoing personal evaluation and serve as the chief methodology that individuals utilize to assess their position within groups and organizations. This process is important for individuals such as women, people with disability, and members of racial and ethnic minority groups who have traditionally been excluded from the mainstream's networks of influence in work organizations.

Explanatory Theories Addressing Question 2: How Can Experiences of Exclusion Influence Employee Attitudes, Behaviors, and Performance?

Sociometer Model of Self-Esteem

A theoretical connection between worker inclusion-exclusion experiences and performance and satisfaction *outcomes* in organizational social systems can be extrapolated from the "sociometer model" of self-esteem (Leary, 2010; Leary & Baumeister, 2000; Leary & Downs, 1995). The authors posit that other people's reactions, particularly the degree to which they accept and include individuals or reject and exclude them, are vital to a person's physical and psychological well-being. Research demonstrates that social and physical pain share common physiological mechanisms and that social exclusion is painful because reactions to rejection are mediated by aspects of the physical pain system (Campbell et al., 2006; Leary, 2010; MacDonald & Leary, 2005; Zhong & Leonardelli, 2008).

Because human beings have always depended on others for their basic needs, they are motivated to maintain connections with significant people and social systems in their lives (Baumeister & Leary, 1995). Leary and Baumeister (2000) note,

> It is safe to conclude that the human organism is characterized by a basic need to belong—a fundamental motivation to form and maintain at least a handful of meaningful social attachments. The power and importance of this motivation are sufficient to think that people might well possess an internal meter to monitor such relationships. (p. 11)

This psychological gauge, or "sociometer," is the individual's self-esteem that acts as a personal indicator that allows people to monitor inclusion or exclusion reactions toward them from their environment (Leary & Baumeister, 2000; Leary, Schreindorfer, & Haupt, 1995; Vohs & Baumeister, 2010). Triggered by an environment that is exclusionary, threats to one's self-esteem produce behavioral outcomes that are aimed at rectifying the situation by, for example, compensatory efforts to assimilate or by disengaging from the exclusionary system and linking with a more inclusive environment. To alleviate the stressful consequences of social exclusion, individuals are willing to go to great lengths and even sacrifice their own needs. For example, excluded participants were more likely to spend money on and consume products strategically in the service of social affiliation compared to the controls in a study of the consequences of social exclusion (Mead, Baumeister, Stillman, Rawn, & Vohs, 2011). The socially excluded participants were more likely to tailor their spending preferences to those of an interaction partner, spend money on an unappealing food item favored by a peer, and even express a willingness to try an illegal drug if those behaviors would boost the likelihood of a desired social relationship.

Box 7.3

OUCH! FACING THE STING OF SOCIAL EXCLUSION

Consider a time when you felt excluded. Perhaps you remember feeling left out of social activities as a child, or you might recall a more recent offense by a fellow coworker or classmate. How did you respond? Research demonstrates that social exclusion can result in three types of behaviors: prosocial (e.g., cooperating), antisocial (e.g., choosing not to cooperate), and even unethical (e.g., cheating) (Baumeister, Brewer, Tice, & Twenge, 2007; Derfler-Rozin, Pillutla, & Thau, 2010; Kouchaki & Wareham, 2015; Lee, Tams, Scott, & Schippers 2015; Narayanan, Tai, & Kinias, 2013; Pfundmair, Graupmann, Frey, & Aydin, 2015; Thau, Derfler-Rozin, Pitesa, Mitchell, & Pillutla, 2015). On the one hand, some studies suggest that social exclusion can encourage more prosocial behavior. Prosocial behavior benefits others—even at a cost to the self—and serves the purpose of fostering group belongingness (Twenge, Baumeister, DeWall, Ciarocco, & Bartels, 2007). In one set of studies, excluded participants conformed more to others' opinions, paid more attention to information related to socially connecting with others, rated neutral faces as more friendly and welcoming, and chose a task that involved working with a partner rather than working alone (Baumeister et al., 2007). On the other hand, laboratory studies described in Baumeister's seminal literature review suggest that social exclusion can cause a person to be more aggressive and less cooperative—in other words, to exhibit antisocial behavior (Baumeister et al., 2007). In one set of experiments, for example, socially excluded participants donated less money to a student emergency fund, were less likely to volunteer for more experiments to help the experimenter with a simple task such as picking up spilled pencils, or cooperated less with a fellow student in a mixed-motive game (Twenge et al., 2007).

This begs the question of *why*. Why does social exclusion cause some people to attempt reconnection, others to disengage, and still others to behave unethically? Recent studies attempt to unpack this complex "black box."

- *Power.* Narayanan et al. (2013) examined the role of power and found that following social exclusion, participants primed with high power were more likely to attempt social connection compared to those primed with low power. These authors note that following exclusion, an individual's promotion (approach) and prevention (avoid) systems are activated. Power has greater "regulatory fit" with approach strategies; thus, excluded individuals with power are more likely to seek reconnection rather than disengage and avoid those who excluded them. Additionally, social exclusion can signal loss of followers (and thus power) to high-powered individuals, thus strengthening the motivation to reconnect.

- *Type of social support.* Using an employee sample, Scott, Zagenczyk, Schippers, Purvis, and Cruz, (2014) looked at how social support influences people's experience of social exclusion by coworkers. Findings from this study show that *type* of support matters. High organizational support acted as a buffer against the effects of coworker exclusion in terms of performance and self-worth. In contrast, support from family and friends exacerbated the negative effects that coworker exclusion had on self-esteem and job-induced tension. These reactions can, in turn, influence whether or not the excluded individual makes an attempt to socially reconnect with the coworkers who excluded him or her.

- *Cultural orientation.* Pfundmair et al. (2015) took a more macro perspective and assessed how cross-cultural differences can explain social exclusion responses. Study findings indicated that participants with an individualist orientation were more likely to behave antisocially following exclusion, whereas behavior did not differ between exclusion and inclusion conditions for those with a collectivist orientation. Pfundmair et al. (2015) suggested that only individualist participants viewed the social exclusion as a threat, whereas collectivist participants had more developed buffering skills and viewed the social exclusion more as a minor incident.

- *Physiological response.* Kouchaki and Wareham (2015) took a different approach and looked at how the body responds to social exclusion. More specifically, these researchers predicted that when socially excluded, people can have both psychological and physical reactions. Kouchaki and Wareham (2015) predicted that the physiological arousal (measured by galvanic skin response) that follows exclusion increases the likelihood of engaging in unethical behavior. Using both student and employee-supervisor samples, results showed that excluded individuals were more likely to behave unethically, and this relationship was explained (or mediated) by the level of physiological arousal experienced after exclusion.

- *Individual need for belonging.* Thau et al. (2015) examined the effect that risk of social exclusion has on unethical behavior. Using both student and employee samples, study findings show that individuals at risk of exclusion were more likely to engage in pro–group unethical behavior (e.g., discrediting out-group members) when the individual had a high need for inclusion. These effects did not hold when the individual's inclusion needs were low. Furthermore, while pro–group unethical behavior increased, unethical behavior that only benefited the self did not increase after exclusion.

Overall, this research highlights the complexity of social exclusion. To be sure, social exclusion is distinct from workplace exclusion. The latter pertains specifically to exclusion from formal and informal organizational processes because of membership to a particular diversity category. That being said, this research helps us understand how an exclusionary work environment can provoke a variety of behavioral responses from employees.

Identity-Based Motivation Theory

Identity-based motivation theory is instrumental in explaining the connection between workplace exclusion and employee attitudinal, behavioral, and performance outcomes. The premise of this theory is that people prefer to act in ways that feel congruent with their identities. Yet people have multiple identities, and which identities are salient and what these identities seem to mean are dynamically constructed in context (Oyserman, 2015; Oyserman & Destin, 2010). Experiences of workplace exclusion can influence outcomes in two ways. First, workplace exclusion can shape which identities (e.g., employee, woman, Latina) are more salient in specific situations. Second, workplace exclusion can shape which norms, values, and behaviors seem to be associated with these identities. According to this theory, experiencing difficulty in the workplace, such as exclusion, can affect employees' motivation to undertake or complete tasks. For example, when an employee experiences difficulties and adversity she or he may conclude that the task is impossible, or "not for me," indicating that effort is a waste of time and that one should turn one's attention elsewhere. Alternatively, the difficulty could signal task importance because worthwhile goals are often difficult to attain—"no pain, no gain." Interpretation of experienced difficulty matters. If the difficulty associated with the behavior is understood as underscoring its importance, then one would feel motivated to act and exert effort. In contrast, if an individual perceives that the difficulty associated with a behavior underscores the base rate for success, then experiencing difficulty indicates that "this is not for me," which can result in disengagement and abandonment of the behavior. Individuals carry multiple identities, and different workplace situational cues make certain identities more or less salient for an employee.

Identity-based motivation theory has been used to understand disparities in academic performance and health outcomes (Oyserman, 2013, 2015; Oyserman & Destin, 2010; Oyserman, Smith, & Elmore, 2014). Each of the elements of identity-based motivation theory has been tested experimentally. As predicted, changing students' interpretation of experienced difficulty with schoolwork changes their academic performance (Smith & Oyserman, 2015). Whether an identity such as gender has a positive or negative impact on school engagement depends on whether school success seems congruent or incongruent with being a boy or a girl in the moment (Elmore & Oyserman, 2012). Furthermore, changing students' understanding of the school context changes whether salient identities have positive or negative effects on school engagement (Oyserman, Destin, & Novin, 2015).

Identity-based motivation theory has direct applicability for understanding the consequences of workplace exclusion. For example, suppose a woman learns of a challenging new leadership position at her organization. How soon and how persistently she advocates for the position—even whether she applies at all—is likely to depend in part on whether her employee identity includes or excludes the sense that she fits in, is valued, and would be taken seriously. In an exclusionary work environment, clues can be lack of women in top positions, comments from supervisors that women generally do not make good leaders, negative responses to women who are in supervisory roles, or a climate in which fitting in and belonging is matched with characteristics she lacks even though overt policy is not gender biased.

Note that identity-based motivation theory also predicts that small changes in the workplace can have powerful effects on behavior if the change focuses on interpretation of experienced difficulty or on how important identities such as gender or race-ethnicity are framed in terms of fitness for and connection to work. Based on this theory, in the example above, the challenge of applying for the new job opening coupled with her awareness of her own gender identity might cause her to feel that the new position is "not for me," and she responds by ignoring the job announcement. This is because exclusionary messages in her work environment communicate negative norms, values, and behaviors associated with her gender identity, and this influences her motivation and response to new situations. Avoiding opportunities like a new leadership position could then affect outcomes including job satisfaction, organizational commitment, and performance evaluations. Identity-based motivation theory helps to explain the relationship between exclusionary work environments and the psychological and behavioral responses of employees belonging to minority or marginalized groups.

Interactional Model of Cultural Diversity

Finally, multiple researchers have used Cox's Interactional Model of Cultural Diversity (IMCD) to explain the relationship between diversity climate and organizational effectiveness (as reviewed by McKay & Avery, 2015). Although diversity climate is distinct from workplace inclusion, elements of this model can be used to link experiences of inclusion-exclusion to organizational outcomes. The IMCD proposes that diversity climate influences experiences in the workplace, and ultimately, organizational effectiveness through two individual level pathways: affective outcomes (such as job satisfaction) and achievement outcomes (such as job performance) (Cox, 1994). In this model, organizational effectiveness includes measures such as turnover and attendance, as well as creativity, problem-solving, workgroup communication, and macro-level factors such as market share and profitability (Cox, 1994). The IMCD has been used in conjunction with social identity theory to explain how diversity climate perceptions vary based on employee identity characteristics (McKay & Avery, 2015).

Explanatory Theories Addressing Question 3:
Why Are There Conflicts Between Groups in the Workplace?

Theories of Intergroup Relations: Realistic Conflict Theory, Equity Theory, Relative Deprivation Theory, and Intergroup Contact Theory

A close examination of workplace miscommunications, conflicts, disputes, and even violence often reveals that they are the product of intergroup relations. The classic definition of intergroup relations is provided by Sherif (1966): "Whenever individuals belonging to one group interact, collectively or individually, with another group or its members in terms of their group identification, we have an instance of intergroup behavior" (p. 12). Given the definition of diversity presented in Chapter 6, theories of intergroup relations should provide us with a deeper understanding of why people create these diversity categories, why they include or exclude members of other groups, and how they affect workplace relationships.

There are several major theories of intergroup relations that are relevant beyond specific national contexts (Brewer, 2003; Burke & Stets, 2009; Taylor & Moghaddam, 1994). A few theories are worth mentioning here: *Realistic conflict theory* (RCT) is an economic theory that assumes that people act in self-interest and that conflict is caused by people's drive to maximize their own or their group's rewards to the detriment of other groups' interests (Sassenberg, Moskowitz, Jacoby, & Hansen, 2007; Savelkoul, Gesthuizen, & Scheepers, 2011; Sherif, 1966); *equity theory* emphasizes people's striving for justice and views perceptions of injustice as the cause for personal distress and intergroup conflict (Adams, 1965; Bell & Martin, 2012; Bolino & Turnley, 2008; Walster, Walster, & Berscheid, 1978); *relative deprivation theory* focuses on perceptions of inequality between one's own access to resources and that of others in the society, resulting in intergroup conflict, and emphasizes the emotional aspects (e.g., anger, outrage, and grievance) of oppression (Carrillo, Corning, Dennehy, & Crosby, 2011; Crosby, 1976; Feldman & Turnley, 2004; Smith, Pettigrew, Pippin, & Bialosiewicz, 2012; Stouffer, Suchman, DeVinney, Star, & Williams, 1949); and *intergroup contact theory* sees the root cause for conflict in lack of contact between groups, or contact under unfavorable conditions, and holds that optimal-contact conditions (e.g., equal status between the groups, common goals, intergroup coalition, and support of authorities, law, or custom) could reduce prejudice and intergroup conflict (Allport, 1954/1979; Brown & Hewstone, 2005; Crisp, Turner, & Rhiannon, 2009; Pettigrew, 1998; Pettigrew & Tropp, 2006; Pettigrew, Tropp, Wagner, & Christ, 2011).

Research on Organizational Demography Documenting Exclusion

Organizational demography has been used as a conceptual framework for diversity research for more than 2 decades (Aparna, 2006; Bell, Villado, Lukasik, Belau, & Briggs, 2010; Choi, 2007; Ely, 1994; Gonzalez & Denisi, 2009; King et al., 2011; Tsui & Gutek, 1999; Wei, Lau, Young, & Wang, 2005). According to Tsui and Gutek (1999), "Organizational demography focuses on the distribution of worker characteristics along dimensions studied by other demographers (i.e., sex, race, ethnicity, national origin, age, migration, and emigration)" (p. 13). However, whereas diversity research focuses primarily on minorities, women, and other disadvantaged groups in the workplace, research on organizational demography is broader, examining the effect of demographic distributions on everyone in the organization. More specifically, the research questions center on the impact of demographic differences between and among worker attitudes and behaviors, and toward the organization as a whole. Its proponents claim that unlike diversity research, which often has a strong policy and practice implication and is action oriented, organizational demography is geared toward explaining the impact of organizational demography on any group in the organization (Aparna, 2006; Bell et al., 2010; Choi, 2007; Gonzalez & Denisi, 2009; Tsui, Porter, & Egan, 2002). The study of organizational demography is, therefore, useful for examining the relationship between diversity and exclusion in work organizations.

Research on organizational demography indicates that being in the minority has significant effects on individuals' affective experiences in the workplace, including feelings of isolation and lack of identification in one-on-one relationships (Barlow, Louis, & Terry, 2010; Mor Barak et al., 2006; Roscigno, Lopez, & Hodson, 2009). Milliken and Martins (1996) indicated a strong and consistent relationship between diversity in gender, ethnicity, and age and exclusion from important workplace interactions. One of the most frequently reported problems faced by women and minorities in organizational settings is their limited access to, or exclusion from, vital and yet informal interaction networks (Gray, Kurihara, Hommen, & Feldman, 2007; McDonald, 2011; McDonald, Lin, & Ao, 2009; McPherson, Smith-Lovin, & Cook, 2001; Petersen, Saporta, & Seidel, 2000). Ella L. J. Edmondson Bell and Stella M. Nkomo (2003) discussed both African American women's and Caucasian women's experiences of exclusion in their book, *Our Separate Ways: Black and White Women and the Struggle for Professional Identity*:

> Another barrier experienced by Black women is limited access to informal and social networks in their organizations. The African American women we interviewed felt they had less access to these networks in their organizations than White men and White women. As a result, they felt cut off from important organizational information and less accepted as full members of the organization. Many of the women spoke of the critical importance of informal networks in career advancement. In most corporations, excellent performance is necessary for advancement but is not the sole criterion. Getting ahead also depends on access to informal networks and the relationships those networks can foster—mentorships, sponsorships, and help from colleagues. Building these relationships requires that the women be part of the social networks within the company. . . . Similarly, the White women managers also believed that exclusion from the "old-boy network" was one of the barriers to women's advancement. (pp. 152–153)

Due to the duality of race and gender, Black university graduate women in France as well as African American women in managerial and executive positions in the United States are more likely to be excluded from informal social networks (Combs, 2003; Diop, 2012; Hall et al., 2012). These networks allocate a variety of instrumental resources that are critical for job effectiveness and career advancement, as well as expressive benefits such as social support and friendship. Information gleaned from informal social networks provides access to valuable job-related information, and can affect job stability and better promotion prospects (Gray et al., 2007; Ibarra, 1993; McDonald, 2011). In the context of gender relations, men's network cohesion with other men can prevent women from access to information, knowledge, and job opportunities and therefore contributes to exclusion of women in the workplace. Men can, therefore, shape rules at work that would help them maintain their advantages over women. They also can change the rules if necessary to keep women in more subordinate positions, often by devaluing the work that women do (DiTomaso, Post, & Parks-Yancy, 2007). As a result, women can feel "out of the loop," or excluded, from important information flows. Often, interactions that take place informally have meaning that can be more consequential to labor market outcomes than formal decision-making processes. Thus, the informality of the promotion system can particularly disadvantage those without well-placed mentors with powerful social networks (Gray et al., 2007, p. 153).

The Federal Glass Ceiling Commission in the United States has identified "information isolation," or the exclusion from information networks, as one of the main barriers that block the career advancement of women, as well as ethnic minorities, particularly in the private sector (Federal Glass Ceiling Commission, 1995). A number of studies have found that women face organizational barriers in promotion to senior management positions (Neale & Özkanli, 2010), and those who do make it to elite positions are often "outsiders on the inside"—that is, they are less integrated in informal discussion networks and outside the influential, central circle of high-level contacts (Fisher, 2006; Ibarra, 1993; Kirshnan, 2009). This isolation means that women are excluded from top networks and informal relationships that are necessary for further career advancement (Gray et al., 2007) and might explain, at least to some extent, the higher turnover rate among women in top management positions (Kirshnan, 2009).

Although women and members of minority groups have made some inroads into traditional nonminority male job domains, organizational jobs remain largely structured along race, gender, and class lines, with the more meaningful and prestigious jobs being held by men of the dominant group and of higher social echelons (Beggs, 1995; Cheung & Halpern, 2010; Sealy & Singh, 2010). For example, recent statistics indicate that women at the highest levels of business organizations are still rare. According to two recent reports, only 20 (4%) women serve as CEOs running the United States' largest 500 publicly traded companies, and only 19.2% of board seats at these companies are held by women (Catalyst, 2015a, 2015b). Some scholars have speculated that the extreme overrepresentation of White men in organizational positions of authority may have a negative impact on women and non-White subordinates (Acker, 2011; Ely, 1994). For example, in most of the developed countries, women constitute less than 10% of engineers, and their turnover rates within those organizations are much higher than those of men. Drawing on data from three large Australian-based multinational engineering companies, Sharp, Franzway, Mills, and Gill (2011) argued that in failing to engage with the sexual politics in male-dominated organizations, managing diversity obscures the systematic nature of women's disadvantage and men's advantage in the workplace. In other words, the authors argue that typical diversity management practices overlook the need to address gender-based power structures that discriminate against women in male-dominated organizational cultures such as engineering organizations (Sharp et al., 2011). Earlier work on women in male-dominated organizations indicated that women may attempt to assimilate—that is, to alter their thoughts, feelings, behaviors, and expectations at work to mirror those typically associated with men (Ely, 1995; Ely & Thomas, 2001). The disproportionate representation of men over women in senior organizational positions may highlight for women their limited mobility and reinforce their perceptions of themselves as lower status than men (Ely, 1994). Analyzing the narratives of 33 prominent women engineers with careers in management, Kyriakidou (2011b) demonstrates that the process of identity construction for women engineers differs in significant ways from that of their male counterparts in that their process is centered on redefinition that allows the women to establish positive professional identities. Ely, Ibarra, and Kolb (2011) focus on leadership development for women, which they conceptualize as identity work, and demonstrate how subtle forms of gender bias in the workplace interfere with the identity work of women leaders.

There is ample evidence of the differential treatment experienced by racial/ethnic minorities and women in the workplace. For example, men believe that gender is a cue to competence and that, in the absence of any definite information to the contrary, the performer's gender becomes relevant in making job-related decisions (Forschi, Lad, & Sigerson, 1994). Women, on the other hand, either do not hold that belief or do so to a lesser degree. Forschi and colleagues (1994) conclude that this double standard is a subtle mechanism through which the status quo of gender inequality in the workplace is maintained. The supervisor-subordinate relationship provides a key insight into the workings of intergroup relations in the organization. The more dissimilar the supervisor and subordinates are in terms of race and gender, the less effective the supervisor perceives the subordinate to be (Avery, Volpone, McKay, King, & Wilson, 2012; Goldberg, Riordan, & Zhang, 2008; Tsui et al., 2002).

Being in the minority in the workplace has significant effects on individuals' behavioral and affective experiences in the workplace, particularly discriminatory experiences and the stress involved in feeling isolated (Stainback, Ratliff, & Roscigno, 2011). Avery, McKay, and Wilson's (2008) findings indicate that both African Americans and Hispanics believe they are more likely to experience race-related discrimination in the workplace than their White counterparts. Similarly, women tend to have less access to a variety of measures of status in the organization, such as income, position, and information, than do men (Kamenou & Fearfull, 2006; McDonald, 2011; McDonald et al., 2009). Potential advancement ladders are shorter for women and less frequently allow them to climb to executive or administrative levels (Cheung & Halpern, 2010; DiTomaso et al., 2007; Gray et al., 2007; Insch et al., 2008; Sealy & Singh, 2010). Because leadership and management qualities are defined mostly in masculine terms, these barriers persist for women. Leadership and management qualities are often defined in masculine terms (think manager, think man), perpetuating barriers for advancement and acceptance of women as managers (Aycan, Bayazit, Berkman, & Boratav, 2012; Kark, Waismel-Manor, & Shamir, 2012; Nkomo & Cox, 1996).

Research thus indicates that individuals from diverse groups commonly find themselves excluded from networks of information and opportunity (Abrams, Hogg, & Marques, 2004; Choi & Rainey, 2010; Gray et al., 2007; McGuire, 2000; Pettigrew & Martin, 1989; Shore et al., 2011). The reasons are varied. First, overt or covert racism, sexism, ageism, as well as other forms of discrimination may be the motivation for exclusionary practices (Larkey, 1996). These behaviors may be in the form of unintentional racism, in which unconscious avoidance behavior is expressed toward an individual or a group, or in the form of blatant racism, in which certain people are consciously excluded from information networks and job opportunities (Bertrand & Mullainathan, 2004; Friedman, 2010; Gaertner & Dovidio, 1986). Second, economic self-interest can be the motivation for preventing access to power and economic resources from certain individuals or groups (Larkey, 1996). Such behaviors result in the continued job segregation of women and minorities, as well as the exclusion of these groups from development and promotion opportunities (Becker, 1957/1971; Feagin & Feagin, 1988; Gray et al., 2007; Prescott & Bogg, 2011). And third, prevalent stereotypical perceptions and general senses of discomfort with those who are perceived as different (e.g., women, members of a minority group) can be the reason for their exclusion from important organizational processes and resources (Kalev, 2009). People tend to feel comfortable with others with whom they share important characteristics, fortifying in-group/out-group perceptions and creating exclusionary behaviors (Abrams et al., 2004; Bernstein, Sacco, Young, Hugenberg, & Cook, 2010; Blau, 1977). Perception patterns of in-group/out-group variability contribute to attitudes that close the door on opportunities for those who are different. People expect fewer variations from the stereotype in out-group members than they do in in-group members because they typically perceive out-groups as more homogeneous on negative stereotypical characteristics (Linville, Fischer, & Salovey, 1989; Rubin & Badea, 2007; Vonk & Van Knippenberg, 1995). An out-group is perceived as a single unit, not a collection of possibly different individuals, and the result is that those who are different are not given opportunities to demonstrate their unique and individual characteristics. They are treated according to preconceived notions and prejudices. Furthermore, this perception of homogeneity among out-group members is increased under conditions of competition (Corneille, Yzerbyt, Rogier, & Buidin, 2001; Sassenberg, et al., 2007). The processes that were previously described increase the likelihood of exclusion of those who are different (i.e., women, ethnic and racial minorities, and members of groups that may be stereotypically defined or labeled as different)—especially in situations of competition that are common in the workplace, such as competition for jobs, salary increases, and promotions.

Theory	Orienting Versus Explanatory	Implications for Understanding Workplace Diversity and Exclusion
Critical race theory	Orienting theory	• Race is socially constructed. • Workplace exclusion may be a common experience for members of certain employee groups. • Maintaining an exclusionary workplace may serve to benefit members of certain employee groups. • Minority status entails a unique ability to communicate issues that dominant group members may not know about or understand in the same way.
Intersectionality theory		• Employees simultaneously carry multiple, complex identities. • Different forms of social inequality, oppression, and discrimination overlap. • As a result, each individual experiences bias and workplace exclusion in a unique way.
Social identity theory		• People often think of themselves and others as members of specific social groups rather than as unique individuals. • The meaning attached to these social categories influences how people interact with those who are both in and out of their own identity group. • People want to belong to groups that enjoy distinct and positive identities. • Employees who belong to groups with higher perceived social status will accept and include those who are like them, while excluding those who are perceived to be different.
Social comparison theory	Explanatory theory: Why do employees feel excluded in their workplace?	• A sense of exclusion can result from the social comparison process. • Social comparison can happen through formal organizational activities and casual workplace interactions. • Employee peer groups act as a reference point for understanding one's status in the organization. • Perceptions of exclusion may arise when individuals compare themselves to relevant others and feel that they are treated differently because they are members of a particular identity group.
Symbolic interaction theory		• A sense of exclusion can result from the symbolic interaction process. • People interpret and synthesize symbols and objects in their environment. • Perceptions of exclusion arise from an ongoing personal evaluation in which employees interpret the meaning attached to the symbols and objects in their workplace environment. • A sense of exclusion can come from this interpretation and the assessment of one's relative standing that results.

(Continued)

TABLE 7.1 ● (Continued)

Theory	Orienting Versus Explanatory	Implications for Understanding Workplace Diversity and Exclusion
"Sociometer model" of self-esteem	Explanatory theory: How can experiences of exclusion influence employee attitudes, behaviors, and performance?	• People monitor others' reactions toward them, especially the degree to which they are accepted or rejected. • The "sociometer" is a psychological gauge that allows employees to monitor inclusive and exclusionary reactions from the workplace environment. • This assessment can influence how employees respond to workplace conditions and situations. • Experiences of exclusion can threaten one's self-esteem and influence employee behavior and performance.
Identity-based motivation theory		• Awareness of one's own identity and the meaning that other people attach to that identity can affect how employees respond to difficulty. • Exclusionary workplaces may express more overtly negative messages about certain identity groups. • A negative association between an identity and a behavior can cause an employee to feel unmotivated and to disengage when faced with difficulty at work (even if he or she does not believe in that association). • This response to difficulty may negatively affect employee attitudes, behaviors, and performance.
Interactional model of cultural diversity (IMCD)		• An exclusionary workplace can negatively influence employees in terms of how they feel (e.g., job satisfaction) as well as their career achievement (e.g., job performance). • Negative attitudes and behaviors at the individual level harm effectiveness at the organizational level (e.g., turnover, attendance, workgroup cohesiveness, profitability, and market share).
Realistic conflict theory	Explanatory theory: Why are there conflicts between groups in the workplace?	• Intergroup conflict arises because people are self-interested and driven to maximize rewards for themselves or their group. • Dominant employee groups may exclude nondominant employee groups in an attempt to maximize opportunities, resources, and rewards in their organization.
Equity theory		• People strive for justice; perceptions of injustice cause distress and create intergroup conflict. • Perceived injustice in the workplace may cause conflict among different employee groups.
Relative deprivation theory		• Intergroup conflict arises when people feel that they have unequal access to resources compared to others. • Workplace conflict may arise when some employees feel that they have different access to organizational resources compared to other employees.
Intergroup contact theory		• Lack of contact or unfavorable contact between groups causes intergroup conflict. • Exclusion in the workplace may be exacerbated by insufficient or negative contact between different employee groups.

Summary and Conclusion

This chapter examines theories that address the following questions: How are differences among groups created, and why? Why are people who are different from the "mainstream" more likely to be excluded from positions of power and influence in work organizations? Over the years of research and scholarly investigation, several theories have been generated that explain the nature of intergroup relations. The need to belong to social groups appears to be universal. The theories discussed in this chapter demonstrate that people are motivated to seek inclusion and avoid exclusion, and that this basic human need transcends cultural and national boundaries. Furthermore, individuals seek to belong to groups that are associated with higher status and prestige in society. Belonging to such groups is central to individuals' identity and their sense of worth.

To unpack different aspects of the inclusion-exclusion construct we presented a typology of theories, as summarized in Table 7.1. We began by introducing two orienting theories—critical race theory and intersectionality theory—which sensitize us to ideas that are integral to our understanding of workplace exclusion. For example, racism is ubiquitous and each employee has his or her own unique and overlapping set of identities. Next, we presented key explanatory theories that answer three driving questions: *Why do employees feel excluded in their workplace? How can experiences of exclusion influence employee attitudes, behaviors, and performance? Why are there conflicts between groups in the workplace?* Social identity theory, social comparison theory, and symbolic interaction theory emphasize the meaning that is attached to different group membership and help to explain why employees feel excluded. The sociometer model of self-esteem, identity-based motivation theory, and Cox's foundational intersectional model of cultural diversity help us understand how exclusionary work environments translate into employee outcomes. For example, awareness of one's own identity and the meaning that other people attach to that identity can affect how employees respond to difficulty. The last set of theories focuses on reasons for intergroup conflict: the desire to maximize resources, perceived injustice, perceived unequal access to resources, and insufficient or negative contact between groups.

The inclusion-exclusion continuum, introduced in this chapter, is linked to important psychological processes such as self-esteem, depression, anxiety, and a general perception that one's life has meaning. This is particularly relevant for members of disadvantaged or stigmatized groups who may suffer the psychological consequences of being excluded. Therefore, this need to be included in social groups is a strong motivator in human behavior. Though one needs to be aware of the inherent competitive nature of identity groups, what one gains in status the other may lose; taken together, these theories tell us that work organizations may gain a more loyal, satisfied, and committed workforce by becoming more inclusive.

Notes

1. For research scales that assess this construct in the context of diversity, see Chapter 17.

2. Dr. Isaac Olawale Albert is from the Peace and Conflict Studies Programme in the Institute of African Studies, University of Ibadan, Nigeria.

8

Culture and Communication in the Global Workplace

The Jack Welch of the future cannot be me. I spent my entire
career in the United States. The next head of General Electric will be somebody
who spent time in Bombay, in Hong Kong, in Buenos Aires. We have to send
our best and brightest overseas and make sure they have the training that will
allow them to be global leaders who will make GE flourish in the future.

—Jack Welch, CEO of U.S.-based General
Electric in a speech to GE employees[1]

To succeed in managing a workforce that is increasingly diverse and multinational, managers
need knowledge about cultural differences and similarities among nations. They also need to
be sensitive to these differences, which can contribute to their effectiveness in cross-cultural
communication. Human behavior and interpersonal interactions are reflective of the values and
norms of specific societies. These cultural values and behavioral norms differ between societies, but
until recently, they have been considered quite stable within societies. In recent decades, however,
this perception started to change as scholars became more aware of the impact of the global trends
of immigration and worker migration on national cultures (see Chapters 4 and 5). In today's global
business world, a manager has to understand cultural differences among societies and their meaning
in business relations. In addition, she or he needs to be sensitive to cultural nuances within societies
that are associated with the diversity of that society. In this chapter, we examine the cultural context
in the global workplace and analyze communication patterns that facilitate or block effective cross-
cultural communication.

The Cultural Context for the Global Workplace

What is *culture?* The Latin origin of the word refers to the tilling of the soil, although its common, everyday use pertains to refinement, particularly through education, literature, and the arts. In this book, we refer to the broader meaning of the word *culture* as used by social scientists. There are many definitions of culture in the social psychological and anthropological literature,[2] but the most widely accepted is that proposed in the mid–20th century by Kroeber and Kluckhohn (1952) after analyzing 160 definitions of the concept of culture and synthesizing the following definition:

> Culture consists of patterns, explicit or implicit, of and for behavior acquired and transmitted by symbols, constituting the distinctive achievements of human groups, including their embodiments in artifacts; the essential core of culture consists of traditional (historically derived and selected) ideas and especially their attached values; culture systems may, on the one hand, be considered as products of action, on the other as conditioning elements of further action. (p. 181)

Culture is defined as "the way of life, especially the general customs and beliefs, of a particular group of people at a particular time" (*Cambridge dictionary*, 2015). Using the analogy of computer programming, Hofstede, Hofstede, and Minkov (2010) call culture "software of the mind," noting that the patterns of thinking, feeling, and acting embedded in a culture are like "mental programs." They define culture as "the collective programming of the mind which distinguishes the members of one group or category of people from another" (p. 6). Although culture does not determine the exact behavior for human beings the way programs dictate how computers function, it does delineate the expectations, actual or anticipated, and behaviors within a specific social context. Others define culture as a "set of beliefs and values about what is desirable and undesirable in a community of people, and a set of formal or informal practices to support the values" (Javidan & House, 2001, p. 292). Understanding societal culture can be complex because it includes two sets of elements at once: The first are the ongoing cultural practices that inform us about the current perceptions of specific cultures, and the second are the strongly held values that inform us about aspirations and direction that cultures wish to develop (Dorfman, Javidan, Hanges, Dastmalchian, & House, 2012; House, Dorfman, Javidan, Hanges, & DeLuque, 2013; Javidan, Stahl, Brodbeck, & Wilderom, 2005).

If culture is the sum of the learned and shared patterns of thought and behaviors that are characteristic of a given people, how are national cultures around the world different from one another? To answer this question, Geert Hofstede, a Dutch social scientist, embarked on a multinational study examining national cultures (Hofstede, 1980, 1997, 2001, 2015; Hofstede & Hofstede, 2005; Hofstede et al., 2010). In his initial book, *Culture's Consequences,* Hofstede (1980) presented a statistical analysis of about 117,000 questionnaires collected in 1967 and 1973 from employees working in IBM subsidiaries in 40 different countries. Studying individuals who worked for the same organization was assumed to provide the researchers with a good environment for studying national cultures because all the employees were thought to share the same organizational culture and environment. This allowed the researchers to focus on the differences in the participants' responses as indicative of national cultural differences. In other words, the researchers assumed that being employed by the same organization (IBM) has created a common organizational culture; therefore, whatever differences in values and norms that would be evident among employees who worked in different countries would be the result of national cultural differences. The most important result of this analysis was a theoretical formulation of four value dimensions for representing differences among national cultures: power distance, uncertainty avoidance, individualism-collectivism, and masculinity/femininity. A fifth dimension—long- versus short-term orientation—was added a decade later (Hofstede, 1997).

It is important to note from the outset that Hofstede's research (e.g., 1980, 1997, 2001) was widely lauded for its breakthrough contribution to the study of culture (e.g., Kirkman, Lowe, & Gibson, 2006; Søndergaard, 1994), yet it was criticized for its lack of scientific rigor and even outright cultural bias (e.g., Ailon, 2008; McSweeney, 2002). Because of its enduring and widespread influence, we devote the following sections to discussing the strengths of the work as well as its limitations.

Cultural Value Dimensions

Social anthropologists have long agreed that all societies face the same basic problems—they differ only in the way they try to solve these problems.[3] Hofstede (1980), based on an earlier framework developed by Inkeles and Levinson (1969), examined culture in the different countries along four axes: (a) *power distance*—the relationship with authority and social inequality; (b) *individualism versus collectivism*—the relationship between the individual and the group; (c) *masculinity versus femininity*—the tendency toward assertiveness in contrast to modesty; and (d) *avoidance of uncertainty*—the control of aggression and expressions of emotions. Interestingly, Hofstede (1980) found that national culture, as measured along these axes, explained more of the differences in work-related values and attitudes than did position within the organization, profession, age, or gender. Following the discovery and writeup of the four original cultural dimensions that were previously stated, Hofstede (2001) decided to add a fifth dimension to his model. This dimension was based on the answers in student samples from 23 countries to the Chinese Value Survey (CVS). The study's instrument was developed by Michael Harris Bond in Hong Kong based on values suggested by Chinese scholars, and seemed to reflect Confucian teachings in both of its poles. The fifth dimension was *long- versus short-term orientation*—the tendency for thrift and perseverance and respect for tradition and fulfilling social obligations. Table 8.1 provides definitions for each dimension, with some country-specific examples.

These five dimensions have clear implications for individual and group expectations related to acceptable behaviors in the workplace. Whether employees expect their supervisor, for example, to be authoritative and give clear instructions that they will closely follow or whether they expect to operate independently and have egalitarian relationships with their supervisors depends to a large extent on the cultural perception of power distance in their society. Next is a description of the cultural differences in expected and acceptable behaviors in the workplace, according to Hofstede's five axes.

Power Distance

In large power distance societies, such as Latin countries (Latin American and Latin European, like France and Spain), as well as Asian and African countries, the hierarchical system in society is considered existential. Applying this principle to the workplace, supervisors and subordinates consider themselves as existentially unequal. There are many supervisors and many layers of management with large salary differentials between people at the top and at the bottom, as well as in between. Subordinates expect to be told what to do, and superiors are entitled to special privileges. Hofstede and his colleagues (2010) note that, in high power distance societies, "The ideal boss, in the subordinates' eyes, is one they feel most comfortable with and who they respect most, is a benevolent autocrat or 'good father'" (p. 73). In contrast, in small power distance societies, such as the United States, Canada, Great Britain, and Denmark, subordinates and supervisors consider themselves as existentially equal. The hierarchical strata in the organizations are considered permeable, providing the possibility for both subordinates and supervisors to move up or down the ladder, and supervisors are expected to be accessible to subordinates. The ideal boss is "a resourceful (and therefore respected) democrat" (Hofstede et al., 2010, p. 74). There is evidence that congruence between managers' societal values of power distance and the culture of the

TABLE 8.1 • Dimensions of Cultural Difference

Dimension	Definition[1]	Country-Specific Examples[2]
Power distance	*Power distance* refers to the extent to which the less powerful members of institutions and organizations within a country expect and accept that power is distributed unequally.	Large power distance: Malaysia, Guatemala, Panama, Philippines, Mexico Small power distance: Austria, Israel, Denmark, New Zealand, Ireland
Individualism versus collectivism	*Individualism* pertains to societies in which the ties between individuals are loose. *Collectivism* pertains to societies in which people are integrated into strong, cohesive in-groups, which throughout a lifetime continue to protect them in exchange for unquestioning loyalty.	High individualism: United States, Australia, Great Britain, Canada, the Netherlands High collectivism: Guatemala, Ecuador, Panama, Venezuela, Colombia
Masculinity versus femininity	*Masculinity* pertains to societies in which gender roles are clearly distinct. *Femininity* pertains to societies in which social gender roles overlap (both men and women are supposed to be modest, tender, and concerned with quality of life).	High masculinity: Japan, Austria, Venezuela, Italy, Switzerland High femininity: Sweden, Norway, the Netherlands, Denmark, Costa Rica
Avoidance of uncertainty	*Avoidance of uncertainty* refers to the extent to which the members of a culture feel threatened by uncertain or unknown situations—the extent to which they need predictability in the form of written and unwritten rules.	Weak uncertainty avoidance: Greece, Portugal, Guatemala, Uruguay, Belgium Strong uncertainty avoidance: Singapore, Jamaica, Denmark, Sweden, Hong Kong
Long-term versus short-term orientation	*Long-term orientation* refers to the fostering of virtues oriented toward future rewards—in particular, perseverance and thrift. *Short-term orientation* refers to the fostering of virtues related to the past and present—in particular, respect for tradition, preservation of "face," and fulfilling social obligations.	Long-term orientation: China, Hong Kong, Taiwan, Japan, Korea Short-term orientation: Zimbabwe, Canada, Philippines, Nigeria, Pakistan

Source: Adapted from Hofstede, 1980, 1997, 2001; Hofstede, G. (1980). Culture's consequences: International differences in work related values. Beverly Hills, CA: Sage; Hofstede G. (1997). Cultures and organizations: Software of the mind. New York: McGraw-Hill; Hofstede, G. (2001). Culture's consequences: Comparing values, behaviors, institutions, and organizations across nations (2nd ed.). Thousand Oaks, CA: Sage.

Notes:

1. Definitions for the four cultural dimensions are drawn from Hofstede (1997, pp. 28, 51, 113), and the fifth cultural dimension is drawn from Hofstede (2001, pp. 356, 359). These definitions are also cited in Hofstede's more recent work with his colleagues (e.g., Hofstede et al., 2010).
2. Country-specific identifications in this table and throughout the chapter are based on Hofstede's study among IBM employees worldwide and Michael Bond's CVS study among students. Scores and rankings for the more than 60 countries included in the original study on each of the four cultural dimensions can be found in Hofstede (1980, 1997; Hofstede et al., 2010), and those for 23 countries included in the CVS study on the fifth dimension can be found in Hofstede (2001; Hofstede et al., 2010).

organization in which the manager works can reduce job-related stress. For example, Joiner (2001) found that managers in Greece, a country characterized by a large power distance, were comfortable with the so-called Eiffel Tower organizational culture, characterized by centralization and formalizations, and that the congruence between this type of organizational culture and the Greek culture contributed to reduced levels of stress among the managers.

Individualism Versus Collectivism

The individualism/collectivism dimension refers to the extent to which people see themselves as an integral part of a social group with primary alliance to the group or as separate individuals with primary responsibility for themselves and their very immediate family only. In collectivist societies, such as many Latin American countries as well as Arab-speaking countries, people are born into extended families or other in-groups, which continue to protect them in exchange for loyalty. This reality is evident in the workplace, where the relationship between the employer and the employees in the organization is seen as a family relationship. There are mutual obligations with strong loyalty on the part of the employee connected to an employer's commitment for protection and security in return. In a strong collectivist-oriented context, there is a clear preference for group-oriented human resource (HR) management practices (Aycan, Al-Hamadi, Davis, & Budhwar, 2007). Employee loyalty in this context refers to an unwritten contract that requires employees to be faithful to their duties, to their managers and coworkers, and to their organization. Loyalty often serves as a mediator between the perception of a familiar (collectivistic) organizational climate and job performance and often means that employees are more likely to follow orders, behave according to expectations, and do the best job they know how to do (Jen, Chou, Lin, & Tsai, 2012; Umiker, 1995). Hiring preference is given to relatives, first to relatives of high-ranking members of the organization and then to others. The assumption underlying this practice is that hiring relatives of employees reduces the company's business risk (due to familiarity with the new hires) and increases employee loyalty. Even when employees do not perform to expectation, they can still expect to hold onto their jobs because of the family loyalty value. A strong collectivist orientation, such as in many countries in the Middle East, often translates into commitment to the work organization (Fischer & Mansell, 2009; Robertson, Al-Khatib, & Al-Habib, 2002). A study of 365 employees from Saudi Arabia, Kuwait, and Oman provides support for the proposition that a collectivist orientation is associated with a strong group commitment and belief in participatory work ethics (Robertson et al., 2002), and two sets of meta-analyses of employee commitment across cultures indicate that greater collectivism was associated with higher organizational commitment and lower intention to leave (Fischer & Mansell, 2009).

In individualist societies, such as the United States, Australia, Great Britain, and Canada, people are expected to act in their best interests. For example, employees in these individualist societies would most likely view their supervisor as rewarding individual efforts, unlike employees in collectivistic societies, who are more likely to perceive supervisory actions as rewarding team or work group collaboration. The relationship between employees and employers is based, therefore, not on group loyalty but on complementing self-interests. Employers' decisions related to hiring and promotions are expected to be based on skills, achievements, and merit; favoritism and nepotism are strongly discouraged. In approaching work assignments, employees in a collectivist society would emphasize working together and will view the relationships as more important than the task, whereas the reverse will be true in the individualist society, where the task will prevail over the relationship. A study comparing social support of employees in a U.S.-based company with that of employees in its former subsidiary in Israel found significant differences that are rooted in the collectivist-individualist leanings, respectively, of these two societies (Mor Barak, Findler, & Wind, 2003). Using the statistical method of factor analysis, which allowed the researchers to identify clusters of relationships between variables, the researchers examined the sources of social support for employees in the two societies. They found that employees in the United States clearly delineated between three types of support providers: (a) their supervisor; (b) their coworkers; and (c) support providers from outside the work environment—their spouses/ partners, family members, and friends. The Israeli employees did not make such distinctions. For the Israeli employees, living in a collectivist society, the lines between supervisors, coworkers, and family/ friends networks were blurred because a coworker—or a supervisor, for that matter—could also have been a friend or a family member.

Masculinity Versus Femininity

The masculinity/femininity dimension refers to the extent to which dominant values in the society emphasize assertiveness, competition, and material achievements, attributes associated with masculine qualities, as compared with feminine qualities such as relationships among people, care for others, and care for quality of life in general. Hofstede (1980, 1997; Hofstede & Hofstede, 2005) justifies anchoring these qualities in the gender-related terminology of the ancient, universal, gender-role differences between men as hunters, fighters, and providers and women as caretakers and nurturers of the family. In masculine societies, such as Japan, Italy, Mexico, and the United States, assertiveness, ambition, and competitiveness are expected and rewarded in the work context. In contrast, employees who show modesty, solidarity, and care for others are valued more in feminine societies such as Sweden, Norway, the Netherlands, and Denmark. In feminine societies, there is a preference for solving work-related conflicts by compromise and negotiation, whereas in masculine societies, power struggles and direct confrontation may be more common in conflict resolution. Managers in feminine societies take into consideration their employees' needs and strive for consensus, whereas managers in masculine societies are expected to be assertive and decisive. The balance between work and family is also very different in both types of societies. In the Scandinavian countries (identified as feminine societies), fathers often take time out from work to take care of a young or sick child. In a review of paternity leave statistics in the European Union (EU), almost all fathers in Sweden and the majority of fathers in Norway and in Finland take paternity leave (Dermott, 2001; O'Brien, 2009). In contrast, in masculine societies, the mother typically takes care of the children, and the father is expected to continue with his work as usual. In some countries, such as Japan and South Korea, the traditional cultural expectation was that women retire completely from the workforce once they had their first child and devote full time to raising their children. When British prime minister Tony Blair limited his schedule but continued to work when his fourth child, Leo, was born in May 2000, a public debate ensued about the justification for such an action, with some criticizing his action as irresponsible and others hailing it as an example of paternal responsibility. Great Britain is, of course, near the masculine end of the scale.

Avoidance of Uncertainty

Avoidance of uncertainty is a dimension that refers to the extent to which people in a society feel anxious about ambiguous situations and the steps that they are willing to take to create stability through formalization of rules and regulations. In high uncertainty avoidance societies, such as Belgium, Japan, and France, there are many rules that govern the behavior of employees as well as the work process. In contrast, in low uncertainty avoidance societies such as Great Britain, Jamaica, and South Africa, there are fewer regulations and a general belief that there should not be more rules than are strictly necessary. High job mobility is prevalent and expected in societies with low uncertainty avoidance, and job stability and lifetime employment are more common and cherished in societies with high uncertainty avoidance. Hofstede and his colleagues (2010) note the importance of the anxiety component of uncertainty avoidance and its impact on time orientation in the work context:

In strong uncertainty avoidance societies people like to work hard, or at least to be always busy. Life is hurried, and time is money. In weak uncertainty avoidance societies people are quite able to work hard if there is a need for it, but they are not driven by an inner urge towards constant activity. They like to relax. Time is a framework to orient oneself in, but not something one is constantly watching. (p. 210)

Long- Versus Short-Term Orientation

The long- versus short-term orientation is the fifth dimension that was added after the introduction of the original four dimensions to address differences in East–West cultural orientations. Designed by Chinese scholars and reflecting Confucian principles, the CVS provided the initial evidence for this dimension among students in 23 different countries (Hofstede, 2007; Hofstede & Bond, 1988). Long-term orientation refers to the fostering of virtues oriented toward future rewards: in particular, perseverance and thrift. Short-term orientation refers to the fostering of virtues related to the past and present: in particular, respect for tradition, preservation of "face," and fulfilling social obligations.

In long-term–oriented cultures, a person's responsibilities for family and for work are not separate and not viewed as in competition. In fact, the two seem to support each other, and therefore family enterprises are very common. The long-term pole on the continuum is associated with persistence, perseverance, and tenacity in pursuit of goals, and this value orientation is seen as supporting entrepreneurial initiatives. These values are paired with the values of thrift and a sense of comfort with hierarchy, all leading to the availability of capital and to a stable work relationship within a family or close-knit work enterprise. At the other end of the continuum, the short-term orientation places great emphasis on personal steadiness and stability, which could suppress risk-seeking behaviors that are required to support entrepreneurial activities.

On the continuum of long- versus short-term orientation, Asian countries scored toward the long-term pole while the rest of the countries scored at the medium- or short-term pole. The top long-term scorers were China, Hong Kong, Taiwan, Japan, and Korea (Hofstede, 2007). No Western countries scored more than medium term; the United States, Britain, and Canada scored in the short-term orientation range, as did countries of Africa. High scores on the long-term dimension were strongly correlated with the countries' economic success in the last quarter of the 20th century (Hofstede & Hofstede, 2005, p. 223). The authors noted that long-term orientation is identified as a major explanation for the explosive growth of the East Asian economies during that period.

Summary and Critique of Hofstede's Framework

Hofstede's original work received wide acclaim for its pioneering nature and has since been cited and used in a vast number of research projects around the world, but it was also criticized for its less than rigorous theoretical framework and less than perfect research methods (e.g., Ailon, 2008; McSweeney, 2002). The strengths of the work included an ambitious effort to measure and quantify the values that distinguish one culture from another along five unified dimensions and a demonstration of the significance of national cultures to management theory and practice. As a result, the books promoted sensitivity to cultural diversity in the workplace at the very time that global businesses were expanding. It also undermined the assumption that management knowledge that originated in the United States could be universally applied and emphasized the need to learn different cultures and adapt management practices to local values and norms. The typology that Hofstede put forth in his work has been widely applied and has become exceptionally influential (e.g., Baskerville, 2003; Bhagat, 2002; Bing, 2004; Chandy & Williams, 1994; Cronje, 2011; Hart, 1999; Kirkman et al., 2006; Søndergaard, 1994; Triandis, 2004; Yoo, Donthu, & Lenartowicz, 2011).

In a retrospective piece, Michale Minkov and Geert Hofstede (2011) summarize what they call "the Hofstede doctrine," noting that Hofstede's body of work has a distinct identity with five major contributions to cross-cultural research: (a) generating a paradigm shift in the study of culture, from treating it as a single (though, admittedly, complex) variable to unpackaging it into independent, measurable dimensions; (b) creating cultural dimensions that are meaningful on a national level, underpinned by variables that correlate across nations, not across individuals or organizations; (c) addressing basic universal problems that all societies have to deal with; (d) reflecting stable national differences that, though evolving, remain quite the same, or move in a similar direction as to render them quite consistent over time; and (e) having been based on a very large data set, demonstrating the importance and relevance of national culture to organizational behavior, management practices, and to society at large.

Hofstede's work has been criticized on several levels, including its limited conceptualization of culture, its less than rigorous methodology, and its inherent Western cultural bias (e.g., Ailon, 2008; Baskerville-Morley, 2003, 2005; Eckhardt, 2002; Engle & Nash, 2015; Eringa, Caudron, Rieck, Xie, & Gerhardt, 2015; Harrison & McKinnon, 1999; Kitayama, 2002; McSweeney, 2002; Robinson, 1983; Singh, 1990).

The work was criticized because it seemed to identify culture with nations and because it has operated under the assumption that within each nation there was a uniformed and relatively static culture. This notion of a unified national culture is particularly problematic in light of the increased diversity within nations. One glaring example from Hofstede's (1980) initial study was the use of an all-White sample (because of the apartheid regime of the time) to represent the totality of the South African national culture. Another stream of criticism related to the validity and reliability of the study's measures as well as the limited research methodology. For example, even though the total number of questionnaires was very large—117,000—this number includes both waves of the questionnaire that were administered in 1968 and 1969 and again from 1971 to 1973. The large number in and of itself does not ensure representativeness. In fact, in some of the countries the samples were very small (e.g., 58 in Singapore and 37 in Pakistan). Hofstede's (2001) claim that the sample sizes were sufficient because of the homogeneity of values within national samples is highly questionable because the basic premise of homogeneous national cultures cannot be substantiated (McSweeney, 2002). Finally, an interesting analysis by Ailon (2008) uses a mirroring technique to deconstruct Hofstede's book *Culture's Consequences* (1980), using the book's own assumptions and logic. The author demonstrates that, despite his explicit efforts to remain "culturally neutral," the book's specific Western cultural lens is evident throughout the chapters. For example, with respect to the uncertainty avoidance dimension, Ailon (2008) notes, "Hofstede strongly disagrees with the claim that company rules should not be broken, thus expressing low uncertainty avoidance value" (p. 423), yet the book itself manifests what appears to be a very high intolerance for the unpredictable, ambiguous, or uncertain. In other words, it manifests very high uncertainty avoidance (p. 893). Ailon found several inconsistencies in both theory and methodology and cautioned against an uncritical reading of Hofstede's cultural dimensions.

A central concern among all of Hofstede's critics is the author's central premise that *national cultures are uniform* and therefore could be represented by relatively small samples (1980, p. 65) and could be measured, quantified, compared, and graphed quite precisely on the continuum of each of the five dimensions. McSweeney (2002) notes that "if the aim is understanding then we need to know more about the richness and diversity of national practices and institutions—rather than merely assuming their 'uniformity' and that they have an already known national cultural cause" (p. 112). Ailon (2008) sums up her criticism with a positive note, highlighting Hofstede's pioneering work on the backdrop of the period of his initial research: "Hofstede, it should be remembered, worked within the discursive limits of the 1970's, and he did so impressively, at least in so far as the popularity of *Culture's Consequences* indicated" (p. 901).

It is important to remember that the cultural dimensions offered by Hofstede's work were in many respects the first attempt to scientifically characterize the very broad concept of culture in a multinational context. Judging by the numerous researchers who found this conceptual framework useful, the author's contribution has been enormous. Yet, as national cultures become more diverse with an influx of immigrants, migrant workers, and the migration of businesses (painstakingly demonstrated in the first part of this book), it is important to pay attention to diversity within national cultures and to the change in the culture of those nations as a result of infusion of other cultures over time. Any manager who attempts to shortcut her or his learning process by looking for broad-brush characterizations of "uniform" and "constant" national cultures may be doing a disservice to herself or himself. It has been the premise of this book all along that in today's increasingly diverse workforce, a more nuanced understanding of, sensitivity to, and proficiency in the cultural differences not only *between* but *within* national cultures is essential.

The GLOBE Study

A different attempt to identify cultural dimensions in an international context is the Global Leadership and Organizational Behavior Effectiveness (GLOBE) research program. GLOBE is a multiyear program of cross-cultural research designed to examine the relationship between societal culture, organizational culture, and organizational leadership effectiveness (Dorfman et al., 2012; House, Dorfman, House, Dorfman et al., 2013; House, Hanges et al., 2004, 2013; Javidan, House, Dorfman, Hanges, & Sully de Luque, 2006). The project was conceived in 1991 by Robert J. House from the Wharton School at the University of Pennsylvania, who assembled a team of approximately 170 social scientists and management scholars from 61 countries representing major geographic regions throughout the world to collaborate on the study. The researchers collected data from over 17,000 middle managers in three industries: financial services, food processing, and telecommunications, as well as archival measures of country economic prosperity and the physical and psychological well-being of the cultures studied.

GLOBE has several distinguishing features. First, it is truly a cross-cultural research program. The constructs were defined, conceptualized, and operationalized by the multicultural team of researchers. Second, the industries were selected through a polling of the country investigators, and the instruments were designed with the full participation of the researchers representing the different cultures. Finally, the data in each country were collected by investigators who were either natives of the cultures studied or had extensive knowledge of and experience in those cultures.

The authors derived nine cultural dimensions from the literature and measured them both as practices (the way things are) and values (the way things ought to be) (Dorfman et al., 2012; House, Dorfman et al., 2013; Javidan, Dorfman, Sully de Luque, & House, 2006). The nine cultural attributes that were described in the study were:

- *Performance orientation:* The degree to which a collective encourages and rewards group members for performance improvement and excellence
- *Assertiveness:* The degree to which individuals are assertive, confrontational, and aggressive in their relationships with others
- *Future orientation:* The extent to which individuals engage in future-oriented behaviors such as delaying gratification, planning, and investing in the future

- *Human orientation:* The degree to which a collective encourages and rewards individuals for being fair, altruistic, generous, caring, and kind to others

- *Institutional collectivism:* The degree to which organizational and societal institutional practices encourage and reward collective distribution of resources and collective action

- *In-group collectivism:* The degree to which individuals express pride, loyalty, and cohesiveness in their organizations or families

- *Gender egalitarianism:* The degree to which a collective minimizes gender inequality

- *Power distance:* The degree to which members of a collective expect power to be distributed equally

- *Uncertainty avoidance:* The extent to which a society, organization, or group relies on social norms, rules, and procedures to alleviate unpredictability of future events

The study authors focused on leadership, which they defined through a process of cross-cultural discussions as "the ability of an individual to influence, motivate, and enable others to contribute toward the effectiveness and success of the organizations of which they are members" (House, Hanges et al., 2004, p. 15). The principal outcome of the study was the development of six universally shared dimensions of leadership: charismatic/value based, team oriented, self-protective, participative, humane oriented, and autonomous.

Cross-Cultural Communication

Effective interactions in today's global business world depend to a great extent on the ability to convey a clear message that people in different cultures can comprehend in the way the communicator intended them to understand it. Business communication can be interpreted very differently, depending on the cultural orientation of a particular country. For example, in masculine societies, an effective manager is one who communicates directly, assertively, and even aggressively. Those from feminine-leaning societies may interpret such behavior as unfriendly, arrogant, and even rude. A Swedish manager reading a help-wanted advertisement for a salesperson in the United States might be taken aback by the requirement that the qualified candidate be "aggressive." On the other hand, British managers may interpret a Chinese manager's modesty and humility in stating his qualifications as a weakness. Although the cross-fertilization of ideas generated from a diverse workforce can be beneficial to organizations, some research indicates that congruence between organizational culture and the culture of the wider society could produce beneficial outcomes. For example, a study of Mexican workers indicates that such congruence, along the axes noted by Hofstede and his colleagues, contributes to job satisfaction and organizational commitment (Madlock, 2012).

An incident in the city of Najaf during the 2003 war in Iraq (see Box 8.1) demonstrates one leader's bold and effective use of nonverbal, cross-cultural communication that probably saved many lives that day. Unable to speak Arabic and with no interpreter on site, the commander of the U.S. Army's 101st Airborne Division was unable to use language to communicate his nonaggressive intentions to the Arabic-speaking crowd. In a spur-of-the-moment decision, he instructed his soldiers to kneel on one knee, smile, and point their weapons to the ground. This vulnerable yet friendly posture was clearly understood by the crowd that responded likewise by smiling and sitting on the ground. Luckily, in the Najaf incident, the nonverbal body language was sufficiently universal to convey the peaceful intentions of the soldiers and to prevent what could have been a deadly incident.

Box 8.1

LEADERSHIP THROUGH EFFECTIVE CROSS-CULTURAL COMMUNICATION SAVES THE DAY IN NAJAF

Early in June 2003 during the U.S. war in Iraq, the U.S. Army's 101st Airborne Division on a mission to secure the area entered the city of Najaf. It was an uneventful patrol. The search turned up nothing. The Shia Muslim population, which traditionally had not supported Saddam's rule, seemed curious and friendly, but didn't get too close. The local population had cautiously welcomed the U.S. troops. Word came from the Grand Ayatollah Sistani that he was willing to meet with the American commander, but he asked first that the U.S. soldiers secure his compound.

As the troops started down the road toward the Ayatollah's compound, the crowd that assembled there to watch the American soldiers mistook their intentions to mean that they were progressing toward the Imam Ali shrine located in Najaf. The Imam Ali shrine is the burial site of the prophet Muhammad's son-in-law and considered one of the holiest sites in the world for Shia Muslims.

The once-friendly crowd became alarmed and chaos ensued. Earlier warm greetings were replaced with angry shouts and gestures as hundreds of people attempted to block the soldiers' way. Clerics appeared with a message from the Grand Ayatollah that the soldiers were progressing at his invitation, but their message was drowned out.

Realizing the explosive situation at hand and unable to verbally convey his peaceful intentions, the colonel told his men to stay calm. He instructed the soldiers to smile, get down on one knee, and point their weapons to the ground. The puzzled soldiers reluctantly complied. A hush fell on the crowd. Then slowly the crowd responded in kind—relaxing, smiling, and sitting on the ground. The tension was diffused, but the colonel realized that the situation was still potentially volatile. "Turn around," he ordered his men, "just turn around and go." The soldiers complied, and as they were leaving, the colonel turned around and bowed apologetically to the crowd as if saying, "Sorry for the misunderstanding." A potentially deadly confrontation was prevented.

Source: Chilcote (2003).

Although in the business world the stakes do not often involve human lives, they do involve people's livelihood. Cross-cultural miscommunication can result in lost opportunities—such as losing a job or a business deal—that could be detrimental to the financial and economic well-being of individuals and organizations. Conversely, effective cross-cultural communication can open up employment and business opportunities that may not otherwise be available to the participants.

Effective Cross-Cultural Communication

Communication, in its most basic form, is the use of symbols to convey meaning. Symbols can include words, tones of voice, gestures, or use of objects (artifacts). It refers to "the process through which people, acting together, create, sustain, and manage meaning through the use of verbal and nonverbal signs and symbols from a particular context" (Conrad & Poole, 2012, p. 5). Even more so, communication is the practice of collective exchange and is fundamentally societal (Greenaway, Wright, Willingham, Reynolds, & Haslam, 2015). Broadly defined, communication is multidimensional (Neuliep, 2008) and relates to three types of goals: (a) instrumental goals (e.g., performing tasks), (b) relational goals (e.g., negotiating conflicts), and (c) identity management (e.g., conveying a desired self-image) (Bernstein, 1975; Clark & Delia, 1979; Halliday, 1978).

Cross-culture is a particularly challenging form of communication. It involves several potential barriers to communication that are related to the use of verbal and nonverbal methods to convey meanings that may or may not be the same in the cultures of origin of the participants (see Figure 8.1 for an illustration).

When people use symbols that elicit meaning in another person, whatever the original intent was, or even without conscious intent, they are still communicating. Often, the message that is received may be different from the one that was intended because of cultural barriers on the part of receivers and transmitters. Take, for example, gender differences in perceptions of sexual meanings. A man may perceive a woman's behavior as flirtatious when her original intent was simply courteous and entirely nonsexual, leading to severe misunderstandings. Add to that the cultural layer when, for example, it is entirely acceptable and even chivalrous for a French businessman to compliment a woman colleague on her dress in the French cultural context. An American businesswoman might perceive the exact same behavior as inappropriate and may even interpret it as sexual harassment. Miscommunication occurs when the original intent of the person transmitting the message is different from the meaning that is received by the other person, and it is more likely to occur between participants who belong to different cultures.

Verbal Communication

The use of different languages often creates a barrier to communication because one or both sides are not as articulate as they could be in their native tongues. For example, a person from Holland who speaks Dutch but is also fluent in French may not be as familiar with the vocabulary, grammar, and idioms of the language as would be a native French speaker. Articulating her thoughts (encoding) would be more

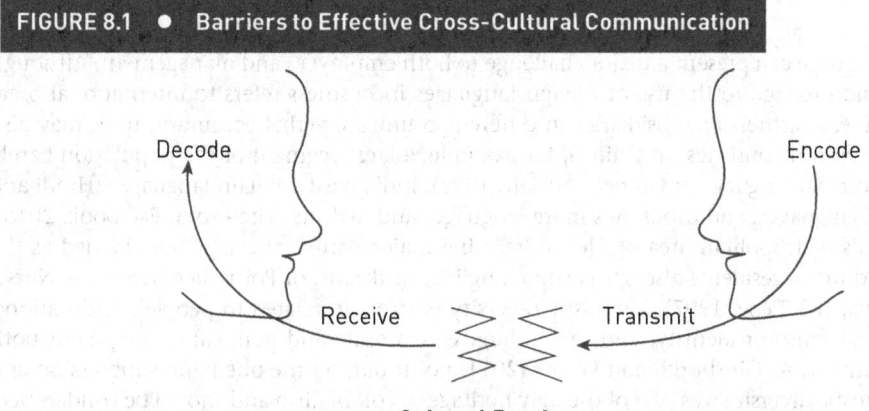

FIGURE 8.1 • Barriers to Effective Cross-Cultural Communication

Decode   Encode

Receive ≷ ≷ Transmit

Cultural Barriers

Verbal		Nonverbal	
Vocabulary	Accent	Tone of voice	Emotions
Grammar	Enunciation	Eye contact	Clothes/artifacts
Idioms	Emphasis in	Body language	Proximity
Volume	sentence	Gesturing	

difficult for her, and the end message may not be exactly what she intended to convey. In addition, her accent, enunciation, and emphasis in sentence intonation (the "music" of the language) may make it difficult for the listener to clearly comprehend what she was saying and to be distracted from the message.

When conducting international business, the choice of which language to use (e.g., one's own or the host country's language) is more than a practical matter. It is a choice of whether to signify national pride on the one hand or to demonstrate respect for the host country's culture on the other. Foreign leaders often speak their own language and communicate through an interpreter, even when they are fluent in the host country's language, to show a sense of national pride. For example, when the supersonic plane the *Concorde* was designed, there was a bitter argument between the French and the British who collaborated on the project, perhaps reflecting the age-old rivalry and animosity between the two countries.[4] At one point, work was halted after the French insisted that the plane should have a Gallic final letter *e* in its name, whereas the British stolidly referred to it as "Concord." Eventually, the French spelling was adopted (Arnold, 2003). On the other hand, saying a few words, such as "hello" or "good evening," in the host country's language can go a long way. When John F. Kennedy gave his famous speech in front of the Berlin town hall and said, "All free men, wherever they may live, are citizens of Berlin, and, therefore, as a free man, I take pride in the words, '*Ich bin ein Berliner*'" (I am a Berliner), more than a million West Berliners responded with a roar of approval.[5] Similarly, when Bill Clinton spoke at the funeral of Yitzhak Rabin, the prime minister of Israel who was assassinated because of his work toward peace in the Middle East, he began his English speech by saying two words in Hebrew, "*Shalom, chaver*" (goodbye [also doubles as peace], my friend). The people of Israel were so touched by this gesture that these words later appeared in poems, in everyday phrases, and on bumper stickers. Willy Brandt, the former German chancellor, once commented, "If I'm selling to you, I speak your language. If I am buying, *dann müssen Sie Deutsch sprechen*" (then you must speak German) (Nurden, 1997, p. 39). After the January 7, 2015, killings of 11 staff members of the *Charlie Hebdo* French satirical weekly newspaper by two brothers from Al Qaeda's branch in Yemen, about 2 million people met in Paris in a rally of national and international unity against the killings. The phrase "*Je suis Charlie*" (I am Charlie) became a slogan of support and freedom of speech.

Linguistic diversity is an important aspect of global diversity. Managing a workforce that does not share a common language can present a major challenge to both employees and management. Although most of the discussion related to the use of foreign languages in business refers to international organizations with business partners or subsidiaries in different countries, verbal communication may also present a challenge within countries. In Guinea, for example, a large segment of the population barely speaks French, the official language of Guinea (Auclair, 1992); India has two main languages (Hindi and English), 14 official languages, and thousands more languages and dialects (The World Factbook, 2015); and in South Africa's metropolitan area of Alexandra, nine major Bantu languages are claimed as the home language, and many residents also speak some English, Afrikaans, or Portuguese (Heine & Nurse, 2000; McCall, Ngeva, & Mbebe, 1997). Linguistic diversity is strongly related to people's and nations' history, heritage, and sense of identity, and can influence economic and political development both positively and negatively. As Ginsburgh and Weber (2011) point out, on the one hand suppression and elimination of linguistic diversity was part of the ugly heritage of colonialism and should be condemned. On the other hand, a plethora of languages within a nation (e.g., 527 languages in Nigeria, 217 in the Democratic Republic of Congo, thousands in India) could cause difficulties such as miscommunication, institutional wastefulness, inefficiencies, and, when tied to strong ethnic, national, or religious identity, even war (Ginsburgh & Weber, 2011).

Often, misunderstandings occur when one person is not familiar with all aspects of the other's language. A classic example of such mistaken translation resulted in a horned Moses holding the Ten

Commandments in the famous Michelangelo statue (circa 1513). The original biblical Hebrew text describes Moses coming down Mount Sinai after meeting God "with his face radiating," or literally with rays of light coming out of his face (Exodus 34:29). However, the Hebrew word for *ray* is the same as the word for *horn—keren*. Michelangelo, relying on Jerome's vulgate translation of the Old Testament, which apparently confused the two meanings, sculpted the famous statue of Moses with two horns protruding from his head. On the other hand, sometimes the use of a foreign language can add a different dimension to the discussion because people who are not native speakers can pick up errors that native speakers will not see. Adler and Gundersen (2008, p. 74) describe an example of a business using this perceptual characteristic to its advantage: For proofreading, the Canadian National Railway gives reports written in English to bilingual francophone employees and reports written in French to bilingual anglophone employees.

Language Fluency and Cultural Fluency

When dealing with foreign languages and different cultures, language fluency and cultural fluency are not the same—although they are related. Language fluency refers to the possession of linguistic skills that allow one to function much like a native speaker of the language. Cultural fluency refers to the ability to identify, understand, and apply the communicative behaviors of members of the other group; it is the ability to go back and forth between two or more cultures; to send and receive messages in a way that ensures that the meanings of the messages of both the sender and receiver regularly match (Glazier, 2003; Molinsky, 2005; Oyserman, 2011; Staub, 2009). Children of immigrants who grow up speaking the language of their parents at home, but without connection to their broader cultural heritage, face great difficulties when returning to their homeland, even though they may speak the language fluently. For example, according to U.S. laws, legal aliens who commit a crime may be deported to their home country. After the 9/11 terrorist attacks of 2001, the United States began enforcing its immigration laws more vigorously, and more immigrants who committed crimes were deported. Among the deportees was a large group of Cambodian nationals who grew up in the United States and were highly acculturated to the American way of life. Although their parents spoke Khmer at home, they did not teach them about their cultural heritage because they wanted to forget the horrors of the Khmer Rouge and Pol Pot regimes. As a result, although they were fluent in Khmer, these deportees experienced great difficulties adjusting to the Cambodian way of life and culture.[6]

Nonverbal Communication

Nonverbal barriers to cross-cultural communication include body language—movements, gestures, and postures—as well as use of artifacts such as personal adornments and the physical setting. Trust and respect are often conveyed through nonverbal rather than verbal communication. A case in point is the controversy in the U.S. media ignited by U.S. president Barack Obama's bow to the Japanese emperor during his Asian tour in November 2009. Some interpreted the bow as a culturally sensitive sign of respect, but others complained it was an indication of subservience unbefitting a U.S. president ("Obama's Bow in Japan," 2009; "The Presidential Bow," 2009). Obama's defenders attributed the bow to his multicultural background and worldly awareness, while his critics, citing a tradition that the U.S. president bows to no one, claimed it was a sign of his naiveté. The supporters also noted that the bow, a typical Asian form of greeting, was also accompanied by a very Western firm handshake, while the critics noted that the very low bow, practically a 90-degree angle, was a gesture of extreme deference and subordination. Either way, it is clear that this one nonverbal gesture spoke volumes. Indeed, it was discussed more than any of the speeches the president and his hosts gave during the tour.

One person who is using nonverbal communication to combat prejudice and discrimination against refugees from predominantly Muslim countries in Europe is comedian filmmaker Firas Alshater. A Syrian refugee himself, Alshater engaged in a street social experiment to test how ordinary Germans react to refugees and if they would give a hug to him as he stood, blindfolded, in the middle of a large public square in Berlin (see Box 8.2). In addition to body gestures, artifacts can be used to transfer important information, and those, too, need to be understood and interpreted in their specific cultural and national contexts (see Box 8.3 for an example of the use of the physical setting to convey respect in different cultures).

Clothing has long been used to communicate rank (e.g., the cardinal robes and the queen's crown), mood (e.g., mourning clothes), occasion (e.g., wedding outfits in different cultures), and even seasons (e.g., the geisha's seasonal kimono colors, or light and dark business attire in the West, depending on the time of year). Clothes are an extension of the body and closely relate to the person's gender, age, socioeconomic status, and national origin. When doing business in a foreign country, one often faces the question of whether to wear the business attire that is common in one's own culture or in the host country. Although in modern times the Western business suit goes a long way for men, it is not the same for women. Western clothes may be perceived as inappropriately revealing by many cultures, and wearing them might be interpreted as disrespectful to the host culture and perceived as offensive. On the other hand, wearing a traditional outfit, such as the Muslim attire of *abaya*, *burqa*, or *hijab*,[7] may be seen as confining or even degrading by Western women. The U.S. Army's policy of "strongly encouraging" army servicewomen to conform to Saudi rules and wear *abayas* while serving in Saudi Arabia has long been controversial.[8] When Madeleine Albright, the U.S. secretary of state during Bill Clinton's presidency, visited Egypt and Saudi Arabia in 1999, she found a middle-ground solution. Although she did not wear the traditional Muslim attire that is expected from women in that country, she wore dresses and skirts that were longer than the ones she wore in Washington. She also donned a wide-brimmed hat, thus walking the fine line between conveying respect for her hosts' culture and her own. In contrast, Mahatma Gandhi, the father of modern India and the leader of its liberation movement from Great Britain, wore just a loincloth during his visit to England in 1931, shocking the conservative British society (Brown &

Box 8.2

HUGS FOR INCLUSION: USING A UNIVERSAL NONVERBAL GESTURE TO COMMUNICATE ACCEPTANCE

In a YouTube video that went viral, Firas Alshater, a comedian and filmmaker, conducted a social experiment to find out how ordinary Germans react to refugees. Alshater stood blindfolded in the middle of the Alexanderplatz square in Berlin next to a sign in German that read, "I am a Syrian refugee. I trust you. Do you trust me? Hug me!" He waited a long time for someone to hug him but after the first person did, many passersby came over and gave Alshater hugs. In the hour and a half that he stood there, about 40 people hugged him. The video, posted on YouTube on January 27, 2016, received more than 700,000 hits. Alshater, who immigrated to Berlin as an asylum seeker in 2013, spent 9 months in jail for documenting the atrocities committed by the Syrian regime. He concludes his video by stating, "I learned that the Germans need a bit of time but then they can't be stopped. That's why I believe the integration will be a success . . . Eventually."

Sources: "Zukar 01—Who Are Those Germans?" Retrieved from https://www.youtube.com/watch?v=ZozLHZFEblY; Ma (2016); Shuster (2016a).

Box 8.3

HOW CAN THE IMPORTANT GUEST SIT AT THE HEAD OF A ROUND TABLE? THE USE OF THE PHYSICAL SETTING TO CONVEY RESPECT IN BUSINESS COMMUNICATION

To convey respect to a high-ranking visitor, Europeans and North Americans have the person sit at the head of a rectangular table. A round table is typically reserved for occasions when the participants are presumed to be equals. A prime example is the famous legend of King Arthur of Camelot and his Knights of the Round Table. King Arthur conveyed the equality among his chosen knights through the use of a round table. Similarly, in modern times, the representatives to the UN Security Council all sit at a round table. The assumption of these Western cultures is that there is no way to identify a more- or less-respected seat at a round table, and therefore no way to indicate the relative ranking of the participants.

In the Chinese culture, on the other hand, the ranking of the participants can be clearly identified by the way they sit at a round table: The highest-ranking participant in a meeting will be seated directly facing the main entrance to the room, and the rest of the participants, in descending order of rank, will be seated to his or her left and right sides until the lowest-ranking person will have his or her back to the entrance. This follows a similar logic of circular-ranked importance expressed in the Chinese perception of geography. The Chinese tradition indicates that the imperial palace is the most important place in the world, and from there, in circles of decreased importance, are the other areas of Beijing, the rest of China, and the rest of the world.

Fee, 2008). The British media interpreted his attire as primitive and disrespectful, but Gandhi was sending a clear message of independence and defiance as well as respect for Indian culture and traditions: "It was a rejection not only of the material products of Europe, but also of the European value system with its criteria of decency" (Tarlo, 1996, p. 75).

Over the years, more work organizations and international bodies relaxed strict clothing requirements to accommodate the traditional or religious attire. For example, Disney allowed a Muslim employee at its Orange County park to wear a specially designed headscarf after initially objecting to her religious head covering. Initially, Noor Abdallah, who worked at a ticket booth in the Disneyland park, was told that she could not wear the hijab and was offered another job away from the public. After she refused, the park worked with her to design a covering—a blue scarf topped with a beret—to match her costume and meet her religious demands ("Disney, Muslim Worker," 2010). In preparation for the 2012 Olympic Games in London, FIFA (Fédération Internationale de Football Association) overturned its ban on women playing football with their heads covered, opening the doors to women athletes from traditional Muslim countries to compete in the Olympics. Other international sports bodies have also relaxed clothing rules in ways that allowed more Muslim women to compete in the games such as Saudi Arabian judo player Wodjan Ali Seraj Abdulrahim, Saudi Arabian runner Sarah Attar, and U.S. fencer Ibtihaj Muhammad (Khaleeli, 2012).

Cross-Cultural Communication Styles

A question that is very relevant for any business transaction is whether and to what extent members of a particular cultural group will alter their preferred communication style when interacting with members from another cultural group. Utilizing the theoretical perspective presented earlier, will members of collectivist cultures become more direct and task oriented in their communication with members of individualist cultures? Will members of individualist cultures become more concerned with the needs of others and in preserving harmony in the transaction? Or will one or both groups become more entrenched in their own communication style?

It is plausible to assume that adapting to the other's communication style will generate a perception of similarity and familiarity that will contribute to creating a positive atmosphere in cross-cultural encounters (e.g., Byrne's 1971 similarity attraction paradigm; Foley, Linnehan, Greenhaus, & Weer, 2006; Lee & Gudykunst, 2001). Intergroup contact theory and research, originally proposed as a "contact hypothesis" by Allport (1954/1979), suggests that intergroup contact typically reduces prejudice (Brown & Hewstone, 2005; Harrington & Miller, 1992; MacInnis & Page-Gould, 2015; Pettigrew, Tropp, Wagner, & Christ, 2011).

Allport's original conditions for optimal contact, such as equal status and common goals, facilitate the effect but are not necessary conditions, and there are other positive outcomes for intergroup contact such as greater trust. Research findings apply to many types of groups including different ages, genders, nations, ethnicities, races, sexual orientations, and abilities, and the major mediators between intergroup contact and such positive outcomes are affective—reduced anxiety and empathy (Pettigrew et al., 2011). On the other hand, because cross-cultural encounters create uncertainty and provoke anxiety, participants may resort to the familiarity of their own cultural norms and even more strongly exhibit their normative communication styles, especially when the contact is nonvoluntary or threatening (Lau, Lam, & Deutsch Salamon, 2008; Laurent, 1984; Pettigrew et al., 2011; Tse, Francis, & Walls, 1994). A study conducted in New Zealand supports the latter (see Box 8.4).

Box 8.4

ARE MEMBERS OF A CULTURAL GROUP INTERACTING WITH A MEMBER OF ANOTHER GROUP MORE LIKELY TO CHANGE THEIR ORIGINAL COMMUNICATION STYLE OR REINFORCE IT?

Pekerti and Thomas (2003) examined intercultural and intracultural communication styles between two groups in New Zealand: Anglo-Europeans, representing a low-context individualist culture, and East Asians, representing a high-context collectivist culture. Participants in the experiment were 96 students at a large New Zealand university, one half of whom were Anglo-European New Zealanders (Pakeha) and one half of whom were students from Asia (primarily from China) who were first generation, with less than 10 years in New Zealand (to control for acculturation). Students were randomly assigned to one of two conditions—interaction with members of their own cultural group or interaction with members of the other cultural group.[9] The assignment was ranking of 15 crimes by their severity, and participants were given no more than 15 minutes to rank the crimes by consensus. The interactions were videotaped and coded by independent observers for the occurrence and intensity of each cultural communication behavior. The results showed that interacting with members of a different culture increased the tendency to use the cultural communication style of their own culture. Specifically, in interactions with Anglo-Europeans, the Asian students were more likely than they were with members of their own culture to accommodate and change their opinions in order to preserve harmony. A similar trend was apparent with the Anglo-European students, who were more likely than they were with members of their own cultural group to be direct and task oriented in their interaction with Asian students. The authors attribute this behavior to the uncertainty involved in cross-cultural interactions, which increases people's tendency to rely on their own cultural norms. The authors conclude that in cross-cultural communication, the dominant tendency is exaggeration of one's own cultural behaviors rather than adaptation.

The tendency to resort to the familiarity of one's own cultural norms may be even stronger when facing a conflict. Sometimes due to misunderstanding, cultural ignorance, or fear of losing face, this behavior can have a toll both in human relationships and in financial outcomes. Mangaliso (2001) describes an incident in a South African mining company that mushroomed into a labor dispute and a prolonged strike that cost the company greatly—all because management was unable to appropriately communicate with its workers. In the beginning of the labor dispute, the workers invited top management to address them on the issue in a public forum. Management denied their request, however, and responded instead by sending messages through envoys and written statements posted on bulletin boards. In the high-context collectivist culture of the South African workers, management's impersonal and task-oriented communication was entirely inappropriate. It failed to take into consideration the South African concept of *ubuntu*, meaning humaneness, consideration for compassion and community—similar to the Chinese concept of *quanxi*, the Korean *chaebol*, and the Spanish *simpatia* (mentioned in Chapter 9), all indicating a cultural emphasis on relationships (Hurwich-Reiss, Wadsworth, & Markman, 2014; Sanchez-Burks & Lee, 2007; Triandis, Marin, Lisansky, & Betancourt, 1984). Frustrated and humiliated, the workers began a strike that lasted more than 2 weeks and resulted in several hundreds of employees being fired and several million dollars of company losses. One of the employee representatives was reported to have said, "The only thing that employees wanted was for top management to come and address us. Just to speak to us" (Mangaliso, 2001, p. 23). In retrospect, the strike and its costly consequences could have been avoided if management understood the cultural context of its workers and was able to communicate with them in an appropriate manner.

Summary and Conclusion

To succeed in managing a workforce that is increasingly diverse and multinational, managers need to understand cultural differences and to become competent in cross-cultural communication. This chapter examines the cultural context of the global workplace and analyzes communication patterns that facilitate or block effective cross-cultural communication.

Research on cultural dimensions and the wealth of studies inspired by Geert Hofstede's pioneering work provide an important context for understanding cross-cultural interactions in the workplace. His four axes of power distance (authority and social inequality), individualism versus collectivism (cohesion and loyalty to the group), masculinity versus femininity (competition in contrast to care for others), avoidance of uncertainty (tolerance for ambiguity), and long- versus short-term orientation (fostering of virtues oriented toward future rewards in contrast to virtues related to the past such as respect for tradition) have clear implications for individual and group expectations related to acceptable behaviors in the workplace. Whether employees expect to be rewarded, for example, for individual excellence or for a team effort depends to a large extent on the cultural perception of individualism versus collectivism in their society. The GLOBE project, led by Robert J. House, examined nine cultural dimensions of leadership worldwide through a longitudinal study in 62 world cultures. The principal outcome of the study was the development of six universally shared dimensions of leadership: (a) charismatic/value based, (b) team oriented, (c) self-protective, (d) participative, (e) humane oriented, and (f) autonomous.

Defined as *the use of symbols to convey meaning*, communication in today's global environment has become largely cross-cultural. Cross-cultural communication involves several potential barriers that are related to the use of verbal and nonverbal methods to convey meanings that may or may not be the same in the cultures of origin of the participants. Miscommunication occurs when the original intent of the person transmitting the message is different from the meaning that is received by the other person, and it is more likely to occur between participants who belong to different cultures. Often, misunderstandings occur when one person is not familiar with all aspects of the other's language, is not fluent or articulate in the language used for the business transaction, or miscommunicates or misreads nonverbal communication such as movement or gestures.

Effective communication with employees, customers, shareholders, regulators, and other business partners presents a serious challenge, even when conducted within the same cultural framework. The challenge is compounded when communication involves two or more diverse cultural contexts. When one partner to a business communication misreads the cultural clues encoded in the other person's message, the transaction can result in a misunderstanding, hurt emotions, conflicts, and lost business opportunities. On the other hand, making the effort to understand other cultures and to communicate effectively within them can go a long way in fostering trust, conveying respect, and eventually securing mutually beneficial business deals.

Notes

1. See Javidan and House (2001, p. 289).

2. For a summary table of key definitions of culture, see Erez and Earley (1993).

3. See, for example, Margaret Mead (1935/2001) and Ruth Benedict (1934/1989).

4. The interesting historical/political context to the inception of the *Concorde* project was that the project was designed in response to the space race between the United States and the Soviet Union in the 1960s. Its goal was to demonstrate the technological abilities of Western Europe as a center of world power, independent from the United States and the Soviet Union. This was the impetus for France and England to put aside their historical animosity and work collaboratively on this project ("History of the Supersonic Airliner," 2001; "The World," 2003).

5. See "Text: Kennedy's Berlin Speech" (2003).

6. See "The World" (2003).

7. *Abaya* is a head-to-toe, traditional Muslim dress made from black, lightweight fabric that has two layers; *burqa* similarly provides cover from head to toe and covers the face so that only the eyes are exposed, sometimes behind a netlike fabric; and *hijab* is a traditional Muslim headscarf.

8. Lieutenant Colonel Martha McSally has led a long struggle to end this policy by the Pentagon. McSally, who was the first woman U.S. service member to fly in combat, was stationed in Saudi Arabia, where she was forced to wear the *abaya* and travel in the rear seats of vehicles in accordance with local custom. Congressman Jim Langevin of Rhode Island joined McSally's fight and called the army's requirement "gender discrimination," saying that "women make first-class soldiers and should not be treated like second-class citizens" ("Langevin Seeks," 2002).

9. The study used a 2×2 (culture × condition) design, and in assignment to the two experimental conditions, the researchers used blocks by gender, age, and culture to control for possible effects of these variables on the outcome variable of communication style.

9

Interpersonal Relationships in a Global Work Context

JEFFREY SANCHEZ-BURKS
AND MICHÀLLE E. MOR BARAK

On his first day back from vacation, Gabriel, a Mexican engineering specialist working for a large multinational corporation based in Germany, received his next project assignment. The automotive plant's assignments typically lasted 6 to 8 months and involved highly interdependent multifunctional teams that worked under intense deadlines. Gabriel glanced at the names of the other people assigned to the team. It was not usual that the members would be unfamiliar with one another, but Gabriel recognized the names of three new team members. He had heard that they were all highly regarded for their skills in their areas of expertise. However, from what he had heard about their previous assignments, he worried that their exclusive and impersonal focus to tasks and time schedules—and, frankly, their unfriendliness—would not work well with the rest of the team. In previous assignments, Gabriel's teams had enjoyed a friendly atmosphere (i.e., they would go out for drinks together, sometimes inviting each other to their homes on weekends). In Gabriel's opinion, that made the team productive and successful. He worried that the new team would experience little harmony and much interpersonal conflict.

With trepidation, Gabriel decided to ask for another assignment, fearing the lack of interpersonal harmony, despite the high level of collective talent, would impede the team's ability to succeed on its core objectives. Upon hearing the request, Iris, the German project coordinator, was

---

Jeffrey Sanchez-Burks, PhD, is a professor of management and organizations at the University of Michigan Stephen M. Ross School of Business.

surprised about Gabriel's concern. For Iris, the issue was straightforward: The new people were excellent professionals who would help the team produce better outcomes with a shorter time schedule; therefore, Gabriel's concern for the team's productivity was unfounded.

As demonstrated by this incident, people from different cultures often bring very different sets of assumptions about appropriate ways to coordinate and communicate in business relationships (Sanchez-Burks & Lee, 2007). Culture infuses meaning into the social situation. Whereas interpersonal harmony may be regarded as essential to task success in one society, such as Mexico, it may be seen as less consequential in another, such as Germany. As we will discuss in this chapter, one's perceptions, values, and behavior in such situations reflect deep-seated beliefs about the nature of interpersonal work relationships. To understand and manage these differences requires understanding the nature of cultural diversity and how it influences relational and communication styles (Chua, Morris, & Mor, 2012; Sanchez-Burks & Lee, 2007).

There are different levels of cultural diversity, as described in Chapter 6. Some levels are more obvious to the observer than others. The most salient level of diversity to workers and scholars alike is demographic differences such as gender, ethnicity, or nationality. These categories are important to the extent that a person's identity and others' perceptions of them are influenced by these social categories. For example, ethnic preferences and prejudices can affect dynamics between a Japanese sales representative and a Peruvian distributor discussing logistics in Lima. The mere perception of differences in demographic category, such as *Japanese* and *Peruvian,* can facilitate or sabotage business relations depending on one's beliefs (see Chapter 7 for a discussion of social categorization's impact on intergroup and interpersonal relationships).

The other, more implicit level of difference that people encounter in a global marketplace entails cultural variation in cognitive, communicative, and relational styles. Although the markers of diversity at this level can be difficult to observe directly, they nonetheless exert a powerful influence on people's preferences and team dynamics, as illustrated in the opening example. Broadly speaking, culture refers to shared understandings made manifest in act and artifact about what is true, good, and efficient (Redfield, 1941; Sanchez-Burks & Lee, 2007; also see Chapter 8 for an expanded discussion on culture). These shared understandings about proper relational styles found within cultures create particular challenges for intercultural business that have less to do with differences in ethnicity and more to do with deep-seated cultural variation between groups (Sanchez-Burks, Nisbett, & Ybarra, 2000). This variation is revealed in how members of two cultures make sense of a situation, the appropriate way to convey bad news, and the extent to which one should or should not mix business and personal matters with colleagues and business partners. As a result, this level of cultural diversity can derail what might otherwise be a promising intercultural partnership.

This chapter begins by describing how culture shapes the mental models people use to coordinate and communicate. We then discuss an organizing framework for these diverse cultural mental models.

We describe how cultural mental models influence people's emotional involvement or detachment with coworkers and business partners and beliefs about the importance of interpersonal harmony and conflict. Finally, we discuss how this diversity shapes communication styles and the challenges this cultural variation presents to creating a worldwide inclusive workplace.

Cultural Styles and Relational Mental Models

There is no such thing as an interpersonal style that is culture neutral. As a result of a cognitive bias social psychologists refer to as *naive realism* (Ross & Ward, 1996), we mistakenly assume that what people in our immediate environment consider appropriate and proper forms of behaving and communicating reflect the natural way things should be and therefore are universally correct. Even when we become aware of cultural differences, this bias often leads us to devalue others' relational work style as "incorrect" and "unprofessional" (Uhlmann, Heaphy, Ashford, Zhu, & Sanchez-Burks, 2013). Indeed, the particular cultural contexts in which people are raised and begin their careers create culturally unique relational mental models.

Relational mental models influence our perceptions and the way we communicate and relate to others. Bartlett (1932, 1958) is credited with first proposing the concept of a relational mental model, which he referred to as a mental model. He arrived at the concept from studies of memory he conducted in which participants misremembered details of stories that were not actually in the original stories. He suggested that participants' use of preexisting mental models to understand the story shaped their interpretation and subsequent recall of the stories' details. Bartlett's work, replicated and elaborated on in subsequent social cognition studies, provides insights into how mental models serve as a framework for encoding, understanding, and remembering information. Later studies (e.g., Knight & Nisbett, 2007; Nisbett & Miyamoto, 2005; Nisbett, Peng, Choi, & Norenzayan, 2001; Quinn & Holland, 1987) have demonstrated the importance of mental models in understanding culturally related variation in thinking styles. Relational mental models refer specifically to thinking styles about interpersonal relationships in specific situations (Baldwin, 1992; Baldwin & Dandeneau, 2005). Cultural mental models allow people to coordinate thought and action by creating shared expectations about how a social interaction should unfold, what behaviors are appropriate, and which elements of an interaction are important to notice (Baldwin, 1992; Baldwin & Dandeneau, 2005; Fiske & Haslam, 1996). In many Latin American societies, for example, it is inappropriate to abruptly end one business meeting in order to avoid being late to another appointment. The relational mental model used in Latin cultures places priority on the relationship in the present moment. This can be contrasted with the relational mental models found in Northern European and European American cultures, where proper social interactions involve strict adherence to punctuality and schedules. (For an illustration of attempts to alter relational mental models for punctuality norms, see Box 9.1.) Within each society, relational mental models facilitate interpersonal harmony by providing shared expectations about, for example, when to end one meeting and begin the next. Problems arise, however, during intercultural encounters when people are guided by different relational mental models. For example, the Mexican is likely to interpret his European American colleague's abrupt ending of the meeting according to the minute hand on the clock as "rude" and impersonal. Likewise, the European American will perceive his Mexican colleague's lack of respect for punctuality as "unprofessional." Both are interested in successful business relationships; however, the relational mental models they bring to the table influence their specific approach toward achieving this goal.

Box 9.1

RELATIONAL MENTAL MODELS ABOUT TIME IN ECUADOR

The Ecuadorian national government once launched a campaign designed to eliminate the social practice of arriving 15 to 30 minutes late to business meetings and social events (jokingly referred to as running on "Ecuadorian time"). Citing the financial costs of tardiness, which is estimated at $724 million a year, the campaign began with a national "clock synchronization ceremony." Hundreds of officials gathered in the heart of Quito's downtown to mark a ceremonious start to the drive. The population was urged by President Lucio Gutiérrez to be on time "for the sake of God, the country, our people, and our consciences" ("Ecuador Punctuality," 2003). The ceremony did not begin on time.

Researchers have documented relational mental models that are unique to a particular culture and mental models that reflect broad cultural dimensions. In China, there is a culture-specific mental model based on *quanxi* (Tsui & Farh, 1997), in which one is expected to attend carefully to the interconnections among business colleagues and partners. In Korea, a mental model reflecting *chaebol* (Kim, 1988), or company familism, structures business relationships to reflect both work and personal features. Mexican business relationships reflect a *simpatia* mental model (Diaz-Guerrero, 1967; Sanchez-Burks, 2002; Triandis, Marin, Lisansky, & Betancourt, 1984), which places importance on proactively creating rapport and personal connections. In contrast, the influence of *Protestant relational ideology* in European American culture (Sanchez-Burks, 2002, 2005; Sanchez-Burks & Uhlmann, 2013; Uhlmann & Sanchez-Burks, 2014) maintains a sharp distinction between the relational mental models used at work and outside work. (For an example of how differences in European American and Mexican relational mental models lead to different memories of "what just happened" in a team meeting, see Box 9.2.)

Box 9.2

WHAT JUST HAPPENED IN THAT MEETING?

In a series of field studies on workgroups, Mexicans, Mexican Americans, and European Americans were asked to view recordings of team meetings and later report what they could remember about what happened in the meeting. Although there were no cultural differences in their ability to recall task-related information such as progress on the agenda or questions raised, there was significant difference in their memory for interpersonal dynamics. European Americans were far less likely than either the Mexicans or Mexican Americans to recall interpersonal and social-emotional dynamics, such as one person being rude or friendly to another or one person being interrupted by another (Sanchez-Burks et al., 2000).

Relational mental models characterized as broad cultural dimensions include independence-interdependence, high/low context, and individualism-collectivism (Hofstede & Hofstede, 2005; Triandis, 1996). The distinction between independent and interdependent self-construals, for example, focuses on a relational mental model in which perceptions, emotions, and behavior are focused on the individual in the situation, compared with a mental model in which the focus is the connection relationships within the group. Both culture-specific and these broader-level mental models serve as the foundation for how people from different cultures interpret, communicate, and approach interpersonal relationships.

The influence of relational mental models is revealed in numerous interpersonal dynamics of business relationships. At the micro level, for example, relational mental models influence the degree of nonverbal coordination between two people interacting. People attentive to relational concerns tend to unconsciously mirror the gestures and posture of their counterparts in a social interaction and as a consequence increase interpersonal rapport (Chartrand & Bargh, 1999; Sanchez-Burks et al., 2000; Van Swol, 2003). For example, if one of the parties to a conversation is speaking softly and not using hand gestures, after a while, the attentive observer is likely to do the same, which will increase the first person's sense of comfort and create more harmony in the relationship. When people are "out of sync" in their nonverbal gestures as a result of diversity in relational mental models, it can increase levels of anxiety and can actually reduce one's performance in the situation. This was demonstrated in a study conducted at a Fortune 500 company in which a European American interviewed a pool of European Americans and Latinos under instructions to subtly mirror the nonverbal gestures of half of the applicants (e.g., lean forward when the applicant leaned forward) and not mirror the gestures of the other half. Videotaped recordings of the interviews were shown to experts who evaluated the performance of the applicants under these two conditions. The study found that interview performance was contingent on level of nonverbal coordination for the Latino applicants but significantly less so for the European American men and women (Sanchez-Burks, Bartel, & Blount, 2009). Thus, subtle cultural differences in relational mental models between interviewer and applicant can sabotage the success of intercultural workplace interactions. Such findings illustrate how important understanding cultural diversity in relational mental models can be for individuals and the organization. For organizations to sustain effective recruiting and selection efforts, and thus an important competitive advantage in the marketplace, they must manage such implicit cultural diversity.

The influence of relational mental models on attention can also affect managers' perceptions of what motivates their subordinates. DeVoe and Iyengar (2004) report in a study on employees of a multinational retail bank that the intrinsic motivation of subordinates (e.g., a desire to work hard because of one's personal interest in the project rather than for financial rewards or threats of punishment) is more likely to be noticed by Japanese and Mexican managers than European American managers, presumably because the latter are guided by relational mental models that are less sensitive to such personal information.

In sum, experience and socialization within different cultural contexts create culturally unique relational mental models. In turn, these relational mental models provide specific templates that guide our perceptions, communication, and behavior in social situations. In organizations, these relational mental models shape a variety of dynamics, including what people notice and take away from business meetings and the degree to which they coordinate their nonverbal behaviors and are affected by the overall level of coordination. These mental models also influence managers' perceptions of what motivates their subordinates and their accuracy vis-à-vis subordinates' actual interests and motivations. Together, the notion of culturally grounded relational mental models provides a foundation for understanding what people from different societies "bring to the table" in diverse organizations and international business ventures. In the next section, we discuss specific organizing frameworks for understanding cultural diversity in relational mental models. These frameworks provide a way to understand how cultural mental models produce variation in beliefs about notions of professionalism, proper networking strategies, and harmony and conflict.

Diversity in Interpersonal Relationships

Emotional Detachment Versus Emotional Involvement

Cultural divides that challenge intercultural relationships often stem from the way individuals integrate or differentiate two types of relational mental models: (a) task-focused mental models and (b) social-emotional mental models. When people are guided solely by a task-focused mental model, they focus exclusively on elements of the situation directly related to the task, such as whether progress on the agenda is being made, steps are being taken to meet upcoming deadlines, and other issues related more to the job than the people involved. In contrast, people guided solely by social-emotional mental models will focus their attention and effort on emotional and interpersonal concerns.

As shown in Figure 9.1, the level of integration of these two mental models varies along a continuum. In cultures where these concerns are combined, people maintain a dual focus on task and interpersonal concerns. Dual attention does not necessarily mean equal attention at all times. That is, emphasis on relational concerns relative to task concerns and vice versa can vary from one culture to the next and between individuals in the same culture. It does mean, however, that there is no sharp distinction between the two areas and that they are intertwined. For example, a manager will coordinate her group's efforts to be productive while closely managing interpersonal harmony. Workers in these societies are more likely to mingle work and personal issues, go out with their coworkers on the weekend, and have a preference to work with their family and friends (Kacperczyk, Sanchez-Burks, & Baker, 2009; Morris, Podolny, & Sullivan, 2008). At the other end of the continuum are societies with more differentiated relational styles. Here, managers work hard to maintain a sharp divide between one's work and personal life. At work, people operate with an implicit understanding to put personal matters aside and to avoid emotions and other concerns believed to harm one's image of the polite but impersonal professional. This approach can be wise, indeed, even when the individual does not personally desire to maintain a strong boundary. Organizations serve as institutional mechanisms that reinforce cultural norms. As such, those that adhere to the prevailing norms are more attractive candidates (Dumas & Sanchez-Burks, 2015; Uhlmann, et al., 2013). One manager with a strong differentiated style reported this in an interview on the meaning of professionalism: "It is a death wish to talk about personal matters or get emotional at work." Pressures to tune out one's own and others' emotions do come at a cost: Individuals in these cultures underutilize their emotional intelligence abilities while at work (Ybarra, Kross, & Sanchez-Burks, 2014).

There is tremendous cultural variation in the form and content of social-emotional mental models. In East Asian societies, workers preserve harmony passively by not "rocking the boat," whereas in Latin societies, people proactively create harmony through open displays of warmth and graciousness, even to strangers. Despite disparate ways of fostering social-emotional ties, interdependent styles are common in much of the world, including East Asian, Latin, and Middle Eastern societies (Ayman & Chemers, 1983; Earley & Erez, 1997; Hampden-Turner & Trompenaars, 1993; Markus & Kitayama, 1991). These differences can be complex, blurring the lines between culture and nationality. For example, immigrants and members of ethnic groups whose culture of origin used the interdependent cultural mental model are highly likely to use it even when living in a different cultural context. Research has provided evidence that Latinos (both Mexicans and Mexican Americans) are guided by a concern with social-emotional aspects of workforce relations to a far greater degree than are Anglo Americans, and the relationship holds true even when the Latinos reside in a differentiated culture such as the United States (Sanchez-Burks et al., 2000).

There can also be gender differences in interpersonal style. For example, women have been found to be more attentive than men to social-emotional aspects of work relationships and therefore more likely

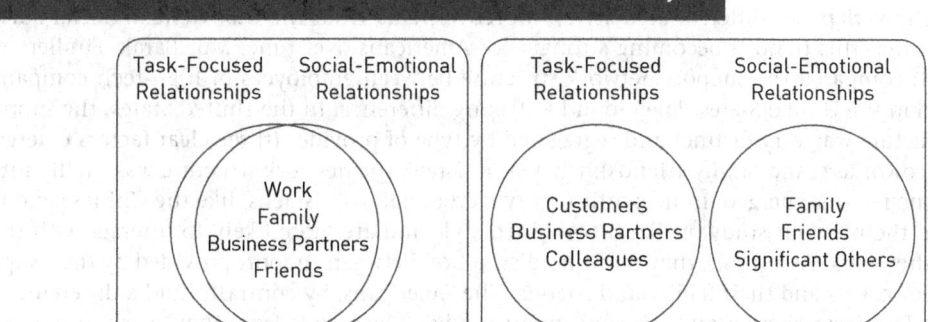

FIGURE 9.1 • Combined Versus Differentiated Relational Styles

Source: Adapted from Sanchez-Burks, J. (1999). Ascetic Protestantism and cultural schemas for relational sensitivity in the workplace. Unpublished doctoral dissertation, Department of Psychology, University of Michigan, Ann Arbor.

to use the interdependent relational style, even in cultural contexts in which the differentiated style is more prevalent, such as in North America (Reardon, 1995). However, in contrast to cultural differences, research suggests that gender differences can be quite inconsistent, emerging in some studies but not others (Holtgraves, 1997; Sanchez-Burks et al., 2003; Tannen, 1990). At this point, it appears that differences in relational styles that may exist between men and women are exhibited within a particular culture, appearing to be smaller in magnitude relative to differences between cultures. For example, although American women may have more interdependent self-construals than American men, they are less interdependent than Japanese men and more independent than Japanese women (Kashima et al., 1995).

An exception in this general tendency toward interdependent relational styles is the United States, particularly among European Americans. Here, acting "professional" means suppressing authentic displays of social emotionality, maintaining a divide between one's work and personal life, and not letting interpersonal issues stand in the way—the "emotional overcoat" theory (Mann, 1999). In fact, professional emotionality is prescribed in these cultures where employees are expected to be courteous in a friendly way and not display strong emotions, either positive or negative, in the workplace. Bringing authentic emotionality to the workplace (e.g., being sad, depressed, or overly happy) is frowned upon and considered unprofessional behavior. Employees may be expected to display "scripted" emotions such as the "Have a nice day" script for many jobs in the service sector in which workers are required to be at all times cheerful and helpful to customers to encourage a positive experience and repeat service (e.g., training programs for telemarketers teach them how to speak on the phone with a smile in their voice so the smile will be obvious to the person on the other end of the phone line). Other organizational positions having less customer contact, as well as jobs such as lawyers, physicians, and nurses, are expected to be cool and emotionally detached in order to project professional competence (Mann, 1999). In either of these cases, the prescribed job-related emotional script typical in the differentiated cultural context requires workers to put effort into acting out emotions they do not feel or to suppress emotions they do feel in order to meet the emotional scripts of their jobs.

Variation in how social and task concerns are structured appears also at the social network level. Morris and his colleagues (2008) investigated the overlap between work and social ties among Citibank employees in Spain, China, Germany, and the United States. They asked bank branch employees how much they interact with coworkers during their time off, for example, on the weekend. Whereas the Spaniards and Chinese indicated it was quite common to interact with the same people inside and outside work (see combined style later in this chapter), Americans were significantly less likely to show such overlap (see differentiated style). Moreover, data from the U.S. General Social Survey (GSS) shows that this trend is becoming stronger for Americans over time. Mor Barak, Findler, and Wind (2003) compared the support network structure between employees of high-tech companies in Israel and in the United States. They found a striking difference. In the United States, the support network structure was very distinct and segregated by type of provider (three clear factors emerged: supervisor, coworkers, and family/friends), whereas in Israel, the network structure was highly interconnected (no factors emerged in the confirmatory factor analysis). Israelis, like the Chinese and the Spaniards in the previous study, utilize a combined style and are more likely to interact with their coworkers after work. As a result, they made no distinction between support provided by their supervisors and coworkers and their family and friends. The Americans, by contrast, hold a differentiated style and make a clear distinction between support provided by people from their work context and those from outside the work context (Dumas & Sanchez-Burks, 2015; Mor Barak et al., 2003).

The relative permeability of the work/nonwork boundary in a culture also has implications for how well individuals and teams are able to develop creative innovative ideas. All new ideas contain elements of previously unrelated ideas that are brought together to create new recombinations. When individuals, working alone or in teams, put out their nonwork unique and diverse experience and identities, they inherently narrow the array of ideas available for recombination (Cheng, Sanchez-Burks, & Lee, 2008; Sanchez-Burks, Karlesky, & Lee, 2015). This may explain why some of the most innovative firms in the United States, such as IDEO and Google, have created unique organizational cultures that explicitly encourage people to bring their nonwork selves into the workplace.

Finally, previous studies point to the fact that cultures of interdependence promote well-being, while cultures of independence tend to foster psychological distress (Bellah, Madsen, Sullivan, Swidler, & Tipton, 1985). Cultures of interdependence are composed of social structures that promote the good of the collective and the group's responsibility for taking care of its own. Social institutions in independent cultures, in contrast, support individual autonomy and personal fulfillment with the expectation that the individual will take care of his or her own needs. The result is a more fragmented support network, with less communication between its various parts and gaps in support that reduce its positive impact on well-being.

In sum, understanding the degree to which an individual's relational mental models reflect a combined versus differentiated style provides a basis for anticipating the challenges that will arise when people from cultures using these two styles attempt to work together (Sanchez-Burks, Lee, Nisbett, & Ybarra, 2007). These challenges include coordinating differences in the beliefs about the importance of social-emotional elements of work relations, their role in defining appropriate and professional behavior, and expectations about blending or differentiated work and nonwork social worlds.

Conflict and Harmony

Relational styles influence one's beliefs about conflict and its consequences (e.g., whether relationship conflict in a team is a threat to task success). The more that social-emotional elements are removed from one's workplace relational mental model (see differentiated style), the less vulnerable the team is perceived to be to social-emotional disruptions. According to Neuman, Sanchez-Burks, Goh, and Ybarra (2004), managers in combined-style cultures interpret conflict as an inherent barrier to success: A team, collaboration, or partnership without interpersonal harmony can rarely be productive (see Gabriel's alarm at the team's composition in the case vignette at the beginning of this chapter). On the other hand, managers in differentiated cultures, although not enjoying interpersonal discord, do not perceive it necessarily to be a limiting factor for a team's success (Iris's attitude to the team's composition in the case vignette demonstrates this approach). In a survey conducted in the United States, China, and

Korea, Neuman and his colleagues (2004) asked managers and business students to what extent task and relationship conflict were a roadblock to success, if at all (see Figure 9.2). Virtually all of the managers believed that task-related conflict was a barrier to success, surprising only in that research demonstrates that under certain circumstances it may provide a source of synergy and remedy to groupthink (for reviews, see Jehn & Bendersky, 2004). However, only the European Americans, particularly men, had a different belief about the effects of relationship conflict—as one manager stated, "It [relationship conflict] is unfortunate but not devastating." Research also demonstrates that the negative effect of process conflict on the other types of conflict (e.g., task, relationship) over time may be limited when members are able to resolve their process conflicts at the start of their time together (Greer, Jehn, & Mannix, 2008). On one hand, this optimism about the ability of a team to put aside interpersonal differences and focus on task may appear misguided, given the evidence that it is more of illusion than optimism (De Dreu & Weingart, 2003). On the other hand, more recent findings reveal that being highly attuned to social emotions can cause one to see relationship conflict even where it does not exist (Bechtoldt, Beersma, Rohrmann, & Sanchez-Burks, 2011).

The broader implication of these different beliefs about relationship conflict is that when conflict does arise in cross-cultural relationships (as it often does whenever people must work closely in interdependent

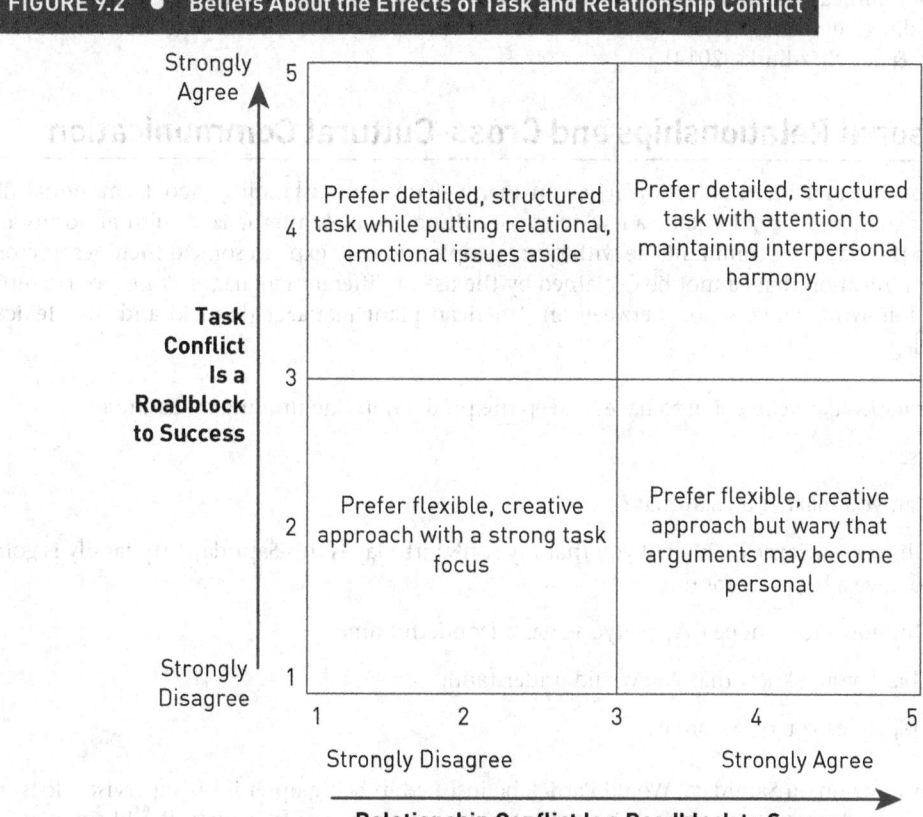

FIGURE 9.2 ● Beliefs About the Effects of Task and Relationship Conflict

Source: Neuman, E., Sanchez-Burks, J., Goh, K., & Ybarra, O. (2004). *Cultural theories about conflict and team performance among European* Americans [working paper]. Ann Arbor: University of Michigan.

tasks), people's reactions will differ likewise, and these different reactions may trigger a spiral downward in dynamics that extends far beyond the initial conflict (Ferguson, Peterson, & Sanchez-Burks, 2012). For example, a Korean manager may become anxious that the team's ability to succeed may be limited because of the interpersonal conflict and, hence, try to exit the team or work hard to restore interpersonal harmony. In contrast, the American is less likely to ruminate over the issue and prefers to "let bygones be bygones" rather than continue to focus on interpersonal difficulties over task-specific issues. Thus, beliefs about relationship conflict rather than actual effects of relationship conflict may pose the more serious threat to cross-cultural working relationships. Decisions about which teams to join, who to invite, and if and when to attempt an exit from the team will all reflect these beliefs about how much interpersonal harmony and relationship conflict affect a team's ability to succeed in its mission.

Relational styles further shape how individuals convey disagreements. In heavily task-focused cultures, there is an assumption that it is better to manage conflict directly. This direct confrontation is intended to quickly resolve the conflict in a manner deemed most efficient. Alternatively, in cultures where the normative relational style is to maintain a dual focus on the task and social-emotional concerns, direct confrontation is considered immature. Instead, conflict management is performed in a manner such that emotions and relationships are carefully woven into the script. Though task-focused cultures commonly refer to this as a less efficient and more indirect form of conflict management, akin to indirect communication (see the next section), it only appears this way to outsiders. The subtle forms of conveying disagreement are actually quite clear to the other party who is keenly attuned to such cues (Brett, Behfar, & Sanchez-Burks, 2014).

Interpersonal Relationships and Cross-Cultural Communication

Successful cross-cultural communication relies on many shared understandings about emotional displays, indirect cues, and face,[1] to name a few. In every culture, people's internalized cultural norms and values inform the way they communicate with other people and may explain some difficulties in cross-cultural communication that cannot be explained by the use of different languages alone. For example, consider the following conversation between an American plant manager (Patrick) and his Mexican supervisor (Diego):

Patrick: It looks like we're going to have to keep the production line running on Saturday.

Diego: I see.

Patrick: Can you make it on Saturday?

Diego: Oh, yes . . . Patrick, did I tell you that my son's birthday is this Saturday? My family is going to have a big party for him.

Patrick: Oh, how nice. I hope that everyone has a wonderful time.

Diego: Thank you, I knew that you would understand.

Patrick: OK, so see you on Saturday.

Will Diego show up on Saturday? Would Patrick be justified in being upset if his supervisor does not appear? Culture and context rather than language, per se, are necessary to explain the likely miscommunication between Patrick and Diego. In the following sections, we describe how culture shapes one's communication style and the implications of this diversity for cross-cultural communication in a global marketplace. We begin by discussing communication patterns that reflect different points along the cultural continuums of high/low context and individualism-collectivism. Next, we describe how these cultural continuums create communication contexts that differ in their orientation toward face and relational concerns versus instrumental concerns and preferences for direct versus indirect communication.

Theoretical Perspectives on Interpersonal Cross-Cultural Communication

All business transactions, whether within the same culture or across different cultures, involve communication. Business-related communication includes activities such as exchanging information and ideas, decision making, motivating, and negotiating (Adler & Gundersen, 2008). An important theoretical construct used to differentiate among cultural communication styles involves the continuum of *low-context to high-context* cultures (Hall, 1959). Members of high-context cultures, such as Japan, China, Mexico, and Chile, exchange information using a communication style in which the content and meaning of the information is derived from contextual cues in the setting, with only minimal information explicitly derived from a literal interpretation of the transmitted message itself. In such communications, the words convey only a small part of the message, and the receiver needs to fill in the gaps based on understanding of the context and of the speaker. In contrast, members of low-context cultures, such as the United States, Australia, and Germany, exchange information through transactions that are the opposite: Most of the information is conveyed within the transmitted message itself. The actual words rather than the context contain the intended meaning (Hall, 1976). Thus, high- and low-context cultures differ in the degree to which one must attend to interpersonal and contextual cues in the situation in order to understand what is taking place and what is being communicated. These cues are essential for understanding in high-context cultures and substantially less important in low-context cultures.

A second theoretical distinction between cultures that is relevant to communication is the continuum of *collectivist to individualist* cultures. These terms are part of a broad theoretical formulation to differentiate cultures across the globe (Hofstede, 1980; Hofstede & Hofstede, 2005; Triandis, 1996, 2003; see Chapter 8). At this point, suffice it to say that individualist cultures are those that value autonomy and independence, whereas collectivist cultures are those that value reciprocal obligations and interdependence. In collectivist societies such as many Latin American, African, and Arab-speaking countries, people are born into extended families or other groups that are structured to remain highly interdependent and loyal to one another in all spheres of life.

In Guinean culture, for example, as is the case in most of Africa, the deep sense of commitment to the extended family intertwines in subtle and complex ways with the working life. It is not uncommon, therefore, to see employees leaving work to settle family matters and to be absent for a couple of days to mourn relatives in remote villages (Auclair, 1992). In societies steeped in individualism such as the United States, Australia, Great Britain, and Canada, people are expected to act according to their self-interests rather than those of the collective and are not viewed as an inextricable part of a larger social group (Bellah et al., 1985; Javidan & House, 2001). In collectivist societies, the group is primary, and individuals are derived from their social relationships and group memberships. In individualist societies, it is the individual who is primary, and social affiliations are proprieties of the individual—each person having a unique collection of memberships and relationships (Wagner, 2002).

Cultures often cluster along the cultural continuums described thus far. Research reveals links between the cultural context continuum of low to high context and the cultural value continuum of individualism and collectivism. That is, cultures that have a collectivist value system (with an emphasis on "we" rather than "I") also tend to have a high-context orientation, whereas individualist cultures (with an emphasis on "I" rather than "we") are often more low context in nature (Gudykunst, Ting-Toomey, & Chua, 1988; Ting-Toomey, 1988, 2007). Moreover, the cultural patterns described earlier as having differentiated versus combined relational styles also tend to covary with these dimensions. High-context collectivists tend to exhibit a combined relational style (blending task and social-emotional ties), whereas low-context individualists more often show a differentiated relational style (Sanchez-Burks & Lee, 2007).

How does the cultural context affect communication styles? We examine this question according to three interrelated dimensions: (a) face and harmony orientation, (b) relationship versus task orientation, and (c) direct versus indirect communication (see Table 9.1).

Face and Harmony Orientation

The concept of "face" refers to "the public self-image that every member of a society wants to claim for him/herself" (Brown & Levinson, 1978, p. 199). Earley (1997) defines it more broadly: "Face refers to both internal and external presentations of oneself, and it is based on both morality defined in a social structure as well as a socially constructed representation by others" (p. 14). Although the concept of face may manifest itself differently in various cultures and has been mistakenly identified as primarily an Asian cultural preoccupation, everyone has a concept of face that influences his or her behavior and action. In collectivist, high-context cultures such as in Indonesia, for example, it would be inappropriate for a manager to praise individuals too highly in front of their peers. Instead, the group as a whole should be praised when things go well (Foster, 1998). Harmony, which too has mistakenly been attributed to only Asian cultures, is the process through which face is regulated in a particular cultural context (Earley, 1997). As described earlier, the Mexican value placed on *simpatia* similarly emphasizes the importance of interpersonal and group harmony (Diaz-Guerrero, 1967; Triandis et al., 1984). In their communication with others, members of low-context individualist cultures are more likely to be concerned with self-face and have a preference for congruence between their private self-image ("authentic self") and their public self-image ("social self"). In contrast, members of high-context collectivist cultures are more likely to be concerned with the other-face in their interpersonal communication and negotiations (Ting-Toomey, 1988, 2007). The roots of this focus on the other-face in the Asian cultures can be found in the Confucian principle that one needs to continually deepen and broaden one's awareness of the presence of the other in one's self-cultivation (Tu, 1985).

Relationship Versus Task Orientation

As indicated earlier in the chapter, different cultures use relational mental models that emphasize by varying degree either instrumental goals or relational goals. Here, we discuss the impact of these relational mental models on cross-cultural communication. Communication in the combined task/relationship mental model or the differentiated mental model focuses on either achieving a task or the relationship as it relates to the task (see Box 9.3).

TABLE 9.1 • Cultural Context and Communication Orientation		
	Cultural Context	
Communication Orientation	**High-Context Collectivist**	**Low-Context Individualist**
Face and harmony	Other-face concern	Self-face concern
Relationship versus task	Relationship oriented	Task oriented
Direct versus indirect	Indirect communication	Direct communication

Box 9.3

COMMUNICATING THROUGH THE EXCHANGE OF BUSINESS CARDS: TASK-ORIENTED VERSUS RELATIONSHIP/TASK-ORIENTED CULTURES

Exchanging business cards is a decades-old tradition within the business community—a tradition that originated in the United States and Europe. The reason for this custom was straightforward: to provide the very basic information about the bearer of the card so that the other person would remember the card owner's name, job title, company affiliation, and contact information for pursuing future business opportunities. Developed within the Western cultural context, it was clearly task oriented.

Businesspeople in Asian countries such as China and Korea have adopted this custom, but with a cultural twist. Whereas Western businesspeople pay no attention to the way they hand out their cards, Chinese people take great care with the process of giving and receiving a business card: They hold the card with both hands and with a bow present the card with the print facing the recipient of the card. Coming from a relationship-oriented cultural mental model, the method of presenting the card is aimed to convey respect and establish trust. Presenting the card with both hands symbolically indicates that the presenter of the card is honest, has nothing to hide, and is not holding back.

An American businessman who was coached ahead of time about this custom found himself in an awkward situation in meeting a Chinese colleague. The two of them were handing their cards to each other at the very same time. Holding their cards in both hands, neither one had a free hand to take the other's card, let alone accept it with both hands as is customary. Finally, the Chinese man graciously put his card on the table and took the American's card; he then picked up his card from the table and handed it to his American colleague, thus completing their "cultural dance."

An example that demonstrates the discrepancy between the Western differentiated task orientation and the Eastern combined relationship/task orientation is the following incident. An American professor was invited to give a series of lectures in several universities in China. Her hosts exhibited the very warm hospitality for which the Chinese people are known by lavishly wining and dining her. On the morning of the last day of the visit, with her flight scheduled for noon, her hosts insisted on showing her a traditional tea ceremony. Although she appreciated their gracious hospitality and the great effort they had made to find a teahouse that would agree to perform the tea ceremony in the morning rather than the typical afternoon/evening time, she was anxious about the risk of missing her flight. Unbeknownst to her, during the tea ceremony, arrangements were made by one of the hosts for a car that would take her to the airport on time for her flight. Relaxing on the plane (which she did not miss, after all), she reflected that a typical American host would have been more concerned about getting her to her plane on time (differentiated task orientation) than spending additional time in developing the relationship in a social atmosphere (interdependent relationship/task orientation).

Direct Versus Indirect Communication

The most universal communication strategy used to preserve face and harmony, particularly when conveying bad news, is the use of indirectness (Brown & Levinson, 1978). Indirect communication refers to the difference between the literal meaning of what one says (semantic meaning) and the intended meaning (see Figure 9.3 for an example of public displays of indirectness). For example, when a coworker proposes an alternative marketing approach that you do not think is particularly well thought out, you

FIGURE 9.3 ● "Keep Off the Grass," Stated Directly (United States), and the Same Message, Stated Indirectly, "Since We Have Broad Road, Why Should We Open Small Paths" (China)

might say, "It sounds interesting" (indirect communication) in order to avoid saying what you really think: "It's a half-baked idea" (direct communication). Thus, you have not hurt your coworker's feelings and allowed her or him to save face.

Indirectness is an important communicative strategy that varies according to cultural context, individualism-collectivism, and relational styles. In cultures where face and harmony are important, people use face-saving communication strategies such as indirectness to avoid conflict and preserve status structures. Members of collectivist, low-context cultures exchange information primarily on the basis of direct, explicit communication that is focused on precise, straightforward words. In contrast, members of individualist, high-context cultures exchange information primarily on the basis of implicit, indirect communication that is focused on shared experiences developed over time (context), utilizing indirect and nonverbal meaning.

Summary and Conclusion

There is no such thing as an interpersonal style that is culture neutral. People hold assumptions and beliefs about the nature of interpersonal work relationships that are rooted in their cultural context. In this chapter, we focused on a continuum of relational mental models that help explain different types of relationships and communication patterns in different cultures. Relational mental models are the mental models that structure our perceptions and the way we communicate and relate to others. At one end of the spectrum is the differentiated relational mental model, where there is a clear division between task-focused relationships in the business environment and the social-emotional relationships with family, friends, and significant others. At the other end of the spectrum is the combined relational mental model, where both task-focused and social-emotional relationships are intertwined in both the work and the family arenas. In organizations, these relational mental models shape a variety of dynamics, including what people notice and take away from business meetings and the degree to which they coordinate their nonverbal behaviors and are affected by the overall level of coordination.

We then examined cross-cultural communication in low-context versus high-context cultures (where information is received primarily in the message itself rather than from sources such as the settings and the relationships) and in collectivist versus individualist cultures (where emphasis is placed on reciprocal obligations and interdependence within the extended family and community rather than on autonomy, independence, and self-interest). We presented an organizing theoretical model that utilizes the concepts of other-face versus self-face, relationship versus task, and indirect versus direct communication in conjunction with high/low and collectivist/individualist cultures.

Finally, we examined communication patterns and the impact of communication styles on cross-cultural interactions in the global workplace. Members of high-context cultures exchange information using a communication style in which the content and meaning of the information is derived from contextual cues in the setting—with only minimal information explicitly derived from a literal interpretation of the transmitted message itself. In contrast, members of low-context cultures exchange information through transactions that are the opposite: Most of the information is conveyed within the transmitted message itself—the actual words rather than the context contain the intended meaning.

In conclusion, even when the parties communicating share a language and belong to the same culture, misunderstandings are not uncommon. Add to that the layers of cultural expectations and beliefs, gender relations, and national loyalties, and the possibilities for misunderstanding and conflict dramatically increase.

Note

1. The concept of "face" refers to "self-definition in the context of social observers," or "self-definition in one's social system" (Earley, 1997, pp. 3–4). Face includes all aspects concerning how we present ourselves and how others perceive us, and at the same time serves as a basis for self-evaluation. We expand on this concept later in the chapter.

Managing a Diverse Workforce in the Global Context

The Inclusive Workplace

PART III

10

Diversity Management

Paradigms, Rationale, and Key Elements

> If we are to achieve a richer culture, rich in contrasting values, we must recognize the whole gamut of human potentialities, and so weave a less arbitrary social fabric, one in which each diverse human gift will find a fitting place.
>
> —Margaret Mead

In this chapter, we analyze diversity management programs and policies and examine organizational leadership as it relates to diversity. We define the concept of diversity management, describe its historical context, analyze two prominent paradigms for diversity management, and conclude by identifying its key characteristics and limitations.

Defining Diversity Management

In response to the growing diversity in the workforce around the world, many companies have instituted specific policies and programs to enhance recruitment, inclusion, promotion, and retention of employees who are different from the privileged echelons of society. Just as the privileged groups may vary from one country to the next (e.g., urban men of Han descent in China, White men in the United States, or Protestant men in Northern Ireland), so too do the disadvantaged groups (e.g., the lower castes in India, North African immigrants in France, or women in Korea). Although equal rights legislation and affirmative/positive action policies have helped disadvantaged groups obtain access to a variety of jobs not previously open to them, it is their exclusion from circles of influence in work organizations that has kept them from fully contributing to and benefiting from their involvement in the workplace. As Viola Davis, the first African American to win best actress in a television drama, illustrates in her 2015 Emmy Awards speech: "The only thing that separates women of color from anyone else is opportunity. You cannot win an Emmy for roles that are simply not there" (Gold, 2015). Diversity management policies and programs are designed to level the playing field and create a welcoming organizational environment and opportunity for those groups that, in the past and through the present, have not had access to employment, in general, and to more lucrative jobs, in particular. A recent *Forbes* article identifies five trends that are encouraging diversity management in 2015: (a) vocal and public support for diversity efforts from CEOs; (b) linking diversity and inclusion to innovation; (c) expanding diversity definitions to include "diversity of thought"; (d) the business case for diversity, including engagement, retention, and the fact that customers themselves will promote a company's diversity philosophy and products; and (e) the development of "diversity technology" that helps HR managers implement diversity management policies in a more targeted way (Rezvani, 2015).

The term *diversity management* originated in North America but has slowly taken hold in other regions and countries of the world (e.g., April, Ephraim, & Peters, 2012; De Vita, 2010; Egerova, Jirincova, Lancaric, & Savov, 2013; Hays-Thomas, 2004; Jamali, Abdallah, & Hmaidan, 2010; Kaiser & Prange, 2004; Kim, Lee, & Kim, 2015; Manoharan, Gross, & Sardeshmukh, 2014; Nyambegera, 2002; Olsen & Martins, 2012; Ozbilgin & Tatli, 2008; Palmer, 2003; Palmi, 2001). Olsen and Martins (2012) define diversity management broadly as "the utilization of human resource (HR) management practices to (i) increase or maintain the variation in human capital on some given dimension(s), and/or (ii) ensure that variation in human capital on some given dimension(s) does not hinder the achievement of organizational objectives, and/or (iii) ensure that variation in human capital on some given dimension(s) facilitates the achievement of organizational objectives." Jonsen and Özbilgin (2014) focus on global diversity management (GDM) and note that it takes into account local context and is defined as "a management approach that seeks to leverage diversity in organizations with international, multinational, global, and transnational workforces and operations" (p. 366). Martins (2015) offers this simple definition: "DM is typically described as a management practice concerned with valuing people as key human resources" (p. 49). Best, Soyode, Muller-Camen, and Boff (2015) further note, "The purpose of diversity management is to ensure that everyone can succeed based on his or her individual characteristics" (p. 45). We offer the following definition that is brief and succinct and, in the spirit of this book, links diversity to inclusion and applies both locally and globally:

Diversity management refers to the voluntary organizational actions that are designed to create greater inclusion of employees from various backgrounds into the formal and informal organizational structures through deliberate policies and programs. (Mor Barak, 2005, 2011, 2014)

Madera (2013) studied diversity management programs in 14 of the organizations chosen for Diversity Inc.'s 2010 list of Top 50 Companies for Diversity. Some of the selected organizations include Marriott International, Bank of America, Verizon Communications, Coca-Cola Company, MGM Mirage, Walt Disney Company, and Kraft Foods. A content analysis of information from the firm's websites, S&P's Register of Corporations, the Human Rights Campaign, the National Association of Female Executives, and the National Minority Supplier Development Council revealed seven common types of diversity management practices. These types are: (a) having a corporate diversity council, (b) implementing diversity training programs, (c) ensuring supplier diversity, (d) having employee networking and mentoring programs (e.g., affinity groups), (e) providing cultural awareness programs (including language proficiency programs), (f) demonstrating support for women (e.g., supporting the movement of women into top management positions), and (g) offering programs for LGBT employees and providing same-sex benefits (Madera, 2013).

With the globalizing economy and the increase in multinational corporations, diversity management no longer refers solely to the heterogeneity of the workforce within one nation but often also to the workforce composition across nations. The first type, *intranational diversity management,* refers to managing a diverse workforce of citizens or immigrants within a single national organizational context.

An example would be a German company instituting policies and training programs for its employees to improve sensitivity and provide employment opportunities to members of minority groups and recent immigrants in its workforce. The second type, *cross-national diversity management,* refers to managing a workforce composed of citizens and immigrants in different countries (e.g., a Korean company with branches in Japan, China, and Malaysia establishing diversity policies and trainings that will be applicable in its headquarters and also in its subsidiaries in these countries). Each of these types of diversity management presents different challenges and dilemmas, and each requires a different set of policies and programs. In addition to practicing within the laws and social norms of its home country, cross-national diversity management requires employers to take into consideration the legislative and cultural context in other countries, depending on where their workforce resides. For example, a company based in South Africa has to abide by the South African equal rights legislation, which compels it to treat men and women equally. If the same company has a branch in Saudi Arabia, however, it will have to treat its employees according to the laws of that country, which are inspired by the *shari'ah* and follow the Islamic tradition of prescribed gender roles. In South Korea, as another example, the cultural norms dictate that married women with young children leave their careers and devote their time to their families. Therefore, while a U.S. company is likely to provide training and promotion opportunities to young women (in compliance with antidiscrimination legislation), its Korean subsidiary may view such policies as a waste of time, considering the Korean cultural norms (Lee, 1997; Park, 2008). Cox (2001) notes, "The challenge of diversity is not simply to have it but to create conditions in which its potential to be a performance barrier is minimized and its potential to enhance performance is maximized" (p. 16).

Diversity management refers not only to those groups that have been discriminated against or that are different from the dominant or privileged groups, but to "the mixture of differences, similarities and tensions that can exist among the elements of a pluralistic mixture" (Thomas, 2005, p. 93). Using a jar of jelly beans (colorful candy) as a metaphor, Thomas (1996) emphasizes that diversity management deals with the collective mixture of all workers, not just the recent additions to the organizational workforce:

> To highlight this notion of mixture, consider a jar of red jelly beans and assume that you will add some green and purple jelly beans. Many would believe that the green and purple jelly beans represent diversity. I suggest that diversity, instead, is represented by the resultant mixture of red, green and purple jelly beans. When faced with a collection of diverse jelly beans, most managers have not been addressing diversity but, instead, have been addressing how to handle the last jelly beans added to the mixture. . . . The true meaning of diversity suggests that if you are concerned about racism, you include all races; if you're concerned about gender, you include both genders; or if you're concerned about age issues, you include all age groups. In other words, the mixture is all inclusive. (pp. 146–147)

Furthermore, diversity management can advance an organization's competitive advantage in areas such as recruitment, retention, marketing, problem solving, resource acquisition, and financial performance (e.g., Cox, 2001; Houkamau & Boxall, 2011; Singal, 2014). Therefore, diversity management is not the sole domain of the HR function in the organization (as has been the case with affirmative or positive action initiatives) primarily aimed at compliance with legal requirements. It is a systematic, organization-wide effort based on the premise that for organizations to survive and thrive there is an inherent value in diversity (Cox, 2001; Kreitz, 2008; Orlando, 2000). However, it is important to note that careful research in a global context suggests that diversity management can have both positive and negative consequences as well as no change at all, and that a more nuanced approach to the link between diversity management and organizational outcomes is in order (Jackson, Joshi, & Erhardt, 2003; Kochan, Bezrukova, Ely, Jackson, & Joshi, 2003; Olsen & Martins, 2012; Thomas, 2005; Tran, Carcia-Pieto, & Schneider, 2011).

From Equal Rights Laws, to Affirmative/Positive Action, to Diversity Management

The current business focus on diversity is quite different from equal rights legislation and from affirmative/positive action programs. The latter are about trying to achieve equality of opportunities by focusing on specific groups and righting past wrongs. Diversity efforts focus on managing and handling the diverse workforce to give the company a competitive advantage. All of these may be viewed as a continuum: Equal employment opportunity (EEO) legislation means that it is against the law to discriminate, affirmative action programs mean that companies need to take positive steps to ensure equal opportunities, and diversity management is proactive and aimed at promoting a diverse and heterogeneous workforce. The emphasis of the latter is on the business advantage that it can provide to organizations. More and more companies are realizing that there could be a business benefit to having diversity management programs, or at the very least, to including language about it in their public relations materials. In a 2015 interview with *USA Today*, Arnold Donald, president and CEO of Carnival Corporation (the world's largest cruise line), stated: "a highly talented team, with a process to work together, that is diverse will out-innovate a homogeneous team 99.9% of the time. . . . Is it the right social justice thing to do? Of course it is. But it's also actually the right thing to do in terms of just flat-out generating return for shareholders and keeping a business sustainably successful" (Jones, 2015). In another example, IBM's chair and CEO, Sam Palmisano, pointed to the link between diversity management and the core business at IBM. Highlighting IBM's long involvement with equal opportunity and diversity initiatives, Palmisano noted that "diversity policies lie as close to IBM's core as they have throughout our heritage. Today, we're building a workforce in keeping with the global, diverse marketplace, to better serve our customers and capture a greater share of the on demand opportunity" (IBM, 2009). As a testament to its long-term commitment to diversity at all levels of the company, IBM's board of directors elected Virginia "Ginni" Rometty as CEO in October 2011, the first woman to serve in this role in the company's 100-year history. At the time of her appointment, IBM was one of only 18 Fortune 500 companies to be led by a woman. The appointment was followed immediately by a high-profile controversy regarding the Augusta National Golf Club's 80-year-old policy of not admitting women as members. The issue came to the fore because IBM has been one of the tournament's three sponsors and, traditionally, the CEOs of the sponsors don the club's signature green member blazer at the tournament. Due to the club's gender discriminatory policies, Ms. Rometty was barred from becoming a member, despite heading one of the tournament's major sponsors. Both President Barack Obama and his Republican challenger for the presidency, Mitt Romney, criticized the club's policy and called for the club to admit women members (Helyar & Buteau, 2012).

The importance of diversity management programs for global companies is a recurrent theme in the statements of many executives (for a sample of statements in speeches by senior officers of Nikkeiren, Japan's Business Federation, see Ozbilgin & Tatli, 2008, pp. 52–56). Emphasizing the global angle of diversity management, Tiane Mitchell Gordon, senior vice president for diversity and inclusion at AOL, noted that diversity management has a strategic role: "It really is about looking at how we can influence and impact our business from a different lens to understand how, as a global company, we have to be more culturally aware" (Schoeff, 2009). Cox (2001) notes that "the globalization of business is a trend that makes diversity competency crucial for many organizations" (p. 124) because both large and small companies increasingly derive a significant portion of their revenues from other countries in the world.

An interesting explanation for the difference between equal opportunity legislation and diversity management comes from Australia and uses the analogy of wild animals in the zoo:[1]

Imagine your organisation is a giraffe house. Equal opportunity has been very effective widening the door of the giraffe house to let the elephant in, but home won't be best for the elephant unless a number of major modifications are made to the inside of the house. Without these changes the house will remain designed for giraffes and the elephant will not "feel at home." (Krautil, 1995, p. 22)

In the United States, where the term diversity management originated, there was a gradual progression over the years from Title VII of the 1964 Civil Rights Act that mandated EEO, to President Lyndon Johnson's 1972 Executive Order 11246 that outlined affirmative action, and culminating in diversity management policies and programs developed in the 1990s and the 2000s. In Australia, the same progressive development took place with antidiscrimination legislation and affirmative action policies requiring the removal of barriers and the implementation of policies that encourage full employment of groups defined by personal characteristics such as gender, race, physical ability, ethnic heritage, and family responsibilities (Kramar, 1998). There, too, diversity management has been seen as the natural next step for effective management in the future competitive business environment (Burton, 1995; De Cieri, 2003),[2] and many of Australia's most profitable companies have adopted productive diversity policies in different ways (Pyke, 2007).

The European Union (EU) as a whole has developed a strong commitment to equality and positive action policies. Across Europe, there is a trend to strengthen legislation against discrimination as indicated by directives on equal treatment of people irrespective of their race and ethnic backgrounds, and on the equal treatment of persons in the labor market, adopted by the EU Council of Ministers in 2004 (EU Directive 2000/43/EC Art 13) and amended in 2006 (2006/54/EC), to include protection against gender discrimination.[3] Different countries within the EU, however, have implemented varying levels of protections and initiatives, and some have adopted affirmative or positive action programs while others have not.[4] Accordingly, companies in different countries may or may not institute, or even aspire to implement, diversity management policies and programs, and those that have been developed will vary in scope and organizational commitment. In a series of comparative studies, the International Labour Organization (ILO) evaluated antidiscrimination and diversity-training initiatives in different countries in the EU (Wrench, 2007). The studies indicated that Spain, for example, was one of the few industrialized migrant-receiving countries that at the time of the study had not introduced antidiscrimination legislation to protect nonnational workers; and, in general, there was very little or no awareness of the potential problem of ethnic or racial discrimination. Even in countries that have already instituted equal rights laws and public policies that promote diversity, the general organizational culture may not have been ready for the next step of diversity management. In the United Kingdom, for example, diversity management was perceived as premature during the 1990s in several cases unless it followed antiracism and equality trainings (Taylor, Powell, & Wrench, 1997).

It is important to remember that the prerequisite for diversity management is having a diverse workforce. Although recruitment of diverse employees can be a goal of diversity management, if there is little diversity in the organization, the focus should be on recruitment strategies and not on diversity management, per se. In the Netherlands, for example, a heterogeneous workforce is still more of an exception than a rule. Although the demographics have changed quite dramatically in the past 2 decades, the workforce is still quite segregated, though the situation is quite different for multinational firms, which are more likely to employ foreign workers and therefore would have a more diverse workforce (Ozgen, Nijkamp, & Poot, 2011). Most business diversity efforts are focused on recruiting customers, not employees. Therefore, companies need to focus on applying positive action policies in workforce recruitment before they can exercise diversity management (Abell, Havelaar, & Dankoor, 1997; Tsogas & Subeliani, 2005).

In some countries such as South Africa, where a nonracial, democratic constitution came into effect in 1996, equal rights legislation was implemented at just about the same time as its affirmative action policies, and many of its companies have been trying almost simultaneously to design and implement diversity management programs. The results of both equal rights laws and the affirmative action policies in South Africa are already evident in the increased proportion of Black managers, though these rates are still far from their representation in the wider society. As the racial and cultural profile of South African organizations continues to change, the process of managing diversity is becoming more important (April et al., 2012; Horwitz, 2002).

The situation in Brazil is quite similar to that of South Africa—with both legislation and government measures to combat employment discrimination taking place relatively recently.[5] Brazil, however, is quite different because it has long been a heterogeneous society, the product of several migration flows relatively early in its development. As a result, Brazilians take pride in their tradition of nonprejudicial national ideology. Nevertheless, inequalities do exist. Despite its considerable population diversity and multiracial composition, diversity management in Brazil is still a nascent field—the concern of Brazilian companies with the practice of managing cultural diversity is quite recent and relatively limited, and those companies that have developed programs are primarily subsidiaries of U.S. enterprises (Fleury, 1999; Jabbour, Gordono, de Oliveira, Martinez, & Battistelle, 2011; Perez-Floriano & Gonzalez, 2007). A study of 15 companies operating in Brazil found that in most companies diversity management is still an emerging issue, and the major challenges are related to discriminatory actions taken by coworkers. Among the 15 companies studied, only 4 had adopted a consistent set of diversity management and HR practices. These four companies were the only companies to affirm that diversity management required the strong support of top management to sustain efforts toward incorporating diversity (Jabbour et al., 2011).

As is evident from this brief review, equal rights legislation and affirmative/positive action policies are prerequisites for the development of diversity management because they create the social, legal, and organizational environment on which diversity management initiatives can be based. In some countries, the development was sequential and took decades, whereas in others, the development was rapid and almost co-occurring.

Diversity Management Paradigms

In recent years, several paradigms have been offered for diversity management that underscore its unique characteristics and purpose. This section highlights two of the prominent approaches—the HR paradigm and the multicultural organization paradigm.

The Human Resource Paradigm in Diversity Management

Conventional HR practices tend to produce and perpetuate homogeneity in the workforce as a result of the A-S-A (attraction-selection-attrition) cycle (Groeneveld, 2011; Schneider, 1987; Schneider, Smith, & Paul, 2001). Typically, individuals are *attracted* to organizations that appear to have members with values similar to their own. In turn, organizations *select* new members who are similar to their existing members because their hiring continues to make everyone feel comfortable (García, Posthuma, & Colella, 2008). Recruiting practices often emphasize hiring people from sources that historically have been reliable and selecting candidates whose characteristics are similar to those employees who have been successful in the past. As a result, employees who do not fit in well with the dominant organizational culture eventually leave or are fired, creating a selective *attrition* process that supports and maintains a workforce that is homogeneous (Groeneveld, 2011; Schneider et al., 2001). In the long run, this trend is unhealthy for organizations in that it limits their talent pool, their long-term growth and renewal, and their ability to adapt to environmental changes and tap into new markets.

In recent decades, HR managers have recognized the need to adopt effective diversity management practices in order to overcome barriers for diversity and reap the rewards of a diverse workforce. Kossek and Lobel (1996a) summarized the three prevailing HR approaches to diversity management and offered an original approach of their own. The authors later expanded on the model and made the connection between HR management practices, workforce diversity, and individual, group, and organizational outcomes (Kossek, Lobel, & Brown, 2006). The four approaches are presented in Table 10.1 and elaborated in the following sections.

Diversity Enlargement

This approach focuses on increasing the representation of individuals of different ethnic and cultural backgrounds in the organization. The goal is to change the organizational culture by changing the demographic composition of the workforce. For example, the Norwegian government backed a draft law that would oblige companies to appoint women to at least 40% of their directorships ("Oslo Push," 2003). The assumption is that the new employees will conform to existing practices and that no additional intervention will be needed. The mere presence of increasing numbers of employees from different backgrounds will result in a culture change that will bring the desired results. Often, this approach is motivated by compliance to laws and public expectations of political correctness rather than a deep understanding of the business need for diversity (Kossek & Lobel, 1996b).

Diversity Sensitivity

This approach recognizes the potential difficulties introduced by bringing together individuals from diverse backgrounds and cultures in the workplace. It attempts to overcome these difficulties through

TABLE 10.1 • The Human Resource Approach to Diversity Management

Human Resource Approach	Goal	Strategy	Assumptions
Diversity enlargement	Change organizational culture through changing the composition of the workforce	Recruit employees from diverse backgrounds	New hires will change the culture by their mere presence—no need for additional intervention.
Diversity sensitivity	Overcome adversity and promote productive communication and collaboration	Train to increase sensitivity and improve communication	Increased sensitivity to differences will affect performance.
Cultural audit	Identify obstacles faced by employees of diverse backgrounds and modify company practices accordingly	Audit current practices through surveys and focus groups and generate changes to address these deficiencies	Problems are caused by the dominant cultural group in the organization and need to be addressed by that group.
Strategy for achieving organizational outcomes	Achieve organizational goals through diversity management	Integrate diversity management with HR policy areas and other company strategic choices	Diversity management practices have to be linked to desired individual and organizational outcomes.

Source: Kossek, E. E., & Lobel, S. A. (1996). Introduction: Transforming human resource systems to manage diversity: An introduction and orienting framework. In E. E. Kossek & S. A. Lobel (Eds.), Managing diversity: Human resource strategies for transforming the workplace. Cambridge, MA: Blackwell.

diversity training that is aimed at sensitizing employees to stereotyping and discrimination while also promoting communication collaboration. The assumption embedded in this approach is that increased sensitivity to differences will improve performance. Although this is sometimes the case, in other instances, particularly when the training is not linked to corporate goals and initiatives and not supported by its long-term policies, it can create more harm than good. Emphasizing differences can backfire by reinforcing stereotypes and highlighting intergroup differences rather than improving communication through understanding and common interests (Kossek & Lobel, 1996b). (See Box 10.1 for an example of a diversity training gone awry.)

Box 10.1

A DIVERSITY TRAINING GONE AWRY: THE TEXACO "JELLY BEAN JAR" INCIDENT

Diversity training ought to be well planned and executed. Sometimes, the efforts to improve openness and understanding between groups may reinforce negative images and even prejudice. Rather than facilitating open communication and improved relationships, the end result might be divisive and offensive. An example of a diversity training gone awry is the infamous Texaco 1994 "jelly beans" incident that was featured in a lawsuit against the company (Eichenwald, 1996). The lawsuit, filed by the company's African American employees, alleged racist remarks as part of the company's culture. Among other incidents of prejudice and discrimination in the company, the lawsuit alleged that in a diversity training sponsored by the company, a comment was made by one of the managers that "All the black jelly beans seem to be glued to the bottom of the bag," a remark that was interpreted as derogatory toward African Americans. In its defense, the company commissioned an independent counsel who reported that there was nothing inherently derogatory in any of the references to jelly beans. Indicating that the jelly beans reference was a common image used in diversity training,[6] the independent counsel suggested that it may have been a reference to inequities imposed upon African Americans by society, rather than a criticism. The case ended with a $176 million settlement announced November 15, 1996. Interestingly, after Texaco had reached this settlement, two shareholder proposals regarding diversity management were submitted, receiving strong support from other shareholders. This is an example of shareholder activism that can force boards of directors to rethink their ambivalence toward diversity, emphasizing the need to prevent future employment discrimination lawsuits and costly settlements (Buckridge, 2006; De Meuse & Hostager, 2001; Olson, 1997; "Texaco Independent Investigator's Report," 1996; "Texaco Investigator," 1996).

Cultural Audit

This approach aims at identifying the obstacles that limit the progress of employees from diverse backgrounds and that block collaboration among groups in the organization. The audit is usually performed by outside consultants who obtain data from surveys and focus groups and then identify areas in which employees who are different from the dominant group feel that they are being blocked from performing to the best of their ability. Although this is a customized approach that is tailored to specific organizational cultures, the recommendations for change are typically based on the notion that the source of the problem is the dominant cultural group (typically, in North America, White males) and that the change must come from within that group (Kossek & Lobel, 1996b). An example of a cultural audit is Ford Motor Company's global employee satisfaction survey. The survey, called PULSE, is distributed annually among all of the company's salaried employees

(71% of employees participated in the survey in 2002). Employee satisfaction with diversity is one of the 12 dimensions assessed by the survey, and the results are used to assess Ford's commitment and performance in achieving a diverse workforce (Ford Motor Company, 2002). In a study of 119 manufacturing organizations in Australia, Fenwick, Costa, Sohal, and D'Netto (2011) found that positive changes in HR diversity management had occurred during the first decade of the 21st century. The survey provides information about HR diversity management practices that include identification of current skills of staff through a cultural audit process, providing the basis for interventions such as education programs to reduce stereotyping, and adoption of cultural sensitivity workshops. The authors indicate that, based on the survey results, diversity management practices in Australia had progressed from a nascent area in the 1990s into an accepted subfield of HR management. They note that the "overall performance of manufacturing organizations in Australia, with respect to the use of human resource diversity management practices is no longer 'mediocre' and can now be classified as 'above average'" (Fenwick et al., 2011, p. 494).

Strategy for Achieving Organizational Outcomes

This approach, proposed by Kossek and Lobel (1996a) as a comprehensive framework for HR diversity management, focuses on diversity management "as a means for achieving organizational ends, not as an end in itself" (p. 4). Using this strategy, managers have to identify the link between diversity management objectives and desired individual and organizational outcomes. Organizational strategic choices are viewed in the context of environmental drivers such as the changing labor market composition, the global economy, the shift to a service economy, and the legal and governmental pressures. The theoretical foundation for this approach is the resource-based theory—recognizing the value of diversity for conceiving an effective business strategy and for implementing the strategy effectively (Yang & Konrad, 2011). Analyzing environmental drivers can help the organization determine the specific benefits it expects to gain from its diversity management and how those are linked to its overall business strategy. For example, if innovation is a business strategy for the company, it is in its best interest to cultivate culturally diverse teams because creativity and responsiveness to new markets, primarily in today's global economy, are more likely to be found in diverse work teams.

The Multicultural Organization Paradigm in Diversity Management

Cox (1994, 2001) proposed a diversity management paradigm that includes three types: (a) the monolithic organization, (b) the plural organization, and (c) the multicultural organization. Diversity management, according to this paradigm, should strive to create multicultural organizations in which members of all sociocultural backgrounds can contribute and achieve their full potential.

The Monolithic Organization

This is an organization that is demographically and culturally homogeneous. For example, most Chinese companies are monolithic from a cultural and ethnic perspective, as the overwhelming majority of their employees are ethnically Han Chinese. They are not, however, monolithic from a gender perspective because there are many women in the companies. Women, though, are more commonly employed at the lower levels of the organization, whereas most of the managers, particularly at the top levels, are men (Powell & Graves, 2003). A monolithic organization in North America or Europe will have a majority of White men and relatively few women and members of ethnic and racial minorities. Typically, women and racial/ethnic members of minority groups, both men and women, will be segregated in low-status jobs such as receptionists and maintenance people who do not have a significant impact on organizational policies and practices (Cox, 1994, 2001). A monolithic organization will have a culture that will perpetuate the homogeneity of its workforce through its hiring and promotion practices. There will be an expectation that members of diverse groups will assimilate into the culture of the majority, with minimal degrees of structural and formal integration. In other words, because one cultural group manages the organization almost exclusively, both the practices and policies of a monolithic organization are biased in favor of the majority group. Not surprisingly, intergroup conflict is expected to be minimal in such an organization because it is basically homogeneous and is composed of one dominant cultural group. Given the globalizing economy, a monolithic organization will be at a competitive disadvantage, and its homogeneity will become more difficult to maintain given the influx of women and members of minority groups into the workforce around the world.

The Plural Organization

This is an organization that has a heterogeneous workforce, relative to the monolithic organization, and typically makes efforts to conform to laws and public policies that demand and expect workplace equality. It will take active steps to prevent discrimination in the workplace such as audits that assure equality of compensation systems and manager trainings on equal opportunity issues and sexual harassment. Although women and members of minority groups are represented in larger numbers, they make up only a small percentage of the management, particularly top management, and are still expected to assimilate into the majority culture. Examples of plural organizations include companies in which members of minority groups constitute a sizable proportion of the workforce but only a small percentage of the managerial positions. Although there is greater structural and formal integration in the plural organization, institutional bias is rather prevalent and intergroup conflict is significant, primarily because the increased presence of women and members of ethnic and racial minority groups is not accompanied by serious efforts to make them a truly integral part of the organization. Cox (1994, 2001) attributes the increased intergroup conflict in plural organizations in the United States to the backlash against affirmative action programs and the resulting sense among majority group members that they are being discriminated against because of no fault of their own. Cox (1994) identifies the plural organization as the most prevalent type in the North American business environment, but this organizational type is also prevalent in other areas of the world such as Europe, Australia, India, and South Africa.

The Multicultural Organization

This is more an ideal than an actual type because very rarely do companies achieve this level of integration. However, Cox (1994, 2001) indicates that it is important to understand this type and to use it to create a vision for effective diversity management. The multicultural organization is characterized by a culture that fosters and values cultural differences—that truly and equally incorporates all members of the organization via pluralism as an acculturation *process,* rather than as an *end* resulting in assimilation. The multicultural organization has full integration, structurally and informally; is free of bias and favoritism toward one group as compared with others; and has only a minimal intergroup conflict, thanks to the previously stated characteristics that result from effective management of diversity.

Cox's (1994) typology of the monolithic-multicultural organizational continuum presents "pure" types that are rarely found in reality but are useful from an analytic standpoint. Although it was generated primarily for the North American context, it is useful for other countries as well because diversity of the workforce is increasingly central, even in traditionally homogeneous societies. By outlining these types, particularly the extremes, Cox's typology is helpful in providing work organizations with a vision of the model they need to strive for in designing their diversity management strategies.

Models of Global Diversity Management

Jonsen and Özbilgin (2014) developed six models of global diversity management (GDM) based on field studies conducted over the last 10 years. Model types include strategic, process, contextual, intervention, house, and communication. Global diversity management takes into account local context and seeks to leverage diversity in organizations with international, multinational, global, and transnational workforces and operations. The *strategic model* essentially maps out three strategies that organizations can use when implementing GDM policies and practices. Organizations that use a localized strategy tailor their diversity management program to the needs and characteristics of the specific local context. Organizations that use a universal strategy implement diversity management through what the authors refer to as a "one best way" approach, which ignores regional and national differences. To address the weaknesses of the localized and universal strategies, organizations can also use the transversal strategy, which allows organizations to create diversity management policies and practices in a "bottom up fashion." With the transversal strategy, a common set of diversity management principles is developed through dialogue and compromise with a global diversity council made up of local country representatives.

As the name implies, the *process model* describes GDM as a sequence of inputs, activities, and outputs over time. Key inputs for successful GDM include leadership support and features of the organizational culture (e.g., openness to change). Jonsen and Özbilgin (2014) identify a range of activities in the GDM process model including building relationships across global units, developing culturally sensitive human resource management practices, using definitions of diversity that make sense with the local context, and encouraging cross-national social networks. Critical outputs in the GDM process model include the organization's reputation, its organizational performance, and its employees' sense of inclusion.

The *contextual model* uses a systems approach and acknowledges multiple layers of influence that can affect GDM activities. The model highlights individual, organizational, sectorial, national, and international levels of influence. The value of the contextual model, according to Jonsen and Özbilgin (2014), is that it can help organizational leaders identify and understand the influence of important stakeholders, individuals, and institutions across systems levels. This knowledge can then help organizational leaders frame and articulate the "why" and "how" of GDM within their specific context.

Next are the *intervention models* of GDM. Jonsen and Özbilgin (2014) describe three categories of GDM interventions. Informational interventions revolve around staff training and education, and might include diversity training or a formal company diversity statement. Structural interventions alter structures and processes within the organization, for example, HR and performance evaluation procedures or the creation of a diversity council. Finally, cultural interventions dig deeper and "challenge the implicit cultural assumptions of the organization with a view to making the organization more welcoming of difference and more inclusive" (Jonsen & Özbilgin, 2014, p. 374). The level of resources and leadership support required increases as an organization moves from informational to structural to cultural GDM interventions. The different types of interventions also reflect the organization's "GDM maturity," with cultural interventions representing the highest level.

The *house model* acts as a useful tool for organizations that want to implement GDM. Jonsen and Özbilgin (2014) depict this model in the shape of an actual house whereby each layer represents considerations that build upon each other as the organization designs its GDM strategy. Diversity metrics and legal compliance represent the first floor of the house model. Recruitment and retention, development and mentoring, and a supportive environment comprise the second floor. The third floor focuses on communication and education, while talent, leadership, and competitiveness make up the top of the house model. Large companies such as Hewlett-Packard, Sodexo, and Royal Dutch Shell have used this model to manage their global diversity and inclusion programs (Jonsen & Özbilgin, 2014). Each layer of the house model takes into account organizational, national, and international requirements and priorities.

Finally, *communication models* of GDM address the issue of how an organization talks about diversity and inclusion compared to actual action, commitment, and organizational change (as the authors note, "rhetoric versus reality"). Jonsen and Özbilgin (2014) describe four scenarios to illustrate how communication models might conceptualize GDM implementation: (a) "walk the talk"—rhetoric (e.g., active information sharing and proactive discussions about the value of diversity and inclusion) aligns with top management commitment; (b) "empty rhetoric"—there is rhetoric but insufficient top management commitment and action; (c) "just do it"—top management commitment exists but there is no rhetoric that officially labels the activities as diversity and inclusion-related; and (d) "low priority"—both rhetoric and commitment are missing. Organizations can use this model to help assess the current state of their GDM program and develop goals for improvement.

The Impetus for Implementing Diversity Management

Why do companies implement diversity management strategies? There are three types of arguments in favor of diversity management, each with its own slogan (see Table 10.2):

1. *Diversity is a reality that is here to stay.* Businesses have to adapt to the new realities of an increasingly diverse workforce. In the United States, it was the report by the Hudson Institute, Workforce 2000, and the one that followed it, Workforce 2020, that served as a wake-up call to businesses, describing in compelling statistical detail the future trends of the workforce (Johnston & Packer, 1987; Judy & D'Amico, 1997). One of their central predictions was that the workforce will grow slowly but will become more diverse because the proportion of older adults, women, and members of minority groups will continue to increase. Complementing these reports, earlier chapters in this book described diversity trends in other countries as well, demonstrating that the global economy contributes to increased diversity in practically every region of the world.

2. *Diversity management is the right thing to do.* This is the moral and ethical reasoning for diversity management. At the heart of this argument is the notion of equal opportunities regardless of individual characteristics such as gender, race, and sexual orientation. This includes providing all potential employees with equal access to jobs in the organization and providing current employees with comparable pay for jobs of comparable worth (Velasquez, 2011). Another ethical principle, compensatory justice, is the foundation of affirmative action programs (Kellough, 2006). This principle suggests that society has an obligation to overcome historical discrimination against specific groups of people to compensate those who have been intentionally and unjustly wronged (Kellough, 2006; Velasquez, 2011). Therefore, work organizations have a social obligation to participate in compensating groups that have been wronged in the past, such as Blacks in South Africa or Catholics in Northern Ireland.

3. *Diversity makes good business sense.* Diversity management can provide businesses with a competitive advantage. Here the logic is that by managing diversity, companies have much to gain (Cox, 2001; Kochan et al., 2003), including (a) cost reductions due to lower absenteeism and turnover; (b) advantages in the competition for talent in the workforce (Thomas, Thomas, Ely, & Meyerson, 2002);[7] (c) reduced risk of discrimination lawsuits due to a more just and nondiscriminating

TABLE 10.2 • Motivation for Implementing Diversity Management	
Slogan	**Argument**
"Diversity is a reality that is here to stay."	The pool of current and future employees is becoming more diverse, and businesses have no choice but to adapt to this new reality.
"Diversity management is the right thing to do."	Companies have an obligation to promote social justice and implement principles of compensatory justice through their policies and programs.
"Diversity makes good business sense."	Diversity management can give companies a competitive advantage in the global economy.

environment; (d) more effective marketing to diverse customer pools (Kossek et al., 2006; Pradhan, 1989); (e) increased creativity and innovation through diverse work teams (Kossek et al., 2006; Weiss, 1992); (f) government contracts for which minority- or gender-balanced businesses are given preference; and (g) improved corporate image, which generates public goodwill.

Elements of this three-pronged rationale for adopting diversity management are evident in the mission statement and corporate ethos of many companies. For example, Jay C. Rising, president of Automatic Data Processing (ADP), states, "Our goal is to have a workplace that is fully inclusive, one that enables us to leverage the talents of a multi-cultural organization" (ADP, n.d.); and the mission statement of Hanes and Boone (one of the largest law firms in the United States) indicates,

Our greatest asset is our people. They make Haynes and Boone a special firm by embracing core values that foster a healthy work environment, a commitment to being the best and an attitude of service to others. While our people make a positive difference for our clients, they do the same for their local communities by dedicating substantial personal time and funds to pro bono work and community service. We are equally proud of the ethnic, gender and cultural diversity of our people and our success in hiring, retaining and promoting women and ethnic minorities. ("About the Firm," 2002–2003)

These types of mission statements have been adopted by companies outside the United States as well. For example, the diversity statement of Woolworths Holdings, a South African–based retail group, pronounces,

Woolworths believes in a diverse workforce and embraces the principles of employment equity to achieve an appropriate balance for the group. The group has demonstrated its commitment to employment equity by adopting a diversity statement forming the basis for implementation. (Woolworths Holdings Limited, 2004a)

Similarly, the corporate statement about diversity from AstraZeneca, a leading U.K.-based pharmaceutical company, proclaims,

Our definition of diversity includes all our different personal skills and qualities as well as race and gender, where advancement depends solely on ability, performance and good teamwork. We encourage our people to share their knowledge and ideas across boundaries—to build high performance teams that recognize and value our differences—teams that celebrate diversity but which also embrace common goals. Across the business, diversity is high on the agenda and continuous improvement is at the heart of our approach. And we have a clear focus on the future—an aspiration to become a true culture of diversity. (AstraZeneca United Kingdom, 2004b)

Characteristics and Limitations of Diversity Management

The goal of diversity management is to transform the organizational culture from a majority-oriented to a heterogeneous-pluralistic culture in which different value systems are heard and thus equally affect the work environment. Diversity management has a dual focus: The first is enhancing social justice by creating an organizational environment in which no one is privileged or disadvantaged due to characteristics such as race or gender; the second is increasing productivity and profitability through organizational transformation (e.g., Cox, 2001; Ozbilgin & Tatli, 2008; Thomas, 2005). Accordingly, diversity management has three key components:

1. *Diversity management is voluntary.* Equal rights legislation is enforced through sanctions (monetary fines or incarceration), and affirmative/positive action policies are enforced through incentives (government contracts); however, diversity management is self-initiated by the companies themselves. It is not enforced or coerced but is entirely voluntary.

2. *Diversity management uses broad definitions of diversity.* Whereas both equal rights legislation and affirmative or positive action policies specify the groups that are to benefit from the laws or public policies (e.g., specific castes in India or Blacks in South Africa), companies that implement diversity management often use broad and open definitions of diversity. One of the reasons for these broad and often vague definitions is that they make diversity programs inclusive and reduce potential objections from members of the majority group.

3. *Diversity management aims at providing tangible benefits to the company.* Diversity management is seen as a business strategy aimed at tapping into the full potential of all employees in the company in order to give the company a competitive advantage, whereas in the past, employees of different backgrounds (e.g., race/ethnicity or gender) were labeled as unqualified by managers if they did not conform to the values and norms of the majority. The logic of diversity management is that it allows every member of the organization to bring to the workplace his or her unique perspective, benefiting the organization as a whole. Expected benefits of diversity management include broad appeal to diverse clients because diverse employees communicate better with diverse clients, better products because diversity of opinions leads to creativity, and improved sales because diverse employees better understand the needs of diverse clients (Cox, 2001; Ozbilgin & Tatli, 2008; Thomas et al., 2002). Ford Australia, for example, realizing that attracting women as customers is imperative for its future growth, sought to increase the proportion of women among its workforce. Since 2000, Ford Australia has funded the Ford of Australia Women in Engineering Scholarship Program, an undergraduate scholarship platform aimed at encouraging more women to enter the field of automotive engineering. As a result of that program, in 2002, women had increased to a 43% share of the company's total university graduate intake. Similarly, in order to attract diverse clients, Telstra Corporation Limited recruited employees who could speak up to seven different languages to staff its multilingual customer service centers. These multilingual sales consultants take an average of about 2,700 calls each month, with increasingly positive feedback from customers who prefer explaining their telecommunication problems in their native tongues.

Though these key components of diversity management—being voluntary, using a broad definition of diversity, and providing tangible benefits to the company—represent strength in the current business context, they can potentially bring the demise of the concept in the long run. First, the *voluntary nature* of diversity management means that it may not survive during difficult economic times. The concern here is that if forced to make a choice among competing expenditures, diversity programs may be cut back or eliminated altogether because their benefits often take a long time to materialize. Second, the *broad definitions of diversity* mean that the most vulnerable groups in society—racial minority groups, people with disabilities, and women—may not receive the protection they deserve because resources will be spread across many groups. The concern here is that the slogan "Everyone is diverse" dilutes the implications of historical injustices and discrimination that have denied certain groups access to opportunities and resources. And finally, the emphasis on the *practical benefits* suggests that once diversity management is no longer perceived as beneficial to companies, it will disappear. It is, therefore, essential that diversity management will be based not only on the principle of providing tangible benefits to the companies but also on a strong moral and ethical commitment to diversity.

Wondrack and Segert (2015) describe four criticisms related to diversity management program implementation. The first criticism is lack of knowledge about diversity management processes and effects. As the authors note, in this case, diversity management efforts "seem hidden in a black box" (Wondrack & Segert, 2015, p. 241). A second criticism is that diversity management activities only result in surface-level changes and do not alter more deeply rooted discriminatory and exclusionary structures and activities in the organization. The third criticism the authors describe is that diversity management programs may not be sustainable because of problems related to implementation or because leaders discontinue them before the benefits are realized. Finally, diversity management is criticized because the specific return on investments attributable to these programs is difficult to measure. To address these issues, Wondrack and Segert (2015) propose the use of a tool called the Diversity Impact Navigator. The Diversity Impact Navigator has seven steps that are tailored to the specific organizational context and stakeholders: (a) describe the organization's business model; (b) assess and identify factors that influence the organization's intellectual capital using human, structural, and relationship capital categories; (c) analyze current diversity strategies, measures, and initiatives to create a DM inventory; (d) conduct a diversity impact analysis to see how diversity currently influences intellectual capital dimensions in the organization; (e) select relevant indicators; (f) identify current and future target values for the selected indicators; and (g) use key findings to inform and refine DM processes (Wondrak & Segert, 2015, pp. 245–246).

Summary and Conclusion

The globalizing economy and the increase in the number of multinational corporations make diversity management a necessity for companies that want not only to survive but thrive during this time of economic, social, and cultural changes. *Diversity management* refers to the voluntary organizational actions that are designed to create through deliberate policies and programs greater inclusion of employees from various backgrounds into the formal and informal organizational structures. Diversity management, compared with its predecessors (equal opportunity legislation and affirmative action programs), is proactive and aimed at creating an organization in which all members can contribute and achieve to their full potential.

The reasons for implementing diversity management include having to adapt to the new reality of a workforce that is increasingly diverse, doing the right and moral thing, and gaining a competitive advantage. Diversity management has three main characteristics: (a) it is voluntary, (b) it uses a broad definition of diversity, and (c) it aims at providing tangible benefits to the company. Finally, implementing diversity management can give companies a competitive advantage in areas such as problem solving, corporate image, and marketing.

The challenge of diversity management is to break the harmful cycle that equates cultural difference with social/economic disadvantages. Therefore, although the emphasis on the business advantage of diversity management is probably a good motivator for companies to enact diversity programs, it does not mean that moral and ethical missions should be neglected or overlooked. To overcome these potential limitations, diversity management has to focus on both enhancing profitability and fostering social justice.

Notes

1. R. Roosevelt Thomas Jr. (1999) used a similar metaphor as the theme for his book *Building a House for Diversity: How a Fable About a Giraffe and an Elephant Offers New Strategies for Today's Workforce.*

2. The Australian Commonwealth Government established the Industry Task Force on Leadership and Management Skills. The task force published a report in 1995 known as the Karpin Report, which included several recommendations associated with promoting equality and diversity. Burton's (1995) article demonstrates that diversity management is consistent with the Karpin Report's recommendations for effective management.

3. See Chapter 2 on international legislation.

4. One has to be careful about broad generalizations with respect to EU countries because legislation and public policies may vary greatly from one country to another. For example, France has long had a policy that implies (when translated) that

"diversity statistics" are illegal to compile. Hence, it is difficult to know for certain whether the goals of diversity, equality, and nondiscrimination are being achieved—in both the private and the public sector.

5. The Brazilian National Program of Human Rights was created in 1996 to implement international human rights declarations, including the ILO 111 convention on employment discrimination, though the latter was ratified by the Brazilian government earlier, in 1965 (Fleury, 1999).

6. See a quote from Thomas (1996, pp. 109–210) earlier in the chapter referring to the jelly bean image with respect to diversity management.

7. For example, during the high-tech boom of the 1990s, countries like Canada, Germany, and the United Kingdom revised their immigration policies to attract skilled workers from other countries like China and India in order to supply the much-needed workforce for their computer and high-tech industries.

Inclusive Leadership

Unlocking the Diversity Potential

An individual has not started living until he can rise above the narrow confines of his individualistic concerns to the broader concerns of all humanity.

—Martin Luther King Jr.

We need to help students and parents cherish and preserve the ethnic and cultural diversity that nourishes and strengthens this community—and this nation.

—Cesar Chavez

In today's global business world, leaders have to understand cultural similarities and differences among their employees and in society at large in order to inspire and manage effectively. Leadership in this environment depends, to a great extent, upon a deep understanding of the contextual culture that provides meaning to verbal and nonverbal communication and determines interpersonal relationships. It is analogous to an iceberg, with the visible part, above the ocean's surface, being the actual behavior manifested by individuals and the invisible part, beneath the surface, representing the meanings that people in specific cultural contexts attribute to the visible part.

Cultural awareness and competence are essential for effective leadership in the context of diversity. Some authors suggest that cultural intelligence is central to understanding effective global leadership. Cultural intelligence is the ability to behave appropriately in cross-cultural settings, an ability that encompasses cognitive (knowledge), emotional (motivational, mindfulness), and behavioral dimensions (Blasco, Feldt, & Jakobsen, 2012). Defined as "a system of interacting knowledge and skills, linked by cultural metacognition that allows people to adapt to, select, and shape the cultural aspects of their environment," cultural intelligence is hypothesized to be linked to effective intercultural interactions, including interpersonal relationships and task performance (Thomas et al., 2008). Some studies found that cultural intelligence allows leaders to share knowledge and information within their organizations, to facilitate active research, and to enhance team learning during cross-cultural interactions (e.g., Groves & Feyerherm, 2011; Ng, Van Dyne, & Ang, 2009; Rockstuhl, Seiler, Ang, Van Dyne, & Annen, 2011).

In order to provide vision and inspire their organizations, effective leaders need to understand the multiplicity of values, perspectives, and worldviews that individuals and groups may hold dear and use their cultural intelligence in different settings to create an inclusive and effective work environment. An effective leader must be able to cope with contrasting economic, political, and cultural practices in both the national and international contexts (Rockstuhl et al., 2011).

A growing literature (cited throughout this book) has suggested that creating an inclusive workplace, particularly in diverse organizational settings, results in positive outcomes such as increased job satisfaction, retention, organizational commitment, trust, well-being, creativity, and innovation while decreasing conflict, intention to leave, stress, job withdrawal, and organizational turnover. Yet not much is known about what leaders can do to increase workplace inclusion, particularly in diverse organizational contexts.

In this chapter, we explore leadership dilemmas related to what has been termed the *diversity paradox*, define organizational leadership as it relates to diversity, determine what constitutes inclusive leadership at the top level as well as at midlevels of supervisor-supervisee relationships, and conclude by providing some suggestions for effective inclusive leadership.

Leadership Dilemmas and the Diversity Paradox

Organizational leaders seeking to take advantage of the competitive edge provided by diversity policies face what has been termed a *paradoxical dilemma* (see Figure 11.1): If they embrace diversity, they risk workplace conflicts, distrust, and tension, but if they avoid diversity, they risk losing their organizational potential for innovation, creativity, and productivity (Bassett-Jones, 2005).

In their efforts to create inclusive organizations, leaders need to remember that inclusion is not about numerical presence alone. If people of diverse backgrounds are allowed in but expected to conform to the existing culture, then "groupthink" will be sustained and the diversity advantage will not be realized. However, if people of diverse backgrounds are invited to actively contribute and change the organizational culture, fresh, contrarian, and creative ideas will flourish and everyone will benefit.

The solution to the diversity paradox is inclusive leadership. If an organization becomes inclusive, it can minimize or even avoid altogether intergroup conflicts, tension, and distrust. One can think of two potential paths as a result of diversity in organizations—one leading to competitive advantage and the other leading to loss of competitive advantage (see Figure 11.2). Based on research, the key is inclusive policies in management.

Transformational Leadership, Inclusive Leadership, and the Organization's Competitive Advantage

Transformational leadership (TL) refers to the leader's ability to motivate and inspire others to follow a particular course of action (Avolio, Gardner, Walumbwa, Luthans, & May, 2004; Bass, 1990).

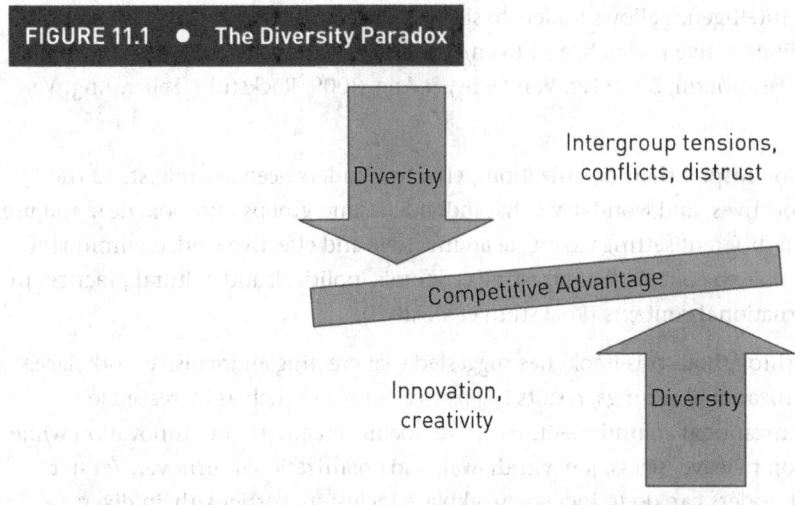

FIGURE 11.1 • The Diversity Paradox

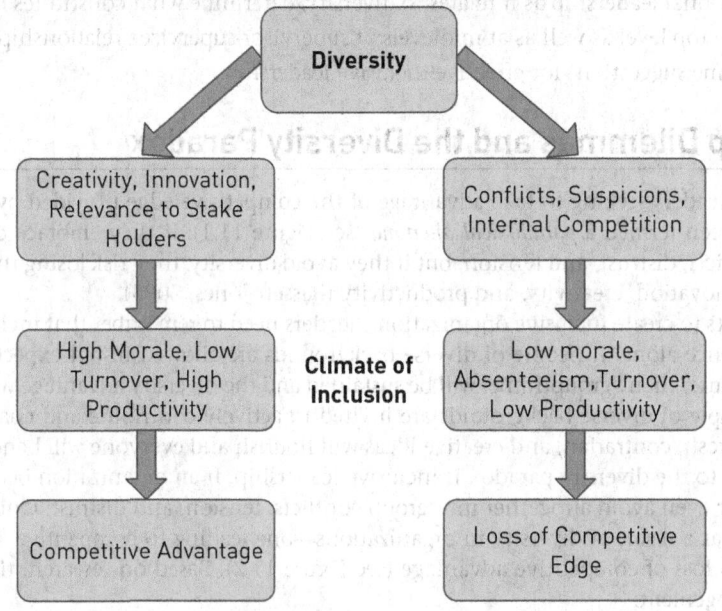

FIGURE 11.2 • Inclusion: The Key to the Diversity Paradox Dilemma

Transformational leaders use self-enhancement courses of action to influence follower behavior. These courses of action have been operationalized as the four components of TL, known briefly as the four I's: (a) individualized consideration; (b) intellectual stimulation; (c) idealized behavior; and (d) inspirational motivation (see Avolio, Bass, & Jung, 1999; Bass & Avolio, 1997; Yukl, 2012). These TL components imply that transformational leaders motivate employees by empowering them and creating opportunities for self-expression and professional development. Consequently, supervisory or organizational-unit TL is expected to increase the strength of the diversity-inclusion climate relationship. Each of the TL components can be linked respectively to each characteristic of inclusive leadership: (a) recognizing each individual's unique characteristics and talents; (b) seeking out different perspectives; (c) creating a shared purpose and common goals; and (d) motivating and inspiring everyone to actively participate in the organizational activities.

Recall that in earlier chapters we noted that according to social identity theory and optimal distinctiveness theory, individuals desire to *belong* to social groups that enjoy distinct and positive identities. At the same time, individuals also need to be recognized for their individual, unique identities. Conceptual development by Shore et al. (2011) has proposed that inclusion is composed of two main elements: *uniqueness*—the desire to be recognized for one's distinctive attributes, and *belonging*—the need to belong to the group and organization. Mor Barak and colleagues proposed three important dimensions to inclusion: (a) in the decision-making process; (b) in information networks; and (c) in the level of participation/involvement in workgroups and in the organization (Mor Barak, 2005, 2014; Mor Barak, Cherin, & Berkman, 1998). Accordingly, we propose the following definition:

> *Inclusive leadership* refers to the ability to recognize and celebrate the uniqueness of the group or organizational members and, at the same time, promote their sense of belonging along the three inclusion dimensions of decision making, information networks and participation in groups and the organization as a whole. (Mor Barak, 2005; Shore et al., 2011)

In our conceptual work we have demonstrated a path by which transformational leadership leads to inclusive leadership and to generating a climate of inclusion in the organization (Brimhall & Mor Barak, 2015; Mor Barak & Brimhall, 2015). More specifically, as outlined in Figure 11.3, transformational leaders provide individualized consideration to each employee, which leads them to recognize each individual's specific characteristics and talents; this promotes the uniqueness aspect of inclusion. Similarly, transformational leaders encourage intellectual simulation, thus promoting an environment in which employees are encouraged to seek different perspectives. This, again, highlights the uniqueness aspect of inclusion.

Organizational Leadership and Inclusion

The Global Leadership and Organizational Behavior Effectiveness (GLOBE) project, noted earlier, in Chapter 8, investigated the complex relationship between societal culture and organizational behavior, with a focus on leadership (Dorfman, Javidan, Hanges, Dastmalchian, & House, 2012). The data generated by this large-scale study, the result of collaboration among more than 200 researchers from multiple academic disciplines located across all parts of the globe for more than 2 decades, are highly relevant for understanding global leadership in the context of diversity. The research team, led by Robert House as the principal investigator along with multiple coordinating teams, defined leadership as "the ability of an individual to influence, motivate, and enable others to contribute toward the effectiveness and success of the organizations of which they are members" (House, Hanges et al., 2004, p. 15).

The GLOBE study found that some leadership behaviors are universally effective, such as charismatic/value-based leadership—broadly defined as the "ability to inspire, motivate, and to expect high performance outcomes from others based on firmly held core values" (Dorfman et al., 2012, p. 3). This universal leadership characteristic includes six primary dimensions: (a) visionary, (b) inspirational, (c) self-sacrifice, (d) integrity, (e) decisive, and (f) performance oriented. Other leadership behaviors

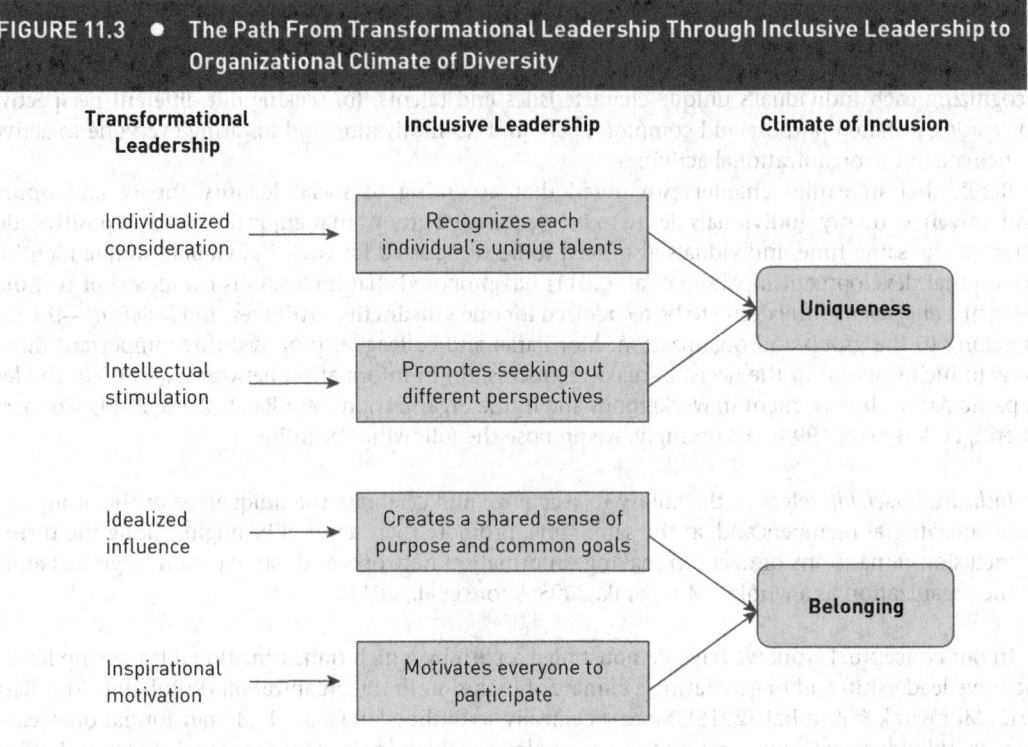

FIGURE 11.3 • The Path From Transformational Leadership Through Inclusive Leadership to Organizational Climate of Diversity

are much more culture specific, such as participative leadership, which is defined as "the degree to which managers involve others in making and implementing decisions" (Dorfman et al., 2012, p. 3). The participative leadership dimension includes two primary dimensions: (a) nonparticipative and (b) autocratic.

A central finding of the GLOBE study is that national culture influences leadership behaviors indirectly, through the leadership expectations of societies. In other words, executives tend to lead in a manner that is quite consistent with the leadership prototypes endorsed within their particular culture. As a result, leaders who behave according to expectations are most effective (Dorfman et al., 2012). Therefore, understanding national culture gives us an insight into which kinds of leadership would likely be enacted and be effective in each society—and, more important, how to bridge those differences in order to generate leadership that would be effective across cultures.

Inclusive Leadership

Leaders can inspire organizations to become more inclusive with respect to their diverse workforce. It is important to remember that ensuring diversity representation in the workforce is only the initial step toward workplace inclusion. Workplace inclusion reflects the extent to which employees perceive that they are part of the communication systems, informal networks, and decision-making processes in the organization. Therefore, increasing diversity representation and achieving workforce inclusion is a two-stage process, with each stage affecting the other in a circular way (see Figure 11.4; Mor Barak & Travis, 2010). The first stage is reactive: Organizations are recruiting and employing a more diverse workforce.

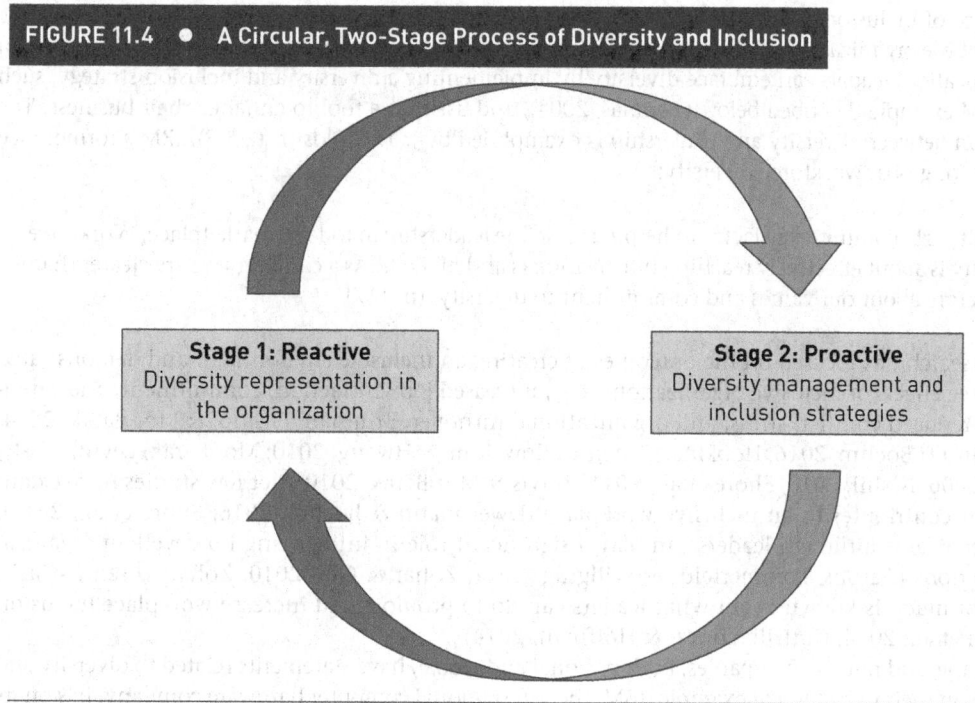

FIGURE 11.4   •   A Circular, Two-Stage Process of Diversity and Inclusion

Stage 1: Reactive
Diversity representation in the organization

Stage 2: Proactive
Diversity management and inclusion strategies

Source: Mor Barak and Travis (2010).

The second stage is proactive: Organizations are investing efforts in active diversity management with the aim of enhancing inclusion and fostering organizational effectiveness in their workforce.

The focus of organizations at the first stage is on capturing the diversity that is available in the workforce. Work organizations at this initial stage are interested in gaining a foothold, in employing qualified individuals in accord with the changing demographics of the available talent and the populations they serve. From this perspective, key considerations include, "Are we able to attract diverse talent into our workforce?" and "To what extent do we reflect our client base?"

At the second stage, organizations invest efforts in creating a culture that accepts and values diversity to increase a sense of inclusion for workers from various identity groups. Key considerations in this stage include the following: "To what extent do our policies and practices attract and retain the most well-qualified and diverse individuals?" "Is our organizational culture inclusive and culturally competent?" "To what extent are employees from different identity groups participating in formal and informal networks and being actively involved in the decision-making process?"

Leadership and global diversity are connected in two complementary ways. First, although some dimensions of organizational leadership are universal, others are culture specific (Dorfman et al., 2012). Given the trends for a more diverse and global workforce, the ability of leaders to manage a diverse workforce and to bridge cross-cultural differences will become central to their ability to perform their jobs effectively. Second, leaders have an important role in inspiring organizations to become more inclusive and in creating an organizational culture of inclusion. For organizations to become truly inclusive, it is not enough that they have policies and guidelines in place; there needs to be a deep conviction in the importance of inclusion. This level of commitment to diversity and inclusion can only come from the very top of the organizations. Rather than ignoring differences between individuals and among groups in the organization, leaders can embrace diversity by implementing a diversity and inclusion strategy, such as the IBM example described below (Thomas, 2004), and use it as a tool to enhance their business. The connection between diversity and leadership is exemplified by J. T. Childs Jr. (2005), IBM's former vice president for global workforce diversity:

> Diversity is becoming a key factor in helping to define leadership in today's marketplace. Workforce diversity is about effectively reaching our customers and markets. As a company we are clearer than ever before about our values and commitment to diversity. (p. 117)

Past research has focused on the outcomes of creating an inclusive environment and demonstrated the positive effects of inclusive organizations (e.g., increased job satisfaction, commitment, and retention and reduced conflict, stress, and organizational turnover; Brimhall, Lizano, & Mor Barak, 2014; Dwertmann & Boehm, 2016; Hopkins, Cohen-Callow, Kim, & Hwang, 2010; Mor Barak, Levin, Nissly, & Lane, 2006; Nishii, 2013; Shore et al., 2011; Travis & Mor Barak, 2010), yet few studies have examined what contributes to an inclusive workplace (Dwertmann & Boehm, 2016; Shore et al., 2011). More specifically, although leaders can play a significant role in influencing how well an organization functions (Aarons, Sommerfeld, & Willging, 2011; Zohar & Gill, 2010; Zohar & Tenne-Gazit, 2008), not much is known about what leaders can do to promote and increase workplace inclusion (Brimhall et al., 2014; Cottrill, Lopez, & Hoffman, 2014).

Most large and midsize companies, both national and global, have statements related to diversity and inclusion on their websites. For example, IBM, the international computer hardware company, has on its website a diversity and inclusion policy statement that starts with the motto, "Diversity of people, diversity of thought. A smarter way to innovate every day" (see IBM Diversity and Inclusion Report, 2015). Hilton Worldwide, an international chain of hotels and resorts, aspires to have "suppliers as diverse as our properties" as one of its inclusion goals. The company states on its website, "The Hilton Worldwide vision is to create supplier relationships that reflect the cultural diversity of local communities. Our commitment is rooted in the belief that relationships with new and diverse suppliers will establish our leadership role in the global marketplace and creates a multitude of benefits for our customers, team members, and stakeholders." Infosys, the Indian multinational information technology consulting company, states, "At Infosys, we welcome people of varying genders, nationalities, and religious beliefs with equal enthusiasm. We believe this is not just the right thing to do, but the smart thing to do if we want to create a work environment that encourages the best talent and ideas."

Placing diversity and inclusion statements on a corporate website, however, does not necessarily mean that the organization's actions support a climate of inclusion. In fact, often the policy messages and statements are different from the actual day-to-day experiences of the employees. We call this *decoupling*—the difference between the policy statement and the practices of the organization (Meyer & Rowan, 1977; Scott, 2008). More specifically, policy-practice decoupling refers to the distinction between *espoused* (or stated) and *enacted* (or practiced) diversity and inclusion policies and procedures (see Figure 11.5). In the present case, decoupling refers to lagging implementation of diversity and inclusion policies, often adopted to gain social legitimacy. Such discrepancy often arises because the implementation of the policy implementation would compete with other organizational goals or affect profitability. For example, if a supervisor thinks that a diverse team would take longer to get organized in working on a project, the supervisor might prefer to choose a nondiverse team, sacrificing not only the policy but also the potential effectiveness of having diverse input into the project. Decoupling, the discrepancy between corporate statements and actual practices, sends a message to employees that the organization "does not really mean it" and therefore employees

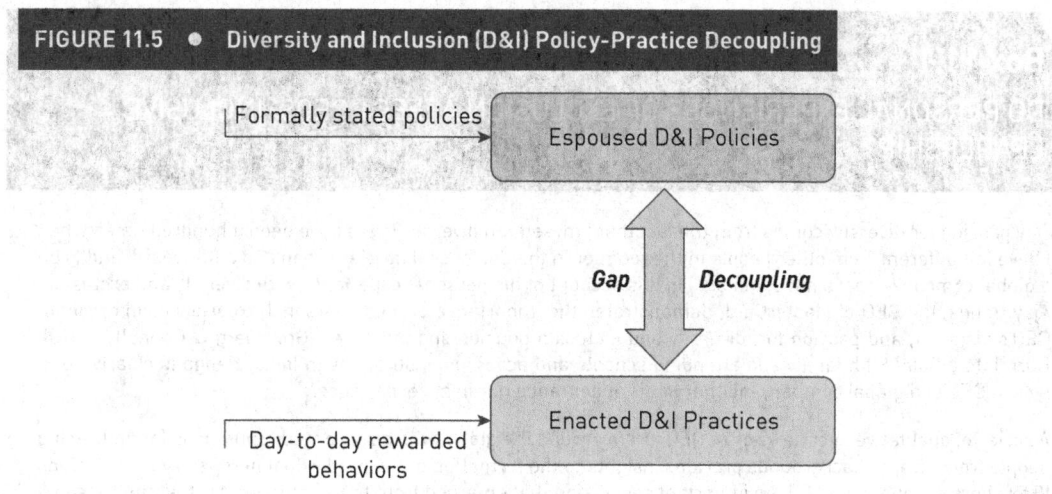

FIGURE 11.5 • Diversity and Inclusion (D&I) Policy-Practice Decoupling

Formally stated policies → Espoused D&I Policies

Gap   Decoupling

Day-to-day rewarded behaviors → Enacted D&I Practices

can disregard these messages or policies. Furthermore, this discrepancy builds frustration into the workforce. Inclusive messages, typically intended to build a committed workforce and a positive public opinion, often do the exact opposite if they are divorced from the reality of the organization.

So how can an organization ensure that inclusion becomes part of its culture rather than an empty slogan or promise? First, the message needs to come from the very top—the CEO, president, and board of the organization. Second, the message needs to be reinforced by behaviors at all levels of the organization, from the supervisors of the larger units all the way to the immediate supervisor of each employee. As workforce diversity continues to grow, it is becoming ever more important to counter decoupling by developing inclusive climates (Mor Barak, 2014; Nishii, 2013; Roberson, 2006). In the next segments we discuss the role of the top leadership of the organization, particularly the CEO, and the supervisors at each level of the organization.

Inclusive Leadership From the Top: The Central Role of CEOs

IBM's chairwoman, president, and CEO, Virginia ("Ginni") Rometty, provides leadership to the company's diversity, inclusion, and engagement initiatives, bringing change both inside and outside the company. For example, IBM's Building Relationships and Influence (BRI) program has over 3,000 women in its alumni network. IBM drove Focus 50 and the Technical Women Pipeline Program in the past 10 years to enable its technical women to progress into executive positions—such as Distinguished Engineer and IBM Fellow—among the company's highest employee technical recognitions. Rometty's leadership was among the reasons why IBM was recognized as one of DiversityInc's Top 50 companies (DiversityInc, 2016). Her personal story of rising from a systems engineer at IBM's Detroit office in 1981 to CEO in 2012 demonstrates the importance of personal narratives of CEOs in affecting their leadership on inclusion initiatives (see Box 11.1). Rometty has been recognized as one of the world's most influential business people (e.g., ranked no. 1 in *Fortune* magazine's list of "50 Most Powerful Women in Business" in 2012, 2013, and 2014, and named one of *Forbes* magazine's "World's 100 Most Powerful People" in 2016). In an interesting twist, Rometty's leadership at IBM has also created a change—toward more inclusion—in an unrelated institution: the prestigious private Augusta National Golf Club, which was forced to accept her as a member as a result of the public outcry regarding its exclusionary policies toward women (see Box 11.2).

Box 11.1

DO PERSONAL EXPERIENCES OF EXCLUSION AFFECT CEOS' INCLUSIVE LEADERSHIP?

"My passion for diversity comes from the fact that I myself am diverse. There have been a hundred times when I have felt different from other people in the room or in the business. I have a turban and a full beard, and I run a global company—that's not common." In this account of his personal experience with diversity and exclusion, Ajay Banga, the CEO of MasterCard, demonstrates the importance of these personal experiences in driving a CEO's vision of, and passion for, diversity and inclusion policies and initiatives (Groysberg & Connolly, 2013). Born into a Saini Sikh family and attending schools and academic institutions in India, Banga is clearly not a typical CEO of a global company, neither in his appearance nor in his experience.

A series of qualitative interviews of 24 CEOs from around the globe, who have earned reputations for embracing people from diverse backgrounds provides insights to the formation of their individual perspectives and visions (Groysberg & Connolly, 2013). An important conclusion that emerged from these interviews is that the personal narratives of CEOs related to exclusion often led them to empathize with different groups who are excluded and drive their passion for implementing diversity and inclusion initiatives. Sometimes the exclusion experiences were of family members and loved ones, rather than the CEO her- or himself.

Carlos Ghosn, the CEO of Nissan Motor Company, told the interviewers how bias had affected his own family. "My mother was one of eight children," he said. "She used to be a very brilliant student, and when the time came to go to college, she wanted to become a doctor. Unfortunately, her mother had to explain to her that there was not enough money in the family, and that the money for college was going to the boys and the girls would instead have to marry. When I was a kid and my mother was telling me this story—without any bitterness, by the way, just matter-of-fact— I was outraged because it was my mother. After hearing that story, I said I would never do anything to hurt someone based on segregation."

Sometimes the experience of exclusion occurs early in the person's career, and at other times it happens when they have already reached a high position of power. Andrea Jung, the former CEO of Avon, shared that as the only woman or Asian sitting around a table with senior executives: "I experienced plenty of meetings outside my organization with large groups of executives, where people assumed that I couldn't be the boss, even though I was."

Even White male CEOs had some personal experiences that helped them develop empathy with groups who are excluded. Jim Rogers of Duke Energy, the electric utility holding company, felt his rural background and southern accent played into negative stereotypes: "When I went to Washington to be a lawyer, I felt like I had to work harder, be better, and prove myself because I had a southern accent and came from a rural state."

Sometimes the "teaching moment" comes when the top manager is, unintentionally, the instigator of exclusion and is called on it. Jim Turley, CEO of Ernst & Young, shared such an experience: "Three women on the board made individual comments that were similar in direction, which I didn't respond to. Not long after they spoke, a fourth person, who happened to be a man, made a comment in line with what the women had been saying, and I said, 'I think Jeff's got it right,' not even aware of what I had just done. To their great credit, the women didn't embarrass me publicly. They pulled me to the side and played it back to me. It was a learning moment for me."

Altogether, these interviews with CEOs who are recognized leaders in diversity and inclusion indicate that personal narratives of exclusion—whether done to them, their loved ones, or even by them—can help top corporate leaders develop self-awareness, insight, and empathy. These experiences, in turn, shape their attitudes toward diversity and inclusion and inform their priorities as leaders.

Source: Adapted from: Mor Barak, M. E. (2000b). The inclusive workplace: An eco-systems approach to diversity management. Social Work, 45(4), 339–354.

Box 11.2

A SECRETARY OF STATE AND A CEO FINALLY BREAK THE GENDER BARRIER AT A PRESTIGIOUS PRIVATE GOLF COURSE

After years of exclusionary practices toward women, the prestigious Augusta club faced a major media storm when it refused to extend membership to IBM's first woman CEO, Virginia ("Ginni") Rometty. Traditionally, the CEOs of the Masters golf event's top corporate sponsors received a membership to Augusta National, the club that hosts the Masters. But for close to a century, since its inception, Augusta National refused to admit women onto its membership rolls (until 1990, the club also excluded Blacks). Therefore, Rometty, despite being CEO of one of the tournament's three lead sponsors—not to mention a Fortune 500 company—was conspicuously excluded. Even the White House press secretary at the time, Jay Carney, weighed in on the issue, saying it was "kind of long past the time when women should be excluded from anything" (Mosle, 2012). Eventually, under pressure from the public and from its male members (including President Barack Obama and presidential candidate Mitt Romney) the club relented and reversed its policy. In August 2012 the private club extended membership to its first woman member, former secretary of state Condoleezza Rice. Rometty was the third woman to receive the Augusta membership (Weinman, 2014). Through her prominent role as CEO of a major global company—a historically male role—Rometty forced a national conversation about respect and equality for women, resulting in a policy reversal. And she did it without ever saying a word about it (Mosle, 2012). This demonstrates that sometimes the mere presence of members of previously excluded groups in prominent non-traditional jobs can bring about inclusion.

CEOs and boards are influential in determining the direction of the organization and the extent to which its leadership supports inclusion. A study of 1,456 nonprofit board CEOs reveals that board governance practices and inclusion behaviors are directly influenced by the gender and racial diversity of the board itself (Buse, Bernstein, & Bilimoria, 2016). The findings suggest that board governance can be improved with more diverse membership, but only if the board behaves inclusively and if there are policies and practices in place to allow the diverse members to have an impact within the organization.

What practices are particularly influential in creating an organizational climate of inclusion? Groysberg and Connolly (2013) note eight such practices, based on in-depth interviews with 24 CEOs of global companies who have been recognized as leaders on diversity and inclusion:

1. *Measure diversity and inclusion.* Metrics are critical to assessing needs and achievements, and most of the leading organizations introduce measures of diversity and inclusion into their employee surveys.

2. *Hold managers accountable.* Many leading organizations make diversity and inclusion goals part of their performance objectives and assessment of managers' achievements.

3. *Support flexible work arrangements.* Balancing work, family, and life is recognized as a cornerstone of inclusive policies, and most leading organizations offer such policies (see Box 11.3 for an example of a CEO reversing the policy, with negative consequences for both employee morale and corporate image).

Box 11.3

A CEO'S CONTROVERSIAL DECISION TO END THE WORK-FROM-HOME POLICY: MARISSA MAYER'S POLICY REVERSAL AT YAHOO

On February 22, 2013, an internal Yahoo memo was leaked to reporters and set up a media storm. The memo revealed a new rule rolled out by CEO Marissa Mayer that requires that Yahoo employees who work remotely relocate to company facilities, *de facto* ending the company's flexibility option. The memo noted "speed and quality are often sacrificed when we work from home. We need to be one *Yahoo!*, and that starts with physically being together" (Swisher, 2013). Mayer reversed the company's flexibility policies in a come-to-work order (Tkaczyk, 2013). Some critics noted as hypocrisy that while banning work-from-home options for her employees, Mayer, who had had a baby a few months earlier, paid to have a nursery built in her office. They noted that, although Mayer was a working mother like many of her employees, she was out of touch with their plight because she was able to bring her baby to work thanks to the nursery in her office (Carlson, 2013). "I wonder what would happen if my wife brought our kids and nanny to work and set them up in the cube next door?" asked the husband of one remote-working Yahoo employee. A couple of months after the media storm that surrounded the new policy erupted, Mayer, in a prescheduled closing keynote address to the Great Place to Work conference in Los Angeles, launched into a speech about Yahoo's vibrant culture. But after a few minutes she surprised the crowd of human resource professionals by saying, "I need to talk about the elephant in the room." At the same time, an image of a purple elephant appeared on the screen behind her, with the large white letters *WFH* (work from home) printed on its side. She then admitted, for the first time since the controversial memo was leaked, that the policy "was wrongly perceived as an industry narrative." Many critics of the policy called it a step backward for workplace flexibility. Mayer acknowledged that people are more productive when they are home alone, but then emphasized that employees are "more collaborative and innovative when they're together. Some of the best ideas come from pulling two different ideas together."

4. *Recruit and promote from diverse pools of candidates*. Diversity begins with a search for talent, and in order to have diversity at all ranks of the company, recruitment needs to focus on finding diverse sources of talent.

5. *Provide leadership education*. Lower levels of organizations tend to be more diverse, and leadership education, such as programs that include leadership training and exposure to higher-level executives, allows members of underrepresented groups a strong preparation for promotion to higher positions within the company.

6. *Sponsor employee resource groups and mentoring programs*. Employee resource groups are networks of employees who share an affiliation (such as women, ethnic minorities, or young professionals) who can provide mentorship, networking, and support for colleagues and assist in identifying promotion opportunities within the organization.

7. *Offer quality role models*. Diversity at the higher levels of the organization provides role models and promotes inclusion throughout the organization.

8. *Make the chief diversity officer position count*. With the proliferation of the relatively new role of chief diversity officer (often also having inclusion in their job title) it is important that the position not only be conspicuous in the organization but that the person holding it be involved and influential in strategic decision making in the organization.

Inclusive Leadership at the Supervisor Level: Leader-Member Exchange (LMX)

Leader-member exchange theory (LMX) is particularly helpful in understanding leadership at the dyadic level—the quality of the relationship between a supervisor and a supervisee—and is, therefore, particularly suitable for the study of diversity relationships in work organizations. The theory focuses on the unique relationship between leaders and each of their subordinates (Graen, 2003; Graen & Uhl-Bien, 1995; Liden, Sparrow, & Wayne, 1997). It challenges the traditional leadership theories that suggest that leaders treat all of their subordinates in a uniform way (Martin, Thomas, Charles, Epitropaki, & McNamara, 2005). For this reason, LMX theory has been claimed to be particularly suited for understanding supervisor-supervisee relationships in the context of contemporary workplace environments that are characterized by diversity. Reflecting on the centrality of the supervisor-supervisee relationship in the context of workforce diversity, Graen (2003) has stated, "LMX relationships are at the core of a successful diversity management initiative."

LMX theory relies on role theory, indicating that an employee's direct supervisor is dominant in the role-making process of the dyad and that the process has three stages: role-taking, role-making, and role-routinization (Graen & Scandura, 1987). At the initial stage of the relationship—the role-taking stage—the supervisor's expectations are central, and these expectations are guided by such factors as the supervisor's previous personal expectations, the supervisee's personal characteristics, and the organizational context (Graen, 2003). If the supervisor has limited or negative experiences with members of diverse groups, it could affect her or his expectations of the supervisee's performance and the quality of their relationship. At the second stage—role-making—the supervisor and supervisee begin to influence each other's attitudes and behaviors. During this stage the supervisor delegates work assignments to the supervisee, whom she or he perceives as being competent and successful in completing the tasks. The supervisee earns the supervisor's respect, and as a result, mutual trust between the two emerges (Goldberg & McKay, 2015). Finally, the third LMX stage—role routinization—occurs when a sense of mutual obligation is formed between the supervisor and the supervisee. Based on mutual services they provide each other, there is a sense of shared understanding regarding goals and behavioral norms and that their career trajectories are interdependent. The relationship at this point is highly predictable and mutually beneficial (Goldberg & McKay, 2015).

The quality of LMX at the group level can influence important employee and organizational outcomes, as demonstrated by a study of 348 supermarket departments that examined LMX as a moderator of the relationships between diversity characteristics and turnover (Nishi & Mayer, 2009). The study findings indicate that group managers created an atmosphere of inclusion through the quality of their relationships with their subordinates. As a result, in groups where the quality of the relationship between the group managers and their subordinates (LMX) was high on average, the positive relationship between diversity and turnover was weaker compared to groups in which the LMX was low. In other words, members of diverse groups were less likely to leave the organization if the quality of the supervisor-supervisee relationships (LMX) in their group was high.

According to LMX theory, the quality of leader-member relationships falls on a continuum ranging from low to high quality. At the low end of the spectrum, the exchange between the leader and the subordinate will be limited to the employment contract and the strict expectations that follow from it. At the high-quality end, on the other hand, the relationship will be based on mutual liking, trust, respect, and influence (Liden & Maslyn, 1998). Based on social exchange theory, we can assume that a relationship at the higher end of the spectrum will be perceived by both parties as mutually beneficial. Employees in the latter type of relationship are more likely to report better working conditions, with more autonomy and more possibilities for participation due to their positive working relationship with their superior. In

Box 11.4

LEADER-MEMBER EXCHANGE AND MANAGING THE MILLENNIALS:
DO THE OLD RULES APPLY?

In his book *Not Everyone Gets a Trophy: How to Manage the Millennials,* Bruce Tulgan identifies the unique qualities of the millennial generation (those born between 1980 and 2000), whom he describes as "confident and self-
possessed" (p. 7). The author shares the story of an experienced nurse-manager in a busy hospital who told him
that she stopped a new young nurse from administering the wrong medicine by intravenous drip to a patient.
"The manager pulled the young nurse aside and explained emphatically how serious a mistake she almost made.
'I explained that this is how patients die unnecessarily.' I told her, 'you need to check the wrist bracelet, then
the patient's chart, then the charge list, then the IV bag. Then you need to check them all again'. Before she
was finished, the young nurse interrupted her. 'Actually, you are doing this conversation wrong' she told her
boss. 'You are supposed to give me some positive feedback before you criticize my work.' What did the manager
respond? 'Okay. Nice shoes. Now, about that IV bag . . . '" (Tulgan, 2016, p. 2).

The millennials are the most diverse generation in history, and as a result, they don't feel the need to conform
for the purpose of gaining entry into institutions, unlike previous generations had to do. In fact, being unique is
a badge of honor, something to take pride in. Tulgan suggests the following nine strategies for managing millennials: (a) bring them on board fast with the right message; (b) get them up-to-speed quickly and turn them
into knowledge workers; (c) practice "in loco parentis" management, and take a strong hand; (d) give them
the gift of context, and help them understand their roles in your company and where they fit in *your* picture;
(e) get them to care about great customer service; (f) teach them how to manage themselves; (g) teach them
how to be managed by you; (h) retain the best of the Millennial Generation one day at a time; and (i) build the
next generation of leaders.

Tulgan emphasizes the importance of the millennials' relationship with their supervisors and managers and
concludes, "They need you to guide, direct, and support them every step of the way. In return, you'll get the
highest-performance workforce in history" (p. 16).

addition, we should assume that they report more social support and good communication with their
leader, and increased affective attachment between the supervisor and the subordinate (Gerstner & Day,
1997).

The most cited and used measure for LMX is the LMX-7 developed by Graen and Uhl-Bien (1995). It uses
a unidimensional scale that contains seven items in which subordinates are asked to rate their relationship
with their leader. In an interesting study using three Norwegian samples, the authors set out to validate the
LMX-7 in the Nordic countries and to find out how quality of leader-member relationships mattered to subordinates (Furunes, Mykletun, Einarsen, & Glaso, 2015). The sample included teachers ($n = 409$), industrial
workers ($n = 406$), and bus drivers ($n = 1024$). The results supported use of the measure LMX-7 as indicated
by factor structure, high-construct validity, sufficient criterion-related validity, discriminant validity, and
internal reliability as measured by Cronbach's alpha above 0.90. In addition, poor-quality relationships, as
indicated by low LMX, were associated with higher levels of role conflict, stress, bullying, turnover intentions, age discrimination, and negative affectivity, as well as lower levels of job satisfaction, commitment,
skills utilization, autonomy, participation, perceived fairness, and social support.

In summary, LMX theory is helpful for understanding leadership in the context of diverse teams
because it focuses on the unique dyadic relationship between the leader and each member of the team

and is based on the quality of relations between leader and followers. In this perspective, the leader provides group members with resources critical to success, and through this relationship shapes the confidence of the followers in attaining shared goals that, in turn, enhance positive outcomes including affective commitment, perceived organizational support, and job satisfaction (Gotsis & Grimani, 2016).

Summary and Conclusion

Organizational leadership is closely connected to diversity management in two complementary ways. First, although some dimensions of organizational leadership are universal, others are culture specific, and the ability of leaders to manage a diverse workforce is becoming central to their ability to perform their jobs effectively. Second, leaders have an important role in inspiring organizations to become more inclusive and in creating an organizational culture of inclusion.

One of the obstacles for reaping the benefits of diversity in organizations has been termed the diversity paradox: If organizations embrace diversity, they risk workplace conflicts, distrust, and tension, but if they avoid diversity, they risk losing their organizational potential for innovation, creativity, and productivity. The solution to the diversity paradox is implementing policies and practices that generate a climate of inclusion in the organization. If an organization becomes inclusive, it can minimize or even avoid altogether intergroup conflicts, tension, and distrust—the downside of diversity—yet enjoy the richness of ideas, creativity, and innovation that is generated by a diverse workforce.

Another obstacle is decoupling—the discrepancy between policies and actual practices related to diversity and inclusion. Leaders have an important role in addressing this gap and minimizing the decoupling. Employees are sensitive to the difference between espoused and enacted policies. Top leadership has to create congruence between the two in order to support a climate of inclusion. Research demonstrates that diversity among top management and boards, together with supporting strong inclusive policies and practices, allow organizations to enjoy the benefits of diversity of talents among their employees.

We define inclusive leadership as "the ability to recognize and celebrate the uniqueness of the group or organizational members and, at the same time, promote their sense of belonging along the three inclusion dimensions of decision making, information networks and participation in groups and the organization as a whole" (Mor Barak, 2005; Shore et al., 2011).

Leader-member exchange theory (LMX) is particularly suited for understanding the supervisor-supervisee relationship in the context of contemporary workplace environments that are characterized by diversity. The theory focuses on the unique relationship between leaders and each of their subordinates; it makes the connection between a high-quality relationship with each subordinate, particularly in a diverse work team, which generates both a climate of inclusion and positive employee and organizational outcomes such as job satisfaction, organizational commitment, and low turnover.

In their efforts to create inclusive organizations, leaders need to remember that inclusion is not about numerical presence alone. If people of diverse backgrounds are allowed in but expected to conform to the existing culture, then "groupthink" will be sustained and the diversity advantage will not be realized. However, if people of diverse backgrounds are invited to actively contribute and change the organizational culture, fresh, contrarian, and creative ideas will flourish and everyone will benefit.

An Overview of the Inclusive Workplace Model

Managing the Globalized Workforce Diversity

Global managers have exceptionally open minds.
They respect how different countries do things, and they have the imagination to
appreciate why they do them that way. . . . *Global managers are made, not born.*

—Percy Barnevick, CEO of Swedish-based Asea Brown Boveri[1]

The economic, social, and demographic trends described earlier in the book create an environment that is a fertile ground for cross-cultural misunderstanding, miscommunication, and intergroup conflicts. The legislative and social policy initiatives taken by individual countries, groups of countries (such as the European Union [EU]), and international organizations (such as the International Labour Organization [ILO]) mitigate potential harmful effects and define "the rules of the game" for work organizations. It is important to understand, though, that these trends are not only a backdrop or context for organizational activities, but they also determine the scope of what companies need to consider as their domain of responsibility when they design diversity policies and programs. In order to avoid the pitfalls and reap the benefits of a diverse workforce, employers need to adopt a broader vision of inclusion, a vision that includes not only the organization itself but also its surrounding community and its national and international context.

The conceptual model for the inclusive workplace introduced here and elaborated on in the next chapters includes both the value base and the practice applications that foster inclusion not only within the organization itself but also within the larger systems that constitute its environment. The process of applying such policies and programs presents several problems and obstacles (Mor Barak, 2000a, 2005, 2014). Some of the barriers to the model's implementation include suspicions and mistrust of those who are different, generational misconceptions (Wong, 2008), cross-cultural misunderstandings, organizational uniformity of thoughts and ideas (Barbosa & Cabral-Cardoso, 2008; Olsen & Martins, 2012), and short-term goals. At the same time, a broad vision for diversity management has a potential for generating important benefits, such as a better work environment for workers and their families (Bond, 2007; Winfeld, 2005), that in turn will contribute to a more productive and loyal workforce. Advantages to the company include recruitment and the competition for talent, positive corporate reputation, legitimacy, firm reputation, and improvement in the public's goodwill toward the company, including customers and stakeholders (Hamdani & Buckley, 2011; Thiederman, 2008).

Diversity Management and the Inclusive Workplace

An organization engaged in diversity management uses policies and programs to accept and capitalize upon the diversity of its own workforce. An inclusive workplace extends beyond diversity management. The inclusive workplace has a strong value base that permeates multiple systems levels to encompass a wider scope of diversity than what is merely represented within the organization's boundaries. The inclusive workplace is active in the community; participates in state and federal programs to include population groups such as immigrants, women, and the working poor; and collaborates across cultural and national boundaries with a focus on global mutual interests (see Box 12.1 for a definition of the inclusive workplace).

It also has policy and practice applications that are unique to each of the levels from the micro to the macro. The more traditional diversity policies and programs have targeted the organization's own workforce, improving the employment opportunities of such groups as women (e.g., Bilimoria, Joy, & Liang, 2008; Kyriakidou, 2011a; Syed & Murray, 2008); members of racial, ethnic (e.g., Smith, 2008; Tatli, 2011), sexual-orientation (e.g., Colgan, Creegan, McKearney, & Wright, 2007), and religious-minority groups (e.g., Menke & Langer, 2011); and people with disabilities (e.g., Ongori, 2012). The concept of an inclusive workplace synthesizes into a cohesive framework the accumulated body of knowledge on diversity within organizations with what we have learned in recent years about business responsibility and involvement with the community along with the projected developments on the global scene. Through programs with the community, such as job preparation workshops or employees volunteering to teach at a local high school, the organization is inclusive of diversity groups that may not be represented in its own workforce; it helps community residents acquire the education and job preparation that will give them access to better jobs; and it helps the community as a whole improve its living conditions. Through collaborations with state and national programs for disadvantaged groups, such as former welfare recipients, domestic violence victims, or recent immigrants, the organization is inclusive of a combination of diversity characteristics that typically bar individuals from even applying for certain classes of jobs or from having a job at all. Finally, through fair and culturally sensitive and respectful international collaborations, the organization is inclusive of cultural diversity that may go beyond national boundaries. These practices are beneficial not only to the recipients of the additional services and programs but also to the organization itself.

In recent decades, the public's expectations for corporate "good citizenship" behaviors have not only increased but also been redefined. The more the public hears of corporate greed, corruption, and faulty

Box 12.1

DEFINITION OF THE INCLUSIVE WORKPLACE

The inclusive workplace is defined as one that	
Micro	• Values and utilizes individual and intergroup differences within its workforce (level I).
↕	• Cooperates with, and contributes to, its surrounding community (level II). • Alleviates the needs of disadvantaged groups in its wider national environment (level III).
Macro	• Collaborates with individuals, groups, and organizations across national and cultural boundaries (level IV).

Sources: Mor Barak (2000a, 2000b, 2005, 2014).

FIGURE 12.1 • Expanding Circles of Inclusion

INCLUSIVE WORKPLACE

Organizational Level

Community Level

National Level

International Level

procedures that result in exploitation and disaster, the less patience it has for corporate indifference and unethical behavior. This sentiment was heightened as a consequence of the global economic crisis of 2008 and generated a very cynical public view of corporate greed and its consequences for both people and the environment. The public often takes corporations' statements about their commitment to ethical conduct with a grain of salt and doubts even the most fundamental statements related to caring for the workforce, the community, and the environment. Even companies that have a strong commitment and track record of conducting their business with integrity and responsibility toward their shareholders find that this is no longer enough. There is a strong expectation among the general public as well as among employees and potential recruits for corporate policies that recognize the importance of the local community and society as a whole. The inclusive workplace offers a model for integration with society via expanding circles of inclusion: Through inclusion of the organization's own workforce, as well as programs with the community—at the state level or across national borders—the organization can be inclusive of diversity groups that may not be represented in its own workforce.

The following chapters introduce each level of the model, identify its value base, and examine policies and practices that make the workplace more inclusive. The barriers and benefits associated with implementing these programs are presented. Each chapter concludes with a case illustration that describes the organizational context and the circumstances that motivate companies to initiate inclusive policies. They illustrate some mistakes that were made and demonstrate interesting and creative programs and initiatives that promote a more inclusive organizational environment. Questions for further analysis and discussion follow each case.

Note

1. Javidan and House (2001, p. 292).

13

The Inclusive
Workplace: Level I
Inclusion Through Diversity Within
the Work Organization

By application of the theory of relativity to the taste of the reader, today in Germany
I am called a German man of science and in England I am represented as a Swiss
Jew. If I come to be regarded as a "Bête noire" the description will be reversed,
and I shall become a Swiss Jew for the German and a German for the English.

—Albert Einstein in a letter to the
London Times, November 28, 1919[1]

The first level of the inclusive workplace, *diversity within work organizations,* relates to the
organization's internal relations with its own employees and reflects the "micro" system level—
that of individuals and groups within the organization. Whereas an exclusionary workplace
is based on the perception that all workers need to conform to preestablished organizational values
and norms (determined by its "mainstream"), the inclusive workplace is based on a pluralistic value
frame that relies on mutual respect and equal contributions of different cultural perspectives to
the organization's values and norms (Cox, 2001; Shore et al., 2011; Stevens, Plaut, & Sanchez-Burks,
2008). For example, an exclusionary workplace will hold a 1-day orientation for new employees,
during which they will be introduced to expectations regarding norms and behaviors in the company
("this is how we do things around here"). An inclusive workplace, on the other hand, will utilize
continuous, multiway communication methods, such as open management-employee meetings and
open e-mail communications, to learn of its employees' concerns and expectations. It will constantly

FIGURE 13.1 • The Inclusive Workplace: The Value Base for Level I

Inclusion and Diversity Within Work Organizations		
System Level	Value Frame	
	Exclusion	Inclusion
	↔	
Individuals and groups within organizations	Conformity to preestablished organizational values and norms that reflect the "majority" or "mainstream"	Pluralistic, coevolving organizational culture that keeps changing to reflect diversity of values and norms

strive to modify its values and norms to reflect the diversity of its workforce. Figure 13.1 illustrates the value base for level I of the inclusive workplace model and identifies the values on either side of the inclusion-exclusion continuum. Note that most organizations will be somewhere along this continuum. Few would be at either extreme.

Inclusive Policies and Practices

A variety of policies and practices constitute inclusion at level I—from recruitment through mentorship and training, to cultural audit and linking diversity practices to strategic goals. What distinguishes an inclusive workplace from an organization that merely implements diversity initiatives is the comprehensive approach to diversity that is part of an overall organizational strategy. This approach includes an organization-wide diversity evaluation, or audit, that should lead to goals that are tailored to the organization's unique culture and will result in implementing appropriate diversity policies and practices. The *cultural audit* is usually performed by outside consultants who obtain data from surveys and focus groups to identify areas in which employees who are different from the dominant group feel that they are blocked from performing to the best of their ability. Based on this assessment, diversity goals are then set forth— with the general purpose of creating a more inclusive work environment and as *a strategy for achieving organizational outcomes* (see Chapter 10 for more details on both cultural audit and diversity management as a strategy for achieving organizational outcomes). In this section, we discuss a variety of diversity policies and practices that an organization can implement to create an inclusive work environment.

Surveys of diversity initiatives in selected multinational corporations indicate that these companies are planning, implementing, and evaluating a large number and variety of diversity initiatives, not only in the United States but also internationally (Cooke & Saini, 2010; Ferner, Almond, & Colling, 2005; Wentling, 2004; Wentling & Palma-Rivas, 2000; Yang & Konrad, 2011). Most of the companies surveyed had diversity statements in their mission as well as their annual reports, and regularly communicated their diversity initiatives to their employees. These diversity and inclusion initiatives typically cover five principal areas: (a) *management leadership,* (b) *education and training,* (c) *performance and accountability,* (d) *work-life balance,* and (e) *career development and planning.*

Through the first type of initiative, *management leadership,* senior management initiate and lead major diversity projects such as using consultants to conduct needs assessments and designing diversity trainings and programs. Groysberg and Connolly (2013) interviewed an international sample of 24 CEOs who ran companies or corporate divisions that had positive reputations for diversity and inclusion (D&I) to understand why and how they executed their D&I goals. Common themes included viewing these initiatives as a "personal mission," passionately linking diversity to a competitive business advantage and stronger ties to a diverse customer base, and tapping into personal experiences (Groysberg & Connolly, 2013). One of the interviewees was Andrea Jung, who was the CEO of Avon at the time of the interview. She described her personal experience this way: "I was often the only woman or Asian sitting around a table of senior executives. I experienced plenty of meetings outside my organization with large groups of executives where people assumed that I couldn't be the boss, even though I was" (Groysberg & Connolly, 2013). CEOs in this study also described an inclusive culture as "one in which employees can contribute to the success of the company as their authentic selves, while the organization respects and leverages their talents and gives them a sense of connectedness" (Groysberg & Connolly, 2013). This description echoes the value base mentioned earlier in this chapter. *Education and training,* the second type of initiative, includes conducting seminars and workshops to increase diversity awareness and skill building to help employees understand the need for, and meaning of, valuing diversity. For example, Sodexo USA's training program called "Spirit of Inclusion"—which includes both raising awareness and skill-building activities—has been given to over 23,000 employees in the United States and Europe (Diversity and Inclusion, 2016). The third type of initiative, *performance and accountability,* requires organizations to develop diversity action plans to meet the goals of specific business units and the organization as a whole, and to hold managers accountable to these goals through various mechanisms including compensation. For example, every quarter at Merck KGaA in Germany, the company compiles and reviews diversity data (e.g., gender distribution) at organizational and group levels to monitor progress toward diversity goals, such as increasing the number of women in top management positions (EMD Group, 2015). Similarly, to ensure senior leader–level accountability for implementing diversity initiatives, AT&T has a Chairman's Diversity Council, led by CEO Randall Stephen (AT&T 2016). *Work-life balance,* the fourth type of initiative, includes offering flexible work arrangements such as telecommuting, job sharing, working at home, and part-time work assignments to accommodate diverse needs and lifestyles of employees. The Adidas Group has a range of what the company refers to as "work-life integration" programs, including flexible work schedules, part-time and telecommuting opportunities, onsite daycare centers, kids' camps during summer holidays, and private nursery rooms for breastfeeding. It even has a parent-child office, which is a workplace with a "kids' corner" that allows parents both to come to work and care for their small children (Work-Life Integration, 2016). Finally, *career development and planning* activities include establishing career development and planning initiatives for women and members of underrepresented groups to ensure fair promotion opportunities for high-potential employees and to increase diversity representation in managerial-level jobs. One example is Goldman Sachs' Emerging Leaders Program, described by the company as "a pipeline development program designed to enhance the progression and retention of strong-performing multi-cultural vice presidents. Through sponsorship assignments, executive coaching and manager engagement, ELP equips participants with the tools to strategically manage their careers" (Goldman Sachs, 2014).

In addition to actively recruiting members of diverse groups, the most common approach to diversity within work organizations is providing sensitivity training and workshops to employees. Often triggered by lawsuits, diversity trainings vary from 1-hour lectures to a series of ongoing seminars. They typically use experiential, emotional, and sometimes confrontational techniques to raise awareness about personal harm caused by the "isms": sexism, racism, ageism, heterosexism, and others. When the training is long term and well conceptualized, the benefits include an increased familiarity and reduced bias against members of out-groups. In the United States, for example, corporate diversity trainings are quite popular, with more than half (71%) of all U.S. companies providing diversity training to their employees (Society for Human Resource Management, 2010). However, often employees resent these diversity-training sessions because they are seen as forced, short-term affairs with no clear connection to the organization's strategic goals (Henderson, 1994; Kalev, Dobbin, & Kelly, 2006; Lynch, 2001; McGuire & Bagher, 2010).

Other efforts to promote diversity and inclusion within organizations include initiatives aimed at (a) establishing organizational responsibility such as appointing a corporate officer to oversee the company's diversity efforts and appointing/electing diversity committees comprised of employees from various departments and levels within the organization, (b) encouraging managers' responsibility for diversity through such mechanisms as evaluating mangers on their diversity performance, and (c) empowering employees of diverse backgrounds through networking and mentorship programs (Colgan, 2011; Groschl, 2011; Kalev et al., 2006). Examples for these efforts include the Commonwealth Bank of Australia's Diversity Council, which is chaired by the company's CEO, with each member of the council acting as an "Executive Sponsor" for a section of the company's diversity and inclusion strategy (Commitment to Diversity, 2016). And General Mills has a variety of affinity networks for underrepresented employees, including the American Indian Council, Asian Heritage, Betty's Family LGBT, Black Champions, and Hispanic, veterans, and women in leadership groups (General Mills, 2016).

Although most diversity efforts in work organizations focus on management initiatives and on developing managerial diversity skills, Thomas (2005) points out that it is just as important to develop the awareness and skills of individual employees at all organizational levels. He advocates that individual employees learn how to become *effective diversity respondents*—people who act with confidence, wisdom, and effectiveness when interacting with others who may be significantly different from them. He further notes that individuals need to develop *diversity maturity*—that is, a combination of knowledge about diversity and a comfort with the dynamics of diversity relationships. In a recent Catalyst report, Prime and Salib (2015) emphasize the important role that psychological safety plays in creating an inclusive workplace. This study uses survey data from over 250 Australian professionals to understand how leaders successfully create workplace inclusion. In this study, inclusive leadership is characterized by four behaviors—empowerment, accountability, courage, and humility—referred to as "EACH" (Prime & Salib, 2015). Findings from this study indicate that "EACH" leadership behaviors create psychological safety among employees, and this in turn creates an environment for successful inclusion initiatives (Prime & Salib, 2015).

Investing in the development of advanced diversity skills is important not only for organizations that will benefit from improved relations and better teamwork among their employees, but also for individuals who will benefit from improved career trajectories. Thomas (2005) argues that "individuals also have a personal responsibility to manage diversity effectively. In fact, unless they do so, the organization as a whole cannot be effective with diversity" (p. 90). It is clearly in the best interest of organizations to elevate their employees' diversity skills while at the same time creating an organizational environment that allows all qualified employees to perform at peak effectiveness (see Box 13.1).

Box 13.1

A COMPANY'S DIVERSITY AND INCLUSION PROGRAMS (LEVEL I): THE CASE OF DCM SHRIRAM INDUSTRIES (INDIA)

DCM Shriram Industries Ltd., headquartered in New Delhi, India, produces a variety of products including sugar, alcohol, fine chemicals, and rayon tire cord. The company's values, stated under its "corporate ethos," indicate a commitment to promoting respectful interactions among all employees and to improving workers' living standards and conditions. In the context of India's past traditions of gender-segregated and caste-oriented society,

DCM Shriram's human resource philosophy includes two components: The first is similar to what U.S.- and European-based companies entitle "diversity training"—a commitment to integration-oriented efforts that include educational and skill-development programs to all employees (regardless of gender and origin) to open up promotion and management opportunities. These efforts also include employee clubs geared toward promoting interaction among employees from different groups and between employees and management. The company's human resource philosophy indicates a belief in "achieving corporate goals through . . . human resource development, career planning and skill-upgrading," and in "building and supporting worker-management relationships."

The second element is more unique to developing countries that are poor in governmental and community services. The company's efforts to promote a positive and inclusive work environment for employees include not only educational, skill-upgrading, and social interaction programs for the company's employees but also family-welfare and community initiatives for the employees and their families. Again, in the context of a traditional class-segregated society such as India's, where a person's identity is largely determined by his or her family of origin, providing services to the family has a deeper meaning than the family-work balance associated with such programs in Western Europe and North America. Under this umbrella, DCM Shriram maintains facilities for housing, sports, and cultural events, as well as libraries and reading rooms for the benefit of employees and their families. Additionally, the company invests in its surrounding communities, where its employees and their families live. One of the company's efforts included the development of a low-cost water purifier especially for rural areas. Through supporting schools, hospitals, and vocational and community centers, and through providing family medical services such as free immunizations and dental/vision treatment programs, the company is investing in its workforce and its community.

Sources: Anand (2003); DCM Shriram Industries Ltd. (2012, 2016); Graham & Whiteside Ltd. (2003); "Why Companies Invest" (2009);

Barriers and Benefits of Implementing the Inclusive Approach at Level I

Organizations that implement inclusive policies and practices may need to overcome barriers on several fronts, but they will be able to reap the benefits both for individual employees and for the organization as a whole.

Barriers

The main barriers have to do with managers' and employees' attitudes and behavior. Specifically, prejudice (biased views) and discrimination (biased behaviors), either overt or covert, are at the core of the barriers for implementing inclusive policies at the workplace. In today's "politically correct" environment, people may be embarrassed to show their ignorance about other cultures, may not want to invest time and energy in learning about those cultures, or may perceive diversity initiatives as a threat to their job security. The barriers traditionally suffered by women, older adults, and ethnic/racial minorities were typically the result of competitive relationships between identity groups in the workplace and often confounded by cross-cultural misunderstandings. These barriers include lack of support in career planning; marginalized status; failure to give nontraditional employees the breadth of experience required for job advancement; social isolation, particularly in management positions; and an unsupportive working environment (Fassinger, 2008; Hyun, 2006; Konrad, 2003; Van Laer & Janssens, 2011). Executives interviewed about the challenges of implementing diversity initiatives reported encountering difficulties in changing attitudes about diversity throughout the workforce, making management more diverse, and changing attitudes or raising diversity competency among managers (Marquis, Lim, Scott, Harrell, & Kavanagh, 2008). Another barrier to creating an inclusive workplace is failing to appropriately address the "people side" of organizational change. Travis and Pollack (2015) used survey data from nearly 900 employees in multinational companies that are operating in China to understand barriers to workplace inclusion. As the authors note, "To create high-performing work cultures, business leaders must pay attention to the people side—how employees connect to company values, its social impact on the broader community, the workplace role models employees are exposed to, and employees' willingness and ability to participate in culture change efforts." When leaders pay attention to this "people side," employees connect to organizational values, are ready and able to contribute, feel that their organization makes a real impact, have opportunities to engage in "holistic dialogue" about culture change in the organization, and see change champions at all organizational levels (Travis & Pollack, 2015). All of these factors increase the likelihood that workplace inclusion efforts will be successful. Figure 13.2 provides a summary illustration of the main barriers and benefits of implementing the inclusive workplace at level I.

An example of a company taking steps to identify and overcome barriers to inclusion is the experience of Sanlam, a financial services company headquartered in Bellville, South Africa. Sanlam developed an employment equity policy as required by the country's 1996 Employment Equity Act. In 1999, the company surveyed its employees and compiled an in-depth report of the barriers to equity within the company. When it was later decided that the company's diversity management initiatives were not progressing quickly enough, the decision was made to link managers' performance bonuses to their diversity management performance (United Nations [UN] Global Compact, 2001). Sanlam continued its efforts to promote diversity through its Human Capital Transformation (HCT) initiative by implementing processes and structures necessary for such a transformation. The group-wide barrier analysis served as a key strategy to Sanlam's HCT initiative, designed to identify barriers to transformation efforts (Sanlam, 2012).

Benefits

By enacting policies that facilitate inclusion of all employees, the employment barriers traditionally suffered by women and members of traditionally disadvantaged groups can be overcome. Such policies open the doors to job advancement and promotions that have clear monetary benefits to individual employees and their families. They also open up channels of communication and enhance employees' decision-making power. Workplace inclusion has been linked to innovation and helpfulness among employees

FIGURE 13.2 ● The Inclusive Workplace: The Practice Model for Level I

Barriers	Benefits	
	Individuals	Organization
• Discrimination • Prejudice • Perception of threat to job security	• Access to advancement and job promotions • Improved income and benefits • More decision-making power	• Business growth and productivity • Cost savings (e.g., lower turnover, less absenteeism) • Positive image with employees, customers, and financial institutions

(Inclusion Matters, 2015). Research into the benefits of diversity for organizations was relatively scarce in the 1980s and early 1990s. Much of the "case for diversity" during that time was built on ideological and deductive reasoning. More research into the benefits of diversity practices has been generated since then, focusing on more clearly defining and measuring diversity and on examining the causal connection between diversity management and organizational outcomes.

There is now accumulating evidence that the benefits of inclusive diversity practices center around three areas: (a) *the opportunity to drive business growth and productivity* by leveraging the many facets of diversity, such as marketing more effectively to minority communities or to senior citizens (e.g., Armstrong et al., 2010; Erhardt, Werbel, & Shrader, 2003; McMahon, 2010; Pitts, 2009; Richard, 2000; "Why Diversity Matters," 2013); (b) *cost savings* due to lower turnover, less absenteeism, and improved productivity—and *winning the competition for talent* by being more attractive to women and members of minority groups (Marquis et al., 2008; "Why Diversity Matters," 2013); and (c) the positive effect that diversity management has on *the company's image and stock prices* (Hollowell, 2007; Robinson & Dechant, 1997; "Why Diversity Matters," 2013; Wright, Ferris, Hiller, & Kroll, 1995).

An example of benefit (a)—that of the connection between diversity and business growth and productivity—is a study conducted in the banking industry that documented an association between racial diversity and improved performance (Richard, 2000). The study's sample included 63 banks from three states—California, Kentucky, and North Carolina—and was based on a combination of financial information (obtained from quarterly reports to the Federal Reserve) and a questionnaire to solicit human resource (HR) information on racial composition (obtained from HR managers in the companies). Although the study's first hypothesis—that racial diversity was positively associated with a company's performance—was not supported, its second hypothesis—that this relationship was moderated by the organization's business strategy—was. More specifically, higher racial diversity was positively related to a company's performance when a company pursued a growth strategy, and it was negatively related to performance when the company pursued a downsizing strategy. Another study investigated the relationship between demographic diversity of the executive board of directors and organizational performance among 127 large U.S. companies. The results indicated that boards of directors' diversity was positively associated with both return on investment and return on assets, thus appearing to have an impact on the overall organizational performance (Erhardt et al., 2003). A third study, utilizing a sample of 68 companies in Spain (or based in Spain), provides evidence for a positive relationship between diversity on corporate boards and firm values (Campbell & Minguez-Vera, 2008). A fourth study in this category is a survey of U.S. federal employees that investigated the relationship between diversity management, job satisfaction, and work group *performance.* The findings indicated that *diversity management* was strongly linked to both work group performance and job satisfaction, and that people of color saw benefits from diversity management above and beyond those experienced by White employees (Pitts, 2009). Two other studies conducted on samples of U.S. federal employees bolster evidence for the importance of diversity management in promoting a satisfied workforce and stable performance.

Choi's (2009) study of U.S. federal employees found greater levels of job satisfaction and less turnover in public organizations with diversity management practices compared to those without. While Choi and Rainey's (2010) study of 150,000 federal workers found that racial diversity alone was negatively related to performance, it also determined that once it was managed through diversity management policies, organizational performance improved. In a 2011 Catalyst study, Fortune 500 companies that had the most women on their boards of directors outperformed those with the fewest by 16% on return of sales (ROS) and by 26% on return on invested capital (ROIC) (Carter & Wagner, 2011).

An example of benefit (b)—that of cost savings that may result from diversity management initiatives—is the experience of Sprint-Nextel Communications. In 2001, Nextel focused its attention on ascertaining the impact of its diversity trainings. The initiative, called the "All-Inclusive Workplace," tracked changes in employee retention and corporate financial benefits that could be attributed to diversity training. The results showed that roughly 10% of the improvement in retention was due to the training; the overall decrease in turnover was 2.2%, or 371 individuals. To put it simply, the training was responsible for 36 people continuing to work at Nextel. This is significant, considering that turnover costs an average of $89,000 per employee, which makes the total savings for the company approximately $3.5 million. Accordingly, based on an impact assessment using the cost of diversity training, Sprint-Nextel figured its saving as a $1.63 net benefit for every dollar spent on the diversity training (Kirkpatrick, Phillips, & Phillips, 2003). Sprint-Nextel's diversity and inclusion efforts have been recognized by several organizations. In 2012, the company was named one of the Top 20 Most Responsible Companies for advanced policies on diversity by *Forbes* as well as one of the 40 Best Companies for Diversity by *Black Enterprise* magazine, in addition to several awards and recognitions in previous years (Sprint-Nextel, 2012).

In general, the literature suggests that diversity initiatives can help companies increase the skill base and range of talent among employees, managers, and executives. In part, this may be because companies that recruit from a wider pool of candidates have access to and are able to hire a larger number of exceptional personnel, thus affecting the organization's bottom line (Marquis et al., 2008). IBM's undeviating commitment to diversity (Clegg, 2012) has certainly resulted in benefits, as indicated by Ted Childs, IBM's former vice president for workforce diversity: "A consistent heritage of diversity translates into a strong reputation that helps us attract and keep talented employees" (Alsop, 2004, pp. 158–159). As mentioned above, cost savings from diversity initiatives can also be attained through attracting and retaining top talent. Gap Inc. recently won a 2016 Catalyst award for its "Women and Opportunity" initiative aimed at enhancing gender inclusion and attracting top female talent across all levels of the organization (Gap Inc., 2016). Gap's efforts have resulted in notable outcomes, including 77% women representation at the highest senior leadership level (up from 33% since 2007), and women of color now represent 40% of all female employees (Gap Inc., 2016).

Finally, examples for benefit (c)—improved company image and stock price—are provided by a study that examined the impact of exemplary versus faulty corporate diversity practices on companies' stock prices (Wright et al., 1995). The study employed event study methodology that is commonly used in financial economics research. This procedure was used to determine if there was a significant change in the price of a company's stock on the days immediately surrounding the announcement of an event of interest, indicating either exemplary or faulty diversity practices. In this study, the event chosen as an indicator of exemplary diversity practices was the announcement of the annual Exemplary Voluntary Efforts Award by the U.S. Department of Labor. Nominees for the award must be free of problems with compliance with the Equal Employment Opportunity Commission (EEOC), must show a commitment to equal employment opportunity (EEO) with demonstrated results, and must show a desire to go beyond "business as usual" practices. Data for this portion of the study included 34 award-winning companies over 7 years. The event chosen as an indicator of faulty diversity practices was the announcement of major settlements by companies found to be guilty of labor discrimination. Data for this portion of the study came from the *Wall Street Journal Index* and the Dow Jones News Retrieval and included 34 companies whose announcements came out during the same 7 years as the award-winning announcements (1986–1992). Companies included in both data sets represented a variety of industries and different sizes, all traded on the New York Stock Exchange during the period of the study. The results indicated that announcements of companies receiving awards for high-quality, voluntary diversity programs were associated with positive and significant stock price changes for those companies, and that announcements conveying that companies were guilty of discriminatory practices were associated with negative and significant stock returns for those companies. Though the association was limited to the days immediately following those announcements, this study demonstrates that high-quality diversity efforts contribute to sustaining a competitive advantage and are valued in the marketplace (Wright et al., 1995).

Creating a hospitable environment for all employees and building a reputation of a company with a diverse workforce can go a long way to improve a company's bottom line. Customers from diverse backgrounds expect the workforce to look like them and are more likely to do business with a company that has a positive image with respect to diversity. Similarly, diversity initiatives and a progressive corporate image can make the stock appealing to socially responsible investors (Alsop, 2004; Bear, Rahman, & Post, 2010). A study on the impact of board diversity on firm reputation found support for the link between gender diversity on corporate boards and corporate social responsibility ratings (Bear et al., 2010). The study drew its sample from companies selected from *Fortune*'s 2009 Most Admired List, which rates companies based on nine criteria including innovation, employee management, use of corporate assets, social responsibility, quality of management, financial soundness, long-term investment, quality of products and/or services, and global competitiveness. *Fortune*'s 2009 Most Admired List was comprised of 689 companies and covered 39 industries in the United States and 25 internationally. Bear and colleagues (2010) focused their study on the health care sector and included companies in areas such as managed care, pharmaceuticals, and medical equipment. Study findings provide evidence to the strengths that women bring to corporate boards including increased sensitivity to corporate social responsibility and participative decision-making styles, subsequently leading to enhanced corporate social responsibility ratings and improved corporate reputation. Soares, Cobb et al. (2011) found similar results—among Fortune 500 companies, gender inclusive leadership was positively associated with charitable giving. For example, contributions from companies that had gender-diverse boards of directors were 28 times higher than companies that had no women on their boards. The authors further note that: "Gender inclusive leadership may also increase the quality of CSR initiatives. Companies with both women and men leaders in the boardroom and at the executive table are poised to achieve sustainable big wins for the company and society" (Soares, Cobb et al., 2011).

Case Illustration: Level I—Inclusion Through Diversity Within Work Organizations—Denny's, Inc.

All human beings have differences. . . . we need to recognize that.

—Rachelle Hood-Phillips,
Chief Diversity Officer, Denny's, Inc.

On December 11, 1991, the Thompsons, an African American family, went to Denny's to celebrate Rachel Thompson's 13th birthday. It wasn't the celebration they had anticipated. After waiting what seemed like an inordinate amount of time to be seated, they told their waitress that it was Rachel's birthday so she was entitled to a free meal under Denny's popular birthday promotion. The waitress ignored the request and the baptismal certificate that the Thompsons presented as proof of their daughter's age. Instead, she went to get her manager. Unfortunately, the manager did not offer a better remedy. The manager asked for proof of Rachel's age but rejected the baptismal certificate. Instead, he said he would accept a school ID card, which Rachel promptly presented. Again, the manager rejected the proof. He asked for the baptismal certificate again, which Mrs. Thompson slid over to the manager. At that point, the manager accused Mrs. Thompson of throwing things at him and started yelling at her. Finally, the Thompsons left Denny's without having eaten. The happy occasion was shattered for both Rachel and the entire Thompson family (story recounted from Adamson, 2000).

The Thompsons' experience is just one of many such accounts from African Americans who visited Denny's in the 1990s (Riesch & Kleiner, 2005). Denny's, once famous for its breakfast menu, became infamous for its discrimination, generating immense negative publicity for denying service to African Americans at several of its restaurants across the United States. In addition to discriminating against its minority customers, Denny's purchased no supplies from minorities and had few minorities in its management.

After paying $54 million to settle a pair of class-action lawsuits, Denny's has undergone a major transformation to change the level of diversity within the company as well as improve the way employees treat customers. Their efforts have been rewarded with widespread praise (Kanso, Levitt, & Nelson, 2012) and numerous awards, including *Fortune* magazine's choice as the number one place for minorities to work. In the words of Denny's former CEO, Jim Adamson, "Denny's has gone from worst to first" (Adamson, 2000). Despite all these changes, however, Denny's still faces a negative public image and continual lawsuits for discrimination.

Homogenous History

Most famous for its "Original Grand Slam Breakfast," Denny's offers a variety of breakfast, lunch, and dinner menu options. Starting in 1953 as a doughnut shop named Danny's Donuts, Denny's has grown into the largest full-service, family-style restaurant chain in the United States, with over 1,000 locations. Denny's became an international company in 1969 when it opened a restaurant in Acapulco, Mexico. It now operates in seven countries, including the United States.

A major stain appeared on Denny's history after two class-action lawsuits for discrimination were filed in 1993 (*Ridgeway v. Flagstar Corporation and Denny's, Inc.* and *United States of America v. Flagstar Corporation and Denny's, Inc.*). The cases accused Denny's (and Denny's parent company at the time, Flagstar) of repeated civil rights violations, primarily against African Americans. Some claimed that Denny's required African Americans to pay for meals prior to consumption. When challenged, employees told customers that other African Americans had left without paying, so prepayment was required. Some African American customers were charged a cover charge prior to being served.

"Blackout" periods were instituted at some restaurants, during which time the number of African American patrons was limited. In many cases, with or without a blackout period, service was refused to African Americans. Denny's employees would simply deny or delay seating, claiming that the restaurant was too full. Frequently during the delay, other later-arriving, non–African American customers were seated or served.

Denny's denied complimentary "birthday meals" for African Americans or in some cases required burdensome proof of a child's age. This was the case for the Thompson family who were denied a birthday meal for their daughter on her 13th birthday.

Denny's sometimes forced the removal of African Americans from its restaurants. This frequently occurred after a customer claimed that he or she was not being treated properly. Denny's employees would then claim the customer was being hostile and order his or her removal, either by security guard or the police (U.S. Department of Justice, 1993).

Although not every Denny's restaurant or employee was guilty of discrimination, the problem was systemic, as evidenced by other practices. Denny's had only one African American franchisee and no minority suppliers in the early 1990s. Denny's board of directors consisted almost exclusively of White men.

Initially, Jerry Richardson, the CEO of Denny's parent company, Flagstar, denied and fought the charges filed in the lawsuits. Faced with growing negative publicity, Richardson signed a pact with the National Association for the Advancement of Colored People (NAACP) in 1993 to help solve the company's problems. He agreed to hire more minorities and increase the number of purchases from minority-owned businesses. Despite these efforts, the evidence continued to mount, eventually causing Denny's to settle the lawsuits.

Denny's losses from the lawsuits and widespread negative publicity were significant. In addition to having to pay $54 million to settle the class-action lawsuits from 1993, many customers refused to patronize Denny's. In a 1996 survey, Denny's found that 66% of African American customers refused to eat at the chain's restaurants (Henderson, 2001). Additionally, in 1996, some 48% of African Americans equated Denny's with discrimination, though by 2004, negative perceptions had dropped to 14% (Speizer, 2004).

Denny's had to absorb operational expenses associated with its class-action settlement. Under the consent decree from the settlement, Denny's was required to perform the following activities for 7 years, starting May 24, 1994 (U.S. Department of Justice, 1993):

- Retain a civil rights monitor, a person experienced with the monitoring and enforcement of civil rights. The monitor was responsible for investigating any new discrimination claims arising after the settlement.

- Develop and administer a nondiscrimination training program. Training was mandatory for every employee of Denny's and Denny's franchises. The training had to be approved by the monitor.

- Test franchise and company-owned restaurants to ensure compliance with the consent decree.

- Notify the public that Denny's will operate in a nondiscriminatory manner. The consent decree mandated the percentage of various ethnicities that were required in Denny's advertisements—with specific rules for counting the seconds of face time for various ethnicities in television commercials.

The New Face of Denny's

Denny's was faced with the daunting task of changing its behavior and image. To accomplish this, Denny's parent company, Flagstar, hired a new CEO, Jim Adamson, in 1995. Adamson has a history of reversing bad company positions, including helping Revco emerge from bankruptcy and improving Burger King's financial woes (Talaski, 2002). Adamson also possessed a unique diversity perspective. When he was a child, Adamson lived in Japan and Europe because of his father's military travels. As a result of his experiences around the world, Adamson has developed a deep appreciation for diversity and considers it important from a business perspective (Adamson, 2000).

One of Adamson's first steps was to create a chief diversity officer position. He recruited Rachelle Hood-Phillips, with whom he worked at Burger King, to fill the role. Hood-Phillips had spent her career successfully building and managing diversity at Fortune 500 companies.

In addition to creating this new position, Adamson denounced discrimination at employee meetings and other events. He publicly warned that he would fire any employee or franchise owner who discriminated or challenged the diversity changes he implemented.

Diversity Changes

Together, Hood-Phillips and Adamson implemented many changes to improve Denny's diversity (Adamson, 2000). As Adamson concedes, the consent decree initiated some of the practices. Denny's, however, added many additional activities. Hood-Phillips developed methods to effectively measure and track diversity at the company. Her work enabled Adamson to tie diversity to managers' bonuses. For example, 25% of the senior management team's incentive bonus was tied to the advancement of women and minorities.

Denny's diversity training may represent some of the company's best efforts to correct its diversity issues. It teaches employees how to empathize with customers. More important, employees are taught how to reflect their empathy back to the customer and show their concern about a problem. Training teaches sensitivity for every culture—not just for African Americans. For example, employees are taught that it is inappropriate to ask a Hispanic customer to show a green card, regardless of the reason.

Security guards are taught to be more sensitive to customers. Many of the security guards are off-duty police officers who believe that early intervention in situations and monitoring of certain customers will prevent problems. However, Denny's teaches the guards that such actions may actually create more problems than they prevent. This point is demonstrated with videos that show various scenarios in which misinterpretations led to disaster when mishandled. For example, in one scene, a security guard follows a patron who doesn't stop at the register to pay. The guard confronts the patron, which leads to a bad situation. In fact, the patron left his money on the table before leaving, as the video later shows. Security guards are trained to watch the restaurant generally, without making guests feel uncomfortable, and respond to situations only when instructed by the store manager.

Every employee must attend diversity training. The consent decree mandates that an employee attend a diversity session within 90 days of joining Denny's and a second session within 270 days. Denny's tightened those requirements to 75 days and 225, respectively. Most employees, however, attend the sessions much sooner than the deadlines.

The diversity training that Denny's uses has a substantial price tag. According to Adamson, Denny's spends several million dollars each year on compliance and training (Adamson, 2000). However, the training has been so effective that Denny's was released from the oversight of its civil rights monitor at the end of 1999, a year earlier than mandated by the consent decree (Adamson, 2000).

Despite being released from oversight, Denny's continues to investigate every incident or claim of discrimination. A toll-free number is posted in every restaurant to help Denny's identify and investigate problems. Denny's policy is not to tolerate any discrimination. It has strict discipline standards for dealing with employees who discriminate or repeatedly perform questionable actions. Furthermore, any customer who discriminates or uses racial slurs is asked to leave the restaurant immediately.

In addition to all of the training that Denny's is providing, the company has also made substantial improvements in the diversity composition of its workforce—from top management to servers and cooks. Denny's started with its board of directors. In the early 1990s, the board was comprised primarily of White men; by 2012, some 40% of the 10 members of the board of directors were women and members of minority groups. Throughout all levels of the organization, the change in diversity has been evident—38% of management and 61% of the workforce are members of minority groups (Diversity Speaks, 2012). In 2015, three of the 10 board members were women, including the board chair, Debra Smithart-Oglesby (Denny's Leadership, 2016). Also in 2015, Denny's started a Women's Leadership Group aimed at creating an internal network of women leaders who support each other's advancement within the company (2014/2015 Diversity Report, 2016).

Denny's has not only increased the number of minority employees, but it also has increased the number of minority franchise owners from 1 in the early 1990s to 120 in 2002. Because the franchisees, on average, own more than one restaurant, the minority franchisees own a total of 472 restaurants, which represents 46% of all Denny's restaurants. In many cases, Denny's has provided funding to help minority owners get started. As of 2015, some 64.1% of the Denny's total workforce were comprised of members of underrepresented groups (Denny's Diversity, 2016). Furthermore, 45% of total restaurants were minority owned, 5% by individuals who identified as LGBT, and 16% by women in 2015 (2014/2015 Diversity Report, 2016). Denny's has increased its purchases from minority-owned suppliers from $0 in 1992 to $90 million in 2002, representing 15% of Denny's annual purchases, four times the national average. As with its minority franchisees, Denny's has helped fund some of the businesses. For example, one of Denny's suppliers was on the verge of bankruptcy. Adamson devised a creative financing arrangement that loaned money monthly to keep the business operating. The business sold items to Denny's and then repaid the loan monthly after receiving payment for the goods. As of 2015, some 13.1% of Denny's total spending went to minority and women-owned suppliers (Denny's Diversity, 2016). Since 1993, Denny's has spent over $1.7 billion on minority and women-owned businesses (2014/2015 Diversity Report, 2016). And in 2013, *Professional Women's Multicultural* magazine named Denny's the "Best of the Best Top Supplier Diversity Program," and *Black EOE Journal* ranked Denny's as one of the "Best of the Best Top Supplier Diversity Program" (Denny's Diversity Awards, 2016).

In 1995, Denny's enacted a Supplier Diversity Initiative that was developed to significantly grow the company's diversity supplier base and provide the essential links between diverse suppliers and corporate entities, thereby ensuring that qualified minority suppliers have an equal opportunity to participate in Denny's procurement process. The initiative supports suppliers in three key areas: (a) mentoring, (b) community outreach, and (c) second-tier development (Denny's Supplier Diversity Initiative, 2012). In 2012, Denny's reported that the diversity initiative spent over $1.4 billion on minority and women-owned business enterprises (Diversity Speaks, 2012).

More than a decade after the initial incident, in 2007, Denny's created an annual Minority and Women-Owned Business (MBE) Summit. Supporting local minority and women-owned businesses, Denny's developed the annual MBE Summit in an effort to place special emphasis on growth opportunities for local businesses. The event provides minority and women-owned businesses with a series of beneficial workshops by leading experts on success strategies during tough economic times. The event also provides connections with some of the nation's largest and most successful minority businesses and corporations to explore new business and partnering opportunities (Diversity in Focus, n.d.).

In addition to changing its business practices, Denny's has been active with philanthropic activities, supporting numerous human and civil rights organizations. For example:

- In 2002, Denny's initiated a 3-year fund-raising campaign to promote human and civil rights. In the first year, Denny's raised $1.2 million for the National Civil Rights Museum. In 2003, Denny's targeted a $1 million donation to the King Center.

- In 2002, Denny's partnered with the Hispanic College Fund to initiate Denny's Scholastic Stars Sweepstakes. Denny's has pledged $250,000 to provide scholarships to Hispanic students over a 3-year period.

- From 1995 to 2001, Denny's was the largest corporate sponsor for Save the Children (STC), contributing nearly $7 million in support of STC activities on behalf of U.S. children. More than three quarters of the population served by STC were minorities (Diversity in Focus, n.d.).

- In 2004, Denny's again partnered with the King Center to fund the creation and promotion of a nonviolence youth service learning curriculum that was distributed to more than 300 youth organizations nationwide.

- In 2005 and 2006, Denny's partnered with the National Urban League and raised $1 million for the National Urban League's educational and after-school programs (Diversity in Focus, n.d.).

- In 2008, Denny's launched a new initiative in partnership with the Tom Joyner Foundation called the Denny's Single Parent Student Scholarship. The scholarship program is aimed at helping single-parent students attending historically Black colleges and universities (HBCUs) meet the challenges of raising a family while earning a postsecondary education ("Denny's Promotes Diversity Leader," 2008).

- Since 2011, Denny's has donated over $2.3 million to Share Our Strength's No Kid Hungry Program (2014/2015 Diversity Report, 2016).

- In 2013, Denny's started the Hungry for Education scholarship program, which offers over $200,000 in scholarship money to high school and college students for their ideas about how Denny's can end childhood hunger in local communities (2014/2015 Diversity Report, 2016).

To let the public know about all of the changes and recapture some of its lost customer base, Denny's spent several million dollars on an ad campaign targeting minority customers. The campaign illustrated the changes at Denny's, especially the increased number of minority franchise owners and suppliers. Although this new campaign was a fulfillment of the consent decree, Denny's delivered more than was required.

Awards and Impact

The efforts at Denny's have been noticed by numerous organizations. Denny's has won awards for being a friendly place for women and minorities to eat and work. Awards have come from *Family Digest* magazine, the National Association for Female Executives, *Asian Enterprise* magazine, *Latina Style* magazine, *Hispanic Business* magazine, *Essence* magazine, and the Center for Responsible Business. More recently, *Asian Enterprise* magazine ranked Denny's one of the top 10 companies for Asian Americans from 1999 to 2010, and Carolinas Minority Supplier Development Council named Denny's "Corporation of the Year" (Denny's Diversity Report, 2010).

However, the most significant awards that recognize Denny's achievements are from *Fortune* magazine and the NAACP. In 1998, *Fortune* ranked Denny's as the second-best place for minorities to work. Denny's went on to rank number one for 2000 and 2001, remaining in the top 10 consistently since 1998. *Fortune* ranks companies based on a comprehensive list of diversity factors including (a) how well minorities are represented in the general workforce, (b) how many are among the most senior officials and highest-paid employees, (c) whether minorities are promoted into management at the same rates as nonminority employees, (d) whether managers are held financially accountable for meeting diversity goals, (e) how successfully people of color have been integrated into succession plans, (f) the strength of purchasing programs with minority-owned businesses, (g) the use of minority-owned underwriters or pension-management firms, and (h) the portion of charity going to minority-benefiting programs ("Best Companies for Minorities," 2003).

In 1997, the NAACP presented Denny's with the Fair Share Corporate Signatory Award for Minority Business Development. The Anne Arundel (Maryland) branch of the NAACP named Denny's "Corporation of the Year" for 1996. Additionally, in 1996, the NAACP named Jim Adamson "CEO of the Year." More recently, Chief Diversity Officer Rachelle Hood-Phillips was presented with the "We Share the Dream Award" at the 18th Annual Dr. Martin Luther King Jr. Awards Dinner in 2006 (Denny's Diversity Report, 2010).

Denny's has also been selected to the 2006 and 2007 *Black Enterprise* 40 Best Companies for Diversity, receiving high honors such as Most Improved Company. In selecting the top 40, *Black Enterprise* conducts a comprehensive outreach effort to the CEOs and diversity executives of the top-grossing 1,000 publicly traded companies and the 50 leading global companies with significant U.S. operations. *Black Enterprise*'s corporate diversity survey focuses primarily on activities related to the participation of African Americans and other ethnic minority groups in four key areas: supplier diversity, senior management, board involvement, and employee base ("Denny's Named Among Top Performers," 2006). In 2013, Denny's was listed among the "Top 10 Best Companies for Asian-Americans" (*Asian Enterprise* magazine) and "Top 100 Companies Providing the Most Opportunities for Latinos" (*LATINO* magazine) (Denny's Diversity Awards, 2016).

In addition to the awards, Denny's efforts have resulted in increased business. In 1998, Hood-Phillips conducted a follow-up survey and found that 39% of African Americans would not eat at Denny's.

Although that number is still significant, it is substantially lower than the findings from 1996, when 66% of African Americans refused to eat at Denny's (Henderson, 2001). The 2-year change in attitude represents an additional 1 million African American customers for Denny's (Adamson, 2000).

Continued Legal Trouble

Despite the changes made at Denny's, legal trouble persists. Numerous lawsuits have been filed against the company since the 1993 class-action cases (Riesch & Kleiner 2005; Texas Civil Rights Project, 1999; "Trooper Sues," 2003). The claims were familiar: denial of service, mistreatment, racial slurs, and other discrimination practices. The plaintiffs ranged from students, to a police officer, to a reverend. Denny's has also faced sexual harassment and discrimination charges from at least one employee (U.S. EEOC, 2002).

One case involved a group of Chinese and African American students from Syracuse University. They claimed that in 1997 they were refused service and then kicked out of the restaurant by one of the security guards. The students claimed that they were then beaten by the security guard and a mob of 10 White customers. Denny's civil rights monitor recommended the dismissal of one of the employees involved in the incident. The franchise owner protested, claiming no discrimination had occurred. However, he agreed to terminate the employee. For many, the story was not only disturbing but also plausible, considering Denny's past. The district attorney, however, threw out the case. Upon reviewing the evidence, he determined that the students orchestrated the entire string of events from beginning to end. Customers reported that the students were obnoxious and intoxicated, directing profanity at employees. The scuffle outside involved only one other customer, who threw a punch at the students. The students refused to cooperate with police who arrived at the restaurant (Tuchman, 1997).

Another case in January 1999 involved two Muslim men who went to a Denny's in Montana for lunch and requested that the cooks use a separate skillet so as not to contaminate their meals with pork. Halfway through their meals they discovered pork hidden in their food. They were offered new meals after complaining to the manager, only to find bacon within the new meals as well. A Montana Human Rights Bureau investigator concluded that the Denny's employees deliberately placed the pork in the Muslim customers' meals. Another case of blatant discrimination occurred in September 2003 when an African American Florida highway patrol officer, Barbara Levy, went to Denny's with five other uniformed officers during her lunch break. When the meals arrived, Officer Levy discovered a small plastic pig on her plate. When the cook was asked about the incident, his response was, "Well, that's what you are, a black pig." The officer filed a discrimination lawsuit (Riesch & Kleiner, 2005).

In a 1999 lawsuit, an African American couple claimed they were ignored for nearly an hour while only White customers were seated and served. However, Denny's had a videotape of the incident, which showed the couple was in the restaurant not for an hour but just 10 minutes. Additionally, the videotape showed several African American and Hispanic customers being seated during those 10 minutes ("Denny's Catches Phony Discrimination Claim," 2000).

More recently, Denny's was sued by the U.S. EEOC on behalf of former restaurant manager Paula Hart and dozens of other former employees who alleged that they experienced discrimination based on a disability. On June 24, 2011, Denny's settled and agreed to pay $1.4 million to the claimants (Kearney, 2011). In 2015, a Denny's restaurant in Deming, New Mexico, was in the news for discrimination against members of the Deming Pride group whose members visited the restaurant after a gay pride parade. Members filed a discrimination claim with the New Mexico Workforce Solutions Department (Reed, 2015). The Denny's franchise owner at this location donated money to the Deming Pride group, provided compensation to an individual member who said she was verbally abused, and said that he would offer extra antidiscrimination training to his employees.

Responding to one of the discrimination lawsuits, Rachelle Hood-Phillips said, "I wish we could have been faster and more efficient. But let's not confuse the delay of service with discrimination." She noted that the number of discrimination lawsuits against Denny's has declined steadily since 1993, with only four filed in the first half of 2001 ("Family Sues Denny's," 2001).

Questions for Discussion and Further Analysis

1. Could Denny's have managed its diversity issues better? Why or why not?

2. Why do you think Denny's is facing continuing discrimination lawsuits? Do the lawsuits indicate that Denny's policies and practices are not working? Are there other explanations? If you were a consultant, what would you advise the company to do at this point?

3. Jim Adamson stated that he would fire anyone who discriminated or challenged his new policies. What message did this statement send to the employees? What impact do you think it had on employee morale and customer relations?

4. Was Jim Adamson effective in improving Denny's diversity and public image? Why or why not?

Summary and Conclusion

This chapter presents level I of the inclusive workplace model: inclusion through diversity within the work organization. It relates to the organization's internal relations with individuals and groups of employees. A variety of policies and practices constitute inclusion at level I—from recruitment, through mentoring and training, to cultural audit and linking diversity practices to strategic goals. What distinguishes an inclusive workplace from an organization that merely implements diversity initiatives is the comprehensive approach to diversity that is part of an overall organizational strategy.

Diversity initiatives typically cover five principal areas and include (a) management leadership, (b) education and training, (c) performance and accountability, (d) work-life balance, and (e) career development and planning. In addition to actively recruiting members of diverse groups, the most common approach to diversity within the work organization is providing sensitivity training and workshops to employees. Although most diversity efforts in work organizations focus on management, it is just as important to develop the awareness and skills of individual employees at all organizational levels.

The main barriers to implementing inclusive policies at this level are attitudes and behaviors of prejudice and discrimination within the company. These barriers include lack of support in career planning, failure to give nontraditional employees the breadth of experience required for job advancement, and a lonely and unsupportive working environment. The main benefits of inclusive policies at this level include (a) the opportunity to drive business growth and productivity by leveraging the many facets of diversity, such as marketing more effectively to minority communities or to senior citizens; (b) cost savings due to lower turnover, less absenteeism, improved productivity, and winning the competition for talent by being more attractive to women and members of minority groups; and (c) the positive effect that diversity management has on the company's image and stock price. The Denny's case provides an opportunity to examine the impact of diversity lawsuits on a company's image and financial stability. It also illustrates some of the practices that make the company more inclusive, as well as the barriers and benefits to implementing such policies.

Note

1. *Bête noire* is French for "black beast" and refers to something or someone dreaded or hated. Note the context of this statement—between World War I and World War II, when tensions were mounting between Germany and England and Jews were being persecuted in Germany. Einstein's statement is quoted in D. Aczel (1999), *God's Equation: Einstein, Relativity and the Expanding Universe*, p. 121.

14

The Inclusive Workplace: Level II

Inclusion Through Corporate-Community Collaborations

We support the communities where we do business because we draw
our employees, customers, and suppliers from those communities.

—A corporate diversity manager in a large multinational corporation[1]

The second level of the inclusive workplace, *inclusion and corporate-community collaborations*, relates to the organization's sense of being a part of its surrounding community and the reciprocity embedded in this relationship. It reflects the "mezzo" system level of organizations and communities. An exclusionary workplace sees minimal or no connection to its community. An inclusive workplace, on the other hand, recognizes the economic and noneconomic consequences of its presence in the community. It acknowledges the responsibility it has to ameliorate the adverse effects of this presence and to make a positive contribution to the community's well-being. For example, an exclusionary organization will view any volunteer work its employees engage in as a private matter that is part of their after-work activities, whereas an inclusive workplace will encourage, support, and finance activities such as teaching computers to elementary school students or mentoring inner-city youth (see Figure 14.1 for an illustration of the value base for level II of the model).

An important construct in the business literature is that of *corporate social performance* (CSP), currently used as one of the criteria to assess Fortune 500's most-admired companies. The other commonly used term is *corporate social responsibility* (CSR). Both terms expand a company's responsibilities beyond

FIGURE 14.1 • The Inclusive Workplace: The Value Base for Level II		
Inclusion and Corporate-Community Collaborations		
Value Frame		
System Level	Exclusion	Inclusion
	←————————————————————————————————→	
Organizations, communities	Organizational focus is intrinsic, with exclusive responsibility to financial stakeholders	Dual intrinsic and extrinsic focus, with recognition of community systems as stakeholders as well

its traditional economic shareholders to that of multiple stakeholders, including the community (Greening & Turban, 2000; Hutchins & Sutherland, 2008; Rowley & Berman, 2000; Shaukat, Qiu, & Trojanowski, 2015; Valiente, Ayerbe, & Figueras, 2012). Carroll (1979) developed one of the earlier versions of a comprehensive view of CSP and has reiterated his opinion (2000) that social performance review should include a comprehensive assessment of actions related to most social issues and stakeholders.

The most well-known criticism of CSR came from the Nobel Prize–winning economist Milton Friedman (1970), who proclaimed in his *New York Times Magazine* article on September 13, 1970, that "the social responsibility of business is to increase its profit." It is important to place Friedman's comment in the context of the time in which it was said. Public expectations from corporations were limited, and employees and consumers alike were not as socially aware and savvy about their power to influence corporate citizenship behavior as they are today. On close observation, Friedman's comment may not be as much of a contradiction to CSR as it may seem. Because of the change in the social context, corporations need to contribute to the welfare of their communities to create goodwill among their customers and to attract talented employees; both are essential for making a profit. It is important to note that both CSP and CSR focus on a direct, business-related role for companies vis-à-vis the community, with an emphasis on the strategic and bottom-line implications of socially responsible corporate practices (Carroll & Shabana, 2010; Heal, 2008; Valiente et al., 2012; Werther & Chandler, 2006).

The constructs of CSP and CSR include more than just the corporate-community collaborations referred to in this level of the inclusive workplace. They apply to a whole host of activities that are socially and environmentally beneficial, and in some respects, relevant to levels III and IV of the model as well. Both constructs stem from the recognition that economic actions of business entities have noneconomic consequences and that business organizations have an impact on other institutions of society above and beyond their economic sphere.

In the past, when businesses abided by the law and exercised fair and honest practices, they were considered to have integrity. However, this is no longer enough, as the public is aware of businesses' obligation to society and expects them to have a strategy in place to fulfill this obligation. Corporations today do not have the luxury of waiting for government instructions; government can be slow to act and/or new legislation may not be effective. The public, therefore, expects firms to be active and proactive in responding to the needs of the community (Schwartz & Gibb, 1999; Werther & Chandler, 2011). As Carroll (2015) notes, "CSR represents a language and a perspective that is known the world over and has become increasingly vital as stakeholders have communicated that modern businesses are expected to do more than make money and obey the law" (p. 87). In this context, the primary role of the corporation as an economic institution is accepted as a given, and the corporation is expected to engage voluntarily in activities that benefit its community (Greening & Turban, 2000; Johnson, 2009). Clearly, businesses recognize their duty not only to protect their physical and social environment but to also to contribute to the welfare of their community. At the same time, there is also accumulating research documenting the connection between a company's social and ethical policies and its financial performance, a connection that has been termed *doing well by doing good* (see, for example, Batruch, 2011; Benioff & Southwick, 2004; Field, 2007).

Inclusive Policies and Practices

Given their economic power, corporations can step in and offer to groups and communities essential resources that would not otherwise be provided by governmental agencies. A wide range of activities falls under the title of CSP, such as supporting educational or cultural institutions in the community, providing mentorship to youth, or tutoring children in local schools (see Box 14.1 for a case example). In an effort to find out if CSR practices can actually bring improvements in financial and social performance, a group of researchers analyzed data from 100 Chinese national state-owned enterprises (CNSOEs; Zhu, Liu, & Lai, 2016). The authors found that the CSR activities of these organizations were related to the environment, labor practices, political responsibility, and human rights, but that more attention needs to be placed on managing the supply chains, fair operating practices, and community development. The authors evaluate the social performance of CNSOEs by using the two performance ranking systems developed by the Chinese Academy of Social Sciences. Their findings, based on regression results and structural equation modeling (SEM), indicate that that CSR practices pertinent to organizational governance, human rights, and the environment were beneficial for their social performance. Similarly, Grosbois (2011) explored CSR among the 150 largest hotel companies in the world. Based on the content analysis of websites and reports published online by the hotel companies, Grosbois found that while a large number of hotel companies report dedication to CSR goals, substantially fewer companies provide information on specific initiatives undertaken to achieve these goals, and an even smaller number report on the goals actually being achieved. Similarly, Werner (2009) studied CSR initiatives in Bangladesh that are intended to decrease social exclusion among minority groups and explored whether CSR projects boost economic and social capabilities while also reducing social exclusion. Werner found that CSR has potential for providing positive and lasting impact on developing countries, especially social exclusion among marginalized populations. CSR initiatives in Bangladesh included job skills and training opportunities for women in addition to rehabilitation and health care services for women and their communities.

Box 14.1

A COMPANY'S COMMUNITY INCLUSION PROGRAMS (LEVEL II)— THE CASE OF NESTLÉ (SWITZERLAND)

Headquartered in Vevey, Switzerland, Nestlé is the largest food and beverage company in the world. The company operates in nearly every country of the world, employing 339,000 individuals and with revenues at $92 billion as of 2015 ("World's Most Admired Companies," 2016; Nestlé 2014). Nestlé was one of *Fortune* magazine's 2015 Global Most Admired Companies. In the company's 2014 Shared Value Report (Nestlé in Society, 2014), the CEO emphasized the company's "firm belief that for a company to prosper over the long term and create value for shareholders, it must create value for society at the same time." Furthermore, the company noted that investing and trading internationally can create new jobs, raise skill levels, and benefit the local economies. However, some of Nestlé's past business actions have attracted widespread criticism (Yamey, 2000). The most prominent and well-documented controversy concerned the company's methods of marketing processed cow's milk or baby formula as a substitute for breastfeeding to mothers across the world, including developing countries. Nestlé's activities attracted worldwide attention during the Nestlé boycott of 1977. Another problem involved child labor (children younger than 15) at cocoa farms connected to Nestlé. A report by the Fair Labor Association (FLA) commissioned by Nestlé, indicates that researchers who visited 260 farms used by the company in the Ivory Coast from September to December 2014 found 56 workers under the age of 18 and about half of them under the age of 15 (Clarke, 2015). The company has worked hard to improve the public perception of its activities, launching some Fair Trade products and focusing on its CSR activities (Nestlé, 2011b).

To those ends, the Nestlé Foundation, an independent organization, was established in 1966 to promote scientific and technical knowledge transfer to developing countries (Nestlé Foundation, 2014). The foundation sponsors the International Fellowship Programs that work to develop nutrition-related research in low-income countries. The foundation also provides research grants on a continuous basis and has recently sponsored research among populations in countries such as China, Senegal, Ethiopia, Vietnam, Pakistan, and Mexico.

Beyond the Nestlé Foundation, the company is involved in numerous other community initiatives and actively encourages employee participation. For example, in Brazil, over half of the Nestlé employees participate in a program that teaches good nutrition to marginalized families. The program's goal is to reach a half million children. A similar program is under way in Russia. In Morocco, Nestlé provides funding for the Zakoura Foundation's elementary education initiative. The company finances the work of 10 schools, allowing for the education of children who cannot enter the public school system (primarily because of their remote locations). In South Africa, Nestlé is teamed with EcoLink to teach people in remote rural communities the skills needed for such activities as trench gardening or accessing drinkable water. In Nigeria and other African countries where HIV/AIDS is pandemic, Nestlé sponsors the Red Cross and Red Crescent Societies' Africa Health Initiative 2010, focused on reducing the spread of HIV (International Federation of Red Cross and Red Crescent Societies, 2002; Nestlé, 2011b). As of 2015, Nestlé was working with nearly 300 community partners to deliver its Healthy Kids Global Programme in 80 countries (Healthy Kids Global Programme, 2015). The goal of this program is to increase children's knowledge and awareness about nutrition and physical activity.

In general, many multinational organizations as well as nationally and locally based ones are actively involved with community initiatives such as mentorship programs for disadvantaged students, internships, sponsorship of local school programs, and participation of company leaders on boards of minority organizations in the community. For example, the University of Southern California (USC), the largest private employer in the city of Los Angeles, initiated a series of community outreach programs in the early 1990s as part of its strategic plan ("Strategic Plan," 2004). The university, located in the Los Angeles downtown area that is home to diverse, partly immigrant, and mostly disadvantaged communities, has launched several community-oriented programs. These programs included the Family of Five Schools—a public-private partnership that provides special educational, cultural, and developmental opportunities for approximately 8,000 children who live close to USC's University Park campus; the Joint Educational Project—sending 1,200 mentors, teaching assistants, and mini-teams into the local schools and agencies; and Civic and Community Relations—encouraging more entrepreneurs, and especially minority entrepreneurs, to establish businesses in the immediate vicinity of the university's campuses (USC Civic and Community Relations, n.d.). The USC follow-up strategic plan ("Strategic Plan," 2011) called for the continuation and expansion of the outreach programs to underserved communities around the campus in the downtown Los Angeles area. The USC State of the Neighborhood Project, launched in 2013, focused on strategic priority areas for USC civic engagement, identified opportunities for interdisciplinary faculty research, and served as a resource and framework for university and community stakeholders in the areas of civic engagement, place-based research, and student service learning (Amaro, 2015).

Another example is the U.S.-based Shell Youth Training Academy (SYTA) and the similar Nigerian Shell Intensive Training Programme (SITP), both sponsored by the Royal Dutch/Shell Corporation, a global group of energy and petrochemical companies. The academy opened in February 1993 to provide high school students in the Los Angeles Unified School District with postsecondary career opportunities and training. The SYTA's and the SITP's goal is also to provide Shell with access to a larger talent pool of prospective employees in the local community (Shell Intensive Training Programme, 2009; Shell Youth Training, 2004). Two similar programs were opened in Chicago and Oakland, with more than 1,000 students taking advantage of them since their inception. Once accepted (based on a 2.2 grade point average and teacher recommendations), 11th- and 12th-grade students attend half-day classes at the SYTA academy for one semester. The program covers consumer service occupations, career planning, job search skills, assessment of personal interests and aptitude, interpersonal skills, effective communication, and other elements of successful career development.

Another example of a corporate-community collaboration is the Native American Professional Network (NAPN), one of Bank of America's 12 employee networks (Native American Professional Network, n.d.). Not only does the group assist with the recruitment and advancement of Native Americans and Alaska Natives within the company, it has also partnered with United National Indian Tribal Youth (UNITY), the largest Native American youth organization in the United States. Through this collaborative effort, members of NAPN provide financial literacy education materials and workshops at UNITY chapter meetings and the group's annual meeting. In 2014, Bank of America also cosponsored the long-standing National Congress of American Indians' (NCAI) 71st annual convention.

Barriers and Benefits of Implementing the Inclusive Approach at Level II

Barriers at Level II

The main obstacle for initiating and maintaining activities that benefit the company's social environment is economic pressure to demonstrate profitability on a short-term basis (e.g., quarterly), which makes it difficult to allocate the money necessary for long-term commitments to social goals. When companies are under pressure to demonstrate short-term profitability, it is difficult for managers to justify the allocation of resources necessary for commitments to social causes that may yield results only in the long run. Businesses often perceive the relationship between social responsibility and financial performance as a trade-off. They view the costs incurred from socially responsible actions as an economic disadvantage compared with other business activities (Greening & Turban, 2000; Valiente et al., 2012; Werther & Chandler, 2006, 2011). For example, many suppliers believe that addressing CSR issues makes them less competitive (Vogel, 2005, p. 95). A secondary but important barrier is that of finding the right leaders to be champions of such programs, people who command authority and respect in the organization and who can initiate and maintain these activities. Often, even when a commitment has been made and money allocated for a social cause, there is no steady leadership to sustain such an effort beyond the initial stages of excitement and self-congratulations.

Figure 14.2 provides a summary illustration of the benefits and the obstacles of implementing the inclusive workplace at level II of the model.

Benefits

In addition to the moral and ethical value of socially responsible corporate policies and programs, accumulating research provides evidence that companies draw tangible benefits from such activities. Early examinations of CSR actions focused on damage control, specifically organizational policies that are aimed at preventing lawsuits (e.g., Frooman, 1997; Werther & Chandler, 2011). Research and scholarly articles are typically focused more on tangible benefits such as advantages in recruitment, creating goodwill among consumers, increased employee loyalty, and improved corporate image (e.g., Aguinis & Glavas, 2012; Batruch, 2011; Du, Bhattacharya, & Sen, 2015; Greening & Turban, 2000; Hutchins & Sutherland, 2008; Valiente et al., 2012; Vogel, 2005; Werner, 2009; Werther & Chandler, 2006, 2011; Zientara, Kujawski, & Bohdanowicz-Godfrey, 2015).

There is accumulating empirical evidence for the link between CSP and financial performance (Flammer, 2015; Wang & Choi, 2013). For example, using a sample of 622 firms, Wang and Choi (2016) found that consistency in social performance, both with respect to the domains and over time, was positively related to financial performance of these organizations. In a meta-analysis of 52

FIGURE 14.2 • The Inclusive Workplace Model: Obstacles and Benefits for Level II		
Inclusion and Corporate-Community		
	Benefits	
Barriers	*Individuals*	*Organization*
Economic pressures to demonstrate profitability	Employment, job training	Improved corporate image and reputation
Limited company vision (shortsighted and internally focused)	Mentorship	Advantage in recruitment and in labor disputes
	Improved services to the community	
Lack of leadership to champion and sustain efforts		Increased employee loyalty
		Strong connection between social performance and economic performance

quantitative studies over 30 years of research, Orlitzky, Schmidt, and Rynes, (2003) found a positive correlation between companies' social performance and their financial performance. Examining the application of this line of research to the banking industry, Simpson and Kohers's (2002) research supports the link between social and financial performance. They measured CSP using two categories from the rating system mandated by the Community Reinvestment Act (CRA)[2]—indicating high versus low social performance. Their outcome measure of financial performance was the banks' rates of return on assets and loan losses to total loans.[3] The results indicate a strong relationship between social and financial performance. More specifically, the return on assets for the high social performers was almost twice the return on assets of the low social performers, and the loan losses experienced by the high performers were almost half of those experienced by the low social performers.[4] All results were statistically significant.

Social programs generate goodwill from employees and customers alike that may result in fewer labor problems and a more favorable customer view of the company's products. Rayton, Brammer, and Millington (2015) explored the positive relationship between CSP and improved organization-employee relationships (as measured in this study by employee affective commitment). This study used employee attitude survey data from 594 employees at a large banking services company in the United Kingdom. The researchers examined both external CSP (involving stakeholders outside of the organization, e.g., philanthropic activities) and internal CSP (the experience of company practices from the employee perspective, e.g., diversity initiatives). Main findings include (a) perceived level of external CSP is significantly and positively related to employee affective commitment, and (b) internal CSP forms part of the psychological contract between the company and employee, that when breached, is significantly negatively related to affective commitment (Rayton et al., 2015).

A firm's demonstrated social concern is an important dimension of its reputation in the long run because publics judge a company's concern for the wider society and its ability to achieve mutual relationships with groups in its environment. One of the most interesting theoretical explanations offered for the connection between social and financial performance is that of the "virtuous cycle"—financially successful businesses have slack resources that can be devoted to social performance as a result of their financial performance, which creates a self-perpetuating cycle of simultaneously superior performance in both areas (Vogel, 2005; Waddock & Graves, 1997).

Community-oriented programs may bring additional economic benefits by improving the company's standing with important constituencies such as bankers, investors, and government officials. Reputations have potentially favorable consequences because they enable companies to improve their standing by charging premium prices and by enhancing their access to capital markets. USC, mentioned earlier for its community-oriented programs, reaped the benefits of its community collaboration efforts when in 2000 it was named College of the Year by the *Time/Princeton Review College Guide*. The *Time/Princeton* editors noted that the award was given primarily because of the university's comprehensive community outreach program that created an exceptional learning environment for students. This recognition boosted the university's image, and although it is difficult to distinguish between the award's impact and other changes that have affected USC's reputation, its student applications and enrollments have increased in the years since the award. A few years earlier, during the 1992 Los Angeles urban uprising, or riots,[5] many businesses in the university's vicinity were devastated, but the campus itself was spared, presumably because of its good relationships and positive image in the local community. In contrast, Shell, which owns many gas stations in the Los Angeles downtown area, was not so lucky. Most of its stations were burned to the ground. Shell's management realized, after the fact, that the company's lack of involvement in local programs put it in disfavor with the community. This realization was the impetus for establishing the SYTA mentioned earlier. The company reports that most of the program participants find employment upon graduation.

Among the company's direct benefits are its improved reputation in the local community and its access to talented and well-trained young people in the local neighborhood who often choose to work at Shell upon graduation (Shell Youth Training, 2004). Similarly, after the 2015 Baltimore riots[6], there was a call to invest in the community, rebuild businesses, and provide employment to the unemployed, particularly to young people. An important mechanism for these private investments was the Community Development Financial Institutions, (CDFIs). CDFIs are private financial institutions that invest in underserved populations and in distressed communities across the United States through financial loans aimed at creating economic opportunities. In Baltimore, the CDFIs have made loans and investments that promoted access to capital to encourage local economic growth.

Case Illustration: Level II—Inclusion Through Corporate-Community Collaboration—Unilever

Companies have a duty to manage all aspects of business in a responsible and sustainable way.
—Antony Burgmans and
Niall FitzGerald, Chairmen, Unilever

Many governments around the world see palm plantations, which produce palm oil, as a cash cow. The demand for palm oil is ever increasing, and its uses are widespread, from food to cosmetics to soap. Faced with heavy foreign debt and poor economies, governments of countries such as Malaysia, Indonesia, and Ghana have introduced palm plantations to improve their economy, but they don't always work as planned. In Malaysia, workers have faced low wages and poor living conditions for decades (Hassan, 2004; Raja, 2012; Ramachandran & Shanmugam, 1995). With the purchase of foreign plantation-owning companies by the Malaysian government in the 1980s, plantation workers (most of whom were Indians) had hoped for security in terms of tenure, higher wages, and better working conditions. Their hopes were crushed, as the new management was only interested in multiplying profits and ensuring that wages remained low (Raja, 2012). Sanitary conditions in some plantations are quite poor. Frequently, running water and electricity, if available at all, are available for only short periods of time during the day. The water is sometimes contaminated by the chemicals and effluent found on the plantations. In some cases, several families share a bucket as their toilet. When the bucket is full, people use the surrounding bushes, and children can be found using open drains around the house as a toilet. When flush toilets are available, waste drains from the septic tank often directly empty into the water supply. Such practices are illegal in Malaysia. The government that promised a better way of life via palm plantations, however, has ignored the plight of the plantation workers. The reason is a matter of definition. Plantations do not fall under any category for which the Malaysian government has planners. As a result, the government has claimed that it is the responsibility of the plantations, not the government, to provide proper working conditions (Ramachandran & Shanmugam, 1995). The plight of the palm oil plantation workers has been documented by global advocacy and conservation organizations (e.g., Hance, 2009).

Unilever and Palm Oil

In 1850, the United Kingdom repealed a tax on soap, which had previously been considered a luxury item. The resultant lower price of soap led to William Lever's entry into the soap business, building a company to mass-produce soap. In 1930, Lever's U.K.-based company, known as Lever Brothers, merged with Margarine Unie, a Dutch margarine producer, to form the Unilever Group. Unilever has evolved into one of the world's largest consumer goods companies, with operations in approximately 100 countries, sales in over 150 countries, and revenue of $45.6 billion in 2002. Unilever specializes in food as well as home and personal care products, owning such widely recognized brand names as Hellmann's, Knorr, Lipton, Bertolli, Slim-Fast, Ben & Jerry's, Dove, Pond's, and Wisk. Despite the 1930 merger, Unilever is still a joint venture between Unilever PLC (United Kingdom) and Unilever NV (the Netherlands), trading separately on the stock market but acting as one company with a single board of directors.

Importance of Palm Oil

Palm oil, derived from the fruit and seeds of the oil palm tree, is one of the more common raw ingredients that Unilever employs throughout its product line. Palm oil is found in soap, margarine, snack foods, cosmetics, cooking oils, and other products. Because of the ubiquitous value of palm oil, Unilever's search for a large, constant supply has a long history. Lever Brothers started looking for palm oil sources in Africa in the early 1900s. In the 1950s, Unilever began operating its own oil palm plantations in Malaysia to complement its African plantations. Today, Unilever each year buys over 1 million tons of palm oil, 6% to 8% of the total world production.

Palm oil offers two major benefits to manufacturers and growers. First, the yield of palm oil is higher than that of any other edible vegetable oil source. Second, the properties of palm oil allow for its use with less processing, saving both time and money.

The Oil Palm Tree Industry

Palm oil is one of the world's most rapidly increasing crops, and more palm oil is produced than any other vegetable oil. Global palm oil production is increasing by 9% every year, prompted largely by expanding biofuel markets in the European Union and by food demands in Indonesia, India, and China. Oil palm trees, used to produce palm oil, grow best in wet tropical conditions (Fitzherbert et al., 2008). Therefore, commercial plantations are usually found in countries within 10 degrees of the equator. Although the palm oil industry originated in Africa, Asia now dominates world production. Malaysia is the world's largest grower of oil palms, producing 50% of the world's supply (over 16 million acres of trees), followed by Indonesia, with 30% of the world's production (nearly 10 million acres).

Current Trends

Oil palm trees are viewed as a cash crop by governments with large foreign debts or struggling economies. As a result, many governments are encouraging the growth of palm plantations in order to increase the country's income and reduce its debt. The expectation is that plantations will double in acreage within 20 years, primarily in West Africa, South America, and Southeast Asia (Sustainable Agriculture Initiative [SAI], 2002). Some countries, such as Malaysia, are already running out of expansion room.

Impact of Palm Plantations

People living in oil palm plantation areas have felt the impact of the industry in numerous ways. First, many environmental influences have directly affected the local people. Second, indigenous people have been relocated to make room for plantations. Finally, the local people have been affected economically.

Environmental

The environments that support palm plantations typically support rain forests as well. In many countries, rain forests have been converted into palm plantations. The exact number of converted acres is hard to determine and rather controversial. Some countries, such as Sri Lanka and Ghana, are converting degraded land (such as rubber plantations or mining land) to palm plantations. Malaysian officials claim that no forests have been converted to palm plantations, but the same cannot be said for other countries. For example, in Indonesia, the minister of forests and estate crop development reported that 815,000 acres of forest were being converted to palm plantations annually (Gautam et al., 2000). In 1998, some 20,273,789 acres of Indonesian forest were about to be approved for conversion to palm plantations (Manurung, 2002).

The impact of such forest conversion includes a rise in pests, changes in the flow of ground surface water, increased land erosion, and pollution of rivers and drinking water due to the use of fertilizers and pesticides. In Malaysia, the number of polluted rivers had increased from 7 in 1990 to 12 in 2001, with the opening of more land for palm plantations being cited as the reason for the increased pollution ("More Rivers," 2002).

Social

The entry of large plantations has often triggered conflict between local communities and estate investors. In Indonesia, "to secure the vast area needed, estate investors usually use whatever means necessary. It is therefore common knowledge that the estate business is engaged in random forest tree felling and forced control of communal land" (Bider, 2003). For example, according to Cameroonian law, peasants do not have customary rights to land, so expropriation does not require indemnification by the state (World Rainforest Movement, 2001).

Amnesty International reported that in Burma, for at least 13 years prior to its report, there was widespread use of forced labor (Ramachandran & Shanmugam, 1995). Primarily ethnic minorities were forced to work for no pay. In many cases, the army was involved in seizing minorities for work. Unpaid wages are common in other countries as well. In Mexico, Guatemalan workers have frequently been unpaid for their work, requiring intervention by the Guatemalan government to recover wages.

Economic

Despite governmental desire to encourage palm plantation growth because of the financial opportunities, the benefits rarely make it to the indigenous people. Wages for palm plantation workers are notoriously low (Bhattacharjee, 2003), typically being determined by several factors: world prices for palm oil, weather, size of the fruit, and yields. Unlike some crops, palm plantations are usually fully harvested. Production, then, often exceeds demand, leading to a reduction in palm oil prices. With the increasing acreage of palm plantations, rising supply will likely lead to further price reductions, spurring a higher demand for the product, especially as a substitute for more expensive vegetable oils. As demand increases, governments and plantation investors increase production even further to maintain their necessary income levels. This cycle keeps constant pressure on prices, resulting in consistently low wages for the workers.

Large nonlocal companies are noted for failing to promote the local economy. For example, in Malaysia, nonlocal companies typically pay an oil palm sales tax, but little else. The main reason for this is the expatriation of earnings; most of the palm plantations are owned by companies based in Kuala Lumpur. Additionally, many of the companies hire foreign laborers to harvest the palm fruit, denying wages to local workers. Finally, many of the companies import supplies such as food, farm supplies, machinery, chemicals, and fertilizers directly from their home offices in other countries ("Plantation Giants," 2003).

Unilever's Sustainability Development

In 1995, Unilever commissioned two studies on sustainable development. The studies revealed a complex set of criteria for sustainable agriculture. From these criteria, Unilever's sustainable agriculture mission statement was formally adopted in 1998, which included the following principles:

- Output must be high enough to meet demand.

- Negative environmental impacts on soil, air, water, and biodiversity must be minimized.

- Quality and safety of products must be guaranteed.

- Changing consumer demands must be met.

- Profitability must be competitive with other industry sectors.

- Agriculture must offer an attractive livelihood to workers (Vis & Standish, 2000).

In 1997, two Unilever employees, Jan-Kees Vis and Hans Broekhoff, were working to translate sustainable development into terms that related to Unilever's business. Vis and Broekhoff developed the concept of the triple bottom line to show that Unilever depended on economic, environmental, and social assets. They used this concept to show why Unilever needed to preserve these assets (Standish, Mehalik, Gorman, & Werhane, 1998). Eventually, Vis and Broekhoff developed a set of strategies to preserve the three assets. The strategies now guide Unilever's worldwide operations.

The same philosophy guided Unilever to create an unusual partnership with Oxfam, a global charity organization to fight poverty and injustice, to engage in a research project that explored links between international business and poverty reduction and use Unilever as a case study. The study examined critically Unilever's impact on its environment and demonstrated, among other things, the mutual benefits to the community and to the company that were derived from the company's sponsored community projects. These projects included a donation to UNICEF to reopen 900 health centers that had been closed when public funding was cut for supportive efforts to reduce water pollution in the Brantas River (Clay, 2005).

Unilever's sustainable development plan has led to several honors: Dow Jones ranked Unilever number four on its sustainability index (Hartmann & SAM Research, 2003, 2015), and *Fortune* magazine listed Unilever among its 50 World's Most Admired Companies ("World's Most Admired Companies," 2009). Unilever was awarded the top ranking in the 2015 Sustainability Leaders survey (published in May 2015) from GlobeScan/SustainAbility for the fifth consecutive year. GlobeScan and SustainAbility asked over 800 expert stakeholders representing business, government, nongovernmental organizations (NGOs), and academia across 82 countries who they considered to be the corporate leaders in the area of sustainability. GlobeScan and SustainAbility said, "Consistent with the past four years, Unilever's global reputation among corporations is judged by experts to be unparalleled, with the leadership gap this year widening even further. This is a remarkable achievement by the company, especially since past leaders have tended to falter or be supplanted by others within a few years of claiming the top of the ranking." Unilever was awarded top position with a 71% score in the latest Oxfam Behind the Brands Scorecard, published in March 2015. The campaign assesses and rates agricultural sourcing policies of the world's 10 largest food and beverage companies.

Sustainable Agriculture Initiative

Unilever employs its sustainable development commitment and experience to facilitate a broader impact. It was one of the three founding companies of the Sustainable Agriculture Initiative (SAI). SAI was created to actively support the development and communication of sustainable agriculture practices worldwide. Like Unilever's sustainable development plan, SAI's initiatives target the triple bottom line: economics, environment, and society (Pretty et al., 2008; SAI, 2002). As of 2015, SAI had over 60 members from industry suppliers, governments, and NGOs (SAI, 2015).

The company came to realize that it could not work on the initiative alone and therefore formed a partnership to move forward on agriculture sustainability and to develop and renovate production systems. In 1998, Unilever developed an internal Sustainable Agriculture Steering Committee to foster focused working groups and activities toward developing sustainability indicators and goals for each crop. A Sustainable Agricultural Advisory Board was later developed and appointed members from agricultural research, policy, and NGOs. The Advisory Board held environmental and policy debates that addressed sustainability-specific indicators for each crop, and the rapidly changing policy environments at national and international levels (Pretty et al., 2008).

In coordination with SAI, Unilever became a founding member of the Roundtable on Sustainable Palm Oil (RSPO) in 2004. The nonprofit association brings together stakeholders from seven sectors of the palm oil industry to address sustainability issues and progress toward sustainability produced palm oil, and was developed to promote "the growth and use of sustainable oil palm products through credible global standards and engagement of stakeholders" (RSPO, 2012). The RSPO currently represents more than 40% of all palm oil producers in the world. Current partnerships involved with Unilever's sustainable agriculture goals are the International Fund for Agriculture Development (IFAD), Solidaridad, The Enhanced Livelihoods Investment Initiative, Scaling Up Nutrition, and The Global Alliance for Improved Nutrition (GAIN) (SAI, 2015).

Implementation of the Sustainable Development Plan

Unilever introduced pilot projects to test its sustainable development plan. It started with five of its strategically important crops: palm oil, peas, spinach, tomatoes, and black tea (Vis & Standish, 2000). The pilot program for palm oil was in Malaysia at the Unilever palm plantation (which it has since sold). Unilever ("Malaysia: Improving Biodiversity," 2003) employed the following sustainable practices:

- Liquid effluent from the mills was used as irrigation and fertilizer for the trees. This reduced the amount of synthetic nutrients needed.

- Leguminous ground cover was grown to prevent soil loss, fix nitrogen, and encourage beneficial insects that are natural predators of tree pests.

- Owls were used to control rats.

- Palm fronds and empty fruit bunches from the mills were left to decompose naturally under the trees. This provided some nutrients (especially potassium) and helped to curb weed growth, restrict beetle pests, and reduce soil loss during rain. Industry practice had been to burn the empty bunches, using them as mulch helped reduce air pollution.

- Steep hillsides were left as natural forest, which provided a wildlife refuge. Hunting was not permitted.

In addition to Unilever's agricultural programs, the company has undertaken numerous social programs ("Environment and Society," 2003; Unilever Annual Progress Report, 2016; Unilever Sustainable Living Plan Progress Report, 2012):

- 45 million people have gained access to safe drinking water from Pureit since its launch in 2005.

- India: Indian School of Business—Unilever has taken a leading role in developing a world-class business school. It has also worked with the government with UNICEF to promote handwashing, building capabilities to sustain the program for the long term.

- South Africa: Nelson Mandela Scholarships—The scholarships aim to improve the leadership in South Africa by helping those from disadvantaged backgrounds.

- Sri Lanka: Unilever Cultural Trust Fund—Started in 1979, this fund was designed to protect indigenous workers in Sri Lanka.

- Vietnam: In partnership with the World Toilet Organization and Domesto, the company trains local entrepreneurs to set up hygienic toilet businesses such as supplying latrines, toilet cleaners, and sanitation education to prevent diseases such as diarrhea that can lead to death. Building Partnerships With Suppliers—Unilever offered financial support and education to help develop quality long-term relationships in Vietnam.

- Indonesia: River cleanup—Unilever organized a community-wide effort to clean the badly polluted Brantas River in Java.

- Bangladesh: Improving health care—Lever Brothers Bangladesh provided an initial $135 million to the Friendship Association to convert an old oil tanker into a hospital and provide operating income.

More recently, social programs that Unilever has undertaken include:

- Brazil: Free Laundry—Since 2004, Unilever fully funds 36 washing machines on land donated by the local municipality and allows people to wash their clothes for free ("Brazil Free Laundry," 2012).

- Kenya : HIV/AIDS Discussion—Advocates from Unilever partnered with seven other companies in 2009 to provide HIV/AIDS education organized through Neighbors Against AIDS, a coalition of companies that provides HIV/AIDS education in the workplace. The goal was to get people to talk openly about HIV/AIDS ("Kenya Fighting HIV/AIDS," 2012).

- Ghana: Education and Development—Started in 1999, Unilever developed the Ghana Foundation for Education and Development. The foundation has awarded 120 scholarships to children of employees to cover 3 years of education at the secondary level. The foundation also focuses on rural communities in Ghana. In 2006, the foundation provided potable, safe water to rural districts in Ghana to improve the health and hygiene of community residents.

- Unilever's Sustainable Living Plan: In November 2010, Unilever put together the Sustainable Living Plan, a 10-year approach toward sustainable growth in eight core areas. These core indicators focus on improving the health and well-being of the people, reducing the impact on the environment, and enhancing people's livelihoods by 2020. The plan involves Unilever and also its suppliers, distributors, and consumers who use its brands. As of 2011, Unilever was on target to meeting its goals (Unilever Progress Report, 2011).

Unilever's Progress Report for 2011 demonstrates the company's current progress in the eight core areas:

- *Health and hygiene*: Unilever is on track to reduce disease through handwashing, improve oral health and self-esteem, and provide safe drinking water.

- *Improving nutrition*: Unilever is on track to meet the 10-year indicator for healthy nutrition standards. This includes reducing salt levels, saturated fats, trans fats, and calories; increasing essential fatty acids; and providing an increase in education on nutrition to the community.

- *Greenhouse gases* (GHG): In the 10-year plan, Unilever will decrease the amount of GHG manufacturing and the amount in clothing.

- *Water*: Unilever is working on reducing the amount of water use on agriculture, in the laundry process, and during the manufacturing process.

- *Waste*: Unilever is working on eliminating waste by reducing/reusing packaging and getting rid of PVC and other manufacturing wastes.

- *Sustainable sourcing*: By 2020, Unilever plans to have 100% of its agricultural raw materials sustainable. These include palm oil, sugar, fruit, rapeseed oil, tea, dairy, cocoa, and vegetables.

- *Better livelihoods*: By 2020, Unilever plans to engage with 500,000 small-holder farmers and 75,000 small-scale distributor companies.

- *The people:* Unilever will work internally to provide a better and healthier working place for its employees. This includes reducing the amount of injuries, accidents, and energy consumption in its office, and increasing employee health and nutrition (Unilever Annual Progress Report, 2016; Unilever Progress Report, 2011).

Unilever's current Sustainable Living Plan has three main areas, with goals to be achieved by 2020: improve human health and well-being; reduce environmental impact; and enhance livelihoods through fairness in the workplace, opportunities for women, and inclusion (Unilever Sustainable Living Plan, n.d.).

Unilever's Current Involvement in Palm Oil

Divesting of Plantations

Unilever has undertaken a refocusing of its business with the intention of focusing solely on promoting its core brands. As a result, the company is divesting all noncore businesses such as its oil palm plantations. In December 2002, Unilever sold its Malaysian palm plantations, which account for over 50,000 acres.

Helping Ghana Grow Oil Palm Plantations

Unilever has a long-standing relationship with Ghana, investing in the country's economy and the skills of its employees. Unilever has also been active with numerous community activities such as implementing the Unilever Foundation for Education and Development. The foundation contributes to education to help Ghana reach its goal of being a middle-income economy by 2020.

In addition to the foundation, Unilever recently pledged its expertise to help the Ghana government implement its oil palm tree initiative ("Ghana: Unilever Ready to Assist," 2002). Ghana, like many other countries, sees a large economic benefit in palm plantations. It wants to convert 568,000 acres of 1,581,000 acres of degraded mining land into palm plantations ("Ghana: Degraded Mining Lands," 2003).

Unilever Foundation. In January 2012, Unilever announced the launch of the Unilever Foundation, created to improve quality of life through changes in hygiene, sanitation, access to clean drinking water, basic nutrition, and enhanced self-esteem. The Unilever Foundation has partnered with five global charitable foundations that are dedicated to creating sustainable changes worldwide ("Unilever Foundation for Education and Development," 2012). These include:

Oxfam: Unilever and Oxfam have been working together on projects for many years. In the United Kingdom, they are providing food parcels to the very poorest people, helping them move from "surviving" to "thriving." Unilever and Oxfam are planning to take this project worldwide.

PSI: Population Services International (PSI) is working with Unilever on an initiative to contribute to and improve the health of children and families through handwashing, clean drinking water, and sanitation. PSI is dedicated to helping people in countries by focusing on specific health issues like HIV/AIDS, children, maternal health, and family planning.

Save the Children (STC): STC is working with Unilever to improve the lives of children around the world by improving access to health care and lifesaving vaccines, and ensuring more children and mothers are reached with high-impact health and nutrition programs. STC is also working on a global movement for child survival.

UNICEF: Unilever is continuing to partner with UNICEF on a project to improve sanitation in developing countries through UNICEF's Community Approaches to Total Sanitation (CATS) initiative, a program that promotes good hygiene practices, helps create demand for toilets, and raises awareness of the sanitation crisis.

World Food Programme (WFP): A public-private partnership that aims to create a scalable and sustainable model to improve nutrition, health, and livelihoods in Bangladesh and Indonesia ("Unilever Foundation for Education and Development," 2012).

Questions for Discussion and Further Analysis

1. What was Unilever's motivation to undertake such ambitious programs for sustainability development?

2. What can Unilever do to improve the wages and living conditions of the oil palm workers worldwide? What impact would such actions have on the triple bottom line of Unilever's sustainable development plan?

3. How can Unilever employ its influence over the government of Ghana to improve worldwide conditions? Should Unilever encourage or discourage Ghana from entering the oil palm industry?

4. What are the impacts of Unilever's divesting itself of oil palm plantations? Will Unilever still have influence over the triple bottom line of the oil palm industry? Why or why not?

Summary and Conclusion

This chapter describes the second level of the inclusive workplace, *inclusion and corporate-community collaborations,* which relates to the organization's sense of being a part of its surrounding community and to the reciprocity embedded in this relationship. Whereas an exclusionary workplace sees minimal or no connection to its community, an inclusive workplace recognizes the economic and noneconomic consequences of its presence there.

Relevant to level II of the inclusive workplace model is the term *CSP,* an emerging construct in the business literature that expands a company's responsibilities beyond its traditional economic shareholders to that of multiple stakeholders, including the community. It stems from the recognition that economic actions of business entities have noneconomic consequences, and that business organizations have an impact on other institutions of society above and beyond their economic sphere.

A wide range of activities falls under the title of CSP, such as supporting educational or cultural institutions in the community, providing mentorship to youth, or tutoring children in local schools. The main obstacles for initiating and maintaining activities that benefit the company's social environment are economic pressures to demonstrate profitability on a short-term basis, limited corporate vision, and lack of leaders who could champion and sustain such initiatives. The benefits include advantages in recruitment, goodwill from employees and customers alike, and improved corporate image. In addition to the moral and ethical importance of such actions, recent research provides evidence that companies draw tangible benefits from socially responsible activities. With all this to take into consideration, corporations today do not have the luxury of waiting for government instructions and regulations that would force them into action; the public expects them to be active and proactive in responding to the needs of the community.

Notes

1. The quote is from one of the interviewees for a study of multinational companies. The survey was based on semistructured interviews with company diversity directors (Wentling & Palma-Rivas, 2000, p. 44).

2. The CRA of 1997 mandated that commercial banks serve their communities by providing private funding for local housing needs and economic development. Under this act, banks are mandated to meet the credit needs of low-income customers.

3. Return on assets measures the ability of bank managers to acquire deposits at a reasonable cost, invest these funds in profitable loans and investments, and profitably perform the daily operations of the bank. The ratio of loan losses to loans is another important measure of success because loan losses can be a major expense for banks.

4. The mean return on assets for corporations that were ranked with outstanding social performance was 1.750%, compared with 0.984% of those ranked as needing improvement,

and the mean for loan losses was 0.478% compared with 0.812%, respectively.

5. On April 29, 1992, a jury in the Los Angeles suburb of Simi Valley acquitted the four White Los Angeles police officers who had been caught on home video repeatedly clubbing Rodney King, an African American motorist who had led them on a car chase after they tried to stop him for speeding. On the video, the policemen were seen repeatedly beating King, who was already lying on the ground without any visible signs of resistance. The verdict outraged much of the city, and all hell broke loose on the streets of Los Angeles barely an hour after the jury came back. The riots that began that afternoon became one of the nation's bloodiest, ending 3 days later with 55 people dead; more than 2,300 injured; and 1,100 buildings destroyed. Some scholars use the term *urban uprising* rather than *riots* because the protesters and looters were members of the city's disadvantaged minority communities and their reaction was not only a spontaneous outrage at the unjust

verdict but a communal response to a much larger set of social-power issues.

6. On April 12, 2015, Baltimore Police Department officers arrested Freddie Gray, a 25-year-old African American resident of Baltimore, Maryland. During his transport in a police vehicle Gray sustained injuries to his neck and spine and went into a coma. in On April 18, 2015, the residents of Baltimore protested in front of the Western district police station. Following Gray's death on April 19, 2015, spontaneous protests started in the city. The civil unrest continued with some twenty police officers injured, about 250 people arrested, 150 vehicle fires, 60 structure fires, and hundreds of businesses damaged.

The Inclusive Workplace: Level III

Inclusion Through State/National Collaborations

> Oneness amongst men, the advancement of unity in
> diversity—this has been the core religion of India.

—Rabindranath Tagore (1861–1941), Indian freedom fighter; composer of "Jana Gana Mana," India's
national anthem; and the first Asian person to be awarded the Nobel Prize for Literature (1913)

The third level, *inclusion of disadvantaged groups through state/national collaborations,* refers to the values that drive organizational policies with regard to disadvantaged populations such as welfare recipients, domestic violence victims, and youth in distress. It reflects the "mezzo/macro," national-system level of the state or the federal government where appropriate. The exclusionary workplace views such populations as in the sole domain of welfare agencies or charity organizations. The inclusive workplace, on the other hand, perceives populations that are often locked out of opportunities, such as welfare recipients seeking work, hourly workers, the long-term unemployed, domestic violence survivors, low-income families, youth in distress, individuals with disabilities and those experiencing mental illness, and individuals with criminal justice backgrounds (e.g., Harris , Matthews, Penrose-Wall, Alam, & Jaworski, 2014; Hill, 2014; Kossek, Huber-Yoder, Castellino, & Lerner, 1997; Kossek, Huber, & Lerner, 2003; Kossek, Pichler, Meece, & Barratt, 2008; Solinas-Saunders, Stacer, & Guy, 2015; Williams & Huang, 2011; W. J. Wilson, 2011) as a potentially stable and upwardly mobile workforce. As a result, the inclusive workplace will be more likely to, for example, invest in on-the-job training and evening educational classes for these groups, whereas the exclusionary organization will more readily dispose of these workers or not hire them in the first place.

This third level refers to companies' involvement with programs aimed at helping disadvantaged groups obtain jobs or move on to better jobs. The main focus here is on social class with the confounding issues of gender and race because women and people of color are disproportionately represented in the lower social echelons of society. In a remarkable book based on several sources of data and hundreds of interviews, W. J. Wilson (2011) argues that an array of social problems related to U.S.-based inner-city poor families all stem from the fact that blue-collar jobs have been relocated to other countries. The lack of access to jobs and retraining for other jobs is at the center of many social ills such as poverty, drugs, violence, and breakup of families. Populations in need include former welfare recipients, the working poor, domestic violence survivors, and youth in distress (see Figure 15.1). For example, following the enactment of welfare reform in the United States (the 1996 Personal Responsibility and Work Opportunity Reconciliation Act, P. L. 104–193), which terminated welfare benefits after a maximum of 60 months, more and more individuals with welfare histories have had to enter the labor force. Welfare reform ended 60 years of public assistance programs in which the sole criterion for continued aid was dependency, poverty, age, or disability. In 1997, Temporary Assistance for Needy Families (TANF) replaced conventional welfare benefits by providing a federal block grant to states, territories, and tribes. The federal funds cover assistance, administrative costs, and services targeting needy families (Administration for Children and Families, 2011).

Active Labor Market Programs (ALMPs) are widely used in European countries. These are government programs that intervene in the labor market to help the unemployed find work and prevent the social problems related to long-term chronic unemployment. Results from a meta-analysis based on a data set that comprises 137 program evaluations from 19 countries indicate that rather than contextual factors such as labor market institutions or the business cycle, it is almost exclusively the program type that seems to make a difference in the program's effectiveness. Wage subsidies and "Services and Sanctions" can be effective in increasing participants' employment probability, more so than direct employment in the public sector. Training programs—the most commonly used type of active policy—showed modestly positive effects. New Zealand, a welfare state with universal entitlements to health care and education coverage, underwent a somewhat similar welfare reform in 1996 (Kingfisher & Goldsmith, 2001). The reduction of the Domestic Purposes Benefit, which was designed to support single parents with dependent children, has facilitated and/or forced the entry of poor, single mothers into the

FIGURE 15.1 ● The Inclusive Workplace: The Value Base for Level III

Inclusion Through State/National Collaborations		
	Value Frame	
System Level	Exclusion	System Level
	←——————————————————————————→	
State, Federal Government	Viewing disadvantaged groups as the domain of welfare agencies and charity organizations and treating them as disposable labor	Treating disadvantaged groups as potentially stable, upwardly mobile employees and investing in their education and training

workforce. A key component of the program was the expectation that benefit recipients would find jobs by the time their benefits were terminated. Barriers to employment of former welfare recipients (the majority of whom are single mothers) included finding reliable, consistent, and affordable childcare and transportation; family issues such as domestic violence and substance abuse; health problems; education, job skills, and labor market situation; and problems at work such as poor working conditions, low pay, and job location (Blumenberg, 2002; Ellerbe et al., 2011; Hildebrandt, 2009; Kossek et al., 1997, 2003; Michalopoulos et al., 2003; Ovwigho, Saunders, & Born, 2008). Lacking the skills to land stable, high-paying, and benefits-rich jobs, most of the working poor remain at or near poverty level, even when employed full time.

Traditionally, employers have had very limited involvement or interest in welfare recipients or in other disadvantaged groups, and they have not viewed the working poor as an element in organizational life worth substantial investment (Kossek et al., 1997, 2003; W. J. Wilson, 2011). Corporate sponsorship and support of former welfare recipients could help these disadvantaged groups overcome the difficulties they face in this transition. Therefore, if corporations take appropriate initiative with respect to disadvantaged groups, social and legislative changes such as the welfare-to-work reform could be conceptualized as an opportunity to, on the one hand, make the workplace more inclusive with respect to social class, and on the other hand, give companies access to untapped human resources. Besides the ethical and moral value of such actions, access to potential job seekers may be particularly important in tight job markets like the one experienced in Japan in the 1980s (1.35 advertised jobs for each person seeking work) and in the 1990s in several other countries around the world. It is much more difficult to make the case for hiring workers from disadvantaged groups during periods of economic downturn, such as the global recession that began in the second half of the first decade in the 21st century. Such periods are characterized by high unemployment and a surplus of skilled workers. One could make the argument, however, that high-skilled workers who may have other options once the recession is over would be less likely to stay with the company than workers who may not have other options and therefore be more likely to stay and provide continuity and stability to the organization.

An inclusive workplace sponsors and supports projects that help former welfare recipients overcome barriers to employment. These programs focus on removing barriers to employment faced by mothers of young children, who constitute the majority of welfare recipients and poor families (Hildebrandt, 2009). They assist former welfare recipients with child care, transportation, housing, and health care expenses, which are the main barriers to employment faced by this group (Hamersma, 2008; Michalopoulos et al., 2003; Schwab, 2008). They also provide on-the-job training to allow them to improve their job skills and increase their wages and benefits. In Thailand, for example, a group of 14 of the country's successful businesses formed The Plan Group, an umbrella organization that initiates innovative programs to help disadvantaged groups in their country. The four founders of the group were students in the 1970s who saw fellow students killed on the street by the security forces of the country's military government. Once they became successful businessmen, their umbrella organization emerged out of their resolve to make a difference in their country through the implementation of extensive community and national projects (Schwartz & Gibb, 1999).

Employment programs to assist the working poor and other socially disadvantaged groups often require a private-public recourse partnership to make them successful. In the United States, for example, two forms of public incentives have been offered to private employers to improve employment rates among former welfare recipients. The first is the Work Opportunity Tax Credit (WOTC), a subsidy to employers who hire new workers from certain disadvantaged groups such as welfare recipients, youth food stamp recipients, poor veterans, youth from disadvantaged geographic areas, Supplemental Security Income (SSI) recipients, and low-income ex-felons. The second is the Welfare-to-Work Tax Credit (WtW), a program that applies specifically to long-term welfare recipients (with at least 18 months of continuous welfare receipt at the time of hire) and provides a larger subsidy. Research demonstrated modest success of these two programs. Although these programs helped former welfare recipients receive and maintain jobs, the author notes that firms' participation in this subsidy program was surprisingly low. The relatively low participation rates could be attributed to lack of information among firms, lack of firms' interest in involvement with government programs, high transaction costs relative to benefits, or difficulty in identifying qualified workers, perhaps because of worker stigma (Hamersma, 2008).

Barriers and Benefits of Implementing the Inclusive Approach at Level III

Barriers

The main obstacle to implementing such programs is a limited corporate vision. Companies often focus only on the immediate needs and objectives of the company rather than consider the bigger picture, which includes moral and ethical values as well as labor force trends and the larger organizational environment. The other obstacles are discrimination as well as stereotypes and prejudices held by management and workers against disadvantaged populations, such as welfare recipients, domestic violence victims, individuals with criminal justice histories, youth in distress, and women and people of color in general (Ellerbe et al., 2011; Hancock, 2004; Harley, 2014).

Figure 15.2 provides a summary of barriers and benefits to implementing level III policies and practices.

Benefits

Including the working poor, domestic violence survivors, youth in need, and those with welfare histories, human resource (HR) planning and policy initiatives of work organizations can benefit companies as well as individuals and their families. Opening up employment and advancement opportunities for these populations may increase their chances of obtaining higher-paying jobs with better benefits that will release them from the vicious cycle of low-paying jobs that barely suffice for basic needs. A by-product will be an increase in the pool of consumers with discretionary income. The economic benefits for companies include gaining a more loyal workforce that is committed to the organization (and has lower turnover rates as a result); expanding employee pools; improving customer relations through better treatment of low-wage employees who are often frontline workers; having a more attractive, value-based corporate image that is more appealing to both customers and investors; and increasing the pool of consumers with discretionary income (Kossek et al., 1997, 2003; Taylor, Carnochan, Pascual, & Austin, 2015; Williams & Huang, 2011; see Box 15.1 for the story of a company that partnered with the government to improve the lot of disadvantaged groups).

FIGURE 15.2 • The Inclusive Workplace Model: Obstacles and Benefits for Level III

Inclusion Through State/National Collaborations		
	Benefits	
Barriers	Individuals	Organization
• Limited company vision (shortsighted and internally focused) • Stereotypes, prejudice, and discrimination against disadvantaged population groups	• Employment benefits • Job training • Advancement opportunities • Improved job prospects	• Expanded potential employee pool • Increased employee loyalty • Improved customer relations • A more attractive value-based corporate image

Box 15.1

A COMPANY'S COLLABORATION WITH GOVERNMENTAL PROGRAMS FOR DISADVANTAGED POPULATIONS (LEVEL III): THE CASE OF HONG YIP SERVICE COMPANY LTD. (HONG KONG)

Hong Yip Service Company Ltd. (Hong Yip), a subsidiary of the Sun Hung Kai Properties Ltd., is one of the largest property management companies in Hong Kong (Hong Yip Service Co. Ltd., n.d.-a). Based in Wanchai, the company manages approximately 100 million sq. ft. of residential and commercial space, including private and public housing, offices, shopping centers, and government properties. Hong Yip is frequently recognized for its commitment to the environment and to social service, having received awards for activities such as its efforts to stop the spread of the SARS virus and its environmentally friendly property management activities (Hong Kong Trade Development Council, 2012). The Hong Kong Council of Social Service recognized Hong Yip as a Caring Company 2002/2003 for demonstrating its willingness to employ individuals from vulnerable groups and for developing partnership projects with the social service sector (Hong Kong Council of Social Services, 2003). Hong Yip has continued to receive the Caring Company Award for 10 consecutive years, including a recent award in 2012 (Hong Yip Service Co. Ltd., n.d.-a).

Hong Yip indicates the belief that issues such as environmental protection, youth employment, and employee retraining are ameliorated when companies partner with government and social services (Hong Yip Service Co. Ltd., n.d.-b those ends, the company has been involved in ongoing partnerships with the government of Hong Kong to assist in creating more job opportunities for vulnerable populations. One such partnership is with the Employees Retraining Board, whose purpose is to provide retraining to eligible workers so they can adjust to changes in the economic environment (Employees Retraining Board, 2003). Service recipients include displaced workers, individuals new to Hong Kong, elderly workers, people with disabilities, and industrial accident victims. Hong Yip has also partnered with the Youth Pre-Employment Training Programme, designed to provide school leavers ages 15–19 with training to enhance their employability (Labour Department, Government of Hong Kong, 2003). After completing training courses offered by the Labour Department, participants receive solid, hands-on experience in the workplace. For Hong Yip, these partnerships constitute a win-win situation: The company is permitted to hire the trainees, should it so choose, upon completion of the program.

Since 2001, Hong Yip has participated in the Hong Kong Social Welfare Department's Volunteer Movement, as well as programs that work to redevelop and support local communities. Hong Yip also sponsors walk/run campaigns, blood drives, children's mentoring programs, educational programs, and programs for the developmentally disabled (Hong Yip Service Co. Ltd., n.d.-a). Current volunteer activities at Hong Yip include food bank donations, used book and clothes recycling efforts, the Elderly Care Program, the Building Homes With Heart redevelopment program, and the Disability and Able-bodied project.

Box 15.2

REGIONAL PROGRAMS THAT CULTIVATE LEVEL III INCLUSION AT MARRIOTT INTERNATIONAL

Marriott International, a hospitality company with over 4,000 managed and franchised hotels globally and over 360,000 employees, has regional programs that exemplify level III of the inclusive workplace model and demonstrate a commitment to enhancing employment opportunities for disadvantaged groups. For example, funded by the Marriott Foundation for People With Disabilities, the Bridges From School to Work Program trains and finds employment for individuals with disabilities in nine major U.S. cities (Bridges, n.d.). Marriott International has also partnered with the Youth Career Initiative (YCI) for nearly 20 years (YCI, 2014b). Marriott supports YCI by providing life and employment skills to vulnerable youth in 19 hotel properties in five continents (Marriott International, Inc., 2015). Participating sites include Hanoi, New Delhi, Mumbai, Budapest, Rio de Janeiro, and Mexico City (YCI, 2014a). And in Dubai, Kuwait, and Doha, Marriott works with the Akilah Institute to help young women find employment, obtain leadership roles, and achieve financial independence (YCI, 2014c). Currently, 41 Akilah Institute graduates are enrolled in the company's hotel training program and will act as supervisors and trainers in the Kigali Marriott Hotel set to open in 2016 (Marriott International, Inc., 2015).

Marriott has won a variety of awards for its diversity and inclusion initiatives. In 2014 alone, Marriott was named one of the Top 50 Companies for Diversity (*DiversityInc.*), 100 Best Companies (*Working Mother*), Top 50 Best Companies for Latinas (*LATINA Style*), World's Best Multinational Workplace (*Great Places to Work Institute*), and Top Corporation of the Year (*Women's Business Enterprise National Council*) (Marriott International, Inc., 2014).

Case Illustration: Level III—Inclusion of Disadvantaged Groups at the National/State Level—Eurest

If we are comparing [Australia's record] with arbitrary arrests and executions and having your arms chopped off, the problems in Australia pale in significance.

—Australian attorney general
Daryl Williams (1996–2003)

For the indignity and degradation thus inflicted on a proud people and a proud culture, we say sorry.
—Australian prime minister Kevin Rudd
in a long-overdue apology to the
Aborigines, February 13, 2008

On October 7, 1830, the "black line" formed in Tasmania. The black line was a human chain of 2,200 soldiers, police, freemen, and convicts stretching across southeastern Tasmania, 200 kilometers in length, to flush out Aboriginals, Australia's native inhabitants. As a result of massive murderous attacks on Aborigine men, women, and children, by 1835 less than 400 Aborigines remained alive of the estimated 1,500 who lived in Tasmania in 1824 (Macintyre, 2016; Madley, 2008).

Prior to the black line incident, settlers would shoot on sight at the 4,000 initial Tasmanian Aboriginals, which caused a decrease of the population to 2,000 by 1820. They would kill the men and take the children from the mothers. Often, the settlers would chase a mother through the bushes until she had to leave her children behind. The children were then used for labor. Though the local government admitted that the aggression originated with the settlers, no settler was ever charged for such crimes. Instead, in 1824 the government permitted Tasmanian settlers to shoot Aboriginals and in 1830 offered a bounty for each captured Aboriginal adult and child (Kiernan, 2000; Macintyre, 2016; Madley, 2008).

History of the Aboriginals

Britain first colonized Australia in 1788 when the native population of Australia, known as Aboriginals, totaled approximately 750,000. As a result of disease and warfare with the settlers, the Aboriginal population dwindled to fewer than 50,000 by 1901 (Macintyre, 2016; Madley, 2008).

Although Britain did not sanction attacks on the Aboriginals, the authorities passed numerous laws that put the native population at a disadvantage. For example, when the island was first colonized, Aboriginals were stripped of their land rights. Additionally, Aboriginals were not considered British subjects. Therefore, the laws, which were written to protect British subjects, did not protect the Aboriginal people from crimes such as murder (Kiernan, 2000).

In 1837, the British House of Commons Select Committee on Aborigines acknowledged some of the killings and further stated that if atonement were to be made to the remaining Aboriginals, it would require no ordinary sacrifice on the part of the British. Since the time of that statement, some British subjects were convicted of murdering Aboriginals. However, injustices continued. For example, by 1856 it was common practice to punish Aboriginals collectively for crimes committed by individuals in their ethnic group, an act that is now considered genocide by international laws (Kiernan, 2000).

The atonement mentioned by the House of Commons began with the passing of several laws ostensibly designed to protect the Aboriginals. The Aboriginal Protection Act of 1869 gave Victoria's governor the right to provide provisions for the Aboriginals. In particular, it gave the governor the right to decide where any Aboriginal could live. It further gave the governor the power to determine the care, custody, and education of Aboriginal children (Kiernan, 2000), a provision that controversially remained in effect until the 1970s.

Building on the 1869 Aboriginal Protection Act, a 1918 Northern Territory ordinance provided for the protection of Aboriginal children. As with the Victorian law, a practice emerged in which children of mixed descent, referred to as half-castes, were removed from their parents and raised by non-Aboriginal "White" parents. This law resulted in the removal of between 50,000 and 100,000 Aboriginal children over the course of the century (Kiernan, 2000).

Despite the controversy surrounding the forced separation of families and the stripping of land rights, the Aborigines were unable to challenge these laws for two reasons: First, they were not citizens. Second, they were non-Christians, who by British definition could not swear an oath. Therefore, the courts rejected any evidence of wrongdoing (Kiernan, 2000; Madley, 2008), essentially leaving no way for the Aborigines to challenge laws or even to testify about crimes committed against them.

The legacy of past injustice persists in the Aboriginal people today. For generations, Aboriginal people were forced to live under segregation, protection, and assimilation policies, and were denied the freedom to determine their own future. The extent of intrusion was wide-ranging and included restrictions on movement, relationships, and marriage; the control of employment; and the removal of Aboriginal children from parents and family members. These policies created dependence, caused great pain, and had devastating and lasting effects on the Aboriginal population. The destruction and devastation caused by colonization has resulted in the breakdown of social structures and traditional values across many generations. Attempts to improve circumstances have been relatively unsuccessful, as there has been little acknowledgement and understanding of the historical context. The fragmentation of family relationships and the learned helplessness has had a crippling effect on successive generations. Deprived of adequate health care, education, and economic independence, many Aboriginal people were left without hope, and some have turned to a life of alcohol, drugs, and crime to survive (Cox, Young, & Bairnsfather-Scott, 2009).

Australia's Plan to Mend the Injustices

New Laws

Past laws, which were designed to protect the Aborigines, created more problems than they solved, such as the forced separation of families to protect the children (Cox et al., 2009; Macintyre, 2016). However, starting in the mid-1900s, tangible progress in the laws began—the most significant of which was Australia's granting citizenship to Aborigines in 1967. Aboriginals were not only granted citizenship, which meant they could now testify in court and challenge laws, but they were also allowed to vote (Zan, 1997).

In 1992, two legal cases led to Australia's reversal of its claim that Australia was *terra nullius,* meaning the land had belonged to no one before settlement. As a result, Australia granted some limited indigenous land rights to the Aboriginal people (Macintyre, 2016; Zan, 1997). In addition to the reversal of the land rights, the Australian government enacted a plan to help families that were forcibly separated. The government allotted AU$63 million (US$49 million) to reunite families and provide counseling ("Australian Government," 2001).

Indigenous Employment Policy

As of June 30, 2011, the Aboriginal population had rebounded to 548,370, representing about 2.5% of the total Australian population of 22.5 million people (Australian Bureau of Statistics, 2007). However, the Aborigines represented a significantly higher proportion of the unemployed. According to the Australian Bureau of Statistics (2008), 15.1% of indigenous people were unemployed, compared with 3.8% for the general population.

Fueled by the indigenous population's high unemployment rate and higher than average population growth rate, the Australian federal government implemented the Indigenous Employment Policy in 1999, which was composed of several key areas (Department of Employment and Workplace Relations, 2003):

- *Wage assistance:* Compensates employers up to AU$4,400 (US$3,406) over 26 weeks for providing long-term employment to indigenous workers.

- *Structured training and employment projects:* Compensates employers offering training programs for indigenous people.

- *Corporate Leaders for Indigenous Employment:* Partners companies and the government with the goal of hiring more indigenous people; the government funds some of the hiring expenses, such as preemployment training, mentoring, cross-cultural training, and other appropriate expenses.

- *National Indigenous Cadetship Program:* Supports companies that sponsor indigenous people as cadets. Cadets, similar to interns in other parts of the world, work during vacation breaks from their school and are usually employed by the sponsoring company.

- *Indigenous Small Business Fund:* Funds indigenous organizations that train indigenous people about business practices. It also funds individuals with good business ideas.

- *Community Development Employment Projects Placement Incentive:* Provides a bonus for each placement of an individual into the general workforce.

- *Voluntary Service to Indigenous Communities:* Matches skilled volunteers with the needs of indigenous communities.

An evaluation of the policy showed that progress has been made in increasing opportunities for indigenous job seekers. In the first 2 years of the policy, around 12,000 indigenous people participated in training and were placed in jobs. In line with the policy focus of the program, there has been a strong shift toward private sector companies' participation compared with the level of participation in previous indigenous programs (Department of Employment and Workplace Relations, 2003).

Eurest

Eurest is the largest food service company in Australia, employing 7,050 people at more than 500 sites as of 2001. Additionally, it has operations in New Zealand and Papua New Guinea. Some of its businesses include catering and managing concession stands and cafeterias across a broad array of industries (e.g., schools, health care facilities, sporting venues, armed forces, and airports).

Eurest was formed in 1997 as a joint venture between Compass Group, the world's leading food service organization, and Accor, the world's largest hotel and tourism service company. Some of the parent company brands include Upper Crust, Harry Ramsden's, Au Bon Pain, Naples 45, Caffe Ritazza, Motel 6, Sofitel, and Red Roof Inns.

Indigenous Training and Employment Program

In 1998, Eurest (part of the Compass Group) was one of the first businesses to begin working with the Australian government to promote employment opportunities for Australia's indigenous population (Compass Group, 2015d; Eurest, 2001). A year later, Australia's Indigenous Employment Policy was born. While the government was busy developing this program, Eurest was busy developing its own—the Indigenous Training and Employment Program (ITEP) (Eurest, 2004). Eurest's ITEP supports the government's goals of indigenous employment. Specifically, ITEP teaches new work skills integrated with consultation and mutual understanding of local communities (Eurest, 2004). The key elements (Northern and Central Land Councils, 2001) that Eurest integrates into the various applications of its plan include the following:

- A dedicated ITEP manager employed by Eurest
- Aboriginal community consultation
- Structured and accredited preemployment training
- A gradual exposure to the workplace
- Mentor support and an on-site buddy system
- Cross-cultural training for non-Aboriginal employees

According to Eurest published figures (2001), Eurest increased its indigenous workforce by 203 people within 18 months of initiating ITEP. Additionally, Eurest helped a dozen students enhance their employment prospects via a prevocational retail hospitality training course operated by Eurest and Mission

Employment (Ellis, 2002). As of 2015, Compass Group directly employed more than 500 indigenous Australians and planned to increase this number to over 1,550 by the year 2018 through Project 1050 (this number represents the difference between the 500 currently employed and the goal of 1,550 indigenous employees to be hired) (Compass Group, 2015c). Explaining the program, Managing Director Mark van Dyck notes, "Our commitment to achieving positive, sustainable and capacity building outcomes for Indigenous people is core to our business. We believe there is tremendous untapped potential for business and Government to realise the significant benefits of increasing Indigenous participation rates and we are proud to be an inaugural partner of the Indigenous Employment Parity Initiative" (Compass Group, 2015b). The goal of the Indigenous Employment Parity Initiative is to get 20,000 more indigenous job seekers employed at large Australian companies by the year 2020, which will better reflect the representation of indigenous individuals in the broader population (Compass Group, 2015b).

In addition to increasing indigenous employment within its existing business units, Eurest has worked to develop joint venture projects specifically designed for employment of indigenous people. An example of this is Eurest's joint venture with the Northern and Central Land Councils. The arrangement was to create extensive Aboriginal employment utilizing the Alice to Darwin railway construction project (Northern and Central Land Councils, 2001).

Eurest secured a $10 to $12 million contract to supply catering, cleaning, retail, canteen, gardening, and general maintenance for construction camps during the railway project, which was expected to last 2 years. The railway project was ideal for Aboriginal people because it ran through remote areas, which is where many Aboriginals live and required skills that are familiar to them (Northern and Central Land Councils, 2001).

Although exact employment figures for the project were not available, all three partners were dedicated to employing as many indigenous people as possible. In addition to Eurest's ITEP manager, each of the land councils had officers dedicated to maximizing Aboriginal participation in the project (Northern and Central Land Councils, 2001).

Awards

The results of Eurest's efforts are not only greater employment opportunities for Australia's indigenous population but also many accolades for the company (Eurest, 2004). For example, in 1999, from the Australian National Training Authority, the Australian Training Award (winner in the industry category for hospitality); from the State Training Board/Department of Training, the Training Excellence Award—Employer of the Year Finalist; and from the Partners in Employment and Training State Summit and Awards, the Aboriginal Programs Industry Excellence Award. In 2000, from the Department for Employment, Workplace Relations and Small Business, the NAIDOC Award; from the Compass Group in the Community Award, the Gold Award, Southern Europe and Development Division; and from the Compass Group in the Community Award, the Global Silver Award. In 2002, from the Corporate Leaders for Indigenous Employment Awards, finalist in the Outstanding Organization Category. In 2003, the Prime Minister's Employer of the Year Award. In 2010, from the Scottish Restaurant Awards, the Healthy Workplace Restaurant of the Year; and from Jones Lang LaSalle, the Supplier of Distinction Award (Eurest Services, 2011). And in 2011, from Jones Lang LaSalle, the Supplier of Distinction Award for Innovation (Eurest Services, 2012). Recent awards include the Supply Nation Corporate Member of the Year in 2014 and the Australian HR Awards for Best Recruitment Strategy in 2013 (Compass Group, 2015a).

Continuing Controversy

Controversy continues for Australia regarding the government's interactions with the Aboriginal people. For example, the Australian parliament believed that the money allocated to help separated families was not enough. It recommended compensating families that had been forcibly separated. However, the Australian government formally rejected that recommendation in 2001 ("Australian Government," 2001).

Part of the reason for the controversy surrounding the family-separation issue is a matter of definition. In a 1997 report, Australia's Human Rights and Equal Opportunity Commission called the forced removal of Aboriginal children an act of genocide. Two months after that report was released, however, the High Court of Australia disagreed. It ruled on a suit filed by several Aboriginals who had been separated from their families as children, ruling unanimously that the separations were not an act of genocide (Zan, 1997).

Regardless of the various laws and definitions of events, the Aboriginal people have had one basic request that for many years went unanswered: that the Australian federal government issue an apology. On February 13, 2008, their request was finally answered. Thousands of Aboriginal Australians gathered in the nation's capital to watch the new prime minister, Kevin Rudd, deliver a formal apology in a speech to the Australian parliament and to the nation. Saying that the Australian government was sorry for the past wrongs caused by successive governments on the indigenous Aboriginal population, the prime minister said, "we apologize for the laws and policies of successive parliaments and government that have inflicted profound grief, suffering, and loss on these, our fellow Australians" ("Australia Apology," 2008; Macintyre, 2016, p. 5).

Closing the Gap

Months after the apology by the prime minister, the Australian government authorized Closing the Gap (CTG), an initiative developed to close the gap and increase health and overall well-being for the Aboriginal population. Altman (2009) argues that the CTG only looks at socioeconomic factors, and therefore it will provide a fractional solution to the indigenous population in Australia and could even exacerbate the problem for indigenous Australians in the future.

Based on the prime minister's speech, Altman (2009) states that unless policies change to go above and beyond the government's goals for the CTG, "the next phase in Indigenous policy making and program investments is as 'destined to fail' as previous approaches." Though the effort to correct past wrongs is commendable, it seems that the government may not have a thorough understanding of the culture and politics of the Aboriginal population and therefore may not be using the best approaches to close the gap (Altman, 2009). The author expresses concern that the cultural differences between the indigenous population and the general population are overlooked by the Australian government; therefore, he says, "Such an approach allows the state to ignore politico-economic relations and the distribution of property and power, and to instead reframe difficult political questions as technical—to close the gap" (Altman, 2009, p. 14).

Such criticisms notwithstanding, the Australian government's efforts to close the gap continue. In October 2008, the Australian Employment Covenant (AEC) was developed to create 50,000 new jobs for indigenous Australians within a 2-year span. AEC provided mentoring and support, while also offering pre- and post-employment training on marketable job skills. At the end of the 2-year period, the plan secured approximately 20,000 job pledges from employers and only approximately 2,800 job placements, which were well short of the AEC's original goal. Data suggest that this was an impossible goal to begin with (Jordan & Mavec, 2010). This example may substantiate Altman's views on the issues pertaining to the CTG. Although the employment plan is no longer in effect, the AEC continues to work on efforts to increase employment for the indigenous populations (Jordan & Mavec, 2010).

Questions for Discussion and Further Analysis

1. What impact might the government's subsidization of Aborigines' employment have in the short term? In the long term?

2. Does the fact that Eurest receives money for training and hiring indigenous employees affect the perceived value of Eurest's action? Why or why not?

3. How might Eurest's Aborigines Employment Plan affect customer perceptions of Eurest? How might it affect employee morale?

4. Eurest's ITEP includes two key elements not specifically addressed in the government's plan: (a) the gradual introduction of indigenous employees to the workplace, and (b) a dedicated ITEP manager. Why do you think Eurest added these elements? What benefits might they offer? What problems might they create? If you were consulting for Eurest, would you recommend that it keep or eliminate these two elements? Why?

5. If during a press interview Eurest were asked for its position regarding the continuing Aboriginal controversies, how would you recommend it respond? What impact might your recommendation have on Eurest's employees, customers, and business and government partners?

Summary and Conclusion

Inclusion of disadvantaged groups through state/national collaborations refers to the values that drive organizational policies with regard to disadvantaged populations such as welfare recipients, domestic violence victims, and youth in distress. Although the exclusionary workplace views disadvantaged populations as in the sole domain of welfare agencies and charity organizations, the inclusive workplace perceives them as a potentially stable and upwardly mobile workforce.

The main obstacle to implementing such programs is a limited corporate vision that is focused on short-term goals. The other obstacles are stereotypes and prejudices held by management and workers against disadvantaged populations. On the other hand, including these population groups in HR planning and in policy initiatives of work organizations can benefit companies as well as individuals and their families. Opening up employment and advancement opportunities for these populations may increase their chances of obtaining higher-paying jobs with better benefits, which will release them from the vicious cycle of low-paying jobs that barely suffice for basic needs. The economic benefits for companies include gaining a more loyal workforce, expanding employee pools, improving customer relations, and having a more attractive, value-based corporate image.

If corporations take appropriate initiative with respect to disadvantaged groups, social and legislative changes such as the welfare-to-work reform can be conceptualized as an opportunity to, on the one hand, make the workplace more inclusive with respect to social class, and on the other hand, give companies access to untapped human resources. Besides the ethical and moral value of such actions, access to potential job seekers may be particularly important in tight job markets.

16

The Inclusive Workplace: Level IV

Inclusion Through International Collaborations

It is the duty of the corporation to make profits for its
shareholders, but to earn them in such a way as to make a real and permanent
contribution to the well being of the people and to the development of South Africa.

—Sir Ernest Oppenheimer,
founder of Anglo American in 1917[1]

L evel IV, *inclusion through international collaborations,* refers to the organization's positions and
practices related to the fair exchange of economic goods and services and the respectful cultural
relationship with individuals and groups in other countries. It reflects the "macro" system level
of international relations. The exclusionary workplace operates from a framework that is ethnocentric,
competition-based, and focused on narrowly defined financial and national interests (see Figure
16.1). The inclusive workplace sees value in collaborating across national borders, being pluralistic,
and identifying global mutual interests. The exclusionary organization, for example, will send local
employees on international assignments to strictly enforce a company's values and norms overseas,
whereas the inclusive workplace will hire local managers and give autonomy to its international
branches.

The combination of business internationalization, worker migration, and workforce diversity creates a challenge for companies engaged in international business. Multinational companies such as
IBM, General Electric, British Petroleum, Siemens, and Eastman Kodak each do business in more than

FIGURE 16.1 ● **The Inclusive Workplace: The Value Base for Level IV Inclusion Through Global Collaborations**

Inclusive Policies and Practices: Inclusion Through Global Collaborations		
	Value Frame	
System Level	Exclusion	Inclusion
	←	→
	Culture-specific	Pluralistic
International	Ethnocentric	Collaboration-based
Global	International focus	Focus on global mutual interests

50 countries. Of the 1,000 largest industrial companies in the United States, 700 expect their growth abroad to exceed their domestic growth in the next 5 years. The process through which people, companies, and countries acquire wealth has undergone major changes in recent decades because of the internationalization of capital markets and advances in technology.

The increasingly more open economic markets create opportunities for countries with surplus workforce and underdeveloped economies to come together with countries that can finance economic endeavors and provide jobs. However, these conditions also open up opportunities for exploitation by companies that take advantage of workers' desperation in poor regions by employing them in abhorrent conditions and subminimal payment. In order to compete in this changing environment, companies must develop intelligent systems of human resource (HR) management and open up opportunities for a diverse workforce across national boundaries (for a case example of such policies and programs, see Box 16.1). If they wish to survive and succeed in today's changing market conditions, companies need to conduct their business in a fair and ethical way while respecting other cultures.

An interesting example of inclusive practices is that of Hindustan Unilever Ltd., the Indian division of Unilever, which, out of business necessity, developed an innovative international initiative. In 1975, the company was almost forced to close its dairy in Etah, not because the villagers did not have enough cows but because, being poverty stricken, they were unable to properly feed their livestock. The management of Hindustan Unilever decided to invest efforts and financial resources in its "integrated rural development initiative," helping some 600 villagers reach self-sufficiency. As a result of the program, the health and income levels of the local people have improved considerably, the dairy has been operating at full capacity, and the villagers are now loyal consumers of Hindustan Unilever products. Furthermore, the company now requires its managers, who typically live in India's cities, to spend 2 months living and working with the villagers in Etah to get to know them better and to make actual contributions to their community. This initiative has built on a long-term policy at Unilever, begun in the 1930s, of emphasizing the connection to the local community and appointing nationals to managerial positions in India and in Ghana (Jones, 2005, p. 173, 2010; Schwartz & Gibb, 1999, pp. 87–88). Hindustan Unilever is currently implementing Project Shakti (Hindustan Unilever Limited, n.d.), a program aimed at helping rural women (Shakti Ammas) achieve financial independence and security. Through Project Shakti, women are given training in IT, accounting, marketing, and health and hygiene skills. They are

Box 16.1

A COMPANY'S INTERNATIONAL INCLUSION INITIATIVES (LEVEL IV): THE CASE OF eSHOPAFRICA (GHANA)

eShopAfrica is a fair trade e-commerce business founded in 1999 in Accra, Ghana. The company's founder, Cordelia Salter-Nour, had worked for several years in the technology arm of aid and development organizations in Africa. Despite the increasing use of technology in Africa, Ms. Salter-Nour felt that technology was not benefiting the ordinary person. Furthermore, she realized that small-business entrepreneurs in many African countries struggled fiercely to get their businesses off the ground. Hence, she decided that technology could be used to aid the development of small businesses in Africa (C. Salter-Nour, personal communication, November 25, 2003). The stated aim of eShopAfrica is to use technology to develop a fair trade marketplace for traditional African artisans, allowing them to build sustainable businesses (eShopAfrica, n.d.-a).

One of the oldest e-commerce businesses in sub-Saharan Africa, this fair trade company, which markets traditionally produced arts and crafts from Ghana, Ethiopia, Zimbabwe, and Mali, started trading online in 2001. The company has grown into a sustainable business while still maintaining traditional supply chain dynamics (Clark, 2011). eShopAfrica sources its products from tradespeople throughout Ghana (eShopAfrica.com, n.d.-b). Product offerings include musical instruments, carvings, jewelry, textiles, fashions, and housewares. So, for example, a customer may have to wait for goods to be produced by the artisan, especially during busy agricultural times when the artisan has to attend to planting or harvesting their crops (Clark, 2011).

Although profitability is as essential to eShopAfrica as it is to any business, the company expresses equal commitment to the businesses and the communities from which it sources merchandise. The company's fair trade charter, applied to dealings with each supplier, includes payment of fair market prices (as agreed upon with suppliers after establishing product quality guidelines), prompt submission of payment, prohibition of forced labor/organized child labor, and refusal to disturb traditional supply and production lines. Each artisan is featured on the company's website, complete with a photo and a biographical sketch. Often, information is provided about the artisan's training and the status of his or her small-business venture. For example, Samuel Naah, the carpenter who has gained international recognition for his Ga-culture decorated chests (Hale, 2003; Karlin, 2005; Phillips, 2002), has been able to pay off his apprenticeship fees and set up his own workshop with the revenues generated by his eShopAfrica sales. To ensure success for the company and the small businesses with which it works, eShopAfrica has partnered with several nongovernmental organizations (NGOs) and governmental agencies, including the Ghana Export Promotion Council (the public agency charged with promoting Ghana's nontraditional products in international markets). The company is also included on the World Bank's list of e-commerce businesses that support grassroots entrepreneurs (World Bank Group, 2003).

also equipped with smartphones that have an Enterprise Resource Package to help them manage their businesses. The program expanded to include husbands and brothers of the Shakti Ammas in 2010. The men can sell products via bicycle, thus expanding the service area of the women who are limited to travel on foot. To date, Project Shakti has assisted more than 70,000 women and 48,000 men in over 165,000 villages (Hindustan Unilever Limited, n.d.). Project Shakti participants reach more than 4 million rural households. The program is currently being translated and adapted to other countries including Bangladesh, Sri Lanka, and Vietnam.

Another example is the corporate social responsibility (CSR) program implemented by Chiquita Brands International, Inc., a producer, distributor, and marketer of fresh and processed foods. Chiquita's banana division accounts for more than half of the company's revenues and employs some 20,000 employees in more than 127 banana farms in five countries in Latin America: Guatemala, Honduras,

Costa Rica, Panama, and Colombia (Wicki & Van der Kaaij, 2007). The rural areas from which Chiquita sources bananas struggle to various degrees with poverty, literacy, access to health care, and other basic social and infrastructure needs. The company went through four stages in the process: (a) raising top-management awareness, (b) formulating a vision and core corporate values, (c) changing organizational behavior, and (d) anchoring the change. Through much of its 100-year history, including those as predecessor companies United Fruit and United Brands, the company has been fiercely competitive and suffered from a less than stellar reputation. Chiquita Brands faced problems of corporate integrity as a result of its dealings with extortion by left-wing guerrilla and right-wing paramilitary groups in Colombia between 1989 and 2004.[2] The extended and systematic dealings with these groups were antithetical to the process of corporate responsibility to which the firm was committed during the time frame of 1998 to 2004, revealing a "divided self" in which major corporate activities diverged dramatically from the core values of the firm (Maurer, 2009). Reconciling this dilemma was the main impetus for implementing the company's socially oriented organizational change (Were, 2003). Formed in 2011, the IUF/COLSIBA/Chiquita Women's Committee represents a partnership between Chiquita and trade unions and is tasked with supporting the women who work on the banana farms (Chiquita Brands International, n.d.-a). As Sue Longley, the International Officer for Agriculture and Plantations (International Union of Food Workers), explained: "The IUF/COLSIBA/Chiquita Women's Committee is a good example that others could follow. It is the outcome of a process of negotiations and joint work between unions and the company that has taken place over more than 10 years. To date, Chiquita is the only company in the sector to make such a commitment. . . . The challenge, as with other parts of the agreement, is to get things applied on the ground so moving ahead with a pilot project on women's employment will be a crucial next step" (Chiquita Brands International, n.d.-b). In October 2014, Chiquita Brands agreed to a $742 million buyout with Brazilian orange juice maker Cutrale Group and its investment firm partner, Safra Group (Dow Jones & Company, Inc., n.d.).

Lotus Corporation, on the other hand, developed its international inclusive initiative out of ideological conviction. In 1992, although there was not yet a democratically elected government in place, Lotus reversed its previous policy not to do business in South Africa and launched a visionary initiative with the purpose of assisting in the development of the Black business community. The company established its South Africa social investment fund (with an annual budget of about $350,000) and has charged its newly hired manager with a mandate to work directly with Black-run information technology projects. The company created an internship program for Black programming trainees in Johannesburg and brought a group of Black computer instructors to Lotus's Massachusetts headquarters for advanced training, including training Black South Africans to assume managerial positions. In addition to the fund and the training opportunities, Lotus also made efforts to conduct its business dealings in the country in a way that will enhance Black businesses. Specifically, it formed a partnership with the only non-White software distributorship and invested time and resources in providing the technical assistance that was needed to bring the distributorship up to the requisite professional level (Alperson, 1993; Makower, 1995).

Barriers and Benefits to Implementing the Inclusive Approach at Level IV

Barriers

There are several obstacles related to applying the principles of the inclusive workplace to international collaborations. The primary barrier is greed, which motivates companies to go beyond a fair economic exchange and take advantage of employees or resources in the host country. Companies exploit uneducated people who live in poor nations with the purpose of gaining economic advantage. The second barrier is discrimination, or inappropriate consideration of age, gender, race, or other personal characteristics with respect to the hiring and employment conditions of both local employees and expatriates (employees who move from one country to the other to do their jobs). And the third is lack of respect for other national cultures, which leads to a forced implementation of the values and norms that are not appropriate for the host country.

Benefits

Companies today can reap the benefits of an increasingly global marketplace by employing workers from different nationalities in or outside their native countries. This expansion creates new jobs, including international job opportunities, for these companies' employees. From a business point of view, diversity and nondiscrimination policies applied to international business contacts are crucial. Skill shortages, underutilized customer potential, and improved market understanding are only a few of the more obvious business reasons. Chiquita Brands International (mentioned earlier) counts among its program's employee benefits (a) the adjustment of payment and benefits to many of its employees to make their compensation fairer, and (b) the improvement of health and safety conditions in its farms. Among the benefits to the company, Chiquita Brands International credits the program with improved sales in Europe as a result of the company's improved image, reduced health insurance costs because of lower accident rates, improved environmental protection, and improved industrial relations, including reduced work disruptions caused by strikes and stoppages (Were, 2003; Wicki & Van der Kaaij, 2007).

Another example comes from Bata International, a maker of shoes.[3] When Bata decided to expand its operations in Thailand, it worked with development experts from the Thai Business Initiative in Rural Development to set up small shoe factories in poor villages of the northeastern province of Buri Ram. The company provided the training in manufacturing and business skills, and the village cooperatives owned and managed the factories, investing the profits back into their communities. The company currently provides employment to almost 500 people in Buri Ram, and this investment has boosted the province's economy and helped in the development of many villages in the area. These small rural factories turned out some of the highest-quality shoes of any Bata factory in the world, with very healthy profits for the company (Schwartz & Gibb, 1999). Bata currently implements the Rural Sales Program, the Aquarella Catalogue Sales Program, and the Bata Children's Program (Bata.com, n.d.). Bata partnered with CARE to start the Rural Sales Program (RSP) in 2005. The RSP provides employment opportunities to women living in poverty in Bangladesh, and the company expects 10,000 participants in 2015 (Bata.com, n.d.). Currently implemented in Colombia, Bolivia, Ecuador, and Peru, the Aquarella Catalogue Sales Program seeks to secure financial independence for Latin American women through flexible work opportunities (Bata.com, n.d.). The women entrepreneurs (called *promotores*) market the Bata catalog at homes and offices, and there were 40,000 participants as of 2015. The Bata Children's Program (BCP) was launched in 2010 and matches Bata employees with volunteer activities that serve disadvantaged children who live in the communities where Bata does business (Bata.com, n.d.). Program focus areas include education, health, sustainable living, and mentoring. The program currently has 3,000 volunteers (Bata.com, n.d.).

Although international businesses have existed for centuries, the world has clearly entered an era of unprecedented global economic activity, including worldwide production, distribution, and—in increasingly large numbers—global strategic alliances. With foreign production currently accounting for more than 25% of their domestic production, multinational companies have a great stake in the international scene. These global ventures and international collaborations allow companies to expand their

FIGURE 16.2 ● The Inclusive Workplace Model: Barriers and Benefits for Level IV Inclusion Through Global Collaborations

Inclusion Through State/National Collaborations		
	Benefits	
Barriers	Individuals	Organization
• Greed—going beyond fair trade and exploiting others • Discrimination • Lack of respect for other nations and cultures	• Job opportunities, both for local residents and for expatriates • Improved health and safety conditions	• Expanded geographic markets • Improved industrial relations and less litigation • Increased economic activities • Better marketing to international customers • Improved corporate image with customers, financial institutions, and stockholders

geographical markets and to increase their economic activities. Given that products and services reach a growing number of men and women in countries throughout the world, sales organizations and supplier communities can improve their access to people with talent by increasing the diversity of their workforce. They can also become more aware of specific needs of their internationally based customers, which can enable them to create valued products and services (United Nations Global Compact, 2001, 2004, 2012).

Figure 16.2 provides a summary illustration of the barriers and benefits of implementing the inclusive workplace at level IV of the model.

Case Illustration: Level IV—Inclusion Through Global Collaborations—Fair Trade Company

If fair trade clothes followed the trends and were designed by the right designer, they would sell as well as any others.

—Alice Fisher, commissioning editor at *Vogue*

Opening the newspaper and seeing stories about sweatshops and child labor violations in developing countries has become a common occurrence. In the December 7, 2003, edition of the *New York Times,* Joseph Kahn reported on the sweatshop conditions in one plant, Kin Ki Industrial, a Chinese factory that makes items such as Etch A Sketch, a popular toy in the United States.

The story begins by illustrating the "official" working conditions at Kin Ki: good salary, respectable hours without night or weekend work, leisure time, work contracts, pensions, medical benefits, and tasty food provided by the factory cafeteria. It sounds like an ideal situation, one that some workers in industrialized countries might envy. These "official" working conditions are outlined on paper and given to workers just prior to inspections so that they know what to tell inspectors. However, if workers are asked for a copy of their work contract or other documents, the paper instructs them to intentionally waste time and then say that they can't find the paperwork.

The reality of the working conditions, however, is very different. As one Kin Ki official admits, the wages and benefits fall short of legal levels. That may be quite an understatement, if the workers' claims are a fair indication. Workers at the Kin Ki plant claim to earn 24 cents per hour, below the legal minimum of 33 cents per hour. Additionally, the workers are required to work 84-hour weeks (12 hours per day, 7 days per week) without the benefit of overtime pay as required by law. Workers are fed an uninspiring diet of boiled vegetables, beans, and rice, and meat is served twice per month. Despite protests by the workers for more pay and more meat, they have received only a few cents extra per day—with no improvements in the food. The employees who led the protests are no longer with the company. One official claimed the "troublemakers" left of their own accord. That may be true because Kin Ki is not a prison; although sometimes it may be hard to tell, based on the guarded front entrance, high walls surrounding the factory, and chicken wire on the dormitory windows (Kahn, 2003).

Fair Trade History

There has been a growing movement to eliminate poor working conditions, as experienced at Kin Ki, not only through laws or trade penalties but through positive trading relations, known as fair trade. Fair trade originated in the late 1950s when a U.K. charity, Oxfam, started selling crafts made by Chinese refugees (Aaronson & Zimmerman, 2006; Ram, 2002). This practice helped bolster Oxfam's organizational goal of offering a lasting solution to poverty and suffering around the world.

Since that time, fair trade practices have emerged to ensure that producers, laborers, and farmers are paid a price that not only covers their costs but also allows them to support their families, invest in their businesses, and invest in social and economic improvements (Ram, 2002). Several organizations have formed with the sole focus of promoting and monitoring fair trade practices, including the following:

- World Fair Trade Organization, originally formed in 1989 as The International Federation of Alternative Trade Organization, operates in over 70 countries across five regions (World Fair Trade Organization, n.d.)

- The Fairtrade Foundation (United Kingdom) in 1992

- Fair Trade Federation (United States) in 1994

- Fair Trade USA, originally formed in 1998 as Transfair

- Fair Trade Association of Australia and New Zealand (2003)

Several of the organizations, such as the Fairtrade Foundation and Fair Trade USA, certify that consumer products meet fair trade guidelines, adding a certification to product packaging such as the Fairtrade Foundation's "fairtrade mark" in the United Kingdom.

Principles of Fair Trade

The key principles of fair trade, as defined by the Fair Trade Federation (2008), are as follows:

- The creation of opportunities for economically disadvantaged producers

- Gender equity—particularly making sure that women are properly paid for their work and empowered within their organizations

- Transparency and accountability—including transparent management and open dialogues between importers and producers

- Capacity building—promoting sustainable business practices by producers and providing management-skill development and financial and technical assistance

- Payment of a fair price—as agreed through dialogue between the importer and producer

- Improved working conditions

- Environmental sustainability

- Promotion of fairer trade by educating consumers about the importance of purchasing fairly traded products

Market Expansion

The fair trade market has grown considerably since its start with craft items in the United Kingdom. Consumers can now buy a wide array of fair trade products including produce, coffee, tea, toys, jewelry, furniture, paper products, clothing, chocolate, rugs, and other items (Fair Trade Federation, 2003). The demand for fair trade products had spread across approximately 58 countries as of 2007, including Europe to the United States, Canada, Australia, New Zealand, and Japan (The Fair Trade Foundation, 2008b). The number and types of fair trade products, however, varies from country to country.

New fair trade products are regularly introduced around the world. In some cases, the products are new to the world. For example, the world's first fair trade mangos purchased from farmers in Ecuador became available in Europe in 2002 (Ram, 2002). In 2008, fair trade Austria introduced organic fair trade mangos, pineapples, and avocados, which were not previously available. Fair trade flowers were made available in Italy, the United States, and Sweden (The Fair Trade Foundation, 2008a). More often, the new products are an expansion into a new country. For example, Wild Oats Markets offered fair trade bananas, sold in Europe for years, for the first time in the United States in 2004 (Horowitz, 2004).

More than any other product, coffee is experiencing strong growth worldwide (Fair Trade Federation, 2003), with expected increases ranging from 23% in the United States to 80% in Japan in 2003. Fair trade coffee was introduced in Europe in 1990 and, as of 2001, had grown to $300 million in sales with over 150 brands in over 35,000 supermarkets (Bojarski, 2002). Now in the United States, large-scale food manufacturers are beginning to offer fair trade coffee for the first time. Procter & Gamble has introduced a fair trade coffee line available via the Internet. Kraft is introducing a fair trade coffee line, focusing on distribution via its food service division (Turcsik, 2003). Other popular companies that source fair trade items include Dole (bananas, pineapples, oranges), Honest Tea (teas, sugar), Ben and Jerry's ice cream (sugar, cocoa, vanilla, coffee, bananas), and Green Mountain Coffee Roasters (coffee) (Ben & Jerry's, n.d.; Dole Food Company, Inc., n.d.; Honest Tea, n.d.).

Example of the Costs of Fair Trade Goods

How much extra do fair trade products cost? That varies by product and company; however, the costs can often be kept relatively close to the price of non–fair trade products, as illustrated by the coffee market. According to Fair Trade USA, coffee importers buy directly from growers at $1.31 per pound (10 cents above prevailing market rates), or $1.51 per pound (20 cents above market rates) for organic coffee (TransFair USA, 2007). Although the prices paid by importers are not much more than the prevailing market rates, the monies go directly to the growers instead of to middlemen. As a result, the growers receive a higher price than the 40 cents per pound that they received via middlemen (Bojarski, 2002). How does that translate into cost differentials for the end consumer? Starbucks, one of the largest coffee chains in the United States, offers 1-lb. bags of fair trade coffee beans (mild blend) for $11.45 per pound compared with $9.95 per pound for comparable non–fair trade beans, a 15% difference. Fair trade products do not categorically cost more than conventional products, and the cost can depend on the extent to which small cooperatives can handle the considerable shipping and logistical requirements of moving their products to market (Fair Trade USA, n.d.-a).

Global Village and Fair Trade Company

Need for Options in Japan

In 1990, Safia Minney moved from Britain to Japan because of her husband's work. While there, she became dismayed with her options for organic foods and recycling. Additionally, she found that Japan's culture was filled with excess packaging and a lack of concern for environmental and human rights issues (People Tree, 2001). As a result, Ms. Minney started distributing pamphlets that indicated where it was possible to buy organic foods and to recycle (Davis, 2003). From this effort grew Global Village, an NGO with the goal of providing information sources for Japanese consumers to recycle and to purchase environmentally and socially friendly products.

In 1995, Ms. Minney formed Fair Trade Company, a natural outgrowth of Global Village. Whereas Global Village was formed to show consumers where to find socially friendly products, Fair Trade Company was formed to actually provide such products to consumers in Japan.

Fair Trade Company formed relationships with underprivileged people from around the world to use indigenous resources to produce clothing and handicrafts. All of the producers were paid a price—approximately 30% above the prevailing market prices—that would allow them to sustain a living for their families and to invest in their businesses (People Tree, 2001). Fair Trade Company primarily sells clothing, a product in a highly competitive and price-conscious market. The company's solution to keeping its prices down is to "work hard" (Trapp, 2002). That method is a common one among fair trade companies, where lowering workforce costs is viewed as the means to competitive pricing. For example, volunteers make up 68% of the total workforce population (excluding supermarkets) in the United States, Canada, and Japan (Fair Trade Federation, 2003) and 98% in Europe (Krier, 2001).

Fair Trade and Gender Inequality in Less-Developed Countries

The issues of fair trade and gender inequalities have been an ongoing battle for some time. According to Rice (2008), women in less-developed countries were not receiving the same working conditions in terms of equality and fairness in the fair trade workforce than those of men. Women were often given jobs that were "easy," low skilled, and less paying. In less-developed countries, the social norm was for women to stay at home and take care of the family. If women were working in fair trade, it was considered temporary until they start raising a family; therefore, management did not put a lot of energy into their training or in developing their job skills. This view contributed to women receiving less-skilled, low-paying jobs with producers (Rice, 2008).

In 2005, women produced 70% of the food for themselves and their families in less-developed countries, although men provided fair trade agriculture production and, in most cases, companies were managed and operated mostly by men (Rice, 2008). It is the view of many that fair trade is biased toward men because of the "social" expectation for women in less-developed countries to stay at home and take care of their families. Although, today, gender inequality is not at the level it once was, Rice (2008) suggested more research is needed in order to fully identify how trade relations perpetuate inequality and what trade relations are necessary to advance global and gender parity. Terstappen, Hanson, and McLaughlin (2013) echo this point in their review of the fair and alternate trade literature. These authors investigated gender, health, and labor inequities in their review and note that "gender equity and the gendered dimensions of fair trade are repeatedly described in the literature as areas in need of further investigation" (pp. 26–27).

Formula for Success

Naturally, some people may be concerned about the quality of the clothing. As Ms. Minney explains, "If people do have an impression . . . they think they're oatmeal and miserable and made of string. The image isn't really sexy. But the clothing looks and feels great" (Davis, 2003).

Not only did Fair Trade Company have to deal with such negative images of fair trade clothes, but it also had to handle higher prices. Despite efforts to keep costs down through hard work, Fair Trade Company's T-shirts sell for about 50% more than a consumer would typically pay for a non–fair trade shirt (Davis, 2003).

Regardless of these hurdles, Fair Trade Company experienced 40% to 50% growth per year over its first several years. Soon it launched a small catalog, which by 1999 developed into a 100-page catalog called People Tree, listing Fair Trade Company's products (People Tree, 2001). By the end of 2002, the catalog had 20,000 customers in Japan, which, combined with sales to about 500 Japanese stores, led Fair Trade Company to annual sales of $7.4 million.

Ms. Minney explains that product quality was the key to her success in Japan. "Japan is very design led. People are not interested unless a product is decently designed and of a certain quality." Ms. Minney adds that Japan's customers are only concerned about how something is produced if it looks good first (Trapp, 2002).

After gaining success in Japan, Fair Trade Company branched into the United Kingdom market in September 2000, naming the company People Tree after its catalog. After 2 years of sales in the United Kingdom with little more than word-of-mouth promotion, sales have climbed to $460,000 (Trapp, 2002). In 2014, People Tree was voted into the U.K.'s Top 5 Most Ethical Companies by *Ethical Consumer* (a not-for-profit U.K. magazine and website) (People Tree, n.d.). As Ms. Minney explains in an April 2015 blog post, "Fair Trade is a long term partnership between producers and traders based on mutual respect and transparency, and the benefits of upholding these values is clear, no matter the industry. It's no secret that here at People Tree we are focused on putting people first and one of the primary ways we achieve this is by ensuring we adhere to Fair Trade practices at all times. In doing so, we are helping people in the world's most marginalised communities to escape poverty, strengthen their communities and promote environmental sustainability" (Fairtrade Cocoa, n.d.).

Fair Trade Future

Fair Trade Product Certifications

Certified fair trade products are common in Europe. According to the European Fair Trade Association, nearly 81% of all products sold in Europe feature a certification on the packaging that assures consumers that proper principles were followed (Krier, 2001). Transfair is working to expand its certifications beyond a few labeled products in the United States, Canada, and Japan. There is general agreement that the certifications are having a profound effect on the industry and will become more common in the coming years (Fair Trade Federation, 2003).

Traidcraft, a fair trade company located in the United Kingdom, offers products without certification. This has to do with the complex process of putting a "mark" on each product. Handcrafted items are not yet fair trade–certifiable because of the uniqueness of each item and the difficulty to set a single price on the item. Since the handcrafted items are not certified, women cannot participate in all the benefits of fair trade (Rice, 2008).

Fair Trade Impact on Producing Countries

Cooperation of Fair Trade recently conducted a survey that reached out to producers in Africa, Asia, and South America. It found that fair trade provides more than 37,500 jobs to people in Africa, with the largest number held by women. According to the survey report, approximately 69% of women and 31% of men were employed by fair trade producers (Boonman, Huisman, Sarrucco-Fedorovtsjev, & Sarrucco, 2011). Roughly 88% of the producers who answered the survey stated that, taking experience into consideration, the pay for men and women was equal.

Fair trade producers in Asia, according to the Cooperation of Fair Trade, provide a total of approximately 215,000 jobs, while South American producers employ approximately 21,000 people. In Asia, 59% of employees are men and 41% are women, while in South America, 83% of workers are female and 17% are male (Boonman et al., 2011).

Fair Trade Cities

In Europe, a growing trend is to have cities certified as a "fair trade city." The Fairtrade Foundation determines the criteria and awards the designation. To earn this designation, a city must prove that shops and suppliers are committed to selling fair trade products (Hart, 2003). The European Union (EU) and the Fairtrade Foundation launched an international Fairtrade Towns website in July 2009, and by the end of 2012 there were 937 Fairtrade towns/cities in 18 countries worldwide (The Fairtrade Towns in Europe Project, n.d.). Wales is leading the pack in the battle for fair trade city designations and has been declared the first Fairtrade nation in the world (The Fairtrade Towns in Europe Project, 2009). Ammanford became Wales's first fair trade city in July 2002. Since then, Swansea and Cardiff have moved close to the designation (Hart, 2003), and Wrexham is aiming to be the first fair trade county borough in the United Kingdom. With all of the fair trade growth in Wales, some are suggesting that Wales may become the first fair trade country in the world. However, the idea is so new that the Fairtrade Foundation has not yet determined criteria for such a designation ("Wales in the Fast Lane," 2003). A number of other cities have achieved fair trade status over the last decade. For example, in 2015, Taipei City, Taiwan, was designated an official fair trade city (Fairtrade, n.d.). As one local fair trade business owner noted, "The concept of ethical consumption and Fairtrade are very new to most of consumers in Taiwan, and it's taken a lot of effort to educate consumers. We've been knocking on the door for a long time, but it was always closed. . . . We still have long way to go. . . . But the launch of Fairtrade Taipei City is a really important milestone for the Fairtrade movement in Taiwan. From the Mayor down, people are starting to understand that fair trade is not only a cultural phenomenon, but a new way of doing business."

Summary and Conclusion

The fourth level, inclusion through international collaborations, refers to the organization's positions and practices related to the fair exchange of economic goods and services and the respectful cultural relationship with individuals and groups in other countries. The exclusionary workplace operates from a framework that is ethnocentric, competition-based, and focused on narrowly defined financial and national interests, but the inclusive workplace sees value in collaborating across national borders, being pluralistic, and identifying global mutual interests.

The combination of business internationalization, worker migration, and workforce diversity creates a challenge for companies engaged in international business. The increasingly more open economic markets create opportunities for the countries with surplus workforce and underdeveloped economies to come together with countries that can finance economic endeavors and provide jobs. These conditions, however, also open up opportunities for exploitation by companies that take advantage of workers' desperation in poor regions by employing them in abhorrent conditions with subminimal payment.

There are several obstacles related to applying the principles of the inclusive workplace to international collaborations. The primary barrier is greed, which motivates companies to go beyond a fair economic exchange and to take advantage of employees or resources of a host country. Other barriers include discrimination in hiring and employment conditions and lack of respect for other national cultures, which leads to a forced implementation of the values and norms that are not appropriate for the host country. On the other hand, implementing inclusive workplace principles can help companies reap the benefits of an increasingly global marketplace by employing workers from different nationalities in their native countries. From a business point of view, diversity and nondiscrimination applied to international business contacts are crucial. Overcoming skill shortages and underutilized customer potential and improving market understanding of foreign markets are only a few of the more obvious business reasons. Finally, applying fair trade principles can improve a company's public image and its standing with customers and stock owners alike.

In order to compete in this changing environment, companies must develop intelligent systems of HR management and open up opportunities for a diverse workforce across national boundaries. If they wish to survive and succeed in today's changing market conditions, companies need to conduct their business in a fair and ethical way while respecting other cultures.

Questions for Discussion and Further Analysis

1. Which method do you think would work better for improving worldwide working conditions: voluntary methods via fair trade products, or laws mandating fair working conditions for imports? What would be the benefits and drawbacks of each approach?

2. What impact do you think Fair Trade Company's higher prices have on sales? What might be some of the reasons why Fair Trade Company is paying a higher premium to producers than that paid by importers of fair trade coffee?

3. If you were consulting for another clothing company that wants to implement fair trade practices, how would you use the experience of People Tree to assist this company? How would you tie the company's diversity management practices to its newly initiated fair trade practices? How would you use both to improve the company's image internally (with its employees) and externally (with customers, financial institutions, and stock owners)?

4. Some might claim that the use of a high percentage of volunteers in the fair trade industry is trading one group of low-wage workers for another. What are your opinions on the topic? Is this a fair analogy? Why or why not?

5. How can we better understand the relationship between fair trade and gender inequality in less-developed countries?

Notes

1. Anglo American is South Africa's largest company and the world's number one in the mining industry. The quote was provided by Anglo American manager Margie Keeton (Schwartz & Gibb, 1999, p. 88).

2. In 2008, Chiquita Brands International admitted it had paid nearly $2 million in protection money to a murderous paramilitary group in Colombia that has killed or massacred thousands of people. The company said it did so to protect its employees there, but families of civilians killed by paramilitaries have faulted the company for contributing to their deaths. The company's admission and the victims' allegations have tarnished the company's image ("The Price of Bananas," 2009).

3. Bata International, founded in 1894 by Tomáš Baťa in Zlim, is in today's Czech Republic. The company is a retailer, manufacturer, and distributor of commercial fashion footwear and accessories. Over the years, the company has grown to over 40,000 employees and over 5,000 stores. It manages a retail presence in over 50 countries and runs 33 production facilities across 22 countries. The Bata shoe organization has traditionally regarded itself as a "multidomestic" rather than a multinational enterprise, and it makes it a priority to contribute to the economy in any new markets it enters.

Practical Steps for Creating an Inclusive Workplace

Climate for Diversity, Climate for Inclusion, and Survey Scales

"If it is true that there are as many minds as there are heads,
then there are as many kinds of love as there are hearts."

—Leo Tolstoy, *Anna Karenina*

Introduction

Organizations aiming to become inclusive need to engage in a continuous four-stage process comprised of the following steps: (a) a self-study/assessment of its diversity climate and of its climate for inclusion; (b) a strategic plan of action relevant to the organization's mission and goals; (c) implementation—actions and corrective actions that address conflicts or dilemmas; and (d) feedback—collecting information regarding diversity and inclusion at the team and organizational levels (depicted in Figure 17.1). In this chapter we will define and elaborate on the constructs of climate

FIGURE 17.1 ● Practical Steps for Creating an Inclusive Workplace

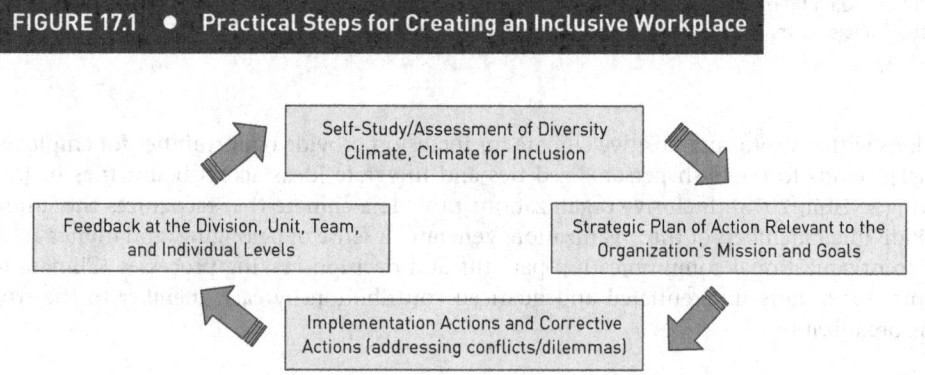

for diversity and climate for inclusion and offer specific practical tools for assessing those two very important types of climates.

Climate for Diversity and Climate for Inclusion

Organizational climate refers to the shared perceptions of employees regarding an organization's policies, procedures, and practices. These shared perceptions typically inform individuals' understanding of the behaviors that are expected from them in their role as employees in the specific organization (Reichers & Schneider, 1990; Schneider, Gunnarson, & Niles-Jolly, 1994; Zohar & Hofmann, 2012).

Broadly, climate for diversity refers to employee perceptions regarding the extent to which the organization's policies reward role behaviors that include employees from diverse backgrounds in organizational processes and social networks. More specifically,

> *Climate for diversity* refers to shared employee perceptions of the extent to which organizational policies and practices encourage and reward: (a) increasing representation of diverse groups in the organization, and (b) implementing equitable practices that apply to everyone in the organization regardless of their demographic characteristics. (Mor Barak, 2014; Mor Barak, Cherin, & Berkman, 1998)

Climate for diversity is the extent to which employees view an organization as integrating employees of diverse backgrounds into the organization and the presence of personnel practices that are applied equitably to everyone in the organization (McKay & Avery, 2015). Organizations with positive and strong climates for diversity not only invite employees of diverse backgrounds on board but also provide them with a level playing field.

Climate for inclusion requires a change in interaction patterns in the organization (Nishii, 2013). Based on Shore et al.'s (2011) and Nishii's (2013) conceptualization of inclusion and of Mor Barak's (2005) definition of inclusion, we offer the following definition of climate for inclusion:

> *Climate for inclusion* refers to shared employee perceptions of the extent to which organizational policies and practices encourage and reward acceptance of demographically diverse employees by (a) recognizing their unique attributes; (b) providing them with a sense of belonging; and (c) encouraging their involvement in organizational communication, decision-making processes, and informal interactions.

Organizations with a strong and positive climate for inclusion provide opportunities for employees of diverse backgrounds to establish personalized ties and integrate ideas across boundaries in joint problem solving (Nishii, 2013). Inclusive organizations provide a climate that recognizes the unique identities of individual members of the organization, generates a sense of belonging, and invites active contribution to organizational communication patterns and decision-making processes. Climate for inclusion allows for a more differentiated and nuanced contribution by each member to the work group and the organization.

As demonstrated throughout this book, although diversity and inclusion are often used interchangeably or as a single combined term (sometimes abbreviated as D&I), they are distinct constructs (Mor Barak, 2014; Nishii, 2013; Roberson, 2006; Shore et al., 2011). Diversity refers to demographic differences among members, including both observable (e.g., gender, race, age) and nonobservable (e.g., culture, cognition, education) attributes (Roberson, 2006). Inclusion, on the other hand, refers to employees' perception that their full participation in communication and decision-making processes is welcomed and that their unique contribution to the organization is appreciated. Diversity can exist without inclusion, and inclusion can exist without diversity. For example, an organization might have strong initiatives to recruit members of diverse groups and provide equal access to jobs yet not have policies in place to ensure that all employees are included in organizational processes and decision making. Similarly, a nondiverse organization, in which employees have great similarities in demographic characteristics, may have inclusive policies yet maintain its nondiverse character. Therefore, diversity and inclusion are distinct constructs that can exist independently of each other.

Most organizations take a limited approach to assessing diversity and inclusion. They administer annual employee surveys ("taking the pulse" of the organization) and typically add a couple of questions related to diversity and inclusion as a way to measure these aspects of their organizational culture. The limitation of this approach is that most of these questions are single items (as opposed to scales) with only face value validity—that is, they look like they measure what they intend to measure but there is no other evidence for their validity or reliability (i.e., that they measure what they say they measure and that they do it consistently). There are a few composite scales available for climate for diversity (e.g., Chrobot-Mason, 2003; Kossek and Zonia, 1993; Mor Barak et al., 1998) and for climate for inclusion (e.g., Mor Barak et al., 1993; Nishii, 2013), though some do not have much information about validity and reliability and not much history of research outcomes over time. In the next section I offer a detailed description of two measures that I developed over the years through research with colleagues and doctoral students. The first is the Climate for inclusion-exclusion scale and the second is the diversity climate scale.

The Climate for Inclusion-Exclusion Scale (MBIE)

Overview

The Mor Barak inclusion-exclusion scale (MBIE) (2005)[1] builds on an earlier measure of inclusion offered by (Mor Barak & Cherin, 1998), with additional items and a more structured conceptual framework. It measures the degree to which individuals feel a part of critical organizational processes such as access to information, involvement and participation with the organization, and influence in the decision-making process. It uses a matrix system of five work-organization system levels (work group, organization, supervisor, higher management, and social/informal) intersected by three inclusion dimensions (decision making, information networks, and participation/involvement). The measure thus includes 15 items that evaluate a worker's sense of inclusion in relation to the following five work-organization system levels:

1. Work group (items 1–3)

2. Organization (items 4–6)

3. Supervisor (items 7–9)

4. Higher management (items 10–12)

5. Social/informal (items 13–15)

In each of these levels, the respondent is asked to assess his or her inclusion across the following three dimensions:

a. The decision-making process (items 1, 4, 7, 10, 13)

b. Information networks (items 2, 5, 8, 11, 14)

c. Level of participation/involvement (items 3, 6, 9, 12, 15)

The 15 scale items are summed to create a composite inclusion-exclusion continuum score with three reverse-scored questions (items 5, 8, 15—noted by the letter *R*) to prevent response sets from systematically answering the questions. Higher scores on the scale reflect a higher sense of inclusion (see below).

SCALE ITEMS

1	2	3	4	5	6
Strongly Disagree	Moderately Disagree	Slightly Disagree	Slightly Agree	Moderately Agree	Strongly Agree

1. I have influence in decisions taken by my work group regarding our tasks... □ 1 □ 2 □ 3 □ 4 □ 5 □ 6

2. My coworkers openly share work-related information with me. .... □ 1 □ 2 □ 3 □ 4 □ 5 □ 6

3. I am typically involved and invited to actively participate in work-related activities of my work group. .... □ 1 □ 2 □ 3 □ 4 □ 5 □ 6

4. I am able to influence decisions that affect my organization. .... □ 1 □ 2 □ 3 □ 4 □ 5 □ 6

5. I am usually among the last to know about important changes in the organization (R). .... □ 1 □ 2 □ 3 □ 4 □ 5 □ 6

6. I am usually invited to important meetings in my organization. .... □ 1 □ 2 □ 3 □ 4 □ 5 □ 6

7. My supervisor often asks for my opinion before making important decisions. .... □ 1 □ 2 □ 3 □ 4 □ 5 □ 6

8. My supervisor does not share information with me (R). .... □ 1 □ 2 □ 3 □ 4 □ 5 □ 6

9. I am invited to actively participate in review and
    evaluation meetings with my supervisor. .... □ 1 □ 2 □ 3 □ 4 □ 5 □ 6

10. I am often invited to contribute my opinion in meetings with
    management higher than my immediate supervisor. .... □ 1 □ 2 □ 3 □ 4 □ 5 □ 6

11. I frequently receive communication from management
    higher than my immediate supervisor
    (i.e., memos, e-mails). .... □ 1 □ 2 □ 3 □ 4 □ 5 □ 6

12. I am often invited to participate in meetings with
    management higher than my immediate supervisor. .... □ 1 □ 2 □ 3 □ 4 □ 5 □ 6

13. I am often asked to contribute in planning social activities
    not directly related to my job function. .... □ 1 □ 2 □ 3 □ 4 □ 5 □ 6

14. I am always informed about informal social activities
    and company social events. .... □ 1 □ 2 □ 3 □ 4 □ 5 □ 6

15. I am rarely invited to join my coworkers when they go
    for lunch or drinks after work (R). .... □ 1 □ 2 □ 3 □ 4 □ 5 □ 6

Psychometric Properties and Previous Research Utilizing the Measure

Accumulating research demonstrates the validity and reliability of the MBIE measure across diverse worker population groups in different countries. The initial version of the measure showed good internal consistency in a sample of 3,400 employees of diverse racial and ethnic backgrounds in a California-based high-tech company with a Cronbach's alpha of .88 (Mor Barak & Levin, 2002). Utilizing the inclusion scale in a multivariate model, the study demonstrated that women and members of racial/ethnic minority groups were more likely to feel excluded, and that exclusion was linked to job dissatisfaction and a lower sense of well-being. A series of cross-national studies demonstrated the resiliency of the measure across cultures. In a cross-cultural study with samples of employees from similar high-tech companies in the United States and Israel, the inclusion-exclusion measure similarly demonstrated good internal consistency with Cronbach's alphas of .90 and .81 for the two national samples, respectively (Mor Barak, Findler, & Wind, 2001). The theoretical factor structure fit both samples well (the Bartlett's Test of Sphericity was 1342.30 and 406.72, each at $p < .001$, and the Kaiser-Meyer-Olkin measure was .87 and .78, respectively, for the two samples). The combined factors accounted for 65% and 67% of the variance in the two samples, respectively.

A second study with these samples tested a multivariate model and demonstrated that ethnicity, inclusion-exclusion, perception of fairness, job stress, social support, and job satisfaction were all significant correlates of employee well-being (Mor Barak, Findler, & Wind, 2003). Utilizing only the national sample drawn from a high-tech corporation in Israel, a third study tested a theoretical model using structural equations statistical methodology. The study utilized the 10 items related to decision-making processes and information networks from a 15-item inclusion-exclusion scale and documented the measure's strong internal consistency with a Cronbach's alpha of .81. The findings demonstrated several significant associations between diversity and organizational culture, such as fairness and inclusion, employee well-being, job satisfaction, and organizational commitment (Findler, Wind, & Mor Barak, 2007). An earlier version of the scale (Mor Barak & Cherin, 1998) showed strong internal consistency (Cronbach's alpha = .87) and appropriate correlations indicating convergent validity (r = .63, p < .05) with Porter and Lawler's (1968) organizational satisfaction, and discriminant validity ($r =\sim$ .32, p < .05) with Porter's work alienation scale (Price & Mueller, 1986).

Examining perception of inclusion among Korean employees, another international study matched a sample of 381 employees with their 320 supervisors in one of the largest corporations in Korea (Cho & Mor Barak, 2008). The inclusion-exclusion scale once again demonstrated good internal consistency with a Cronbach's alpha of .83. Findings from the study indicated that perception of inclusion was strongly related to job satisfaction, organizational commitment, and job performance (as evaluated by the employees' supervisors) among the Korean employees. In another study conducted in Korea, Kang and Mo (2010) investigated the role of organizational inclusion-exclusion in relation to perceived organizational support, organizational commitment, and turnover intention. The findings showed that organizational inclusion-exclusion was positively associated with perceptions of organizational support. The MBIE scale showed good reliability in a sample of 353 child welfare workers. Cronbach's alphas of the three subscales ranged from .66 to .85 (Kang & Mo, 2010). Lauring and Selmer's (2010) study examining the associations between common language and group cohesiveness including group involvement, group conflict, and group trust in multicultural organizations in Denmark found the involvement subscale of the MBIE measure to be reliable. The five items of the group involvement subscale produced a Cronbach's alpha of .88. The findings showed that consistency in English management communication and frequency of communication were strongly associated with group involvement (Lauring & Selmer, 2010).

Another study examining how perceived inclusion affected teen volunteers' organizational satisfaction illustrated the good internal consistency of the MBIE scale (Bortree & Waters, 2008). Cronbach's alphas of the three distinct factors ranged from .70 to .82. The finding showed that inclusion was strongly associated with organizational satisfaction. Using the 15-item inclusion-exclusion scale, Waters and Bortree (2010) conducted a series of studies to explain the role of inclusion in retaining teen volunteers. They used the eight subscales of the measure—five system levels of work group, organization, supervisor, higher management, and social/informal, and the three dimensions of decision-making process, information networks, and level of participation/involvement. Waters and Bortree (2010) demonstrated that trust as a predictor of teen volunteers' retention was positively associated with their perception of inclusion in work groups and decision making. The reliability coefficients of seven subscales were between .70 and .82, while that of the eighth subscale, the social group, was lower than .70 (Waters & Bortree, 2010). Waters and Bortree (2010) additionally showed that gender was a predictor for retaining teen volunteers. For female volunteers, social group inclusion and participation in informal/social meetings appeared to be the strongest factors contributing to their retention as volunteers, while inclusion in information networks and decision making appeared to be the strongest factors for male volunteers. Cronbach's alphas of the eight factors ranged from .73 to .79 (Waters & Bortree, 2010). Acquavita, Pittman, Gibbons, and Castellanos-Brown (2009) demonstrated similar high internal consistency of the inclusion-exclusion scale with a Cronbach's alpha of .91. The authors examined the relationship among minority status, workplace racial composition, perceived inclusion, organizational diversity, and job satisfaction for social work professionals employed in organizations through the use of a national Internet-based survey. The results showed that perceived inclusion was positively associated with job satisfaction (Acquavita et al., 2009).

The Age & Generations Study, carried out by the Sloan Center on Aging & Work at Boston College, gathered data from employees in nine U.S. workplaces in 2007–2008. The data included information on employees' work experiences focusing on their perceptions of inclusion using the MBIE scale. To date, three research reports and one peer-reviewed article examining the role of inclusion in the workplace have been published utilizing these data. Findings from a study carried out by Matz-Costa, Pitt-Catsouphes, Besen, and Lynch (2009) suggested that perceived inclusion diminished after the 2007 economic downturn and appeared to be lower among individuals who had decreased job security resulting from the economic crisis. The study used six of the 15 inclusion-exclusion scale items. Pitt-Catsouphes, Matz-Costa, and Besen (2009) examined whether perceptions concerning quality of employment vary by age/generation, career stage, dependent care, and tenure groups. As one quality of employment factor, team inclusion was measured using 11 items of the inclusion-exclusion scale. Workers providing child and elder care and workers with 3–10 years of job tenure were likely to have low levels of team inclusion, but there were no significant variations by age, generation, and career-stage groups for team inclusion (Pitt-Catsouphes et al., 2009). In a follow-up study, Pitt-Catsouphes and Matz-Costa (2009) examined the engagement of multigenerational employees and utilized the MBIE scale to demonstrate that employee feelings of being included were a predictor of worker engagement for younger-boomers but not for other, older age groups (Pitt-Catsouphes & Matz-Costa, 2009).

In a later study, Matz-Costa, Carapinha, and Pitt-Catsouphes (2012) examined the effects of relational age (employee perception of personal age relative to the age distribution of his or her work team) in work team members' perceptions of inclusion in a multi worksite sample of 1,778 employees, ages 17–77. The authors adapted a shorter version of the MBIE with seven items comprising two factors—assessment of employees' inclusion in team decision making and inclusion in information sharing. The reliability coefficients of the two factors were .81 and .84, respectively. Results indicate that employees who felt they were age dissimilar from their work teams—where the majority of their team members were in a different age cohort— reported being less included in both decision making and information sharing than those on age-diverse work teams—where the work team is heterogeneous in terms of age, without a clear age majority (Matz-Costa et al., 2012).

Reliability for the inclusion-exclusion scale has been consistently documented in child welfare studies. Using a sample of 359 child welfare workers, Travis and Mor Barak (2010) examined what factors affected workers' responses to challenging situations—seeking positive change or disengaging from their jobs—in child welfare organizations. They used the five-item subscale of the inclusion in decision making from the original 15 items of the inclusion-exclusion scale. The Cronbach's alpha reliability measure of the scale was .71, indicating good internal consistency. The findings suggested that workers who feel included in decision making are more likely to speak up (exercise voice) and less likely to disengage psychologically (neglect) (Travis & Mor Barak, 2010). Hopkins, Cohen-Callow, Kim, and Hwang (2010) shed light on predictors of job withdrawal, work withdrawal, job search behavior, and exit from the organization in child welfare. Four items were adapted from the inclusion-exclusion scale to measure inclusion in the decision-making process as a predictor of organizational disengagement. The subscale showed good internal consistency with a Cronbach's alpha of .88. Unexpectedly, the findings indicated that feelings of inclusion in the decision-making process were positively related to job withdrawal. This finding contradicted the assumption that being part of the decision-making process would contribute to staying in the organization. The authors provide a possible explanation, indicating that it may not be just participation in the decision making but the outcomes of that process. In other words, if participating in decision making does not translate to sufficient changes in the workplace, then it could be perceived by workers as a futile waste of time (Hopkins et al., 2010). Another study was carried out to examine the mediating role of organizational commitment between inclusion and turnover intention (Hwang & Hopkins, 2012). The findings indicate that the negative relationship between inclusion and intention to leave was mediated by organizational commitment. To measure inclusion, the authors used the full 15 items of the inclusion-exclusion scale and documented good internal consistency for the scale items with a Cronbach's alpha of .78 (Hwang & Hopkins, 2012).

Inclusion was a central variable in Cottrill's (2012) study of authentic leadership, organizational climate for organizational ethics, organization-based self-esteem (OBSE), and organizational citizenship behavior (OCB). Using an employee sample of 107 primary respondents and 213 peer respondents in the United States, the findings indicated that authentic leadership and organizational climate for ethics were positively linked to inclusion. The findings also elucidated the mediating impact of inclusion on the relationship between authentic leadership and OCB. The study reports high internal consistency for the MBIE with Cronbach's alphas ranging from .81 to .90 (Cottrill, 2012).

Longitudinal studies conducted in three locations in the United States—California, Massachusetts, and Texas—demonstrated viable relationships among diversity, inclusion, and employee retention in nonprofit public agencies. One of these studies used structural equations modeling to provide empirical support for a comprehensive theory-based model of the relationship among diversity, inclusion, individual well-being, job satisfaction, organizational commitment, and turnover, controlling for stress, perception of fairness, and social support (Mor Barak, Levin, Nissly, & Lane, 2006). Another longitudinal study focused on the relationship between perception of dissimilarity and the inclusion dimension of work group involvement, using the five-item participation/involvement dimension from the original 15-item inclusion-exclusion measure. The study demonstrated high internal consistency for the scale items with Cronbach's alphas of .89 and .90 for Time 1 and Time 2, respectively. The findings suggested that visible and informational dissimilarity were negatively related to work group involvement, while group openness to diversity was found to moderate the relationship between visible and informational dissimilarity and work group involvement (Hobman, Bordia, & Gallois, 2004).

Using a data set comprised of more than 500 public child welfare workers, Hwang and Hopkins (2015) used the full 15-item inclusion-exclusion scale to examine relationships among diversity characteristics, inclusion, and several organizational outcomes including organizational commitment, job satisfaction, and intention to leave. In this study, perceptions of inclusion were significantly and positively associated with organizational commitment and job satisfaction. Brimhall, Lizano, and Mor Barak, (2014) also explored the relationship between perceptions of inclusion and job satisfaction and intention to leave among public child welfare workers. This study used two-wave longitudinal data from 363 child welfare workers and full versions of the inclusion-exclusion and diversity climate scales (described in the next section) to see if inclusion is a mechanism through which leader-member exchange and diversity climate influence organizational outcomes. Findings highlighted the importance of inclusion in understanding both job satisfaction and intention to leave within this unique employee group. One key study finding was that inclusion perceptions were a pathway for explaining how diversity climate and leader-member exchange positively influence job satisfaction.

Bortree and Waters (2014) used the 15-item inclusion-exclusion scale to understand the role that inclusion plays in future volunteer intention among volunteers with diverse racial and ethnic backgrounds. This study used survey data from 634 individuals who volunteer at three library systems. Overall, findings suggested that positive inclusion perceptions influenced relationship quality, which then affected the individuals' intention to volunteer in the future. Relationship quality was assessed in terms of trust, control mutuality (power), commitment, and satisfaction. Results showed significant differences among non-Hispanic Caucasians and the three minority groups included in this study (African Americans/Blacks, Asians, and Hispanics/Latinos). Minority groups expressed significantly lower perceptions of inclusion, which were associated with lower relationship quality (in terms of trust and power) and reduced future volunteer intentions.

To understand job satisfaction among peer providers in community-based behavioral health agencies, Davis (2013) used items from the inclusion-exclusion scale in a survey of 100 members of the National Association of Peer Specialists. Peer providers are individuals who have experienced mental health issues themselves and then receive training to collaborate with and provide treatment alongside mental health professionals. This study explored the influence of five factors—role clarity, psychological empowerment, supervisory alliance, coworker support, and inclusion-exclusion—on job satisfaction among peer providers. From the inclusion-exclusion scale, nine items were included in the final survey. In this study, role clarity and psychological empowerment emerged as significant job satisfaction predictors.

The Mor Barak et al. Diversity Climate Scale

Overview

The diversity climate scale examines employees' views about the diversity climate in the organization (Mor Barak et al., 1998). It includes 16 items with two dimensions: the organizational and the personal, each containing two factors, as follows (see Figure 17.2):

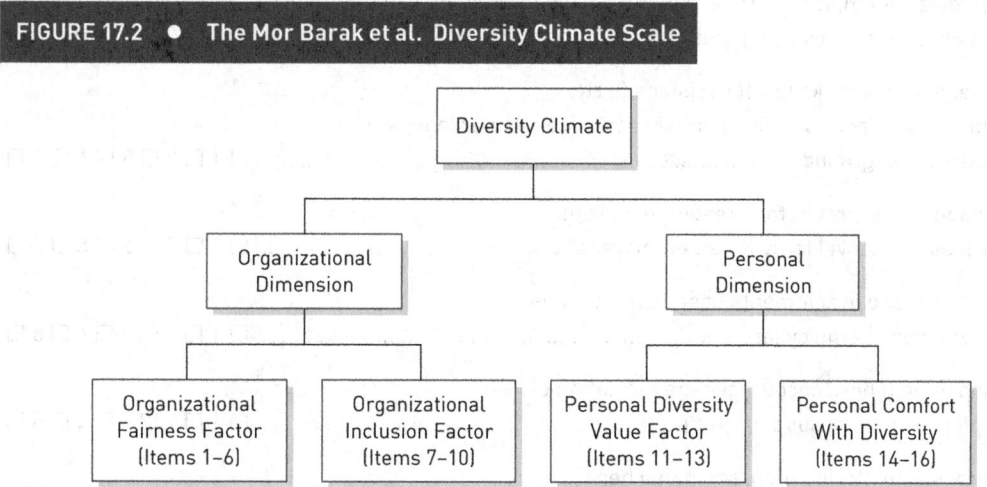

FIGURE 17.2 ● The Mor Barak et al. Diversity Climate Scale

The organizational dimension refers to the perception of management's policies and procedures that affect members of minority groups and women—such as discrimination or preferential treatment in hiring and promotion procedures (factor a). It also refers to management actions that affect inclusion or exclusion of women and members of minority groups—such as mentorship programs or the preservation of the "old boys' network" (factor b). The personal dimension refers to individuals' views of the importance of diversity to work groups and to the organization (factor c) and their level of comfort in interactions with members of other groups (factor d).

The 16 scale items are summed to create a composite diversity perceptions score with four reverse-scored questions (items 1, 9, 15, and 16, noted by the letter *R*) to prevent response sets in answering the questions. Higher scores on the scale reflect a positive perception of diversity climate. The dimensions and factors can be separately summed and analyzed to gain insight into the composition of employees' views of the diversity climate.

Diversity Climate Scale Items

1	2	3	4	5	6
Strongly Disagree	Moderately Disagree	Slightly Disagree	Slightly Agree	Moderately Agree	Strongly Agree

1. I feel that I have been treated differently here because of my race, gender, sexual orientation, religion, or age (R). .... □ 1 □ 2 □ 3 □ 4 □ 5 □ 6

2. Managers here have a track record of hiring and promoting employees objectively, regardless of their race, gender, sexual orientation, religion, or age. .... □ 1 □ 2 □ 3 □ 4 □ 5 □ 6

3. Managers here give feedback and evaluate employees fairly, regardless of employees' race, gender, sexual orientation, religion, age, or social background. .... □ 1 □ 2 □ 3 □ 4 □ 5 □ 6

4. Managers here make layoff decisions fairly, regardless of factors such as employees' race, gender, age, or social background. .... □ 1 □ 2 □ 3 □ 4 □ 5 □ 6

5. Managers interpret human resource policies (such as sick leave) fairly for all employees. .... □ 1 □ 2 □ 3 □ 4 □ 5 □ 6

6. Managers give assignments based on the skills and abilities of employees. .... □ 1 □ 2 □ 3 □ 4 □ 5 □ 6

7. Management here encourages the formation of employee network support groups. .... □ 1 □ 2 □ 3 □ 4 □ 5 □ 6

8. There is a mentoring program in use here that identifies and prepares all minority and female employees for promotion. .... □ 1 □ 2 □ 3 □ 4 □ 5 □ 6

9. The "old boys' network" is alive and well here (R). .... □ 1 □ 2 □ 3 □ 4 □ 5 □ 6

10. The company spends enough money and time on diversity awareness and related training. .... □ 1 □ 2 □ 3 □ 4 □ 5 □ 6

11. Knowing more about cultural norms of diverse groups would help me be more effective in my job. .... □ 1 □ 2 □ 3 □ 4 □ 5 □ 6

12. I think that diverse viewpoints add value. .... □ 1 □ 2 □ 3 □ 4 □ 5 □ 6

13. I believe diversity is a strategic business issue. .... □ 1 □ 2 □ 3 □ 4 □ 5 □ 6

14. I feel at ease with people from backgrounds different from my own. .... □ 1 □ 2 □ 3 □ 4 □ 5 □ 6

15. I am afraid to disagree with members of other groups for fear of being called prejudiced (R). .... □ 1 □ 2 □ 3 □ 4 □ 5 □ 6

16. Diversity issues keep some work teams here from performing to their maximum effectiveness (R) .... □ 1 □ 2 □ 3 □ 4 □ 5 □ 6

Psychometric Properties and Previous Research Utilizing the Measure

The measure focuses on employee perceptions in that it has been documented that behavior in the workplace is driven by perceptions of reality. For example, Eisenberger, Fasolo, and Davis-LaMastro (1990) found that employees' perceptions of being valued by an organization were associated with their conscientiousness, job involvement, and innovativeness. What people believe is of vital importance, whether or not their beliefs are consistent with reality, and appears to influence their behavior.

The assessment tool was developed based on a review of the literature, similar surveys used in other companies, and items solicited from members of the organization reflecting issues that they felt were important to understanding the organizational diversity environment. Items covered the personal dimension (e.g., "I am afraid to disagree with members of other groups for fear of being called prejudiced") and the organizational dimension (e.g., "Management takes seriously the opinions, ideas, and viewpoints of minorities and women"). Item contributors included men and women of diverse racial/ethnic backgrounds working as human resource managers, project managers, midlevel managers, and line workers. After the first pool of about 100 items was collected, a pretest of the items was conducted by asking a selected group of workers (representing various levels of management, occupations, genders, and racial/ethnic backgrounds) to answer the questions and critique the content, wording, and style. A diversity committee of a California-headquartered international company composed of representatives of ethnic groups and men and women from different functions in the organization, reviewed the items for face validity. This committee served as a representative liaison group to advise on development of an empathic survey (Alderfer, 1980; Alderfer & Brown, 1972). This process occurred twice and resulted in a pool of 16 items using a five-point Likert-type scale ranging from "strongly agree" to "strongly disagree," with one additional category of "can't answer," which was not included in determining mean scores.

The scale, as well as each of its factors, showed strong to adequate internal consistency with Cronbach's alphas of .83, .86, .80, .77, and .71, respectively (Mor Barak et al., 1998). The factor structure was tested on a sample of 2,686 employees in a California-headquartered international high-tech company with a diverse workforce. The factors fit the data well—Bartlett's Test of Sphericity was 4593.15 at $p < .001$, and the Kaiser-Meyer-Olkin measure was .90 (Kaiser, 1970; Norusis, 1993). The four factors had Eigen values between 1.2 and 5.4, explaining 57.1% of the variance (factor I—29.9%; factor II—13.1%; factor III—7.4%; factor IV—6.6%).

The results of the study examining ethnic and gender differences in employee perceptions of organizational diversity climate revealed that, overall, members of the majority group of the organization (White men) had more positive overall perceptions ("Things are good as they are") than women and members of racial and ethnic minority groups ("More needs to be done"). White men specifically perceived the organization as more fair and inclusive than did White women or members of racial and ethnic minority groups (men and women). Conversely, White women and members of racial and ethnic minority groups saw more value in, and felt more comfortable with, diversity than did White men (Mor Barak et al., 1998).

The measure has been used by researchers in various studies in different contexts and with diverse population groups (e.g., testing management skills, examining diversity climate in health care organizations, testing leadership in a global context).

Caldwell, Mack, Johnson, and Biderman (2002) utilized the diversity perception scale in a sample of 202 African American women employed at a national organization. The study examined the relationships among diversity, affective commitment, job satisfaction, and intention to leave. The measures used in the study included three of the four scale factors, with the exception of the personal comfort with diversity factor. The organizational fairness and organizational inclusion factors were found to have good internal consistency, with Cronbach's alphas of .81 and .67, respectively. However, the personal diversity value dimension yielded a low Cronbach's alpha of .35. The study's findings indicated that there are significant relationships among organizational fairness, inclusion, job satisfaction, affective commitment, and turnover intention. Examining interaction effects, the researchers report that respondents who reported high perceived personal diversity also reported strong associations between perceived organizational fairness and perceived organizational inclusion, as well as between affective commitment and intention to leave (Caldwell et al., 2002).

The diversity climate scale has been shown to have high levels of internal consistency in both national and international samples. Sia and Bhardwaj (2009) examined the impact of psychological contract on diversity climate among 207 employees at the lower and middle management levels of two public sector units in Orissa, India. The study used three of the four subscales of the diversity climate scale—inclusion, fairness, and personal diversity value—and the 12-item scale demonstrated good internal consistency with a Cronbach's alpha of .71. The authors found that incompatibility between the worker's expectations and the organizational reality with respect to the psychological contract were negatively linked to diversity climate in the organization (Sia & Bhardwaj, 2009). Using a sample of 391 Australian government workers, Soldan (2009) investigated whether there were worker differences in perceived management receptivity to diversity management (PMRDM) by demographic and job-related characteristics, and whether diversity climate affected PMRDM. Organizational fairness and inclusion appeared to be predictors of PMRDM. Cronbach's alphas of the four subscales of the diversity climate scale ranged from .71 to .86 (Soldan, 2009).

Several studies have used one or two subscales of the diversity climate scale. Of the four subscales, the organizational fairness scale has been most frequently used in several research fields to date. Maranto and Griffin (2011), examining factors affecting exclusion for women faculty, demonstrated that procedural fairness was a strong factor that promoted an inclusive organizational climate for men and women. The reliability of the five-item organizational fairness scale was .84 (Maranto & Griffin, 2011). Buttner, Lowe, and Billings-Harris (2010) also used the organizational fairness scale to examine the effect of diversity climate on professional employee of color outcomes, organizational commitment, and turnover intentions. The study's results indicate that diversity climate affects organizational commitment and turnover intentions, and that interactional and procedural justice played mediating roles between diversity climate and employee outcomes. Specifically, when a diversity climate was perceived to be fair, racially aware respondents reported lower levels of psychological contract violation. The organizational fairness subscale showed good internal consistency with a Cronbach's alpha of .92 (Buttner et al., 2010).

Focusing on diversity climate dimensionality, Buttner and her colleagues (2012) examined the relative effect of diversity climate dimensions captured by the Mor Barak et al. (1998) diversity climate scale and the Chrobot-Mason (2003) diversity promise fulfillment scale. The authors hypothesized that the two scales would measure different aspects of diversity climate and that the different climate dimensions would interactively affect professional employee of color outcomes: organizational commitment and turnover intentions. The results indicated that the diversity climate dimension, as measured by the Mor Barak et al. scale, mediated between diversity promise fulfillment and the outcomes. The authors also found complete mediated moderation between the interaction of the diversity climate measure and the diversity fulfillment scale and turnover intentions by organizational commitment. Ten items from the diversity climate scale, comprising the fairness and inclusion subscales, were used in this study, and the Cronbach's alpha reliability coefficient for the scale was .89 (Buttner, Lowe, & Billings-Harris, 2012).

Gonzalez and Denisi (2009) have shed light on the significance of diversity climate in the organization by examining the impact of demographic diversity on individual attachment and firm unit performance in a relatively diverse organization. The authors found that at the individual level, diversity climate moderated the impact of relational and categorical demography on affective organizational commitment, organizational identification, and intention to quit, and at the organizational level, diversity climate moderated the impact of organizational diversity on firm productivity and return on profit. The study assessed diversity climate by using the 10 items comprising the organizational dimension of the Mor Barak et al. diversity climate scale. The Cronbach's alpha reliability measure was .80 (Gonzalez & Denisi, 2009).

The personal diversity value factor of the diversity climate scale was used by Triana, Wagstaff, and Kim (2012) in investigating the impact of personal value of diversity on perceptions of discriminatory treatment among members of minority groups in the United States. The findings suggested that a high personal diversity value led to strong negative reactions to the mistreatment of women and racial minorities in the workplace. The Cronbach's alpha reliability coefficient of the scale was .70 (Triana et al., 2012).

Several studies have utilized the diversity climate scale as criteria for the development of other scales measuring diversity perception (e.g., McKay, Avery, & Morris, 2008, 2009; McKay et al., 2007; Pugh, Dietz, Brief, & Wiley, 2008). For example, McKay et al. (2007) used nine items to assess how managers perceive the value of diversity in organizations and considered the similarity of their scale to the earlier version of this diversity scale. One item utilized by McKay et al., (2008, 2009) was similar to the organizational fairness subscale. The authors reported that the association between their measure and the diversity perceptions scale provides support for the validity of their scale. Similarly, Pugh, et al., (2008) used the diversity perceptions scale as a guide to obtain the validity of their scale. Johnson (2008) suggests using the diversity perceptions scale as a self-assessment tool to gauge one's ethical leadership with respect to the moral aspects of diversity and exclusion (pp. 308–311). DeLia (2010) also used and revised two items of the diversity perception scale to develop a scale of heterogeneity norm: "This team believes different viewpoints add value," and "The differences on this team seem to keep us from performing at our maximum effectiveness." Triana and Garcia (2009) used one item of the diversity perceptions scale—"My organization spends enough money and time on diversity awareness and related training"—to measure perceived organizational efforts to support diversity. Triana, Kim, and Garcia (2011) gauged personal value for diversity by using one item of the diversity perceptions scale: "I think that diverse viewpoints add value."

More recently, Paolillo, Pasini, Silva, and Magnano (2016) tested the psychometric properties of an Italian adaptation of the diversity climate scale. This study consisted of a small qualitative pilot study and larger quantitative survey using 389 Italian employees across a range of sectors and organizational sizes. In this study's sample, 50% were male, 96% were Italian workers, 52% came from companies in northern Italy, 87% were between 26 and 55 years of age, 70% had completed 8 to 13 years of school, 73% had a permanent contract, and two-thirds of the study were blue-collar workers. Confirmatory factor analysis indicated that a three-factor solution using 12 of the 16 original items best fit this data set. The adapted scale excluded the personal comfort dimension, which highlights the fact that the diversity climate construct may operate differently across cultural contexts.

Summary and Conclusion

This chapter provided a four-stage intervention and implementation model for creating a diverse and inclusive work organization. We introduced the construct of organizational climate and applied it to both climate for diversity and climate for inclusion. We provided differential definitions for each of the terms. We then introduced two measures, one for climate for diversity and the other for climate for inclusion; introduced their respective conceptual structures and specific items; and provided detailed psychometric properties for each.

Note

1. Revised and expanded from the earlier versions of the inclusion-exclusion and diversity perceptions scales (Mor Barak & Cherin, 1998; Mor Barak et al.,1998; Mor Barak et al., 2001; Mor Barak & Levin, 2002).

18

Toward a Globally Inclusive Workplace

Putting the Pieces Together

There is only one caste—humanity.

—Pampa, 9th-century Indian poet and writer

The previous chapters described the value basis, the practice applications, and the barriers and benefits of implementing each system level of the inclusive workplace. From the micro to the macro, these levels begin with inclusion within the organization, proceed through corporate-community relations and collaborations with state/national initiatives, and culminate with international collaborations (see Figure 18.1). In this chapter, we put the different aspects of the inclusive workplace together and examine the implications for a broader vision of managing global diversity.

The Value Base for the Inclusive Workplace

The inclusive workplace is guided by a set of values that propels its policies and practices. An organization's actions, like a person's behavior, are informed by its values, whether explicit or implicit, and affect its policies, programs, and actions. In order to become inclusive, organizations need to evaluate their current values and norms and initiate new policies and programs that can bring about needed change. For the sake of clarity, our discussion in the previous chapters highlighted the values that drive the exclusionary workplace on the one hand and those that drive the inclusive workplace on the other. In reality, rarely do we find these extreme cases, as most organizations will be somewhere along the continuum. The chart presented in Figure 18.2 provides a summary illustration of the value schemes presented earlier for each of the system levels of the inclusive workplace. The model examines the organization's value frame on each of the four system levels (the vertical y-axis) and at the two extremes of the inclusion-exclusion continuum (the horizontal x-axis).

FIGURE 18.1 • The Inclusive Workplace Model

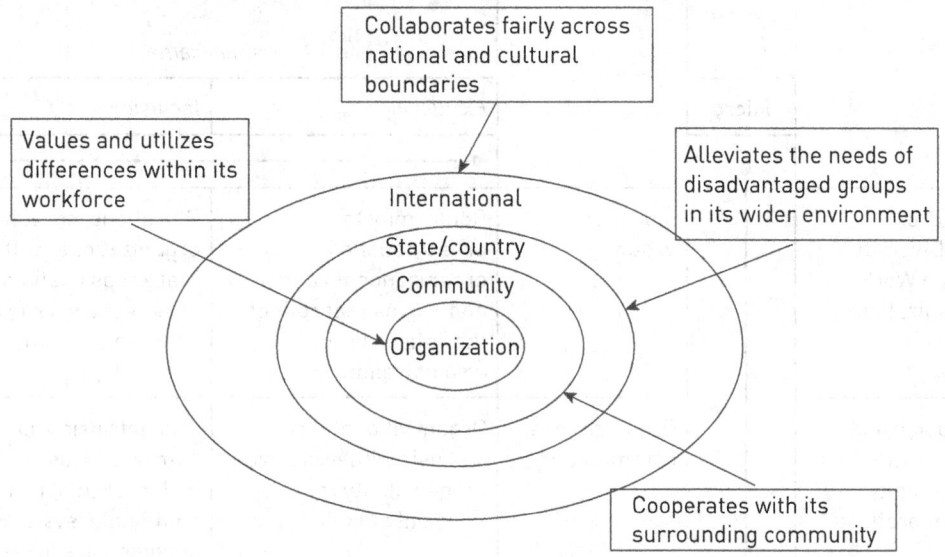

The first level, *inclusion and diversity within work organizations,* relates to the organization's internal relations with its own employees. Whereas an exclusionary workplace is based on the perception that all workers need to conform to preestablished organizational values and norms (determined by its "mainstream"), the inclusive workplace is based on a dynamic, coevolving value frame that relies on mutual respect and equal contributions of different cultural perspectives to the organization's values and norms. The second level, *inclusion and corporate-community collaborations,* relates to the organization's sense of being a part of its surrounding community and the reciprocity embedded in that relationship. An exclusionary workplace sees minimal or no connection to its community. An inclusive workplace, on the other hand, recognizes the economic and noneconomic consequences of its presence in the community. It acknowledges the responsibility it has to ameliorating the adverse effects of this presence and to making a positive contribution to the community's well-being. The third level, *inclusion through state/national collaborations,* refers to the values that drive organizational policies with regard to disadvantaged populations such as welfare recipients, domestic violence victims, and youth in distress. The exclusionary workplace views these populations as being in the sole domain of welfare agencies and charity organizations. The inclusive workplace perceives welfare recipients seeking work, domestic violence survivors, and youth in distress as a potentially stable and upwardly mobile workforce. Finally, the fourth level, *inclusion through global collaborations,* refers to the organization's positions and practices related to the fair exchange of economic goods and services and the respectful cultural relationship with individuals, groups, and organizations in other countries. The exclusionary workplace operates from a framework that is ethnocentric and focused on narrowly defined financial and national interests. The inclusive workplace sees value in collaborating across national borders, being pluralistic, and identifying global mutual interests.

FIGURE 18.2 • The Value Base for the Inclusive Workplace

	System Level		Value Frame	
	Micro		Exclusion	Inclusion
	↑		← →	
Inclusion and Diversity Within Work Organizations		Individuals, groups	Conformity to preestablished organizational values and norms that reflect the "majority" or "mainstream."	Pluralistic, coevolving organizational culture that keeps changing to reflect diversity of values and norms.
Inclusion and Corporate-Community Collaborations		Organizations, communities	Organizational focus is intrinsic with exclusive responsibility to financial stakeholders.	Dual intrinsic and extrinsic focus with recognition of community systems as stakeholders as well.
Inclusion Through State/ National Collaborations		State, federal government	Viewing disadvantaged groups as the domain of welfare agencies and charity organizations and treating them as disposable labor.	Treating disadvantaged groups as potentially stable, upwardly mobile employees and investing in their education and training.
Inclusion Through Global Collaborations	↓	International, global	Culture-specific. Ethnocentric. Intranational focus.	Pluralistic. Collaboration-based. Focus on global mutual interests.
	Macro			

Implementation of the Inclusive Workplace

Implementing the inclusive workplace can have substantial benefits to the organization and to its employees but will present considerable barriers in the process (see Figure 18.3).

At level I—*inclusion through diversity within the work organization*—an inclusive workplace allows, encourages, and facilitates the inclusion of individual employees who are different from the mainstream in the organizational information networks and decision-making processes. The main benefits at this level include better access to promotion and benefits as well as improved job satisfaction and well-being for individual employees. At the organizational level, companies may experience lower turnover and reduced absenteeism as a result of improved job satisfaction among employees, better access to high-potential employees

FIGURE 18.3 ● Implementing the Inclusive Workplace Model

	Principles	Barriers	To Individuals	Benefits — To Organization
Micro				
Inclusion Through Diversity Within the Work Organizations	Encouraging and facilitating inclusion of employees who are different from the "mainstream"	• Discrimination • Prejudice • Perception of threat to job security	• Access to advancement and job promotions • Improved income and benefits • More decision-making power	• Business growth and productivity • Cost savings (e.g., lower turnover, less absenteeism) • Positive image with employees, customers, and financial institutions • Improved corporate image and reputation • Advantage in recruitment and in labor disputes
Inclusion Through Corporate-Community Collaborations	Recognizing the community as a stakeholder and directly contributing to its welfare	• Economic pressures to demonstrate profitability • Limited company vision • Lack of leadership to champion and sustain efforts	• Employment, job training • Mentorship • Improved services to the community • Employment benefits	• Increased employee loyalty • Strong connection between social performance and economic performance • Expanded potential employee pool
Inclusion Through State/National Collaborations	Extending services through programs and policies aimed at assisting disadvantaged groups in society	• Shortsighted and internally focused company vision • Stereotypes, prejudice, and discrimination of disadvantaged population groups	• Job training • Advancement opportunities • Improved job prospects	• Increased employee loyalty • Improved customer relations • A more attractive value-based corporate image
Inclusion Through Global Collaborations	Conducting business fairly through respecting and accommodating other national cultures	• Greed—going beyond fair trade and exploiting others • Discrimination • Lack of respect for other nations and cultures	• Job opportunities, both for local residents and for expatriates • Improved health and safety conditions	• Expanded geographic markets • Improved industrial relations and preventing litigation • Increased economic activities • Better marketing to international customers • Improved corporate image with customers, financial institutions, and stock owners
Macro				

who will be attracted to their organizational culture, a more committed workforce, and greater appeal to clients of diverse backgrounds. The likely obstacles to implementing inclusive policies and practices at level I include prejudice, overt and covert discrimination, misunderstanding of groups from diverse backgrounds, and employees' perceptions, as well as actual group competition for access to power within the organization.

At level II—*inclusion through corporate-community collaborations*—an inclusive workplace recognizes the community as a legitimate stakeholder and directly and actively collaborates with community organizations in an effort to contribute to the community's welfare, realizing that the corporation's own well-being is tied to it. Benefits to individuals in the community include access to opportunities like job training, employment, and additional services that community members would not otherwise have. The organization's tangible rewards include improved corporate image within as well as outside the community, which can translate into advantages in recruitment and avoiding or mitigating the potentially negative results of labor disputes. Shortsighted and internally focused corporate vision and economic pressures to demonstrate short-term profitability are among the main barriers to implementing inclusive policies and programs at this level.

At level III—*inclusion through state/national collaborations*—companies are extending services through programs and policies aimed at assisting disadvantaged groups in society. The focus of the inclusionary policies and programs at this level is on social class—though social class is often related to gender and race/ethnicity group membership. Benefits to individuals often include job training that may lead to employment with the company or improved job prospects with other employers. Work organizations may expand their potential employee pool as a result of these policies, gain a loyal workforce, and improve customer relations—particularly among the disadvantaged groups but also among other clients who care about social issues. The main barriers to implementing inclusive policies at this level include shortsighted and internally focused company vision and stereotyping disadvantaged groups as unstable and disposable labor.

Finally, at level IV—*inclusion through international collaborations*—a company is inclusive toward its *entire* workforce, both locally and overseas, particularly in developing countries. It avoids the temptation to exploit uneducated employees in poor regions and conducts business in a fair and ethical way that respects and accommodates other cultures. Benefits to individuals in the host countries include access to job training and employment that may otherwise not be available and improved life conditions for individuals, their families, and the communities in which they live. Treating their employees fairly and respectfully also benefits organizations, as they are able to generate goodwill from both their employees and potential customers, gain a loyal and committed workforce, and expand their economic activities. The main barriers related to applying the principles of the inclusive workplace with respect to the international collaborations are greed, cultural and national difficulties in communication, and unfair or inappropriate consideration of diversity in employment conditions of both local employees and expatriates.

Conclusion

The economic, social, and demographic trends described in Part I of the book create an environment that is fertile ground for intergroup conflicts, as explained in Part II of the book. The legislative and social policy initiatives taken by individual countries, and by the international community as a whole, mitigate potential harmful effects and define "the rules of the game" for work organizations. It is important to understand, though, that these trends are not only a backdrop or context for organizations to consider; they also define the *scope* of what companies need to consider as their domain when they design diversity policies and programs. In order to avoid the pitfalls and reap the benefits of a diverse workforce, employers need to adopt a *broader vision of inclusion,* a vision that encompasses not only the organization itself but also its surrounding community and its national and international environment.

An inclusive workplace allows, encourages, and facilitates the inclusion of individual employees who are different from the mainstream in the organizational information networks and decision-making

Box 18.1

MY WATERCOLORS METAPHOR FOR DIVERSITY

As a child, I spent a week of my summer vacation at my cousins' magnificent villa overlooking the Mediterranean. We walked in the gardens collecting flowers of different colors—blues, reds, pinks, lilacs, purples, yellows—and placed them in glass jars with water, each color separately. By the end of the week, we had produced a magnificent collection of rainbow-colored water in individual containers. We placed the glass jars in a row on a shelf and proudly admired our creation. Using a painter's brush, we created beautiful pictures using these home-made watercolors. We enjoyed watching how some colors maintained their original brilliance while others merged to create new ones—the blue and yellow created a new shade of green and the red and blue created a beautiful purple. Then we got a creative idea for an experiment: If the individual jars had such brilliant colors, what an amazing color could all of them produce together? We poured a sample from each jar into one big container and held our breaths. To our chagrin, the result was a dull gray. That image stayed with me and now serves as a metaphor for what happens to people who are forced to blend in and give up their unique identities. Their brilliant distinctive ideas will fade into an assimilated dull gray. Yet, if they are allowed to maintain their unique identity they will create new ideas and, together, form a work of art.

processes at each of the four levels—from the organization, through the community and state, to the international. Full-fledged inclusion as opposed to, for example, sensitivity training initiatives necessitates a radical upending of basic assumptions, patterns, and structures. An organization that does not confront the daunting and complex task of moving toward an inclusive workplace cannot set appropriate diversity-related goals. Valuing diversity goes beyond the golden rule of treating others as you wish to be treated yourself because it involves a higher behavior, one that is receiver-centered rather than self-centered. Sometimes called the "platinum rule," valuing diversity involves treating others as *they* wish to be treated.

This inclusive workplace offers a broad vision for managing diversity in today's global economy, one that contains individuals and groups that have a direct or indirect stake in the organization, such as potential future employees, customers, and investors, all of whom are also increasingly diverse. Although some companies, primarily in North America and Europe, have already introduced diversity initiatives, the inclusive workplace offers a comprehensive and multilevel approach that ensures fair and inclusive treatment of individuals who are different from the mainstream. Changing the organization's culture from merely "diversity tolerant" or "respectful of diversity" to *truly inclusive* can be done through deliberate actions at the four system levels suggested in this book. The limitation of this approach is rooted in its ambitious scope. As demonstrated in the case studies, although some smaller companies can and do adopt inclusive initiatives, it is primarily midsize to large companies with adequate resources that are able to engage in all four levels of inclusion. With the growing number of larger and multinational companies all over the world, however, this model can potentially benefit individual employees, their families and communities, and work organizations.

The goal of diversity management is not to assimilate people of diverse characteristics into the dominant culture, on the one hand, nor to create segregated groups or communities of similar backgrounds, on the other hand, but to create a social, legislative, and organizational environment that respects and values individual differences. The old conventional assimilation paradigm utilized the industrial melting pot image—individuals were expected to shed their unique group affiliations and cultural characteristics in order to take on the majority culture's values, norms, and behaviors. In depicting diversity management, I propose an image from the art world—the *painter's palette* (see Box 18.1). *Like colors, when people are forced to blend and give up their unique characteristics, the result is a dull gray. Allowed to display their true colors, they shine brightly and together create an inspiring work of art.*

• References •

Aarons, G. A., & Sommerfeld, D. H. (2012). Leadership, innovation climate and attitudes towards evidence-based practices during a statewide implementation. *Journal of the American Academy of Child & Adolescent Psychiatry, 51*, 423–431.

Aarons, G. A., Sommerfeld, D. H., & Willging, C. E. (2011). The soft underbelly of system change: The role of leadership and organizational climate in turnover during statewide behavioral health reform. *Psychological Services, 8*(4), 269–281.

Aaronson, S. A., & Zimmerman, J. M. (2006). Fair trade: How Oxfam presented a systemic approach to poverty, development, human rights, and trade. *Human Rights Quarterly, 28*(4), 998–1030.

Abell, J. P., Havelaar, A. E., & Dankoor, M. M. (1997). *The documentation and evaluation of anti-discrimination training in the Netherlands.* Geneva: International Labour Office.

About the Firm. (2002–2003). Retrieved December 8, 2003, from www.haynesboone.com/about/about.asp

Abrams, D. (1992). Processes of social identification. In G. M. Breakwell (Ed.), *Social psychology of identity and the self concept* (pp. 57–99). London: Academic/Survey University Press.

Abrams, D., & Hogg, M. A. (1988). Comments on motivational status of self esteem in social identity and intergroup discrimination. *European Journal of Social Psychology, 18*, 317–332.

Abrams, D., Hogg, M. A., & Marques, J. M. (2004). A social psychological framework for understanding social inclusion and exclusion. In D. Abrams (Ed.), *Social psychology of inclusion and exclusion.* Abingdon, UK: Psychology Press.

Acker, J. (2011). Theorizing gender, race and class in organizations. In E. Jeanes, D. Knights, & P. Martin (Eds.), *Handbook of gender, work and organizations.* New York: Wiley.

Acquavita, S. P., Pittman, J., Gibbons, M., & Castellanos-Brown, K. (2009). Personal and organizational diversity factors' impact on social workers' job satisfaction: Results from a national Internet-based survey. *Administration in Social Work, 33*(2), 151–166.

Aczel, D. (1999). *God's equation: Einstein, relativity and the expanding universe.* New York: Four Walls Eight Windows.

Adams, J. S. (1965). Inequity in social exchange. In L. Berkowitz (Ed.), *Advances in experimental social psychology* (Vol. 2, pp. 267–299). New York: Academic.

Adamson, J. (2000). *The Denny's story: How a company in crisis resurrected its good name.* New York: Wiley.

Adarand Constructors v. Peña, 515 U.S. 200 (1995).

Adler, N. J., & Gundersen, A. (2008). *International dimensions of organizational behavior* (5th ed.). Mason, OH: Thomson South-Western.

Administration for Children and Families. (2011). *Temporary Assistance for Needy Families.* Retrieved August 21, 2012, from www.acf.hhs.gov/programs/ofa/tanf/about.html

Afiouni, F., Karam, C. M., & El-Hajj, H. (2013). The HR value proposition model in the Arab Middle East: Identifying the contours of an Arab Middle Eastern HR model. *The International Journal of Human Resource Management, 24*(10), 1895.

Afiouni, F., Ruël, H., & Schuler, R. (2014). HRM in the Middle East: Toward a greater understanding. *The International Journal of Human Resource Management, 25*(2), 133–143.

Aguinis, H., & Glavas, A. (2012). What we know and don't know about corporate social responsibility: A review and research agenda. *Journal of Management, 38*(4), 932–968.

Ahmad, F. (2012). Graduating towards marriage? Attitudes towards marriage and relationships among university-educated British Muslim women. *Culture and Religion: An Interdisciplinary Journal, 13*(2).

Ailey, S. H., Brown, P., Friese, T. R., & Dugan, S. (2016). Building a culture of inclusion: Disability as opportunity for organizational growth and improving patient care. *Journal of Nursing Administration, 46*(1), 9–11.

Ailon, G. (2008). Mirror, mirror on the wall: Culture's consequences in a value test of its own design. *Academy of Management Review, 33*(4), 885–904.

AKILAH Institute for Women. (n.d.). *Overview.* Retrieved from http://www .akilahinstitute.org/overview/

Alba, R., & Silberman, R. (2002). Decolonization immigrations and the social origins of the second generation: The case of North Africans in France. *The International Migration Review, 36*(4), 1169–1193.

Alderfer, C. P. (1980). The methodology of organizational diagnosis. *Professional Psychology, 11*(3), 459–468.

Alderfer, C. P., & Brown, L. D. (1972). Designing an empathic questionnaire for organizational research. *Journal of Applied Psychology, 56*(6), 456–460.

Alderfer, C. P., & Smith, K. K. (1982). Studying intergroup relations embedded in organizations. *Administrative Science Quarterly, 27*(1), 35–65.

Allport, G. W. (1979). *The nature of prejudice* (25th anniversary ed.). Reading, MA: Addison-Wesley. (Original work published 1954)

Alon, S. (2015). *Race, class, and affirmative Action.* New York: Russell Sage Foundation.

Alperson, M. (1993, May 2). Profile/ Mackie McLeod; Helping Lotus do the right thing in South Africa. *New York Times.* Retrieved December 5, 2009, from www.nytimes.com/1993/05/02/ business/profile-mackie-mcleod-helping-lotus-do-the-right-thing-in-south-africa.html

Alsop, R. J. (2004). *The 18 immutable laws of corporate reputation: Creating, protecting, and repairing your most valuable asset.* New York: Free Press.

Altman, J. C. (2009, April). *Beyond closing the gap: Valuing diversity in indigenous Australia.* CAEPR Working Paper No. 54/2009. Center for Aboriginal Research, Canberra, ACT: Center for Aboriginal Research, The Australian National University.

Amaro. (2015). *USC state of the neighborhood report.* Retrieved from https://issuu.com/uscedu/docs/usc_ state_of_the_neighborhood_repor/1

Amnesty International. (2012). *Report the state of the world's human rights.* London: Author.

Anand, S. (2003, May 14). *Beat those blues.* Retrieved December 3, 2003, from www.hindustantimes.com/2003/ May/14/674_248122,00310003.htm

Ansell, R., & Tinsley, A. (2011). Bhopal's never ending disaster. *The Environmentalist.* Retrieved from www.environmentalistonline.com/ article/2011-10-13/bhopal-s-never-ending-disaster#Video

Aparna, J. (2006). The influence of organizational demography on the external networking behavior of teams. *Academy of Management Review, 31*(3), 583–597.

Appelrouth, S., & Desfor Edles, L. (2007). *Classical and contemporary sociological theory* (Chapter 8, pp. 311–347). Thousand Oaks, CA: Pine Forge Press.

April, K., Ephraim, N., & Peters, K. (2012). Diversity management in South Africa: Inclusion, identity, intention, power and expectations. *African Journal of Business Management, 6*(4), 1749–1759.

Aramovich, N. P. (2014). The effect of stereotype threat on group versus individual performance. *Small Group Research, 45*(2), 176–197.

Archibong, U., & Sharps, P. W. (2011). A comparative analysis of affirmative action in the United Kingdom and United States. *Journal of*

Psychological Issues in Organizational Culture, 2, 17–38.

Arcidiacono, P., Aucejo, E., & Hotz, V. J. (2013). University differences in the graduation of minorities in STEM fields: Evidence from California. *National Bureau of Economic Research.* Retrieved March 6, 2016, from http:// www.nber.org/papers/w18799

Armstrong, C., Flood, P., C., Guthrie, J. P., Liu, W., Maccurtain, S., & Mkamwa, T. (2010). The impact of diversity and equality management on firm performance, beyond high performance work systems. *Human Resource Management, 49,* 977–998.

Arnold, J. (2003, October 10). Why economists don't fly Concorde. *BBC News.* Retrieved September 12, 2004, from http://news.bbc.co.uk/2/hi/ business/2935337.stm

Arnold, W. (2002, October 16). Scandal lets Malaysia prove its mettle. *New York Times,* p. W1. [An excerpt of the article can be found at http://query.nytimes.com/gst/]

Arrow, K. J. (1973). The theory of discrimination. In O. Ashenfelter & A. Rees (Eds.), *Discrimination in labor markets* (pp. 3–33). Princeton, NJ: Princeton University Press.

Arrow, K. J. (1998). What has economics to say about racial discrimination? *The Journal of Economic Perspective, 12*(2), 91–100.

Arsu, S., & Bilefsky, D. (2013, October 8). Turkey lifts longtime ban on head scarves in state offices. *New York Times.*

Ashford, J. B., LeCroy, C. W., & Lortie, K. L. (2009). *Human behavior in the social environment: A multidimensional perspective.* Belmont, CA: Brooks/Cole.

Ashforth, B. E., & Mael, F. S. (1989). Social identity theory and the organization. *Academy of Management, 14,* 20–39.

Asian Business Coalition on AIDS. (2003). *Case study 2: Haiha-Kotobuki Export Company.* Retrieved December 4, 2003, from www.abconaids.org/asp/view.asp? PageID=47&SiteID= 6&LangID=0&MenuID=108&SponsorID=50

AstraZeneca United Kingdom. (2004a). *About us.* Retrieved May 26, 2004, from www.astrazeneca.co.uk/azcareers/workinghere/diversity.asp

AstraZeneca United Kingdom. (2004b). *Diversity and inclusion at AstraZeneca.* Retrieved February 21, 2016, from http://www.astrazenecacareers.com/about-us/culture/diversity-inclusion/

AT&T. (2016). Diversity. Retrieved March 31, 2016, from http://www.att.com/gen/corporate-citizenship?pid=17725

Athreya, B. (2011). White man's "burden" and the New Colonialism in West African cocoa production—race/ethnicity. *Multidisciplinary Global Contexts, 5*(1), 51–59.

Athukorala, P. (1986). *Sri Lanka's experience with international contract migration and the reintegration of return migrants* (working papers of the ILO International Migration Programme). Geneva: International Labour Office.

Auclair, M. (1992). Out in Africa: Going where no communicator has gone before. *Communication World, 9*(3), 43–45.

Australia apology to Aborigines. (2008, February 13). BBC News. Retrieved December 4, 2009, from http://news.bbc.co.uk/2/hi/7241965.stm

Australian Bureau of Statistics. (2007). Population distribution, Aboriginal and Torres Strait Islander Australians, 2006. Retrieved December 4, 2009, from www.abs.gov.au/AUSSTATS/abs@.nsf/Latestproducts/4705.0Media%20Release12006?open document&tabn

ame=Summary&prodno=4705.0&issue=2006&num=&view=

Australian Bureau of Statistics. (2008). *Population projections, Australia 2006 to 2101.* Canberra, Aus.: Author.

Australian Employment Services. (2002, September 5). Eurest—a natural corporate leader. *Corporate Leaders for Indigenous Employment Bulletin.*

Australian government rules out Aboriginal compensation. (2001, June 28). *Agence France Presse.* Retrieved September 13, 2004, from http://web.lexis-nexis.com/ universe/document

Automatic Data Processing. (n.d.). *Diversity statement.* Retrieved December 8, 2003, from http://nas.adp.com/about/diversity_statement.html

Avery, D. R., McKay, P. F., & Wilson, D. C. (2008). What are the odds? How demographic similarity affects the prevalence of perceived employment discrimination. *Journal of Applied Psychology, 93*(2), 235–249.

Avery, D. R., Volpone, S. D., McKay, P. F., King, E. B., & Wilson, D. C. (2012). Is relational demography relative? How employment status influences effects of supervisor-subordinate demographic similarity. *Journal of Business and Psychology, 27,* 83–98.

Avolio, B. J., Gardner, W. L., Walumbwa, F. O., Luthans, F., & May, D. R. (2004). Unlocking the mask: A look at the process by which authentic leaders impact follower attitudes and behaviors. *The Leadership Quarterly, 15,* 801–823.

Award over racism upheld. (2001, October 25). *The Los Angeles Times,* Pt. 2, p. 1.

Aycan, Z., Al-Hamadi, A. B., Davis, A., & Budhwar, P. (2007). Cultural orientations and preferences for HRM policies and practices: The case

of Oman. *The International Journal of Human Resource Management, 18*(2), 11.

Aycan, Z., Bayazit, M., Berkman, Y., & Boratav, H. B. (2012). Attitudes towards women managers: Development and validation of a new measure with Turkish samples. *European Journal of Work and Organizational Psychology, 21*(3), 426–455.

Ayman, R., & Chemers, M. M. (1983). Relationship of supervisory behavior ratings to work group effectiveness and subordinate satisfaction among Iranian managers. *Journal of Applied Psychology, 68,* 338–341.

Baga-Reyes, V. (2003, November 2). Caregiving is Filipinos' new ticket to overseas jobs. *Philippine Daily Inquirer.* Retrieved September 12, 2004, from www.inq7.net/lif/ 2003/nov/02/lif_1-1.htm

Baldwin, M. W. (1992). Relational schemas and the processing of social information. *Psychological Bulletin, 112*(3), 461–484.

Baldwin, M. W., & Dandeneau, S. D. (2005). Understanding and modifying the relational schemas underlying insecurity. In M. W. Baldwin (Ed.), *Interpersonal cognition* (pp. 33–61). New York: Guilford.

Barbosa, I., & Cabral-Cardoso, C. (2008). Managing diversity in academic organizations: A challenge to organizational culture. *Women in Management Review, 22*(4), 274–288.

Barefoot College. (2015). *Indian college turns rural women into engineers.* Retrieved March 29, 2016, from http://www.barefootcollege.org/indian-college-turns-rural-women-into-engineers/

Barefoot College provides model of self-development at village level. (2003, March 10). *Global Village News and Resources Issue 57.* Retrieved

December 11, 2003, from http://gvnr .com/57/1.htm

Barlow, F. K., Louis, W. R., & Terry, D. J. (2010). Minority report: Social identity, cognitions of rejection and intergroup anxiety predicting prejudice from one racially marginalized group towards another. *European Journal of Social Psychology, 40*(5), 805–818.

Barnes, R. (2009, June 30). Justices rule for White firemen in bias lawsuit. *The Washington Post*. Retrieved July 24, 2009, from www.washingtonpost.com/ wp-dyn/ content/article/2009/06/29/ AR2009062901608.html

Bar-Tal, D. (1997). Formation and change of ethnic and national stereotypes: An integrative model. *International Journal of Intercultural Relations, 21*(4), 491–523.

Bar-Tal, D., & Labin, D. (2001). The effect of a major event on stereotyping: Terrorist attacks in Israel and Israeli adolescents' perceptions of Palestinians, Jordanians and Arabs. *European Journal of Social Psychology, 31*, 1–17.

Bartlett, C., & Beamish, P. (2010). *Transnational management: Text, cases, and readings in cross-border management* (6th ed.). Boston: McGraw-Hill.

Bartlett, C., & Ghoshal, S. (1998). Beyond strategic planning to organization learning: Lifeblood of the individualized corporation. *Strategy & Leadership, 21*(1), 34–39.

Bartlett, C., & Ghoshal, S. (2002a). Building competitive advantage through people. *MIT Sloan Management Review, 43*(2), 34–41.

Bartlett, C. A., & Ghoshal, S. (2002b). *Managing across borders: The transnational solution* (2nd ed.). Boston: Harvard Business School Press.

Bartlett, C., Ghoshal, S., & Beamish, P. (2007). *Transnational management: Text, cases, and readings in cross-border management* (5th ed.). Boston: McGraw-Hill.

Bartlett, F. C. (1932). *Remembering: An experimental and social study.* Cambridge, UK: Cambridge University Press.

Bartlett, F. C. (1958). *Thinking.* New York: Basic Books.

Basford, T. E., Offermann, L. R., & Behrend, T. S. (2014). Do you see what I see? Perceptions of gender microaggressions in the workplace. *Psychology of Women Quarterly, 38*(3), 340–349.

Baskerville, R. F. (2003). Hofstede never studied culture. *Accounting, Organizations and Society, 28*, 1–14.

Baskerville-Morley, R. F. (2005). A research note: The unfinished business of culture. *Accounting, Organizations and Society, 30*(4), 389–391.

Bass, B.M. (1990). *Bass and Stogdill's Handbook of Leadership: Theory, research and management applications* (3rd ed.). New York: Free Press.

Bass, B. M., & Avolio, B. J. (1997). *Full range leadership development: Manual for the multifactor leadership questionnaire*. Palo Alto, CA: Mind Garden Inc.

Bassett-Jones, N. (2005). The paradox of diversity management, creativity and innovation, diversity management. *Creativity and Innovation Management, 14*(2), 169–175.

Bata.com. (n.d.). Retrieved from http://batalife.com/thinking-long-term/our-programmes/

Batruch, C. (2011). Does corporate social responsibility make a difference? *Global Governance Insights, 17*, 155–159.

Baugh, J. (1983). *Black street speech: The history, structure, and survival.* Austin: University of Texas Press.

Baumeister, R. F., Brewer, L. E., Tice, D. M., & Twenge, J. M. (2007). Thwarting the need to belong: Understanding the interpersonal and inner effects of social exclusion. *Social and Personality Psychology Compass, 1*(1), 506–520.

Baumeister, R. F., & Leary, M. R. (1995). The need to belong: Desire for interpersonal attachments as a fundamental human motivation. *Psychological Bulletin, 117*(3), 497–529.

Bear, S., Rahman, N., & Post, C. (2010). The impact of board diversity and gender composition on corporate social responsibility and firm reputation. *Journal of Business Ethics, 97*, 207–221.

Bechtoldt, M. N., Beersma, B., Rohrmann, S., & Sanchez-Burks, J. (2011). A gift that takes its toll: Emotion recognition and conflict appraisal. *European Journal of Work and Organizational Psychology*, 1–20.

Becker, G. S. (1971). *The economics of discrimination* (2nd ed.). Chicago: University of Chicago Press. (Original work published 1957)

Beggs, J. J. (1995). The institutional environment: Implications for race and gender inequality in the U.S. labor market. *American Sociological Review, 60*, 612–633.

Bell, A. R., Engle, N. L., & Lemos, M. C. (2011). How does diversity matter? The case of Brazilian river basin councils. *Ecology and Society, 16*(1), 42.

Bell, E. (1990). The bicultural life experience of career-oriented Black women. *Journal of Organizational Behavior, 11*, 459–478.

Bell, E. L. (1992). Myths, stereotypes, and realities of Black women: A personal reflection. *Journal of Applied Behavioral Sciences, 28*(3), 363–376.

Bell, E. L. (2004). Myths, stereotypes and realities of Black women. *Journal of Applied Behavioral Science, 40*(2), 146–159.

Bell, E. L. J. E., & Nkomo, S. M. (2003). *Our separate ways: Black and White women and the struggle for professional identity.* Boston: Harvard Business School Press.

Bell, R. L., & Martin, J. S. (2012). The relevance of scientific management and equity theory in everyday managerial communication situations. *Journal of Management Policy and Practice, 13*(3), 106–115.

Bell, S. T., Villado, A. J., Lukasik, M. A., Belau, L., & Briggs, A. L. (2010). Getting specific about demographic diversity variable and team performance relationships: A meta-analysis. *Journal of Management, 37*(3), 709–743.

Bellah, R. N., Madsen, R., Sullivan, W. M., Swidler, A., & Tipton, S. M. (1985). *Habits of the heart: Individualism and commitment in American life.* New York: Harper & Row.

Ben & Jerry's. (n.d.). *Fairtrade progress.* Retrieved from http://www .benjerry.com/values/issues-we-care-about/fairtrade

Benedict, R. (1989). *Patterns of cultures.* Boston: Mariners Books. (Original work published 1934)

Bengtson, V. L. (2005). *Sourcebook of family theory and research.* Thousand Oaks, CA: Sage.

Bengtson, V. L., & Settersten, R. A. (2016). Chapter 1: Theories of age, aging, and the aged. In V. L. Bengtson & R. A. Settersten (Eds.), *Handbook of theories of aging* (3rd ed.; pp. 1–8). New York: Springer Publishing Co.

Benioff, M., & Southwick, K. (2004). *Compassionate capitalism: How corporations can make doing good an integral part of doing well.* Franklin Lakes, NJ: Career Press.

Bennington, L., & Wein, R. (2000). Anti-discrimination legislation in Australia: Fair, effective, efficient or irrelevant? *International Journal of Manpower, 21*(1), 21–32.

Benz v. Compania Naviera Hidalgo, S. A., 353 U.S. 138, 147 (1957).

Bergsieker, H. B., Leslie, L. M., Constantine, V. S., & Fiske, S. T. (2012). Stereotyping by omission: Eliminate the negative, accentuate the positive. *Journal of Personality and Social Psychology, 102*(6), 1214–1238.

Berlyne, D. E. (1968). American and European psychology. *American Psychologist, 23*, 447–452.

Berndt, A. (2014). *Essay about Christopher A. Bartlett, Sumantra Ghoshal: Managing across borders: The transnational solution.* Munich: GRIN Verlag GmbH.

Bernstein, B. (1975). *Class, codes, and control: Theoretical studies toward a sociology of language.* New York: Schoken.

Bernstein, M. J., Sacco, D. F., Young, S. G., Hugenberg, K., & Cook, E. (2010). Being "in" with the in-crowd: The effects of social exclusion and inclusion are enhanced by the perceived essentialism of ingroups and outgroups. *Personality and Social Psychology Bulletin, 36*(8), 999–1009.

Bertossi, C. (2010). Mistaken models of integration? A critical perspective on the crisis of multiculturalism in Europe. In A. Silg (Ed.), *European multiculturalism revisited* (pp. 235–251). London: Zed Books.

Bertrand, M., & Mullainathan, S. (2004). Are Emily and Greg more employable than Lakisha and Jamal? *American Economic Review, 94*(4), 991–1013.

Best companies for minorities. (2003, July 7). *Fortune,* pp. 103–120.

Best, S., Soyode, A., Muller-Camen, M., & Boff, A. (2015). The complex concept of sustainable of diversity management. *Human Resource Management International Digest, 23*(5), 45–48.

Better Work Indonesia. (2013). *Guidelines on the Prevention of Workforce Harassment.* Better Work Indonesia.

Bhagat, R. S. (2002). Book review of *Culture's consequences: Comparing values, behaviors, institutions, and organizations across nations* (2nd ed.). *Academy of Management Review, 27,* 460–462.

Bhargava, A. (1986). The Bhopal incident and Union Carbide: Ramifications of an industrial accident. *Bulletin of Concerned Asian Scholars, 18*(4), 1–18.

Bhattacharjee, A. (2003, May 3). *The price of Malaysia's palm oil expansion.* Retrieved December 6, 2003, from www.earthisland.org/borneo/news/articles/030502article.html

Bider, B. (2003, November 18). Oil palm estates damage environment. *The Jakarta Post.* Retrieved September 12, 2004, from www.thejakartapost.com/yesterdaydetail.asp? fileid=20031118.Q03

Bilimoria, D., Joy, S., & Liang, X. (2008). Breaking barriers and creating inclusiveness: Lessons of organizational transformation to advance women faculty in academic science and engineering. *Human Resource Management, 47*(3), 423–441.

Billig, M., & Tajfel, H. (1973). Social categorization and similarity in intergroup behavior. *European Journal of Social Psychology, 3*(1), 27–52.

Bing, J. W. (2004). Hofstede's consequences: The impact of his work on consulting and business practices. *Academy of Management Executive, 18*(1), 80–87.

Birch, N. (2008, January 28). Turkey divided over headscarf ban decision. *The Independent.* Retrieved July 15,

2009, from www.independent.co .uk/news/europe/turkey-divided-over-headscarf-ban-decision-774865.html

Blair, G. (2010). *Japan sinks (even) lower on gender discrimination report.* Retrieved June 29, 2012, from www.csmonitor.com/World/Asia-Pacific/2010/0511/Japan-sinks-even-lower-on-gender-discrimination-report

Blair, I. V. (2002). The malleability of automatic stereotypes and prejudice. *Personality and Social Psychology Review, 6*(3), 242–261.

Blasco, M., Feldt, L. E., & Jakobsen, M. (2012). If only cultural chameleons could fly too: A critical discussion of the concept of cultural intelligence. *International Journal of Cross Cultural Management, 12,* 229–245.

Blascovich, J., Wyer, N., Swart, L., & Kibler, J. (1997). Racism and racial categorization. *Journal of Personality and Social Psychology, 72,* 1364–1372.

Blau, P. M. (1977). *Inequality and heterogeneity: A primitive theory of social structure.* New York: Free Press.

Block, R. N. (2007). Work-family legislation in the United States, Canada, and Western Europe: A quantitative comparison. *Pepperdine Law Review, 34*(2), 333–358.

Block, R. N., & Roberts, K. (2000). A comparison of labour standards in the United States and Canada. *Relations Industrielles/Industrial Relations, 55*(2), 273–307.

Blommaert, L., Coenders, M., & Van Tubergen, F. (2014). Discrimination of Arabic-named applicants in the Netherlands: An Internet-based field experiment examining different phases in online recruitment procedures. *Social Forces.* Advance online publication. doi:10.1093/sf/sot124

Bloom, D. E., & Brender, A. (1993). Labor and the emerging world economy. *Population Bulletin, 48*(2). Washington, DC: Population Reference Bureau.

Bloom, D. E., Canning, D., & Lubet, A. (2015). Global population aging: Facts, challenges, solutions and perspectives. *Daedalus, 144*(2), 80–92.

Bloom, H. (2002, March/April). Can the United States export diversity? *Across the Board,* 47–51.

Blumenberg, E. (2002). On the way to work: Welfare participants and barriers to employment. *Economic Development Quarterly, 16*(4), 314–325.

Blumiller, E. (2008, October 10). McCain draws line on attacks as crowds cry "Fight back." *New York Times.*

Bodenhausen, G. V. (2010). Diversity in the person, diversity in the group: Challenges of identity complexity for social perception and social interaction. *European Journal of Social Psychology, 40,* 1–16.

Boekhorst, J. A. (2015). The role of authentic leadership in fostering workplace inclusion: A social information processing perspective. *Human Resource Management, 54*(2), 241–264.

Bojarski, S. (2002, May 1). Do you know where your coffee comes from? *Daily Campus.* Retrieved from www .dailycampus.com

Bolino, M. C., & Turnley, W. H. (2008). Old faces, new places: Equity theory in cross-cultural contexts. *Journal of Organizational Behavior, 29*(1), 29–50.

Bond, M. A. (2007). *Workplace chemistry: Promoting diversity through organizational change.* Hanover, NH: University Press of New England.

Boonman, M., Huisman, W., Sarrucco-Fedorovtsjev, E., & Sarrucco, T. (2011). Fair trade facts and figures: A success story for producers and consumers. *The Dutch Association of Worldshops.* Retrieved from www.european-fair-trade-association.org/efta/Doc/FT-E-2010.pdf

Booysen, L. (2007). Societal power shifts and changing social identities in South Africa: Workplace implications. *South African Journal of Economic and Management Sciences, 10*(1), 1–20.

Bortree, D. S., & Waters, R. D. (2008). The value of feeling included: The impact of inclusion on teen volunteers' organizational satisfaction. *International Journal of Volunteer Administration, 25,* 17–26.

Bortree, D. S., & Waters, R. D. (2014). Race and inclusion in volunteerism: Using communication theory to improve volunteer retention. *Journal of Public Relations Research, 26*(3), 215–234.

Bosnia women protest at ban on headscarf. (2016, February 7). BBC News. Retrieved February 17, 2016, from www.bbc.com/news/world-europe-35518768

Boston, T., & Nair-Reichert, U. (2003). Affirmative action: Perspectives from the United States, India, and Brazil. *Western Journal of Black Studies, 27*(1), 3–14.

Bostwick, W., & Hequembourg, A. (2014). "Just a little hint": Bisexual-specific microaggressions and their connection to epistemic injustices. *Culture, Health & Sexuality, 16*(5), 488–503.

Bourhis, R. Y., Sachdev, I., & Gagon, A. (1994). Intergroup research with the Tajfel matrices: Methodological notes. In M. P. Zanna & J. M. Olson (Eds.), *The psychology of prejudices: The Ontario Symposium* (Vol. 7, pp. 209–232). Hillsdale, NJ: Lawrence Erlbaum.

Boxenbaum, E., Gjuvsland, M., & Leon, C. E. (2011). Diversity management in Denmark: Evolutions from 2002 to 2009. In S. Groschl (Ed.), *Diversity in the workplace: Multi-disciplinary and international perspectives.* Brookfield, VT: Gower.

Branscombe, N. R., Schmitt, M. T., & Harvey, R. D. (1999). Perceiving pervasive discrimination among

African Americans: Implications for group identification and well-being. *Journal of Personality and Social Psychology, 77,* 135–149.

Braun, S. (1998, June 12). Mitsubishi to pay $34 million in sex harassment case. *The Los Angeles Times.* Retrieved June 28, 2012, from http://articles.latimes.com/1998/jun/12/news/mn-59249

Brazil free laundry and volleyball in the favelas. Case Studies. (2012). Unilever. Retrieved from www.unilever.co.id/sustainability/case studies/health-nutrition-hygiene/brazilfreelaundryandvolleyballinthe favelas.aspx

Brett, J., Behfar, K., & Sanchez-Burks, J. (2014). Managing cross-cultural conflicts: A close look at the implication of direct versus indirect confrontation. In N. Ashkanasy & K. Jehn (Eds.), *The handbook of conflict management* (pp. 136–154). London, England: Edward Edgar.

Brewer, M. (2003). *Intergroup relations.* Philadelphia: Open University Press.

Brewer, M. B., & Gardner, W. (1996). Who is this "we"?: Levels of collective identity and self-representations. *Journal of Personality and Social Psychology, 71*(1), 83–93.

Bridges. (n.d.). *What we do.* Retrieved from http://www.bridgestowork.org/about-bridges/what-we-do/

Brigham, J. C. (1971). Ethnic stereotypes. *Psychological Bulletin, 76,* 15–38.

Brimhall, K. C., Lizano, E. L., & Mor Barak, M. E. (2014). The mediating role of inclusion: A longitudinal study of the effects of leader-member exchange and diversity climate on job satisfaction and intention to leave among child welfare workers. *Children and Youth Services Review, 40,* 79–88.

Brimhall, K. C., & Mor Barak, M. E. (2015). *Leadership and inclusion among public child welfare workers.* Manuscript in progress.

Brimhall, K. C., Mor Barak, M. E., Hurlburt, M., McArdle, J. J., Palinkas, L., & Henwood, B. (under review). Increasing workplace inclusion: The promise of leader-member exchange. *Human Service Organization.*

Broughton, E. (2005). The Bhopal disaster and its aftermath: A review. *Environmental Health, 4,* 6.

Brown, P., & Levinson, S. (1978). Universals in language usage: Politeness phenomenon. In E. Goody (Ed.), *Questions and politeness: Strategies in social interaction* (pp. 56–289). Cambridge, UK: Cambridge University Press.

Brown, R., & Hewstone, M. (2005). An integrative theory of intergroup contact. In M. P. Zanna (Ed.), *Advances in experimental psychology* (Vol. 37, pp. 256–284). Elsevier Academic Press.

Brown, T. M., & Fee, F. (2008). Spinning for India's independence. *American Journal of Public Health, 98*(1), 39. doi:10.2105/AJPH.2007.120139

Browne, A. (2004, January 19). Belgium next in line as Europe's veil ban spreads. *The Times* (London). Retrieved September 12, 2004, from www.headscarf.net/veil% 20ban%20 spreads.jpg

Bruce Jenner: "I'm a woman." (2015). ABC News.Retrieved March 27, 2016, from www.abcnews.go.com/Entertainment/bruce-jenner-im-woman/story?id=30570350

Buckridge, H. (2006). Merging without purging: Incentivizing boards of directors to promote diversity through M & A. *Journal of Civil Rights and Economic Development, 20*(2), Art. 5. Retrieved from http://scholarship.law.stjohns.edu/jcred/vol20/iss2/5

Buengeler, C., & Den Hartog, D. N. (2015). National diversity and team performance: The moderating role of interactional justice climate. *The International Journal of Human Resource Management, 26*(6), 831–855.

Bureau of Democracy, Human Rights and Labor. (n.d.). *2007 country reports on human rights practices.* Retrieved August 10, 2009, from www.state.gov/g/drl/rls/hrrpt/2007/index.htm

Burke, P. J., & Stets, J. E. (2009). *Identity theory.* New York: Oxford University Press.

Burkley, M., & Blanton, H. (2009). The positive (and negative) consequences of endorsing negative self-stereotypes. *Self and Identity, 8*(2–3), 286–299.

Burton, C. (1995). Managing for diversity: Report to Karpin. In E. M. Davis & C. Harris (Eds.), *Making the link: Affirmative action and industrial relations* (pp. 66–71). Sydney, Australia: Affirmative Action Agency and Labour Management Studies Foundation.

Buse, K., Bernstein, R. S., & Bilimoria, D. (2016). The influence of board diversity, board diversity policies and practices, and board inclusion behaviors on nonprofit governance practices. *Journal of Business Ethics, 133*(2), 179–191.

Buttner, E. H., Lowe, K. B., & Billings-Harris, L. (2010). Diversity climate impact on employee of color outcomes: Does justice matter? *Career Development International, 15*(3), 239–258.

Buttner, H. E., Lowe, K. B., & Billings-Harris, L. (2012). An empirical test of diversity climate dimensionality and relative effects on employee of color outcomes. *Journal of Business Ethics, 110*(3), 247–258.

Buzinger, M. (2007). Positive action declared unconstitutional. *Indian Journal of Constitutional Law, 1*(1), 198–210.

Byrd, M. Y. (2007). The effects of racial conflict on organizational performance: A search for theory. *New Horizons in Adult Education & Human Resource Development, 21*(1/2), 13–28.

Byrne D. (1971). *The attraction paradigm.* New York: Academic.

Caldwell, Q. S., Mack, D., Johnson, C. D., & Biderman, M. D. (2002, April). *Value for diversity as a moderator of organizational relationships.* Poster presented at the 17th Annual Meeting of the Society for Industrial and Organizational Psychology, Toronto, Canada.

Cambridge Dictionary. (2015). *Culture.* Retrieved from www.dictionary. cambridge.org/us/dictionary/english/

Campbell, K., & Minguez-Vera, A. (2008). Gender diversity in the boardroom and firm financial performance. *Journal of Business Ethics, 83,* 435–451.

Campbell, W. K., Krusemark, E. A., Dyckman, K. A., Brunell, A. B., McDowell, J. E., Twenge, J. M., et al. (2006). A magnetoencephalography investigation of neural correlates for social exclusion and self-control. *Social Neuroscience, 1,* 124–134.

Capuano, S. (2011, March 17). The south–north mobility of Italian college graduates. An empirical analysis. *European Sociological Review.*

Carbado, D. W., & Roithmayr, D. (2014). Critical race theory meets social science. *Annual Review of Law and Social Science, 10*(1), 149–167.

Caria, F. M. dos Santos Torrao. (2012, March). *Case study: Product-specific sustainable marketing audit: Delta Q.* Master's thesis in Marketing, Instituto Superior de Economia e Gestao, Universidade Technica de Lisboa.

Carlson, N. (2013, February 26). *Marissa Mayer, who just banned working from home, paid to have a nursery built at her office.* Retrieved from http://www.businessinsider.com/ marissa-mayer-who-just-banned-working-from-home-paid-to-have-a-nursery-built-at-her-office-2013-2

Carrell, M. R., Mann, E. E., & Sigler, T. H. (2006). Defining workforce diversity programs and practices in organizations: A longitudinal study. *Labor Law Journal, 57*(1), 5–12.

Carrillo, J., Corning, A. F., Dennehy, T. C., & Crosby, F. J. (2011). Relative deprivation: Understanding the dynamics of discontent. In D. Chadee (Ed.), *Theories of social psychology*, pp. 140–160. Oxford, UK: Wiley-Blackwell.

Carroll, A. B. (1979). A three-dimensional model of corporate social performance. *Academy of Management Review, 4,* 497–505.

Carroll, A. B. (2000). A commentary and an overview of key questions on corporate social performance measurement. *Business and Society, 39,* 466–478.

Carroll, A. B. (2015). Corporate social responsibility. *Organizational Dynamics, 44*(2), 87–96.

Carroll, A. B., & Shabana, K. M. (2010). The business case for corporate social responsibility: A review of concepts, research and practice. *International Journal of Management Review, 12*(1), 85–105.

Carter, N. M., & Wagner, H. M. (2011, March). *The bottom line: Corporate performance and women's representation on boards (2004–2008).* New York: Catalyst. Retrieved April 2, 2016, from http://www.catalyst .org/system/files/the_bottom_ line_corporate_performance_and_ women%27s_representation_on_ boards_%282004-2008%29.pdf

Caruso, D. (2003, Summer). Limits of the classic method: Positive action in the European Union after the new equality directives. *Harvard International Law Journal, 44*(2). Retrieved July 20, 2009, from http:// papers.ssrn.com/s013/papers .cfm?abstract_id=437202

Casad, B. J., & Bryant, W. J. (2016). Addressing stereotype threat is critical to diversity and inclusion in organizational psychology. *Frontiers in Psychology, 7,* 8.

Castano, E., Yzerbyt, V., Bourguignon, D., & Seron, E. (2002). Who may enter? The impact of in-group identification on in-group/out-group categorization. *Journal of Experimental Social Psychology, 38,* 315–322.

Casteel, P. D. (2015). Diversity in the workplace (sociology). *Research Starters: Sociology* (Online), 10.

Catalyst. (2015). *Lesbian, gay, bisexual, transgender workplace issues.* Retrieved from http://www .catalyst.org/knowledge/lesbian-gay-bisexual-transgender-workplace-issues

Catalyst. (2015a, January 13). *2014 Catalyst census: Women board directors.* New York: Catalyst.

Catalyst. (2015b, April 3). *Women CEOs of the S&P 500.* New York: Catalyst.

Caudron, S. (1993). Employees use diversity-training exercise against Lucky Stores in intentional-discrimination suit. *Personnel Journal, 72*(4), 52.

Cave, D. (2011, July 6). Better lives for Mexicans cut allure of going north. *New York Times.*

Chaaban, J., & Cunningham, W. (2008). *Measuring the economic gain of investing in girls: The girl effect dividend.* World Bank. Retrieved May 23, 2012, from http://econ.worldbank .org/exter nal/default/main?menuPK =633473&pagePK=64165395&piPK= 64165418&theSitePK=469372

Chandy, P. R., & Williams, T. G. E. (1994). The impact of journals and authors on international business. *Journal of International Business Studies, 25,* 715–728.

Chartrand, T. L., & Bargh, J. (1999). The chameleon effect: The perception-behavior link and social interaction. *Journal of Personality and Social Psychology, 76*(6), 893–910.

Chater, R. E. J., & Chater, C. V. (1992). Positive action: Towards a strategic approach. *Women in Management Review, 7*(4), 3–14.

Chatman, C. M., & Von Hippel, W. (2001). Attribution Mediation of in-group bias. *Journal of Experimental Social Psychology, 37,* 267–272.

Chatman, J. A., & Flynn, F. J. (2001). The influence of demographic heterogeneity on the emergence and consequences of cooperative norms in work teams. *Academy of Management Journal, 44,* 956–974.

Cheng, C.-Y., Sanchez-Burks, J., & Lee, F. (2008, August). Taking advantage of differences: Increasing team innovation through identity integration. *Research on Managing Groups and Teams, 11,* 55–73.

Chesnais, J.-C. (2000, November). The decolonization of Europe. In L. Maurawiec & D. Adamson (Eds.), *Demography and national security: Proceedings of a workshop* (pp. 14–15). Santa Monica, CA: RAND. Retrieved September 12, 2004, from www.rand.org/ publications/CF/ CF169/CF169.pdf

Cheung, F. M., & Halpern, D. F. (2010). Women at the top: Powerful leaders define success as work + family in a culture of gender. *American Psychologist, 65*(3), 183–193.

Chilcote, R. (2003, June 4). *Cooler heads prevail in Najaf.* Retrieved May 25, 2004, from www.cnn.com/2003/ WORLD/meast/04/03/otsc.irq. chilcote.najaf/

Childs, J. T., Jr. (2005). Managing workforce diversity at IBM: A global HR topic that has arrived. *Human Resource Management, 44,* 73–77.

Chingos, M. M. (2013). Redirecting students to less demanding colleges not a strategy for success in the sciences. *Brookings.* Retrieved March 6, 2016, from http://www.brookings .edu/research/papers/2013/03/13-science-minorities-chingos

Chiquita Brands International. (n.d.-a). *Equal rights protection.* Retrieved from http://www.chiquita .com/The-Chiquita-Difference/ Improving-Lives/Equal-Rights-Protection.aspx

Chiquita Brands International. (n.d.-b). *Our renewed purpose.* Retrieved from http://www.chiquita .com/getattachment/4dedce2f-c4ac-4183-9e14-c87a6202e511/CORP13_ CSR_Report_Complete_Reduced_ File_Size_R2.pdf.aspx

Chirac on secular society. (2003, December 18). BBC News. Retrieved September 12, 2004, from http://news .bbc.co.uk/2/hi/europe/3330679.stm

Cho, S., Crenshaw, K. W., & McCall, L. (2013). Toward a field of intersectionality studies: Theory, applications, and praxis. *Signs, 38*(4), 785–810.

Cho, S., & Mor Barak, M. E. (2008). Understanding diversity and inclusion in a perceived homogeneous culture: A study of organizational commitment and job performance among Korean employees. *Administration in Social Work, 32*(4), 100–126.

Choi, J. N. (2007). Group composition and employee creative behavior in a Korean electronics company: Distinct effects of relational demography and group diversity. *Journal of Occupational and Organizational Psychology, 80,* 213–234.

Choi, N. G. (2001). Diversity within diversity: Research and social

work practice issues with Asian American elders. In N. G. Choi (Ed.), *Psychological aspects of the Asian-American experience: Diversity within diversity* (pp. 301–319). New York: The Haworth Press.

Choi, S. (2009). Diversity in the US federal government: Diversity management and employee turnover in federal agencies. *Journal of Public Administration Research and Theory, 19,* 603–630.

Choi, S., & Rainey, H. G. (2010). Managing diversity in U.S. federal agencies: Effects of diversity and diversity management on employee perceptions of organizational performance. *Public Administration Review, 70*(1), 109–121.

Cholewinski, R. (1997). *Migrant workers in international human rights law: Their protection in countries of employment.* Oxford, England: Oxford University Press.

Christiansen, K. (1994). *Italian painting.* Westport, CT: Hugh Lauter Levin Associates Publishers.

Chrobot-Mason, D. L. (2003). Keeping the promise: Psychological contract violations for minority employees. *Journal of Managerial Psychology, 18*(1), 22–45.

Chua, R. J., Morris, M. W., & Mor, S. (2012). Collaborating across cultures: Cultural metacognition and affect-based trust in creative collaboration. *Organizational Behavior and Human Decision Processes, 118,* 116–131.

Cisneros, S. (1984). *The house on Mango Street.* New York: Vintage Books.

Claringbould, I., & Knoppers, A. (2007). Finding a "normal" woman: Selection processes for board membership. *Sex Roles, 56,* 495–507.

Clark, R. A., & Delia, J. G. (1979). Topoi and rhetorical competence. *Quarterly Journal of Speech, 65,* 165–206.

Clark, V. (2011, July 5). Making money online in Africa through e-commerce. *African Business Review.* Retrieved from www.africanbusinessreview .co.za/money_matters/making-money-online-in-africa-through-e-commerce

Clarke, J. S. (2015, September 2). Child labour on Nestlé farms: Chocolate giant's problems continue. *The Guardian.* Retrieved from http://www.theguardian.com/ global-development-professionals-network/2015/sep/02/child-labour-on-nestle-farms-chocolate-giants-problems-continue

Clay, J. (2005). *Exploring the links between international business and poverty reduction: A case study of Unilever.* Netherlands: OxfamGB and Unilever.

Clegg, A. (2012, April 1). On my agenda. *People Management,* 44–47.

Coale, A. J., & Zelnik, M. (2015). *New estimates of fertility and population in the United States.* Princeton, NJ: Princeton University Press.

Coates, T. P. (2007, February 1). Is Obama Black enough? *Time.*

Cohen, C., & Sterba, J. P. (2003). *Affirmative action and racial preference: A debate.* New York: Oxford University Press.

Coleman, B. D. (2012). What if?: A study of seminal cases as if decided under a Twombly/Iqbal Regime. *Oregon Law Review, 90*(4), 1147–1180.

Colgan, F. (2011). Equality, diversity and corporate responsibility: Sexual orientation and diversity management in the UK private sector. *Equality, Diversity and Inclusion: An International Journal, 30,* 719–734.

Colgan, F., Creegan, C., McKearney, A., & Wright, T. (2007). Equality and diversity policies and practices at work: Lesbian, gay and bisexual workers. *Equal Opportunities International, 26*(6), 590–609.

Collier, M. J., & Thomas, M. (1988). Cultural identity: An interpretive perspective. In Y. Y. Kim & W. B. Gudykunst (Eds.), *Theories in intercultural communications* (pp. 99–122). Newbury Park, CA: Sage.

Combs, G. M. (2003). The duality of race and gender for managerial African American women: Implications of informal social networks on career advancement. *Human Resource Development Review, 2*(4), 385–405.

Comer, K. (2002, August 8). Black employees to file discrimination lawsuit against Xerox. *The Associated Press State & Local Wire.* Retrieved August 14, 2002, from http://web .lexis-nexis.com/universe/printdoc

Commission for the Study of International Migration and Cooperative Economic Development. (1990). *Unauthorized migration: An economic development response.* Washington, DC: Government Printing Office.

Commission of the European Communities. (1999). Communication from the Commission to the Council, the European Parliament, the Economic and Social Committee and the Committee of the Regions on Certain Community Measures to Combat Discrimination. COM 564 final.

Commitment to Diversity. (2016). *Commitment to diversity and inclusion.* Retrieved March 31, 2016, from https://www.commbank.com .au/about-us/who-we-are/our-company/our-approach-to-diversity/ commitment-to-diversity.html

Committee for Asian Women. (2000, April). Survey on the legal provisions for protection and prevention of sexual harassment. *Asian Women Workers Newsletter.* Retrieved October 27, 2002, from http://caw.jinbo.net/

Comparative advantage: The boomerang effect. (2012, April 21).

The Economist. Retrieved from www .economist.com/node/21552898

Compass Group. (2015a). *Awards.* Retrieved from http://www.compass-group.com.au/news/awards

Compass Group. (2015b). *Compass group to hire 1,050 indigenous jobseekers over next three years.* Retrieved from http://compass-group.com.au/news/media-centre/2015/03/19/compass-group-to-hire-1-050-indigenous-jobseekers-over-next-three-years

Compass Group. (2015c). *Indigenous strategy.* Retrieved from http://www .compass-group.com.au/being-responsible/corporate-responsibility/ indigenous-strategy

Compass Group. (2015d). *Indigenous training and employment.* Retrieved from http://www.compass-group .com.au/who-we-are/our-people/ indigenous-training-employment

Conrad, C., & Poole, M. S. (2012). *Strategic organizational communication in a global economy* (7th ed.). New York: Wiley-Blackwell.

Constantine, M. G. (2007). Racial microaggressions against African American clients in cross-racial counseling relationships. *Journal of Counseling Psychology, 54*(1), 1–16.

Constitution of the Kingdom Saudi Arabia. (n.d.). Retrieved May 15, 2004, from www.saudiinstitute.org/ const.htm

Constitution of the Republic of South Africa. (1996). Retrieved May 26, 2004, from www.polity.org.za/html/ govdocs/constitution/saconst .html?rebookmark=1

Cook, J. (2004, Feb. 11). Debate over outsourcing heats up. *Seattle Post-Intelligencer.* Retrieved from www.seattlepi.com/business/article/ Debate-over-outsourcing-heats-up-ignited-by-1136780.php

Cooke, A. L. (1999). Oppression and the workplace: A framework for understanding. *Diversity Factor, 8*(1), 6.

Cooke, F. L., & Saini, D. S. (2010). Diversity management in India: A study of organizations in different ownership forms and industrial sectors. *Human Resource Management, 3,* 477–500.

Corcoran, K., Crusius, J., & Mussweiler, T. (2011). Social comparison: Motives, standards, and mechanisms. In D. Chadee (Ed.), *Theories of social psychology* (pp. 119–139). Oxford, UK: Wiley-Blackwell.

Corneille, O., Yzerbyt, V. Y., Rogier, A., & Buidin, G. (2001). Threat and the group attribution error: When threat elicits judgments of extremity and homogeneity. *Personality and Social Psychology Bulletin, 27*(4), 437–446.

Cornelissen, J. P., Haslam, S. A., & Balmer, J. M. T. (2007). Social identity, organizational identity and corporate identity: Towards an integrated understanding of processes, patternings and products. *British Journal of Management, 18*(S1), S1–S16.

Corrigan, P. (2004). How stigma interferes with mental health care. *American Psychologist, 59*(7), 614–625.

Cottrill, K. R. (2012). *Antecedents and outcomes of inclusion: Exploring authentic leadership, organizational climate for ethics, organization-based self-esteem, and organizational citizenship behaviors.* Doctoral dissertation, Alliant International University, Alhambra, CA.

Cottrill, K., Lopez, P. D., & Hoffman, C. C. (2014). How authentic leadership and inclusion benefit organizations. *Equality, Diversity and Inclusion, 33,* 275–292.

Council of Europe. (2000). *Recent demographic developments in Europe.* Strasbourg, France: Council of Europe Publishing.

Council of Labor Affairs. Executive Yuan Taiwan R.O.C. (2009). Retrieved from www.cla.gov.tw/cgi-bin/siteMaker/SM_theme?page=48e31c0e

Council of Labor Affairs. Executive Yuan Taiwan R.O.C. (2012). *Gender equality in employment and prohibition of employment discrimination.* Retrieved November 30, 2012, from www.cla.gov.tw/cgi-bin/siteMaker/SM_theme?page=48f2ba69

Cowell, A. (2000, October 31). Dublin is a magnet for technology and young people. *New York Times,* p. C1.

Cox, D., Young, M., & Bairnsfather-Scott, A. (2009). No justice without healing: Australian aboriginal people and family violence. *The Australian Feminist Law Journal, 30,* 151–161.

Cox, T. (1994). *Cultural diversity in organizations: Theory, research, and practice* (1st ed.). San Francisco: Berrett-Koehler.

Cox, T. (2001). *Creating the multicultural organization: A strategy for capturing the power of diversity.* San Francisco: Jossey-Bass.

Crenshaw, K. W. (1989). *Demarginalizing the intersection of race and sex: A black feminist critique of antidiscrimination doctrine, feminist theory and antiracist politics.* University of Chicago Legal Forum 139–167.

Crisp, R. J., Turner, R. N., & Rhiannon, N. (2009). Can imagined interactions produce positive perceptions? Reducing prejudice through simulated social contact. *American Sociologist, 64*(4), 231–240.

Cristaldi, F., & Darden, J. T. (2011). The impact of immigration policies on transnational Filipino immigrant women: A comparison of their social and spatial incorporation in Rome and Toronto. *Journal of Urban History, 37,* 694–709.

Cronje, J. C. (2011). Using Hofstede's cultural dimensions to interpret cross-cultural blended teaching and learning. *Computers & Education, 56*(3), 596–603.

Crosby, F. (1976). A model of egoistical relative deprivation. *Psychological Review, 83,* 85–113.

Cuberes, D., & Teignier-Baqué, M. (2011). *Gender inequality and economic growth.* World Development Report 2012. Gender Quality and Development. Retrieved March 26, 2016, from http://siteresources.worldbank.org/INTWDR2012/Resources/7778105-1299699968583/7786210-1322671773271/cuberes.pdf

Cummings, A., Zhou, J., & Oldham, G. R. (1993). *Demographic differences and employee work outcomes: Effects on multiple comparison groups.* Paper presented at the annual meeting of the Academy of Management, Atlanta, GA.

Cunningham, G. B. (2007). Perceptions as reality: The influence of actual and perceived demographic dissimilarity. *Journal of Business and Psychology, 22*(7), 79–89.

Daniels, T. P. (2010). Urban space, belonging, and inequality in multi-ethnic housing estates of Melaka, Malaysia. *Identities: Global Studies in Culture and Power, 17,* 176–203.

Darity, W., Jr. (1999, Fall). Experts speak on G-7 summit. *Earth Island Journal, 14*(3), 81.

Darity, W. A., & Deshpande, A. (2000). Tracing the divide: Intergroup disparity across countries. *Eastern Economic Journal, 26*(1), 75–87.

Darwin, C. (1995). *The origin of species.* New York: Gramercy. (Original work published 1859)

Davis, J. (2003, September 28). Fashion special: Ethics girl. *Independent on Sunday* (London).

Davis, J. B. (2009). Identity and individual economic agents: A narrative approach. *Review of Social Economy, 67*(1), 71–94.

Davis, J. K. (2013). Predictors of job satisfaction among peer providers on professional treatment teams in community-based agencies. *Psychiatric Services (Washington, DC)*, 64(2), 181–184.

Davis, S. (2009, January 29). President's first law: Obama signs Lilly Ledbetter wage bill. *Wall Street Journal*.

DCM Shriram Industries Ltd. (2012). *Annual report 2011–12*. New Delhi, India: Author.

DCM Shriram Industries Ltd. (2016). Corporate social responsibility. Retrieved from www.dcmshriram.com/csr-policy

De Cieri, H. (2003). *Human resource management in Australia: Strategy, people, performance*. Sydney: McGraw-Hill Australia.

De Dreu, C. K. W., & Weingart, L. R. (2003). Task versus relationship conflict, team performance, and team member satisfaction: A meta-analysis. *Journal of Applied Psychology*, 88(4), 741–749.

De Meuse, K. P., & Hostager, T. J. (2001). Developing an instrument for measuring attitudes toward and perceptions of workplace diversity: An initial report. *Human Resource Development Quarterly*, 12(1), 33–51.

De Vita, L. (2010). The diversity management approach: New implications for gender policies in Italy. *Equality, Diversity and Inclusion: An International Journal*, 29(8), 724–742.

Deaux, K., Reid, A., Martin, D., & Bikman, N. (2006). Ideologies of diversity and inequality: Predicting collective action in groups varying in ethnicity and immigrant status. *Political Psychology*, 27(1), 123–146.

Delgado, R., & Stefancic, J. (2012). *Critical race theory: An introduction* (2nd ed.). New York: New York University Press.

DeLia, E. (2010). *Complexity leadership in industrial innovation teams: A field study of leading, learning and innovating in heterogeneous teams*. Doctoral dissertation, Rutgers, The State University of New Jersey, New Brunswick, NJ.

Deloitte. (2015). *The Deloitte millennial survey 2016*. Retrieved from http://www2.deloitte.com/global/en/pages/about-deloitte/articles/gx-millennials-one-foot-out-the-door.html#report

Denny's catches phony discrimination claim on video. (2000, August 28). Retrieved November 3, 2003, from www.newsmax.com/articles/?a=2000/8/26/131812

Denny's Diversity. (2016). *Diversity*. Retrieved March 31, 2016, from https://www.dennys.com/diversity/

Denny's Diversity Awards. (2016). *Denny's diversity awards and recognitions*. Retrieved March 31, 2016, from http://www.dennysdiversity.com/files/Dennys-Diversity-Awards.pdf

Denny's Diversity Report. (2010). Retrieved from www.dennysdiversity.com/report/DennysDiversityReport.pdf

Denny's Leadership. (2016). *Leadership*. Retrieved March 31, 2016, from https://www.dennys.com/company/leadership/#board

Denny's named among top performers in *Black Enterprise* list of the 40 Best Companies for Diversity. (2006, June 12). *Business Wire*. Retrieved December 3, 2009, from www.encyclopedia.com/doc/1G1-146914889.html

Denny's promotes diversity leader April Kelly-Drummond. (2008, March 31). *Westside Gazette*, p. 14A.

Denny's Supplier Diversity Initiative. (2012). Retrieved from www.dennyssupplierdiversity.com/

Denzin, N. K. (2007). *Symbolic interactionism and cultural studies: The politics of interpretation*. Cambridge, MA: Wiley-Blackwell.

Department of Employment and Workplace Relations. (2003). *Indigenous Employment Policy Evaluation Stage Two: Effectiveness Report, Commonwealth of Australia*.

Derfler-Rozin, R., Pillutla, M., & Thau, S. (2010). Social reconnection revisited: The effects of social exclusion risk on reciprocity, trust, and general risk-taking. *Organizational Behavior and Human Decision Processes*, 112(2), 140–150.

Dermott, E. M. (2001). New fatherhood in practice? Parental leave in the U.K. *The International Journal of Sociology and Social Policy*, 21(4–6), 145.

Deshpande, A. (2007). Overlapping identities under liberalization: Gender and caste in India. *Economic Development and Cultural Change*, 55, 735–760.

Devine, P. G. (2001). Implicit prejudice and stereotyping: How automatic are they? Introduction to the special section. *Journal of Personality and Social Psychology*, 81(5), 757–759.

DeVoe, S. E., & Iyengar, S. S. (2004). Managers' theories of subordinates: A cross-cultural examination of manager perceptions of motivation and appraisal of performance. *Organizational Behavior and Human Decision Processing*, 93(1), 47–62.

Dew, E. M. (1994). *The trouble in Suriname, 1975–1993*. Westport, CT: Praeger.

Dias, T. (1997, October 1–3). *The disaster and its aftermath: The Hiroshima of the chemical industry*. Paper presented at the Conference on Environmental Justice: Global Ethics for the 21st Century, Melbourne, Australia. Retrieved November 10, 2003, from www.arbld.unimelb.edu.au/envjust/papers/allpapers/dias/home.htm

Diaz-Guerrero, R. (1967). *Psychology of the Mexican.* Austin: University of Texas Press.

Dijkstra, P., Gibbons, F. X., & Buunk, A. P. (2010). Social comparison theory. In J. E. Maddux & J. P. Angney (Eds.), *Social psychological foundations of clinical psychology* (pp. 195–211). New York: Guilford.

Diller, J. V. (2010). *Cultural diversity: A primer for the human services.* Belmont, CA: Brooks/Cole.

Diop, C. (2012, August 1–4). *Black graduate women in the workplace in France: Experiences of exclusion and marginalization.* Paper presented at the Second ISA Forum of Sociology, Buenos Aires, Argentina.

Disney, Muslim worker agree on hijab substitute. (2010, September 29). *USA Today.* Retrieved from www.usatoday.com/news/religion/2010-09-29-disney-muslim_N.htm

DiTomaso, N., Post, C., & Parks-Yancy, R. (2007). Workforce diversity and inequality: Power, status, and numbers. *The Annual Review of Sociology, 33,* 473–501.

Diversity and Inclusion. (2016). *How we act.* Retrieved March 31, 2016, from http://www.sodexo.com/en/corporate-responsibility/diversity-inclusion/actions/training.aspx

Diversity in Focus. (n.d.). Retrieved from www.strategicdiversity.com/Diverse_Company_Profiles_Dennys.htm

Diversity speaks. (2012). Retrieved from www.dennysdiversity.com

The Diversity Task Force. (2001). *Best practices to achieving workforce diversity.* U.S. Department of Commerce and Vice President Al Gore's National Partnership for Reinventing Government Benchmarking Study. Retrieved August 22, 2009, from http://govinfo.library.unt.edu/npr/initiati/benchmk/workforce-diversity.pdf

DiversityInc. (2016). *Why it's on the list.* Retrieved from http://www.diversityinc.com/ibm/

Dobbs, M. F. (1996). Managing diversity: Lessons from the private sector. *Public Personnel Management, 25*(3), 351.

Doki, G. A. (2012). The drama in cross-cultural marriages and stereotypes in central Nigeria. The tiv-igede paradigm in the global age. *CreativeArtist: A Journal of Theater and Media Studies,* 186–200.

Dole Food Company, Inc. (n.d.). *Fairtrade.* Retrieved from http://dolecrs.com/performance/certifications/fairtrade/

Donnelly, R. (2015). Tensions and challenges in the management of diversity and inclusion in IT services multinationals in India. *Human Resource Management, 54*(2), 199–215.

Dorfman, P., Javidan, M., Hanges, P., Dastmalchian, A., & House, R. (2012). GLOBE: A twenty year journey into the intriguing world of culture and leadership [Special issue]. *Journal of World Business, 47*(4), 504–518.

Dothard v. Rawlinson, 433 U.S. 321 (1977).

Dotsch, R., Wigboldus, D. H. J., Langner, O., & Van Knippenberg, A. (2008). Ethnic out-group faces are biased in the prejudiced mind. *Psychological Science, 19*(10), 978–980.

Douglas, C., Ferris, G. R., Buckley, M. R., & Gundlach, M. J. (2003). Organizational and social influences on leader-member exchange processes: Implications for the management of diversity. In G. B. Graen (Ed.), *Dealing with diversity* (pp. 59–90). Greenwich, CT: Information Age Publishing.

Dow Jones & Company, Inc. (n.d.). *Chiquita agrees to $742 million buyout.* Retrieved from http://www.wsj.com/articles/chiquita-agrees-to-sale-1414412730

Drabe, D., Hauff, S., & Richter, N. F. (2015). Job satisfaction in aging workforces: An analysis of the USA, Japan and Germany. *The International Journal of Human Resource Management, 26*(6), 783–805.

Drajem, M. (2004, March 31). Offshoring aids economy, says business study. Retrieved from www.dfw.com/mld/dfw/business/8319303.htm?1c

Drydakis, N., & Vlassis, M. (2010). Ethnic discrimination in the Greek labour market: Occupational access, insurance coverage and wage offers. *Manchester School, 78,* 201–218.

Du, S., Bhattacharya, C. B., & Sen, S. (2015). Corporate social responsibility, multi-faceted job-products, and employee outcomes. *Journal of Business Ethics, 131*(2), 319–335.

Dulebohn, J. H., Bommer, W. H., Liden, R. C., Brouer, R. L., & Ferris, G. R. (2012). A meta-analysis of antecedents and consequences of leader-member exchange: Integrating the past with an eye toward the future. *Journal of Management, 38,* 1715–1759.

Dumas, T., & Sanchez-Burks, J. (2015). The professional, the personal and the ideal worker: Pressures and objectives shaping the boundary between life domains. *Academy of Management Annals, 9*(1), 1–42.

Dunham, Y., Baron, A. S., & Carey, S. (2011). Consequences of "minimal" group affiliations in children. *Child Development, 82,* 793–811.

Durkheim, E. (2014). *The division of labor in society.* New York: Simon and Schuster. (Original work published 1893)

Dutton, J. E., & Dukerich, J. M. (1991). Keeping an eye on the mirror: Image and identity in organizational adaptation. *Academy of Management Journal, 34,* 517–554.

DW. (2013). *Indian firms take little notice of law against sexual harassment.* Retrieved March 29, 2016, from http://www.dw.com/en/indian-firms-take-little-notice-of-law-against-sexual-harassment/a-17298779

Dwertmann, D., & Boehm, S. (2016). Status matters: The asymmetric effects of supervisor-subordinate disability incongruence and climate for inclusion. *The Academy of Management Journal, 59*(1), 44–64.

Earley, P. C. (1997). *Face, harmony, and social structure.* Oxford, UK: Oxford University Press.

Earley, P. C., & Erez, M. (1997). *The transplanted executive: Why you need to understand how workers in other countries see the world differently.* New York: Oxford University Press.

Eckhardt, G. (2002). Book review of *Culture's Consequences: Comparing values, behaviors, institutions, and organizations across nations* (2nd ed.). *Australian Journal of Management, 27,* 89–94.

ECtHR, Leyla Sahin vs Turkey, Judgement of 19 June 2004, Application No. 44774/98. Retrieved May 3, 2007, from http://cmiskp.echr.coe.int/tkp197/view.asp?item=2&portal=hbkm&action=html&highlight=leyla&sessionid=9750942&skin=hudoc-en

Ecuador punctuality. (2003, October 2). *Reuters.*

Edwards, A. (2014, June 20). *World Refugee Day: Global forced displacement tops 50 million for first time in post-World War II era.* Retrieved from www.unhcr.org/news/latest/2014

Edwards, R. D. (2011). Changes in world inequality in length of life. *Population and Development Review, 37*(3), 499–528.

Edwards, T. (2010). The nature of international integration and human resource policies in multinational companies. *Cambridge Journal of Economics, 35*(3), 483–498.

EEOC. (2009). *Education racism and colorism from employment.* U.S. Equal Employment Opportunity Commission. Retrieved from http://www1.eeoc.gov/eeoc/initiatives/e-race/caselist.cfm?renderforprint=1

EEOC v. Patterson-UTI Drilling Co. No. 15-CV-600 (D. Colo. Mar. 24, 2015).

Egerova, D., Jirincova, M., Lancaric, D., & Savov, R. (2013). Applying the concept of diversity management in organizations in the Czech Republic and the Slovak Republic—a research survey. *Technological and Economic Development of Economy, 19*(2), 350.

Eichenwald, K. (1996, November 1). Texaco to make record payout in bias lawsuit. *New York Times,* p. 1.

Eisenberger, R., Fasolo, P., & Davis-LaMastro, V. (1990). Perceived organizational support and employee diligence, commitment, and innovation. *Journal of Applied Psychology, 75*(1), 51–59.

Elamin, A. M., & Omair, K. (2010). Males' attitudes towards working females in Saudi Arabia. *Personnel Review, 39*(6), 746–766.

Eleven tips on getting more efficiency out of women employees. (1943, July). *Mass Transportation.*

Ellemers, N., & Haslam, S. A. (2012). Social identity theory. In P. A. M. Van Lange, A. W. Kruglanski, & E. T. Higgins, *Handbook of theories of social psychology* (Vol. 2, pp. 379–398). Thousand Oaks, CA: Sage.

Ellerbe, T., Carlton, E. L., Ramlow, B. E., Leukefeld, C. J., Delaney, M., & Staton-Tindall, M. (2011). Helping low-income mothers overcome multiple barriers to self-sufficiency. *Families in Society, 92*(3), 289–294.

Ellis, G. (2002, September 11). Training increases job hopes. *Illawarra Mercury.*

Elmore, K. C., & Oyserman, D. (2012). If "we" can succeed, "I" can too: Identity-based motivation and gender in the classroom. *Contemporary Educational Psychology, 37*(3), 176–185.

Elson, D. (1999). Labor markets as gendered institutions. *World Development, 27*(3), 611–627.

Ely, R. (1994). The effects of organizational demographics and social identity on relationships among professional women. *Administrative Science Quarterly, 39,* 203–238.

Ely, R. (1995). The power in demography: Women's social constructions of gender identity at work. *Academy of Management Journal, 38,* 589–634.

Ely, R. J., Ibarra, H., & Kolb, D. M. (2011). Taking gender into account: Theory and design for women's leadership development programs. *The Academy of Management Learning and Education, 10*(3), 474–493.

Ely, R. J., & Roberts, L. M. (2008). Shifting frames in team-diversity research: From difference to relationships. In A. P. Brief (Ed.), *Diversity at work.* New York: Cambridge University Press.

Ely, R., & Thomas, D. (2001). Cultural diversity at work: The effects of diversity perspectives on work group processes and outcomes. *Administrative Science Quarterly, 46*(2), 229–273.

EMD Group. (2015, April 16). Corporate responsibility report 2014: Diversity and inclusion. Retrieved March 31, 2016, from http://reports.emdgroup.com/2014/cr-report/employees/diversity-and-inclusion.html

Employees Retraining Board. (2003). *About ERB.* Retrieved November 26, 2003, from www.erb.org/english/index3.html

Engle, R. L., & Nash, B. (2015). Does it matter if researchers use individual dimension constructs or only aggregated constructs of cultural distance and cultural intelligence? *Journal of International Business Research, 14*(2), 47–65.

Enteman, W. (1996). Stereotyping, prejudice, and discrimination. In P. M. Lester (Ed.), *Images that injure pictorial stereotypes in the media* (pp. 9–14). Westport, CT: Praeger.

Environment and society. (2003). Unilever. Retrieved December 3, 2003, from www.unilever.com/environmentsociety

Equal Employment Opportunity Commission. (2015, October). Retrieved March 26, 2016, from http://www.eeoc.gov/eeoc/litigation/selected/aapi.cfm

Equal Employment Opportunity Commission. (n.d.). *What you should know about EEOC and the enforcement protections for LGBT workers.* Retrieved from http://www.eeoc.gov/eeoc/newsroom/wysk/enforcement_protections_lgbt_workers.cfm

Equal Employment Opportunity Commission v. Arabian American Oil Co. et al., 499 U.S. 244, 89–1838 (1991).

Equal Employment Opportunity Commission v. Mitsubishi Motor Manufacturing of America, 102 F.3d 869 (7th Cir. December 16, 1996)

Erez, M., & Earley, P. C. (1993). *Culture, self-identity and work.* Oxford, UK: Oxford University Press.

Erhardt, N. L., Werbel, J. D., & Shrader, C. B. (2003). Board of director diversity and firm financial performance. *Corporate Governance, 11*(2), 102–111.

Eringa, K., Caudron, L. N., Rieck, K., Xie, F., & Gerhardt, T. (2015). How relevant are Hofstede's dimensions for inter-cultural studies? A replication of Hofstede's research among current international business students. *Research in Hospitality Management, 5*(2), 187–198.

eShopAfrica. (n.d.-a). *eShopAfrica .com: Fair trade direct from Africa.* Retrieved August 12, 2012, from www.eShopAfrica.com

eShopAfrica.com. (n.d.-b). *Meet our artisans.* Retrieved from http://www.eshopafrica.com/PBCPPlayer.asp?ID=1417269

Essed, P. (1991). *Understanding everyday racism: An interdisciplinary theory.* Newbury Park, CA: Sage.

Essed, P. (1995). *Understanding everyday racism.* Thousand Oaks, CA: Sage.

Essed, P. (1996). *Diversity: Gender, color, and culture.* Amherst: University of Massachusetts Press.

Essed, P. (2002). Cloning cultural homogeneity while talking diversity: Old wine in new bottles in Dutch work organizations? *Transforming Anthropology, 11*(1), 1–19.

Essed, P., & de Graaff, M. (2002). *The topicality of diversity.* Municipal Policy in Focus den Haag: E-Quality and Utrecht: Forum, p 149.

Essed, P., & Trienekens, S. (2008). "Who wants to feel white?" Race, Dutch culture and contested identities. *Ethnic and Racial Studies, 31*(1), 52–72.

Eurest. (2001, April). *Media release: Minister backs national indigenous initiative.* Rose Bay, NSW, Australia: Author.

Eurest. (2004). *Indigenous training and employment project.* Retrieved February 27, 2004, from www.eurest.com.au/Second/indigenoustraining andemploymentprogram.html

Eurest Services. (2011, May 19). *Compass Group's recently recognized as Jones Lang LaSalle Supplier of Distinction.* Retrieved December 6, 2012, from www.eurestservices.us/news/

Eurest Services. (2012, June). *Compass Group receives 2011 Jones Lang LaSalle Supplier of Distinction*

Award for Innovation. Retrieved December 6, 2012, from www.eurestservices.us/news/

European Business Awards. (2011). *Country representative—Portugal.* Retrieved August 31, 2012, from www.businessawardseurope.com/download/EBA_case_study_Delta_final.pdf

European Commission. (2008). *Geographic mobility in the European Union: Optimising its economic and social benefits.* Retrieved July 14, 2014, from http://ec.europa.eu/social/home.jsp?langId=en

European Commission. (2012). *Tackling discrimination.* Retrieved June 27, 2012, from http://ec.europa.eu/justice/discrimination/index_en.htm

European Commission. (2016). *Tackling discrimination.* Retrieved from www.ec.europa.eu/justice/discrimination/index_en.htm

European Commission for Justice. (2011, April 5). Communication on an EU Framework for National Roma Integration Strategies by 2020.

European Commission for Justice. (2012, May 21). National Roma Integration Strategies: A first step in the implementation of the EU Framework.

European Union Agency for Fundamental Rights. (2014, April). *Handbook on European Data Protection Law.* Luxembourg: Publications Office of the European Union.

European Union Agency for Fundamental Rights & the European Court of Human Rights. (2011). *Handbook on European non-discrimination law.* Strasbourg, France: Author. Retrieved from www.fra.europa.eu

European Union Law Database. (2016). *Council Directive 2000/43/EC of 29 June 2000 implementing the principle of equal treatment between persons irrespective of* racial or ethnic origin. Retrieved February 21, 2016, from http://eur-lex.europa.eu/legal-content/EN/TXT/?uri=CELEX%3A32000L0043

Fair Trade Federation. (2003). *2003 report on fair trade trends in U.S., Canada and the Pacific rim.* Washington, DC: Author.

Fair Trade Federation. (2008a). *Fair trade federation interim trends report.* Washington, DC: Author.

The Fair Trade Foundation. (2008b, May 22). *Global fair trade sales increase by 47%.* Retrieved August 13, 2009, from www.fairtrade.org.uk/press_releases_and_statements_may_2008

Fair Trade USA. (n.d.-a). *Frequently asked questions.* Retrieved from http://fairtradeusa.org/what-is-fair-trade/faq

Fair Trade USA. (n.d.-b). *Green Mountain Coffee Roasters, Inc. celebrates ongoing commitment to fair trade certified and sustainable coffee.* Retrieved from http://fairtradeusa.org/press-room/press-release/green-mountain-coffee-roasters-inc-celebrates-ongoing-commitment-fair-trade

Fairtrade. (n.d.). *Join the world's largest coffee break, 13–15 May!* Retrieved from http://www.fairtrade.net/single-view+M53d8bd027b2.html

Fairtrade Canada. (n.d.). *Co-op profiles.* Retrieved August 31, 2012, from http://fairtrade.ca/en/get-involved/co-op-profiles#LS

Fairtrade Cocoa. (n.d.). Retrieved from http://blog.peopletree.co.uk/fairtrade-cocoa/

The Fairtrade Towns in Europe Project. (2009). *3rd European fair-trade towns conference report.* Lyon, France. 6–7 February 2009. Retrieved August 16, 2009, from www.fairtradetowns.org/news

The Fairtrade Towns in Europe Project. (n.d.). *Fairtrade towns.*

Retrieved December 2, 2012, from www.fairtradetowns.org

Family sues Denny's, alleges bias. (2001, June). Global diversity @ work. Retrieved November 3, 2003, from www.diversityatwork.com/news/sept01/Family.htm

Farndale, E., Biron, M., Briscoe, D. R., & Raghuram, S. (2015). A global perspective on diversity and inclusion in work organisations. *The International Journal of Human Resource Management, 26*(6), 677–687.

Fassinger, R. E. (2008). Workplace diversity and public policy: Challenges and opportunities for psychology. *American Psychologist, 63*(4), 252–268.

Feagin, J. R., & Feagin, C. B. (1988). Theories of discrimination. In P. S. Rothenberg (Ed.), *Racism and sexism: An integrated study* (pp. 41–48). New York: St. Martin's Press.

Federal Glass Ceiling Commission. (1995). *Good for business: Making full use of the nation's human capital. The environmental scan. A fact-finding report of the Federal Glass Ceiling Commission.* Washington, DC: Government Printing Office.

Feldman, D. C., & Turnley, W. H. (2004). Contingent employment in academic careers: Relative deprivation among adjunct faculty. *Journal of Vocational Behavior, 64*(2), 284–307.

Fenwick, M., Costa, C., Sohal, A. S., & D' Netto, B. (2011), Cultural diversity management in Australian manufacturing organisations. *Asia Pacific Journal of Human Resources, 49,* 494–507.

Ferdman, B. M., & Deane, B. (2014). *Diversity at work: The practice of inclusion* (1st ed.). San Francisco: Jossey-Bass.

Ferguson, A., Peterson, R., & Sanchez-Burks, J. (2012). *Causes and consequences of perceptions of intragroup conflict asymmetry.*

Unpublished manuscript, London Business School.

Fernandez, J. P. (1991). *Managing a diverse workforce.* Lanham, MD: Lexington Books.

Ferner, A., Almond, P., & Colling, T. (2005). Institutional theory and the cross-national transfer of employment policy: The case of "workforce diversity" in US multinationals. *Journal of International Business Studies, 36*(3), 304–321.

Festinger, L. (1954). A theory of social comparison processes. *Human Relations, 7,* 117–140.

Field, L. M. (2007). *Business and the Buddha: Doing well by doing good.* Somerville, MA: Wisdom Publications.

Figart, D. M. (2005). Rereading Becker: Contextualizing the development of discrimination theory. *Journal of Economic Issues, 39*(2), 475–484.

Fiji Islands Constitution Amendment Act of 1997. (n.d.). Retrieved May 15, 2004, from http://confinder.richmond.edu/fijiislands.htm

Filartiga v. Pena-Irala, 630F.2d 876 (U.S. Court of Appeals, Second Circuit, 1980).

Findler, L. Wind, L., & Mor Barak, M. E. (2007). The challenge of workforce management in a global society: Modeling the relationship between diversity, organizational culture, and employee well-being, job satisfaction and organizational commitment. *Administration in Social Work, 31*(3), 63–94.

Fischer, R., & Mansell, A. (2009). Commitment across cultures: A meta-analytical approach. *Journal of International Business Studies, 40,* 1339–1358.

Fisher, M. (2006). Wall Street women: Navigating gendered networks in the new economy. In M. Fisher & G. Downey (Eds), *Frontiers of capital:*

336

Ethnographic reflections on the new economy. Durham, NC: Duke University Press.

Fisher v. the University of Texas, No. 11-345 (2012).

Fiske, A. P., & Haslam, N. (1996). Social cognition is thinking about relationships. *Current Directions in Psychological Science, 5*(5), 143–148.

Fitzherbert, E. B., Struebig, M. J., Morel, A., Danielsen, F., Carsten, A., Brühl, C. A., et al. (2008). How will oil palm expansion affect biodiversity? *Trends in Ecology & Evolution, 23*(10), 538–545.

Flammer, C. (2015). Does corporate social responsibility lead to superior financial performance? A regression discontinuity approach. *Management Science, 61*(11), 2549–2568.

Fleury, J. (2012). Wandering through the borderlands of the social sciences: Gary Becker's *Economics of Discrimination. History of Political Economy, 44*, 1–40.

Fleury, M. T. (1999). The management of culture diversity: Lessons from Brazilian companies. *Industrial Management and Data Systems, 99*(3), 109–117.

Flinn, C. J. (2015). Gary Becker's contributions to the analysis of discrimination. *Journal of Demographic Economics, 81*(1), 45–50.

Flore, P. C., & Wicherts, J. M. (2015). Does stereotype threat influence performance of girls in stereotyped domains? A meta-analysis. *Journal of School Psychology, 53*(1), 25–44.

Foley, S., Linnehan, F., Greenhaus, G. H., & Weer, C. H. (2006). The impact of gender similarity, racial similarity, and work culture on family-supportive supervision. *Group & Organization Management, 31*(4), 420–441.

Foley Bros., Inc. v. Filardo, 336 U.S. 281, 284–285 (1949).

Fonseca, I. (1996). *Bury me standing: The gypsies and their journey.* New York: Vintage Books.

Ford, A., & Lee, H. H. (1991, March 20). Racial tensions blamed in girl's death shooting: Prolonged distrust, insults and violence between the Korean store owners and their Black neighbors are cited by both sides. *The Los Angeles Times,* p. B1.

Ford Motor Company. (2002). *2002 corporate citizen report (how we did in 2002: employees).* Retrieved May 26, 2004, from www.ford.com/en/company/about/corporateCitizenship/principlesProgressPerformance/our-principles/relationships-2002-employees.htm

Forschi, M., Lad, L., & Sigerson, K. (1994). Gender and double standards in the assessment of job applicants. *Social Psychology Quarterly, 57*(4), 326–339.

Foster, D. (1998). Waiting and winning in Indonesia. *Workforce, 3*(5), 28–30.

Fowler, E. (1996). *San'ya blues: Laboring life in contemporary Tokyo.* Ithaca, NY: Cornell University Press.

Freedom to Work. (2015, July). *Historic victory: Sexual orientation discrimination is barred by existing law, federal commission rules.* Retrieved from http://www.freedomtowork.org/?p=923, http://time.com/3962469/lgbt-discrimination-eeoc/

Frempomaa, Y. Y. (1986). *Migrant workers in West Africa, with special reference to Nigeria and Ghana* (Working Papers of the ILO International Migration Programme). Geneva: ILO.

Friedman, J. W. (2010). *Employment discrimination: Examples and explanations.* New York: Aspen Publishers.

Friedman, M. (1970, September 13). The social responsibility of business is to increase its profit. *New York Times Magazine*

Frooman, J. (1997). Socially irresponsible and illegal behavior and shareholder wealth. *Business and Society, 36*, 221–249.

Fudge, J. (2011). Global care chains, employment agencies, and the conundrum of jurisdiction: Decent work for domestic workers in Canada. *Canadian Journal of Women and the Law, 23*, 235–264.

Fulton, L. (2015). Worker representation in Europe. Labour Research Department and ETUI. Produced with the assistance of the SEEurope Network. Retrieved from http://www.worker-participation.eu/National-Industrial-Relations/Across-Europe/Workplace-Representation2

Furunes, T., Mykletun, R. J., Einarsen, S., & Glasø, L. (2015). Do low-quality leader-member relationships matter for subordinates? Evidence from three samples on the validity of the Norwegian LMX scale. *Nordic Journal of Working Life Studies, 5*(2), 71–87.

Gaertner, S. L., & Dovidio, J. F. (1986). The aversive form of racism. In J. F. Dovidio & S. L. Gaertner (Eds.), *Prejudice, discrimination, and racism.* San Diego, CA: Academic.

Gap Inc. (2016, January). *Women and opportunity.* Retrieved April 2, 2016, from http://www.catalyst.org/knowledge/gap-inc-women-and-opportunity

García, M. F., Posthuma, R. A., & Colella, A. (2008). Fit perceptions in the employment interview: The role of similarity, liking, and expectations. *Journal of Occupational and Organizational Psychology, 81*(2), 173–189.

Gautam, M., Lele, U., Hyde, W., Kartodihardjo, H., Khan, A., Erwinsyah I., et al. (2000). *The challenges of World Bank involvement in forests: An* evaluation of Indonesia's forests and World Bank assistance. Preliminary report. Washington, DC: The World Bank Group.

Geidner, C. (2010). Don't Ask, Don't Tell Repeal Act of 2010 is law. Retrieved June 9, 2012, from www .metroweekly.com/poliglot/2010/12/ dont-ask-dont-tell-repeal-act.html

Geisel, T. S. [Dr. Seuss]. (1961). The sneetches and other stories (pp. 3–4, 21–24). New York: Random House.

General Mills. (2016). Diversity and inclusion. Retrieved March 31, 2016, from https://generalmills.com/ Responsibility/diversity-and-inclusion

German courts uphold Muslim headscarf ban in schools. (2008, March 18). Der Spiegel. Retrieved July 15, 2009, from www.spiegel.de/international/ germany/0,1518, 542211,00.html

Gerstner, C. R., & Day, D. D. (1997). A meta-analytic review of leader-member exchange theory: Constructs and issues. Journal of Applied Psychology, 82(6), 827–844.

Ghana: Degraded mining lands to be turned into oil palm plantations. (2003, September 25). Africa News. Retrieved from www.allafrica.com/ stories/200309250729.html

Ghana: Unilever ready to assist PSI on oil palm. (2002, September 19). Africa News. Retrieved from www .allafrica.com

Giangreco, A., Carugati, A., Sebastiano, A., & Altamimi, H. (2012), War outside, ceasefire inside: An analysis of the performance appraisal system of a public hospital in a zone of conflict. Evaluation and Program Planning, 35(1), 161–170.

Gielen, U. P. (2016). The changing lives of 2.2 billion children: Global demographic trends and economic disparities. In U. P. Gielen & J. L. Roopnarine (Eds.), Childhood and adolescence: Cross-cultural

perspectives and applications (2nd ed., pp. 63–96). Santa Barbara, CA: Praeger.

Gilbert, J., Carr-Ruffino, N., Ivancevich, J. M., & Lownes-Jackson, M. (2003). An empirical examination of inter-ethnic stereotypes: Comparing Asian American and African American employees. Public Personnel Management, 32(2), 251–266.

Giles, H., & Coupland, N. (1991). Language: Contexts and consequences. Bristol, PA: Open University Press.

Giles, W., & Johnson, P. (1986). Perceived threat, ethnic commitment and interethnic language behavior. In Y. Y. Kim (Ed.), Interethnic communications: Current research (pp. 91–116). Beverly Hills, CA: Sage.

Ginsburgh, V., & Weber, S. (2011). How many languages do we need? The economics of linguistic diversity. Princeton, NJ: Princeton University Press.

Glastra, F. J., Meerman, M., Schedler, P. E., & De Vries, S. (2000). Broadening the scope of diversity management. Strategic implications in the case of the Netherlands. Industrial Relations/Relations Industrielles, 50(4), 698–724.

Glazier, J. A. (2003). Developing cultural fluency: Arab and Jewish students engaging in one another's company. Harvard Educational Review, 73(2), 141–163.

Global most admired companies. (2012, July 23). Fortune. Retrieved August 18, 2012, from http://money .cnn.com/magazines/fortune/ global500/2012/snapshots/6126.html

Gocłowska, M. A., Crisp, R. J., & Labuschagne, K. (2012). Can counter-stereotypes boost flexible thinking? Group Processes Intergroup Relations, 1–15.

Gold, M. (2015, September 20). Viola Davis's Emmy speech. The New York

Times. Retrieved from http://www .nytimes.com/live/emmys-2015/ viola-daviss-emotional-emmys-acceptance-speech/

Goldberg, C., & McKay, P. F. (2015). Diversity and LMX development. In T. N. Bauer & B. Erdogan (Eds.), The Oxford handbook of leader-member exchange. Oxford, England: Oxford Library of Psychology.

Goldberg, C., Riordan, C. M., & Zhang, L. (2008). Employees' perception of their leaders: Is being similar always better? Group Organization Management, 33(3), 330–355.

Goldman Sachs. (2014, November 17). Goldman Sachs diversity program receives innovative leadership award. Retrieved March 31, 2016, from http://www .goldmansachs.com/careers/blog/ posts/gld-leadership-award.html

Gomez, E. T. (2009). The rise and fall of capital: Corporate Malaysia in historical perspective. Journal of Contemporary Asia, 39(3), 345–381.

Gonzales, L., Davidoff, K. C., Nadal, K. L., & Yanos, P. T. (2014). Microaggressions experienced by persons with mental illnesses: An exploratory study. Psychiatric Rehabilitation Journal, 38(3), 234–241.

Gonzalez, J. A., & Denisi, A. S. (2009). Cross-level effects of demography and diversity climate on organizational attachment and firm effectiveness. Journal of Organizational Behavior, 30, 21–40.

The good life in a Bombay call center. (2003, Feb. 2). Retrieved from http://www.bloomberg.com/news/ articles/2003-02-02/online-extra-the-good-life-in-a-bombay-call-center

Goodman, P. S., & Haisley, E. (2007). Social comparison processes in an organizational context: New directions. Organizational Behavior and Human Decision Processes, 102, 109–125.

Gorman, F. (2000). Multinational logistics: Managing diversity. *Air Force Journal of Logistics, 24*(3), 8.

Gotsis, G., & Grimani, K. (2016). Diversity as an aspect of effective leadership: Integrating and moving forward. *Leadership & Organization Development Journal, 37*(2), 241–264.

Goujon, A., & Lutz, W. (2004). Future human capital: Population projections by level of education. In W. Lutz, W. Sanderson, & S. Scherbov (Eds.), *The end of world population growth in the 21st century* (pp. 121–157). London, England: Earthscan.

Government of India. (2015). *Handbook on sexual harassment of women at workplace.* New Delhi: Government of India.

Graen, G. B. (Ed.), (2003). *Dealing with diversity.* Greenwich, CT: Information Age Publishing.

Graen, G. B., & Scandura, T. A. (1987). Toward a psychology of dyadic organizing. In L. L. Cummings & B. M. Staw (Eds.), *Research in organizational behavior, 9,* 175–208. Greenwich, CT: JAI Press.

Graen, G. B., & Uhl-Bien, M. (1995). Relationship-based approach to leadership: Development of leader-member exchange (LMX) theory of leadership over 25 years: Applying a multi-level multi-domain perspective. *Leadership Quarterly, 6,* 219–247.

Graham & Whiteside Ltd. (2003). DCM Shriram Industries Ltd. *The Major Companies Database.* Company profile retrieved December 4, 2003, from LexisNexis database.

Grant, B. Z., & Kleiner, B. H. (1997). Managing diversity in the workplace. *Equal Opportunities International, 16*(3), 26–32.

Gratz v. Bollinger, 539 U.S. 244 (2003).

Gray, M., Kurihara, T., Hommen, L., & Feldman, J. (2007). Networks of exclusion: Job segmentation and social networks in the knowledge economy. *Equal Opportunities International, 26*(2), 144–161.

Greenaway, K. H., Wright, R. G., Willingham, J., Reynolds, K. J., & Haslam, S. A. (2015). Shared identity is key to effective communication. *Personality and Social Psychology Bulletin, 41*(2), 171–182.

Greenberg, J., Ashton-James, C. E., & Ashkanasy, N. M. (2007). Social comparison processes in organizations. *Organizational Behavior and Human Decision Processes, 102,* 22–41.

Greening, D. W., & Turban, D. B. (2000). Corporate social performance as a competitive advantage in attracting a quality workforce. *Business and Society, 39*(3), 254–280.

Greenwald, A. G., & Banaji, M. R. (1995). Implicit social cognition: Attitudes, self-esteem, and stereotypes. *Psychological Review, 102*(1), 4–27.

Greer, L. L., Jehn, K. A., & Mannix, E. A. (2008). Conflict transformation: A longitudinal investigation of the relationships between different types of intergroup conflict and the moderating role of conflict resolution. *Small Group Research, 39*(3), 278–302.

Griffin, J. J., & Mahon, J. F. (1997). The corporate social performance and corporate financial performance debate: Twenty-five years of incomparable research. *Business and Society, 36,* 5–31.

Griggs v. Duke Power Company, 420 F. 2d 1225 (4th Cir. 1970).

Groeneveld, D. (2011). Diversity and employee turnover in the Dutch public sector: Does diversity management make a difference? *International Journal of Public Sector Management, 24*(6), 594–612.

Grosbois, D. (2011). Corporate social responsibility reporting by the global hotel industry: Commitment, initiatives and performance. *International Journal of Hospitality Management, 31*(2), 896–905.

Groschl, S. (2011). Diversity management strategies of global hotel groups. *International Journal of Contemporary Hospitality Management, 23,* 224–240.

Groves, K. S., & Feyerherm, A. E. (2011). Leader cultural intelligence in context: Testing the moderating effects of team cultural diversity on leader and team performance. *Group & Organization Management, 36*(5), 535–566.

Groysberg, B., & Connolly, K. (2013). Great leaders who make the mix work. *Harvard Business Review.* Retrieved March 31, 2016, from https://hbr.org/2013/09/great-leaders-who-make-the-mix-work

Grutter v. Bollinger, 539 U.S. 306 (2003).

Gudykunst, W. B., Ting-Toomey, S., & Chua, E. (1988). *Culture and interpersonal communication.* Newbury Park, CA: Sage.

Guerin-Gonzales, C., & Strikwerda, C. (1993). *The politics of immigrant workers: Labor activism and migration in the world economy since 1830.* New York: Homes & Meier.

Guimond, S. (2006). *Social comparison and social psychology: Understanding cognition, intergroup relations, and culture.* Cambridge, UK: Cambridge University Press.

Gutiérrez, R. A. (2013). Higher education and equity: Historical narratives, contemporary debates. *Diversity and Democracy, 16*(2). Retrieved from https://www.aacu.org/publications-research/periodicals/higher-education-and-equity-historical-narratives-contemporary

Guveli, A. (2011). Social and economic impact of the headscarf ban on women in Turkey. *European Societies*, 171–189.

Hai Ha-Kotobuki. (2012). *Company profile*. Retrieved August 25, 2012, from http://companies.globalmarket .com/haiha-kotobuki-confectionery-co-ltd-118714.html

Hale, B. (2003, February 3). African crafts go online. *BBC News*. Retrieved September 12, 2004, from http://news.bbc.co.uk/1/hi/business/2688323.stm

Hall, E. T. (1959). *The silent language of business*. Garden City, NJ: Doubleday.

Hall, E. T. (1976). *Beyond culture*. New York: Anchor Press.

Hall, J. C., Everett, J. E., & Hamilton-Mason, J. (2012). Black women talk about workplace stress and how they cope. *Journal of Black Studies, 43*(2), 207–226.

Halliday, M. A. K. (1978). *Language as social semiotic*. Baltimore: University Park Press.

Hallinan, M. T. (2001). Sociological perspectives on Black–White inequalities in American schooling. *Sociology of Education*, 50–70.

Hamdani, M. R., & Buckley, M. R. (2011). Diversity goals: Reframing the debate and enabling a fair evaluation. *Business Horizons, 54*, 33–40.

Hamersma, S. (2008). The effects of an employer subsidy on employment outcomes: A study of the work opportunity and welfare-to-work tax credits. *Journal of Policy Analysis and Management, 27*(3), 498–520.

Hampden-Turner, C., & Trompenaars, A. (1993). *The seven cultures of capitalism: Value systems for creating wealth in the United States, Japan, Germany, France, Britain, Sweden, and the Netherlands*. New York: Doubleday.

Hance, J. (2009, November 19). *Oil palm workers still below poverty line, despite minister's statements, mongabay.com*. Retrieved December 6, 2009, from http://news .mongabay.com/2009/1119-hance_ oilpalmworkers.html

Hancock, A. (2004). *The politics of disgust: The public identity of the welfare queen*. New York: New York University Press.

Hanna, B. (2015). Just like any other city: The de-gasification of the Bhopal gas relief system. *Social Justice, 41*(1/2), 38.

Harley, D. A. (2014). Adult ex-offender population and employment: A synthesis of the literature on recommendations and best practices. *Journal of Applied Rehabilitation Counseling, 45*(3), 10.

Harrington, H. J., & Miller, N. (1992). Research and theory in intergroup relations: Issues of consensus and controversy. In J. Lynch, C. Modgil, & S. Modgil (Eds.), *Cultural diversity and the schools* (Vol. 2, pp. 159–178). London: Falmer.

Harris, D. (2001). *In the eye of the beholder: Observed race and observer characteristics*. (Population Studies Center Research Report 02–522). Ann Arbor: University of Michigan.

Harris, L. M., Matthews, L. R., Penrose-Wall, J., Alam, A., & Jaworski, A. (2014). Perspectives on barriers to employment for job seekers with mental illness and additional substance-use problems. *Health & Social Care in the Community, 22*(1), 67–77.

Harris, T. E. (2011). Toward effective employee involvement: An analysis of parallel and self-managing teams. *Journal of Applied Business Research, 9*(1), 25–33.

Harrison, D. A., & Klein, K. J. (2007). What's the difference? Diversity constructs as separation, variety, or disparity in organizations. *Academy of Management Review, 32*, 1199–1228.

Harrison, D. A., & Sin, H. (2006). What is diversity and how should it be measured. In A. M. Konrad, P. Prasad, & J. K. Pringle (Eds.), *Handbook of workplace diversity* (pp. 191–216). Thousand Oaks, CA: Sage.

Harrison, G. L., & McKinnon, J. L. (1999). Cross-cultural research in management control systems design: A review of the current state. *Accounting, Organizations and Society, 24*, 483–506.

Harshbarger, R. (2015). MTA outreach to homeless focusing on the end of subway lines, trains in motion. *amNew York*. Retrieved from http://www.amny.com/transit/mta-outreach-to-homeless-focusing-on-the-end-of-subway-lines-trains-in-motion-1.11013462

Hart, A. (2003, October 29). Cities playing fair. *South Wales Evening Post*, p. 22.

Hart, W. B. (1999). Interdisciplinary influences in the study of intercultural relations: A citation analysis of the *International Journal of Intercultural Relations*. *International Journal of Intercultural Relations, 23*, 575–589.

Hartenian, L. S., & Gudmundson, D. E. (2000). Cultural diversity in small business: Implications for firm performance. *Journal of Developmental Entrepreneurship, 5*(3), 209.

Hartmann, G. G., & SAM Research, Inc. (2003, November 20). *Profile of Unilever: Market Sector Leader, DJSI World*. Zurich: SAM Research, Inc.

Hartmann & SAM Research. (2015). *Awards & recognition*. Retrieved from https://www.unilever.com/news/awards-and-recognition/

Harvey, C. (2012). Contextualised equality and the politics of legal mobilization: Affirmative action in Northern Ireland. *Social & Legal Studies, 21*, 23–50.

Harzing, A. W. (2000). An empirical test and extension of the Bartlett and Ghoshal typology of multinational companies. *Journal of International Business Studies, 31*(1), 101–120.

Haslam, S. A., & Ellemers, N. (2005). Social identity in industrial and organizational psychology: Concepts, controversies and contributions. *International Review of Industrial and Organizational Psychology, 20*, 39–118.

Hassan, A. A. G. (2004). *Growth, structural change and regional inequality in Malaysia*. Aldershot, UK: Ashgate.

Haub, C., & Riche, M. F. (1994). Population by the numbers: Trends in population growth and structure. In L. A. Mazur (Ed.), *Beyond the numbers: A reader on population, consumption, and the environment* (pp. 95–108). Washington, DC: Island Press.

Haynes and Boone. (2016). *Diversity and inclusion mission statement*. Retrieved February 21, 2016, from http://www.haynesboone.com/firm/diversity

Hays-Thomas, R. (2004). Why now? A contemporary focus on managing diversity. In M. S. Stockdale & F. J. Crosby, *The psychology and management of workplace diversity* (pp. 3–30). Malden, MA: Blackwell Publishing.

Head, J. (2010, December 31). *Quiet end to Turkey's college headscarf ban*. Retrieved June 27, 2012, from www.bbc.co.uk/news/world-europe-11880622

Heal, G. (2008). *When principles pay: Corporate social responsibility and the bottom line*. New York: Columbia University Press.

Healey, J. F. (2009). *Diversity and society: Race, ethnicity, and gender* (3rd ed.). Thousand Oaks, CA: Pine Forge Press.

Healthy Kids Global Programme. (2015). *The Nestlé healthy kids global programme*. Retrieved from http://www.nestle.com/nutrition-health-wellness/kids-best-start/children-family/healthy-kids-programme

Heath, A. (2014). *Affirmative action policies to remedy ethnic minority disadvantage in the labour market*. Robert Schuman Centre for Advanced Studies, Research Paper No. PP 2014/01.

Heine, B., & Nurse, D. (Eds.). (2000). *African languages: An introduction*. Cambridge, England: Cambridge University Press.

Helyar, J., & Buteau, M. (2012, April 8). *CEOs praising diversity stay silent on no-women Augusta*. Bloomberg News.

Henderson, G. (1994). *Cultural diversity in the workplace*. Westport, CT: Praeger.

Henderson, T. P. (2001, June). Perception that some merchants practice racial profiling generates debate. *Stores Magazine*. Retrieved November 3, 2003, from www.stores.org/archives/jun01edit.asp

Herman, J., Mallory, C., & Wilson, B. (2016). *Estimates of transgender populations in states with legislation impacting transgender people*. The Williams Institute. Retrieved March 27, 2016, from http://williamsinstitute.law.ucla.edu/wp-content/uploads/Estimates-of-Transgender-Populations.pdf

Herrnstein, R., & Murray, C. (1994). *The bell curve: Intelligence and class structure in American life*. New York: Free Press.

Hildebrandt, E. (2009). Impoverished women with children and no welfare benefits: The urgency of researching failures of the temporary assistance for needy families program. *American Journal of Public Health, 99*(5), 793–801.

Hill, H. (2014). The $1,000 tipping point: What can be achieved with this sum to break down employment barriers for people with disability? *International Journal of Disability Management, 9*. doi:10.1017/idm.2014.21

Hiller, N. J., DeChurch, L. A., Murase, T., & Doty, D. (2011). Searching for outcomes of leadership: A 25-year review. *Journal of Management, 37*, 1137–1177.

Hilton Worldwide. *Suppliers as diverse as our properties*. Retrieved from http://www.hiltonworldwide.com/development/performance-advantage/supply-management/supplier/diversity/

Hiltzik, M. (2003, October 20). Silicon Valley: Visas down, job exports up. *The Los Angeles Times*. Retrieved December 8, 2003, from www.latimes.com/classified/jobs/career/la-fi-golden200ct20,0,7510486.column?coll=la-class-employ-career

Hindustan Unilever Limited. (n.d.). *Enhancing livelihoods through Project Shakti*. Retrieved from https://www.hul.co.in/sustainable-living/case-studies/enhancing-livelihoods-through-project-shakti.html

Hirst, G., van Dick, R., & van Knippenberg, D. (2009). A social identity perspective on leadership and employee creativity. *Journal of Organizational Behavior, 30*, 963–982.

History of immigration in France. (n.d.). Retrieved October 27, 2003, from www.fritz-karsen.de/comenius/1999_00/history.html

History of the supersonic airliner. (2001, July 5). CNN [television broadcast].

Hitlan, R. T., Cliffton, R. J., & DeSoto, M. C. (2006). Perceived exclusion in the workplace: The moderating effects of gender on work-related attitudes and psychological health. *North American Journal of Psychology, 8*(2), 217–235.

Hobman, E. V., Bordia, P., & Gallois, C. (2004). Perceived dissimilarity and work group involvement: Moderating effects of group openness to diversity. *Group & Organization Management, 29*(5), 560–587.

Hodges-Aeberhard, J. (1999). Affirmative action in employment: Recent court approaches to a difficult concept. *International Labour Review, 138*(3), 247.

Hofstede, G. (1980). *Culture's consequences: International differences in work related values.* Beverly Hills, CA: Sage.

Hofstede, G. (1997). *Cultures and organizations: Software of the mind.* New York: McGraw-Hill.

Hofstede, G. (2001). *Culture's consequences: Comparing values, behaviors, institutions, and organizations across nations* (2nd ed.). Thousand Oaks, CA: Sage.

Hofstede, G. (2007). Asian management in the 21st century. *Asia Pacific Journal of Management, 24*, 411–420.

Hofstede, G. (2011). Dimensionalizing cultures: The Hofstede model in context. *Online Readings in Psychology and Culture, 2*(1). doi:10.9707/2307-0919.1014

Hofstede, G. J. (2015). Culture's causes: The next challenge. *Cross Cultural Management, 22*(4), 545–569.

Hofstede, G., & Bond, M. H. (1988). The Confucius connection: From cultural roots to economic growth. *Organizational Dynamics, 16*(4), 4–21.

Hofstede, G., & Hofstede, G. J. (2005). *Cultures and organizations: Software of the mind* (2nd ed.). New York: McGraw-Hill.

Hofstede, G., Hofstede, G. J., & Minkov, M. (2010). *Cultures and organizations: Software of the mind: Intercultural cooperation and its importance for survival* (3rd ed.). New York: McGraw-Hill.

Hogg, M. A. (2006). Social identity theory. In J. Burke (Ed.), *Contemporary social psychological theories* (pp. 111–136). Stanford, CA: Stanford University Press.

Hogg, M. A., & Reid, S. A. (2006). Social identity, self-categorization, and the communication of group norms. *Communication Theory, 16*(1), 7–30.

Hogg, M. A., & Terry, D. J. (2000). Social identity and self-categorization processes in organizational contexts. *The Academy of Management Review, 25*(1), 121–140.

Hogg, M. A., & Terry, D. J. (2001). *Social identity processes in organizational contexts.* Philadelphia: Psychology Press.

Hollowell, B. J. (2007). Examining the relationship between diversity and firm performance. *Journal of Diversity Management, 2*, 51–60.

Holtgraves, T. (1997). Styles of language use: Individual and cultural variability in conversational indirectness. *Journal of Personality and Social Psychology, 73*(3), 624–637.

Holvino, E. (2010). Intersections: The simultaneity of race, gender and class in organization studies. *Gender, Work & Organization, 17*, 248–277.

Honest Tea. (n.d.). *Help us celebrate Fair Trade Month and enter for a chance to win Honest Tea.* Retrieved from https://www.honesttea.com/blog/help-us-celebrate-fair-trade-month-and-enter-for-a-chance-to-win-honest-tea/

Hong Kong Council of Social Services. (2003). *Caring company scheme.* Retrieved November 26, 2003, from www.hkcss.org.hk/partnership/caring_com_e.htm

Hong Kong Legal Information Institute. (n.d.). *Sex Discrimination Ordinance.* Retrieved November 30, 2012, from www.hklii.hk/cgi-bin/sinodisp/eng/hk/legis/ord/480/index.html?stem=&synonyms=&query=Sex%20Discrimination%20Ordinance

Hong Kong Trade Development Council. (2012). Retrieved August 21, 2012, from www.hktdc.com/sourcing/hk_company_directory.htm?locale=en&companyid=1X02FC4W

Hong Yip Service Co. Ltd. (n.d.-a). Company website. Retrieved August 21, 2012, from www.hongyip.com.hk/Pages/home

Hong Yip Service, Co. Ltd. (n.d.-b). Dedication to environmental and social affairs. Retrieved from http://www.hongyip.com.hk/Services/social_commitments

Hookway, J. (2009, July 8). Affirmative action spurs Asian debate. *The Wall Street Journal*, p. A1.

Hopkins, A. (2006). Price Waterhouse v. Hopkins: A personal account of a sexual discrimination plaintiff. *Hofstra Labor & Employment Law Journal, 22*, 357–416.

Hopkins, K. M., Cohen-Callow, A., Kim, H. J., & Hwang, J. (2010). Beyond intent to leave: Using multiple outcome measures for assessing turnover in child welfare. *Children and Youth Services Review, 32*(10), 1380–1387.

Hopkins v. Price Waterhouse, 618 F.Supp. 1109 (D.D.C.1985).

Hopkins v. Price Waterhouse, 825 F.2d 458 (D.C. Cir. 1987).

Hordes, M. W., Clancy, J. A., & Baddaley, J. (1995). A primer for global start-ups. *The Academy of Management Executive (1993–2005), 9*(2), 7–11.

Hornsey, M. J. (2008). Social identity theory and self-categorization theory: A historical review. *Social and Personaltiy Psychology Compass, 2*(1), 204–222.

Horowitz, M. (2004). *Attitudes towards wage fairness in the Maquiladora Zone: Social identities, reference groups, and the sale of labor power.* Doctoral dissertation, University of Kansas, Lawrence, KS.

Horwitz, F. M. (2002). Whither South African management? In N. Warner & P. Joynt (Eds.), *Managing across cultures: Issues and perspectives* (2nd ed., pp. 203–214) London: Thomson.

Houkamau, C., & Boxall, P. (2011). The incidence and impacts of diversity management: A survey of New Zealand employees. *Asia Pacific Journal of Human Resources, 49*(4), 440–460.

House, R. J., Dorfman, P. W., Javidan, M., Hanges, P. J., & Sully de Luque, M. (2013). *Strategic leadership across cultures: GLOBE study of CEO leadership behavior and effectiveness in 24 countries.* Thousand Oaks, CA: Sage.

House, R. J., Hanges, P. J., Javidan, M., Dorfman, P. W., & Gupta, V. (Eds.). (2004). *Culture, leadership, and organizations: The GLOBE Study of 62 Societies* (3rd ed.). Thousand Oaks: Sage Publications.

House, R. J., Hanges, P. J., Javidan, M., Dorfman, P. W., & Gupta, V. (2013). *Culture, leadership, and organizations: The GLOBE study of 62 societies.* Thousand Oaks, CA: Sage.

House Bill No. 663 (2016). *Restroom facilities; Use of facilities in public buildings or schools.* Retrieved March 25, 2016, from https://www.richmondsunlight.com/bill/2016/hb663/

Howard, J. M., & Rothbart, M. (1980). Social categorization and memory for in-group and out-group behavior. *Journal of Personality and Social Psychology, 38,* 301–310.

Hsu, T. (2013, May 9). Wet Seal to pay $7.5 million to settle race discrimination suit. *Los Angeles Times.* Retrieved March 24, 2016, from http://www.latimes.com/business/la-fi-mo-wet-seal-naacp-lawsuit-20130509-story.html

Huber, M. E., Seitchik, A. E., Brown, A. J., Sternad, D., & Harkins, S. G. (2015). The effect of stereotype threat on performance of a rhythmic motor skill. *Journal of Experimental Psychology: Human Perception and Performance, 41*(2), 525–541.

Hull, G. (2015). Affirmative action and the choice of amends. *Philosophia: Philosophical Quarterly of Israel, 43*(1), 113–134.

Hurwich-Reiss, E., Wadsworth, M. E., & Markman, H. J. (2014). Cultural adaptation of a family-strengthening intervention low-income Spanish-speaking families. *Journal of Latina/o Psychology, 2*(1), 21–36.

Hutchings, K., Metcalfe, D., & Cooper, B. K. (2010). Exploring Arab Middle Eastern women's perceptions of barriers to, and facilitators of, international management opportunities. *The International Journal of Human Resource Management, 21*(1), 61–83.

Hutchins, M. J., & Sutherland, J. W. (2008). An exploration of measures of social sustainability and their application to supply chain decisions. *Journal of Cleaner Production, 16,* 1688–1698.

Hwang, J., & Hopkins, K. (2012). Organizational inclusion, commitment, and turnover among child welfare workers: A multilevel mediation analysis. *Administration in Social Work, 36*(1), 23–39.

Hwang, J., & Hopkins, K. M. (2015). A structural equation model of the effects of diversity characteristics and inclusion on organizational outcomes in the child welfare workforce. *Children and Youth Services Review, 50,* 44–52.

Hyun, J. (2006). *Breaking the bamboo ceiling: Career strategies for Asians.* New York: Harper.

Ibarra, H. (1993). Personal networks of women and minorities in management: A conceptual framework. *Academy of Management Review, 18,* 56–87.

IBM. (2009). Retrieved July 26, 2009, from www-03.ibm.com/employment/us/diverse/50/sp.shtml

IBM. (2015). *Diversity and inclusion report: Diversity of people. Diversity of thought. A smarter way to innovate every day.* Retrieved from http://www-03.ibm.com/employment/us/diverse/downloads/ibm_diversity_brochure.pdf

IBM. (2016). *Lesbian, gay, bisexual, transgender, intersex.* Retrieved March 25, 2016, from http://www-07.ibm.com/employment/au/diversity/glbt.html

ILGA. (2014). *A world survey of laws: Criminalisation, protection and recognition of same-sex love.* Retrieved from http://old.ilga.org/Statehomophobia/ILGA_SSHR_2014_Eng.pdf

Immigration and Refugee Board of Canada. (2008, May 20). *Turkey: Situation of women who wear headscarves.* Canada: Author. Retrieved July 15, 2009, from www.unhcr.org/refworld/type,QUERYRESPONSE,,TUR,4885a91a8,0.html

Inclusion matters. (2015, March). New York: Catalyst. Retrieved March 31, 2016, from http://www.catalyst.org/system/files/inclusion_matters_print_1.pdf

Infosys. *Creating a diverse workplace.* https://www.infosys.com/careers/culture/diversity-inclusivity/

Inkeles, A., & Levinson, D. J. (1969). National character: The study of modal personality and sociocultural systems. In G. Lindzey & E. Aronson (Eds.), *The handbook of social psychology* (2nd ed.). Reading, MA: Addison-Wesley.

Insch, G. S., McIntyre, N., & Napier, N. K. (2008). The expatriate glass ceiling: The second layer of glass. *Journal of Business Ethics, 83*(1), 19–28.

International Federation of Red Cross and Red Crescent Societies. (2002,

November 13). *Implementation of the declaration of commitment on HIV/AIDS*. Statement delivered by Encho Gospodinov, Head of International Federation Permanent Observer Office to the United Nations in New York, to the United Nations General Assembly, Third Committee, New York. Retrieved September 12, 2004, from www.ifrc .org/docs/news/speech02/eg131102.asp

International Gay and Lesbian Human Rights Commission. (1999, April). *Antidiscrimination legislation: A worldwide summary.* IGLHRC Fact Sheet. Retrieved October 28, 2002, from www.iglhrc.org/news/factsheets/990604-antidis.html

International Gay and Lesbian Human Rights Commission. (2012). *Argentina adopts landmark legislation in recognition of gender identity.* Retrieved December 2, 2012, from www.iglhrc.org/cgi-bin/iowa/article/pressroom/pressrelease/1526.html

International Labour Organization. (2000). *World labour report 2000: Income security and social protection in a changing world.* Geneva: International Labour Office.

International Labour Organization. (2005). Retrieved September 7, 2009, from www.ilo.org/public/libdoc/ILO-Thesaurus/english/tr2351.htm

International Labour Organization. (2007). *Equality at work: Tackling the challenges.* Global Report under the follow-up to the ILO Declaration of fundamental principles and rights at work. International Labour Conference 96th Session 2007. Retrieved June 26, 2009, from www.ilo.org

International Labour Organization. (2010). *World social security report: Providing coverage in times of crisis and beyond.* Geneva: International Labour Office.

International Labour Organization (ILO). (2011). *Key indicators of the labour market (KILM)* (7th ed.). Geneva: ILO. Retrieved from www.ilo.org

International Labour Organization. (2012). *LABORSTA Internet.* Retrieved May 29, 2012, from http://laborsta .ilo.org/

International Labour Organization (ILO). (2014). *Database of national labour, social security and related human rights legislation.* Geneva: ILO.

The Islamic veil across Europe. (2011, September 22). BBC News. Retrieved June 27, 2012, from www.bbc.co.uk/news/world-europe-13038095

The Islamic veil across Europe. (2014, July 11). BBC News. Retrieved March 24, 2016, from www.bbc.com/news/world-europe-13038095

Jabbour, C. J. C, Gordono, F. S., de Oliveira, J. H. C., Martinez, J. C., & Battistelle, R. A. G. (2011). Diversity management: Challenges, benefits, and the role of human resource management in Brazilian organizations. *Equality, Diversity and Inclusion: An International Journal, 30*(1), 58–74.

Jackson, S. E., & Joshi, A. (2011). Work team diversity. In S. Zedeck (Ed.), *APA handbook of industrial and organizational psychology: Volume II.* Washington, DC: American Psychological Association.

Jackson, S. E., Joshi, A., & Erhardt, N. L. (2003). Recent research on team and organizational diversity: SWOT analysis and implications. *Journal of Management, 29,* 801–830.

Jackson, S. E., May, K. E., & Whitney, K. (1995). Understanding the dynamics of diversity in decision making teams. In R. A. Guzzo & E. Salas (Eds.), *Team effectiveness and decision making in organizations* (pp. 204–261). San Francisco: Jossey-Bass.

Jamali, D., Abdallah, H., & Hmaidan, S. (2010). The challenge of moving beyond rhetoric: Paradoxes of diversity management in the Middle East. *Equality, Diversity and Inclusion: An International Journal, 29*(2), 167–185.

Javidan, M., Dorfman, P., Sully de Luque, M., & House, R. J. (2006). In the eye of the beholder: Cross cultural lessons in leadership from project GLOBE. *Academy of Management Perspective, 20*(1), 67–90.

Javidan, M., & House, R. (2001). Cultural acumen for the global manager: Lessons from Project GLOBE. *Organizational Dynamics, 29*(4), 289–305.

Javidan, M., House, R., Dorfman, P. W., Hanges, P. J., & Sully de Luque, M. (2006). Conceptualizing and measuring cultures and their consequences: A comparative review of GLOBE's and Hofstede's approaches. *Journal of International Business Studies, 37,* 897–914.

Javidan, M., Stahl, G. K., Brodbeck, F., & Wilderom, C. P. M. (2005). Cross-border transfer of knowledge: Cultural lessons from project GLOBE. *Academy of Management Executive 19*(2), 59–76.

Jehn, K. A., & Bendersky, C. (2004). Intragroup conflict in organizations: A contingency perspective on the conflict-outcome relationship. In R. Kramer & B. Staw (Eds.), *Research in organizational behavior: An annual series of analytical essays and critical reviews* (Vol. 25, pp. 187–242). San Diego, CA: Elsevier.

Jen, C., Chou, L., Lin, C., & Tsai, M. (2012). The influence of the perception of a familial climate on job performance: Mediation of loyalty to supervisors and moderation of filial behavior. *International Journal of Psychology, 47*(3), 169–178.

Jensen, E. (2015, May 1). *China replaces Mexico as the top sending country for immigrants to the United States.* U.S. Census Bureau. Retrieved from http://

researchmatters.blogs.census .gov/2015/05/01/china-replaces-mexico-as-the-top-sending-country-for-immigrants-to-the-united-states/

Jensenius, F. R. (2015). Development from representation? A study of quotas for the scheduled castes in India. *American Economic Journal: Applied Economics, 7*(3), 196–220.

Jimenez-Cook, S., & Kleiner, B. H. (2005). Nursing at the cross roads: Increasing workforce diversity and addressing health disparities. *Equal Opportunities International, 24*(7/8), 1–10.

John-Henderson, N. A., Rheinschmidt, M. L., & Mendoza-Denton, R. (2015). Cytokine responses and math performance: The role of stereotype threat and anxiety reappraisals. *Journal of Experimental Social Psychology, 56*, 203–206.

Johnson, C. E. (2008). *Meeting the ethical challenges of leadership: Casting light or shadow.* Thousand Oaks, CA: Sage.

Johnson, H. H. (2009). Corporate social responsibility: Determining your position. In E. Biech (Ed.), *The 2010 Pfeiffer Annual: Consulting* (pp. 141–147). San Francisco: Pfeiffer.

Johnston, W. B., & Packer, A. E. (1987). *Workforce 2000.* Indianapolis, IN: Hudson Institute.

Joiner, T. A. (2001). The influence of national culture and organizational culture alignment on job stress and performance: Evidence from Greece. *Journal of Managerial Psychology, 16*(3), 229.

Jones, C. (2015, January 22). Carnival CEO steers cruise giant in new directions. *USA Today.* Retrieved from http://www.usatoday.com/story/travel/cruises/2015/01/22/carnival-ceo-putting-his-stamp-on-worlds-biggest-cruise-company/21867385/

Jones, D., Pringle, J., & Shepherd, D. (2000). Managing diversity meets Aotearoa/ New Zealand. *Personnel Review, 29*(3), 364–380.

Jones, G. (2005). *Renewing Unilever: Transformation and tradition.* New York: Oxford University Press.

Jones, G. (2010). *Multinational strategies and developing countries in historical perspective.* Harvard Business School Working Paper, 10-076.

Jonsen, K., Maznevski, M. L., & Schneider, S. C. (2011). Diversity and its not so diverse literature: An international perspective. *International Journal of Cross Cultural Management, 11*(1), 35–62.

Jonsen, K., & Özbilgin, M. (2014). Models of global diversity management. In B. M. Ferdman & B. Deane (Eds.), *Diversity at work: The practice of inclusion* (1st ed., pp. 364–385). San Francisco: Jossey-Bass.

Joplin, J. R. W., & Daus, C. S. (1997). Challenges of leading a diverse workforce. *Academy of Management Executive, 11*(3), 32.

Jordan, K., & Mavec, D. (2010, October). *Corporate initiatives in indigenous employment: The Australian employment covenant two years on.* CAEPR Working Paper No. 74/2010. Canberra, Aus.: Center for Aboriginal Research, The Australian National University.

Joseph Rowntree Foundation, research report, pp. 1–27. Retrieved from www.jrf.org.uk/

Joshi, A., & Roh, H. (2009). The role of context in work team diversity research: A meta-analytic review. *Academy of Management Journal, 52*(3), 599–627.

Judd, C. M., Blair, I. V., & Chapleau, K. M. (2004). Automatic stereotypes vs. automatic prejudice: Sorting out the possibilities in the possibilities of the weapon paradigm. *Journal of Experimental Social Psychology, 40*(1), 75–81.

Judy, R. W., & D'Amico, C. (1997). *Workforce 2020.* Indianapolis, IN: Hudson Institute.

Kaas, L., & Manger, C. (2012). Ethnic discrimination in Germany's labour market: A field experiment. *German Economic Review, 13*(1), 1–20.

Kabeer, N. (2000). *The power to choose.* London, England: Verso.

Kacperczyk, A., Sanchez-Burks, J., & Baker, W. (2009). *Social isolation in the workplace: A cross-cultural and longitudinal analysis.* Paper submitted for publication.

Kahn, J. (2003, December 7). Ruse in toyland: Chinese workers' hidden woe. *New York Times*, p. 1.

Kaiser, H. F. (1970). A second generation little Jiffy. *Psychometrika, 35*, 401–415.

Kaiser, R., & Prange, H. (2004). Managing diversity in a system of multi-level governance: The open method of co-ordination in innovation policy, *Journal of European Public Policy, 11*(2), 249–266.

Kalev, A., (2009). Cracking the glass cages? Restructuring and ascriptive inequality at work. *American Journal of Sociology, 114*(6), 1591–1643.

Kalev, A., Dobbin, F., & Kelly, E. (2006). Best practices or best guesses? Assessing the efficacy of corporate affirmative action and diversity policies. *American Sociological Review, 71*(4), 589–617.

Kamen, A. (1992, June 22). Myth of "model minority" haunts Asian Americans; Stereotype eclipses diverse group's problems. *The Washington Post*, p. A1.

Kamenou, N., & Fearfull, A. (2006). Ethnic minority women: A lost voice in HRM. *Human Resource Management Journal, 16*(2), 154–172.

Kamenou, N., Netto, G., & Fearfull, A. (2012). Ethnic minority women in the Scottish labour market: Employers' perceptions. *British Journal of Management, 22*(2), 286–304.

Kang, H., & Mo, S. (2010). Linking child welfare workers' organizational inclusion-exclusion to perceived organizational support, organizational commitment and turnover intention. *Journal of Adolescent Welfare, 12*(4), 69–89.

Kang, H. H., & Tran, L. C. (2003, December 29). Filipino workers in Taiwan: A status report. *BusinessWorld,* 22–26.

Kanso, A. M., Levitt, S. R., & Nelson, R. A. (2012). Public relations and reputations management in a crisis situation: How Denny's restaurants reinvigorated the firm's corporate identity. In T. W. Coombs & S. J. Holladay's (Eds.), *The handbook of crisis communication* (pp. 359–377). Oxford, UK: Wiley Blackwell.

Kanter, R. M. (1992). Power failure in management circuits. In J. M. Shafritz & J. S. Ott (Eds.), *Classics of organization theory* (3rd ed., pp. ix, 534). Pacific Grove, CA: Brooks/Cole.

Kark, R., Waismel-Manor, R., & Shamir, B. (2012). Does valuing androgyny and femininity lead to a female advantage? The relationship between gender-role, transformational leadership and identification. *The Leadership Quarterly, 23*(3), 620–640.

Karlin, S. (2005, February 1). Coffins to die for. *Fortune Small Business Magazine.* Retrieved December 5, 2009, from http://money.cnn.com/magazines/fsb/fsb_archive/2005/02/01/8250629/index.htm

Kashima, Y., Yamaguchi, S., Kim, U., Choi, S. C, Gelfand, M. J., & Yuki, M. (1995). Culture, gender, and self:

A perspective from individualism-collectivism research. *Journal of Personality and Social Psychology,* 925–937.

Katz, D., & Braly, K. (1935). Racial prejudice and racial stereotypes. *Journal of Abnormal and Social Psychology, 30,* 175–193.

Kearney, B. (2011, June 26). Denny's to pay $1.3 million to former employees. *The Daily Record.*

Kearney, E., Gebert, D., & Voelpel, S. (2009, June 1). When and how diversity benefits teams: The importance of team members' need for cognition. *Academy of Management Journal, 52*(3), 581–598.

Kellough, E. J. (2006). *Understanding affirmative action: Politics, discrimination, and the search for justice.* Washington, DC: Georgetown University Press.

Kennedy, S., Schrier, J., & Rogers, S. (1984). The price of our success: Our monocultural science. *American Psychologist, 39,* 996–997.

Kennedy Dubourdieu, E. (2007). From positive discrimination to equality of opportunity: Building cohesion in Britain another way? *Revue Française de Civilisation Britannique,* 51–64.

Kent, M., & Wade, P. (2015). Genetics against race: Science, politics and affirmative action in Brazil. *Social Studies of Science, 45*(6), 816–838.

Kenya fighting HIV/AIDS. Case Studies. (2012). Unilever. Retrieved from www.unilever.co.id/sustainability/casestudies/health-nutrition-hygiene/kenyafightinghivaids.aspx

Keyton, J., Cano, P., Clounch, T. L., Fischer, C. E., Howard, C., & Topp, S. S. (2012). Ethical storm or model workplace? In S. K. May (Ed.), *Case studies in organizational communication: Ethical perspectives and practices* (2nd ed., pp. 157–168). Thousand Oaks, CA: Sage.

Khaleeli, H. (2012, July 23). Sports hijabs help Muslim women to Olympic success. *The Guardian.*

Kidder, W., & Lempert, R. (2015). The mismatch myth in U.S. higher education: A synthesis of empirical evidence at the law school and undergraduate levels. In U. M. Jayakumar & L. M. Garces (Eds.), *Affirmative action and racial equity: Considering the evidence in Fisher to forge the path ahead* (pp. 105–129). New York: Routledge.

Kiernan, B. (2000, September 10). Australia's Aboriginal genocides. *Bangkok Post.*

Kim, H. K., Lee, U. H., & Kim, Y. H. (2015). The effect of workplace diversity management in a highly male-dominated culture. *Career Development International, 20*(3), 259–272.

Kim, Y. Y. (1988). On theorizing intercultural communication. In Y. Y. Kim & W. B. Gudykunst (Eds.), *Theories in intercultural communication* (pp. 11–21). Newbury Park, CA: Sage.

King, E. B., Dawson, J. F., West, M. A., Gilrane, V. L., Peddie, C. I., & Bastin, L. (2011). Why organizational and community diversity matter: Representativeness and the emergence of incivility and organizational performance. *Academy of Management Journal, 54*(6), 1103–1118.

King, R. B. (1999). Time spent in parenthood status among adults in the United States. *Demography, 36,* 377–385.

Kingfisher, C., & Goldsmith, M. (2001). Reforming women in the United States and Aotearoa/New Zealand: A comparative ethnography of welfare reform in global context. *American Anthropologist, 103*(3), 714–732.

Kirkman, B. L., Lowe, K. B., & Gibson, C. B. (2006). A quarter century of *Culture's consequences: A review of empirical research incorporating Hofstede's cultural values framework. Journal of International Business Studies, 37,* 285–320.

Kirkpatrick, D., Phillips, J. J., & Phillips, P. P. (2003, October). Getting results from diversity training—in dollars and cents. *HR Focus, 80*(10), 3–4.

Kirshnan, H. A. (2009). What causes turnover among women on top management teams? *Journal of Business Research, 62*(11), 1181–1186.

Kirton, G., & Greene, A. (2002). The dynamics of positive action in UK trade unions: The case of women and black members. *Industrial Relations Journal, 33,* 157–172.

Kitayama, S. (2002). Culture and basic psychological processes— Toward a system view of culture: Comment on Oyserman et al. *Psychological Bulletin, 128,* 89–96.

Klarsfeld, A., Booysen, L. A., Ng, E., Roper, I., & Tatli, A. (Eds.). (2014). *9.78 E+ 12: Country perspectives on diversity and equal treatment.* Cheltenham, England: Edward Elgar Publishing.

Klasen, S. (1999). *Does gender inequality reduce growth and development? Evidence from cross-country regressions.* World Bank. Retrieved September 12, 2004, from www.worldbank.org/gender/prr/ wp7.pdf

Knight, N., & Nisbett, R. E. (2007). Culture, class and cognition: Evidence from Italy. *Journal of Cognition and Culture, 7,* 283–291.

Kochan, T., Bezrukova, K., Ely, R., Jackson, S., & Joshi, A. (2003). The effects of diversity on business performance: Report of the diversity research network. *Human Resource Management, 42*(1), 3–21.

Konrad, A. M. (2003). Special issue introduction: Defining the domain of workplace diversity scholarship. *Group & Organization Management, 28*(4), 4–17.

Konrad, A. M., & Hartmann, L. (2001). Gender differences in attitudes toward affirmative action programs in Australia: Effects of beliefs, interests, and attitudes toward women. *Sex Roles, 45*(5/6), 415–432.

Kossek, E. E., Huber, M. S. Q., & Lerner, J. V. (2003). Sustaining work force inclusion and well-being of mothers on public assistance: Individual deficit and social ecology perspectives. *Journal of Vocational Behavior, 62*(1), 155–175.

Kossek, E. E., Huber-Yoder, M., Castellino, D., & Lerner, J. (1997). The working poor: Locked out of careers and the organizational mainstream? *Academy of Management Executive, 11*(1), 76–92.

Kossek, E. E., & Lobel, S. A. (1996a). Introduction: Transforming human resource systems to manage diversity: An introduction and orienting framework. In E. E. Kossek & S. A. Lobel (Eds.), *Managing diversity: Human resource strategies for transforming the workplace* (pp. 1–19). Cambridge, MA: Blackwell.

Kossek, E., & Lobel, S. (1996b). *Managing diversity: Human resource strategies for transforming the workplace.* Cambridge, MA: Blackwell.

Kossek, E. E., Lobel, S., & Brown, J. (2006). Human resource strategies to manage work force diversity: Examining "the business case." In A. M. Konrad, P. Prasad, & J. K. Pringle (Eds.), *Handbook of workplace diversity* (pp. 53–74). Thousand Oaks, CA: Sage.

Kossek, E. E., Pichler, S., Meece, D., & Barratt, M. (2008). Family, friend, neighbor child care providers and maternal well-being in low-income systems: An ecological social perspective. *Journal of Occupational and Organizational Psychology, 81,* 369–391.

Kossek, E. E., & Zonia, S. C. (1993). Assessing diversity climate: A field study of reactions to employer efforts to promote diversity. *Journal of Organizational Behavior, 14,* 61–81.

Kouchaki, M., & Wareham, J. (2015). Excluded and behaving unethically: Social exclusion, physiological responses, and unethical behavior. *Journal of Applied Psychology, 100*(2), 547–556.

Kramar, R. (1998). Managing diversity: Beyond affirmative action in Australia. *Women in Management Review, 13*(4), 133–146.

Kramar, R. (2012). Diversity management in Australia: A mosaic of concepts, practice and rhetoric. *Asia Pacific Journal of Human Resources, 50,* 245–261.

Krautil, F. (1995). Managing diversity in Esso Australia. In E. M. Davis & C. Harris (Eds.), *Making the link: Affirmative action and industrial relations.* Sydney, Australia: Affirmative Action Agency and Labour Management Studies Foundation.

Kray, L. J., Galinsky, A. D., & Thompson, L. (2002). Reversing the gender gap in negotiations: An exploration of stereotype regeneration. *Organizational Behavior and Human Decision Processes, 87*(2), 386–409.

Kreitz, P. A. (2008). Best practices for managing organizational diversity. *The Journal of Academic Librarianship, 34*(2), 101–120.

Krier, J. M. (2001). *Fair trade in Europe 2001: Facts and figures on the fair trade sector in 18 European countries.* Maastricht, the Netherlands: EFTA (European Fair Trade Association).

Kroeber, A. L., & Kluckhohn, C. (1952). *Culture: A critical review of concepts and definitions.* Cambridge, MA: Harvard University Press.

Kurowski, L. (2002). Cloaked culture and veiled diversity: Why theorists ignored early US workforce diversity. *Management Decision, 40*(2), 183–191.

Kyriakidou, O. (2011a). Gender, management and leadership. *Equality, Diversity and Inclusion: An International Journal, 31*(1), 4–9.

Kyriakidou, O. (2011b). Negotiating gendered identities through the process of identity construction: Women managers in engineering. *Equality, Diversity and Inclusion: An International Journal, 31*(1), 27–42.

La Siembra Co-Operative. (2015). *Trader of the year.* Retrieved from lasiembra.com/camino/la-sembras-awards

La Siembra Co-Operative. (n.d.-a). *Camino.* Retrieved August 31, 2012, from www.lasiembra.com/camino/

La Siembra Co-Operative. (n.d.-b). *Camino awards.* Retrieved August 31, 2012, from www.lasiembra.com/camino/en/camino-awards

La Siembra Co-Operative. (n.d.-c). *Fair trade.* Retrieved August 31, 2012, from www.lasiembra.com/camino/en/fairtrade

La Siembra Co-Operative. (n.d.-d). *Family farmers.* Retrieved from http://www.lasiembra.com/camino/en/family-farmers

La Siembra Co-Operative. (n.d.-e). *2012 international year of the co-op.* Retrieved August 31, 2012, from www.lasiembra.com/camino/en/2012-international-year-of-the-co-op

Labour Department, Government of Hong Kong. (2003). *Youth pre-employment training program.* Retrieved November 20, 2003, from www.yptp.com.hk/

Lai, Y., & Kleiner, B. H. (2001). How to conduct diversity training effectively. *Equal Opportunities International, 20*(5/6/7), 14–18.

Langevin seeks to author legislation to ban forced wearing of the abaya by American servicewomen in Saudi Arabia. (2002, May 8). Congressman Langevin [Press release]. Retrieved from www.house.gov/apps/list/press/ri02_langevin/050802abayaamend.htm

Larkey, L. K. (1996). Toward a theory of communicative interactions in culturally diverse workgroups. *Academy of Management Review, 21*(2), 463–491.

Lau, D. C., Lam, L. W., & Deutsch Salamon, S. (2008). The impact of relational demographics on perceived managerial trustworthiness: Similarity or norms? *The Journal of Social Psychology, 148*(2), 187–209.

Lau, D. C., & Murnighan, J. K. (1998). Demographic diversity and faultiness: The compositional dynamics of organizational groups. *Academy of Management Review, 23*(2), 325.

Laurent, A. (1984). The cultural diversity of Western conceptions of management. *International Studies of Management and Organizations, 13,* 75–96.

Lauring, J., & Selmer, J. (2010). Multicultural organizations: Common language and group cohesiveness. *International Journal of Cross Cultural Management, 10*(3), 267–284.

Lawler, E. E., III. (1992). *The ultimate advantage: Creating the high-involvement organization.* San Francisco: Jossey-Bass.

Lawler, E. E., III. (2008). *Talent: Making people your competitive advantage.* San Francisco: Jossey-Bass.

Leane, G. W. G. (2011). Rights of ethnic minorities in liberal democracies: Has France gone too far in banning Muslim women from wearing the burka? *Human Rights Quarterly, 33*(4), 1032–1061.

Leary, M. R. (2010). Affiliation, acceptance, and belonging: The pursuit of interpersonal connection. In S. Fiske, D. T. Gilbert, & G. Lindzey (Eds.), *Handbook of social psychology.* New York: Wiley.

Leary, M. R., & Baumeister, R. F. (2000). The nature and function of self-esteem: Sociometer theory. *Advances in Experimental Social Psychology, 32,* 1–62.

Leary, M. R., & Downs, D. L. (1995). Interpersonal functions of the self-esteem motive: The self-esteem system as a sociometer. In M. H. Kernis (Ed.), *Efficacy, agency, and self-esteem.* New York: Plenum.

Leary, M. R., Schreindorfer, L. S., & Haupt, A. L. (1995). The role of low self-esteem in emotional and behavioral problems: Why is low self-esteem dysfunctional? *Journal of Social and Clinical Psychology, 14*(3), 297–314.

Lee, C. M., & Gudykunst, W. B. (2001). Attraction to interethnic interactions. *International Journal of Intercultural Relations, 25,* 373–387.

Lee, H. (2012). Affirmative action in Malaysia: Education and employment outcomes since the 1990s. *Journal of Contemporary Asia, 42,* 230–254.

Lee, K., Tams, S., Scott, K. L., & Schippers, M. C. (2015). Opening the black box: Why and when workplace exclusion affects social reconnection behaviour, health, and attitudes. *European Journal of Work and Organizational Psychology, 24*(2), 239–217.

Lee, M. (1997). Why do some women participate in the labor force while others stay at home? *Korea Journal of Population and Development, 26*(2), 33–54.

Lee, S., Juon, H., Martinez, G., Hsu, C. E., Robinson, E. S., Bawa, J., et al. (2009). Model minority at risk: Expressed needs of mental health by Asian American young adults. *Journal of Community Health, 34*(2), 144–152.

Leiter, S., & Leiter, W. M. (2011). *Affirmative action in antidiscrimination law and policy: An overview and synthesis* (2nd ed.). Albany: State University of New York Press.

Lengnick-Hall, M. L., Gaunt, P. M., & Kulkarni, M. (2008). Overlooked and underutilized: People with disabilities are an untapped human resource. *Human Resource Management, 47*(2), 255–273.

Lennox, C., & Waiters, M. (2013). *Human rights, sexual orientation and gender identity in the commonwealth: Struggles for decriminalisation and change.* Retrieved March 27, 2016, from http://sas-space.sas .ac.uk/4824/#undefined

Lent, R. (1970). Binocular resolution and perception of race in the United States. *British Journal of Psychology, 61*, 521–533.

Lestaeghe, R. (2010). The unfolding story of the second demographic transition. *Population and Development Review, 36*(2), 211–252.

Leung, A. K.-Y., Chiu, C.-Y., & Hong, Y.-Y. (Eds.). (2011). *Cultural processes.* New York: Cambridge University Press.

Lev, M. A. (1997, September 21). The sexism stain at Mitsubishi. *Chicago Tribune.* Retrieved from http:// articles.chicagotribune.com/1997- 09-21/news/9709210157_1_sexual- harassment-mitsubishi-motors- japanese-experts

Levy, B. R., & Leifheit-Limson, E. (2009). The stereotype-matching effect: Greater influence on functioning when age stereotypes correspond to outcomes. *Psychology and Aging, 24*(1), 230–233.

Levy, S. R. (1999). Reducing prejudice: Lessons from social- cognitive factors underlying perceiver differences in prejudice. *Journal of Social Issues, 55*(4), 745–765.

Li, S. X., Dogan, K., & Haruvy, E. (2011). Group identity in markets. *International Journal of Industrial Organization, 29*, 104–115.

Libertella, A., Sora, A., & Natale, S. (2007). Affirmative action policy and changing views. *Journal of Business Ethics, 74*, 65–71.

Liden, R. C., & Maslyn, J. (1998). Multidimensionality of leader- member exchange: An empirical assessment through scale development. *Journal of Management, 24*(1), 43–72.

Liden, R. C., Sparrow, R. T., & Wayne, S. J. (1997). Leader-member exchange theory: The past and potential for the future. *Research in Personnel and Human Resources Management, 75*, 47–119.

Linder, M. (1992). *Migrant workers and minimum wages: Regulating the exploitation of agricultural labor in the United States.* Boulder, CO: Westview Press.

Linnehan, F., & Konrad, A. M. (1999). Diluting diversity: Implications for intergroup inequality in organizations. *Journal of Management Inquiry, 8*(4), 399–414.

Linnehan, F., Konrad, A., Reitman, F., Greenhalgh, A., & London, M. (2003). Behavioral goals for a diverse organization: The effects of attitudes, social norms, and racial identity for Asian Americans and Whites. *Journal of Applied Social Psychology, 33*(7), 1331–1359.

Linville, P. W., Fischer, G. W., & Salovey, P. (1989). Perceived distributions of characteristics of ingroup and outgroup members: Empirical evidence and a computer simulation. *Journal of Personality and Social Psychology, 57*(2), 165–188.

Littrell, R. F., & Nkomo, S. M. (2005). Gender and race differences in leader behavior preferences in South Africa. *Women in Management Review, 20*(8), 562–580.

Lock up gays, says Ugandan president. (1999, September 29). BBC News. Retrieved September 14, 2003, from http://news.bbc.co.uk/1/hi/ world/africa/460893.stm

Locksley, A., Ortiz, V., & Hepburn, C. (1980). Social categorization and discriminatory behavior: Extinguishing the minimal intergroup discrimination effect. *Journal of Personality and Social Psychology, 39*, 773–783.

Lonsmann, D. (2014). Linguistic diversity in the international workplace: Language ideologies and processes of exclusion. *Multilingua, 33*(1-2), 89–116.

Lopez, S. H., Hodson, R., & Roscigno, V. J. (2009). Power, status, and abuse at work: General and sexual harassment compared. *The Sociological Quarterly, 50*, 3–27.

Lowery, B. S., Hardin, C. D., & Sinclair, S. (2001). Social influence effects on automatic racial prejudice. *Journal of Personality and Social Psychology, 81*(5), 842–855.

Lucas, O., & Jarman, N. (2016, February 19). Poverty and ethnicity: Key messages for Northern Ireland. York, England: Joseph Rowntree Foundation.

Lutz, H., Herrera Vivar, M. T., & Supik, L. (2011). Framing intersectionality. In H. Lutz, M. T. Herrera Vivar, & L. Supik (Eds.), *Framing intersectionality: Debates on a multi-faceted concept in gender studies.* Burlington, VT; Ashgate.

Lutz, W., & Goujon, A. (2001). The world's changing human capital stock. *Population and Development Review, 27*(2), 323–339.

Lutz, W., & Gui, Y. C. (2000). *China's unfolding educational revolution.* International Institute for Applied Systems Analysis, POPNET, No. 33.

Lynch, F. R. (2001). *The diversity machine: The drive to change the white male workplace.* New Brunswick, NJ: Transaction Publishers.

Ma, A. (2016). Meet the Syrian YouTube star who's making Germany laugh. *The Huffington Post.* Retrieved June 14, 2016, from http://www.huffingtonpost.com/entry/firas-alshater-zukar-asylum-seeker-video-series_us_56b4c783e4b04f9b57d94a16

Maatman, G. L. (2000, September 11). Harassment, discrimination laws go global. *National Underwriter,* 34–35.

Maatman, M. E. (2015, December 24). Echoes from the segregationist past at oral argument. *The News Journal* (Wilmington DE), p. A13.

MacDonald, G., & Leary, M. R. (2005). Why does social exclusion hurt? The relationship between social and physical pain. *Psychological Bulletin, 131*(2), 202–223.

MacInnis, C. C., & Page-Gould, E. (2015). How can intergroup interaction be bad if intergroup contact is good? Exploring and reconciling an apparent paradox in the science of intergroup relations. *Perspectives on Psychological Science, 10*(3), 307–327.

Macintyre, S. (2016). *A concise history of Australia* (Cambridge Concise Histories). (4th ed.). Cambridge, England: Cambridge University Press.

MacPherson, K. (2004, March 27). Kaptur criticizes overseas phone jobs. *Toledo Blade.* Retrieved from www.toledoblade.com/Politics/2004/03/27

Madera, J. M. (2013). Best practices in diversity management in customer service organizations: An investigation of top companies cited by Diversity Inc. *Cornell Hospitality Quarterly, 54*(2), 124–135.

Madley, B. (2008). From terror to genocide: Britain's Tasmanian penal colony and Australia's history wars. *Journal of British Studies, 47,* 77–106.

Madlock, P. E. (2012). The influence of cultural congruency, communication, and work alienation on employee satisfaction and commitment in Mexican organizations. *Western Journal of Communication, 76*(4), 380–396.

Makower, J. (1995). *Beyond the bottom line: Putting social responsibility to work for your business and the world.* New York: Simon & Schuster.

Malaysia: Improving biodiversity at our palm oil plantations. (2003). Unilever. Retrieved December 3, 2003, from www.unilever.com/environmentsociety/environmentalcasestudies/biodiversity/Malaysia_PalmOil.asp

Malaysian Labour Law: Regulation of Employment. (n.d.). Retrieved June 9, 2012, from http://my.jobsdb.com/my/en/v6html/jobseeker/handbook/regulation-of-employment/sexual-harassment_4.htm

Mangaliso, M. P. (2001). Building competitive advantage from Ubuntu: Management lessons from South Africa. *Academy of Management Executive, 15*(3), 23–33.

Mann, S. (1999). *Hiding what we feel, faking what we don't.* New York: HarperCollins.

Manoharan, A., Gross, M. J., & Sardeshmukh, S. R. (2014). Identity-conscious vs. identity-blind: Hotel managers' use of formal and informal diversity management practices. *International Journal of Hospitality Management, 41,* 1–9.

Manton, K. G., Corder, L., & Stallard, E. (1997, March 18). Chronic disability trends in elderly United States populations: 1982–1994. *Proceedings of the National Academy of Sciences, USA, 94*(6), 2593–2598.

Manton, K. G., & Gu, X. (2001). Changes in the prevalence of chronic disability in the United States black and nonblack population above age 65 from 1982 to 1999. *PNAS, 98*(11), 6354–6359.

Manton, K. G., Gu, X., & Lowrimore, G. R. (2008). Cohort changes in active life expectancy in the U.S. elderly population: Experience from the 1982–2004 National Long-Term Care Survey. *Journals of Gerontology, Series B: Psychological Sciences and Social Sciences, 63,* P269–P281. doi:10.1093/geronb/63.5.S269

Manurung, E. G. T. (2002, October 9). Loss from oil palm estates. *Jakarta Post.* Retrieved August 31, 2009, from www.thejakartapost.com/search/news/loss+from+ oil+palm+estates

Maranto, C. L., & Griffin, A. E. C. (2011). The antecedents of a "chilly climate" for women faculty in higher education. *Human Relations, 64*(2), 139–159.

Markus, H., & Kitayama, S. (1991). Culture and the self: Implications for cognition, emotion, and motivation. *Psychological Review, 98*(2), 224–253.

Marmenout, K., & Lirio, P. (2014). Local female talent retention in the Gulf: Emirati women bending with the wind. *The International Journal of Human Resource Management, 25*(2), 144–166.

Marquis, J. P., Lim, N., Scott, L. M., Harrell, M. C., & Kavanagh, J. (2008). Managing diversity in corporate America: An exploratory analysis. *Occasional Paper, Labor and Population.* Santa Monica, CA: RAND.

Marriott International, Inc. (2014). *The world's favorite travel company.* Retrieved from http://files.shareholder.com/downloads/MAR/1014994386x0x819614/987062c0-247a

-422a-b2ee-5a76ff60e1ed/Marriott_2014AR.pdf

Marriott International, Inc. (2015). *Global diversity and inclusion*. Retrieved from http://www.marriott.com/diversity/cultural-diversity.mi

Martin, P. L. (1994). Germany: Reluctant land of immigration. In W. A. Cornelius, J. F. Hollifield, & P. L. Martin (Eds.), *Controlling immigration: A global perspective* (pp. 189–225). Stanford, CA: Stanford University Press.

Martin, R. L. (2003). The virtue matrix: Calculating the return on corporate social responsibility. In *Harvard Business Review on Corporate Responsibility*. Boston: Harvard Business School Press.

Martin, R., Thomas, G., Charles, K., Epitropaki, O., & McNamara, R. (2005). The role of leader-member exchanges in mediating the relationship between locus of control and work reactions. *J. Occupational and Organizational Psychology, 78*, 141–147.

Martinez Lucio, M., & Perrett, R. (2009). The diversity and politics of trade unions' responses to minority ethnic and migrant workers: The context of the UK. *Economic and Industrial Democracy, 30*, 324–347.

Martins, L. (2015). HR leaders hold the key to effective diversity management. *Human Resource Management International Digest, 23*(5), 49–53.

Martins, V. A., & Martins, M. R. (2012). Outsourcing operations in project management offices: The reality of Brazilian companies. *Project Management Journal, 43*(2), 68–83.

Massey, D. S., Arango, J., Hugo, G., Kouaouci, A., Pellegrino, A., & Taylor, J. E. (2005). *Worlds in motion: Understanding international migration at the end of the millennium*. New York: Oxford University Press.

Matz-Costa, C., Carapinha, R., & Pitt-Catsouphes, M. (2012). Putting age in context: Relational age and inclusion at the workplace. *Indian Journal of Gerontology, 26*(1), 50–74.

Matz-Costa, C., Pitt-Catsouphes, M., Besen, E., & Lynch, K. (2009). *The difference of downturn can make: Assessing the early effects of the economic crisis on the employment experiences of workers* (Issue Brief No. 22). Boston: Boston College.

Maurer, V. G. (2009). Corporate social responsibility and the "divided corporate self": The case of Chiquita in Colombia. *Journal of Business Ethics, 88*(4), 595–603.

McBride, A., Hebson, G., & Holgate, J. (2015). Intersectionality: Are we taking enough notice in the field of work and employment relations? *Work, Employment & Society, 29*(2), 331.

McCall, G. J., Ngeva, J., & Mbebe, M. (1997). Mapping conflict cultures: Interpersonal disputing in a South African black township. *Human Organization, 56*(1), 71–78.

McDonald, F., & Potton, M. (1997). The nascent European policy towards older workers: Can the European Union help the older worker? *Personnel Review, 26*(4), 293–306.

McDonald, S. (2011). What you know or who you know? Occupation-specific work experience and job matching through social networks. *Social Science Research, 40*(6), 1664–1675.

McDonald, S., Lin, N., & Ao, D. (2009). Networks of opportunity: Gender, race, and job leads. *Social Problems, 56*(3), 385–402.

McElhaney, K. A. (2008). *Just good business: The strategic guide to aligning corporate responsibility and brand*. San Francisco: Berrett-Koehler Publishers.

McGoldrick, D. (2006). *Human rights and religion: The Islamic headscarf in Europe*. London: Hart Publishing.

McGregor, J. (2006). The pervasive power of man-made news. *Pacific Journalism Review, 12*(1), 21–34.

McGregor, J., & Gray, L. (2002). Stereotypes and older workers: The New Zealand experience. *Social Policy Journal of New Zealand, 18*, 163–177.

McGuire, D., & Bagher, M. (2010). Diversity training in organisations: An introduction. *Journal of European Industrial Training, 34*, 493–505.

McGuire, G. M. (2000). Gender, race, ethnicity, and networks: The factors affecting the status of employee's network members. *Work and Occupation, 27*(4), 501–523.

McKay, P. F., & Avery, D. R. (2015). Diversity climate in organizations: Current wisdom and domains of uncertainty. *Research in Personnel and Human Resources Management, 33*, 191–233.

McKay, P. F., Avery, D. R., & Morris, M. A. (2008). Mean racial-ethnic differences in employee sales performance: The moderating role of diversity climate. *Personnel Psychology, 61*(2), 349–374.

McKay, P. F., Avery, D. R., & Morris, M. A. (2009). A tale of two climates: Diversity climate from subordinates' and managers' perspectives and their role in store unit sales performance. *Personnel Psychology, 62*(4), 767–791.

McKay, P. F., Avery, D. R., Tonidandel, S., Morris, M. A., Herandez, M., & Hebl, M. R. (2007). Racial differences in employee retention: Are diversity climate perceptions the key? *Personnel Psychology, 60*(1), 35–62.

McMahon, A. M. (2010). Does workplace diversity matter? A survey of empirical studies on diversity management and firm performance,

2000–2009. *Journal of Diversity Management, 5,* 37–48.

McPherson, M., Smith-Lovin, L., & Cook, J. M. (2001). Birds of a feather: Homophily in social networks. *Annual Review of Sociology, 27,* 415–444.

McSweeney, B. (2002). Hofstede's model of national cultural differences and their consequences: A triumph of faith—a failure of analysis. *Human Relations, 55*(1), 89–118.

Mead, G. H. (1982). In D. Miller (Ed.), *The individual and the social self: Unpublished works of George Herbert Mead.* Chicago: University of Chicago Press.

Mead, M. (2001). *Sex and temperament in three primitive societies.* New York: HarperCollins. (Original work published 1935)

Mead, N. L., Baumeister, R. F., Stillman, T. F., Rawn, C. D., & Vohs, K. D. (2011). Social exclusion causes people to spend and consume strategically in the service of affiliation. *Journal of Consumer Research, 37*(5), 902–919.

Menke, I., & Langer, P. C. (Eds.). (2011, March). Muslim service members in non-Muslim countries: Experiences of difference in the armed forces in Austria, Germany and the Netherlands. *Forum International, 29.*

Merriam-Webster's collegiate dictionary (11th ed.). (2002). *Discrimination.* Springfield, MA: Merriam- Webster.

Meyer, J. W., & Rowan, B. (1977). Institutionalized organizations: Formal structure as myth and ceremony. *American Journal of Sociology, 83,* 340–363.

Michalopoulos, C., Edin, K., Fink, B., Landriscina, M., Polit, D., Polyne, J., et al. (2003). *Welfare reform in Philadelphia: Implementation, effects, experiences of poor families and neighborhoods.* New York: Manpower Demonstration and Research Corporation.

Microaggressions. (n.d.). Retrieved from http://www.microaggressions .com/

Migration Policy Institute. (2012, November 15). *Belgium: A country of permanent immigration.* Retrieved March 26, 2016, from http://www .migrationpolicy.org/article/belgium-country-permanent-immigration

The Millennial beard: Why boomers need their younger counterparts. (2015, December 3). *Time Magazine.* Retrieved March 27, 2016, from www .time.com/4134381/millennials-boomers-workplace-dependency/

Milliken, F. J., & Martins, L. L. (1996). Searching for common threads: Understanding the multiple effects of diversity in organizational groups. *The Academy of Management Review, 21*(2), 402–433.

Ministry of Labor in Korea. (n.d.). *The Act on Equal Employment and Support for Work-Family Reconciliation.* Retrieved November 30, 2012, from www.moel.go.kr/ english/topic/laborlaw_view .jsp?tab=Equal&idx=224

Minkov, M., & Hofstede, G. (2011). The evolution of Hofstede's doctrine. *Cross Cultural Management: An International Journal, 18*(1), 10–20.

Mississippi University for Women v. Hogan, 458 U.S. 718 (1982).

Mitchell, R., Boyle, B., Parker, V., Giles, M., Chiang, V., & Joyce, P. (2015). Managing inclusiveness and diversity in teams: How leader inclusiveness affects performance through status and team identity. *Human Resource Management, 54*(2), 217–239.

Moffatt, M. (2015). *An untouchable community in South India: Structure and consensus.* Princeton, NJ: Princeton University Press.

Molinsky, A. L. (2005). Language fluency and the evaluation of cultural faux pas: Russians interviewing for jobs in the United States. *Social Psychology Quarterly, 68*(2), 103–120.

Moore, S. (1999). Understanding and managing diversity among groups at work: Key issues for organisational training and development. *Journal of European Industrial Training, 23*(4/5), 208.

Mor Barak, M. E. (2000a). Beyond affirmative action: Toward a model of organizational inclusion. In M. E. Mor Barak & D. Bargal (Eds.), *Social services in the workplace.* New York: Haworth.

Mor Barak, M. E. (2000b). The inclusive workplace: An eco-systems approach to diversity management. *Social Work, 45*(4), 339–354.

Mor Barak, M. E. (2005). *Managing diversity: Toward a globally inclusive workplace.* Thousand Oaks, CA: Sage.

Mor Barak, M. E. (2011). *Managing diversity: Toward a globally inclusive workplace* (2nd ed.). Thousand Oaks, CA: Sage.

Mor Barak, M. E. (2014). *Managing diversity: Toward a globally inclusive workplace* (3rd ed.). Thousand Oaks, CA: Sage Publications.

Mor Barak, M. E. (2015, January). Inclusion is the key to diversity management, but what is inclusion? *Human Service Organizations Management, 39*(2), 83–88.

Mor Barak, M. E., & Brimhall, K. C. (2015). *Inclusive leadership and climate for inclusion: A conceptual model of transformational leadership in diverse teams.* Manuscript in progress.

Mor Barak, M. E., & Cherin, O. A. (1998). A tool to expand organizational understanding of workforce diversity: Exploring a measure of inclusion-exclusion. *Administration in Social Work, 22*(1), 47–65.

Mor Barak, M. E., Cherin, D. A., & Berkman, S. (1998). Ethnic and gender differences in employee diversity perceptions: Organizational and personal dimensions. *Journal of Applied Behavioral Sciences, 34*(1), 82–104.

Mor Barak, M. E., Findler, L., & Wind, L. (2001). International dimensions of diversity, inclusion, and commitment in work organizations. *Journal of Behavioral and Applied Management, 2*(2), 72–91.

Mor Barak, M. E., Findler, L., & Wind, L. (2003). Cross-cultural aspects of diversity and well-being in the workplace: An international perspective. *Journal of Social Work Research and Evaluation, 4*(2), 49–73.

Mor Barak, M. E., & Levin, A. (2002). Outside of the corporate mainstream and excluded from the work community: A study of diversity, job satisfaction and well-being. *Community, Work & Family, 5*(2), 133–157.

Mor Barak, M. E., Levin, A., Nissly, J. A., & Lane, C. J. (2006). Why do they leave? Modeling child welfare workers' turnover intentions. *Children and Youth Services Review, 28,* 548–577.

Mor Barak, M. E., & Travis, D. J. (2010). Diversity and organizational performance. In Y. Hasenfeld (Ed.), *Human services as complex organizations* (pp. 341–378). Thousand Oaks, CA: Sage.

More rivers in the country are polluted, says law. (2002, July 20). Bernama: The Malaysian National News Agency.

Moreton-Robinson, A. (2011). The White man's burden: Patriarchal White epistemic violence and aboriginal women's knowledge within the academy. *Australian Feminist Studies, 26*(70), 413–431.

Morris, M. W., Podolny, J., & Sullivan, B. N. (2008, July–August). *Organization Science, 19*(4), 517–532.

Moscovici, S. (1972). Society and theory in social psychology. In J. Israel & H. Tajfel (Eds.), *The context of social psychology* (pp. 17–68). London: Academic.

Moses, M. S. (2010). Moral and instrumental rationales for affirmative action in five national contexts. *Educational Researcher, 39,* 211–228.

Mosle, A. (2012, April 13). The quiet sounds of power. *The Huffington Post.* Retrieved from http://www .huffingtonpost.com/anne-mosle/ virginia-rometty_b_1423794.html

The most powerful women in business. (2012). *Fortune.* Retrieved from http://fortune.com/most-powerful-women/2014/ginni-rometty-1/

Moussouris v. Microsoft Corporation (2015).

Muller, H. J., & Parham, P. A. (1998). Integrating workforce diversity into the business school curriculum: An experiment. *Journal of Management Education, 22*(2), 122.

Murphy, S. E., & Ensher, E. A. (1999). The effects of leader and subordinate characteristics in the development of leader-member exchange quality. *Journal of Applied Social Psychology, 29,* 1371–1394.

Mussweiler, T., & Strack, F. (2000). The "relative self": Informational and judgmental consequences of comparative self-evaluation. *Journal of Personality and Social Psychology, 79,* 23–38.

A Muslim woman beat Abercrombie & Fitch. Why her Supreme Court victory is a win for all Americans. (2015, June 1). *The Washington Post.* Retrieved from http://www. washingtonpost.com/news/acts-of-faith/wp/2015/06/01/a-muslim-woman-beat-abercrombie-fitch-why-her-supreme-court-victory-is-a-win-for-all-americans/

Muttarak, R., Hamill, H., Heath, A., & McCrudden, C. (2013).

Does affirmative action work? Evidence from the operation of fair employment legislation in Northern Ireland. *Sociology, 47*(3), 560–579.

Myrskylä, M., Goldstein, J. R., & Cheng, Y. A. (2013). New cohort fertility forecasts for the developed world: Rises, falls, and reversals. *Population and Development Review, 39*(1), 31–56.

NAACP. (2012). *Cogdell v. Wet Seal.* Retrieved March 24, 2016, from http://www.naacpldf.org/case-issue/ cogdell-v-wet-seal

Nadal, K. L. (2012). Subtle and overt forms of islamophobia: Microaggressions toward Muslim Americans. *Journal of Muslim Mental Health, 6*(2), 15–37.

Nadal, K. L., Davidoff, K. C., Davis, L. S., Wong, Y., Marshall, D., & McKenzie, V. (2015). A qualitative approach to intersectional microaggressions: Understanding influences of race, ethnicity, gender, sexuality, and religion. *Qualitative Psychology, 2*(2), 147–163.

Nahrgang, J. D., Morgeson, F. P., & Ilies, R. (2009). The development of leader-member exchange: Exploring how personality and performance influence leader and member relationships over time. *Organizational Behavior and Human Decision Processes, 108,* 256–266.

Narayanan, J., Tai, K., & Kinias, Z. (2013). Power motivates interpersonal connection following social exclusion. *Organizational Behavior and Human Decision Processes, 122*(2), 257–265.

Nath, D. (2000). Gently shattering the glass ceiling: Experiences of Indian women managers. *Women in Management Review, 15*(1), 44–55.

National Gay and Lesbian Task Force. (2012). Retrieved June 5, 2012, from www.thetaskforce.org/reports_and_ research/nondiscrimination_laws

Native American Professional Network. (n.d.). *A culture of diversity and inclusion*. Retrieved from http://about.bankofamerica.com/en-us/global-impact/native-american-professional-network.html#fbid=HKaL_BNC_1B

NATLEX, International Labour Organization. (n.d.). Retrieved April 30, 2004, from www.ilo.org/dyn/natlex/natlex_browse.home

Nazario, S. (2002, September 29). Enrique's journey. *The Los Angeles Times*, pp. A1–A10.

Nazario, S. (2007). *Enrique's journey: A story of a boy's dangerous odyssey to reunite with his mother*. New York: Random House.

Nazario, S. (2014). Enrique's journey. *Update on the family*. Retrieved March 26, 2016, from http://www.enriquesjourney.com/about-the-family/update-2/

Neale, J., & Özkanli, O. (2010). Organisational barriers for women in senior management: A comparison of Turkish and New Zealand universities. *Gender and Education, 22*(5), 547–563.

Nelson, S. S. (2003, December 10). Turkish women fighting head-scarf ban. *Knight Ridder/Tribune News Service*.

Nembhard, I. M., & Edmondson, A. C. (2006). Making it safe: The effects of leader inclusiveness and professional status on psychological safety and improvement efforts in health care teams. *Journal of Organizational Behavior, 27*, 941–966. doi:10.1002/job.413

Nestlé. (2011a). *Annual report: The world's leading nutrition, health and wellness company*. Retrieved August 18, 2012, from www.nestle.com/Common/NestleDocuments/Documents/Library/Documents/Annual_Reports/2011-Annual-Report-EN.pdf

Nestlé. (2011b). *Nestle creating shared value report 2011*. Retrieved August 17, 2012, from www.nestle.com/Common/NestleDocuments/Documents/Library/Documents/Corporate_Social_Responsibility/2011-CSV-Report.pdf

Nestlé. (2014). *Annual Report 2014*. Retrieved from https://www.nestle.com/asset-library/documents/library/documents/annual_reports/2014-annual-report-en.pdf

Nestlé Foundation. (2012). *About the foundation*. Retrieved August 17, 2012, from www.nestlefoundation.org/e/about.html

Nestlé Foundation. (2014). Retrieved from file:///C:/Users/morbarak/Documents/Book%20e4%20edition/Revised%20book%20chapters/Chapter%2014/Nestle%20AnnualReport2014.pdf

Nestlé in Society. (2014). *Nestlé in society summary report 2014*. Retrieved from http://www.nestle.com/asset-library/documents/library/documents/corporate_social_responsibility/nestle-in-society-summary-report-2014-en.pdf

Neuliep, J. W. (2008). *Intercultural communication: A contextual approach* (4th ed.). Thousand Oaks, CA: Sage.

Neuman, E., Sanchez-Burks, J., Goh, K., & Ybarra, O. (2004). *Cultural theories about conflict and team performance among European Americans* (working paper). Ann Arbor: University of Michigan.

New Economy Development Group. (2006, January 5). La Siembra Co-Operative, Inc.—Balancing social justice and business principles. Retrieved August 31, 2012, from www.coop.gc.ca/COOP/display-afficher.do?id=1235072330684&lang=eng#t1

New Zealand Ministry of Social Development. (2009). *The social report 2009*. Wellington: Ministry of Social Development.

Ng, K., Van Dyne, L., & Ang, S. (2009). From experience to experiential learning: Cultural intelligence as a learning capability for global leader development. *Academy Of Management Learning & Education, 8*(4), 511–526.

Nica, E. (2013). Organizational culture in the public sector. *Economics, Management and the Financial Markets, 8*(2), 179–184.

Nigeria—Watchdog goes back to school. (2002, October 8). *AllAfrica, Inc. Africa News*. LexisNexis Academic. Retrieved from http://web.lexis-nexis.com/universe

Nisbett, R. E., & Miyamoto, Y. (2005). The influence of culture: Holistic versus analytic perception. *Trends in Cognitive Sciences, 9*(10), 467–473.

Nisbett, R. E., Peng, K., Choi, I., & Norenzayan, A. (2001). Culture and systems of thought: Holistic versus analytic cognition. *Psychological Review, 108*(2), 291–310.

Nishii, L. H. (2013). The benefits of climate for inclusion for gender-diverse groups. *Academy of Management Journal, 56*(6), 1754–1774.

Nishii, L. H., & Mayer, D. M. (2009). Do inclusive leaders help reduce turnover in diverse groups? The moderating role of leader-member exchange in the diversity to turnover relationship. *Journal of Applied Psychology, 94*, 1412–1426.

Nixon, J. C., & West, J. F. (2000). American addresses work force diversity. *Business Forum, 25*(1/2), 4.

Nkomo, S. (2001, July). *Much to do about diversity: The muting of race, gender and class in managing diversity practice*. Paper presented at the International Cross-Cultural Perspectives on Workforce Diversity: The Inclusive Workplace, Bellagio, Italy.

Nkomo, S., & Cox, T., Jr. (1996). Diverse identities in organizations.

In S. R. Clegg, C. Hardy, & W. R. Nord (Eds.), *Handbook of organizations studies* (pp. 338–356). London: Sage.

No Ceilings Report: The Full Participation Project. (2015). The Economic Intelligence Unit & World Policy Analysis Center. Retrieved from No Ceilings, noceilings.org/report/report.pdf.

North Carolina passes law blocking measures to protect LGBT people. (2016). NPR. Retrieved March 25, 2016, from http://www.npr.org/sections/thetwo-way/2016/03/24/471700323/north-carolina-passes-law-blocking-measures-to-protect-lgbt-people

Northern and Central Land Councils. (2001, January 19). *Media release: Land Councils and Eurest in benchmark agreement for Aboriginal employment on the railway project.* Casuarina and Alice Springs, NT, Australia: Authors. Retrieved February 27, 2004, from www.nlc.org.au/html/files/01_01_railway.pdf

Northern Ireland Assembly. (2012, August 10). *Fair employment in Northern Ireland: The decades of change (1990–2010).* Research and Information Service Research Paper 121/12.

Norusis, M. J. (1993). *SPSS for Windows, release 6.0.* Chicago: SPSS.

Number of female "Fortune" 500 CEOs at record high. (2011, October 26). *USA Today.* Retrieved June 29, 2012, from www.usatoday.com/money/companies/management/story/2011-10-26/women-ceos-fortune-500-companies/50933224/1

Nurden, R. (1997, October 30). Teaching tailored for business people's every demand. *The European*, p. 9.

Nyambegera, S. M. (2002). Ethnicity and human resource management practice in sub-Saharan Africa: The relevance of the managing diversity discourse. *The International Journal of Human Resource Management, 13*(7), 1077–1090.

Obama's bow in Japan sparks some criticism. Conservative commentators accuse president of groveling to foreign leader. (2009, November 26). MSNBC News. Retrieved November 30, 2009, from www.msnbc.msn.com/id/33978533/ns/ politics-white_house/

O'Brien, M. (2009). Fathers, parental leave policies, and infant quality of life: International perspectives and policy impact. *The ANNALS of the American Academy of Political and Social Science, 624*(1), 190–213.

Ocholla, D. N. (2002). Diversity in the library and information workplace: A South African perspective. *Library Management, 23*(1/2), 59.

Offermann, L. R., Basford, T. E., Graebner, R., Basu DeGraaf, S., & Jaffer, S. (2013). Slights, snubs, and slurs: Leader equity and microaggressions. *Equality, Diversity and Inclusion: An International Journal, 32*(4), 374–393.

Offermann, L. R., Basford, T. E., Graebner, R., Jaffer, S., De Graaf, S. B., & Kaminsky, S. E. (2014). See no evil: Color blindness and perceptions of subtle racial discrimination in the workplace. *Cultural Diversity & Ethnic Minority Psychology, 20*(4), 499–507.

O'Keeffe, V. (2016, April). Saying and doing: CALD workers' experience of communicating safety in aged care. *Safety Science, 84*, 131–139.

Olden, D. R. (2015). Shifting the lens: Using critical race theory and Latino critical theory to re-examine the history of school desegregation. *Qualitative Inquiry, 21*(3), 250–261.

O'Leary, V. E., & Ickovics, J. R. (1992). Cracking the glass ceiling: Overcoming isolation and discrimination. In U. Sekeran & F. Leong (Eds.), *Womanpower: Managing in times of demographic turbulence* (pp. 7–30). Newbury Park, CA: Sage.

Olsen, J. E., & Martins, L. L. (2012). Understanding organizational diversity management programs: A theoretical framework and directions for future research. *Journal of Organizational Behavior, 33*(8), 1168–1187.

Olson, W. (1997, February). Framing Texaco: How lawyers and the *New York Times* concocted a scam. *The American Spectator.* Retrieved May 26, 2004, from http://walterolson.com/articles/texacotp.html

Ongori, H. (2012). Rhetoric and reality of disabilities management in organisations: A strategy to manage employee turnover. *International Journal of Learning & Development, 2*(1), 509–519.

O'Niell, B., Gidengil, E., Cote, C., & Young, L. (2015). Freedom of religion, women's agency and banning the face veil: The role of feminist beliefs in shaping women's opinion. *Ethnic and Racial Studies*, 1886–1901.

Organisation for Economic Co-operation and Development. (2000). *Trends in international migration* (Annual Report of the Continuous Reporting System on Migration, SOPEMI). Paris: OECD.

Organisation for Economic Co-operation and Development. (2009). *International migration outlook* (2008 ed.). Paris: OECD.

Organisation for Economic Co-operation and Development. (2010). *International migration outlook* (2010 ed.). Paris: OECD.

Organisation for Economic Co-operation and Development. (2011). *OECD FACTBOOK 2011.* Paris: Author.

Organisation for Economic Co-operation and Development.

(2013, October 3–4). *World migration in figures*. A joint contribution by UN-DESA and the OECD to the United Nations High-Level Dialogue on Migration and Development.

Organisation for Economic Co-operation and Development. (2014). *International migration outlook* (2014 ed.). Retrieved June 15, 2015, from http://www.oecd.org/migration/international-migration-outlook-1999124x.htm

Organisation for Economic Co-operation and Development. (2015, Sept.). *Is this humanitarian migration crisis different?* Retrieved from www.oecd.org/migration

Orlando, R. C. (2000). Racial diversity, business strategy, and firm performance: A resource-based view. *Academy of Management Journal, 43*(2), 164–177.

Orlitzky, M., Schmidt, F. L., & Rynes, S. L. (2003). Corporate social and financial performance: A meta-analysis. *Organization Studies, 24*(3), 403–431.

Ortman, J. M., Velkoff, V. A., & Hogan, H. (2014, May). *An aging nation: The older population in the United States population: Estimates and projections*. U.S.Census Bureau. Retrieved from http://www.census.gov/prod/2014pubs/p25-1140.pdf

Osborne, B. (2005). *Fair employment in Northern Ireland: A generation on*. Belfast, Northern Ireland: Blackstaff Press.

Oslo push for women directors. (2003, June 13). *BBC News*. Retrieved May 2004, from http://news.bbc.co.uk/1/hi/business/2988992.stm

Ovwigho, P. C., Saunders, C., & Born, C. E. (2008). Barriers to independence among TANF recipients: Comparing caseworker records and client surveys. *Administration in Social Work, 32*(3), 84–110.

Oyserman, D. (2013). Not just any path: Implications of identity-based motivation for disparities in school outcomes. *Economics of Education Review, 33*, 179–190.

Oyserman, D. (2015). *Pathways to success through identity-based motivation*. New York: Oxford University Press.

Oyserman, D. (2011). Culture as situated cognition: Cultural mindsets, cultural fluency, and meaning making. *European Review of Social Psychology, 22*(1), 164–214.

Oyserman, D., & Destin, M. (2010). Identity-based motivation: Implications for intervention. *The Counseling Psychologist, 38*, 1001–1043.

Oyserman, D., Destin, M., & Novin, S. (2015). The context-sensitive future self: Possible selves motivate in context, not otherwise. *Self and Identity, 14*(2), 173–188.

Oyserman, D., Smith, G. C., & Elmore, K. (2014). Identity-based motivation: Implications for health and health disparities. *Journal of Social Issues, 70*(2), 206–225.

Ozbilgin, M., & Tatli, A. (2008). *Global diversity management: An evidence based approach*. London: Palgrave Macmillan.

Ozgen, C., Nijkamp, P., & Poot, J. (2011). *The impact of cultural diversity on innovation: Evidence from Dutch firm-level data*. IZA Discussion Paper No. 6000. Retrieved from http://ssrn.com/abstract=1941152

Palmer, G. (2003). Diversity management, past, present and future. *Asia Pacific Journal of Human Resources, 41*(1), 13–24.

Palmi, P. (2001). The management of diversity in public administration: The European approach. *Economic Research, 14*(1), 49–58.

Pamuk, H. (2013, October 8). Turkey lifts generations-old ban on Islamic head scarf. Reuters.

Paolillo, A., Pasini, M., Silva, S. A., & Magnano, P. (2016). Psychometric properties of the Italian adaptation of the Mor Barak et al. diversity climate scale. *Quality & Quantity, 50*, 1–18. doi:10.1007/s11135-016-0316-3

Parham, P. A., & Muller, H. J. (2008). Review of workplace diversity content in organizational behavior texts. *Academy of Management Learning and Education, 7*(3), 424–428.

Park, K. (2008). "I can provide for my children": Korean immigrant women's changing perspectives on work outside the home. *Gender Issues, 25*(1), 26–42.

Park, S., Sturman, M. C., Vanderpool, C., & Chan, E. (2015). Only time will tell: The changing relationships between LMX, job performance, and justice. *Journal of Applied Psychology, 100*, 660-680.

Partnership for a New American Economy. (2012). *Not coming to America: Why the U.S. is falling behind in the global race for talent*. Retrieved May 23, 2012, from http://www.renewoureconomy.org/not-coming

Passel, J., Cohn, D., & Gonzalez-Barrera, A. (2012). *Net migration from Mexico falls to zero—and perhaps less*. Washington, DC: Pew Hispanic Center.

Patel, V. (2005). *A brief history of the battle against sexual harassment at the workplace*. Retrieved July 26, 2009, from http://infochangeindia.org/20051101160/Women/Analysis/A-brief-history-of-the-battle-against-sexual-harassment-at-the-workplace.html

Patrick, H. A., & Kumar, V. R. (2012). *Managing workplace diversity: Issues and challenges*. Thousand Oaks, CA: Sage.

Pekerti, A. A., & Thomas, D. C. (2003). Communication in intercultural interaction: An empirical investigation of idiocentric and sociocentric communication styles.

Journal of Cross-Cultural Psychology, 34(2), 139–154.

Pelleschi, A. (2016). *Transgender rights and issues*. Edina, MN: ABDO.

Penderson, M. H. (2012). Going on a class journey: The inclusion and exclusion of Iraqi refugees in Denmark. *Journal of Ethnic and Migration Studies, 38*(7), 1101–1117.

People Tree. (2001, July). *Company Newsletter*, 1 (London).

People Tree. (n.d.). *People Tree awards & recognition*. Retrieved from http://www.peopletree.co.uk/about-us/our-credentials/awards

Perez-Floriano, L. R., & Gonzalez, J. A. (2007). Risk, safety and culture in Brazil and Argentina: The case of TransInc Corporation. *International Journal of Manpower, 28*(5), 403–417.

Perraton, J., Goldblatt, D., Held, D., & McGrew, A. (2000). Economic activity in a globalizing world. In D. Held, A. McGrew (Ed.), *The global transformations reader*. Cambridge, England: Polity Press.

Perry, B. A. (2007). *The Michigan affirmative action cases*. Lawrence: University Press of Kansas.

Petersen, P., Saporta, I., & Seidel, M. L. (2000). Offering a job: Meritocracy and social networks. *American Journal of Sociology, 106*(3), 763–816.

Pettigrew, T. F. (1986). The intergroup contact hypothesis reconsidered. In M. Hewstone & R. Brown (Eds.), *Contact and conflict in intergroup encounters*. New York: Blackwell.

Pettigrew, T. F. (1998). Reactions toward the new minorities of western Europe. *Annual Review of Sociology, 24*, 77–103.

Pettigrew T. F., Allport, G. W., & Barnett, E. O. (1958). Binocular resolution and perception of race in South Africa. *British Journal of Psychology, 49*, 265–278.

Pettigrew, T. F., & Martin, J. (1989). Organizational inclusion of minority groups: A social psychological analysis. In J. P. Van Oudenhoven & T. M. Willemsen (Eds.), *Ethnic minorities: Social psychological perspectives*. Berwyn, PA: Swets North America.

Pettigrew, T. F., & Tropp, L. R. (2006). A meta-analytic test of intergroup contact theory. *Journal of Personality and Social Psychology, 90*, 751–783.

Pettigrew, T. F., Tropp, L. R., Wagner, U., & Christ, O. (2011). Recent advances in intergroup contact theory. *International Journal of Intercultural Relations, 35*(3), 271–280.

Pew Research Center. (2016). *The millennials*. Retrieved from http://www.pewresearch.org/topics/millennials/

Pfundmair, M., Graupmann, V., Frey, D., & Aydin, N. (2015). The different behavioral intentions of collectivists and individualists in response to social exclusion. *Personality and Social Psychology Bulletin, 41*(3), 363–378.

Phillips, M. (2002, May 22). Ghana's tech frontier, Internet start-up flourishes. *The Wall Street Journal*. Retrieved September 13, 2004, from www.busyinternet.com/site/about/pr/wsj/WSJ_com%20-%20Technology.htm

Pitt-Catsouphes, M., & Matz-Costa, C. (2009). *Engaging the 21st century multi-generational workforce: Findings from the age and generations study* (Issue Brief 20). Boston: Boston College. Retrieved July 26, 2012, from www.bc.edu/content/dam/files/research_sites/agingandwork/pdf/publications/IB20_Engagement.pdf

Pitt-Catsouphes, M., Matz-Costa, C., & Besen, E. (2009). *Age & generations: Understanding experience at the workplace* (Issue Brief 6). Boston: Boston College. Retrieved July 26, 2012, from www.bc.edu/content/dam/files/research_sites/agingandwork/pdf/publications/RH06_Age_Generations.pdf

Pitts, D. (2009). Diversity management, job satisfaction and performance: Evidence from U.S. federal agencies. *Public Administration Review, 69*(2), 328–338.

Plantation giants should plough back earnings, says PBS. (2003, July 13). Bernama: The Malaysian National News Agency. Retrieved September 13, 2004, from www.pbs-sabah.org/pbs3/html/news/2003/130703bernama.html

Point, S., & Singh, V., (2003). Defining and dimensionalising diversity: Evidence from corporate websites across Europe. *European Management Journal, 21*(6), 750–761.

Pollack, A. (1996, May 7). It's see no evil, have no harassment in Japan. *New York Times*. Retrieved from www.nytimes.com/1996/05/07/business/it-s-see-no-evil-have-no-harassment-in-japan.html?pagewanted=all&src=pm

Ponterotto, J. G., Utsey, S. O., & Pedersen, P. (2006). *Preventing prejudice: A guide for counselors, educators, and parents*. Thousand Oaks, CA: Sage.

Population Reference Bureau. (2011). *2011 World population data sheet*. Washington, DC: Author.

Population Reference Bureau. (2016). *Human Population: Population Growth*. Retrieved from www.prb.org/publications/Lesson-Plans/HumanPopulation/PopulationGrowth.aspx

Port Authority. (2000). *Port Authority to enhance social services it provides for homeless*. Retrieved December 15, 2003, from www.panynj.gov/pr/113-00.html

Port Authority of New York and New Jersey. (2004, April 13). *Port Authority* renews partnership with urban pathways. Press Release Number: 43-2004.

Porter, L., & Lawler, E. E., III. (1968). *Managerial attitudes and performance.* Homewood, IL: Irwin.

Posthuma, R. A., & Campion, M. A. (2009). Workplace age stereotypes: Common stereotypes, moderators and future research directions. *Journal of Management, 35*(1), 158–188.

Powell, G. N., & Graves, L. M. (2003). *Women and men in management* (3rd ed.). Thousand Oaks, CA: Sage.

Pradhan, A. (1989, November 6). Ethnic markets: Sales niche of the future. *National Underwriter,* 18.

Pramualratana, A., & Rau, B. (2001). *HIV/AIDS programs in private sector businesses.* Bangkok: Thailand Business Coalition on AIDS.

Prasad, P., Pringle, J. K., & Konrad, A. M. (2006). Examining the contours of workplace diversity: Concepts, contexts and challenges. In A. M. Konrad, P. Prasad, & J. K. Pringle (Eds.), *Handbook of workplace diversity* (pp. 1–22). London: Sage.

Prescott, J., & Bogg, J. (2011). Segregation in a male-dominated industry: Women working in the computer games industry. *International Journal of Gender, Science and Technology, 3*(1), 205–227.

The presidential bow. (2009, November 16). National Public Radio. Retrieved November 30, 2009, from http://minnesota.publicradio.org/collections/special/columns/news_cut/ archive/2009/11/the_presidential_bow.shtml?refid=0

Preston, J. (2015, June 3). Pink slips at Disney. But first, training foreign replacements. *The New York Times.* Retrieved March 22, 2016, from http://www.nytimes.com/2015/06/04/us/last-task-after-layoff-at-disney-train-foreign-replacements.html

Preston, S. H., & Stokes, A. (2012, June).Sources of population aging in more and less developed countries. *Population and Development Review, 38*(2), 221–236.

Pretty, J., Smith, G., Goulding, K. W. T., Groves, S. J., Henderson, I., Hine, R. E., et al. (2008). Multi-year assessment of Unilever's progress towards agricultural sustainability I: Indicators, methodology, and pilot farm results. *International Journal of Agricultural Sustainability, 6,* 3–62.

Price, J. L., & Mueller, C. W. (1986). *Handbook of organizational measurement.* Marshfield, MA: Pittman.

The price of bananas. (2009, August 9). CBS *60 Minutes.* Retrieved December 5, 2009, from www.cbsnews.com/stories/1998/07/08/60minutes/main4080920.shtml

Price Waterhouse v. Hopkins, 490 U.S. 228 (1989).

Prime, J., & Salib, E. R. (2015). *The secret to inclusion in Australian workplaces: Psychological safety.* New York: Catalyst. Retrieved March 31, 2016, from http://www.catalyst.org/system/files/the_secret_to_inclusion_in_australian_workplaces.pdf

Pugh, S. D., Dietz, J., Brief, A. P., & Wiley, J. W. (2008). Looking inside and out: The impact of employee and community demographic composition on organizational diversity climate. *Journal of Applied Psychology, 93*(6), 1422–1428.

Pyke, J. (2007). *Productive diversity in Australia—How and why companies make the most of diversity.* Saarbrücken, Germany: VDM Verlag Dr. Müller.

Qin, J., Smyrnois, K., & Deng, L. (2012). An extended intervening process model: Diversity, group, processes, and performance. *Human Resource Development Review, 11*(1), 1–30.

Quinn, N., & Holland, D. (1987). *Cultural models of language and thought.* New York: Cambridge University Press.

Raja, S. S. (2012). The London Dawn Raid and its effect on Malaysian plantation workers. *Indonesia and the Malay World, 40*(116), 74–93.

Ram, H. (2002, March 9). The A-Z of fair trade: Harry Ram explains why the decision to make the switch to fair trade produce should be as easy as ABC. *Independent* (London).

Ramachandran, S., & Shanmugam, B. (1995). Plight of plantation workers in Malaysia: Defeated by definitions. *Asian Survey, 35*(4), 394–407.

Rašković, M., Brenčič, M. M., & Jaklič, M. (2013). Antecedents and evolution of the Bartlett and Ghoshal transnational typology. *Multinational Business Review, 21*(2), 3–3.

Rayton, B. A., Brammer, S. J., & Millington, A. I. (2015). Corporate social performance and the psychological contract. *Group & Organization Management, 40*(3), 353–377.

Rea, D., & Eastwood, J. (1992). Legislating for Northern Ireland's fair employment problem. *International Journal of Manpower, 13*(6–7), 31–39.

Reed, E. (2015, June 16). *LGBT group resolves discrimination complaint with NM Denny's.* Retrieved March 31, 2016, from http://www.kob.com/article/stories/s3827332.shtml#.VjFk07erTBQ

Reardon, K. K. (1995). *They don't get it, do they? Communication in the workplace: Closing the gap between women and men* (pp. 183–191). New York: Little, Brown.

Redfield, R. (1941). *The folk culture of Yucatan.* Chicago: University of Chicago Press.

Read, J. G. (2002). Challenging myths of Muslim women: The influence of

Islam on Arab-American women's labor force participation. *Muslim World, 96*, 19–39.

Regev, D. (2007, August 25). The Department of Commerce "Harassment Project": Inspectors will visit work organizations starting next month. Yediot Aharonot (Hebrew).

Reichers, A. E., & Schneider, B. (1990). Climate and culture: An evolution of constructs. In B. Schneider (Ed.), *Organizational climate and culture* (pp. 5–39). San Francisco: Jossey-Bass.

Reverse mentoring: What it is and why it's beneficial. (2011). *Forbes*. Retrieved March 27, 2016, from http://www.forbes.com/sites/work-in-progress/2011/01/03/reverse-mentoring-what-is-it-and-why-is-it-beneficial/#73df1ee653aa

Reverse outsourcing is a new trend. (2010, May 12). *Newsweek*.

Rezvani, S. (2015, February 3). Five trends driving workplace diversity in 2015. *Forbes*. Retrieved from http://www.forbes.com/sites/work-in-progress/2015/02/03/20768/

Ricci v. DeStefano, Nos. 07-1428 and 08-328. 530 F. 3d 87, reversed and remanded (2009). Retrieved November 30, 2012, from www.law.cornell.edu/supct/html/07-1428.ZS.html

Rice, J. (2008). Free trade, fair trade, and gender inequality in less developed countries. *Sustainable Development, 18*, 42–50.

Richard, O. C. (2000). Racial diversity, business strategy, and firm performance: A recourse-based view. *Academy of Management Journal, 43*(2), 164–177.

Richburg, K. (2004, March 4). French senate approves ban on religious attire. *The Washington Post*, p. A14.

Richmond v. J. A. Croson Co., 488 U.S. 469 (1989).

Riesch, C., & Kleiner, B. H. (2005). Discrimination towards customers in the restaurant industry. *Equal Opportunities International, 24*(7/8), 29–37.

Rikleen, L. (2015). *Creating tomorrow's leaders: The expanding roles of millennials in the workplace.* Retrieved from https://www.bc.edu/content/dam/files/centers/cwf/pdf/BCCWF%20EBS-Millennials%20FINAL.pdf

Riley, K. (2015). *Strategies for transitioning workforces from baby-boomer to millennial majorities.* Walden University ScholarWorks. Retrieved from http://scholarworks.waldenu.edu/cgi/viewcontent.cgi?article=3029&context=dissertations

Ro, H. K., & Loya, K. I. (2015). The effect of gender and race intersectionality on student learning outcomes in engineering. *The Review of Higher Education, 38*(3), 359–396.

Roberge, M., & Dick, R. (2010). Recognizing the benefits of diversity: When and how does diversity increase group performance? *Human Resource Management Review, 20*, 295–308.

Roberson, L., Deitch, E. A., Brief, A. P., & Block, C. J. (2003). Stereotype threat and feedback seeking in the workplace. *Journal of Vocational Behavior, 62*, 176–188.

Roberson, L., & Kim, R. (2014). Stereotype threat research hits the sweet spot for organizational psychology. *Industrial and Organizational Psychology, 7*(3), 450–452.

Roberson, L., & Kulik, C. (2007). Stereotype threat at work. *Academy of Management Perspectives, 21*(2), 24–40.

Roberson, Q. M. (2006). Disentangling the meanings of diversity and inclusion in organizations. *Group & Organization Management, 31*(2), 212–236.

Roberts, L., & White, J. (2000). DaimlerChrysler to cut thousands of jobs in North America. *World Socialist Website, International Committee of the Fourth International.* Retrieved September 12, 2004, from www.wsws.org/articles/2000/nov2000/chry-n28.shtml

Robertson, C. J., Al-Khatib, J. A., & Al-Habib, M. (2002). The relationship between Arab values and work beliefs: An exploratory examination. *Thunderbird International Business Review, 44*(5), 583.

Robinson, G., & Dechant, K. (1997). Building a business case for diversity. *Academy of Management Executive, 11*(3), 21–31.

Robinson, R. V. (1983). Book review of *Culture's Consequences:* International differences in work-related values. *Work and Occupations, 10*, 110–115.

Rocco, T. S., Bernier, J. D., & Bowman, L. (2014). Critical race theory and HRD: Moving race front and center. *Advances in Developing Human Resources, 16*(4), 457–470.

Rockstuhl, T., Seiler, S., Ang, S., Van Dyne, L., & Annen, H. (2011). Beyond general intelligence (IQ) and emotional intelligence (EQ): The role of cultural intelligence (CQ) on cross-border leadership effectiveness in a globalized world. *Journal of Social Issues, 67*(4), 825–840.

Roemer, J. E. (2002). Equality of opportunity: A progress report. *Social Choice Welfare, 19*, 455–471.

Roscigno, V. J., Lopez, S. H., & Hodson, R. (2009). Supervisory bullying, status inequalities and organizational context. *Social Forces, 87*(3), 1561–1589.

Ross, L., & Ward, A. (1996). Naive realism: Implications for social conflict and misunderstanding. In T. Brown, E. Reed, & E. Turiel (Eds.), *Values and knowledge* (pp. 103–105). Hillsdale, NJ: Lawrence Erlbaum.

Roundtable on Sustainable Palm Oil. (2012). Retrieved from www.rspo.org/

Rowley, T., & Berman, S. (2000). A brand new brand of corporate social performance. *Business & Society, 39*(4), 397–418.

Roy, B. (2011). *TED talk: Learning from a barefoot movement.* Retrieved March 29, 2016, from https://www.ted.com/talks/bunker_roy/transcript?language=en#t-147000

Rubin, M., & Badea, C. (2007). Why do people perceive ingroup homogeneity on ingroup traits and outgroup homogeneity on outgroup traits? *Personality and Social Psychology Bulletin, 33*(1), 31–42.

Rugman, A. M., Verbeke, A., & Yuan, W. (2011). Re-conceptualizing Bartlett and Ghoshal's classification of national subsidiary roles in the multinational enterprise. *Journal of Management Studies, 48*(2), 253–277.

Russon, M. (2015, April 27). Google faces age discrimination class action lawsuit from 64-year-old engineer Robert Heath. *International Business Times.*

Sahu v. Union Carbide, 04-cv-08825, U.S. Court of Appeals for the Second Circuit (Manhattan) (2009).

Sanchez-Burks, J. (1999). *Ascetic Protestantism and cultural schemas for relational sensitivity in the workplace.* Unpublished doctoral dissertation, Department of Psychology, University of Michigan, Ann Arbor.

Sanchez-Burks, J. (2002). Protestant relational ideology and (in)attention to relational cues in work settings. *Journal of Personality and Social Psychology, 83*(4), 919–929.

Sanchez-Burks, J. (2005). Protestant relational ideology: The cognitive underpinnings and organizational implications of an American anomaly. *Research in Organizational Behavior*

(R. Kramer & B. Staw, Eds), *26,* 265–305.

Sanchez-Burks, J., Bartel, C., & Blount, S. (2009). Performance in intercultural interactions at work. *Journal of Applied Psychology, 94*(1), 216–229.

Sanchez-Burks, J., Karlesky, M., & Lee, F. (2015). Psychological bricolage and the creative process. In C. Shalley, M. Hitt, & J. Zhou (Eds.), *Oxford handbook of creativity, innovation and entrepreneurship* (pp. 93–102). New York: Oxford University Press.

Sanchez-Burks, J., & Lee, F. (2007). Culture and workways. In S. Kitayama & D. Cohen (Eds.), *Handbook of cultural psychology* (Vol. 1, pp. 346–369). New York: Guilford.

Sanchez-Burks, J., Lee, F., Choi, I., Nisbett, R., Zhao, S., & Jasook, K. (2003). Conversing across cultures: East-west communication styles in work and nonwork contexts. *Journal of Personality and Social Psychology, 85*(2), 263–372.

Sanchez-Burks, J., Lee, F., Nisbett, R., Ybarra, O. (2007). Cultural training based on a theory of relational ideology. *Basic and Applied Social Psychology, 29*(3), 257–268.

Sanchez-Burks, J., & Uhlmann, E. (2013). Outlier nation: The cultural psychology of American workways. In M. Yuki & M. Brewer (Eds.), *Culture and group processes* (pp. 121–142). Oxford, England: Oxford University Press.

Sanchez-Burks, J., Nisbett, R. E., & Ybarra, O. (2000). Cultural styles, relational schemas and prejudice against outgroups. *Journal of Personality and Social Psychology, 79*(2), 174–189.

Sander, R., & Taylor, S., Jr. (2012). *Mismatch: How affirmative action hurts students it's intended to help, and why universities won't admit it.* New York: Basic Books.

Sanlam. (2012). *Sustainability report 2011—Material pillars—Responsibility for developing our people—Workplace transformation and diversity.* Retrieved from http://sanlam.sustainabilityreporting.co.za/workplace_ transformation.php

Sardar, Z. (2001, July 30). More hackney than Hollywood. *New Statesman, 14*(667), 14–16.

Sarkozy vows to continue expulsions of Roma from France. (2010, August 26). BBC News. Retrieved January 8, 2013, from www.bbc.co.uk/news/world-europe-11080315

Sassen, S. (1988). *The mobility of labor and capital: A study in international investment and labor flow.* Cambridge, England: Cambridge University Press.

Sassen, S. (1999). *Guests and aliens.* New York: New Press.

Sassenberg, K., Moskowitz, G. B., Jacoby, J., & Hansen, N. (2007). The carry-over effect of competition: The impact of competition on prejudice towards uninvolved outgroups. *Journal of Experimental Social Psychology, 43*(4), 529–538.

Savage, C. (2009, June 10). Videos shed new light on Sotomayor's positions. *New York Times.* Retrieved from www.nytimes.com/2009/06/11/us/politics/ 11judge.html?_r=1

Savelkoul M., Gesthuizen, M., & Scheepers, P. (2011). Explaining relationships between ethnic diversity and informal social capital across European countries and regions: Tests of constrict, conflict and contact theory. *Social Science Research, 40,* 1091–1107.

Saz-Carranza, A., & Ospina, S. M. (2011). The behavioral dimension of governing interorganizational goal-directed networks—managing the unity-diversity tension. *Journal of Public Administration Research and Theory, 21,* 327–365.

Scandura, T. A., & Graen, G. B. (1984). Moderating effects of initial leader-member exchange status on the effects of a leadership intervention. *Journal of Applied Psychology, 69*, 428–436.

Schiffman, R., & Wicklund, R. A. (1992). The minimal group paradigm and its minimal group psychology: On equating social identity with arbitrary group membership. *Theory and Psychology, 2*(1), 29–50.

Schmader, T., & Hall, W. M. (2014). Stereotype threat in school and at work: Putting science into practice. *Policy Insights from the Behavioral and Brain Sciences, 1*(1), 30–37.

Schmitt, M. T., Branscombe, N. R., Silvia, P. J., Garcia, D. M., & Spears, R. (2006). Categorizing at the group-level in response to intragroup social comparisons: A self-categorization theory integration of self-evaluation and social identity motives. *European Journal of Social Psychology, 36*, 297–314.

Schmitt, M. T., Spears, R., & Branscombe, N. R. (2003). Constructing a minority group identity out of a shared rejection: The case of international students. *European Journal of Social Psychology, 33*, 1–12.

Schneider, B. (1987). The people make the place. *Personnel Psychology, 40*, 437–453.

Schneider, B., Gunnarson, S. K., & Niles-Jolly, K. (1994). Creating the climate and culture of success. *Organizational Dynamics, 23*, 17–29. doi:10.1016/0090-2616(94)90085-X

Schneider, B. D., Smith, B., & Paul, M. C. (2001). P-E fit and the attraction-selection-attrition model of organizaitonal functioning; Introduction and overview. In M. Erez, U. Kleinbeck, & H. Thierry (Eds.), *Work motivation in the context of a globalizing economy*. Mahwah, NJ: Lawrence Erlbaum.

Schoeff, M., Jr. (2009). Diversity's strategic role. *Workforce Management*. Retrieved July 26, 2009, from www.workforce.com/section/06/feature/25/37/81/index.html

Schwab, K. (2008). Global corporate citizenship: Working with governments and civil society. *Foreign Affairs, 87*(1), 107–118.

Schwartz, P., & Gibb, B. (1999). *When good companies do bad things*. New York: Wiley.

Schyns, B., Paul, T., Mohr, G., & Blank, H. (2005). Comparing antecedents and consequences of leader-member exchange in a German working context to findings in the U.S. *European Journal of Work and Organizational Psychology, 14*, 1–22.

Scott, K. L., Zagenczyk, T. J., Schippers, M., Purvis, R. L., & Cruz, K. S. (2014). Co-worker exclusion and employee outcomes: An investigation of the moderating roles of perceived organizational and social support. *Journal of Management Studies, 51*(8), 1235–1256.

Scott, W. R. (2008). *Institutions and organizations: Ideas and interests* (3rd ed.). Thousand Oaks, CA: Sage.

Sealy, R. H. V., & Singh, V. (2010). The importance of role models and demographic context for senior women's work identity development. *International Journal of Management Reviews, 12*(3), 284–300.

Seol, D. H. (1999). *Foreign labor and Korean society*. Seoul: Seoul National University.

Sexton, V. S., & Misiak, H. (1984). American psychology and psychology abroad. *American Psychologist, 39*, 1026–1031.

Shackelford, W. G. (2003). The changing definition of workplace diversity. *Black Collegian, 33*(2), 53.

Sharma, S. (2015). Indian media and the struggle for justice in Bhopal. *Social Justice, 41*(1/2), 146.

Sharp, R., Franzway, S., Mills, J., & Gill, J. (2011). Flawed policy, failed politics? Challenging the sexual politics of managing diversity in engineering organizations. *Gender, Work & Organization, 19*(6), 555–572.

Shaukat, A., Qiu, Y., & Trojanowski, G. (2015). Board attributes, corporate social responsibility strategy, and corporate environmental and social performance. *Journal of Business Ethics, 175*, 1–17. doi:10.1007/s10551-014-2460-9

Shell Intensive Training Programme. (2009). Retrieved December 6, 2009, from www.shell.com/home/content/nigeria/society_environment/youth/sitp.html

Shell Youth Training. (2004). Retrieved May 31, 2004, from www.countonshell.com/community/involvement/shell_youth_training.html

Shen, J., Chanda, A., D'Netto, B., & Monga, M., (2009). Managing diversity through human resource management: An international perspective and conceptual framework. *The International Journal of Human Resource Management, 20*(2), 235–251.

Shenoy-Packer, S. (2015). Immigrant professionals, microaggressions, and critical sensemaking in the US workplace. *Management Communication Quarterly, 29*(2), 257–275.

Sheppard, C. (2012). Mapping anti-discrimination law onto inequality at work: Expanding the meaning of equality in international labour law. *International Labour Review, 151*(1–2), 1–19.

Sherif, M. (1966). *In common predicament: Social psychology of intergroup conflict and cooperation*. New York: Houghton Mifflin.

Shinnar, R. S. (2008). Coping with negative social identity: The case of Mexican immigrants. *The Journal of Social Psychology, 148*(5), 553–575.

Shore, L. M., Randel, A. E., Chung, B. G., Dean, M. A., Ehrhart, K. H., & Singh, G. (2011). Inclusion and diversity in work groups: A review and model for future research. *Journal of Management, 37*(4), 1262–1289.

Shorter-Gooden, K. (2004). Multiple resistance strategies: How African American women cope with racism and sexism. *Journal of Black Psychology, 30*(3), 406–425.

Shuster, S. (2016a, June 13). Firas Alshater—crossing cultures with laughter. *Time,* p. 47.

Shuster, S. (2016b) *Time* magazine. Refugees could be the next victims of the Brussels attack. Retrieved from http://time.com/4268072/brussels-attack-refugees-greece/

Sia, S. K., & Bhardwaj, G. (2009). Employees' perception of diversity climate: Role of psychological contract. *Journal of Indian Academy of Applied Psychology, 35,* 305–312.

Simpson, G. W., & Kohers, T. (2002). The link between corporate social and financial performance: Evidence from the banking industry. *Journal of Business Ethics, 35,* 97–109.

Singal, M. (2014). The business case for diversity management in the hospitality industry. *International Journal of Hospitality Management, 40,* 10–19.

Singer, S. (2008, April 11). Xerox settles lawsuit over race discrimination for $12M. *USA Today.* Retrieved from www.usatoday30.usatoday.com/money/industries/manufacturing/2008-04-11-xerox-discrimination-suit_N.htm

Singh, J. P. (1990). Managerial culture and work-related values in India. *Organization Studies, 11,* 75–101.

Slabbert, A. (2001). Cross-cultural racism in South Africa—dead or alive? *Social Behavior and Personality, 29*(2), 125–132.

Sluss, D. M., & Ashforth, B. E. (2007). Relational identity and identification: Defining ourselves through work relationships. *Academy of Management Review, 32,* 9–32.

Smeesters, B., Arrijn, P., Feld, S., & Nayer, A. (2000). The occurrence of discrimination in Belgium. In Zegers de Beijl (Ed.), *Documenting discrimination against migrant workers in the labour market.* Geneva: International Labour Office.

Smith, G. C., & Oyserman, D. (2015). Just not worth my time: Experienced difficulty and time investment. *Social Cognition, 33,* 86–103.

Smith, H. J., Pettigrew, T. F., Pippin, G. M., & Bialosiewicz, S. (2012). Relative deprivation: A theoretical and meta-analytic review. *Personality and Social Psychology Review, 16*(3), 203–232.

Smith, P. B., & Fischer, R. (2003). Reward allocation and culture. *Journal of Cross-Cultural Psychology, 34*(3), 251–268.

Smith, P. M. (2008). Culturally conscious organizations: A conceptual framework. *Libraries and the Academy, 8*(2), 141–155.

Smith, R. K. M. (2007). Religion and education: A human rights dilemma illustrated by the recent "headscarf case." *Globalisation, Societies and Education, 5*(3), 303–314.

Soares, R., Cobb, B., Lebow, E., Regis, A., Winsten, H., & Wojnas, V. (2011). *2011 Catalyst census: Fortune 500 women board directors.* Retrieved June 29, 2012, from www.catalyst.org/file/533/2011_fortune_500_census_wbd.pdf

Soares, R., Marquis, C., & Lee, M. (2011). *Gender and corporate social responsibility: It's a matter of sustainability.* New York: Catalyst. Retrieved April 2, 2016, from http://www.catalyst.org/system/files/gender_and_corporate_social_responsibility.pdf

Society for Human Resource Management. (2010). *SHRM poll: Workplace diversity weathers the recession* [Press release]. Retrieved from www.shrm.org/about/pressroom/pressreleases/pages/workplacediversitypoll.aspx

Soldan, Z. (2009). Does management walk the talk? Study of employee perceptions. *Journal of Diversity Management, 4*(4), 1–12.

Soldan, Z., & Nankervis, A. (2014). Employee perceptions of the effectiveness of diversity management in the Australian Public Service: Rhetoric and reality. *Public Personnel Management, 43*(4), 543–564.

Solinas-Saunders, M., Stacer, M. J., & Guy, R. (2015). Ex-offender barriers to employment: Racial disparities in labor markets with asymmetric information. *Journal of Crime and Justice, 38*(2), 249–269.

Søndergaard, M. (1994). Research note: Hofstede's consequences: A study of reviews, citations and replications. *Organization Studies, 15,* 447–456.

Sotomayor found her "competitive spirit" in gold starts. (2013, January 14). NPR. Retrieved March 26, 2016, from http://www.npr.org/series/169151509/the-sotomayor-interview

Sowell, T. (1996). *Migrations and cultures: A world view.* New York: Basic Books.

Sowell, T. (2004). *Affirmative action around the world: An empirical study.* New Haven, CT: Yale University Press.

Speizer, J. (2004). Diversity on the menu. *Workforce Management,* pp. 41–45.

Sprint-Nextel. (2012). Awards & recognition: Citizenship, diversity and workplace excellence. Retrieved from www.sprint.com

Sri Lanka, no to sexual harassment. (2007). *The Sunday Times.* Retrieved March 26, 2010, from http://communicatinglabourrights.wordpress.com/2007/12/17/sri-lanka-no-to-sexual-harassment/

Stainback, K., Ratliff, T. N., & Roscigno, V. J. (2011). The context of workplace sex discrimination: Sex composition, workplace culture and relative power. *Social Forces, 89*(4), 1165–1188.

Standish, M., Mehalik, M. M., Gorman, M. E., & Werhane, P. H. (1998). *General dilemma: Should Unilever and Vis pursue sustainable agriculture?* Retrieved December 1, 2003, from http://repo-nt.tcc.virginia.edu/ethics/Cases/unilever/ UnileverC.doc

Stanecki, K. (2002). *The AIDS pandemic in the 21st century* (draft report prepared for the XIV International Conference on AIDS). Washington, DC: U.S. Census Bureau.

Statistics New Zealand. (n.d.). *2006 Census.* Retrieved November 20, 2012, from www.stats.govt.nz/Census/2006CensusHomePage.aspx

Staub, K. J. (2009). Facilitating supervisee cultural fluency for a multicultural society. *Perspectives on Administration and Supervision, 19,* 45–50.

Steele, C. M. (2011). *Whistling Vivaldi: How stereotypes affect us and what we can do.* New York: Norton.

Steele, C., & Aronson, J. (1995). Stereotype threat and the intellectual test performance of African Americans. *Journal of Personality and Social Psychology, 69,* 797–811.

Stephan, W. G., Ybarra, O., & Martinez, C. (1998). Prejudice toward immigrants to Spain and Israel: An integrated threat theory analysis. *Journal of Cross-Cultural Psychology, 29,* 4, 559–576.

Sterba, J. P. (2011). *Affirmative action for the future.* Ithaca, NY: Cornell University Press.

Stevens, F. G., Plaut, V. C., & Sanchez-Burks, J. (2008). Unlocking the benefits of diversity: All-inclusive multiculturalism and positive organizational change. *Journal of Applied Behavioral Science, 44*(1), 116–133.

Stewart, J. (2015, July 1). Exxon lumbers along to catch up with gay rights. *New York Times.* Retrieved from www.nytimes.com/2015/07/02/business/exxon-lumbers-along-to-catch-up-with-gay-rights.html?_r=0

Stone, B. (2004, April 19). Should I stay or should I go? Newsweek. Retrieved from www.newsweek.com/should-i-stay-or-should-i-go-124855

Stotzer, R. L., & Hossellman, E. (2012). Hate crimes on campus: Racial/ethnic diversity and campus safety. *Journal of Interpersonal Violence, 27*(4), 644–661.

Stouffer, S. A., Suchman, E. A., DeVinney, L. C., Star, S. A., & Williams, R. M. (1949). *The American soldier: Adjustment during army life* (Vol. 1). Princeton, NJ: Princeton University Press.

Strachan, G., & Jamieson, S. (1999). Equal opportunity in Australia in the 1990s. *New Zealand Journal of Industrial Relations, 24*(3), 319–341.

Strategic Plan for the University of Southern California. (2004). Retrieved from https://about.usc.edu/files/2011/07/StrategicPln_12_10_04.pdf

Strategic Plan for the University of Southern California. (2011). Retrieved August 17, 2012, from http://strategic.usc.edu/USC%20Strategic%20Vision%20Dec%202011.pdf

Strunsky, S. (2014, July 7). Policing the homeless at Port Authority bus terminal, but not as criminals. *NJ.com.* Retrieved from http://www.nj.com/news/index.ssf/2014/07/policing_homelessness_at_the_port_authority_bus_terminal_but_not_as_a_crime.html

Sue, D. W. (2010). *Microaggressions in everyday life: Race, gender, and sexual orientation.* Hoboken, NJ: Wiley.

Sue, D. W., Capodilupo, C. M., Torino, G. C., Bucceri, J. M., Holder, A. M. B., Nadal, K. L., & Esquilin, M. (2007). Racial microaggressions in everyday life: Implications for clinical practice. *American Psychologist, 62*(4), 271–286.

Sue, D. W., Lin, A. I., Torino, G. C., Capodilupo, C. M., & Rivera, D. P. (2009). Racial microaggressions and difficult dialogues on race in the classroom. *Cultural Diversity and Ethnic Minority Psychology, 15*(2), 183–190.

Sunstein, C. R. (1999). Affirmative action, caste, and cultural comparisons. *Michigan Law Review I, 97,* 1311–1320.

Supreme Court releases audio of Justice Antonin Scalia saying maybe Black students don't belong at elite universities. (2015, December 11). CNN. Retrieved February 24, 2016, from http://www.cnn.com/2015/12/11/politics/supreme-court-antonin-scalia-african-americans-audio/

Sustainable Agriculture Initiative. (2002). *High-level pan-European conference on agriculture and biodiversity: Towards integrating biological and landscape diversity for sustainable agriculture in Europe.* Strasbourg, France: Council of Europe Press.

Sustainable Agriculture Initiative. (2015). *Mainstreaming sustainable agriculture.* Retrieved from https://www.unilever.com/sustainable-living/

transformational-change/
mainstreaming-sustainable-
agriculture/

Svehla, T. (1994). Diversity
management: Key to future
success. *Frontiers of Health Services
Management, 11*(2), 3.

Swift, M. (2010, August 5). Age-bias
case vs. Google can move forward,
state supreme court rules. *The
Mercury News.*

Swisher, K. (2013, February 22).
"Physically together": Here's the
internal Yahoo no-work-from-home
memo for remote workers and
maybe more. *All Things D.* Retrieved
from http://allthingsd.com/20130222/
physically-together-heres-the-
internal-yahoo-no-work-from-home-
memo-which-extends-beyond-
remote-workers/

Syed, J., Burke, R. J., & Pinar Acar,
F. (2010). Re-thinking tanawwo
(diversity) and musawat (equality) in
the Middle East. *Equality, Diversity
and Inclusion: An International
Journal, 29*(2), 144–149.

Syed, J., & Murray, P. A. (2008). A
cultural feminist approach towards
managing diversity in top management
teams. *Equal Opportunities
International, 27*(5), 413–432.

Tabuchi, H. (2015, August 2). Chinese
textile mills are now hiring in places
where cotton was king. *The New York
Times.* p. A1.

Tajfel, H. (1957). Values and
perceptual judgment of magnitude.
Psychological Review, 64, 192–204.

Tajfel, H. (1959). Quantitative
judgment in social perception. *British
Journal of Psychology, 50,* 16–29.

Tajfel, H. (1978). *Differentiation
between social groups.* New York:
Academic.

Tajfel, H. (2010). *Social identity and
intergroup relations.* Cambridge, UK:

Cambridge University Press. (Original
work published 1982)

Tajfel, H., Flament, C., Billing, M.
G., & Bundy, R. F. (1971). Social
categorization and intergroup
behaviour. *European Journal of Social
Psychology, 1,* 149–177.

Tajfel, H., & Turner, J. C. (1979).
An integrative theory of intergroup
conflict. In W. G. Austin &
S. Worchel (Eds.), *The social
psychology of intergroup relations* (pp.
33–47). Monterey, CA: Brooks/Cole.

Tajfel, H., & Turner, J. C. (1986).
The social identity theory of
intergroup behavior. In S. Worchel
& W. G. Austin (Eds.), *Psychology
of intergroup relations* (pp. 7–24).
Chicago: Nelson-Hall.

Tajfel, H., & Wilkes, A. L. (1963).
Classification and quantitative
judgment. *British Journal of
Psychology, 54,* 101–113.

Talaski, K. (2002, January 23). New
chief could be Kmart's savior. *USA
Today.* Retrieved November 3, 2003,
from www.usatoday.com/money/
retail/2002-01-23-kmart-adamson
.htm

Talesh, S. (2015). Legal
intermediaries: How insurance
companies construct the meaning of
compliance with antidiscrimination
laws. *Law & Policy, 37*(3), 209–239.

Tang, N., Jiang, Y., Chen, C. C., Zhou,
Z., Chen, C., & Yu, Z. (2015). Inclusion
and inclusion management in the
Chinese context: An exploratory
study. *The International Journal of
Human Resource Management, 26*(6),
856–874.

Tannen, D. (1990). *You just don't
understand: Women and men in
conversation.* New York: Morrow.

Tarlo, E. (1996). *Clothing matters:
Dress and identity in India.* Chicago:
University of Chicago Press.

Tatli, A. (2011). A multi-layered
exploration of the diversity
management field: Diversity
discourses, practices and
practitioners in the UK. *British
Journal of Management, 22,* 238–253.

Tavris, C., & Aronson, E. (2007).
*Mistakes were made (but not by me):
Why we justify foolish beliefs, bad
decisions, and hurtful acts.* Orlando,
FL: Harcourt.

Taylor, D. M., & Moghaddam, F.
M. (1994). *Theories of intergroup
relations.* Westport, CT: Praeger.

Taylor, P., Powell, D., & Wrench,
J. (1997). *The evaluation of antidiscrimination training activities
in the United Kingdom.* Geneva:
International Labour Office.

Taylor, S., Carnochan, S.,
Pascual, G., & Austin, M. J. (2015,
January 16). *Engaging employers as
partners in subsidized employment
programs.* Paper presented at the
Society for Social Work Research
(SSWR), New Orleans, LA.

Teigen, M. (2011). Gender quotas in
corporate boards. In K. Niskanen
(Ed.), *Gender and power in the Nordic
countries—with focus on politics and
business* (pp. 87–108). Oslo: Nordic
Gender Institute.

Terstappen, V., Hanson, L., &
McLaughlin, D. (2013). Gender,
health, labor, and inequities: A review
of the fair and alternative trade
literature. *Agriculture and Human
Values, 30*(1), 21–39.

Tetteh, V. (2015). Diversity in the
workplace. *Research Starters:
Business.* Retrieved from www
.enotes.com/research-starters/
diversity-workplace

*Texaco independent investigator's
report.* (1996, November 11). Court TV
Online. Retrieved May 26, 2004, from
www.courttv.com/archive/legaldocs/
business/ texaco/report.html

Texaco investigator: Tape analysis shows no racial slur. (1996, November 11). Retrieved September 13, 2004, from www.cnn.com/US/9611/11/texaco/

Texas Civil Rights Project. (1999, October 12). *TCRP files 4th lawsuit in campaign against local restaurants for racial discrimination (2nd suit against a Denny's restaurant).* Retrieved November 3, 2003, from www.texascivilrightsproject.org/Press_Releases/1999/2nd_Denny's_lawsuit.htm

Text: Kennedy's Berlin speech. (2003, June 26). BBC News, UK edition. Retrieved May 23, 2004, from http://news.bbc.co.uk/2/hi/europe/3022166.stm

Thau, S., Derfler-Rozin, R., Pitesa, M., Mitchell, M. S., & Pillutla, M. M. (2015). Unethical for the sake of the group: Risk of social exclusion and pro–group unethical behavior. *Journal of Applied Psychology, 100*(1), 98–113.

Theodorakopoulos, N., & Budhwar, P. (2015). Guest editors' introduction: Diversity and inclusion in different work settings: Emerging patterns, challenges, and research agenda. *Human Resource Management, 54*(2), 177–119.

Theological students fail their classes because of headscarf ban. (2002, May 28). *Turkish Daily News.* Retrieved September 13, 2004, from www.turkishdailynews.com/

Thibodeau, P. (2015, April 23). Median age at Google is 29, says age discrimination lawsuit. *Computerworld.*

Thiederman, S. (2008). *Making diversity work: 7 steps for defeating bias in the workplace.* New York: Kaplan Publishing.

A third industrial revolution (special report). (2012, April 21). *The Economist,* p. 8.

Thomas, D. A. (2004). *Diversity as strategy. Harvard Business Review,* 1–10.

Thomas, D. C., Elron, E., Stahl, G., Ekelund, B. Z., Ravlin, E. C., Cerdin, J.-L., et al. (2008). Cultural intelligence: Domain and assessment. *International Journal of Cross Cultural Management, 8*(2), 123–143.

Thomas, R. R., Jr. (1991). *Beyond race and gender: Unleashing the power of your total work force by managing diversity.* New York: American Management Association.

Thomas, R. R., Jr. (1996). A diversity framework. In M. M. Chemers, S. Oskamp, & M. A. Costanzo (Eds.), *Diversity in organizations: New perspectives for a changing workplace* (pp. 245–263). Thousand Oaks, CA: Sage.

Thomas, R. R., Jr. (2005). *Building on the promise of diversity: How we can move to the next level in our workplaces, our communities, and our society.* New York: AMACOM.

Thomas, R. T., Thomas, D. A., Ely, R. J., & Meyerson, D. (2002). *Harvard Business Review on managing diversity.* Boston: Harvard Business School Press.

Ting-Toomey, S. (1988). Intercultural conflict styles. In Y. Y. Kim & W. B. Gudykunst (Eds.), *Theories in intercultural communication* (pp. 22–38). Newbury Park, CA: Sage.

Ting-Toomey, S. (2007). Intercultural conflict training: Theory-practice approaches and research challenges. *Journal of Intercultural Communication Research, 36*(3), 255–271.

Tire Business. (2015, October 24). NTB to settle EEOC religious harassment suit. Retrieved from http://www.tirebusiness.com/article/20151024/NEWS/151029956/ntb-to-settle-eeoc-religious-harassment-suit

Tiwari, T. (2016). India's new HR challenge: Managing a multi-generational workforce. *Journal of Business and Human Resource Management, 1*(1), 1–6. Retrieved from http://crescopublications.org/pdf/JBHRM/JBHRM-1-003.pdf

Tkaczyk, C. (2013, April 19). Marissa Mayer breaks her silence on Yahoo's telecommuting policy. *Fortune.* Retrieved from http://fortune.com/2013/04/19/marissa-mayer-breaks-her-silence-on-yahoos-telecommuting-policy/

Tolbert, K. (1999, December 14). Japan officials cited for harassment. *The Washington Post Foreign Service,* p. A31.

Tomei, M. (2003). Discrimination and equality at work: A review of the concepts. *International Labour Review, 42,* 401–417.

Tompkins, R. C. (2011). Working for change: Gender inequality in the labor force in Japan, South Korea, and Taiwan. Master's thesis, *Trinity College Digital Repository.*

Top doc axed in bust-up after reporting Muslim surgeon's hijab was "spotted with blood" before an NHS operation. (2016). *The Sun.* Retrieved March 23, 2016, from http://www.thesun.co.uk/sol/homepage/news/6981906/Top-doc-axed-after-reporting-Muslim-surgeon-hijab-was-spotted-with-blood-before-op.html

Torres, L., Driscoll, M. W., & Burrow, A. L. (2010). Racial microaggressions and psychological functioning among highly achieving African-Americans: A mixed-methods approach. *Journal of Social and Clinical Psychology, 29*(10), 1074–1099.

Tran, V., Carcia-Pieto, P., & Schneider, S. C. (2011). The role of social identity, appraisal, and emotion in determining responses to diversity management. *Human Relations, 64*(2) 161–176.

Transcript: President Obama's Cairo address to the Muslim world. (2009, July 4). *The Washington Post*. Retrieved July 15, 2009, from www.washingtonpost.com/wpdyn/content/article/2009/06/04/AR2009060401117.html

TransFair USA. (2007, June 14). *Social and organic premium increase for Fair Trade Certified coffee: Direct and positive impact for farmers*. Retrieved March 26, 2010, from www.transfairusa.org/pdfs/certification/FTC_price.pdf

Trapp, R. (2002, December 7). The commercial challenge of fair trade: More people are buying ethical goods—and not just because they feel they should, says Roger Trapp. *Independent* (London).

Travis, D. J., & Mor Barak, M. E. (2010). Fight or flight? Factors influencing child welfare workers' propensity to seek positive change or disengage from their jobs. *Journal of Social Service Research, 36*(3), 188–205.

Travis, D. J., & Pollack, A. (2015, July). *Think people, not programs to build inclusive workplaces*. New York: Catalyst. Retrieved March 31, 2016, from http://www.catalyst.org/system/files/think_people_not_just_programs_to_build_inclusive_workplaces.pdf

Triana, M. C., & García, M. F. (2009). Valuing diversity: A group-value approach to understanding the importance of organizational efforts to support diversity. *Journal of Organizational Behavior, 30*(7), 941–962.

Triana, M. C., Kim, K., & García, M. F. (2011). To help or not to help? Personal value for diversity moderates the relationship between discrimination against minorities and citizenship behavior toward minorities. *Journal of Business Ethics, 102*(2), 333–342.

Triana, M. C., Wagstaff, M. F., & Kim, K. (2012). That's not fair! How personal value for diversity influences reactions to the perceived discriminatory treatment of minorities. *Journal of Business Ethics*, 1–8.

Triandis, H. C. (1996). *Individualism and collectivism*. Boulder, CO: Westview Press.

Triandis, H. C. (2003). The future of workforce diversity in international organisations: A commentary. *Applied Psychology: An International Review, 52*(3), 486–495.

Triandis, H. C. (2004). The many dimensions of culture. *Academy of Management Executive, 18*(1), 88–93.

Triandis, H. C., Marin, G., Lisansky, J., & Betancourt, H. (1984). Simpatia as a cultural script of Hispanics. *Journal of Personality and Social Psychology, 47*, 1363–1375.

Trooper sues, claims bias in Ocala Denny's. (2003, June 19). *Star-Banner*. Retrieved September 13, 2004, from www.sptimes.com/2003/06/21/news_pf/State/Trooper_sues_claims_.shtml

Tse, D. K., Francis, J., & Walls, J. F. (1994). Cultural differences in conducting intra- and inter-cultural negotiations: A Sino-Canadian comparison. *Journal of International Business Studies, 25*, 537–555.

Tsogas, G., & Subeliani, D. (2005). Managing diversity in the Netherlands: A case study of Rabobank. *International Journal of Human Resource Management, 16*(5), 831–851.

Tsui, A. S., Egan, T. D., & O'Reilly, C. A. (1992). Being different: Relational demography and organizational attachment. *Administrative Science Quarterly, 37*, 549–579.

Tsui, A. S., & Farh, J. L. (1997). Where gunaxi matters: Relational demography and gunaxi in the Chinese context. *Work and Occupations, 24*(1), 56–79.

Tsui, A. S., & Gutek, B. (1999). *Demographic differences in organizations*. Lanham, MD: Lexington Books.

Tsui, A. S., Porter, L. W., & Egan, T. D. (2002). When both similarities and dissimilarities matter: Extending the concept of relational demography. *Human Relations, 55*(8), 899–929.

Tu, W. M. (1985). Selfhood and otherness in Confucian thought. In A. Marsella, G. DeVos, & F. Hsu (Eds.), *Culture and self: Asian and western perspectives* (pp. 231–251). New York: Tavistock.

Tuchman, G. (1997, September 4). DA: Denny's didn't discriminate against Asian Americans. The Associated Press. Retrieved November 3, 2003, from www.cnn.com/US/9709/04/dennys.dropped

Tulgan, B. (2016). *Not everyone gets a trophy: How to manage the Millennials*. Hoboken, NJ: Wiley.

Tummala, K. K. (1999). Policy of preference: Lessons from India, the United States and South Africa. *Public Administration Review, 59*(6), 495–508.

Tung, C. (2000). The cost of caring: The social reproductive labor of Filipina live-in home health caregivers. *Frontiers, 21*(1), 61–82.

Turcsik, R. (2003, December 1). Supermarket grocery business: Full steam ahead. *Progressive Grocer: The Publication of Strategic Management*.

Turner, J. C. (1987). *Rediscovering the social group: A self-categorization theory*. Oxford, UK: Basil Blackwell.

Turner, J. C., & Giles, H. (1981). *Intergroup behavior*. New York: Basil Blackwell.

Twenge, J. M., Baumeister, R. F., DeWall, N. C., Ciarocco, N. J., & Bartels, M. J. (2007). Social exclusion decreases prosocial behavior. *Journal of Personality and Social Psychology, 92*(1), 56–66.

25 years, 25 success stories. (n.d.). Retrieved December 15, 2009, from www.caic.ca/25stories.html

2014/2015 Diversity Report. (2016). *Guests first*. Retrieved March 31, 2016, from http://dennysdiversity .com/files/DDR2014-15.pdf

Twyman, C. M. (2002). Finding justice in South African labor law: The use of arbitration to evaluate affirmative action. *Case Western Reserve Journal of International Law, 33*, 307–342.

Tyler Prize for Environmental Achievement. (2009). *2004 Tyler Laureates: Barefoot College and Red Latinoamericans de Botánica*. Retrieved September 24, 2012, from http://www.usc.edu/dept/LAS/ tylerprize/laureates/tyler2004.html

U.S. Bureau of Labor Statistics. (2009). *Employment status of the civilian noninstitutional population by age, sex, and race*. Retrieved September 29, 2008, from www.bls .gov/cps/

U.S. Census Bureau. (2000). *Projection of the total resident population by 5-year age groups, and sex with special age categories middle series, 2050–2070*. Retrieved August 16, 2009, from www.census .gov/population/projections/nation/ summary/ np-t3-g.txt

U.S. Census Bureau. (2001). *Age: 2000*. Census 2000 Brief.

U.S. Census Bureau. (2010). *American community survey, 2006–8, public use microdata sample (PUMS)*. Retrieved from http://www.census.gov/acs/

U.S. Census Bureau. (2012). *American factfinder*. Retrieved May 16, 2012, from www.census.gov

U.S. Department of Homeland Security. (2015). Retrieved July 22, 2015, from http://www.uscis .gov/news/alerts/uscis-completes-

h-1b-cap-random-selection-process-fy-2016

U.S. Department of Justice. (1993). *United States of America v. Flagstar Corporation and Denny's, Inc.*, No. 93–20208-JW, consolidated with *Ridgeway v. Flagstar Corporation and Denny's, Inc.*, No. 93–20202-JW. Retrieved November 3, 2003, from www.usdoj.gov/crt/housing/ documents/dennysettle2.htm

U.S. Equal Employment Opportunity Commission. (2002, October 30). *EEOC settles sexual harassment lawsuit against Denny's*. Retrieved November 5, 2003, from www.eeoc .gov/press/10–30-02.html

U.S. Equal Employment Opportunity Commission. (2015). *Jury awards $240,000 to Muslim truck drivers in EEOC religious discrimination suit*. Retrieved from http://www.eeoc .gov/eeoc/newsroom/release/10-22-15b.cfm

Uggen, C., & Shinohara, C. (2009). Sexual harassment comes of age: A comparative analysis of the United States and Japan. *The Sociological Quarterly, 50*, 201–234.

Uhlmann, E., Heaphy, E., Ashford, S., Zhu, L., & Sanchez-Burks, J. (2013). Acting professional: An exploration of culturally bounded norms against nonwork role referencing. *Journal of Organizational Behavior, 34*(6), 866–886.

Uhlmann, E., & Sanchez-Burks, J. (2014). The implicit legacy of American Puritanism. *Journal of Cross-Cultural Psychology, 45*(6), 991–1005.

Umiker, W. (1995). Workplace loyalty in the 1990s. *The Health Care Supervisor, 13*(3), 30–35.

Unilever Annual Progress Report. (2016). *Our latest annual report showcases growth, innovation and sustainability*. Retrieved from https://www.unilever.co.za/news/ news-and-features/2016/our-latest-

annual-report-showcases-growth-innovation-and-sustainability.html

Unilever Foundation for Education Development. (2012). *Case studies*. Retrieved from www.unilever .co.id/sustainability/casestudies/ education/unilever-foundation-for-education-development.aspx

Unilever Progress Report. (2011). *Unilever sustainable living plan progress report 2011*. Retrieved from www.unilever.com/images/ uslp-Unilever_Sustainable_Living_ Plan_Progress_Report_2011_tcm13-284779.pdf

Unilever Sustainable Living Plan. (2012.) Progress Report. Retrieved from www.unilver.com/

Unilever Sustainable Living Plan. (n.d.). *The Unilever Sustainable Living Plan*. Retrieved from https://www .unilever.com/sustainable-living/the-sustainable-living-plan/

United Nations. (1999). *Demographic yearbook, 1999*. New York: Author.

United Nations. (2000a). *Replacement migration* (ESA/P/WP.160). New York: Author. Retrieved September 13, 2004, from www.un.org/esa/ population/publications/ migration/ cover-preface.pdf

United Nations. (2000b). *The world's women 2000*. New York: Author.

United Nations. (2011a). *International migration report 2009: A global assessment*. New York: United Nations.

United Nations. (2011b). *The millennium development goals report 2011*. New York: United Nations.

United Nations. (2011c). *World population prospects* (2010 revision). Retrieved from http://esa.un.org/ unpd/wpp/Excel-Data/population.htm

United Nations. (2012). *Migrants by origin and destination: The role of South-South migration. Population Facts 2012/13*. New York: Author.

United Nations. (2015a). *World investment report 2015.* Retrieved July 29, 2015, from www.unctad.org/

United Nations. (2015b). *World Populations Prospects.* Retrieved from esa.un.org/unpd/wpp/Pulibcations/files/key_Findings_WPP_2015.pdf

United Nations, Human Rights. (2016). *The Committee on Elimination of Discrimination Against Women.* Retrieved March 20, 2016, from http://www.ohchr.org/en/hrbodies/cedaw/pages/cedawindex.aspx

United Nations, Treaty Collection. (1966). *Chapter IV: Human Rights—International Covenant on Economic, Social and Cultural Rights.* Retrieved from https://treaties.un.org/Pages/ViewDetails.aspx?src=TREATY&mtdsg_no=IV-3&chapter=4&lang=en

United Nations Committee on the Elimination of Racial Discrimination. (2009). Consideration of reports submitted by States parties under article 40 of the Covenant: International Covenant on Civil and Political Rights : information provided by the Government of Belgium on the implementation of the concluding observations of the Committee on the Elimination of Racial Discrimination (CERD/C/BEL/CO/15)

United Nations Discrimination (Employment and Occupation) Convention. (1958). No. 111. Retrieved July 20, 2009, from www.unhchr.ch/html/menu3/b/d_i10111.htm

United Nations Economic and Social Commission for Asia and the Pacific. (2003). *Saving our futures: Multi-ministerial Action Guide HIV/AIDS in Asia and the Pacific.* United Nations, ST/ESCAP/2250 No. E.03.II.F.26.

United Nations Educational, Scientific, and Cultural Organization (UNESCO). (2009). *Key statistical tables on education.* Retrieved September 29, 2009, from www.uis.unesco.org/

United Nations Educational, Scientific, and Cultural Organization (UNESCO). (2015). *Educational attainment by ISCED level.* Retrieved July 30, 2015, from http://www.uis.unesco.org/Education/Pages/educational-attainment-data-release.aspx

United Nations Environment Programme, International Fund for Agricultural Development. (2004). *The Barefoot College project, Tilonia, Rajasthan, India.* Retrieved May 5, 2004, from www.unep.org/unep/envpolimp/techcoop/19.htm

United Nations Fact Sheet No. 2 (Rev. 1). (2012). *The International Bill of Human Rights.* Office of the United Nations High Commissioner for Human Rights. Retrieved September 29, 2002, from www.unhchr.ch/html/menu6/2/fs2.htm

United Nations General Assembly. (2009). *Japan tells women's anti-discrimination committee efforts to meet treaty obligations bearing fruit, but progress slow by international standards.* Retrieved June 29, 2012, from www.un.org/News/Press/docs/2009/wom1742.doc.htm

United Nations Global Compact. (2001). *Discrimination is everybody's business: From discrimination to diversity.* New York: Volvo Cars in collaboration with the UN High Commissioner on Human Rights. Retrieved May 27, 2004, from http://research.dnv.com/csr/PW_Tools/PWD/1/00/L/1-00-L-2001-01-0/lib2001/Diversity_report.pdf

United Nations Global Compact. (2004, March 30). *Corporate social responsibility and diversity management.* Keynote address at the MIA Award Ceremony, Copenhagen, by George Kell, United Nations. Retrieved December 5, 2009, from www.unglobalcompact.org/WebsiteInfo/search_global_compact.html?cx=017867615180777054248%3Arbjhpb8rvpy&cof=FORID%3A11&q=Discrimination+is+everybodys+business#1311

United Nations Global Compact. (2012, February 14). Remarks by Secretary-General Ban Ki-moon to KMPG Summit: Business perspective for sustainable growth.

United States Executive Order 11246 (1965). Retrieved from www.eeoc.gov/eeoc/history/35th/thelaw/eo-11246.html

Universal Declaration of Human Rights. (1948, December 10). United Nations. Retrieved September 26, 2012, from www.ohchr.org/EN/UDHR/Pages/Introduction.aspx

Unzueta, M. M., & Binning, K. B. (2012). Diversity is in the eye of the beholder: How concern for the in-group affects perceptions of racial diversity. *Personality and Social Psychology Bulletin, 38*(1), 26–38.

Unzueta, M. M., Knowles, E. D., & Ho, G. C. (2012). Diversity is what you want it to be: How social-dominance motives affect construals of diversity. *Psychological Science, 23*(3), 303–309.

Urban Pathways. (2012a). *40 years of helping New Yorkers.* Retrieved from http://www.urbanpathways.org/history/

Urban Pathways. (2012b). *PATH Outreach Program.* Retrieved August 25, 2012, from www.urbanpathways.org/or_path.asp

US Muslim in Abercrombie hujab court win. (2015, June 1). BBC News. Retrieved from www.bbc.com/news/world-us-canada-32967135

USC Civic and Community Relations. (n.d.). *Our communities.* Retrieved April 2010, from http://communities.usc.edu/programs/#21

Vakalahi, H. (2012). Cultural context of health and well-being among Samoan and Togan American elders. *Indian Journal of Gerontology, 26*(1), 75–93.

Vakulenko, A. (2007). Islamic headscarves and the European Convention on Human Rights: An intersectional perspective. *Social and Legal Studies, 16*, 183–199.

Valiente, J. M. A., Ayerbe, C. G., & Figueras, M. S. (2012, November). Social responsibility practices and evaluation of corporate social performance. *Journal of Cleaner Production, 35*, 25–38.

van den Bos, A., & Stapel, D. A. (2012). Why people stereotype affects how they stereotype: The differential influence of comprehension goals and self-enhancement goals on stereotyping. *Personality and Social Psychology Bulletin, 35*(1), 101–113.

Van Dijk, T. A. (1987). *Communicating racism.* Newbury Park, CA: Sage.

Van Dijk, T. A. (2006, November 16–17). *Racism and the European press.* Presentation prepared for the European Commission against Racism and Intolerance (ECRI).

Van Dijk, T. A. (2007, November 16–17). *Racism, the press and freedom of expression: A summary of ten theses.* Presentation made in the ECRI meeting, Strasbourg, France. To be published by the European Commission against Racism and Intolerance (ECRI).

Van Knippenberg, D., De Dreu, C. K. W., & Homan, A. C. (2004). Work group diversity and group performance: An integrative model and research agenda. *Journal of Applied Psychology, 89*, 1008–1022.

Van Knippenberg, D., & Schippers, M. C. (2007). Work group diversity. *Annual Review of Psychology, 58*, 515–541.

Van Laer, K., & Janssens, M. (2011). Ethnic minority professionals' experiences with subtle discrimination in the workplace. *Human Relations, 64*, 1203–1227.

Van Swol, L. (2003). The effects of nonverbal mirroring on perceived persuasiveness, agreement with an imitator, and reciprocity in a group discussion. *Communication Research, 30*, 46–56.

Van Voris, B., & Hurtado, P. (2012, June 27). Union Carbide wins dismissal of suit over Bhopal plant. *Bloomberg Business week.* Retrieved from www .businessweek.com/news/2012-06-27/ union-carbide-wins-dismissal-of-suit-over-bhopal-plant

Vaupel, J. W. (2001). Demographic insights into longevity. *Population, 13*(1), 245–260.

Vaupel, J. W., Carey, J. R., Christensen, K., Johnson, T. E., Yashin, A. I., Holm, N.V., et al. (1998). Biodemographic trajectories of longevity. *Science, 280*, 5365, 855–860.

Velasquez, M. G. (2011). *Business ethics: Concepts and cases* (7th ed.). Upper Saddle River, NJ: Prentice Hall.

Verdicchio, P. (1999). *Bound by distance: Rethinking nationalism through the Italian diaspora.* Madison, NJ: Farleigh Dickson University Press.

Vietnam Business Forum. (2013). *Hai Ha-Kotobuki: Well-established brand name.* Retrieved from http://vccinews.com/news_detail.asp? news_id=27988

Virgin Group. (2012). *Company overview.* Retrieved from https://www.virgin.com/about-us

Vis, J. K., & Standish, M. (2000). How to make agri-food supply chains sustainable: Unilever's perspective. *Sustainable Development International, 3*, 111–117.

Vishaka guidelines against sexual harassment in the workplace. (2009). Retrieved July 26, 2009, from http://

peoplefriendlypolice.wordpress.com/supreme-court-guidelines-against-sexual-harassment/

Vogel, D. (2005). *The market for virtue: The potential and limits of corporate social responsibility.* Washington, DC: Brookings Institution Press.

Vohs, K. D., & Baumeister, R. F. (2010). *Handbook of self-regulation* (2nd ed.). New York: Guilford.

Volmer, J., Spurk, D., & Niessen, C. (2012). Leader-member exchange (LMX), job autonomy, and creative work involvement. *Leadership Quarterly, 23*, 456–465.

Von Hippel, C., Issa, M., Ma, R., & Stokes, A. (2011). Stereotype threat: Antecedents and consequences for working women. *European Journal of Social Psychology, 41*(2), 151–161.

Vonk, R., & Van Knippenberg, A. (1995). Processing attitude statements from in-group and out-group members: Effects of within-group and within-person inconsistencies on reading times. *Journal of Personality and Social Psychology, 68*(2), 215–227.

Waddington, L., & Bell, M. (2011). Exploring the boundaries of positive action under EU law: A search for conceptual clarity. *Common Market Law Review, 48*, 1503–1526.

Waddock, S., & Graves, S. M. (1997). The corporate social performance-financial performance link. *Strategic Management Journal, 18*(4), 303–319.

Wagner, J. A. (2002). Utilitarian and ontological variation in individualism-collectivism. In B. M. Staw & R. M. Kramer (Eds.), *Research in organizational behavior.* Oxford, UK: JAI /Elsevier Science.

Wales in the fast lane to sign up to idea of fair trade. (2003, March 6). *Western Mail* (Cardiff, Wales).

Walker, S. (2002, May/June). Africanity vs. Blackness: Race, class and culture in Brazil. *NACLA Report on the Americas, 35*(6), 16–20, 50.

Wallulis, J. (2012). The "different mirror" of multicultural history. *Widening Participation and Lifelong Learning, 13,* 87–92.

Walster, E., Walster, G. W., & Berscheid, E. (1978). *Equity: Theory and research.* Boston: Allyn & Bacon.

Wang, H., & Choi, J. (2013). A new look at the corporate social-financial performance relationship: The moderating roles of temporal and interdomain consistency in corporate social performance. *Journal of Management, 39*(2), 416–441.

Wang, H., & Choi, J. (2016, February). Slack resources and the rent-generating potential of firm-specific knowledge. *Journal of Management, 42,* 500–523.

Wards Cove Packing Co., Inc. v. Atonio, 490 U.S. 642, No. 87–1387 (1989).

Waters, R. D., & Bortree, D. S. (2010). Building a better workplace for teen volunteers through inclusive behaviors. *Nonprofit Management & Leadership, 20*(3), 337–355.

Waters, R. D., & Bortree, D. S. (2012). Improving volunteer retention efforts in public library systems: How communication and inclusion impact female and male volunteers differently. *International Journal of Nonprofit and Voluntary Sector Marketing, 17,* 92–107.

Watt, D. (2012). The urgency of visual media literacy in our post-9/11 world: Reading images of Muslim women in the print news media. *Journal of Media Literacy Education, 4*(1), 32–43.

Wei, L. Q., Lau, C. M., Young, M. N., & Wang, Z. (2005). The impact of top management team demography on firm performance in China. *Asian Business & Management, 4,* 227–250.

Weinman, S. (2014, November 13). IBM CEO Ginni Rometty is Augusta National's third female member. *Golf Digest.* Retrieved from http://www.golfdigest.com/story/ibm-ceo-ginni-rometty-is-augus

Weiss, S. (1992). Inland Steel Industries California. *The Business Enterprise Trust,* 1–21. Retrieved from www.caseplace.org/cases3117/cases_show.htm?doc_id=81989

Wells, C. C., Gill, R., & McDonald, J. (2015). "Us foreigners": Intersectionality in a scientific organization. *Equality, Diversity and Inclusion: An International Journal, 34*(6), 539–553.

Wentling, R. M. (2004). Factors that assist and barriers that hinder the success of diversity initiatives in multinational corporations. *Human Resource Development International, 7*(2), 165–180.

Wentling, R. M., & Palma-Rivas, N. (2000). Current status of diversity initiatives in selected multinational corporations. *Human Resource Development Quarterly, 11*(1), 35–60.

Were, M. (2003). Implementing corporate responsibility: The Chiquita case. *Journal of Business Ethics, 44*(2–3), 247–260.

Werner, W. (2009). Corporate social responsibility initiatives: Addressing social exclusion in Bangladesh. *Journal of Health, Population, and Nutrition, 27*(4), 545–562.

Werther, W. B., & Chandler, D. (2006). *Strategic corporate social responsibility.* Thousand Oaks, CA: Sage.

Werther, W. B., & Chandler, D. (2011). *Strategic corporate social responsibility* (2nd ed.). Thousand Oaks, CA: Sage.

What are CDFIs? (n.d.). CDFIs in Baltimore. Retrieved July 22, 20016, from https://baltimorecdfis.org/what-are-cdfis

What "model minority" doesn't tell? (1998, January 3). *The Chicago Tribune,* p. 18.

White, C. M. (2001). Affirmative action and education in Fiji: Legislation, contestation, and colonial discourse. *Harvard Educational Review, 71*(2), 240–268.

White, K. M., & Preston, S. H. (1996). How many Americans are alive because of twentieth century improvements in mortality? *Population and Development Review, 22,* 415–429.

The White House. (2016). *Remarks by the President at Islamic Society of Baltimore.* Retrieved from https://www.whitehouse.gov/the-press-office/2016/02/03/remarks-president-islamic-society-baltimore

Why companies invest in rural India. (2009, July 1). *Wall Street Journal.* Retrieved December 3, 2009, from http://online.wsj.com/article/SB124643327175778655.html

Why diversity matters. (2013, July). New York: Catalyst. Retrieved March 31, 2016, from http://www.catalyst.org/system/files/why_diversity_matters_catalyst_0.pdf

Wicki, S., & Van der Kaaij, J. (2007). Is it true love between the octopus and the frog? How to avoid the authenticity gap. *Corporate Reputation Review, 10*(4), 312–318.

Wiedmer, T. (2015). Generations do differ: Best practices in leading traditionalists, boomers, and generations X, Y, and Z. *Delta Kappa Gamma Bulletin: International Journal for Professional Educators, 82*(1), 51.

Williams, J. C., & Huang, P. (2011, January 27). *Improving work-life fit in hourly jobs: An underutilized cost-cutting strategy in a globalized world.* Retrieved from http://ssrn.com/abstract=2126291

Williams Institute in California. (2016). Retrieved March 26, 2016, from http://williamsinstitute.law .ucla.edu/

Williamson, J. G. (1998). Globalization and the labor market: Using history to inform policy. In P. Aghion & J. G. Williamson (Eds.), *Growth, inequality, and globalization: Theory, history, and policy.* Cambridge, UK: Cambridge University Press.

Wilson, C. (2011) Understanding global demographic convergence since 1950. *Population and Development Review, 37*(2), 375–388.

Wilson, C., Sobotka, T., Williamson, L., & Boyle, P. (2013). Migration and intergenerational replacement in Europe. Population and Development Review, 39(1), 131–157.

Wilson, W. J. (2011). *When work disappears.* New York: Random House.

Winet, E. D. (2012). Face-vail bans and anti-mask laws: State interests and the right to cover the face. *Hastings International and Comparative Law Review, 217.*

Winfeld, L. (2005). *Straight talk about gays in the workplace: Creating an inclusive, productive environment for everyone in your organization* (3rd ed.). New York: Harrington Park.

Winkielman, P., Halberstadt, J., Fazendeiro, T., & Catty, S. (2006). Prototypes are attractive because they are easy on the mind. *Psychological Science, 17*(9), 799–806.

Winkler, A. (2012, February 21). Will the Supreme Court end affirmative action with *Fisher vs. University of Texas? The Daily Beast.*

Women and Global Migration Working Group. (2016). *Bea, Philippines/ Denmark—Undocumented migrant woman.* Retrieved March 26, 2016, from http://wgmwg.org/ wp-content/uploads/2016/03/Bea-Philippines-Denmark.pdf

Women CEOs slowly gain on corporate America. (2009, January 2).

USA Today. Retrieved August 31, 2009, from http://www.usatoday.com/ money/companies/management/ 2009 -01 -01-women-ceos-increase_N.htm

Wondrak, M., & Segert, A. (2015). Using the diversity impact navigator to move from interventions towards diversity management strategies. *Journal of Intellectual Capital, 16*(1), 239–254.

Wong, S. (2008). Diversity—Making space for everyone at NASA/GODDARD space flight center using dialogue to break through barriers. *Human Resource Management, 47*(2), 389–399.

Wood, G. (2008). Gender stereotypical attitudes: Past, present and future influences on women's career development. *Equal Opportunities International, 27*(7), 613–628.

Woolworths Holdings Limited. (2004a). *Corporate governance.* Retrieved May 26, 2004, from www.woolworthsholdings.co.za/ commentary/corporate_governance .html

Woolworths Holdings Limited. (2004b). *Good business journey report.* Retrieved February 21, 2016, from http://www.woolworthsholdings .co.za/investor/annual_reports/ ar2015/whl_2015_gbj.pdf

Work-life integration. (n.d.). Retrieved March 31, 2016, from http://www.adidas-group.com/en/ sustainability/employees/work-life-integration/#/family-and-work-no-conflict-at-the-adidas-group/

The World. (2003, October 23). National Public Radio [Radio broadcast].

World Bank. (1995). *Workers in an integrating world* (World Development Report 1995). Washington, DC: World Bank.

World Bank. (2001). *Engendering development.* New York: Oxford University Press.

World Bank. (2012). *Sustainability report: The diversity of the business case.* Retrieved August 25, 2012, from http://ifcext .ifc.org/ifcext/sustainability .nsf/AttachmentsByTitle/p_ DevelopingValue_Ch3/$FILE/ Developing_Value_Chapter3.pdf

World Bank Group. (2003). *Global coalitions for voices of the poor web guide: E-commerce to support grassroots entrepreneurs.* Retrieved October 31, 2003, from www .worldbank.org/wbp/voices/globcoal/ webguide/ecom.htm

World Business Council for Sustainable Development. (n.d.). *Sonae: Delta Cafés socially responsible coffee.* Retrieved from http://www.delta-cafes.com/en/ media/news/european-business-awards_8db764c27a3e

The World Factbook. (2015). *Languages, Central Intelligence Agency.* Retrieved from www.cia .gov/library/publications/the-world-factbook/fields/2098.html

World Fair Trade Organization. (n.d.). Retrieved from http://wfto.com/ about-us/history-wfto; http://wfto .com/about-us/about-wfto

World Rainforest Movement. (2001). *The bitter fruit of oil palm.* Montevideo, Uruguay: Author.

World's most admired companies. (2009). *Fortune.* Retrieved from http:// money.cnn.com/magazines/ fortune/ mostadmired/2009/snapshots/6127 .html

World's most admired companies. (2016). *Fortune.* Retrieved from http://fortune.com/worlds-most-admired-companies/nestle-33/

The world's most powerful people. (2016). *Forbes.* Retrieved from http://www.forbes.com/ powerful-people/list/#tab:overall_ search:Rometty

Wrench, J. (2007). *Diversity management and discrimination.* Burlington, VT: Ashgate.

Wright, P., Ferris, S. P., Hiller, J. S., & Kroll, M. (1995). Competitiveness through management of diversity: Effects on stock price valuation. *Academy of Management Journal, 38*(1), 272–287.

Wright, S. C., & Tropp, R. (2002). Collective action in response to disadvantage: Intergroup perceptions, social identification, and social change. Relative deprivation: Specification, development, and integration. In I. Walker & H. J. Smith (Eds.), *Relative deprivation: Specification, development, and integration* (pp. 200–236). New York: Cambridge University Press.

Yamey, G. (2000, July 1). Nestlé violates international marketing code, says audit. *BMJ, 321*(8).

Yang, C., D'Souza, G. C., Bapat, A. S., & Colarelli, S. M. (2006). A cross-national analysis of affirmative action: An evolutionary psychological perspective. *Managerial and Decision Economics, 27,* 203–216.

Yang, Y., & Konrad, A. M. (2011). Understanding diversity management practices: Implications of institutional theory and resource-based theory. *Group & Organization Management, 36*(1), 6–38.

Yarhouse, M. A. (2000). Review of social cognition research on stereotyping: Application to psychologists working with older adults. *Journal of Clinical Geropsychology, 6*(2), 121–131.

Ybarra, O., Kross, E., & Sanchez-Burks, J. (2014). The "big idea" that is yet to be: Towards a more motivated, contextual and dynamic model of emotional intelligence. *Academy of Management Perspectives, 28*(2), 93–107.

Yearwood, E. L. (2013). Microaggression. *Journal of Child and Adolescent Psychiatric Nursing, 26*(1), 98–99.

Yogyakarta Principles. (2006). Principles on the application of international human rights law in relation to sexual orientation and gender identity. Retrieved March 27, 2016, from http://www .yogyakartaprinciples.org/principles_ en.pdf

Yoo, B., Donthu, N., & Lenartowicz, T. (2011). Measuring Hofstede's five dimensions of cultural values at the individual level: Development and validation of CVSCALE. *Journal of International Consumer Marketing, 23*(3–4), 193–210.

Youth Career Initiative. (2014a, May 14). *Marriott expands YCI support to include guest donations.* Retrieved from http://www .youthcareerinitiative.org/marriott-expands-yci-support-to-include-guest-donations/

Youth Career Initiative. (2014b, October 15). *Marriott rewards insiders, features YCI for charitable giving.* Retrieved from http://www .youthcareerinitiative.org/marriott-rewards-insiders-features-yci-for-charitable-giving/

Youth Career Initiative. (2014c). *Youth career initiative search.* Retrieved from http://www.youthcareer initiative.org/page/3/?s=marriott&sty pe=default#038;stype=default

Yosso, T. J., Smith, W. A., Ceja, M., & Solórzano , D. G. (2009, Winter). Critical race theory, racial microaggressions, and campus racial climate for Latina/o undergraduates. *Harvard Educational Review, 79*(4), 659–690.

Yukl, G. (2012). *Leadership in organizations* (8th ed.). New York: Pearson.

Zacharias, A., & Vakulabharanam, V. (2011). Caste stratification and wealth inequality in India. *World Development, 39,* 1820–1833.

Zagenczyk, T. J., Scott, K. D., Gibney, R., Murrell, A. J., & Thatcher, J. B. (2010). Social influence and perceived organizational support: A social network analysis. *Organizational Behavior and Human Decision Processes, 111*(2), 127–138.

Zan, M. (1997, August 22). Aborigines fight for justice. *Jakarta Post.*

Zanoni, P., Janssens, M., Benschop, Y., & Nkomo, S. (2010). Unpacking diversity, grasping inequality: rethinking difference through critical perspectives. Introduction. *Organization, 17*(1), 9–29.

Zegers de Beijl, R. (Ed.). (1999). *Documenting discrimination against migrant workers in the labour market.* Geneva: International Labour Office.

Zegers de Beijl, R. (Ed.). (2000). *Documenting discrimination against migrant workers in the labour market: A comparative study of four European countries.* Geneva: International Labour Organization.

Zhong, C. B., & Leonardelli, G. J. (2008). Cold and lonely: Does social exclusion literally feel cold? *Psychological Science, 19,* 838–842.

Zhu, Q., Liu, J., & Lai, K. (2016). Corporate social responsibility practices and performance improvement among Chinese national state-owned enterprises. *International Journal of Production Economics, 171,* 417–426.

Zientara, P., Kujawski, L., & Bohdanowicz-Godfrey, P. (2015). Corporate social responsibility and employee attitudes: Evidence from a study of Polish hotel employees. *Journal of Sustainable Tourism, 23*(6), 859–880.

Zinn, D. L. (1994). The Senegalese immigrants in Bari: What happens when the Africans peer back. In R. Benmayor & A. Skotnes (Eds.), *Migration and identity* (pp. 53–68). Oxford, England: Oxford University Press.

Zlotnick, H. (1994). International migration: Causes and effects. In L. A. Mazur (Ed.), *Beyond the numbers: A reader on population, consumption, and the environment* (pp. 53–68). Washington, DC: Island Press.

Zlotnick, H. (1996). Migration to and from developing regions: A review of past trends. In W. Lutz (Ed.), *The future population of the world: What can we assume today?* (2nd ed., pp. 299–335). London: Earthscan.

Zohar, D., & Gill, L. (2010). Group leaders as gatekeepers: Testing safety climate variations across levels of analysis. *Applied Psychology, 59*, 647–673.

Zohar, D., & Hofmann, D. A. (2012). Organizational culture and climate. In S. W. J. Kozlowski (Ed.), *The Oxford handbook of organizational psychology* (Vol. 1, pp. 643–666). New York: Oxford University Press.

Zohar, D., & Tenne-Gazit, O. (2008). Transformational leadership and group interaction as climate antecedents: A social network analysis. *Journal of Applied Psychology, 93*, 744–757.

Zweifel, P., & Eisen, R. (2012). Challenges confronting insurance. In P. Zweifel & R. Eisen (Eds.), *Insurance economics* (pp. 393–422). New York: Springer.

• Index •

NOTE: Page references with boxes, figures, and tables are referred to as (box), (fig.), and (table).

• About the Author •

Michàlle E. Mor Barak, PhD, is a professor at the University of Southern California (USC) with a joint appointment at the School of Social Work and the Marshall School of Business. She holds the Dean's Endowed Professorship of Social Work and Business and serves as the Department Chair of Community, Organization, and Business Innovation (COBI). A principal investigator on several large research projects, she has published extensively in the areas of global diversity, inclusion, work-life balance, and leadership. Her research was funded by national and international foundations and corporations, including Nike, TRW, Edison, the Rockefeller Foundation, and the Wellness Foundation. Professor Mor Barak received awards of distinction, including a Fulbright award, the Lady Davis award, the University of California Regents Award, the Academy of Management Gender and Diversity in Organizations Division's Scholarly Contributions to Educational Practice Advancing Women in Leadership Award, and the Franklin C. Sterlin Distinguished Faculty Award.

Mor Barak was invited to give keynote addresses at national and international gatherings such as the International Monetary Fund (IMF) Global Inclusion Conference; Equity, Diversity and Inclusion (EDI) International Conference; and the Women's Global Forum on the Economy and Society. She received grants to lead prestigious conferences around the world, including the Rockefeller Foundation's grant to lead an international conference on global workforce diversity in Bellagio, Italy, and the Borchard Foundation's grant to lead a global think tank of scholars on diversity management at the Château de la Bretesche, France. Her recent book *Managing Diversity: Toward a Globally Inclusive Workplace* received accolades in academic journals and won the Cholice Award for Best Academic Titles and the Academy of Management's Terry book award for "the most outstanding contribution to management knowledge."